Financial Strategy

Second Edition

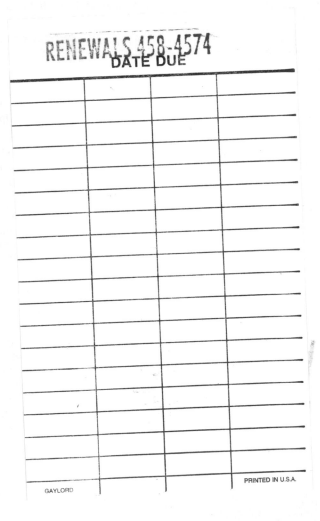

Financial Strategy brings together some of the best articles from leading writers in the field of financial strategy. The increased emphasis on adding value for organisations is reflected in the writings in this book, each of which looks at a particular aspect of how to add value: through investment, financing, and risk management. This volume also covers the debate on corporate governance and performance measurement and reflects both the coming together of issues in accounting and finance as well as the application of financial strategy to organisations in the private and public sectors worldwide.

The Open University Business School offers a three-tier ladder of opportunity for managers at different stages of their careers: the Professional Certificate in Management; the Professional Diploma in Management; and the Masters Programme.

Financial Strategy is the prescribed MBA Course Reader for the Financial Strategy module of the Open University Business School MBA course and for the Issues in International Finance and Investment module of the Masters in International Finance and Management. Designed to meet the needs of students studying at advanced undergraduate and postgraduate levels, it will also appeal to practitioners wishing to keep abreast of the latest thinking in the field of financial strategy. Opinions expressed in this Reader are not necessarily those of the Course Team or of the Open University.

The editors are Janette Rutterford, Professor of Financial Management, Martin Upton and Devendra Kodwani, Lecturer in Finance, at the Open University Business School.

Further information on Open University Business School courses and qualifications may be obtained from Open University Business School, PO Box 197, Walton Hall, Milton Keynes, MK7 6BJ, United Kingdom; tel. OU Business School Information Line: +44 (0) 8700 100311.

Alternatively, much useful course information can be obtained from the Open University Business School's website at http://www.oubs.open.ac.uk.

Financial Strategy
Second Edition

Edited by

Janette Rutterford,
Martin Upton and
Devendra Kodwani

John Wiley & Sons, Ltd

OU Business School

First edition published 1998
This second edition published in 2006 by John Wiley & Sons Ltd, The Atrium, Southern Gate, Chichester,
West Sussex PO19 8SQ, England
Telephone: (+44) 1243 779777

Email (for orders and customer service enquiries): cs-books@wiley.co.uk
Visit our Home Page on www.wiley.com

Other Wiley Editorial Offices

John Wiley & Sons Inc., 111 River Street, Hoboken, NJ 07030, USA

Jossey-Bass, 989 Market Street, San Francisco, CA 94103-1741, USA

Wiley-VCH Verlag GmbH, Boschstr. 12, D-69469 Weinheim, Germany

John Wiley & Sons Australia Ltd, 42 McDougall Street, Milton, Queensland 4064, Australia

John Wiley & Sons (Asia) Pte Ltd, 2 Clementi Loop #02-01, Jin Xing Distripark, Singapore 129809

John Wiley & Sons Canada Ltd, 22 Worcester Road, Etobicoke, Ontario, Canada M9W 1L1

Wiley also publishes its books in a variety of electronic formats. Some content that appears in print
may not be available in electronic books.

Library of Congress Cataloging-in-Publication Data
Financial strategy / edited by Janette Rutterford, Martin Upton, and Devendra Kodwani. – 2nd ed.
    p.   cm.
  Includes bibliographical references and index.
  ISBN 0-470-01655-8 (cloth : alk. paper) – ISBN 0-470-01656-6 (pbk. : alk. paper)
  1. Corporations – Finance.   2. Corporations – Accounting.   3. Value added.   I. Rutterford,
Janette.   II. Upton, Martin.   III. Kodwani, Devendra.
  HG4026.F513 2006
  658.15 – dc22

2005035000

British Library Cataloguing in Publication Data

A catalogue record for this book is available from the British Library

ISBN-13 978-0-470-01655-8 (cloth)
ISBN-10 0-470-01655-8 (cloth)
ISBN-13 978-0-470-01656-5 (paperback)
ISBN-10 0-470-01656-6 (paperback)

Typeset in Times New Roman 11/12pt by SNP Best-set Typesetter Ltd., Hong Kong
Printed and bound in Great Britain by Antony Rowe Ltd, Chippenham, Wiltshire
This book is printed on acid-free paper responsibly manufactured from sustainable forestry in which at
least two trees are planted for each one used for paper production.

Contents

Introduction

Janette Rutterford

It has long been acknowledged that finance plays a vital role within the organisation, with accounting systems designed to help organisation decision-making and control, and financial techniques, such as discounted cash flow, providing tools for valuing projects and investments.

However, in recent years, it has become clear that financial strategy on its own can have a major impact on organisations. For example, choosing the right capital structure can add value, independently of production or marketing decisions. Private equity firms are able to add value simply by buying companies and restructuring their finances. Derivatives can be used to alter the risk-return profile for risks such as currency, interest rate or credit risk, to suit individual organisations' risk and return preferences. The valuation of a new issue can vary according to the state of the stock market. This book will outline the major ways in which financial strategy can add value, looking in particular at adding value through investment decisions, financing decisions and risk management decisions.

Most finance texts concentrate on either accounting or finance and fail to recognise the dilemma facing managers in practice. This is how to motivate managers and employees and measure their performance internally, at the same time ensuring that the performance is valued by external stakeholders, such as creditors and shareholders. Internal performance measures have typically been accounting-focused, whilst stock market measures have been cash-flow linked. This collection of articles will show how the traditional split between accounting – typically historic in focus – and finance – which is forward-looking – is being broken down through the use of measures such as Economic Value Added (EVA®), the balanced scorecard, and, in the public sector, measures such as Best Value.

Indeed, advances have been made in performance measurement in a number of areas. First, the traditional split between analysts concentrating on earnings and corporate financiers concentrating on cash flows had been eroded, with analysts now valuing companies using cash flows, and financiers aware of the impact of earnings announcements on share prices. Accounting regulators, both the International Accounting Standards Board, covering companies in the European Union, and the Financial Accounting Standards

Board, covering companies in the United States, have been moving towards a discounted cash flow valuation of assets approach and away from the historic cost approach in an attempt to reduce the gap between financial market value and accounting book value.

Second, as globalisation of markets has taken place, the need for common accounting standards to ensure compatibility of financial reporting has been recognised, and investors are no longer so confused between, say, Japanese, German and US differences in accounting methods. Investors have become more aware, with company crises such as those experienced by Enron in the US, Royal Ahold in the Netherlands, Parmalat in Italy, Marconi in the UK, of the ability of management to be creative in their reporting of profits and assets, and regulators have moved to stamp out the worst practices. As a result of these changes, there is a trend towards a common set of international accounting standards to which firms seeking finance in international capital markets are required to adhere.

Third, the use of financial performance measures has become more widespread, particularly in the light of the massive privatisation programme, begun in the UK in the 1980s, and still continuing around the world as monopolies are dismantled and replaced by competing organisations. Newly privatised companies whose objectives and performance measures had been stated in non-financial terms are now required to report to investors, creditors and regulators who assess performance in financial terms. But this trend towards financial performance measurement has also taken place within the public sector, with public services required to compare their performance with that of equivalent private sector enterprises. The notion of *value for money* has become commonplace. Public sector projects are now being evaluated using private sector methodologies and sometimes financed and managed by the private sector.

Internationalisation has also widened the financial strategy debate in terms of financial objectives. The Anglo-Saxon corporate governance approach, of managers' role being to maximise *shareholder* value, came into conflict with the so-called Franco-German or continental European model of maximising *stakeholder* value, with stakeholders including managers, employees, pensioners, customers, the local community, as well as creditors and shareholders. Although Jensen and Meckling's 1976 paper on agency theory[1] pointed out that, under the Anglo-Saxon model, managers may not all be trying single-mindedly to maximise shareholder value, the emphasis until recently has been how best to make sure that managers did adopt that approach, in particular through well-structured incentive schemes, typically involving share options. Also, with the dramatic rise in stock market values in the US in the 1990s, the Continental European model of corporate governance came under fire, with major companies such as Siemens introducing management incentive schemes along US lines. However, recent corporate scandals have highlighted some problems with the Anglo-Saxon model, such as the ability of management to window-dress financial performance to enhance the – short-term – value of their executive options, and how this may not be in the interests of stakeholders such as shareholders, employees and pensioners.

The traditional dominance of classical finance theories, such as Modigliani and Miller's models of optimal capital structure and dividend policy, has also been brought into question, being replaced by more considered research into why managers and investors behave in apparently non-rational ways. Part of the answer may be to do with the inadequacies of the relatively simplistic assumptions underlying these models. For example, the net present value of cash flow approach to valuing projects fails to take into account such complexities as the ability of managers to change their minds. For this, the theory of real options has been developed, where managers are deemed not just to have fixed forecast cash flows for each project, but the option to delay, abandon or alter the scale of the project, with consequent effects on their value to the firm. However, another explanation of the failure in practice of some traditional theories may be to do with behaviour. Investors may indeed be irrational, for example, buying in boom markets, and failing to sell in bear markets, instead holding on to losses in the hope the market will go back up. This is a whole new area of research into financial strategies which allows a much richer analysis of the real world.

NOTE

1. M.C. Jensen and W.H. Meckling (1976) "Theory of the Firm: Managerial Behavior, Agency Costs and Ownership Structure," *Journal of Financial Economics*, 3(4), pp. 305–60.

Section 1

Trends in Finance Theory

Section Overview

Janette Rutterford

The typical approach to teaching finance today is to cover the classic theories underpinning the subject area – portfolio theory, the Capital Asset Pricing Model, optimal capital structure and dividend policy, and the valuation of derivatives. The assumption is that managers behave – and have always behaved – in a way which these models predict. Finance theory now has a relatively long history and it is instructive to look at how management and investor behaviour has changed as finance theories have evolved.

The Trends in Finance Theory section to the book examines how finance theory has evolved over the last 100 years or more. The papers and cases in this section chart a trend away from a subjective and intuitive approach to finance problems a hundred years ago to a more rigorous modern approach to finance, with theoretical models backed by empirical analysis. This section also looks at a more recent development, behavioural theory, which takes a step back from theoretical models such as portfolio theory and the Capital Asset Pricing Model and tries to explain stock market phenomena which are anomalies in the context of efficient markets and rational investors.

The first article, "The World was their Oyster", goes back to pre-World War I days to look at how British investors constructed investment portfolios. This was fifty years or more before Markowitz formalised portfolio theory and the concept of "optimal" portfolios in a risk/return sense, and also well before Sharpe *et al.* developed the Capital Asset Pricing Model which led to the development of performance benchmarks for investment portfolios. What emerges from this paper is that investors pre-World War I had, without access to Markowitz's model, developed what they called a "scientific" approach to portfolio construction. This was, in today's terminology, a top-down "naïve" diversification strategy. They divided the world into ten geographic regions and invested equal amounts in one stock from each region. They chose stocks of similar yield for their portfolios, varying the

1

yield according to how much risk they wanted to take on. In those days, risk was not measured by the standard deviation of returns, it was simply measured by yield. The higher the yield, the higher must be the risk. By using this "scientific" approach, investors adopted a passive strategy, investing in the "market" portfolio. But in their case, the market was the world, not just the UK or US stock markets.

By the end of the twentieth century, investors were well aware of both the portfolio theory model elaborated by Markowitz and the Capital Asset Pricing Model (CAPM) developed by Sharpe and others. The CAPM, as with the "scientific" investment approach, shows that, given certain underlying assumptions, an optimal passive investment strategy is to buy and hold the market. Developed by American academics, the CAPM can only with difficulty be applied to an international portfolio. But the CAPM does lead to a linear equation explicitly linking the expected return to the risk of a portfolio or of an individual stock in a particular market. This means that managers and investors can estimate the expected return, and hence the cost, of equity at a market, portfolio or individual company level. This in turn can be used in the Weighted Average Cost of Capital (WACC) formula, derived by Modigliani and Miller, to discount, and hence value, forecast cash flows for equity valuation or project appraisal purposes.

Although the CAPM is simple and elegant, estimating the cost of equity still requires empirical analysis to provide estimates of the coefficients in the risk/return equation; in particular, the equity Beta[1] and what is called the equity risk premium, that is, the difference between the expected return on a stock market, and the risk-free rate of return in that market, usually measured by the return on a long-term government bond. The higher the equity risk premium, the higher will be the corporate cost of capital, and the lower the net present value of project cash flows discounted using the WACC. The lower the equity risk premium, the higher share prices will be. One of the arguments put forward for the stock market boom of the 1990s was that the equity risk premium required by investors had fallen; in other words, that investors viewed equities as less risky than in the past, and were as a result prepared to accept a relatively lower rate of return. So the size of the equity risk premium is one of the important inputs to corporate financial strategy. But it is exceedingly difficult to know, even with a model to put it in, what the correct value for the equity risk premium should be.

Case Study 1, "Global Evidence on the Risk Premium", by Elroy Dimson, Paul Marsh and Mike Staunton, attempts to measure the long run equity risk premium across different countries. The paper highlights how the equity risk premium varies across countries as well as over time, an important issue for both domestic and international companies. It gives us an indication of how, even with a simple and elegant model such as the CAPM, using it in practice is fraught with estimation difficulties. We are not so far away, after all, from the pre-World War I "scientific" investors.

The second article in this section relates to behavioural finance – or "Behavioral Finance" as it is spelt by its US author, Jay Ritter. This new stream of finance literature tries to explain – using investor behaviour – stock market phenomena which cannot be explained by classical finance theory. One of the most puzzling phenomena is stock market bubbles. Why is it that stock markets rise to very high levels, as happened at the end of the 1990s, and then fall back dramatically, as happened in 2000–2002. What can explain the dot.com or "new economy" boom, where companies with less than five years' track record, and still not profitable, could be worth more in stock market terms than long-established blue chip companies? What is it about investor behaviour which can lead to such price trends? Or, more prosaically, how can a company such as Royal Dutch Shell, quoted on the Amsterdam and London Stock Exchanges, be quoted at different prices for the same underlying assets? Are investors irrational? And what about managers? Why is it that mergers and acquisitions are cyclical? When stock market prices are high, merger and acquisition activity is also high. When stock market prices are low, so is M&A activity. Why are companies bought when their prices are high? Are managers, too, irrational? The article sums up the current thinking on behavioural finance and shows that, at yet, researchers have only scratched the surface of this very promising area of research.

Case Study 2 is a McKinsey article, "Do Fundamentals – or Emotions – Drive the Stock Market?", by Marc Goedhart, Timothy Koller and David Wessels. It looks at some of the classic apparently irrational stock market phenomena, such as the Royal Dutch Shell example, and discusses the impact for managers of firms quoted on the stock market.

NOTE

1. The Beta is a measure of the relative cyclicality of a share compared to the stock market as a whole. Beta is 1 when its cyclicality is the same as that of the market; less than 1 when less cyclical than the market; greater than 1 when more cyclical; and 0 when risk-free.

1

The World was their Oyster: International Diversification Pre-World War I

Janette Rutterford

Bernstein (1996), in his history of risk, suggests that our forebears were relatively unsophisticated when it came to managing portfolio risk, or indeed quantifying it:

> Throughout most of the history of stock markets – about 200 years in the United States and even longer in some European countries – it never occurred to anyone to define risk with a number. Stocks were risky and some were riskier than others, and people let it go at that. Risk was in the gut, not in the numbers. For aggressive investors, the goal was simply to maximise return; the faint-hearted were content with savings accounts and high-grade long-term bonds. (p. 247)

Diversification, in the mid- to late nineteenth century, happened more through luck than judgment, as a means of enhancing income in the face of declining yields on British Government bonds. As overseas markets developed, with higher-yielding investment opportunities in their wake, so investors bought the securities on offer. Investment trusts and insurance companies, for example, bought bonds from different parts of the world, with very different risk characteristics, according to historical accident or opportunism. However, by the first decade of the twentieth century, British investors, both institutional and retail, had become more sophisticated in their approach to diversification. They were aware that holding a portfolio of international securities meant improved yields and increased capital safety, achieved by exploiting low correlation between different countries, markets, types of security and types of industry.

By World War 1, recommended portfolios covered the entire globe, the reasoning being that, whilst one country, market or sector might suffer, the world as a whole would continue to grow in economic terms. Buying the global portfolio was deemed to be the most efficient portfolio strategy in risk-return terms. Investors clearly followed this advice since, by 1914, British investors as a whole had almost half of long-term negotiable portfolio capital invested outside their home country and were investing two-thirds of new money overseas (Edelstein 1982, p. 113; Davis and Huttenback 1987, p. 38). A significant number of individual investors had only limited exposure to British securities in their investment portfolios. By contrast, as Graham and Dodd (1934) observed of this period, "the idea of world-wide geographical distribution had never exerted a powerful appeal upon the provincially-minded Americans" (p. 311). Even today, the levels of diversification in US investors' portfolios "present a puzzle" (Statman 2004, p. 44).

DEFINING RISK AND RETURN

Today, investors are assumed to want to maximise investment return, generally agreed to be the total of income and capital gain over a particular period. The measure most commonly used to quantify risk is the standard deviation of returns. The relationship between individual securities is measured by the correlation coefficient. The less correlated the securities in a portfolio, the greater the benefits from diversification. Markowitz diversification optimises the risk-return trade-off by maximising return for a given level of risk, or minimising risk for a given level of return, taking into account each security's expected return, risk level, and correlation coefficient with every other security in the portfolio. The amount to be invested in each security will depend not only on its own risk and return characteristics but how it interacts with other securities. Naïve diversification, which assumes equal amounts invested in each security, achieves a less satisfactory risk-return trade-off than full Markowitz optimisation.

How did nineteenth century investors think about investment risk and return? With French investors called "rentiers" and their British equivalents "capitalists" or "annuitants", the primary aim of these investors was to live off their capital. The vast majority of British investors came from a class which placed constancy of income as their number one priority, as did Jane Austen's Mrs Bennett, in the novel *Pride and Prejudice*, describing their new neighbour, Mr Bingley, to her husband, "A single man of large fortune; four or five thousand a-year. What a fine thing for our girls".[1] Capital gain was not relevant to investors who lived on their income until they died and passed on their income to their heirs.

Early government borrowing was in the form of annuities, which offered investors a guaranteed income until death. Undated British government bonds, known as Consols, provided investors and their heirs with a guaranteed income. Alternatives to government bonds were also analysed with a long-term perspective. Insurance companies were accused of never willingly selling investments and they clearly preferred long-term investments to short-term. A British actuary observed that he thought "it would be agreed that what a life office required was not so much a high yield as a permanent one. A railroad bond producing $4\frac{1}{2}$ per cent for fifty years was obviously preferable to a first-rate industrial debenture yielding even 6 per cent or more for ten years, because by the choice of a long-term security the office could render itself independent of the general course of interest for perhaps the next forty or fifty years" (May 1912, pp. 151, 156).

These investors, when they thought of risk, thought of the risk of capital loss. For example, Bailey, in an 1862 paper addressed to insurance companies, laid out a set of investment "canons". The first was that the main consideration should invariably be the security of capital; the second, that the highest practicable rate of interest should be obtained, but that this principle should always be subordinate to the previous one, the security of the capital (May 1912, p. 153). If the capital value was certain on repayment day, it was argued that price volatility between now and then could be ignored.[2] Bailey also recommended mortgages and non-marketable securities as suitable investments for insurance companies because, being unquoted, prices would not fluctuate.

MANAGING RISK

Today's investment texts advise the use of statistical techniques to manage risk. Historical risk estimates are used, together with expected return forecasts, to generate asset allocation strategies and portfolios that are optimal in the risk/return sense. Previous generations of investors decided on the appropriate risk level indirectly, by choosing a security with the required income yield and an acceptable level of risk of capital loss. For truly risk-averse investors, Three per cent government Consols were the risk-free benchmark, against which all other securities could be compared. "The higher the rate of interest, the worse the security" (Beeton, 1870, p. 26). The risk hierarchy moved up the scale from government-guaranteed bonds, through priority corporate securities, to shares on dividend-paying stocks. The key point was the desired level of yield. Once this had been determined, all that the investor could do was to minimise risk in a number of ways.[3] The first was to avoid investing in categories of security that were considered too high up the risk scale, the higher yield being deemed not worth the risk of interrupted income and/or capital loss. The second was to spend time investigating each security in depth, by studying the accounts and reading newspapers, or by consulting advisers. The third method of reducing risk was to spread risk across different securities. Initially done as an ad hoc "extension" to a limited portfolio, by the early twentieth century a sophisticated global diversification strategy had been developed.

INTERNATIONAL INVESTMENT

International diversification happened partly by default as securities in new enterprises were offered to investors. Whole new industries sprang up, for example, canals, railroads, the telegraph, steam shipping, gas, electricity, bicycles, as well as gold mining opportunities in Australia and California, railways in Japan and South America, and ruby mines in India. In addition to private enterprise, governments and municipalities the world over turned to London to finance their debts. By 1914, there were 5000 securities listed on the London Stock Exchange, at that time the largest in the world, and the vast majority were foreign or Empire stocks. Currency risk was deemed irrelevant. As Capie and Wood (1974, p. 214) point out: "The years 1870 to 1914 were years of monetary tranquillity, the heyday of the classical gold standard. Britain was on the standard and more and more countries were joining it". Loans were in sterling or backed by gold. Cotton, explaining to female investors in 1898 how to write a sterling cheque commented: "remittances in this way can be sent to almost every town in the civilised world" (p. 146).

There is general agreement that one motive for overseas investment was to improve income. For example, Michie (1986) observed that the increased investment in overseas mining shares was encouraged "both by the expanding press and declining interest rates on older more established forms of investment like mortgages and Consols" (pp. 149–50). In particular, during the last two decades of the nineteenth century and up to 1906, yields on Consols fell. The yield on Three per cent Consols reached a low of 1.96% in 1897 and New Groschen Consols issued in 1888 paid $2\frac{3}{4}$ per cent up to April 1903 and $2\frac{1}{2}$ per cent thereafter (Harley 1976, pp. 101, 105). Wages did not fall to reflect the fall in investment income, so investors turned to overseas investments offering higher yields to bridge the income gap.

Colonial government bonds, such as those issued by the Indian government, were considered to be as low risk as home government bonds. "The security of the Indian Government is scarcely, if at all, inferior to that of the British Government itself; for where would be the prestige of the British name were we to allow our Indian empire to be wrested from us by any power whatever?" (*Chadwicks' Investment Circular* 1870, p. 52). Other overseas government and municipal bonds were clearly riskier than British or Colonial bonds, but offered highly attractive rates. For example, *Chadwicks* reported amongst new foreign issuers in London in 1870, the City of Boston, Massachusetts offering 5 per cent coupon at a price of 87 per cent of par, Russia offering 5 per cent at 80, the Mississippi Bridge financing paying 7 per cent and offered at 90, with Alabama paying 8 per cent and offered at $94\frac{1}{2}$. Japan came to the market for the first time in that year, with a 9 per cent offering at 98 (1871, p. 38). Such offers were very attractive in yield terms compared to Three per cent Consols.

Overseas government bonds came highly recommended – in preference to domestic equities – not just by sponsoring banks and brokers but also by investment authors. As *Beeton's Guide* observed: "as a rule, foreign stocks pay a higher rate of interest than other securities, and have this advantage over shares in companies – that only the capital invested can be lost" (1898, p. 54). However, as can be seen from the pricing of these bonds, they were not considered interchangeable. *Beeton's Guide* recommended that investors consider not the countries' willingness but their ability to pay and listed four risk categories: good security and low interest (including France, Belgium, Holland and Russia); middling security with higher interest (Argentine, Brazil, Peru, Egypt, and Turkey); doubtful security and high interest (Austria, Danube, Italy, Portugal and Spain) and finally those which had ceased to pay interest (Greece, Mexico, and Venezuela) (p. 26). Failure to pay did not deter investors who believed that, in the long run, countries would pay up. France's position as low risk might surprise given that 1870 was the year in which it was defeated by Germany. *Chadwicks'* also took a sanguine view of "country" risk as applied to France. Discussing the £10,000,000 debenture issued to indemnify the Germans, *Chadwicks'* commented: "Foreigners will act upon the wise faith that so great a nation and so rich a country will always pay and be solvent somehow – no matter what may be the temporary difficulty" (1871, p. 50). The money was raised at 85 per cent, offering a 6 per cent coupon. Germany, in the same year, as victor, was able to raise money on better terms – five per cent interest at 96½. Although the French risk was higher, the additional yield was deemed more than sufficient to compensate. Even with delayed interest payments or capital depreciation, the return would, it was believed, more than exceed that on risk-free British government bonds.

Political or country risk was not always limited to overseas investment. Indeed, overseas investment could be a means of reducing avoiding political risk at home. Even the British were not immune. In the early part of the nineteenth century, before the passing of the Reform Act, anxious Tories, "withdrew their savings from consols and purchased American bonds, determined to secure a pittance in some foreign country upon which they could live when the wreck took place" (Jenks 1963, p. 80). By the beginning of the twentieth century, the British "burdened with a floating pauper population, and . . . subject to recurring waves of socialism" were being positively encouraged to export their savings: "Indeed, to-day there is no section of the globe in which invested capital stands in such imminent peril as it does in England. In the present Parliament legislation has been largely confined to efforts to disendow the property-holder and to endow Labour at Capital's expense" (Investment Critic 1908, p. 32).

EARLY DIVERSIFICATION STRATEGIES

Initially, there was no particular strategy underlying portfolio construction. Each individual security was judged on its own merits, and bought in what seemed an appropriate amount, given the size of the issue, the amount available at the time, and the over-riding view that most money should be invested in relatively safe securities. An early example is that of Samuel Greg. Rose (1979) argues that the cotton mill owner sought alternative investments to the vicissitudes of the trade cycle by investing £21,000 in Prussian bonds, £5,500 in French rentes, and £3,000 in Peruvian bonds during the period 1813 to 1819. However, for safety, he still kept the majority, 69% in 1824, in Consols. Diversification was also helped by requiring company directors to own shares in the companies on whose boards they sat, as Jefferys (1938) pointed out:

> The multiplication of companies meant multiplication of directorates, and a man of wealth and reputation had no difficulty in obtaining a seat on the board of a company and at the same time was not expected to invest extensively in the company. Directors share qualifications tended to fall. If he wanted income, then distribution of investments was a sounder basis for this than concentration and a prerequisite of distribution was marketability of shares (pp. 208–9).

A cautious approach to diversification was adopted by insurance companies. A survey by May (1912) of the investment portfolios of four insurance companies in 1857 shows between 46% and 87% invested in mortgages, with up to 24% invested in railway bonds, mostly British. In addition to these traditional investments, Metropolitan Life held 5.5% in Turkish government bonds whereas Rock Life had invested 13.5% of its cash in Canadian bonds. In terms of yield, these overseas bonds yielded more than the less than $3\frac{1}{2}\%$ on Consols. May observed that this approach was not diversification, more the principle of "extension of securities", and deplored this method of portfolio construction:

> Since all of our assurance business is based on the law of averages one would naturally have thought that this principle would have been given full weight when considering the question of the investment of funds. I am afraid, however, that in the past very little attention was paid to this point; the ruling consideration appears to have been to endeavour to satisfy oneself as to the safety of the capital in each investment considered by itself (pp. 136–7)

The key driver for international diversification was the quest for higher yield. Individuals were often under more pressure than institutions to generate high incomes. As *Chadwicks' Investment Circular* remarked, in 1870, "As we all know, very many people are constantly on the lookout for good investments, and when we come to inquire what it really is they want, we often find that they are in search of 'a safe five per cent'. Less than five per cent, they say, they cannot live upon." Although acknowledging the British investor's preference for none but British securities, *Chadwicks' Investment Circular* then went on to argue that:

> We are now too much alive to our own interests to place our trust in Consols alone; for indeed the British Government Funds cannot accommodate a tithe of the money that is always pressing forward for investment. Moreover, Railways, and even Foreign Stocks, have been found to pay better in the long run. We hold that, by a careful selection from the various media of investment, very remunerative returns in the shape of interest may be obtained; while, by a proper division of risks, not only may the *security* for the principal be rendered perfectly satisfactory, but there may be a good prospect that the invested capital will steadily increase in value (pp. 30–1).

The authors provided an empirical example (Table 1.1) of how such "proper division" of risks might work. Choosing four securities then dealt on the Stock Exchange, of very different types, they showed that, had one invested £1,000 each in Three per cent Consols, Spanish Three per cents, Turkish Six per cents, and London and Western railway shares ten years before, the annual income yield would have ranged from $3\frac{1}{4}$% for Consols to $10\frac{3}{4}$% for Turkish bonds. They also took the change in principal value over the ten years into account, and showed how the total annual (simple interest) return on investment would have been 3 per cent for Consols, the same for Spanish Three per cents, $8\frac{1}{4}$% per cent for Home Railway Stocks, and a sizeable $11\frac{3}{8}$% on Turkish Six per Cents. They concluded: "The best mode of employing money would thus appear to consist in making a judicious selection amongst Home Railways and Foreign Stocks" (p. 32).

Table 1.1 Chadwicks' Investment Circular's diversified portfolio, 1870

	Consols, at 93	Spanish 3 per Cts., at 47 1/2	Turkish, 6 per Cts., at 56	Lon. & N.W. Rail., at 100
Stock purchased ten years ago	£1,075	£2,100	£1,800	£1,000
The ten years' dividends would have amounted to:				
1861 First half	£16.10	£31.50	£54.00	£26.30
Second half	£16.10	£31.50	£54.00	£18.70
1862 First half	£16.10	£31.50	£54.00	£23.80
Second half	£16.10	£31.50	£54.00	£18.70
1863 First half	£16.10	£31.50	£54.00	£22.50
Second half	£16.10	£31.50	£54.00	£21.20
1864 First half	£16.10	£31.50	£54.00	£30.00
Second half	£16.10	£31.50	£54.00	£28.80
1865 First half	£16.10	£31.50	£54.00	£35.00
Second half	£16.10	£31.50	£54.00	£30.00
1866 First half	£16.10	£31.50	£54.00	£36.20
Second half	£16.10	£31.50	£54.00	£30.00
1867 First half	£16.10	£31.50	£54.00	£33.80
Second half	£16.10	£31.50	£54.00	£26.20
1868 First half	£16.10	£31.50	£54.00	£33.70
Second half	£16.10	£31.50	£54.00	£26.20
1869 First half	£16.10	£31.50	£54.00	£33.80
Second half	£16.10	£31.50	£54.00	£22.50
1870 First half	£16.10	£31.50	£54.00	£35.00
Second half	£16.10	£31.50	£54.00	£30.00
Total dividends	£322.00	£630.00	£1,080.00	£562.8*
Present value of the principal:				
	Consols, at 92 1/2	Spanish 3 per Cts., at 31	Turkish, 6 per Cts., at 61	Lon. & N.W. Rail., at 126 1/2
Total value	£994	£651	£1,098	£1,265

* typographical error as actual total of these dividends is £562.40
Source: Chadwicks Investment Circular 1870, p. 32

Similar advice was also offered in *Beeton's Guide to Investing Money with Safety and Profit*, published in the same year. "If an investor wishes to secure a high rate of interest, he should divide his capital among a number of stocks that can be bought to pay a high rate of interest – the more the better. Supposing he has £500 to invest, let him invest £100 in each of the following – Turkish, Italian, Spanish, Egyptian, Guatemalan, or Argentine. By dividing his capital in this way, the investor reduces risk to a minimum, as it is unlikely that all these countries could stop paying their interest, although it is not unlikely that any one might do so". Although appearing to limit investor choice to government bonds, *Beeton's Guide* allowed choice from a wide range of countries and types of security. For example, the author showed how a five per cent yield could be achieved in a number of different ways, by investing in two, three or more securities and a similar approach could be used to lock in any desired rate of interest. Five per cent could be achieved, for example, by buying half Russian bonds yielding 6% and half English railway debentures, yielding 4%. Alternatively, the same overall yield could be obtained from one-third Turkish bonds yielding $6\frac{1}{2}$%, one-third London and North Western Stock paying $5\frac{1}{4}$%, and one-third in new Three per cent Consols yielding $3\frac{1}{4}$%. A third method of gaining the magic five per cent was one-half in new Three per cent Consols, one-quarter in $7\frac{3}{4}$% Argentine bonds and one-quarter in Brazilian $5\frac{3}{4}$% bonds. The key point was that "it is only necessary to invest a small portion of the whole in a high dividend-paying stock to bring the rate up to 5% and that the greater part is invested in perfectly safe securities. The more the capital is divided the better, so that there may be a smaller amount in each security" (p. 56).

As the nineteenth century drew to a close, the problem of income became more acute, with yields on domestic securities falling. Private investors were forced into overseas securities to obtain higher, or even similar yields to those achieved in earlier years. Fortunately for them, supply was not wanting. Even cautious insurance companies substantially increased their overseas exposure. By 1912, May was able to comment that "the tendency at present was to invest almost exclusively abroad" and that "Canada, South America, China and Japan" were countries in which most assurance companies held securities (pp. 157, 163). Investment trusts were also adventurous in their investment policies. For example, by 1900, Foreign and Colonial Investment Trust held over 300 securities in its portfolio (McKendrick and Newlands 1999, p. 69). However, with increased overseas investment, there began to be a switch from ad hoc "extension" of securities to a more organised portfolio diversification strategy.

"SCIENTIFIC" APPROACH TO DIVERSIFICATION

A key development by the beginning of the twentieth century was a more "scientific" approach to global portfolio diversification. Instead of adding as many risky securities as required to generate the required yield, some investors began to realise that a more top-down approach to portfolio construction was desirable. By World War I, these investors were constructing international portfolios on a top-down basis, targeting a particular level of yield, and minimising capital risk through the choice of relatively uncorrelated securities. Historical analysis of returns, price volatility and correlation were all taken into account in the choice of the optimal portfolios. The need for rebalancing was also allowed for by ensuring that only marketable securities were considered for inclusion. By 1914, only the mathematical optimisation of Markowitz' model was lacking in terms of portfolio best practice. Nevertheless, investors chose more diversified, less correlated portfolios than is the case today, where, despite the implications of Markowitz' model, domestic securities dominate the portfolios of most investors, whether institutional or individual.

An early twentieth century example of the top-down approach is from a 1908 Pamphlet entitled "Women as Investors". In a list of important principles and rules, the author recommends that women readers:

1. "spread the capital over a number of concerns, and do not keep to one class of investment, so that if one or more are failures, there may remain others which are not.

2. do not invest more than about one tenth of the capital in any one concern, unless personally occupied in its management and control" (p. 29).

More complex diversification strategies were actively promoted by the *Financial Review of Reviews*, a monthly magazine first published in 1905, and in textbooks such as "Investment an Exact Science", published by the *Financial Review of Reviews* and written by a frequent contributor, Henry Lowenfeld. Lowenfeld (1911) recommended the following simple rules:

1. "The capital must be divided evenly over a number of sound securities.

2. All the stocks must be identical in quality.

3. Each stock must differ, in respect of the risk to which capital invested in it is exposed, from every other stock in the same list" (pp. 7–8).

The key point behind the recommendations, as made by Crozier (1911), was that, by diversifying according to certain rules, "if this be accurately and skilfully done, there is no reason why the prudent investor should not be certain of getting a *larger* yield of income, with *equal* stability and security, from a Geographical Distribution of Capital than from any other mode of investment. It is thoroughly scientific in character" (my italics) (p. 118). May (1912) held the same view: "the investment of funds in relatively high yielding securities, carefully selected, not only gives more satisfactory return than that shown by the lower yielding stocks, but on the average gives greater security for the capital" (pp. 35–6).[4]

Both Lowenfeld, for individual investors, and May, for life assurance companies, produced schedules to encourage a *full* global diversification.[5] Table 1.2 shows May's suggested schedule, with countries or regions on the

Table 1.2 May's international portfolio template for life assurance companies, 1912

GEOGRAPHICAL DIVISION	MORTGAGES		GOVERNMENTS		MUNICIPAL		RAILWAYS		&C		MISCELLANEOUS	
	Amount authorized £	Amount held £	Amount authorized £	Amount held £	Amount authorized £	Amount held £	Amount authorized £	Amount held £	Amount authorized £	Amount held £	Amount authorized £	Amount held £
Great Britain							A	B				
British Colonies, &c. { India { Canada { &c.												
Europe. { France { Germany { &c.												
Asia. { China { Japan { &c.												
Africa. { Egypt { &c.												
United States of America												
South America. { Argentine, { Brazil { &c.												

Source: May 1912, p. 144

left-hand side and types of security along the top. Table 1.3 shows that put forward by the *Financial Review of Reviews*.

May recommended choosing countries, then types of securities and deciding an amount authorized for each type/country according to individual preference. Speaking in front of fellow actuaries, he felt that these decisions "were so much a question of individual opinion that I am afraid it would be quite out of place for me to put forward any scheme". May divided the world into seven regions; Lowenfeld had nine regions by dividing Europe into North and South, as well as adding an "international" grouping, made up of companies operating on a global scale: international trusts, shipping, telegraph, marine insurance, etc. Such proposals recommended investing in each region of the world, and in a variety of types of security in each region, should funds permit. Crozier (1911), for example, suggested spreading the securities of any one country across a number of different types such as government, railways, shipping, banks and industrials. Different types of financial instrument were also allowed, although preference shares and debentures were preferred to equities, the latter deemed more exposed to market volatility (p. 113).

The thinking behind full global coverage was that, overall, the global population was growing, as was international trade. A global portfolio would therefore reap the benefits of this growth, whilst if one country suffered, another would benefit: "the wider the distribution of one's capital in every respect . . . the wider the distribution of risk run, and consequently the less likelihood of becoming stranded financially, since only a world-wide catastrophe . . . could arise to affect adversely the whole of the world's securities at one time" (Stacey 1923, pp. 38–9). Allen (1906), in the *Financial Review of Reviews* concurred: "While it is impossible to predict the future of any single investment, it is claimed that such a distribution of capital gives a means of forecasting with accuracy the result of a number of investments embracing the world's area, since the controlling factor of the value of such a group of investments being the whole world's trade, which according to previous assumption is unaffected as a whole by cycles of variation, the tendency is to the removal of the speculative element" (p. 27).

The attraction of global diversification was that it ensured that different types of risk were diversified away, improving the risk/return trade-off. Crozier (1911) recommended spreading investments across countries which varied in terms of different types of produce, different "trade currents", supply and demand for investment capital, high interest rate and low interest rate, and so on. Specific security, sector risk and market risk, issues that are still not fully resolved today, were well understood:

> Like the horses in a race, the number of stocks in an investment list are few in number; while the quality of the horses, their past records and present form, the jockeys that ride them, the length of the course, the nature of the ground, etc., correspond to the past history and present quotations of the stocks, and

Table 1.3 *Financial Review of Reviews'* global portfolios for achieving $5\frac{1}{2}$ % and $4\frac{1}{4}$ % annual yield

$5\frac{1}{2}$% INVESTMENT SCHEME.

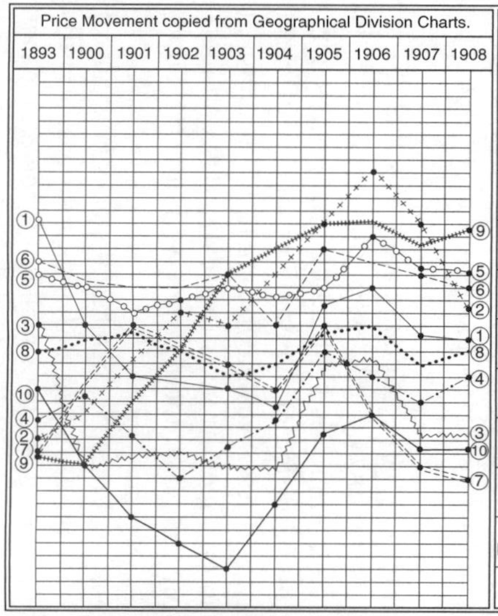

NOTE–The lines In this Chart are identical with the lines given in each separate Geographical Division Chart.

Geographical Division.	Name and Quantity of Stock.	Denoting NUMBER.	Table showing Annual Values at average prices of year.										Table showing Annual Income.									
			1899	1900	1901	1902	1903	1904	1905	1906	1907	1908	1899	1900	1901	1902	1903	1904	1905	1906	1907	1908
BRITISH.	50 Shares Alliance and Dublin Consumers' Gas	(1)	1112	987	967	965	962	960	1075	1062	1025	981	$52\frac{1}{2}$	$52\frac{1}{2}$	$52\frac{1}{2}$	$52\frac{1}{4}$	$52\frac{1}{2}$	$52\frac{1}{2}$	$52\frac{1}{2}$	$52\frac{1}{2}$	$51\frac{1}{4}$	50
BRITISH COLONIES	£1,300 Toronto Mortgage Company Common Stock … … … … …	(2)	975	1007	1111	1199	1176	1248	1355	1436	1324	1371	50	50	50	50	50	60	60	60	60	60
EUROPE, NORTH.	12 Shares Hamburg Electric Supply Ordinary	(3)	984	870	879	882	873	870	954	960	909	906	54	48	42	42	45	45	48	48	48	48
EUROPE, SOUTH.	50 Shares Vienna Bank Verein … …	(4)	1040	1080	1000	920	984	1040	1136	1096	1072	1100	64	60	52	56	56	60	60	60	60	60
ASIA.	£1,000 Nagasaki Harbour Improvement Loan 6% Bonds … … … …	(5)	900	880	840	870	900	870	900	980	940	930	60	60	60	60	60	60	60	60	60	60
AFRICA.	£1,000 Upper Congo Belgian Trading Company 6% Preference Stock …	(6)	1060	1050	1040	1040	1060	980	1080	1060	1050	1050	60	60	60	60	60	60	60	60	60	60
NORTH AMERICA.	£1,000 Laclade Gas Light 5% Cumulative Preferred Stock … …	(7)	930	980	1030	1010	990	975	1030	950	900	900	50	50	50	50	50	50	50	50	50	50
CENTRAL AMERICA.	£1,000 New Trinidad Lake Asphalts 6% Debentures … … … … …	(8)	980	985	1000	980	950	960	1020	1030	1000	1020	60	60	60	60	60	60	60	60	60	60
SOUTH AMERICA.	£1,500 Brazil Great Southern Railway 6% 1st Debentures … … … …	(9)	1095	1065	1200	1305	1440	1485	1530	1545	1470	1485	90	90	90	90	90	90	90	90	90	90
INTER-NATIONAL	£1,500 Anglo-American Telegraph Ordinary Stock … … … …	(10)	975	892	787	735	727	787	900	945	900	870	$55\frac{1}{8}$	$46\frac{7}{8}$	$45\frac{3}{4}$	$45\frac{5}{8}$	$45\frac{3}{4}$	$41\frac{1}{4}$	$48\frac{3}{4}$	$58\frac{1}{8}$	$52\frac{1}{2}$	$52\frac{1}{2}$
Totals of Annual Values and Annual Income		£	10051	9796	9854	9906	10062	10175	10980	11064	10590	10613	$595\frac{5}{8}$	$577\frac{3}{8}$	$562\frac{1}{4}$	$565\frac{7}{8}$	$569\frac{1}{4}$	$578\frac{3}{4}$	$589\frac{1}{4}$	$598\frac{5}{8}$	$591\frac{3}{4}$	$590\frac{1}{2}$

◻ Estimated.

NOTE–The Interest allowance for contingencies is £40 in 1908.

BRITISH INVESTMENT 4¼% SCHEME.

Description of Enterprise.	Name and Quantity of Stock	Descripting Number	Table showing Annual Values at average prices of year.										Table showing Annual Income.									
			1899	1900	1901	1902	1903	1904	1905	1906	1907	1908	1899	1900	1901	1902	1903	1904	1905	1906	1907	1908
CORPORATION.	£1,000 Southampton Corporation 3½% Stock, Redeemable 1945	①	1024	1005	1004	1001	996	987	999	990	975	975	35	35	35	35	35	35	35	35	35	35
RAILWAY.	£800 Furness Railway 4% Consolidated Preference Stock	②	1048	996	920	898	856	820	836	852	824	780	32	32	32	32	32	32	32	32	32	32
TRAMWAY.	200 Shares City of Birmingham Trams 5% Cumulative Preference	③	1090	1080	1075	1025	1020	975	1030	1055	950	925	50	50	50	50	50	50	50	50	50	50
GAS.	50 Shares Alliance & Dublin Consumers' Gas 10% Standard	④	1112	987	967	965	962	960	1075	1062	1025	981	52½	52½	52½	52½	52½	52½	52½	52½	51¼	50
BANK.	12 Shares Parr's Bank	⑤	1074	1068	1026	1014	1008	1005	1023	1056	1020	1020	45 7/16	48	48	48	48	48	48	48	48	48
ELECTRICITY.	£1,200 London Electric Supply Corporation 4% 1st Mortgage Debenture Stock	⑥	1260	1212	1170	1164	1194	1158	1162	1176	1110	1098	48	48	48	48	48	48	48	48	48	48
COTTON.	£1,300 English Sewing Cotton 4% 1st Mortgage Debenture Stock	⑦	1345	1319	1235	1098	1059	1053	1170	1248	1241	1235	52	52	52	52	52	52	52	52	52	52
IRON, COAL AND STEEL.	£800 Vickers, Sons & Maxim 5% Preferred Stock	⑧	1060	1028	1012	1012	936	888	920	936	872	848	40	40	40	40	40	40	40	40	40	40
SOAP.	700 Shares Pears (A. & F.) Ordinary	⑨	1006	964	950	929	922	922	1010	1024	940	940	70	70	70	70	70	70	70	70	70	70
	Totals of Annual Values and Annual Income.	£	10019	9659	9359	9104	8953	8768	9245	9399	8957	8802	425	427½	427½	427½	427½	427½	427½	427½	426¼	425

The nine other Investment Schemes included in the first set of Charts would have shown equal want of stability of capital to the above Investment holding, and this example is given in order to show how the others would compare with the geographically distributed Investment schemes.

to the Money Markets, Stock Exchanges and Trade Currents which ride and dominate them (p. 120).

In terms of how much to invest in each security, the preferred number recommended for the private investors was ten securities, with equal nominal[6] amounts to be initially invested in each. This number tallied nicely with Lowenfeld's nine regions of the globe plus one "international" sector. Withers (1908) argued that, with ten securities, individual investments were large enough for the investor to have the power to realise a substantial portion of his invested capital whilst being few enough to allow the investor to monitor his portfolio and watch for any investments which required replacing (pp. 40–41). Viscount Midleton, writing in the *Financial Review of Reviews* in 1908, complained that insurance companies, with hundreds of investments in their portfolios, had too many securities to be effectively managed and tended to review their portfolios "perhaps only when a quinquennial bonus has to be declared" (p. 11).

The *Financial Review of Reviews*, in their 1909 issue from which Table 1.3 is extracted, produced a number of portfolios of ten securities, each with a different income target, and each aiming to protect the capital value of the portfolio over a ten year period. For each required yield level, securities with similar initial yields were chosen from each geographical area. In the $5\frac{1}{2}\%$ Investment Scheme, for example, African Preference Stock, Central American Debentures and International Ordinary Stock are chosen, each offering an initial yield of between 5% and 6%. As "The Investment Critic", commenting on these portfolios, observed, the British Investment Scheme, limited to British securities, targeted a lower yield of around $4\frac{1}{4}\%$ "owing to the fact that England's accumulated wealth is greater than that of any other nation, capital invested in England commands a lower rate than it does in any other country" (p. 25).

The historical data shown in Table 1.3 are for the period 1899 to 1908, the longest and strongest period when overseas investments outperformed British investments pre-World War I. This ten-year historical analysis tallies with the approach of *Chadwicks' Investment Circular*, forty years earlier. Both use historical data as the basis of their recommendation for full global approach to diversification. Indeed, Lowenfeld argued that his sound principles of investment were based on "centuries of statistics and decades of practical experience" (1911, p. 15). Today, ten years, or more commonly five years, of historical data is still the most commonly-used method of modelling optimal portfolios for the future.

The portfolio analysis of the *Financial Review of Reviews* went further than an analysis of historical returns. It attempted to show graphically the impact of correlation on investment performance by plotting the price movements of the ten securities in each portfolio over the ten-year period. An article by Professor Chapman in the *Financial Review of Reviews* explained positive correlation or lack of it by saying that some industries were complements, such as the pen and pencil industries, whereas others were independent, such as the pen and boot industries (1908, p. 27). From Table 1.3, the positive correlation between stocks in the British Investment scheme is evident. These securities, it was argued, were subject to the same stock market influences, and had all depreciated over the period in question more or less in parallel. In contrast, authors such as Rolleston believed that, by diversifying internationally, as in the $5\frac{1}{2}$% Investment Scheme, the rises and falls of individual investments would "counterbalance each other and thus maintain an equilibrium in value" (1909, p. 38). These rises and falls could be explained by negative correlation between the securities. The counterbalancing effect was due to the fact that the securities were chosen to have equal "quality" or price volatility. In order to achieve this volatility balance, Lowenfeld required that yields on securities in any single portfolio should vary by no more than $1\frac{1}{4}$% (1911, p. 12).

Using diagrams rather than maths, the portfolios proposed by the *Financial Review of Reviews*, and other authors of the time, took expected income, capital safety, price volatility and correlation into account, when determining recommended portfolios. The only theoretical difference between these investment strategies and those suggested by Markowitz, writing fifty years later, was that using an optimisation model might lead to more "efficient" investment portfolios, with amounts to be invested in each security chosen mathematically rather than via a "naïve" strategy of equal nominal amounts in each. However, the portfolios proposed by publications such as the *Financial Review of Reviews*, combined government bonds, corporate bonds and equities into single portfolios, rather than optimising within asset classes as is more common today.

DIVERSIFICATION IN PRACTICE

The main practical difference with today's approach to portfolio diversification is that the *Financial Review of Reviews* felt able to suggest optimal portfolios with only 10% in the British stock market, for example the $5\frac{1}{2}$% yield portfolio shown in Table 1.3. Such a strategy would now be viewed as too risky, even if the Markowitz model were to assume that most domestic securities, as was true in the first decade of the twentieth century for British investors, were inefficient in a risk/return sense. Today, the Markowitz model is rarely applied in a fully global context. Investors prefer to place the bulk of their money in domestic securities, using a constrained (and therefore sub-optimal) Markowitz optimisation process to determine their overseas investments. In the US, for example, pension funds held only 15% of their portfolios in non-UK securities in 2003; for UK pension funds, the equivalent figure was 30%.[7] The UK benchmark APCIMS index, used for private investor portfolios, recommends that a maximum 25% be held in overseas securities.

These figures are in strong contrast to the situation in 1913 when, of all British-held long-term negotiable portfolio capital, foreign investment portfolio holdings accounted for 45% of the total (Edelstein 1982, p. 113). International diversification, as recommended by the *Financial Review of Reviews* and other influential people, such as Lowenfeld, May, academics and politicians – as numerous articles in the *Financial Review of Reviews* from 1905 to World War I testify – was clearly carried out in practice. The advice provided by the *Financial Review of Reviews* was also backed up with practical help. The periodical was published by a company called the Investment Registry which analysed stocks globally and, from these, prepared lists of acceptable stocks for each of the ten regions of the world. Investors could write in to the *Financial Review of Reviews* with their existing portfolio, and be given advice as to how to "internationalise" it or hand over responsibility for investment to the fund managers employed by the Investment Registry. The Investment Registry managed over £30 million in 1913, with over 9500 shareholders and customers (*Financial Review of Reviews* 1913, No. 98, p. 1006).

Merchant bank archives hold information on pre-World War I portfolios of relatively wealthy private individuals. Table 1.4 itemises the investments of three clients of N.M. Rothschild & Co. Limited from the period 1907 to 1909, drawn from a file containing details relating to the estates on death of Rothschild clients. All the estates in the archive file had internationally diversified portfolios, as do the three shown in Table 1.4, with balanced amounts, in nominal terms, spread across major geographical regions. In all three cases shown, the predominant currency of investment was the pound sterling, with the smallest exclusively in sterling-denominated assets. The largest portfolio, that of the Honourable Mrs Clive Behrens, was the most geographically diversified, with investments (of similar quality) in Europe, Asia, the Colonies, Africa, North and South America, Ireland and 20% in British negotiable assets. The second portfolio, that of Lady Crewe, had been switched from a portfolio fully invested in British Trustee stocks, primarily British railway debentures, to a portfolio that held no British securities at all. The smallest portfolio of the three, the estate of Mr Boardman, included 15% invested in Asia, 37% in Latin America, 15% in South Africa and 32% in British securities, although the South African securities were listed under British funds in the Stock Exchange Official Intelligence. All three portfolios concentrated on fixed interest securities, with the overseas securities all offering higher coupons than British Government Consols.[8] By choosing high-yielding overseas securities which were less correlated with each other than were British securities, British investors, certainly those wealthy enough to bank with Rothschilds[9], had pre-World War I investment portfolios which may, in practice, have been close to or exceeded in risk/return efficiency terms, today's constrained Markowitz portfolios.

CONCLUSION

This paper has looked at how pre-World War I British investors thought about and managed risk with respect to their investment portfolios, by examining

Table 1.4 Examples of individuals' internationally diversified portfolios

	Currency***	Nominal	Nominal	% of Total
1907 Trust account for Hon. Mrs Clive Behrens*		Local	£	Nominal
2 3/4% Irish Land	£		20,067	8
4% Industrial Dwellings Debentures 1930	£		27,500	12
4 1/2% Chilli 1886	£		20,000	8
5% Chinese Shanghai Nankin Rwy	£		20,000	8
4% Egypt Unified	£		50,000	21
3% Egypt Preference Bonds	£		15,000	6
4 1/2% Japanese Sterling bond Second Series	£		50,000	21
Burma Railways	£		10,000	4
3% Grand Trunk Pacific Guar. 1st Mort. 1962	$	50,000	10,000	4
3 1/2% Italian Converted	L	43,600	1,744	1
3 1/2% Indian Rupee 1854/5	R	50,000	3,333	1
3 1/2% Bavarian Rwy 1896	M	100,000	4,902	2
3% Belgian First Series 1895	Fc	100,000	4,000	2
Total			236,546	100
1909 Trust account for Lady Crewe**				
5% Brazil bonds 1907	£		10,000	17
5% Argentine bonds 1909	£		10,000	17
5% Chilian bonds 1909	£		10,000	17
4 1/2% Japanese Sterling bond Second Series	£		11,220	19
4% Lake Shore Michigan Sthn gold debs 1931	$	30,000	6,000	10
4% Louisville, Nashville, Atlantic and Knoxville bonds 1955	$	25,000	5,000	9
4% gold bonds Baltimore, Ohio, Pittsburg, Lake Erie, W. Va.	$	30,000	6,000	10
Total			58,220	100
1909 Estate Mr Boardman**				
2 1/2% Consolidated Stock	£		2,000	31
3% Transvaal Guaranteed Stock	£		1,000	15
5% Rio Tinto Preference Shares of £5 each	£		70	1
5% Argentine Buenos Ayres Water Supply Stock	£		1,000	15
4 1/2% Japan Sterling bond Second Series	£		1,000	15
5% Chilian bonds 1909	£		700	11
5% Brazil bonds 1908	£		700	11
Total			6,470	100

* *Source*: N.M. Rothschild Archive, Ref 000/131
** *Source*: N.M. Rothschild Archive, Ref 000/132
*** Currency £ Pound Sterling, $ US Dollar, R Indian Rupee, M Mark, Fc Belgian Florins, L Lire
Exchange rate details taken from 1908 (for 1907) and 1910 (for 1909) Stock Exchange Official Intelligence

contemporary periodicals and investment texts as well as examples of actual investment strategy. The paper argues that these investors sought to maximise yield, whilst minimising long-term income uncertainty and capital deprecia-tion. International investment, encouraged by low yields available at home, by lack of currency risk, and by promotion in the financial literature and by some of the major merchant banks, took off in the mid-nineteenth century and reached a peak immediately prior to World War I.

Whilst being attracted to international investments, investors sought also to minimise risk in a number of ways. They concentrated on senior securi-ties, such as debentures and preference shares, rather than risky ordinary shares. Where possible, they bought securities with which they had some connection, although this was possible only for the informed few. As an alter-native approach to risk reduction, investors, encouraged by their advisers, turned to extensive global diversification, creating world-wide investment portfolios which they believed would benefit from global growth in popula-tion and trade, whilst being protected from difficulties in individual regions, markets, sectors and types of security. Such diversification was "naïve" in a Markowitz sense, since most investors, whether institutional or private, were encouraged to invest equal amounts in each security. However, the global reach of the portfolios ensured greater use of low correlation between sectors such as mining, railroads, retail stores, and countries such as Canada and Chile. Although in practice, many investors may not have been as global as the recommendations encouraged, evidence from archival research points to highly diversified portfolios. The equanimity with which British investors, both institutional and private, invested globally contrasts with the predomi-nantly domestic bias of quantitatively oriented, modern-day institutional investors.

NOTES

1. Jane Austen 1934, p. 2, first published in 1813.
2. US investors agreed with Bailey, viewing undated Consols as more risky than long-dated government bonds. See William Cotton 1898, p. 13.
3. For further discussion of how investors, in particular British investors, valued securities before World War I, see Janette Rutterford 2004.
4. It is not clear whether George May believed that risk reduction would be achieved through the process of diversification itself or through finding more undervalued securities by allowing a broader range of investments.
5. Indeed, in 1912, the *Financial Review of Reviews* published George May's article in full, and published several articles in later issues discussing the role of diver-sification in insurance company strategy.
6. The emphasis on nominal rather than market value reflected the relative disre-gard for capital gain or loss compared with yield as a source of return. Some publications were unsophisticated as to the number of securities to choose and the difference between nominal and market values as far as diversification was

concerned. For example, the weekly *Investors' Review*, in 1905, recommended a model trust with four securities of nominal value £100 each, with market prices varying from £102½ for Buenos Ayres Railway Debentures paying 5% nominal to £280 for Nobel Dynamite shares paying 10% nominal yield (November 11, p. 594).

7. Source: Callan Associates; The WM Company.
8. The Rothschild Archive, St. Swithin's Lane, London, 000/131 and 000/132.
9. There is some evidence that the "middle classes and females" preferred home firms, whereas the "elite" favoured foreign assets. See Samuel Pollard (1985), p. 499. Lance Davis and Robert Huttenback (1987) also point to higher than average overseas investments by the social elite and by businessmen, the former preferring empire and the latter "foreign" stocks (pp. 202–3).

REFERENCES

Allen, Sidney S. 1906. "'Investment an Exact Science' Reviewed." *Financial Review of Reviews*, No. 3 (January): 24–28.

Austen, Jane. 1934. *Pride and Prejudice*. London: Everyman's Library.

B., W. 1908. *Women as Investors*. Birmingham: Cornish Bros.

Beeton, Samuel Orchart. 1870. *Beeton's Guide to the Stock Exchange and Money Market*. London: Ward, Lock, and Tyler.

Bernstein, Peter L. 1996. *Against the Gods: The Remarkable Story of Risk*. New York: John Wiley & Sons Inc.

Capie, Forrest and Douglas Wood. 1974. "Money in the Economy, 1870–1939," in *The Economic History of Britain since 1700*. R. Floud and D. McCloskey eds. Cambridge: Cambridge University Press.

Chadwicks' Investment Circular, issued monthly by Chadwicks, Collier & Co., etc., London 1870–1975.

Chapman, Stanley J. 1908. "Investment Risks and the Geographical Distribution of Capital." *Financial Review of Reviews*, No. 37 (November): 26–33.

Cotton, William. 1898. *Everybody's Guide to Money Matters*. London: Fredrick Warne & Co.

Crozier, J. Beattie. 1911. *The First Principles of Investment*. London: The Financial Review of Reviews.

Davis, Lance E. and Robert A. Huttenback. 1987. *Mammon and the Pursuit of Empire: The Political Economy of British Imperialism, 1860–1912*. Cambridge: Cambridge University Press.

De Foville, Alfred. 1908. "Geographical Distribution and French Investment Success." *Financial Review of Reviews*, No. 27 (January): 20–24.

Edelstein, Michael. 1982. *Overseas Investment in the Age of High Imperialism: The United Kingdom, 1850–1914*. London: Methuen & Co. Ltd.

Graham, Benjamin and David L. Dodd. 1934. *Security Analysis*. New York: McGraw-Hill Book Company, Inc.

Harley, C.K. 1976. "Goschen's Conversion of the National Debt and the Yield on Consols." *Economic History Review*, Vol. 39, Second Series: 101–6.

Investment Critic. 1908. "Factors Determining the Value of Corporation Stocks."
    Financial Review of Reviews, No. 36 (October): 25–32.

Jefferys, J.B. 1938. "Trends in Business Organisation in Great Britain since 1856,
    with special reference to the financial structure of companies, the mechanism of
    investment and the relationship between the shareholder and the company."
    Ph. D. Thesis, University of London.

Jenks, Leland H. 1963. *The Migration of British Capital to 1875*. London: Thomas
    Nelson and Sons Ltd.

Lowenfeld, Henry. 1911. "The Rudiments of Sound Investment." *Financial Review
    of Reviews*, No. 63 (January): 5–17.

Markowitz, Harry. 1952. "Portfolio Selection." *Journal of Finance*, Vol. 7, No. 1
    (March): 77–91.

May, George E. 1912. "The investment of life assurance funds." *Journal of the Insti-
    tute of Actuaries*, Vol. 46:134–68.

McKendrick, Neil and John Newlands. 1999. *'F&C': A History of Foreign & Colo-
    nial Investment Trust*. London: Foreign & Colonial Investment Trust PLC.

Michie, Ranald C. 1986. "The London and New York Stock Exchanges, 1850–1914."
    The Journal of Economic History, Vol. 46, No.1: 71–87.

Midleton, Hon. Viscount. 1908. "British Life Assurance and American Models."
    Financial Review of Reviews, No. 35 (September): 5–12.

Pollard, Sidney. 1985. "Capital Exports, 1870–1914: Harmful or Beneficial." *The
    Economic History Review*, Second Series, Vol. 38, No. 4: 489–514.

Rolleston, Sir John F.L. 1909. "Scientific Investment in Daily Practice." *Financial
    Review of Reviews*, No. 40 (February): 36–51.

Rose, Mary B. 1979. "Diversification of Investment by the Greg Family, 1800–1914."
    Business History, Vol. 21, No.1: 79–95.

Rutterford, Janette. 2004. "From Dividend Yield to Discounted Cash Flow: A History
    of US and UK Equity Valuation Techniques." *Accounting, Business and Finan-
    cial History*, Vol. 14, No. 2: 115–49.

Stacey, H. 1923. *Stacey's Guide to Stock Exchange Investment*, London: The Basing
    Syndicate.

Statman, Meir. 2004. "The Diversification Puzzle." *Financial Analysts Journal*, Vol.
    60, No. 4 (July/August): 44–53.

Treble, J.H. 1980. "The Pattern of Investment of the Standard Life Assurance
    Company 1875–1914." *Business History*, Vol. 22, No. 2: 170–88.

Withers, Hartley. 1908. "The Best Market for Capital." *Financial Review of Reviews*,
    No. 36 (October): 33–41.

CASE STUDY 1

Global Evidence on the Equity Risk Premium

Elroy Dimson, Paul Marsh and Mike Staunton

Today, investors have more cause than ever to ask what returns they can expect from equities, and what the future risk-reward tradeoff is likely to be. Corporate managers, too, need to know what returns their shareholders require for projects of differing risk. And regulators have to know the cost of equity capital in order to set "fair" rates of return for regulated industries. In fact, the magnitude of the equity risk premium – the incremental return that shareholders require to hold risky equities rather than risk-free securities – is one of the most important issues in corporate finance. It drives future equity returns and is a key determinant of the cost of capital.

This article sheds light on the equity risk premium by addressing two fundamental questions: How big has the equity risk premium been historically? And what can we expect for the future? To answer these questions, we need to look at long periods of capital market history, and to extend our horizons beyond just the United States. We start by examining equity returns in 16 different countries over the 103-year period from 1900 to 2002.

THE NEED FOR A LONG-RUN PERSPECTIVE

The dangers of focusing just on recent stock market history are easily demonstrated. Over the last decade of the 20th century, U.S. equity investors achieved a total return (capital gain plus reinvested dividends) of 17.6% per annum, thus increasing their initial stake by a factor of five. During the last five years of the 1990s, U.S. equities achieved high returns every year, ranging from 21% in 1996 to as much as 36% in 1995. Investors became convinced that high corporate growth rates could be extrapolated into the foreseeable future. In fact, surveys suggested that many investors expected long-run stock market returns to continue at double-digit percentage rates indefinitely. With strong growth rates, equity risk appeared lower. As a result, the premium sought by investors to compensate for exposure to equity market risk seemed to decline. This drove stock prices further onward and upward.

Then the technology bubble burst. Because growth projections had proved unrealistic, high growth was perceived to be associated with high risk. Investors demanded a larger reward for equity market risk exposure. Stock prices fell for three successive years from 2000–2002. With markets falling, investors started to project lower returns for the future. Yet it is wrong to overreact to recent stock market performance in projecting future required returns. Just because equities had delivered poor returns since 2000 did not mean that there had been a substantial change in the long-term expected equity premium.

Figure C1.1 compares U.S. real equity returns to those in 15 other countries and a world index. The figure shows annualized real equity returns over 2000–2002, and in all 16 countries, equities suffered negative returns. In contrast, government securities (not shown in Figure C1.1) generally performed well, so that equities markedly underperformed both bonds and bills in all 16 countries over 2000–2002. Estimating the expected risk premium from the performance of equities relative to bills or bonds over this period would clearly be nonsense. Investors cannot have required or expected a negative return for assuming risk. Instead, this was simply a very disappointing period for equities. Yet it would be equally misleading to estimate future risk premiums from data for 1990–1999. Figure C1.1 shows that over this period, equity returns (except in Japan and South Africa) were quite high. The 1990s represented a golden age for stocks, and golden ages, by definition, recur only infrequently.

To understand the risk premium – which is the principal objective of this article – we need to examine periods that are much longer than a few years or even a decade. Stock markets are volatile, with significant variation in year-to-year returns. In order to make inferences, we need a long time series that incorporates bad times as well as good. Figure C1.1 shows real equity returns over the 103-year period 1900–2002 (and which we describe in more detail later); these data provide insight into the perspective that longer

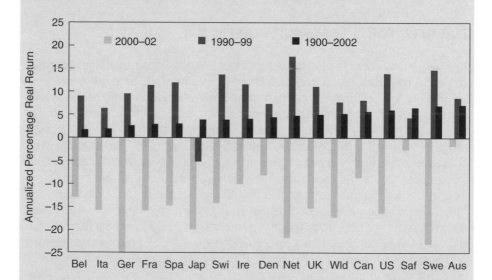

Figure C1.1 Short-term and long-run real returns on equities around the world

The country names listed in abbreviated form along the horizontal axis are (from left to right) Belgium, Italy, Germany, France, Spain, Japan, Switzerland, Ireland, Denmark, The Netherlands, The United Kingdom, the world (the weighted average of the 16 individual countries), Canada, The United States, South Africa, Sweden, and Australia.

Source: E. Dimson, P. Marsh, and M. Staunton, *Triumph of the Optimists: 101 Years of Global Investment Returns* (New Jersey: Princeton University Press, 2002) and *Global Investment Returns Yearbook* (ABN AMRO/London Business School, 2003).

periods of history can bring. Clearly, these 103-year returns are much lower than the returns during the 1990s, but they also contrast favorably with the disappointing returns over 2000–2002.

PRIOR ESTIMATES OF THE RISK PREMIUM

To be fair, financial economists generally measure the equity premium over quite long periods. Standard practice, however, draws heavily on the United States, with most textbooks citing only the U.S. experience. By far the most widely cited U.S. source prior to the end of the technology bubble was Ibbotson Associates,[1] whose equity premium history started in 1926. For the period 1926–1999, they estimated an annualized return on equities of 11.3%, and a risk-free return of 3.8%. This implies a geometric premium relative to bills of 7.3% (1.113/1.038 = 1.073). References to other countries are few and far between, although some textbooks also cite U.K. evidence. Before the publication of our research, the most widely cited sources for the United Kingdom were studies published by Barclays Capital and Credit Suisse First Boston (CSFB)[2] which estimated annualized equity and risk-free returns from start-1919 to start-1999 of 12.2% and 5.5%, respectively, implying a geometric risk premium relative to bills of 6.4%.

In citing these estimates, financial economists are generally making the implicit assumption that the historical risk premium, measured over many decades, offers an unbiased estimate of the future premium, provided the data are of sufficient quality. Yet the 20th century proved to be a period of remarkable growth in U.S. economy, probably exceeding the expectations held in 1926 by U.S. investors. Similar arguments apply to the United Kingdom and the likely expectations of U.K. investors in 1919.

In recent years, practitioners and researchers alike have become increasingly suspicious that these widely cited estimates are too high. Apart from biases in index construction, the finger of suspicion has pointed mainly at success and survivorship bias.[3] One influential study asserted "the high equity premium obtained for U.S. [and, by implication, U.K.] equities appears to be the exception rather than the rule."[4] Recently, well-known finance scholar Zvi Bodie argued that high U.S. and U.K. premiums are likely to be anomalous, and underlined the need for comparative international evidence. He pointed out that long-run studies are always of U.S. or U.K. premiums: "There were 36 active stock markets in 1900, so why do we only look at two? I can tell you – because many of the others don't have a 100-year history, for a variety of reasons."[5]

What Do the Experts Say?

The question of the equity premium has thus been a source of controversy even among the "experts." In late 1998, Ivo Welch studied the opinions of 226 financial economists who were asked to forecast the average annual risk premium over the next 30 years.[6] Their mean forecast was 7.1%; the median was 7.0%; and the range ran from 1% to 15%. Interestingly, the spread in their distribution of forecasts indicated that the uncertainty among financial experts about the risk premium was as great as the uncertainty that arises from standard statistical analysis of historical returns.

Most respondents to the Welch survey would have regarded the Ibbotson Associates Yearbook as the definitive study of the historical U.S. risk premium. At that time, the most recent Yearbook was the 1998 edition, covering the period 1926–1997. The first bar of Figure C1.2 shows that the arithmetic mean risk premium based on the Ibbotson Yearbook data was 8.9% per year.[7] The second bar shows that the key finance textbooks were on average suggesting a premium of 8.5%, a little below the Ibbotson mean. The textbook authors may have based their views on earlier, slightly lower, Ibbotson estimates, or perhaps they were simply shading the Ibbotson estimates downward. The Welch survey mean is in turn lower than the textbook figures, but since the respondents claimed to lower their forecasts when the equity market rises, this difference may be attributable to the market's strong performance in the 1990s.

The survey and textbook figures represent what was being taught at the end of the 1990s in the world's leading business schools and economics departments in the United States and around the world. As such, these estimates were widely used by investors, finance professionals, corporate executives, regulators, lawyers, and consultants. Their influence extended from the classroom to the deal room, to the boardroom, and to the courtroom.

By 2001, however, longer-term estimates of the U.S. arithmetic mean equity premium were gaining publicity. Our own estimate[8] of a 7.7% mean premium over the longer period from 1900–2000 was 1.2% lower than the Ibbotson estimate of 8.9% for 1926–1997. In August 2001, Welch updated his earlier survey, receiving responses from 510 finance and economics professors.[9] He found that the respondents to the follow-up questionnaire had revised their estimates downward by an average of 1.6%. They now estimated an equity premium averaging 5.5% over a 30-year horizon, and 3.4% over a one-year horizon (see Figure C1.2). Those who had participated in the earlier survey and those who were taking part for the first time estimated the same mean premiums. Although respondents to the earlier survey had indicated that, on average, a bear market would raise their equity premium forecast, Welch reports that "this is in contrast with the observed findings: it appears as if the recent bear market correlates with lower equity premium forecasts, not higher equity premium forecasts."

Still, predictions of the long-term equity premium should not be so sensitive to short-term stock market fluctuations. The changing consensus might reflect new approaches to estimating the premium or new facts about long-term stock market performance, such as evidence that other countries have typically had historical premiums that were lower than in the United States.

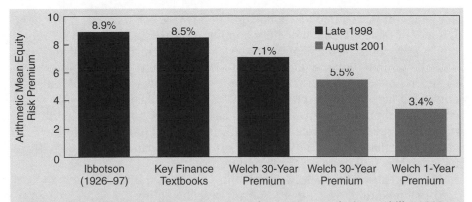

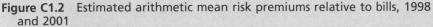

Figure C1.2 Estimated arithmetic mean risk premiums relative to bills, 1998 and 2001

NEW EVIDENCE

The wide dispersion of estimates, together with the dramatic decline in the "expert" consensus premium between 1998 and 2001, reinforces the need to better understand the historical record. Our research helps fill the gap by providing a 103-year history of risk premiums for markets in 16 countries. The evidence on long-run risk premiums presented in this article is derived from a unique new database comprising annual returns on stocks, bonds, bills, inflation, and currencies for 16 countries over the period 1900–2002. The countries include the United States and Canada, the United Kingdom, seven markets from what is now the Euro currency area, three other European markets, two Asia-Pacific markets, and one African market. Together, these countries made up 94% of the free float market capitalization of all world equities at the beginning of 2003, and we estimate that they constituted over 90% by value at the start of our period in 1900.[10]

To compile this database, we assembled the best quality indexes and returns data available for each national market from previous studies and other sources.[11] Many early equity indexes measure just capital gains and ignore dividends, thereby introducing a serious downward bias. Similarly, many early bond indexes record just yields, ignoring price movements. Unlike most previous long-term studies of global markets, however, our investment returns include reinvested gross income as well as capital gains. Our database is thus more comprehensive and accurate than previous research and spans a longer period.[12] Furthermore, we can now set the U.S. risk premium data alongside comparable 103-year risk premiums for 15 other countries, and make international comparisons that help put the U.S. experience in perspective.

Table C1.1 shows the historical equity risk premiums for the 16 countries over the 103-year period 1900–2002. We also display equity premiums for our world equity index, which is a 16-country, common-currency (here taken as U.S. dollars) equity index with each country weighted by its beginning-of-period market capitalization or (in earlier years) its GDP.[13] The left half of Table C1.1 shows equity premiums measured relative to the return on Treasury bills or the nearest equivalent short-term instrument; the right half shows premiums calculated using the same equity returns, but relative to the return on long-term government bonds. Since the world index is computed here from the perspective of a U.S. (dollar) investor, the world equity risk premium relative to bills is calculated with reference to the U.S. risk-free (Treasury bill) rate. The world equity premium relative to bonds is calculated relative to a GDP-weighted, 16-country, common-currency (here taken as U.S. dollars) world bond index.

In each half of the table we show three measures. These are the annualized risk premium, or geometric mean, over the entire 103 years; the arithmetic mean of the 103 one-year premiums; and the standard deviation of the 103 one-year premiums. While the United States and the United Kingdom

Table C1.1 Equity risk premiums* around the world 1900–2002

	Equity Risk Premiums (Percent per Year)					
	Relative to Bills			Relative to Bonds		
	Geometric Mean	Arithmetic Mean	SD	Geometric Mean	Arithmetic Mean	SD
Australia	6.8	8.3	17.2	6.0	7.6	19.0
Belgium	2.2	4.4	23.1	2.1	3.9	20.2
Canada	4.2	5.5	16.8	4.0	5.5	18.2
Denmark	2.2	3.8	19.6	1.5	2.7	16.0
France	6.4	8.9	24.0	3.6	5.8	22.1
Germany	3.9	9.4	35.5	5.7	9.0	28.8
Ireland	3.6	5.5	20.4	3.2	4.8	18.5
Italy	6.3	10.3	32.5	4.1	7.6	30.2
Japan	6.1	9.3	28.0	5.4	9.5	33.3
The Netherlands	4.3	6.4	22.6	3.8	5.9	21.9
South Africa	5.9	7.9	22.2	5.2	6.8	19.4
Spain	2.8	4.9	21.5	1.9	3.8	20.3
Sweden	5.2	7.5	22.2	4.8	7.2	22.5
Switzerland	3.2	4.8	18.8	1.4	2.9	17.5
United Kingdom	4.2	5.9	20.1	3.8	5.1	17.0
United States	5.3	7.2	19.8	4.4	6.4	20.3
Average	4.5	6.9	22.8	3.8	5.9	21.6
World	4.4	5.7	16.5	3.8	4.9	15.0

* The equity risk premium is measured here as 1 + equity rate of return divided by 1 + risk-free return, minus 1. The statistics reported in this table are based on 103 annual observations for each country, except Germany which excludes 1922–23, when bill and bondholders experienced returns of –100% due to hyperinflation. The row labeled "Average" is a simple, unweighted average of the statistics for the 16 individual countries. The row marked "World" is for the World index (see text). *Source:* E. Dimson, P. Marsh, and M. Staunton, *Triumph of the Optimists: 101 Years of Global Investment Returns* (New Jersey: Princeton University Press, 2002), and *Global Investment Returns Yearbook* (ABN AMRO/London Business School, 2003)

have indeed performed well, there is no indication that they are hugely out of line compared to other markets.

Over the entire 103-year period, the annualized (geometric) equity risk premium, relative to bills, was 5.3% for the United States and 4.2% for the United Kingdom. Averaged across all 16 countries, the risk premium relative to bills was 4.5%, while the risk premium on the world equity index was 4.4%. Relative to long bonds, the story is similar. The annualized U.S. equity risk premium relative to bonds was 4.4%, and the corresponding figure for the United Kingdom was 3.8%. Across all 16 countries, the risk premium relative to bonds averaged 3.8%, and for the world index it was also 3.8%.[14]

The annualized equity risk premiums are plotted in Figure C1.3. In this figure, countries are ranked by the equity premium relative to bonds, displayed as bars. The line-plot presents each country's risk premium relative to bills. It can be seen that the United States does indeed have a historical risk premium above the world average, but it is by no means the country with the largest recorded premium. The equity premium for the United Kingdom is closer to the worldwide average. While U.S. and U.K. equities have performed well, both countries are toward the middle of the distribution of worldwide equity premiums.

Commentators have suggested that survivor bias may have led to unrepresentative equity premiums for the United States and the United Kingdom. While legitimate, these concerns are somewhat overstated. Rather, the critical factors are the period over which the risk premium is estimated, together with the quality of the index series. Investors have therefore probably not been greatly misled by a focus on the U.S. and U.K. experiences.

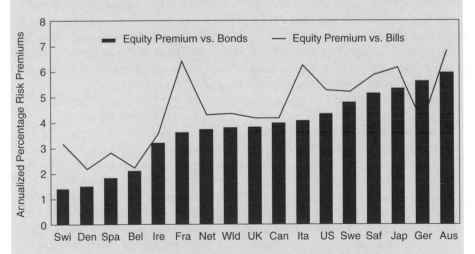

Figure C1.3 Worldwide annualized equity risk premiums 1900–2002 Germany excludes 1922–23.
Source: Dimson, Marsh, and Staunton, *Triumph of the Optimists: 101 Years of Global Investment Returns* (Princeton University Press, 2002) and *Global Investment Returns Yearbook* (ABN AMRO/London Business School, 2003).

The 103-year historical estimates of equity premiums reported here are lower than was previously thought and other studies suggest. Nonetheless, the historical record may still overstate expectations. First, even if we have been successful in avoiding survivor bias within each index, we still focus on *markets* that survived, omitting countries such as Poland, Russia, or China whose compound rate of return was −100%. Although these markets were relatively small in 1900,[15] their omission probably leads to an overestimate of the worldwide risk premium.[16] Second, our premiums are measured relative to bills and bonds, which in a number of countries yielded markedly negative real returns. Since these "risk-free" returns likely fell below investor expectations, the corresponding equity premiums are probably overstated.[17]

Although there is certainly room for debate, we do not consider market survivorship to be the most important source of bias when inferring expected premiums from the historical record. There are cogent reasons for suggesting that investors expected a lower premium than they actually received. However, this has more to do with a failure to fully anticipate improvements in business and investment conditions during the second half of the last century, an issue that we will return to later.

VARIATION IN RISK PREMIUMS OVER TIME

The historical equity premiums shown in Figure C1.3 are the annualized or geometric means of 103 separate one-year premiums that vary a great deal. The bars in Figure C1.4 show the year-by-year premiums on U.S. equities relative to bills.[18] The lowest was −45% in 1931, when equities earned −44% and Treasury bills 1.1%; the highest was 57% in 1933, when equities earned 57.6% and bills 0.3%. Over the 103-year period spanned by Figure C1.4, the mean annual excess return was 7.2%, while the standard deviation was 19.8% (see Table C1.1). On average, therefore, U.S. investors received a positive, and quite large, reward for exposure to equity market risk.

Because the range of excess returns encountered on a year-to-year basis is very broad, however, it can be misleading to label them "risk premiums." As already noted, investors cannot have expected, let alone required, a negative risk premium from investing in equities, otherwise they would simply have avoided them. All of the negative and many of the very low premiums plotted in Figure C1.4 must therefore reflect unpleasant surprises. Nor could investors have required premiums as high as the 57% achieved in 1933. Such numbers are implausible as a required reward for risk, and the high realizations must therefore reflect *pleasant* surprises. As a result, many writers choose not to refer to historical excess returns as "risk premiums." To avoid confusion, we refer to the *expected* or "prospective" risk premium when we are looking to the future. When we measure the excess return over a period in the past, we generally refer to it as the "historical" risk premium.

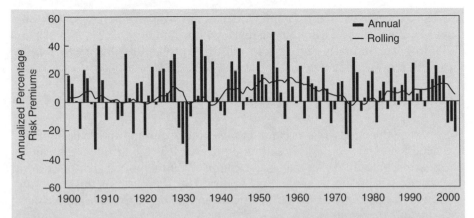

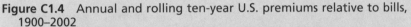

Figure C1.4 Annual and rolling ten-year U.S. premiums relative to bills, 1900–2002

Source: E. Dimson, P. Marsh, and M. Staunton, *Triumph of the Optimists: 101 Years of Global Investment Returns* (New Jersey: Princeton University Press, 2002) and *Global Investment Returns Yearbook* (ABN AMRO/London Business School, 2003).

Because one-year excess returns are so variable, we need to examine longer periods in the hope that good and bad luck might cancel out. A common choice of time frame is a decade. Figure C1.4 therefore also shows the U.S. equity risk premium measured over a sequence of rolling ten-year periods, superimposed on the annual returns since 1900. This line-plot shows that there is clearly less volatility in the ten-year measures.

Even over ten-year periods, however, historical excess returns were sometimes negative, most recently in the 1970s and early 1980s. Figure C1.4 also reveals several cases of double-digit ten-year premiums. Clearly, a decade is still too short a period for good and bad luck to cancel out, or for drawing inferences about investor expectations. Indeed, even with a full century of data, market fluctuations have an impact. Taking the United Kingdom as an illustration, we find that the arithmetic mean annual excess return for the first half of the 20th century was only 3.1%, compared to 8.6% from 1950 to date. As over a single year, all we are reporting is the excess return that was realized over a period in the past.

Imprecise Estimates

We have seen that very long series of stock market data are needed for estimating risk premiums. But even with 103 years of data, the potential inaccuracy in historical risk premiums is still fairly high. The standard error is a measure of this inaccuracy. It equals approximately one-tenth of the annual standard deviation of returns reported in Table C1.1. The standard error for the United States is 1.9%, and the range runs from 1.7% (Australia and Canada) to 3.5% (Germany). This means that while the U.S. arithmetic mean premium (relative to bills) has a best estimate of 7.2% (from Table C1.1), we can be only two-thirds confident that the true mean lies within one standard error of this estimate, namely within the range 7.2% ± 1.9%, or 5.3% to 9.1%. Similarly, there is a 19-out-of-20 probability that the true mean lies within two standard errors – that is, 7.2% ± 3.8%, or 3.4% to 11.0%.

FROM THE PAST TO THE FUTURE

To estimate the equity risk premium to use in discounting future cash flows, we need the expected *future* risk premium, which is the arithmetic mean of the possible premiums that may occur. Suppose future returns are drawn from the same distribution as those that occurred in the past. In this case, the expected risk premium is the arithmetic mean (or simple average) of the one-year historical premiums.

In Figure C1.5, the gray bars show the historical arithmetic mean premium relative to bills for each country. The U.S. equity premium is 7.2%, while the world equity risk premium is 5.7%. The arithmetic mean premiums are noticeably higher than the geometric mean premiums (shown by the grey bars) because whenever there is any variability in annual premiums, the arithmetic mean will exceed the geometric mean (or annualized) risk premium.[19] The difference is largest (in both absolute terms and relative to the geometric mean) for the countries that experienced the greatest volatility of returns over the last century (see Table C1.1).

When returns are lognormally distributed, the arithmetic mean return will exceed the geometric mean return by half the variance. The historical arithmetic means plotted in Figure C1.5 are obviously affected by the historical variances. The latter, however, can be poor predictors of future volatility. This will be especially true for countries with very high levels of historical volatility, where some sources of extreme volatility (such as those arising from

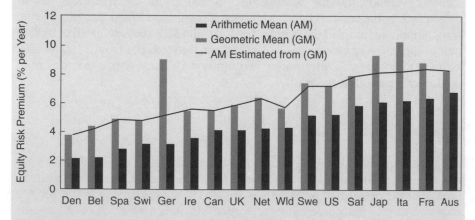

Figure C1.5   Adjustments to historical arithmetic mean equity risk premiums relative to bills, 1900–2002

Source: E. Dimson, P. Marsh, and M. Staunton, *Triumph of the Optimists: 101 Years of Global Investment Returns* (New Jersey: Princeton University Press, 2002) and *Global Investment Returns Yearbook* (ABN AMRO/London Business School, 2003).

hyperinflation and the world wars) are unlikely to recur. We therefore need estimates of expected future risk premiums that are conditional on current predictions of market volatility.

In looking to the future, let us assume for the moment that investors in each country expect the same annualized (geometric mean) risk premium that they have received in the past. We can then estimate the expected future arithmetic mean premium for each country by replacing the historical difference between the geometric and arithmetic means with a difference based on a contemporary, rather than the historical, risk estimate.

Historically, the U.S. and U.K. markets both had volatility levels of 20%. If we take this figure as our contemporary risk estimate, and assume that all countries with historical volatilities in excess of this will have a future volatility of 20%, we can then estimate the expected future arithmetic mean premium for each country. The resulting estimates are shown by the line-plot in Figure C1.5. Note that we have left the historical estimates unchanged for countries with historical volatilities of 20% or below.

For those wishing to forecast future arithmetic mean risk premiums by extrapolating from the long-run historical annualized premiums, the adjusted premiums shown by the line-plot in Figure C1.5 are superior to the raw historical arithmetic means. Using historical volatility estimates, the figures for the United States and the world index remain unchanged at 7.2% and 5.7%, respectively. However, Figure C1.5 shows that the downward adjustments needed for several other countries, such as Japan, Italy, France, and especially Germany, are quite large.

REVISITING HISTORY

But since history may have turned out to be unexpectedly kind to (or harsh on) stock market investors, there are cogent arguments for going beyond raw historical estimates. First, the whole idea of using the achieved risk premium to forecast the future required risk premium depends on having a long enough period to iron out good and bad luck – yet as we noted earlier, our estimates are imprecise even with 103 years of data. Second, the expected equity risk premium could for good reasons vary over time. Third, we must take account of the fact that stock market outcomes are influenced by many factors, some of which (like removal of trade and investment barriers) may be nonrecurring, which implies projections for the future premium that differ from the past.

A comparison of equity returns between the first and second halves of our 103-year period makes the point. Over the first half of the 20th century, the arithmetic average annual real return on the world equity index was 5.1%, whereas over the period 1950–2002 it was 8.4%. Fourteen of the 16 countries had lower mean premiums in the first half-century,[20] with Australia and South Africa being the only exceptions. The 16-country (unweighted) mean annual real return on equities in the first half of the 20th century was 5.1%, versus 9.0% over the next 53 years.

The larger equity returns earned during the second half of the 20th century are attributable to at least four factors. First, there was rapid technological change, unprecedented growth in productivity and efficiency, and enhancements to the quality of management and corporate governance. As Europe, North America, and the Asia-Pacific region emerged from the turmoil of World War II, expectations for improvement were limited to what could be imagined. Reality almost certainly exceeded investor expectations. Corporate cash flows grew faster than investors anticipated, and this higher growth is now known to the market and reflected in higher stock prices. Second, transaction and monitoring costs fell over the course of the century, and this underpinned rising stock prices.[21] Third, in the last two decades of the century, inflation rates generally declined and real interest rates rose, and this had a further impact on the stock market.

Finally, stock prices have also risen because of a fall in the required rate of return due to diminished business and investment risk. Business risk declined as the economic and political lessons of the 20th century were absorbed, international trade flows increased, and the Cold War ended. Investment risk diminished over time as investors gained the benefits of diversification, both domestically (through a wider range of quoted securities and industries, and through intermediaries such as mutual funds[22]) and internationally (with the disappearance of impediments to foreign investment). Diversification allows investors to lower their risk exposure without detriment to expected returns. Factors such as these, which led to a reduction in the required risk premium, have contributed further to the upward re-rating of stock prices.

To convert a pure historical estimate of the risk premium into a forward-looking projection, we would like to reverse-engineer the factors that drove up stock markets over the last 103 years. In principle, we need to identify the influence of factors such as those described above – cash flow improvements, cost reductions, interest rate shocks, and improved diversification opportunities. To illustrate the latter, consider the dramatic change since 1900 in the valuation basis for equity markets. The price/dividend ratio (the reciprocal of the dividend yield) at the start of 1900 was 23 in both the United States and the United Kingdom; but by the start of 2002, the U.S. ratio had risen to 64 and the U.K. ratio to 32. Undoubtedly, this change is in part a reflection of expected future growth in earnings and thus real dividends, so we could in principle decompose the impact of this valuation change into two elements: one that reflects changes in required rates of return and one that reflects enhanced growth expectations.

To keep things simple, assume that the increase in the price/dividend ratio is attributable solely to a long-term fall in the required risk premium for equity investment.[23] Given this assumption, the stock price impact of the re-rating since 1900 is estimated to be 1.0% per year in the United States and 0.3% per year in the United Kingdom. For the world portfolio, based on all 16 countries, the impact of the re-rating of equities is 0.8%. To estimate expected risk premiums, we deduct from our historical premiums the estimated impact of the re-rating of equities. For the U.S., U.K., and world, this adjustment gives rise to estimated risk premiums of 4.3%, 3.9%, and 3.5% respectively. On a forward-looking basis, these expected geometric risk premiums are similar to the estimates obtained recently by Eugene Fama and Kenneth French using a related approach.[24]

EXPECTED RISK PREMIUMS

If they are to be used as prospective risk premiums, however, our annualized figures need to be converted into arithmetic means. Using a projected standard deviation for U.S. and U.K. equities equal to their historical standard deviation of 20%, the prospective arithmetic risk premium for the United States is 6.3% (i.e., 4.3 + 2.0%),[25] while the premium for the United Kingdom is 5.9% (i.e., 3.9 + 2.0%). Using a slightly lower standard deviation for the world index of 16%, again in line with the historical experience, the prospective arithmetic risk premium for the world index is 4.8% (i.e., 3.5 + 1.3%). If stock market volatility in the future is expected to be lower than in the past, then the risk premium estimates would be lower than those presented above. But even without any further downward adjustment, our forward-looking predictions for the equity risk premium are lower than the historically based projections reviewed earlier, whichever country one focuses on.

Further adjustments should almost certainly be made to historical risk premiums to reflect long-term changes in capital market conditions. Since, in most countries, corporate cash flows historically exceeded investor expectations, a further downward adjustment to the equity risk premium is in order. A plausible, forward-looking risk premium for the world's major markets would probably be on the order of 3% on a geometric mean basis, while the corresponding arithmetic mean risk premium would be around 5%.[26]

A literal interpretation of country-by-country historical averages might suggest that France has a higher equity risk premium, while Denmark's is lower. But while there are certainly differences in risk between markets, they are unlikely to account for cross-sectional differences in historical premiums. Indeed, much of the cross-country variation in historical equity premiums is attributable to country-specific historical events that are unlikely to recur. When making future projections, there is a strong case, particularly given the increasingly integrated nature of international capital markets, for taking a global rather than a country-by-country approach to determining the prospective equity risk premium.

However, just as there must be some true differences across countries in their riskiness, there must also be variation over time in levels of stock market risk. It is well known that stock market volatility wanders over time, and it is likely that the "price" of risk – namely the risk premium – also fluctuates over time. In the days following September 11, 2001, for example, financial market risk was high, and the equity premium demanded by investors was probably also high. This depressed the market. If the terror had escalated, the market may have collapsed; but Armageddon did not arrive and the market recovered. Clearly, risk premiums at such times are above average. However, it is difficult to infer changes in expected premiums from any analysis of historical excess returns. For corporate capital budgeting purposes, it may be better to use a "normal" equity premium most of the time, and to deviate from this predication only when there are compelling economic reasons to suppose that expected premiums are unusually high or low.

CONCLUSION

The equity risk premium is the difference between the return on risky stocks and the return on safe bonds or bills; it is central to corporate finance and investment, and it is often described as the most important number in finance. Yet it is not clear how big the equity premium has been in the past or how large it is today.

This article presents new evidence on the historical risk premium for 16 countries over 103 years. Our estimates are lower than frequently quoted historical averages such as the Ibbotson Associates Yearbook figures for the United States, and the earlier Barclays Capital and CSFB studies for the United Kingdom.[27] The differences arise from bias in previous index construction for the United Kingdom and, for both countries, from our use of a longer time frame (1900–2002) that incorporates the earlier part of the 20th century as well as the opening years of the new millennium. Our global focus also results in rather lower risk premiums than hitherto assumed. Prior views have been heavily influenced by the experience of the United States, yet we find that the U.S. risk premium is somewhat higher than the average for the other 15 countries.

The historical equity premium is often presented as an annualized geometric mean rate of return, which summarizes past performance in one number. Looking ahead, for capital budgeting purposes, what is required is the arithmetic mean of the distribution of possible equity premiums. The arithmetic mean of past equity premiums may exceed the geometric mean premium by several percentage points due to market volatility. In forecasting the future arithmetic mean premium, then, investors or corporate managers who believe they can expect the same annualized risk premium that they have observed in the past still need to adjust for differences in volatility. And, for many countries, the volatility that we might anticipate today is probably very different from historical market volatility.

More fundamentally, however, we have argued that past returns have been advantaged by a re-rating due to a general decline in the risk faced by investors as the scope for diversification has increased. We have illustrated one approach that can be used to obtain an estimate of the amount by which the required rate of return has fallen. In addition, we have argued that past returns have also been inflated by the impact of good luck. Since the middle of the last century, equity cash flows have almost certainly exceeded expectations. Stock markets have therefore risen for reasons that are unlikely to be repeated. This means that when developing forecasts for the future, investors and managers should adjust historical risk premiums downward for the impact of these factors.

A plausible, forward-looking risk premium for the world's major markets would be on the order of 3% on a geometric mean basis, while the corresponding arithmetic mean risk premium would be around 5%. These estimates are lower than the historical premiums quoted in most textbooks or cited in surveys of finance academics. Nonetheless, they represent our best estimate of the equity risk premium for corporate capital budgeting and valuation applications.

NOTES

This paper draws on, extends, and updates the research that underpinned our recent book, *Triumph of the Optimists: 101 Years of Global Investment Returns* (New Jersey: Princeton University Press, 2002). We are very grateful to ABN AMRO for their extensive support and to our many international data contributors – too numerous to mention here, but all of whom are listed and cited in our book. We also benefited from the many helpful comments received from participants at numerous academic and practitioner seminars held around the world.

1. See Ibbotson Associates, *Stocks, Bonds, Bills and Inflation Yearbook* (Chicago: Ibbotson Associates, 2000).
2. Barclays Capital, *Equity-Gilt Study* (1999); and Credit Suisse First Boston, *The CSFB Equity-Gilt Study* (1999).
3. The U.K. evidence turned out to be based on a retrospectively constructed index whose composition up to 1955, was tainted by survivor bias and narrow coverage.
4. P. Jorion and W. Goetzmann, "Global Stock Markets in the Twentieth Century," *Journal of Finance*, Vol. 54 (1999), pp. 953–980.
5. Z. Bodie, "Longer Time Horizon 'Does Not Reduce Risk,'" *Financial Times*, January 26, 2002.
6. I. Welch, "Views of Financial Economists on the Equity Premium and Other Issues," *Journal of Business*, Vol. 73 (2000), pp. 501–537.
7. This figure is the arithmetic mean of the one-year geometric risk premiums. The arithmetic mean of the one-year arithmetic risk premiums, i.e., the average annual difference between the equity return and the Treasury bill return was slightly higher at 9.1%.
8. E. Dimson, P. Marsh, and M. Staunton, *Millennium Book II: 101 Years of Global Investment Returns* (ABN AMRO/London Business School, 2001).
9. I. Welch, "The Equity Premium Consensus Forecast Revisited," Working paper, Yale School of Management, September 2001.
10. The Dimson-Marsh-Staunton Global Returns data module is available from Ibbotson Associates, Chicago, IL.
11. Details of our data sources for all 16 countries together with full citations are provided in E. Dimson, P. March, and M. Staunton, *Triumph of the Optimists:*

101 Years of Global Investment Returns (New Jersey: Princeton University Press, 2002) and *Global Investment Returns Yearbook* (ABN AMRO/London Business School, 2003). Where possible, we used data from peer-reviewed academic papers, although some studies were previously unpublished. To span the full period from 1900 onward, we typically linked more than one index series. For the United Kingdom, we constructed our own indexes, since hitherto there was no satisfactory record of long-run returns. For the period since 1955, we used the London Business School Share Price Database to construct an index covering the entire U.K. equity market (see E. Dimson and P. Marsh, "U.K. Financial Market Returns 1955–2000," *Journal of Business*, Vol. 74, pp. 1–31). From 1900–1955, we constructed an index of the performance of the largest 100 companies by a process of painstaking financial archaeology, collecting data from archives in the City of London. We also used archive data to construct indexes for several other countries (such as Canada, Ireland, South Africa, and Switzerland) for periods for which no data were previously available.

12. Interestingly; after publication of our research, Barclays Capital (but not CSFB) corrected their pre-1955 estimates of U.K. equity returns for bias and extended their index series back to 1900.

13. We use market capitalization weights from 1968 onward and GDP (gross domestic product) weights before then due to the lack of reliable comprehensive data on country capitalizations prior to that date.

14. Table C1.1 shows that the annualized world equity risk premium relative to bills was 4.4%, compared with 5.3% for the United States. Part of this difference, however, reflects the strength of the dollar over the period 1900–2002. The world risk premium is computed here from the world equity index expressed in dollars, in order to reflect the perspective of a U.S.-based global investor. Since the currencies of most other countries depreciated against the dollar over the 20th century, this lowers our estimate of the world equity risk premium relative to the (weighted) average of the local-currency-based estimates for individual countries.

15. See R. Rajan and L. Zingales, "The Great Reversals: The Politics of Financial Development in the 20th Century," Working paper No. 8178. (Cambridge MA: National Bureau of Economic Research, 2001), and our book, cited earlier.

16. We say omitting non-surviving markets "probably" gives rise to overestimated risk premiums because of the possibility that some defaulting countries have returns of −100% on bonds, while equities retain some residual value. For such countries, the ex post equity premium would be positive.

17. We again say low risk-free rates "probably" give rise to overstated risk premiums because equity returns would presumably have been higher if economic conditions had not given rise to markedly negative real fixed-income returns. If economic conditions had been better, it is possible that the equity premium would then have been larger.

18. Our U.S. equity returns data are described in E. Dimson, P. Marsh, and M. Staunton, *Triumph of the Optimists: 101 Years of Global Investment Returns* (New Jersey: Princeton University Press, 2002). From 1900–1925, we use the equity returns reported in J. Wilson and C. Jones. "An Analysis of the S&P

500 Index and Cowles's Extensions: Price Indexes and Stock Returns, 1870–1999," *Journal of Business*, Vol. 75 (2002), pp. 505–533; from 1926–1970, we use the CRSP capitalization-weighted index; and from 1971 onward, we employ the Wilshire 5000 Index.

19. For example the arithmetic mean of two equally likely returns of +25% and −20% is (+25 − 20)/2 = 2½%, while their geometric mean is zero since (1 + 25/100) × (1 − 20/100) − 1 = 0.

20. Because year-to-year stock returns are very volatile (see Table C1.1), these differences are statistically significant at the 95% level for only three of these 14 countries. In economic terms, however, the differences are clearly large.

21. See Y. Amihud and H. Mendelsohn, "The Liquidity Route to a Lower Cost of Capital," *Journal of Applied Corporate Finance*, Vol. 12, No. 4 (1999).

22. At the start of our research period in 1900, U.S. domestic investors would have found it much harder than today to construct a well-diversified portfolio. At the start of 1900, there were just 123 stocks listed on the New York Stock Exchange, and the railroad industry alone accounted for 63% of their total market value. See Chapter 2 of our book.

23. In the United States, a confounding factor is the rapid growth of stock repurchases and the trend toward lower dividends; see, for example, E. Fama and K. French, "Disappearing Dividends: Changing Firm Characteristics or Lower Propensity to Pay," *Journal of Financial Economics*, Vol. 60 (2001), pp. 3–43. However, in contrast with the United States, stock repurchases have been far less prevalent in the other countries. In Europe, the United Kingdom has the highest level of buybacks, but even U.K. repurchases are rather small (see Section 11.6 of our book).

24. E. Fama and K. French, "The Equity Premium," *Journal of Finance*, Vol. 57 (2002), pp. 637–659. In their examination of dividend yields and dividend growth estimates, Fama and French use the Gordon model to compute the U.S. equity premium from 1872–1999. They find a premium of 3.8% before 1949, and a premium of 3.4% for the subsequent period. They argue that the difference between these estimates and the larger ex post risk premium based on historical realized returns is attributable to a reduction since 1949 in investors' required rates of return.

25. Assuming lognormally distributed returns, the arithmetic mean exceeds the geometric mean by $½ × variance = ½ × 0.20^2 = 0.02 = 2\%$.

26. For illustrative estimates, see Section 13.7 of our book.

27. Note that these organizations have recently lowered their single-country estimates of the equity risk premium. See R. Ibbotson and P. Chen, "Long-Run Stock Returns: Participating in the Real Economy," *Financial Analysts Journal*, Vol. 59 (2003), pp. 88–98, and the 2003 updates to the reports cited in footnote 2.

2

Behavioral Finance

Jay R. Ritter

1. INTRODUCTION

Behavioral finance is the paradigm where financial markets are studied using models that are less narrow than those based on Von Neumann-Morgenstern expected utility theory and arbitrage assumptions. Specifically, behavioral finance has two building blocks: cognitive psychology and the limits to arbitrage. Cognitive refers to how people think. There is a huge psychology literature documenting that people make systematic errors in the way that they think: they are overconfident, they put too much weight on recent experience, etc. Their preferences may also create distortions. Behavioral finance uses this body of knowledge, rather than taking the arrogant approach that it should be ignored. Limits to arbitrage refers to predicting in what circumstances arbitrage forces will be effective, and when they won't be.

Behavioral finance uses models in which some agents are not fully rational, either because of preferences or because of mistaken beliefs. An example of an assumption about preferences is that people are loss averse – a $2 gain might make people feel better by as much as a $1 loss makes them feel worse. Mistaken beliefs arise because people are bad Bayesians. Modern finance has as a building block the Efficient Markets Hypothesis (EMH). The EMH argues that competition between investors seeking abnormal profits drives prices to their "correct" value. The EMH does not assume that all *investors* are rational, but it does assume that *markets* are rational. The EMH does not assume that markets can foresee the future, but it does assume that markets make unbiased forecasts of the future. In contrast, behavioral finance assumes that, in some circumstances, financial markets are informationally inefficient.

Not all misvaluations are caused by psychological biases, however. Some are just due to temporary supply and demand imbalances. For example, the *tyranny of indexing* can lead to demand shifts that are unrelated to the future cash flows of the firm. When Yahoo was added to the S&P 500 in December 1999, index fund managers had to buy the stock even though it had a limited public float. This extra demand drove up the price by over 50% in a week and over 100% in a month. Eighteen months later, the stock price was down by over 90% from where it was shortly after being added to the S&P.

If it is easy to take positions (shorting overvalued stocks or buying under-valued stocks) and these misvaluations are certain to be corrected over a short period, then "arbitrageurs" will take positions and eliminate these mispricings before they become large. But if it is difficult to take these positions, due to short sales constraints, for instance, or if there is no guarantee that the mispricing will be corrected within a reasonable timeframe, then arbitrage will fail to correct the mispricing.[1] Indeed, arbitrageurs may even choose to avoid the markets where the mispricing is most severe, because the risks are too great. This is especially true when one is dealing with a large market, such as the Japanese stock market in the late 1980s or the U.S. market for technology stocks in the late 1990s. Arbitrageurs that attempted to short Japanese stocks in mid-1987 and hedge by going long in U.S. stocks were right in the long run, but they lost huge amounts of money in October 1987 when the U.S. market crashed by more than the Japanese market (because of Japanese government intervention). If the arbitrageurs have limited funds, they would be forced to cover their positions just when the relative misvaluations were greatest, resulting in additional buying pressure for Japanese stocks just when they were most overvalued!

2. COGNITIVE BIASES

Cognitive psychologists have documented many patterns regarding how people behave. Some of these patterns are as follows:

Heuristics

Heuristics, or rules or thumb, make decision-making easier. But they can sometimes lead to biases, especially when things change. These can lead to suboptimal investment decisions. When faced with N choices for how to invest retirement money, many people allocate using the 1/N rule. If there are three funds, one-third goes into each. If two are stock funds, two-thirds goes into equities. If one of the three is a stock fund, one-third goes into equities. Recently, Benartzi and Thaler (2001) have documented that many people follow the 1/N rule.

Overconfidence

People are overconfident about their abilities. Entrepreneurs are especially likely to be overconfident. Overconfidence manifests itself in a number of ways. One example is *too little diversification*, because of a tendency to invest too much in what one is familiar with. Thus, people invest in local companies, even though this is bad from a diversification viewpoint because their real estate (the house they own) is tied to the company's fortunes. Think of auto industry employees in Detroit, construction industry employees in Hong Kong or Tokyo, or computer hardware engineers in Silicon Valley. People invest way too much in the stock of the company that they work for.

Men tend to be more overconfident than women. This manifests itself in many ways, including trading behavior. Barber and Odean (2001) recently analyzed the trading activities of people with discount brokerage accounts. They found that the more people traded, the worse they did, on average. And men traded more, and did worse than, women investors.

Mental Accounting

People sometimes separate decisions that should, in principle, be combined. For example, many people have a household budget for food, and a household budget for entertaining. At home, where the food budget is present, they will not eat lobster or shrimp because they are much more expensive than a fish casserole. But in a restaurant, they will order lobster and shrimp even though the cost is much higher than a simple fish dinner. If they instead ate lobster and shrimp at home, and the simple fish in a restaurant, they could save money. But because they are thinking separately about restaurant meals and food at home, they choose to limit their food at home.

Framing

Framing is the notion that how a concept is presented to individuals matters. For example, restaurants may advertise "early-bird" specials or "after-theatre" discounts, but they never use peak-period "surcharges." They get more business if people feel they are getting a discount at off-peak times rather than paying a surcharge at peak periods, even if the prices are identical. Cognitive psychologists have documented that doctors make different recommendations if they see evidence that is presented as "survival probabilities" rather than "mortality rates," even though survival probabilities plus mortality rates add up to 100%.

Representativeness

People underweight long-term averages. People tend to put too much weight on recent experience. This is sometimes known as the "law of small numbers." As an example, when equity returns have been high for many years (such as 1982–2000 in the U.S. and western Europe), many people begin to believe that high equity returns are "normal."

Conservatism

When things change, people tend to be slow to pick up on the changes. In other words, they *anchor* on the ways things have normally been. The conservatism bias is at war with the representativeness bias. When things change, people might underreact because of the conservatism bias. But if there is a long enough pattern, then they will adjust to it and possibly overreact, under-weighting the long-term average.

Disposition Effect

The disposition effect refers to the pattern that people avoid realizing *paper losses* and seek to realize *paper gains*. For example, if someone buys a stock at $30 that then drops to $22 before rising to $28, most people do not want to sell until the stock gets to above $30. The disposition effect manifests itself in lots of small gains being realized, and few small losses. In fact, people act as if they are trying to *maximize* their taxes! The disposition effect shows up in aggregate stock trading volume. During a bull market, trading volume tends to grow. If the market then turns south, trading volume tends to fall. As an example, trading volume in the Japanese stock market fell by over 80% from the late 1980s to the mid-1990s. The fact that volume tends to fall in bear markets results in the commission business of brokerage firms having a high level of systematic risk.[2]

One of the major criticisms of behavioral finance is that by choosing which bias to emphasize, one can predict either underreaction or overreaction. This criticism of behavioral finance might be called "model dredging." In other words, one can find a story to fit the facts to *ex post* explain some puzzling phenomenon. But how does one make *ex ante* predictions about which biases will dominate? There are two excellent articles that address this issue: Barberis and Thaler (2002), and Hirshliefer (2001). Hirshliefer (p. 1547) in particular addresses the issue of when we would expect one behavioral bias to dominate others. He emphasizes that there is a tendency for people to excessively rely on the *strength* of information signals and under-rely on the *weight* of information signals. This is sometimes described as the *salience* effect.

3. THE LIMITS TO ARBITRAGE

Misvaluations of financial assets are common, but it is not easy to reliably make abnormal profits off of these misvaluations. Why? Misvaluations are of two types: those that are recurrent or arbitrageable, and those that are non-repeating and long-term in nature. For the recurrent misvaluations, trading strategies can reliably make money. Because of this, hedge funds and others zero in on these, and keep them from ever getting too big. Thus, the market is pretty efficient for these assets, at least on a relative basis. For the

long-term, nonrepeating misvaluations, it is impossible in real time to identify the peaks and troughs until they have passed. Getting in too early risks
losses that wipe out capital. Even worse, if limited partners or other investors
are supplying funds, withdrawals of capital after a losing streak may actually result in buying or selling pressure that exacerbates the inefficiency.

Just who are these investors who make markets efficient? Well, one
obvious class of investors who are trying to make money by identifying misvaluations are hedge funds. A relative value hedge fund takes long and short
positions, buying undervalued securities and then finding highly correlated
securities that are overvalued, and shorting them. A macro hedge fund, on
the other hand, takes speculative positions that cannot be easily hedged, such
as shorting Nasdaq during the last two years.

How well do efforts by arbitrageurs to make money work in practice at
making markets more efficient? As Shleifer and Vishny argue in their 1997
"Limits to Arbitrage" article, the efforts of arbitrageurs to make money will
make some markets more efficient, but they won't have any effect on other
markets.

Let's look at an example, that of a giant hedge fund, Long Term Capital
Management. LTCM was founded about nine years ago by Myron Scholes,
Robert Merton, John Meriwether, and others. For their first three or
four years, they were spectacularly successful. But then, four years ago,
they had one bad quarter in which they lost $4 billion, wiping out their
equity capital and forcing the firm to liquidate. But they were right in the
long run!

LTCM mainly traded in fixed income and derivative markets. But one of
the ways that they lost money was on the Royal Dutch/Shell equity arbitrage
trade.

In 1907, Royal Dutch of the Netherlands and Shell of the UK agreed to
merge their interests on a 60-40 basis, and pay dividends on the same basis.
It is easy to show that whenever the stock prices are not in a 60-40 ratio,
there is an arbitrage profit opportunity. Finance theory has a clear prediction.
Furthermore, these are large companies. Until July 2002, Royal Dutch was
in the S & P 500, and Shell is in the FTSE.

How well does this prediction work?

For the last 22 years, from 1980 to 2001, Figure 2.1 demonstrates that
there have been large deviations from the theoretical relation. In 1998, LTCM
shorted the expensive stock and bought the cheap one. Did they make
money? No, they lost money when prices diverged further from their theoretical values during the third quarter of 1998. To meet liquidity needs,
LTCM and other hedge funds were forced to sell out their positions, and this
selling pressure made markets more inefficient, rather than more efficient.
So the forces of arbitrage failed.

The data plotted in Figure 2.1 end in December 2001, with the price ratio
close to its theoretical value. Has it stayed there? In July 2002, Standard &
Poors announced that Royal Dutch would be dropped from the S&P 500
because they were deleting non-American companies. Royal Dutch dropped

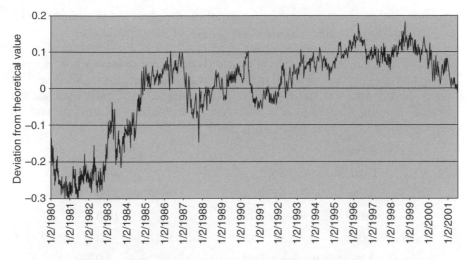

Figure 2.1 Deviations from Royal Dutch/Shell parity from January 1980 to December 2001, as computed by Froot and Dabora (1999) and updated by Ken Froot.

by 17% in the week of the announcement, although there is no suggestion that the present value of dividends changed.

So what is the bottom line on market efficiency? It is useful to divide events into two categories – high-frequency events, which occur often, and low-frequency events, which occur only infrequently, and may take a long time to recover from.

The high-frequency evidence supports market efficiency. It is hard to find a trading strategy that is reliably profitable. And mutual funds have difficulty beating their benchmarks. The low-frequency evidence, however, does not support market efficiency. Examples of enormous misvaluations include:

1. The undervaluation of world-wide stock markets from 1974–1982.
2. The Japanese stock price and land price bubble of the 1980s.
3. The Taiwanese stock price bubble that peaked in February 1990.
4. The October 1987 stock market crash.
5. The technology, media, and telecom (TMT) bubble of 1999–2000.

4. APPLICATIONS OF BEHAVIORAL FINANCE

I would now like to talk about some specific applications of behavioral finance. While I could choose from many applications, I am going to briefly discuss two of my recent publications. The first application concerns inflation and the stock market. I'm going to start out with a simple valuation question. Below, I list some specific assumptions about a hypothetical firm, and the question is, "How much is the equity of this firm worth?"

Assumptions: The inflation rate is 6%, and the equity risk premium is zero, so the nominal cost of capital is 10% (a real cost of capital of 4%). The firm wants to keep the real value of its debt unchanged, so it must increase the nominal amount of debt by 6% each year. There is no real growth, and all free cash flow (if any) is paid out in dividends.

Revenue	$1,200,000
Cost of Goods Sold	$600,000
Administrative Expenses	$400,000
Interest Expense	$200,000
Taxes	$0
After-tax profits	$0
Debt	$2,000,000
Book Equity	$1,500,000
Shares outstanding	10,000
Interest rate on debt	10%

With inflation at 6% and $2 million in debt, the firm must issue $120,000 more debt next year to keep the real value of its debt constant. This cash can be used to pay dividends. This is $12 per share, and using the growing perpetuity formula

$$P = \mathrm{Div}_1/(r - g)$$

with r = 10% and g = 6%, P = $12/(0.10 − 0.06) = $300 per share.

So the equity is worth $3 million, or $300 per share. Earnings are zero because the accountants treat nominal interest expense as a cost, but they don't treat the inflation-induced decrease in the real value of debt as a benefit to equity holders. In other words, the true economic earnings are higher than the accounting earnings, because accountants measure the cost, but not the benefit to equityholders, of debt financing when there is inflation.

This is an example of where framing makes a difference. Nominal interest expense appears on the income statement. The decrease in the real value of nominal liabilities due to inflation does not appear on the income statement. Because it doesn't appear, I would argue that investors don't take it into account, and hence undervalue equities when inflation is high. If you find this implausible, ask yourself "how many finance professors with PhDs get the valuation correct?" If the market makes this mistake, then stocks become riskier, because they fall more than they should when inflation increases, and they rise more than they should when inflation decreases. Over a full inflation cycle, these two effects balance out, which is why stocks are less risky in the long run than they are in the short run (Siegel (1998), Chapter 2).

Modigliani and Cohn (1979) argued that the U.S. stock market was grossly undervalued in the mid- and late 1970s because investors had irrational beliefs about earnings, given the high inflation that existed then. Richard Warr and I, in our March 2002 *JFQA* article on the decline of inflation and the bull market of 1982–1999, conduct an out-of-sample test of the Modigliani-Cohn hypothesis. We argue that part of the bull market of the 1980s was attributable to a recovery from the undervaluation. We also argue that the continued stock market rise in the 1990s was an overshooting – the stock market became overvalued – and we predicted that 2000–2002 would have low stock returns. Fortunately, I believe in my research, and I've had much of my retirement assets in inflation-indexed bonds the last three years. These have been the best-performing asset class.

The second application of behavioral finance that I would like to briefly discuss concerns the underpricing of IPOs.

Prospect theory is a descriptive theory of choice under uncertainty. This is in contrast to expected utility theory, which is *normative* rather than descriptive. Prospect theory focuses on *changes* in wealth, whereas expected utility theory focuses on the *level* of wealth. Gains and losses are measured relative to a reference point. Prospect theory also assumes loss aversion. Prospect theory also incorporates framing – if two related events occur, an individual has a choice of treating them as separate events (segregation) or as one (integration). For example, if a person goes to the racetrack and makes two bets, winning one and losing one, the person may integrate the outcome and focus on the net payoff. If the net payoff is positive, a gain has occurred, and focusing on this makes the better happy. If there is a net loss, segregating the two bets allows the better to feel disappointed once, but happy once.

Tim Loughran and I use prospect theory in our 2002 *RFS* paper "Why Don't Issuers Get Upset About Leaving Money on the Table in IPOs?" to explain the severe underpricing of some IPOs. If an IPO is underpriced, pre-issue stockholders are worse off because their wealth has been diluted. We argue that if an entrepreneur receives the good news that he or she is suddenly unexpectedly wealthy because of a higher than expected IPO price, the entrepreneur doesn't bargain as hard for an even higher offer price. This is because the person integrates the good news of a wealth increase with the bad news of excessive dilution. The individual is better off on net. Underwriters take advantage of this mental accounting and severely underprice these deals. It is these IPOs where the offer price has been raised (a little) that leave a lot of money on the table when the market price goes up a lot.

5. CONCLUSIONS

This brief introduction to behavioral finance has only touched on a few points. More extensive analysis can be found in Barberis and Thaler (2003), Hirshliefer (2001), Shefrin (2000), and Shiller (2000).

It is very difficult to find trading strategies that reliably make money. This does not imply that financial markets are informationally efficient, however.

Low frequency misvaluations may be large, without presenting any opportunity to reliably make money. As an example, individuals or institutions who shorted Japanese stocks in 1987–1988 when they were substantially overvalued, or Taiwanese stocks in early 1989 when they were substantially overvalued, or TMT stocks in the U.S., Europe, and Hong Kong in early 1999 when they were substantially overvalued, all lost enormous amounts of money as these stocks became even more overvalued. Most of these short-sellers, who were right in the long run, were wiped out before the misvaluations started to disappear. Thus, the forces of arbitrage, which work well for high frequency events, work very poorly for low frequency events.

Behavioral finance is, relatively speaking, in its infancy. It is not a separate discipline, but instead will increasingly be part of mainstream finance.

NOTES

1. Technically, an arbitrage opportunity exists when one can *guarantee* a profit by, for example, going long in an undervalued asset and shorting an overvalued asset. In practice, almost all arbitrage activity is risk arbitrage – making trades where the expected profit is high relative to the risk involved.
2. During the bear market beginning in April 2000 in the U.S., aggregate stock market volume has not dropped. This is apparently due to increased trading by institutions, since stock trading by individuals has in fact declined. The significant drop in transaction costs associated with the move to decimalization and technological advances partly accounts for this. Another reason is that many firms split their shares in late 1999 and the first half of 2000, which, *ceteris paribus*, would have resulted in higher trading volume. The drop in commission revenue from individuals (predicted by the disposition effect) has resulted in revenue declines for retail-oriented brokerage firms such as Charles Schwab & Co.

REFERENCES

Barber, Brad, and Terry Odean, 2001. "Boys will be boys: Gender, overconfidence, and common stock investment." *Quarterly Journal of Economics* 116, 261–292.

Barberis, Nicholas, and Richard Thaler, 2003. "A survey of behavioral finance." In G. Constantinides, M. Harris, and R. Stulz (editors) *Handbook of the Economics of Finance*, North-Holland, Amsterdam.

Benartzi, Shlomo, and Richard Thaler, 2001. "Naïve diversification strategies in defined contribution savings plans." *American Economic Review* 91, 79–98.

Froot, Kenneth A., and Emil A. Dabora, 1999. "How are stock prices affected by the location of trade?" *Journal of Financial Economics* 53, 189–216.

Hirshleifer, David, 2001. "Investor psychology and asset pricing." *Journal of Finance* 56, 1533–1597.

Loughran, Tim, and Jay R. Ritter, 2002. "Why don't issuers get upset about leaving money on the table in IPOs?" *Review of Financial Studies* 15, 413–443.

Modigliani, Franco, and Richard Cohn, 1979. "Inflation, rational valuation and the market." *Financial Analysts Journal* 35, 24–44.

Ritter, Jay R., and Richard Warr, 2002. "The decline of inflation and the bull market of 1982–1999." *Journal of Financial and Quantitative Analysis* 37, 29–61.

Shefrin, Hersh, 2000. *Beyond Greed and Fear*, Harvard Business School Press, Boston.

Shiller, Robert J., 2000. *Irrational Exuberance*, Princeton University Press, Princeton.

Shleifer, Andrei, and Robert Vishny, 1997. "The limits of arbitrage." *Journal of Finance* 52, 35–55.

Siegel, Jeremy J., 1998. *Stocks for the Long Run*, *Second Edition*, McGraw-Hill, New York.

Reproduced, with minor modifications, from the *Pacific-Basin Finance Journal*, Vol. 11, No. 4 (September 2003), pp. 429–37.

Do Fundamentals – or Emotions – Drive the Stock Market?

Marc Goedhart, Timothy Koller and David Wessels

There's never been a better time to be a behaviorist. During four decades, the academic theory that financial markets accurately reflect a stock's underlying value was all but unassailable. But lately, the view that investors can fundamentally change a market's course through irrational decisions has been moving into the mainstream.

With the exuberance of the high-tech stock bubble and the crash of the late 1990s still fresh in investors' memories, adherents of the behaviorist school are finding it easier than ever to spread the belief that markets can be something less than efficient in immediately distilling new information and that investors, driven by emotion, can indeed lead markets awry. Some behaviorists would even assert that stock markets lead lives of their own, detached from economic growth and business profitability. A number of finance scholars and practitioners have argued that stock markets are not efficient – that is, that they don't necessarily reflect economic fundamentals.[1] According to this point of view, significant and lasting deviations from the intrinsic value of a company's share price occur in market valuations.

The argument is more than academic. In the 1980s the rise of stock market index funds, which now hold some $1 trillion in assets, was caused in large part by the conviction among investors that efficient-market theories were valuable. And current debates in the United States and elsewhere about privatizing Social Security and other retirement systems may hinge on assumptions about how investors are likely to handle their retirement options.

We agree that behavioral finance offers some valuable insights – chief among them the idea that markets are not always right, since rational investors can't always correct for mispricing by irrational ones. But for managers, the critical question is how often these deviations arise and whether they are so frequent and significant that they should affect the process of financial decision making. In fact, significant deviations from intrinsic value are rare, and markets usually revert rapidly to share prices commensurate with economic fundamentals. Therefore, managers should continue to use the tried-and-true analysis of a company's discounted cash flow to make their valuation decisions.

WHEN MARKETS DEVIATE

Behavioral-finance theory holds that markets might fail to reflect economic fundamentals under three conditions. When all three apply, the theory predicts that pricing biases in financial markets can be both significant and persistent.

Irrational behavior. Investors behave irrationally when they don't correctly process all the available information while forming their expectations of a company's future performance. Some investors, for example, attach too much importance to recent events and results, an error that leads them to overprice companies with strong recent performance. Others are excessively conservative and underprice stocks of companies that have released positive news.

Systematic patterns of behavior. Even if individual investors decided to buy or sell without consulting economic fundamentals, the impact on share prices would still be limited. Only when their irrational behavior is also systematic (that is, when large groups of investors share particular patterns of behavior) should persistent price deviations occur. Hence behavioral-finance theory argues that patterns of overconfidence, overreaction, and overrepresentation are common to many investors and that such groups can be large enough to prevent a company's share price from reflecting underlying economic fundamentals – at least for some stocks, some of the time.

Limits to arbitrage in financial markets. When investors assume that a company's recent strong performance alone is an indication of future performance, they may start bidding for shares and drive up the price. Some investors might expect a company that surprises the market in one quarter to go on exceeding expectations. As long as enough other investors notice this myopic overpricing and respond by taking short positions, the share price will fall in line with its underlying indicators.

This sport of arbitrage doesn't always occur, however. In practice, the costs, complexity, and risks involved in setting up a short position can be too high for individual investors. If, for example, the share price doesn't return to its fundamental value while they can still hold on to a short position – the so-called noise-trader risk – they may have to sell their holdings at a loss.

MOMENTUM AND OTHER MATTERS

Two well-known patterns of stock market deviations have received considerable attention in academic studies during the past decade: long-term reversals in share prices and short-term momentum.

First, consider the phenomenon of reversal – high-performing stocks of the past few years typically become low-performing stocks of the next few. Behavioral finance argues that this effect is caused by an overreaction on the part of investors: when they put too much weight on a company's recent performance, the share price becomes inflated. As additional information becomes available, investors adjust their expectations and a reversal occurs. The same behavior could explain low returns after an initial public offering (IPO), seasoned offerings, a new listing, and so on. Presumably, such companies had a history of strong performance, which was why they went public in the first place.

Momentum, on the other hand, occurs when positive returns for stocks over the past few months are followed by several more months of positive returns. Behavioral-finance theory suggests that this trend results from systematic underreaction: overconservative investors underestimate the true impact of earnings, divestitures, and share repurchases, for example, so stock prices don't instantaneously react to good or bad news.

But academics are still debating whether irrational investors alone can be blamed for the long-term-reversal and short-term-momentum patterns in returns. Some believe that long-term reversals result merely from incorrect measurements of a stock's risk premium, because investors ignore the risks associated with a company's size and market-to-capital ratio.[2] These statistics could be a proxy for liquidity and distress risk.

Similarly, irrational investors don't necessarily drive short-term momentum in share price returns. Profits from these patterns are relatively limited after transaction costs have been deducted. Thus, small momentum biases could exist even if all investors were rational.

Furthermore, behavioral finance still cannot explain why investors overreact under some conditions (such as IPOs) and underreact in others (such as earnings announcements). Since there is no systematic way to predict how markets will respond, some have concluded that this is a further indication of their accuracy.[3]

PERSISTENT MISPRICING IN CARVE-OUTS AND DUAL-LISTED COMPANIES

Two well-documented types of market deviation – the mispricing of carve-outs and of dual-listed companies – are used to support behavioral-finance theory. The classic example is the pricing of 3Com and Palm after the latter's carve-out in March 2000.

In anticipation of a full spin-off within nine months, 3Com floated 5 percent of its Palm subsidiary. Almost immediately, Palm's market capitalization was higher than the entire market value of 3Com, implying that 3Com's other businesses had a negative value. Given the size and profitability of the rest of 3Com's businesses, this result would clearly indicate mispricing. Why did rational investors fail to exploit the anomaly by going short on Palm's shares and long on 3Com's? The reason was that the number of available Palm shares was extremely small after the carve-out: 3Com still held 95 percent of them. As a result, it was extremely difficult to establish a short position, which would have required borrowing shares from a Palm shareholder.

During the months following the carve-out, the mispricing gradually became less pronounced as the supply of shares through short sales increased steadily. Yet while many investors and analysts knew about the price difference, it persisted for two months – until the Internal Revenue Service formally approved the carve-out's tax-free status in early May 2002. At that point, a significant part of the uncertainty around the spin-off was removed and the price discrepancy disappeared. This correction suggests that at least part of the mispricing was caused by the risk that the spin-off wouldn't occur.

Additional cases of mispricing between parent companies and their carved-out subsidiaries are well documented.[4] In general, these cases involve difficulties setting up short positions to exploit the price differences, which persist until the spin-off takes place or is abandoned. In all cases, the mispricing was corrected within several months.

A second classic example of investors deviating from fundamentals is the price disparity between the shares of the same company traded on two different exchanges. Consider the case of Royal Dutch Petroleum and "Shell" Transport and Trading, which are traded on the Amsterdam and London stock markets, respectively. Since these twin shares are entitled to a fixed 60–40 portion of the dividends of Royal Dutch/Shell, you would expect their share prices to remain in this fixed ratio.

Over long periods, however, they have not. In fact, prolonged periods of mispricing can be found for several similar twin-share structures, such as Unilever (Figure C2.1). This phenomenon occurs because large groups of investors prefer (and are prepared to pay a premium for) one of the twin shares. Rational investors typically do not take positions to exploit the opportunity for arbitrage.

Thus in the case of Royal Dutch/Shell, a price differential of as much as 30 percent has persisted at times. Why? The opportunity to arbitrage

Relative difference in valuation between dual-listed companies,[1] %

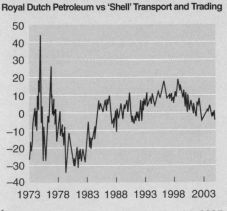

Royal Dutch Petroleum vs 'Shell' Transport and Trading

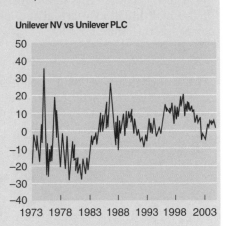

Unilever NV vs Unilever PLC

[1]Data shown from Jan 1, 1973, to Jan 24, 2005.

Figure C2.1 Mood swings
Source: Thomson

dual-listed stocks is actually quite unpredictable and potentially costly. Because of noise-trader risk, even a large gap between share prices is no guarantee that those prices will converge in the near term.

Does this indict the market for mispricing? We don't think so. In recent years, the price differences for Royal Dutch/Shell and other twin-share stocks have all become smaller. Furthermore, some of these share structures (and price differences) disappeared because the corporations formally merged, a development that underlines the significance of noise-trader risk: as soon as a formal date was set for definitive price convergence, arbitrageurs stepped in to correct any discrepancy. This pattern provides additional evidence that mispricing occurs only under special circumstances – and is by no means a common or long-lasting phenomenon.

MARKETS AND FUNDAMENTALS: THE BUBBLE OF THE 1990S

Do markets reflect economic fundamentals? We believe so. Long-term returns on capital and growth have been remarkably consistent for the past 35 years, in spite of some deep recessions and periods of very strong economic growth. The median return on equity for all US companies has been a very stable 12 to 15 percent, and long-term GDP growth for the US economy in real terms has been about 3 percent a year since 1945.[5] We also estimate that the inflation-adjusted cost of equity since 1965 has been fairly stable, at about 7 percent.[6]

We used this information to estimate the intrinsic P/E ratios for the US and UK stock markets and then compared them with the actual values.[7] This analysis has led us to three important conclusions. The first is that US and UK stock markets, by and large, have been fairly priced, hovering near their intrinsic P/E ratios. This figure was typically around 15, with the exception of the high-inflation years of the late 1970s and early 1980s, when it was closer to 10 (Figure C2.2).

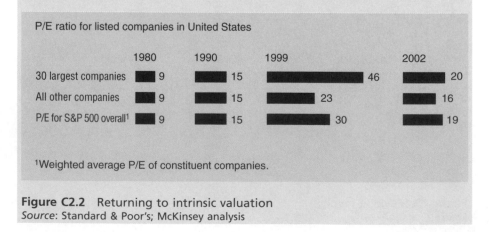

Figure C2.2   Returning to intrinsic valuation
Source: Standard & Poor's; McKinsey analysis

Second, the late 1970s and late 1990s produced significant deviations from intrinsic valuations. In the late 1970s, when investors were obsessed with high short-term inflation rates, the market was probably undervalued; long-term real GDP growth and returns on equity indicate that it shouldn't have bottomed out at P/E levels of around 7. The other well-known deviation occurred in the late 1990s, when the market reached a P/E ratio of around 30 – a level that couldn't be justified by 3 percent long-term real GDP growth or by 13 percent returns on book equity.

Third, when such deviations occurred, the stock market returned to its intrinsic-valuation level within about three years. Thus, although valuations have been wrong from time to time – even for the stock market as a whole – eventually they have fallen back in line with economic fundamentals.

FOCUS ON INTRINSIC VALUE

What are the implications for corporate managers? Paradoxically, we believe that such market deviations make it even more important for the executives of a company to understand the intrinsic value of its shares. This knowledge allows it to exploit any deviations, if and when they occur, to time the implementation of strategic decisions more successfully. Here are some examples of how corporate managers can take advantage of market deviations.

■ Issuing additional share capital when the stock market attaches too high a value to the company's shares relative to their intrinsic value

■ Repurchasing shares when the market under-prices them relative to their intrinsic value

■ Paying for acquisitions with shares instead of cash when the market over-prices them relative to their intrinsic value

■ Divesting particular businesses at times when trading and transaction multiples are higher than can be justified by underlying fundamentals

Bear two things in mind. First, we don't recommend that companies base decisions to issue or repurchase their shares, to divest or acquire businesses, or to settle transactions with cash or shares solely on an assumed difference between the market and intrinsic value of their shares. Instead, these decisions must be grounded in a strong business strategy driven by the goal of creating shareholder value. Market deviations are more relevant as tactical considerations when companies time and execute such decisions – for example, when to issue additional capital or how to pay for a particular transaction.

Second, managers should be wary of analyses claiming to highlight market deviations. Most of the alleged cases that we have come across in our client experience proved to be insignificant or even nonexistent, so the evidence should be compelling. Furthermore, the deviations should be significant in both size and duration, given the capital and time needed to take advantage of the types of opportunities listed previously.

Provided that a company's share price eventually returns to its intrinsic value in the long run, managers would benefit from using a discounted-cash-flow approach for strategic decisions. What should matter is the long-term behavior of the share price of a company, not whether it is undervalued by 5 or 10 percent at any given time. For strategic business decisions, the evidence strongly suggests that the market reflects intrinsic value.

NOTES

1. For an overview of behavioral finance, see Jay R. Ritter, "Behavioral finance," *Pacific-Basin Finance Journal*, 2003, Volume 11, Number 4, pp. 429–37; and Nicholas Barberis and Richard H. Thaler, "A survey of behavioral finance," in *Handbook of the Economics of Finance: Financial Markets and Asset Pricing*, G. M. Constantinides et al. (eds), New York: Elsevier North-Holland, 2003, pp. 1054–123.
2. Eugene F. Fama and Kenneth R. French, "Multifactor explanations of asset pricing anomalies," *Journal of Finance*, 1996, Volume 51, Number 1, pp. 55–84.
3. Eugene F. Fama, "Market efficiency, long-term returns, and behavioral finance," *Journal of Financial Economics*, 1998, Volume 49, Number 3, pp. 283–306.
4. Owen A. Lamont and Richard H. Thaler, "Can the market add and subtract? Mispricing in tech stock carve-outs," *Journal of Political Economy*, 2003, Volume 111, Number 2, pp. 227–68; and Mark L. Mitchell, Todd C. Pulvino, and Erik Stafford, "Limited arbitrage in equity markets," *Journal of Finance*, 2002, Volume 57, Number 2, pp. 551–84.
5. US corporate earnings as a percentage of GDP have been remarkably constant over the past 35 years, at around 6 percent.
6. Marc H. Goedhart, Timothy M. Koller, and Zane D. Willams, "The real cost of equity," *McKinsey on Finance*, Number 5, Autumn 2002, pp. 11–15.
7. Marc H. Goedhart, Timothy M. Koller, and Zane D. Williams, "Living with lower market expectations," *McKinsey on Finance*, Number 8, Summer 2003, pp. 7–11.

Section 2

Adding Value Through Investment

SECTION OVERVIEW

Janette Rutterford

In this section, we look at corporate investment – both in projects and in companies. In a sense, the company can be thought of as a collection of projects, and the Capital Asset Pricing Model teaches us that managers should evaluate each project as a standalone investment, using the hurdle rate appropriate to the project activity and financing rather than using, as many companies in practice do, a company-wide discount rate.

As far as investment in projects or companies is concerned, the use of discounted cash flow techniques and the theoretical dominance of the Net Present Value rule as a decision tool for investment appraisal have long been part of finance textbooks. In this section of the book, we look at the investment decision from different perspectives from that of the methodology of decision-making. First, we explore what happens in the real world when investment decisions are being made and why managers do not in practice always follow the theoretically optimal model. Second, we explore how option valuation, in particular the valuation of "real" options, can be used to improve project appraisal. Third, we look at mergers and acquisitions and why managers keep on buying companies, when the evidence as to their success is fairly thin on the ground.

Isabelle Royer, in "Why Bad Projects Are So Hard to Kill", shows that, despite a better understanding of the financial tools available for project decision making than in the past, managers still do not take theoretically optimal decisions when looking at potential projects. The article, from the *Harvard Business Review*, includes a number of case studies of US firms, and looks at reasons why managers find it so hard to abandon projects which do not meet the required hurdle rates. This article is an example of behavioural research discussed in Section 1 on "Trends in Finance Theory" – a willingness to recognise that managers do not always follow the theoretically optimal path (in this case the positive NPV rule) but may sometimes be apparently irrational in their behaviour.

In the second article in this section, "Realizing the Potential of Real Options: Does Theory Meet Practice?", Alexander Triantis looks at whether real options can actually help when making investment decisions – in other words, do real options add value to the traditional positive NPV approach? Although options to delay projects, abandon projects, scale projects up or down are relatively easy to model, the practical difficulty lies in being able to value real options which differ from financial options by being on real rather than financial assets and so do not have an easy-to-determine market price or, indeed, volatility. Real options became very popular in the late 1990s, being used to explain high valuations of companies such as Amazon or Microsoft, which had, in a sense, options to expand across traditional business boundaries. In the market crash of the early 2000s, real options have somewhat fallen from grace.

However, real options do still have a role to play. They are particularly useful for oil and pharmaceutical companies, both of which have projects which require initial and then subsequent investment, so that the option to abandon at later stages of the project has obvious value. Case Study 3, a *McKinsey Quarterly* article by K. Leslie and M. Michaels, "Real Options", looks at two case studies in which the concept if not the detail of real options was applied to two different industries – electricity generation and oil. They illustrate how the process of thinking through investment decisions in a real options framework is a powerful tool in financial strategy, and in adding value to the organisation.

The remaining article and case study in this section are concerned with mergers and acquisitions. There are essentially two types of article in the classical M&A literature. The first type looks at whether mergers and acquisitions have added value. This type of article takes a database of mergers and acquisitions, for different time periods, industries, countries or even cross-border, and looks at a period of years after the deal to see whether value has been added or, to use a picturesque term, destroyed. A typical result is to show that little or no value is added by M&A, and what value is added tends to accrue to the disposing shareholders rather than to those of the acquiring company.[1] Of course, the method of financing affects these results. If companies use their equity to buy companies, the disposing shareholders essentially share the benefits or costs of the merger. The second type of article looks at the M&A cycle phenomenon. It has long been recognised that M&A takes place in waves, peaking when the stock market is high, and with few deals when the market falls.[2] If buying a company whose shares are quoted on the stock market, this seems to imply that managers are paying over the odds. However, if they are using their own shares, which might also be overvalued, to pay for the acquisition, managers might actually be more rational than they initially appear. Recently, authors such as Andreas Shleifer and Robert Vishny[3] have applied behavioural finance concepts to looking at whether markets or managers are rational or irrational when they issue new equity.

However, there are problems with including articles from either of these "typical" debates. The first approach generates papers which are long, methodologically complicated and whose results vary according to which period, country, etc. is used. The second literature is still in a state of flux. Behavioural finance and classical finance have yet to come to terms with M&A. Classical finance would imply that few deals would be done given the results, and this is clearly not the case. Behavioural finance would imply that, once factors such as the finance method and the timing of the deals are taken into account, there may be method in managers' apparent madness. In this book, we look at a recent article which is outside both these literatures. "Mergers, MNEs and Innovation – the Need for New Research Approaches", by Christian Berggren, considers mergers by multinationals and attempts to use alternative approaches to traditional research to look more deeply at why managers undertake M&A. It comes up with some interesting results. Case Study 4, a *Financial Times* article by Simon London, looks at the recent, rather depressing results on the value added by cross-border mergers and acquisitions. Perhaps the insights provided by Berggren can help to explain these results.

NOTES

1. For example, see E.L. Black, T.A. Carnes and T. Jandik (2001), "The Long-Term Success of Cross-Border Mergers and Acquisitions", Working Paper, available on http://papers.ssrn.com/paper.taf?abstract_id=270188.
2. This was discussed in R.A. Brealey and S.C. Myers (1996), *Principles of Corporate Finance,* 5th edn (New York: John Wiley & Sons Inc.).
3. A. Shleifer and R.W. Vishny (2003), "Stock Market Driven Acquisitions", *Journal of Financial Economics,* 70(3), pp. 295–311.

3

Why Bad Projects Are So Hard to Kill

Isabelle Royer

YOU CAN STILL FIND THEM on eBay, sleek and gleaming videodisc players with LP-sized discs. The product: RCA's SelectaVision – one of the biggest consumer electronics flops of all time.

But it isn't simply the monumental failure in the marketplace that makes the SelectaVision story worth remembering. It's that RCA insisted on plowing money into the product long after all signs pointed to near certain failure. When the company developed its first prototype in 1970, some experts already considered the phonograph-like technology obsolete. Seven years later, with the quality of VCRs improving and digital technology on the horizon, every one of RCA's competitors had abandoned videodisc research. Even in the face of tepid consumer response to SelectaVision's launch in 1981, RCA continued to developed new models and invest in production capacity. When the product was finally killed in 1984, it had cost the company an astounding $580 million and had tied up resources for 14 years.

Companies make similar mistakes – if on a somewhat more modest scale – all the time. Of course, hindsight is 20/20; it's easy after the fact to criticize bold bets that didn't pay off. But too often managers charge ahead in the face of mounting evidence that success is pretty well unachievable.

Why can't companies kill projects that are clearly doomed? Is it just poor management? Bureaucratic inertia? My research has uncovered something quite different. Hardly the product of managerial incompetence or entrenched bureaucracy, the failures I've examined resulted, ironically, from a fervent and widespread belief among managers in the inevitability of their projects' ultimate success. This sentiment typically originates, naturally enough, with a project's champion; it then spreads throughout the organization, often to the highest levels, reinforcing itself each step of the way. The result is what I call collective belief, and it can lead an otherwise rational organization into some very irrational behavior.

Of course, a strongly held conviction and the refusal to let inevitable setbacks undermine it are just what you need to get a project up and running. But there is a dark side: As the project moves forward, faith can blind you to increasingly negative feedback – from the lab, from vendors and partners, from customers.

To better understand why this happens and what can be done to prevent it, I analyzed two failed product innovations at two large French companies. (For a brief description of my research, see Box 3.1 "What Were They Thinking?") One was a new lens created by Essilor, the world's largest maker of corrective lenses for eyeglasses. The other was an industrial additive used in manufacturing paper, paint, and plastics, developed by Lafarge, the largest producer of building materials. In both cases, the projects absorbed millions of dollars of investment before the companies finally abandoned them.

My analysis revealed a number of practices that can help companies avoid this kind of disaster. For one, they can assemble project teams not entirely composed of people enthusiastically singing from the same hymnbook. They can put in place a well-defined review process – and then follow it. Perhaps most important, companies need to recognize the role of "exit champions": managers with the temperament and credibility to question the prevailing belief, demand hard data on the viability of the project, and, if necessary, forcefully make the case that it should be killed. While the importance of project champions is well documented, the value of someone who is able to pull the plug on a project before it becomes a money sink hasn't generally been appreciated.

FAITH THAT WOULDN'T BE SHATTERED

Essilor has long been proud of its research. In 1959, it invented the Varilux "progressive" lens, for instance, which corrects both near- and farsightedness without the telltale lines that denote traditional bifocals. But this story starts in the summer of 1979, when a similar break-through appears possible. Since 1974, the company has been working on a composite glass-and-plastic material that's lightweight, shatter resistant, scratch resistant, and light sensitive. Now a researcher has come up with a way to make a lens from this material. Essilor's research manager immediately takes a personal interest in the idea, and he orders the creation of a trial lens. Two days later, it's done.

The news spreads quickly throughout the company and is greeted enthusiastically. The research manager seeks and gets approval to proceed with additional research. The CEO himself helps select the managers who will oversee the project, many of whom have worked together on the Varilux lens and other successful projects.

Early on, some questions are raised about the potential cost of this new composite lens, as well as its durability. It's common for layers of any composite material to separate. Indeed, the director of research and manufacturing questions whether the product is even viable. But his concern isn't heeded because he is, as one colleague says, "always skeptical." No initial marketing studies are conducted, but none had been done for Varilux, either; in both cases, the projects are driven by the exciting technology. Based on the current sales of other Essilor products, internal estimates predict sales of nearly 40 million units a year by 1985. In April 1980, the project is accepted for development and a target launch date is set for late 1981. Excitement is high.

In September 1980 though, some bad news arrives: Corning, which supplies the glass for the composite lens, says that meeting the U.S. Food and Drug Administration's test for shatter resistance is proving more difficult than expected. If this continues to be the case, company estimates indicate that sales in 1985 will total just 10 million units. Then, pilot tests in January 1981 reveal a number of other problems, including a tendency of the lens to crack as it's mounted into the frame. Researchers are confident that this problem can be solved (though the company later decides it will offer an exchange guarantee to opticians). Despite the problems revealed in the pilot test, production facilities are built, and trial manufacturing begins. But now another issue arises: Production costs turn out to be twice what was forecast, which will make the lens as much as six times as expensive as normal lenses.

Essilor proudly launches the lens in June 1982. The president of the company sends a sample to the French Ministry of Industry. One researcher tucks a prototype away in his attic so that he can someday show his son "how you do innovation." The manager who unveils the lens at a press conference says he feels a sense of "real jubilation."

Customers are less enthusiastic: Opticians complain about the price and the difficulties of mounting the lens. Essilor has forecast sales of 200,000 units by the end of 1982, a number limited solely by initial production capacity. But sales reach just 20,000 by that date. What's more, concerns about the tendency of the lens's layers to separate are proving justified.

Box 3.1   What were they thinking?

How do you get an accurate picture of an organization's belief in a project, especially after the fact? My study of Essilor and Lafarge, which was conducted several years after the two projects analyzed in this article were abandoned, lasted two years. It included several dozen interviews with middle managers and senior executives involved in the projects. I also had access to a range of company documents: reports, memos, written notes, test results, marketing studies, business plans, and, in each case, the analysis of an outside consultant. Finally, for each company, I asked two executive – each with a different view of the project – to review the lengthy written summary of the project history I had prepared.

Researching events long after the fact can provide perspective that would be absent from contemporary research. But there is the danger that people's perceptions and conclusions will be colored because the project's outcome is known. To guard against this, all technical evaluations came from documents written during the course of the project. In interviews, I asked people what their opinions and feelings were at the time, not what they thought now. Later, I cross-checked the interview data with the written record. When there was a conflict, I went back to interviewees to ask for more details until the data were consistent.

These setbacks are an emotional blow to those involved in the project but are not enough to destroy their belief. "It felt like a knockout," one recalls. "Still, although we were in shock, we knew failure was impossible." After all, those involved point out, initial sales of Varilux had also been slow, because people found the progressive lens difficult to get used to.

The problems continue. In 1985, Essilor launches a second-generation lens meant to fix the separation problems, but it fails to do so. Sales drop below 15,000 units a year. In 1986, a modified composite material solves the separation problem, but the lens remains difficult for opticians to mount in the frame. Researchers are asked to fix this problem before the company will commit itself to launching a third-generation lens.

After a year of further research, the problem still isn't solved. But the research manager argues to the executive committee that, since the separation problem has been corrected, the third-generation lens should be launched. The company does so at the end of 1987, and, in 1988, sales grow to a lackluster 50,000 units.

Then, in the spring of 1989, because of retirements and a restructuring of the company's overall research and production activities, four new managers join the project. A new research manager replaces the lens's foremost champion. In September, the new research manager completes his own evaluation of the project. Sales are still low, and the U.S. market remains out of reach because the lens still hasn't passed the FDA test. The investment needed to develop a full range of products, including a progressive lens, could double what has been spent so far. He recommends that the lens be abandoned.

Top management rejects his recommendation. The company does decide, however, to conduct a thorough evaluation of the project. To no one's surprise, a business analysis shows that the lens currently doesn't generate a profit. But a marketing study further concludes that even if the quality problems are ironed out, potential sales will reach only 1.5 million units per year, a fraction of the 40 million originally predicted. The implication: The lens will never be very profitable.

In September 1990, with quality problems still unsolved and no prospect of passing the FDA test, the company decides to call an immediate halt to research on the lens and stop production within a year. It's been ten years since the first warning signs arose. It has cost Essilor Fr 300 million, or more than $50 million in 1990 dollars.

A BELIEF IN CRYSTALS

Lafarge, like Essilor, has a big stake in the success of the product it is developing. It's early 1985, and research that Lafarge has done on the crystallization of gypsum, a mineral commonly used in the company's core building-materials businesses, looks like it is about to bear fruit. The engineering manager of the gypsum division has concluded that the crystals could serve as a superior substitute for the ground-up minerals commonly used in making paper and paint. The market could be large: One internal forecast puts potential annual sales at Fr 400 million, or about $40 million at the time. And pride as well as profit is at stake. Lafarge has typically grown through acquisition; here is a chance for the company to prove it can grow organically by leveraging its resources into new businesses.

Later that year, the engineering manager of the gypsum division begins research on the use of the crystals as a paper filler (something added to paper stock to improve such physical or optical properties as texture or opacity). He finds a partner in a big paper producer, Aussedat Rey. The engineering manager and his boss, the division's director of operations, seek and receive project backing from Lafarge's top management. Because the crystal-based approach is so innovative, enthusiasm quickly grows.

Over the next several years, the project enjoys both successes and setbacks. The paper filler product is superior in a number of ways to existing fillers, and the crystals turn out to have another potential application in plastics manufacturing. Aussedat Rey agrees to pay for further paper filler tests.

These highlight several problems. The product has the potential to clog certain papermaking machines. And it is not concentrated enough, making it relatively expensive for customers to use. Researchers are confident, however, that these problems can be solved. Lafarge's top management accepts the project for development, including applications for paper, paint, and plastics, and sets 1990 as the target launch date.

Aussedat Rey's first production trial of the paper filler in December 1987 is a technical success, although the paper company still wants a more concentrated version. The successful trial heightens Lafarge's optimism; informal estimates of annual sales grow to Fr 1 billion, or about $190 million in 1988 dollars. To be sure, projections indicate that the paper filler itself probably won't be profitable. But the full range of products for paper, paint, and plastics taken together should be. Unfortunately, only the paper filler has advanced beyond the laboratory stage.

Still, people are eager to get the product to market. To begin production in 1990, the gypsum division's director of operations needs funding to break ground on the plant in 1989. At the end of 1988, Lafarge's top management, aware that tests on the more-concentrated version of the paper filler have not yet been run, approves funding for the plant, so long as certain criteria are met. Before the money is released, the project team must have "verified the feasibility of the manufacturing process in the pilot workshop and the product's quality and acceptability to customers."

This tentative go-ahead is greeted enthusiastically by project members. A lone dissenting voice is Lafarge's new mineral-fillers manager, recently recruited from a consumer products company. He raises concerns about remaining technical challenges, especially after a more-concentrated version of the paper filler fails a new test at Aussedat Rey. But his concerns are generally ignored because of his lack of experience in industrial products. In fact, others involved in the project repeatedly remind him of this fact. He stops raising questions – and ultimately resigns.

Meanwhile, Aussedat Rey is showing less interest in the paper filler and repeatedly delays further trials. (It later will sever its relationship with Lafarge because the price of the paper filler is too high.) The paper filler's "quality and acceptability to customers" – the criteria that must be met to receive funding for the plant – seem far from assured. And yet, after a presentation by members of the project, top management gives the plant a green light, and it is inaugurated in September 1990. Several weeks later, at Lafarge's annual meeting of researchers from labs across the company, the paper filler researchers and their managers present the project as an example of a successful internal research initiative.

But the new plant remains idle, as no product has yet emerged from the lab that is ready for production and no customer or partner has been found to fund further tests.

Meanwhile, one of the project's champions, the gypsum division's director of operations, has left Lafarge for health reasons and has been replaced by an operations director from another division of the company. He forms a task force to formally evaluate the viability of the project. This isn't easy because of the lack of data. For example, although an initial market study was done, there have been no follow-ups to gauge demand for a product that is now likely to lack some of the features originally envisioned. Still, in April 1991, the task force's report confirms that the paper filler itself won't be profitable and estimates that two years and another Fr 30 million (about $5.3 million in 1991 dollars) would be needed to get other products ready for pilot testing. The new director of operations recommends terminating the project.

Most team members agree with the factual findings, but many reject the recommendation that the project be killed. So, although top management stops development of the paper filler, it authorizes continued research on products to be used in paper coating and plastics manufacturing. At the end of 1991, however, a test of the paper-coating product produces poor results and offers little hope that it can be improved. In early 1992, the plant is sold and the entire project is stopped, having cost a total of Fr 150 million (nearly $30 million in 1992 dollars) over seven years.

THE SEDUCTIVE APPEAL OF COLLECTIVE BELIEF

So what got into the decision makers at these two companies? Why did Essilor persist with the development of its new lens in the face of so much negative evidence? Why did Lafarge build a brand-new production facility before determining whether its gypsum crystal additive had a future in the marketplace?

These were not cases of bureaucratic inertia. If anything, the procedures and controls over these projects were too lax rather than too unresponsive or inflexible. Nor were these cases in which project champions were flogging a dead horse to justify their original touting of it. What the many interviews and myriad contemporary documents reveal in both companies is the power, and troublesome implications, of a very human impulse: the desire to believe in something – in these situations, in the projects' ultimate success. In both companies, this belief was held not just by a handful of individuals but by much of their organizations.

How does that happen? Collective belief arises because individual belief is often contagious, particularly when it reinforces others' perceptions and desires. When this is the case, the belief can spread easily among the various decision makers who control a project's fate. Here's how that played out at Lafarge and Essilor.

The Emergence of Belief. The original true believer is a project champion, who holds an unyielding conviction – based, often as not, on a hunch rather than on strong evidence – that a project will succeed. This belief then spreads to others; how quickly and with intensity depends on a number of factors. Some of these are organizational and some are particular to the champion – for example, his personal credibility and charisma and the robustness and range of his social network within the company. Indeed, if the champion's reputation is strong enough, the belief can pass from person to person until it is shared by individuals who don't even know the champion and know little of the project. At Lafarge, two project members candidly admitted that they couldn't truly assess the potential of the new product but took the word of one of the project's champions that it was a winner.

Belief in a project is all the more contagious when its ultimate success is something that people greatly desire. For both Essilor and Lafarge, the two projects furthered important companywide goals: the development of products that embodied a strong technological tradition of "research for the sake of vision" at Essilor, and the desire to generate organic growth rather than growth through acquisition at Lafarge.

But a project can also satisfy individual desires, ones that are often quite various and even potentially conflicting. Some at Essilor reported they saw the lens as something "that would permanently eliminate competitors." Others hoped the project would maintain employment levels in the glass factories as plastic lenses grew in popularity. Some senior executives saw the composite glass-and-plastic lens as a way to strengthen corporate culture: Essilor was born from the merger of Essel, a glass-lens manufacturer, and Silor, a rival that made plastic lenses, and the two division still competed against each other.

At Lafarge, some viewed the new additive as a way to enhance the reputation of the company's R&D function. Other saw it as a strategically important move beyond building materials. In both companies, the collective belief served as an umbrella that sheltered an array of hopes and dreams; those, in turn, worked together to reinforce the collective belief.

The Persistence of Belief. Once a collective belief takes hold, it tends to perpetuate itself. For one thing, groups have a way of drowning out dissent. At Essilor and Lafarge, both lone initial dissidents – Essilor's director of research and manufacturing and Lafarge's mineral-fillers manager – were generally ignored or told that the questions they raised reflected their lack of experience or competence. Eventually, they stopped raising questions. This self-censorship gave the groups an illusion of unanimity and invulnerability, which in turn helped sustain individual belief. One manager at Essilor said that the lens's failure in the market in 1982 raised doubts in his mind. But he chose not to voice these and, because of the group's apparent unanimity, soon forgot them.

Curiously, setbacks, rather than undermining faith, often drive people to work all the harder to maintain it. Despite the Essilor lens's poor market performance, the company continued to produce it in vast quantities, consistently more than were sold. Since project members believed the market failure was only a prelude to ultimate success, they exhibited what one manager called "technological relentlessness" in their pursuit of both improvements and customers.

This intensity is not surprising, given the emotional attachment people feel for a project they passionately believe in. As one Essilor manager said of an early version of the lens: "It was a dream, and a dream come true on top of that! The product existed! It was beautiful." Another manager, recalling a setback in lens development, observed, "We didn't dare wonder whether we should stop or not. It was too hard."

Box 3.2   The exit champion and the project champion

At both Essilor and Lafarge, some of the projects' champions opposed the exit champions who successfully pulled the plugs on their projects. Although no public confrontations occurred in either case, the project champions raised with other project participants questions about the exit champions' intentions.

Such conflicts are interesting because in many ways the roles of the traditional project champion and the exit champion are similar. Just as innovations are unlikely to be implemented without champions, failing projects are unlikely to be halted without exit champions. In fact, the types of individuals who gravitate toward those roles are also similar.

Both project champions and exit champions must show initiative; after all, they have by definition assumed their roles rather than been assigned them. And they need to be energetic and determined enough to overcome the obstacles and inevitable skepticism they face. Given their similar personal traits, it's not surprising that, at a number of companies I studied, exit champions had been project champions at other points in their careers.

Differences between project champions and exit champions appear, however, in the particulars. For one thing, while project champions necessarily operate in an environment of uncertainty and ambiguity, exit champions need to remove ambiguity. They must gather hard data that will be convincing enough to overcome the opposition of believers. They need clear criteria for deciding whether to kill the project. When existing procedures don't include such criteria, they need to reach an agreement with believers on the criteria for assessing the new data; otherwise, reaching an agreement on the decision will be impossible. Thus, while project champions often violate procedures, exit champions typically have to introduce or restore them.

Project champions' reputations are often put at risk by their choice to champion what may turn out to be a failed project. Exit champions also put their reputations at risk, but the threat is of a different nature. Project champions run a long-term risk of being wrong – something that will become clear only if a project ultimately fails. Exit champions face the immediate risk that comes from challenging a popular project. That risk exists even if the exit champion is, in fact, ultimately right.

The Consequences of Belief. The greatest danger posed by an organization's collective belief in a project is that problems, even if acknowledged, won't be seen as signs of failure – or at least as issues that should be resolved before moving on to the next stage of development. At Essilor, some managers explained away the lukewarm initial demand for the lens as an aberration related to the soon-to-be-solved technical problem of layer separation, forgetting that the market was generally unaware of this problem. At Lafarge, one manager knew that the decision to build the plant was probably premature, given the available test results for the product, but he said nothing because he was eager to move forward on an enterprise everyone was certain would succeed. Managers at both companies referred to the blindness that resulted from their faith in the projects.

This blindness persists in part because collective belief undermines normal organizational procedures and safeguards. For one thing, the enthusiasm generated by faith in a project can lead to an unrealistically tight development timetable. Essilor canceled some tests and substituted shorter, less reliable ones in order to stick to its aggressive development schedule. A test to see how durable the lenses remained over time, for example, was shortened from two years to six months. Lafarge's desire to remain on schedule was the driving force in the construction of the plant before necessary tests on the additive had been completed.

Enthusiasm also can result in lenient procedures for reviewing the viability of a product throughout its development. For instance, scratch-resistance specifications for Essilor's new lens were not defined until 1990, eight years after the product was initially launched. Furthermore, widespread enthusiasm can lead to the formation of a project team filled with, and overseen by, uncritical boosters of the initiative.

Together, these factors can create a reinforcing chain that perpetuates collective belief. Decision makers' faith in the project results in an absence of clear decision criteria, which leads to ambiguous information, which in turn favors wishful thinking by those decision makers and further bolsters their belief in the project's success. In a sense, the project takes on a life of its own.

AVOIDING THE DANGERS OF BLIND FAITH

In your own company, you have undoubtedly known projects that dragged on but went nowhere. You may be aware of a handful of bad projects that are grinding along, or even picking up speed, right now. How can companies prevent this sort of thing? How could the managers at Essilor, for example, have known that the composite lens project wouldn't turn out the way the Varilux lens effort did?

They probably couldn't, at least for a while. But they could have done a number of things that would have made them better able to judge their progress and counteract the distorting effects of collective belief. Two kinds of safeguards can be build into a project before it even gets under way. Another one requires a manager involved in a project to play an important, new role.

Beware of cheerleading squads. All too often, project teams are self-selected. They include people who have volunteered because they share an initial enthusiasm for the project. They may even have worked together on successful projects in the past. They know the drill and can anticipate one another's moves. In fact, they know them too well. As they interact, there are none of the awkward missteps or misunderstandings that can produce unexpected insights – or signs of trouble. Warning flags that do appear may be ignored; after all, everyone is rooting for something they believe in.

Executives launching a project would do well, then, to include skeptics along with believers in the project teams from the outset, paying particular attention to those who will be directly involved in making decisions. Then, over the course of the initiative, some decision makers should be replaced with others, who will look at the project with fresh eyes.

At Essilor and Lafarge, top management populated the projects with true believers. In fact, in both cases, the sole initial critics joined the projects somewhat by chance. Essilor's director of research and manufacturing was involved only because he was the immediate supervisor of the manager of the plant where the lens would be made. Lafarge's mineral-fillers manager had originally been hired for another job and joined the project only because Lafarge had difficulty finding someone with both minerals and project expertise to fill out the team. At Essilor, personal relationship also came into play; some members had been friends for 20 years – a further reason that robust criticism, which might jeopardize those friendships, didn't emerge.

Only when turnover occurred for reasons unrelated to the project – retirement, health problems, the restructuring of a companywide research function – was the cohesiveness of the project groups disrupted and some measure of objectivity introduced.

Establish an early warning system. From the start, no matter how exciting or important a project is, a company needs to make sure that its control procedures and criteria for evaluating project viability at each stage of development are truly working – that they are clearly defined, rigorous, and actually met. Big companies like Essilor and Lafarge typically have these kinds of effective internal control for all sorts of processes – for example, "stage gates" that companies must go through as they proceed with a potential acquisition. But they can easily forget to establish such structures at the beginning of a project that seems bound for glory. Or even if they do establish processes for good decision making, they can end up ignoring them - or the results – amid the excitement generated by a new project.

Lafarge executive concede that they failed to adhere to their own decision criteria when they went ahead and built the plant – although the criteria were vague enough to make this fairly easy to do. Essilor had several clear procedures for testing the lens during development that weren't followed; others produced negative results, which were ignored. As one Essilor manager said: "The decision to launch was implicit. It was just a question of when."

Recognize the role of the exit champion. Sometimes it takes an individual, rather than growing evidence, to shake the collective belief of a project team. If the problem with unbridled enthusiasm starts as an unintended consequence of the legitimate work of a project champion, then what may be needed is a countervailing force – an exit champion. These people are more than devil's advocates. Instead of simply raising questions about a project, they seek objective evidence showing that problems in fact exist. This allows them to challenge – or, given the ambiguity of existing data, conceivably even to confirm – the viability of a project. They then take action based on the data. At both Essilor and Lafarge, exit champions – the new research manager at Essilor, and the new operations director at Lafarge – joined the projects as evidence of their unpromising futures was mounting. But supporters were still clinging to the shreds of positive evidence that occasionally emerged – or ignoring the evidence altogether. Had it not been for these exit champions, team members said later, the projects probably would have continued for months or even years.

To be effective, an exit champion needs to be directly involved in the project; a negative assessment from someone based elsewhere in the company is too easy to dismiss as ill-informed or motivated by organizational rivalry. The exit champion also needs a high degree of personal credibility. The managers at Essilor and Lafarge who had raised questions about the lens and paper filler during the early development stages lacked this credibility. Essilor's director of research and manufacturing was known within the organization as a naysayer; Lafarge's mineral-fillers manager, who came from another company, appeared to lack industry experience. The exit champions, by contrast, had been with their companies for a long time and were well regarded by top management. Both had a strong network of people at different levels of the company ready to provide support when they decided the project should be killed.

What kind of person would willingly assume such a role? Even if killing a project doesn't put an exit champion out of a job – the individuals at Essilor and Lafarge had responsibilities beyond the projects in question – the role, unlike that of a traditional project champion, seems to offer little in the way of prestige or other personal rewards. (For a discussion of the differences between the two roles, see Box 3.2 "The Exit Champion and the Project Champion.") In fact, the exit champion faces inevitable hostility from project supporters; those at Essilor and Lafarge were variously described as villains or dream breakers.

Consequently, exit champions need to be fearless, willing to put their reputations on the line and face the likelihood of exclusion from the camaraderie of the project team. They need to be determined: Both Essilor's and Lafarge's exit champions failed in their first attempts to stop their projects. Perhaps most important, exit champions need to have some incentive for putting themselves out to halt a bad project. For many, this will simply be an acute distaste for wasted effort. As one exit champion at another company I researched said, "When I work, I need to believe in what I do. I don't want to waste time on something that is worthless."

It is important to understand that an exit champion is not a henchman sent by top management to kill the project. The exit champions at Essilor and Lafarge certainly weren't: They were assigned their positions only because their predecessors had left the company, and they simply took the initiative to determine if their projects were likely to be successful. Indeed, it wasn't initially clear to either of them that their respective projects *should* be killed. Although signs that the projects wouldn't succeed were accumulating, in neither case was the evidence conclusive because it wasn't based on hard data.

Senior executives need to recognize the exit champion as a defined role that someone might play in the organization – otherwise, they may not know an exit champion for who he is and give him the support he will need. And they can take steps to create an environment in which such a savior would be more likely to emerge. Just as companies celebrate and recount stories of the great successes of product champions, they could perhaps identify and spread tales of courageous exit champions in their midst (or at other companies) who saved their organizations millions of dollars. Top managers should at the least make it clear that challenges to a popular project would be welcome or even rewarded. At the same time, though, they need to demand from the exit champion strong evidence of the project's weaknesses – just as they should have earlier demanded growing evidence of its viability.

IT COULDN'T HAPPEN HERE

When all is said and done, do Essilor's and Lafarge's experiences – not to mention RCA's in the case of its ill-fated SelectaVision – simply reflect bad business judgment? Were they nothing more nor less than dumb business moves? Aren't situations like these unlikely to be repeated at your company?

Don't bet on it. Although they may not always be played out on such a grand scale, stories like these are all too familiar in business. That's because belief is a powerful sentiment, and collective belief is even more powerful. Clearly, any project has to start with faith because there typically isn't much objective evidence, if any, at the beginning to justify it. But, as a project unfolds and investments increase, this faith has to be increasingly tested against the data. Indeed, the challenge for managers in the "can-do" culture of business is to distinguish between belief as a key driver of success – and belief as something that can blind managers to a project's ultimate failure.

4

Realizing the Potential of Real Options
Does Theory Meet Practice?

Alexander Triantis

The Annual Real Options Conference, now in its seventh year, has been a useful forum for the exchange and debare of new ideas about corporate strategy and valuation. The tag line for the conference, "Theory Meets Practice," reflects the goal of bringing together academics and practitioners to explore new approaches for making capital investment decisions and adapting such approaches for practical application. And given the presence of both academics and practitioners in this audience, a natural topic for my talk today comes from simply transforming the tag line into a question, "Does Theory Meet Practice?" Is the gap between theory and practice closing, and what can we do to speed this up?

The idea of viewing corporate investment opportunities as "real options" has been around for more than 25 years – in fact, it dates back to Stewart Myers' use of the phrase in his well-known 1977 article.[1] Since then, the idea has had a huge impact on academic research. Based on a literature database that I've maintained since the late 1990s, I estimate there are now nearly 1,000 research papers that incorporate real options ideas.[2] Real options concepts and techniques have not only become prevalent in research in finance and economics, but have also more recently influenced research in virtually every business discipline, including strategy, organizations, management science, operations management, information systems, accounting, and marketing. Real options has thus become a truly cross-disciplinary area of research, with great potential to improve corporate decision-making while promoting better understanding of the role of uncertainty on investment activity in various sectors of our economy.

Given this wide acceptance and activity in academia, one might expect commensurate interest in the practitioner realm. Real options has indeed been used by many companies in evaluating investment opportunities and associated risks, and many managers can point to improvements in decision-making as a result of adopting real options. But even so, the extent of acceptance and application of real options today has probably not lived up to the expectations created in the mid- to late-1990s, when real options first began to take hold at a broad cross-section of companies.

In their 2001 survey of the CFOs of some 400 Fortune 1000 companies, John Graham and Campbell Harvey reported that about a third of the CFOs said they "always" or "almost always" use real options when evaluating new investments.[3] But in another recent survey of Fortune 1000 CFOs, the authors reported a significantly smaller fraction of CFOs – around 10–15% – using real option techniques "always" or "often."[4] And a survey conducted by Bain & Co. in 2000 found that only 9% of the senior executives polled had used real options.

Much of the differences in these survey findings could reflect differing interpretations of the term "real options." In an interview-based survey of 40 corporate managers that I conducted with Adam Borison in 2001, we found that there were indeed significant differences in the ways in which managers were using real options in their organizations. For many firms, real options served primarily as a conceptual tool for strategic planning and framing of decision problems. However, for the majority of firms in our sample, real options valuation techniques, ranging from simple to very rigorous, were being used to evaluate investment opportunities.[5]

Regardless of the exact numbers, it appears that many companies have incorporated real options analysis to varying degrees into their decision-making processes. Even a 10–20% adoption rate over the period of a decade may be quite promising, given the very gradual acceptance of other corporate decision-making techniques, including NPV. Nevertheless, the question remains whether the initial rate of corporate adoption of real options is sustainable. If early successes have led to positive feedback within and across corporations, one would expect the trend to continue. But there is at least one sign that this may not in fact be the case. The Bain survey in 2000 found a very high defection rate (32%) among those senior executives who said that they had used real options. Though this is the only, and perhaps unreliable, statistic we have that might help us calibrate the trajectory of real options adoption, it does not bode well. It is certainly cause to pause and reflect on why theory may not in fact be meeting the needs of practice.

I will begin by discussing some of the key successes of real options to date. Next I will present some critiques of real options raised by practitioners. This will lead in turn to a proposed research agenda, based on five key themes, that I believe can help bridge the current gap between theory and practice.

NEW INSIGHTS AND A NEW VOCABULARY

The interest in real options has helped to focus corporate managers' attention on the value of flexibility. Specifically, in planning a company's investment and operating strategies, managers are increasingly aware that they can respond to new information over time, and that this kind of flexibility affects not only their future decisions, but also their present ones. Viewing corporate strategy in a real options framework is likely to make management both more *reactive*, in the sense of responding effectively as uncertainties are resolved over time, and more *proactive* in building flexibility into projects.

What kinds of strategic insights and recommendations come from viewing projects in this more dynamic framework?

Some of the earliest and best-known insights stem from our knowledge of the pricing of financial options. For example, financial options that are "out-of-the-money" – those where the cost of purchasing the underlying asset is greater than the value of the asset – often sell at high premiums based on the possibility that the asset value could increase beyond the exercise cost before the expiration date. By analogy, corporate real investment opportunities that appear unprofitable when managerial flexibility is ignored in the evaluation analysis *often* have positive value when viewed as growth options – options that can be exploited if and when underlying value drivers, such as input and output prices, move in a profitable direction. For this reason, early-stage projects – or companies that are burning cash and may even have dubious long-term potential under the most likely scenarios – may still have considerable value owing to the possibility of future favorable events, particularly if the underlying uncertainty is large.

A second important lesson from financial options is that growth options that are "in-the-money" (that is, the investment outlay is lower than the present value of the project) are often best left unexercised at the current time. The key insight here is that unfavorable investment situations can be avoided by waiting, and this potential benefit may outweigh the loss due to foregone profits or competitor entry.

While knowledge of these basic facts about options has influenced managerial decision-making, the real impact on shareholder value creation has come more from a change in the corporate mindset about uncertainty and risk. Rather than treating risk as something to be avoided, real options thinking encourages managers to view volatility as a potential source of value, with profound implications for the design of projects and corporate strategy. For example, valuable options can be created in a variety of ways:

■ by dividing up large projects into a number of stages;
■ by investing in information acquisition or production;
■ by introducing "modularity" in manufacturing and design;
■ by developing competing prototypes for new products; or
■ by investing in infrastructure that provides a platform for potential future growth.[6]

In general, the concept of strategic foresight has become more formalized as managers focus less on the "most-likely" scenario and more on the distribution of possible outcomes, taking explicit account of the uncertainties that lie ahead and incorporating flexibility into project design in order to respond to future events. In addition to restructuring R&D, manufacturing, and supply chain processes, managers now consider "selling" flexibility by providing customers with options that they value more than the firm's cost of providing them.[7]

From a risk-and-return perspective, there is also growing recognition that the risk profiles of projects differ considerably based upon whether the projects are early-stage investments in creating options or later-stage expenditures that involve exercising options to complete investment in a project. Furthermore, as suggested above, the real options mindset forces corporate managers to consider more carefully the opportunity cost of investing. For instance, by choosing to invest in new technology infrastructure today, the firm may be passing up the opportunity to invest in a potentially superior, but mutually exclusive, technology in the near future.

These insights seem to resonate with corporate management. Many managers view the insights that emerge from the options analogy as confirming, and perhaps further honing, their instincts, while others find that these insights transform the way they plan and operate at their level of the organization. In fact, a common tendency of managers on first becoming acquainted with the concepts is to see "real options everywhere." And over time, such managers also generally develop an options-based, shorthand vocabulary that does a better job of communicating strategic objectives internally and, in some cases, to the firm's shareholders and the analyst community.

THE SEARCH FOR KILLER APS

Any new technology needs "killer aps," applications that are particularly well suited for the technology and thus help to "sell" the tool in practice. In the case of real options, the first major area of application was in valuing investments in the exploration and development of natural resource reserves, particularly minerals and oil and gas. But the range of applications has increased considerably, particularly in the last decade. The use of real options to evaluate research and development programs has spread well beyond the energy and mineral industries. The pharmaceutical industry and, indeed, the entire life sciences area, together with the technology industry, have provided many examples of successful implementations of real options. Real options analysis is also frequently used in operations management in manufacturing and power generation, especially in capacity planning and the evaluation of operating flexibility. More recently, real options tools have been applied in valuations of various kinds of corporate restructurings, including mergers and acquisitions, joint ventures, and divestitures, and in the planning of infrastructure investments, both brick and mortar as well as IT.

These main applications have some common features that make them particularly well suited to – and often most in need of – real options analysis. They all involve significant up-front investments that often don't lead to immediate cash flows. They also tend to have well-defined stages where the framing of the problem can be logically laid out and where there are major, well-defined sources of uncertainty whose resolution is expected to contribute significantly to the outcome and ultimate value of the projects. In addition, in most cases, data is readily available to estimate key parameters of the model. In the case of natural resources, for example, this data comes directly from financial markets, such as futures and options markets. Real options can also be modeled more accurately in firms that have proprietary opportunities, such as the right to develop a piece of physical or intellectual property, yet operate in perfectly competitive input and output markets, where prices fluctuate independently of the decisions of any particular firm in the industry. Finally, real options seems to have gained more traction in companies where the majority of managers and other employees have science or engineering backgrounds, and are thus comfortable dealing with the basics of probability theory and quantitative modeling.

While the projects or situations in which real options analysis is most widely used have several common characteristics, there are many differentiating features among these applications. For instance, some projects involve a capacity decision, while others require a simple go/no go decision. In some cases, investment decisions may be contingent on one key source of uncertainty that resolves in a continuous fashion over time, while in other cases there may be several variables whose uncertainty is resolved only if the firm invests in information acquisition. Not surprisingly, many of the more recent studies of real options have focused on tailoring real options analysis to better suit applications according to the specific structure and unique characteristics of each type of investment decision. Such studies serve both to refine and to reinforce our intuitive sense of the effect of real options on the strategy, value, and risk of projects and companies in different industries.

REAL OPTIONS IN THE CROSSHAIRS

Despite the growing number of successful implementations, real options has its fair share of critics among practitioners. And as the profile of real options has increased in recent years, the critics have become both more numerous and more vocal. The criticisms aimed at real options seem to fall into four main categories.

First, real options has on occasion been identified as one of the causes of the Internet bubble – and it has even been blamed for the demise of Enron. Loose talk about growth options may well have been used to justify what we now know were sky-high valuations of certain technology-related firms, particularly early-stage Internet ventures. While this type of hot air may be capable of inflating a late-90s-style equity bubble, there were plenty of other plausible suspects, from aggressive accounting to media hype to the proliferation of inexperienced "day traders."

In the only published valuation model of an Internet company that I'm aware of, Eduardo Schwartz and Mark Moon developed a carefully calibrated real options analysis to value Amazon at the end of 1999.[8] The stock price they obtained was roughly one-sixth of Amazon's traded price at the close of 1999, and reasonably close to the post-crash stock price. Thus, while a real options "mindset" can be useful, there is no substitute for careful analysis.

As for Enron, it became one of the more prominent poster children for real options. The company had successfully implemented real options in various facets of its operations, at least from a tactical perspective. But, as has become clear, the demise of Enron had to do with many factors quite unrelated to the use of real options – and thus those critics of real options who point to Enron, or more generally to energy trading companies, appear to be throwing the baby out with the bathwater.

A very different type of critique comes from a separate camp, namely decision analysts, who question the originality and, in some cases, the appropriateness of real options analysis. After all, the idea of systematically mapping out a range of scenarios over time and analyzing how managers should react under these different scenarios was developed by decision analysts four decades ago. Furthermore, some real options analyses have been criticized as inappropriately bundling together "private" and "market" risks, thereby sacrificing some of the specific information that pertains to each of these types of uncertainties.[9]

There is clearly some merit to this "old wine, new bottles" critique. And there are undoubtedly circumstances where decision analysis represents a perfectly reasonable, and considerably more straightforward, approach. But having made that concession, I would argue that real options has at least four significant advantages over conventional decision analysis. First, it has focused attention on the objective of shareholder value maximization. Second, and related to the first point, to the extent that investors' value expectations, and their tradeoffs between risk and return, are reflected in equity and derivatives markets, information from these markets can be used to get more precise estimates of the value that would be created by projects under consideration *from the perspective of the firm's shareholders*. Third, the conceptual framework and shorthand vocabulary of options has helped to simplify the framing of investment decisions. Fourth, at least some decision analysts concede that real options has placed more emphasis than earlier frameworks on "downstream" decisions, such as decisions to abandon uneconomic projects or to expand projects that have become more promising with time.

Now I turn to what I believe are the two significant critiques of real options that both academics developing models and practitioners implementing these models should consider quite seriously. The first is that real options models tend to reflect "perfection" rather than economic reality. Managers are assumed to be completely rational and loyal to the firms' shareholders. They can be counted on to make the right decisions at exactly the right time. The right times to invest in options and to exercise them are in turn all based on managers having perfect information about the relevant parameters that determine the underlying project's value and volatility. On top of these assumptions, the execution of all projects is assumed to be completely unaffected by the firm's other projects, its capital structure, its hedging activities, or by the actions of other firms that may invest in and exercise similar options. While such assumptions clearly simplify the job of modeling investment decisions, they obviously fail to capture important realities of corporate decision-making.

The other – and to me the most formidable – objection to real options would appear to come from the opposite direction. That is, rather than criticizing the simplicity and artificiality of the models, many practitioners view the existing models as too complicated to use and even more so to explain. I call this the "Real Options as an Extreme Sport" critique. Although it may be impressive to see a real options analysis being performed with all its subtle maneuvers, this is not something that you would feel comfortable trying in your own business, let alone trying to explain to a corporate board of directors. Senior management is understandably leery of any black box presented to them by the champions of a project.

BRIDGING THE GAP BETWEEN THEORY AND PRACTICE

The last two critiques of real options by practitioners lead me to cite five key challenges that need to be addressed by future researchers so that our collective research efforts can achieve the goal of providing sound guidance to improve the practice of decision-making. The five main challenges are these: (1) refining the models of perfection; (2) splitting options; (3) modeling managerial behavior; (4) developing heuristics; and (5) valuing the whole firm.

Refining the Models of Perfection

As mentioned earlier, many of our existing models, and certainly the ones that have made their way into practice, reflect a set of assumptions based to a large extent on "perfect markets" and "value-maximizing managers." These models draw on the analogy between real options and financial options, without recognizing some of the key differences between them. For example, the underlying assert in most real options models is effectively (if not explicitly) assumed to be traded in liquid markets with a readily observable price. Option holders are assumed to exercise their options at the optimal time, and to ignore the actions of holders of identical options. Each option is treated as completely separable from other securities in the investor's portfolio. While these assumptions are fairly standard when dealing with financial options, they are clearly much less appropriate in the context of real options.

While we certainly need to address the fundamental differences between real options that are held as part of a corporate entity and financial options that are held within a portfolio of traded securities – and I will discuss some of these differences shortly – there are a number of important ways in which real option valuation models can be further refined from a technical perspective. This line of research parallels in many ways the significant advances that have been made in the financial option pricing realm over the last couple of decades, and that continue to be pursued.

First, and I believe foremost, we need to be careful about specifying the distribution for each of the underlying assets in our model, whether that be a specific commodity price or demand, or a "bundled" uncertainty in the form of the underlying project value. In many of the applications in which real options analysis is used, the distributions of the uncertainties differ significantly from the standard lognormal distribution that is assumed in Black-Scholes and other related models. There may be mean-reversion or jumps in the process for the underlying variables, and the volatility and convenience yields may be stochastic. In the case where there is more than one uncertainty, the correlation may also be stochastic.

Models based on new distribution specifications will continue to be an important contribution to academic literature and to practice, as will research that provides better guidance on how to estimate the nature of the distribution and the key parameters involved. Since the distributions assumed will define the scenarios through time and the cash flows in each scenario, these distributions may have a very significant effect on the valuation of the investment opportunity and the decisions made over time. Given this first-order effect, this presents a very important focal point for future research.

The second main ingredient driving the valuation and exercise of real options is the specification of the price of risk or, more formally, the state-contingent prices assumed for cash flows received at different points in time and under different scenarios. We all recognize that properly reflecting the way in which investors discount a future cash flow stream for its risk is a big challenge. It is also no easy task to explain clearly what techniques we are using to accomplish this. Nonetheless, the proper treatment of risk from the shareholder's perspective is one of the key features of real options that we are extolling, so we can't ignore this important challenge.

In the very specific case where we value real options using a set of commodity futures prices – take petroleum futures, for instance – the risk-return relationship is implicitly embedded in the certainty-equivalent values that the futures prices represent. However, the maturity of these futures contracts typically stop far short of the horizon of the projects we are trying to value, creating challenges in accurately valuing the cash flows at the far end of the project's life. Furthermore, the petroleum-based project is unlikely to have the same liquidity as the package of futures contracts used to replicate the project, and this issue should be considered somehow in the valuation of the project.

For the majority of real options applications, relevant futures markets do not exist and thus futures prices can't be used. Instead, the price of risk that we need to account for in the valuation is effectively obtained by finding "comparable" investment opportunities in the market. This is the essence of the standard DCF procedure we have used in corporate finance for decades. The main difference in this regard between what we do in real options versus in a standard DCF calculation is that, rather than finding a comparable for the investment opportunity we are ultimately trying to value – the real option – we obtain a comparable for an underlying, or option-free, project. We do this because the risk profile of the underlying project is much more stable and straightforward, and thus we have a better chance of matching it with a comparable in the market.

But when we then go to the market to find comparable firms, we rarely find nice, clean, "pure-play" investments that resemble the option-free underlying project. Instead, we tend to find companies very much like the one whose real option we are trying to value – companies that consist of both cash-generating "assets-in-place" and less tangible future growth options. Another approach for a company valuing its real options is to use its own WACC to value the underlying project. The problem with this common practice, however, is that because the WACC presumably represents a blend of the expected rates of return on both lower-risk assets-in-place and higher-risk options, it is likely to overstate the risk of the underlying project.

The key point here is that we haven't yet provided consistent guidance on how to get clean estimates of discount rates for underlying projects and, thus, for most investment opportunities for which real options techniques are used – and so risk is not properly being accounted for. We need to work on this deficiency, which clearly limits the precision of valuations in practice.

The third way in which our models of perfection can be further refined is to develop superior computational methods to obtain accurate solutions in an efficient manner. One significant advance in this direction is the development of more flexible Monte Carlo simulation models that can be used to value American-style options. Since Monte Carlo simulation readily accommodates multiple uncertainties and complex distributions, its ability to handle problems with multiple decision points has created a powerful solution method that can be used with most real option problems that occur in practice.

Splitting Options

Turning away from our models of perfection, let's now consider the various features that make real options different from financial options. One of the key differences is that many real options, particularly growth options, are not held exclusively or completely by just one company. Rather, the potential gains from these options are split across more than one party.[10] There are a couple of ways in which this happens.

The first, and the one that receives the most attention, stems from competition between two or more companies involved in the same type of business – for instance, technology companies that are planning to launch similar new products. There have been numerous models of competition developed in the real options literature, and this will continue to be one of the key research avenues in this area. The complexities of game theory are further complicated by the dynamic nature of real options problems. In addition to elegant models that allow us to derive interesting insights about corporate behavior in a context where companies compete to exercise similar growth options, we have extensive tree-based game theory/real options models that, while more cumbersome, are potentially more applicable in practice. Yet, there is significantly more to be done in this area, particularly since the results of game theory models are often quite sensitive to the underlying assumptions of the model.

The second way in which real options are split between parties is across the different links of a value chain. While some growth options may lie entirely within vertically integrated companies, most growth options in the economy are created and exercised by the cooperative activity of more than one firm. For instance, the option to expand capacity in the airline industry is split across the airlines and the aircraft manufacturers, not to mention airports and other entities. The manner in which options are split between parties is governed by the contractual agreements between those parties. The appropriate design of those contracts is critical to ensuring that the investment in, and exercise of, the overall growth options are done in an optimal fashion so that the options' values are maximized. The contract design, which involves remedies in the case of breach, and may itself involve option features, will determine whether the parties pursue their own conflicting objectives, such as investing at the wrong time or at too high or low a level, or instead work to maximize the value of the partnership.[11] Thus, providing guidance on how to design contracts is essential to extracting the full value of growth options and other real options that exist in the economy.

Government regulation may also determine how growth options are split in many industries, both horizontally across direct competitors and vertically across the value chain, including consumers. For instance, regulation of the power and energy industries, and broader anti-trust and patent regulation and enforcement, will affect how companies invest in and exercise their growth options, and thus should be carefully designed to promote efficient creation and exploitation of growth options.

Modeling Managerial Behavior

To borrow a well-known saying about guns, decision tools don't make decisions, people do. Unless we can appropriately understand managerial behavior, and either modify it or compensate for it through our decision-making tools, the decision support tools that we design may not necessarily yield the results we expect. The two key issues of managerial behavior that need to be addressed are unintended mistakes stemming from "cognitive biases" and intentional actions arising from misaligned incentives.

In virtually all corporate investment evaluation situations, even if there are some variables that can be accurately assessed from financial markets (such as the spot and futures prices of oil), other variables will need to be subjectively estimated (such as the expected volume of reserves). Of course, one of the lessons of real options is that we need to infuse rigor into the evaluation process, and that means attempting to make the estimates of our evaluation inputs as objective as possible. But it is widely recognized that the cognitive biases of managers, subject matter experts, and analysts tend to creep into the analysis, creating more or less predictable distortions.

It is difficult to ignore these and other cognitive biases of managers, since they can have a significant impact on the recommendations produced by a real options analysis. Moreover, a company's culture and its organizational structure may influence this behavior – for instance, by encouraging optimism as a generally positive managerial attribute. The emergent field of behavioral corporate finance has started to address some of these issues.[12]

While cognitive biases may lead to inadvertent inefficiencies in investment policy, the incentive structure that drives managerial behavior will have a more deliberate impact on managerial decision-making. Compensation systems that reward short-term earnings and cash flow, either directly or indirectly (say, by being tied to short-term stock performance) may discourage investment in early-stage options (such as R&D) that will consume cash, while encouraging premature exercise of later-stage growth options that will produce earnings and cash.[13]

Aside from near-term compensation, managers will also clearly consider the implications of their project choices on their careers. Managers' decisions to take on projects may be influenced more by the projects' expected effects on the size of their business units, or on their future allocations of the corporate budget, than on their ability to generate shareholder value. For similar reasons, managers are also likely to prefer to stick with a losing project as long as possible (with the hope that things will improve) instead of exercising their abandonment option.

The cognitive bias and misaligned incentives of managers have two important implications for real options models. The first is that we need to incorporate actual managerial behavior into our models. While one could also make this comment in the context of standard capital budgeting techniques, it is much more relevant here. After all, the key underpinning of real options is the existence of managerial flexibility – and while this flexibility can be used to create value for shareholders, it can also be used by managers to benefit themselves at the expense of shareholders.[14]

The second key implication of the managerial behavior I have described is that we need to provide guidance on how to redesign compensation systems, organizational structures, and investment evaluation processes that account for managers' cognitive biases and their incentive-driven behavior, and that reflect the type of complex investment decisions that managers control over time. The ability to distinguish ex post between good outcomes and good decisions will always be a challenge, and managers will always try to rationalize bad outcomes and claim credit for good outcomes. Two promising ways to address these issues are indexing performance metrics to industry outcomes and delaying compensation to match the duration of projects, at the very least by lengthening the vesting period for equity-linked compensation.

Developing Heuristics

For the most part, academics focus on making models accurate rather than simple. However, theoretically accurate models are often poorly executed in practice *because of* their complexity, while simple models can often be quite effectively employed despite their lack of precision. In the end, it is not clear which is better. One could certainly argue that simpler real options models are more likely to be employed in practice, thus reducing the use of less accurate valuation models such as NPV and so resulting in better (though not optimal) decision-making. Yet relatively little is being done to develop better heuristics, or simpler approaches, to evaluate real options and their associated exercise strategies.

This does not imply that we shouldn't attempt to refine our already complex models in order to make them more theoretically sound. But in the end, those models may serve more as benchmarks to gauge the accuracy of simpler models rather than as the models that are ultimately used in practice. We can then carefully evaluate which heuristics seem to work best in different situations.

Consider three valuation heuristics that are now widely used in practice. The first, and by far most popular, is the NPV rule, which uses a company's WACC to discount expected earnings or cash flows. The NPV technique works quite well under some conditions – namely, if the project's risk is similar to that of the overall firm, if a constant leverage ratio will be maintained throughout the life of the project, and if there is little option value embedded in the project (either because the project is a now-or-never opportunity or there is little flexibility to alter the course of the project over time). But given the restrictiveness of these conditions, it is also clear that NPV will not work in many cases, and it is for these situations that we may need better heuristics.

Another heuristic involves a simple modification to the standard NPV rule – one that involves raising the discount rate above the firm's cost of capital. This has been proposed for situations where there is a valuable option to delay a project.[15] While this may not lead to the exact optimal exercise policy, the error is often small in terms of its impact on the value of the investment opportunity – and, perhaps surprisingly, the error does not appear to be all that sensitive to the gap between the assumed rate and the company's WACC.

This heuristic is used in practice, perhaps not only as a way of accounting for the option to delay, but also as a crude means of offsetting excessively optimistic cash flow forecasts for projects.

Another frequently used class of NPV-based heuristics includes sensitivity, scenario, and simulation analyses. These types of analyses try to overcome one of the major shortcomings of standard NPV that real options analysis directly addresses – notably, the near-exclusive focus on average or most-likely values, with little attention to the potential distribution of outcomes. Sensitivity and simulation analyses help decision makers better understand the effect of the entire distributions of the different input variables on the value of a project. But unlike real options, these techniques fail to take account of managerial flexibility to respond to new information over time.

Scenario analysis, by contrast, lays out a few possible paths of future development, and then devotes considerable attention to exploring the ways that managers can respond to each. But, in addition to focusing on only a few possible outcomes, scenario analysis has two major shortcomings vis-à-vis real options analysis. First, in scenario analysis, a decision taken at any particular point in time is based on the implicit assumption that only one particular path of uncertainty resolution will materialize in the future. In real options analysis, by contrast, *all* possible future paths are effectively considered when making the decision. Second, as with traditional decision tree analysis, scenario analysis does not do a good job of accounting for the effects of risk on the valuation of a project. Despite such limitations, however, scenario analysis is a useful supplement to standard NPV analysis and can lead to better decision-making.

Given the wide use of NPV and its variations, there is clearly a demand in practice for simple techniques that can address the impact of uncertainty and managerial flexibility when making capital investment decisions. If one objective of academic research is to provide practitioners with sound methods to use in practice, it is not enough for academics to simply generate complex analytic techniques and then allow practitioners to figure out how to simplify them for implementation. Rather, academics should formally evaluate different heuristics to figure out which ones are reasonably accurate, and which have the greatest potential to mislead management in their investment or strategic evaluation process. We need to better understand which complexities in real option models are necessary for specific applications, and which add little in the way of accuracy while detracting from the transparency of the valuation methodology. If management finds real options analysis to be too complex a tool, or suspects that the tool can be deliberately or unintentionally misused in ways that are difficult to detect, it simply won't be used – and the gains we expect from the better framing and evaluation of projects will not be realized.

Finally, an important ingredient in enabling the technology transfer from ivory towers to corporate headquarters is the development of software that facilitates the framing of the decision problem, the computations involved in the solution process, and, critically important, the presentation of results. User-friendly software will undoubtedly help to promote the use of real options in organizations. There are already several software packages in use and in development. Some are based primarily on decision tree or binomial lattice frameworks, while others employ simulation as the underlying modeling technique, which works particularly well for investment situations where there is a single decision point. I expect that we will see much more software design activity in the near future.

Valuing and Managing the Firm

Corporate executives are very responsive to the ways in which their companies are evaluated by their investors and by the financial intermediaries who supply information to investors. If EPS is the key metric followed by analysts, managers will focus on ensuring stable growth in EPS, even if this results in decisions that reduce the fundamental long-term value of the company. Thus, in order for more companies to focus on enhancing the value of their real options, and thus on evaluating their options accurately, more analysts and sophisticated investors will need to adopt real option analysis as at least one of the tools they use for assessing shareholder value. But this unfortunately appears a long way off.

To get to that point, the previous four research agenda items need to be addressed, especially the development of simpler models. But there are other issues as well that need to be considered in determining the overall valuation of a company. For instance, how do the various projects or options to invest within the company's portfolio interact with each other? The exercise of each growth option in a company may affect the value of the company's current assets and its other growth options, and thus the incremental value of each growth option is difficult to assess accurately. Another important challenge is to capture the effect of a company's financing and risk management strategies on the exercise and value of the firm's options. Since a company's financing policy, like its investment strategy, is likely to be dynamic rather than static, it is challenging to value the tax shields associated with the company's portfolio of current and future investment. Furthermore, to the extent that external financing is needed to exercise the firm's growth options, the costs and constraints associated with external financing will affect the value of the firm's options.

Given the complexity of the task, it is not surprising that real options analysis hasn't yet hit its stride as a leading method for corporate valuation. Part of the problem, of course, is the difficulty in obtaining the type of detailed information required to perform an accurate valuation analysis. However, more analysis now appreciate the importance of viewing companies as portfolios that must be disaggregated to be valued properly. There is also growing awareness of the shortcomings of standard DCF analyses that rely on most-likely scenarios rather than accounting for the full range of possible scenarios for a company's future. Thus, real options has already piqued the interest of many analysts who are looking for better valuation techniques.

As interest in the analyst community grows, it seems inevitable that companies will increasingly adopt a real options-based framework for looking at corporate decisions in which uncertainty and managerial flexibility are key considerations. Companies will revisit not only how they allocate capital, but also how they should structure dynamic financing and risk management policies, and how they should design incentive compensation systems so that managers are more likely to carry out the optimal policies.

GOING FORWARD

Real options provides an important opportunity to improve the science of valuation and the practice of management. Nevertheless, there is – and will always be – much that is art rather than science in this process. Organizations don't adapt very readily to applying any new tool, particularly one as sophisticated as real options. Corporate acceptance and implementation will require senior-level buy-in and strong leadership, careful adoption of simpler versions of the tool, user-friendly software that can handle the modeling complexity, significant investment in training analysts and managers, deliberate alignment of managerial and shareholder incentives, and the creation of appropriate controls in the capital investment process. Despite these challenges, I believe that there will continue to be a gradual and consistent diffusion of real options analysis throughout business organizations over the next few decades, and that real options will eventually become a standard part of corporate strategic planning and the valuation of capital investment projects. When this happens, NPV will assume its rightful role as a special case of capital investment decision-making, as will other special cases to be used for particular applications – and real options will no longer be considered a "supplementary" capital budgeting tool.

But it would be naïve to think that there will not continue to be a lot of resistance. Academics must listen carefully to the critiques of practitioners and allow them to influence the kinds of problems that are addressed in academic research. To the extent that we can be responsive to the concerns of practitioners, and improve the normative models we offer them, real options will have the type of profound impact that we have long been expecting, but which has not yet been realized.

NOTES

1. Stewart Myers, "Determinants of Corporate Borrowing," *Journal of Financial Economics*, Vol. 5(1977), pp. 147–175.
2. This database is available at www.rhsmith.umd.edu/finance/atriantis, and can be searched based on author name, keywords, journals, or date.

3. John Graham and Campbell Harvey, "The Theory and Practice of Corporate Finance: Evidence from the Field," *Journal of Financial Economics*, Vol. 60 (2001).

4. Patricia and Glenn Ryan's survey of 205 Fortune 1000 CFOs found that, at the 75th percentile level (categorized as "always or often"), 1.6% of the CFOs used Real Option techniques, 5.3% used Option Pricing techniques, 7.6% used Complex Mathematical Models, and 7.9% used Decision Trees. All of these categories overlap somewhat or completely with real options analysis. For example, the category "complex mathematical models" included real options models. For further details, see Patricia Ryan and Glenn Ryan, "Capital Budgeting Practices of the Fortune 1000: How Have Things Changed?" *Journal of Business and Management* (October 2002).

5. Further distinctions in the way that real options analysis is implemented in different organizations are discussed in Alex Triantis and Adam Borison, "Real Options: State of the Practice," *Journal of Applied Corporate Finance* (Summer 2001).

6. I provide further examples and detail in A. Triantis, "Creating and Managing Shareholder Value: A View through a Real Options Lens," in *Real Options and Business Strategy: Applications in Decision Making* (London: Risk Books, 1999), pp. 39–58. For an example of the value of modular plant design, see Tom Copeland an Vladimir Antikarov, "Meeting the Georgetown Challenge," *Journal of Applied Corporate Finance*, this issue.

7. For instance, Dell and HP have built flexibility into their supply chain systems that allows customers to configure their own hardware; see my article with Corey Billington and Blake Johnson, "A Real Options Perspective on Managing Supply Chain Risk in High Technology," *Journal of Applied Corporate Finance*, Vol. 15, No. 2 (Winter 2003).

8. Eduardo Schwartz and Mark Moon, "Rational Pricing of Internet Companies," *Financial Analysts Journal*, Volume 56 (May/June 2000).

9. See Adam Borison, "Real Options Analysis: Where Are the Emperor's Clothes?" In *Journal of Applied Corporate Finance*, Volume 17 Number 2, pp. 17–31.

10. See Peter Miller and Ted O'Leary, "Managing Operational Flexibility in Investment Decisions: The Case of Intel," *Journal of Applied Corporate Finance*.

11. Under the frequently used expectations damages remedy for breach, a growth option shared by two parties will be suboptimally exercised, and the loss in value can be quite significant; see A. Triantis and G. Triantis, "Timing Problems in Contract Breach Decisions," *Journal of Law and Economics*, Vol. 41 (1998).

12. See Hersh Shefrin, "Behavioral Corporate Finance," *Journal of Applied Corporate Finance*, Vol. 14, No. 3 (Fall 2001).

13. See John Graham, Campbell Harvey, and Shiva Rajgopal, "The Economic Implications of Corporate Financial Reporting," *Journal of Accounting and Economics* (2005).

14. It is in this line of research where empirical studies on real options could prove to be most useful. For instance, by observing corporate investment behavior

and comparing it to our rational models of creating and exercising real options, we might be able to calibrate the degree of suboptimality of exercise decisions in practice. But this will clearly be extremely challenging, since it assumes that the researcher is able to estimate both the true parameters of the underlying valuation model as well as managers' estimates of those parameters. Only then would we be able to conclude whether the exercise decisions are being driven by managerial incentives that differ from those of shareholders, or whether management unknowingly misestimated the input parameters to the model.

15. See Robert McDonald, "Real Options and Rules of Thumb in Capital Budgeting," in M. J. Brennan and L. Trigeorgis, Eds, *Project Flexibility, Agency and Competition* (London: Oxford University Press, 2000).

This article is based on my keynote address at the 7th Annual International Conference on Real Options held at the McDonough School of Business, Georgetown University, July 10–12, 2003. Reproduced from *Journal of Applied Corporate Finance*, Vol. 17 No. 2 (Spring 2005), pp. 8–16.

Real Options

K. Leslie and M. Michaels

BEST PRACTICE IN MANAGING REAL OPTIONS

Two UK companies, BP and PowerGen, exemplify the benefits of real-options thinking. Between 1990 and 1996, BP increased its market value from $18 billion to $30 billion, representing a total return to shareholders of 167%. Over the same period, PowerGen raised its market value from $1.4 billion to $3.8 billion, a return of almost 300%.

In both cases, most assets and earnings were in mature industries. BP's exploitation of North Sea oil and gas field development options took place against a background of falling reservoir sizes and volatile oil and gas prices – quite unlike the boom days of the 1970s and early 1980s. PowerGen, for its part, has had to deal with barely rising demand, a saturated market and increasing competition to build new capacity.

Both companies managed to earn extraordinary returns in unfavourable environments because they followed a strategy of making incremental investments to secure the upside while insuring against the downside. They also delayed committing to investment until they had confirmed that it would be worth while, usually by acting on the six levers of option value.

Extending the Field of Vision

The application of real options steers management towards maximizing opportunity while minimizing obligation, encouraging it to think of every situation as an initial investment against future possibility. As a result, management's field of vision is extended beyond long-term plans too rarely properly reexamined, to encompass the full range of opportunities available to it at any moment. Real-options thinking achieves this through its most basic contribution and its most striking departure from the dicta of net present value: the attitude it fosters to uncertainty.

For BP, the economics of a prospective oil or gas field are highly uncertain in terms of margins (oil prices fluctuate, operating costs are unpredictable) and volume (recoverable reserves are difficult to estimate at the start of the licensing, exploration, appraisal and development process). The company has responded by embracing uncertainty. It has increased its exposure to volatile undeveloped prospects by accumulating licences that exploit the flexibility to respond to new technology and operating practices in order to make currently uneconomic prospects profitable. It is a strategy that has transformed BP's view of the North Sea's potential.

For PowerGen, the electricity pool is uncertain in terms of price and volume. The company's strategy evolved from "secure baseload with minimal uncertainty" to "explore opportunistic operating strategies." The outcome was a shift from a net present value approach that would have maximized the baseload volume of a few plants and closed all the others, to a policy of increasing operational flexibilities to respond to the market – and capturing marginal volumes at high prices.

In an increasingly uncertain world, real options have broad application as a management tool. They will change the way you value opportunities. They will change the way you create value – both reactively and proactively. And they will change the way you think.

HOW BP MAXIMIZES THE VALUE OF ITS OILFIELDS

As noted earlier, the sequence of spending decisions that leads to the development of an oil or gas field constitutes a classic real option. First, a company acquires a licence to explore; then it engages in low-cost seismic exploration. If the results are promising, exploratory drilling is undertaken.

If the exploratory well is positive, appraisal drilling takes place. Full development – and most expenditure – goes ahead only if these preliminary stages are completed satisfactorily.

While correct, this description captures no more than the value of the real option's reactive flexibility. Had BP acted on reactive flexibilities alone, it would probably not be earning superior returns in mature provinces like the North Sea, where profitable low-risk investment opportunities were exhausted long ago. By the same token, new opportunities such as those west of Shetland and in certain high-pressure/high-temperature areas of the UK continental shelf require heavy capital investment and carry geological and technical risks, so they usually appear uneconomic under net present value analysis. But because cumulative holding costs are so low and the payoff can be huge if the geological, technical and partnership uncertainties are resolved, almost any option value justifies holding on to such leases.

BP paid the penalty for taking a limited, reactive flexibility approach when it developed the giant Magnus field in the early 1980s. It took an overcautious view of the forecast production plan and built too small a platform. Had proactive flexibilities been considered, higher production might have been achieved. As it was, production was constrained, and Magnus was obliged to pump for an expensive extended period, rather than following the optimal path of build-up, brief peak and long decline.

When the company has taken proactive flexibilities into account, however, the results have been remarkable.[1] Its handling of the Andrew Field is an example. The field was discovered in the mid-1970s but not developed at the time because it was small and, given the drilling technology of those days, required huge investment. The oil price collapse of the mid-1980s and subsequent market volatility made the prospect of development even dimmer. Yet by the mid-1990s, through the application of so-called breakthrough thinking, experimentation, the creation of learning networks and bench-marking, BP had developed radical approaches to drilling, field development, project management, and the sharing of benefits with the contracting indus-try. What the company did, in effect, was to buy an out-of-the-money option to develop the Andrew Field, defer exercising the option until it had proac-tively driven down the exercise price (that is, the investment in development), and then exercise an option that it had turned into an in-the-money one.

Exploiting proactive flexibility in the case of oilfield development licences involves all the steps to reduce capital costs that BP took in the case of the Andrew Field, along with measures to minimize the cost of the real option. The licence bid and its holding cost are the option price – as critical a part of the management equation as the six levers of option value (the same is true in financial options). The holding cost can be reduced by renegotiating spending obligations such as a commitment to a government to drill explo-ration wells, or a commitment to a partner.

As always, it is worth comparing real-options thinking, reactive and proactive, with net present value along the six levers of the options model. The most sensitive levers are increasing the present value of expected cash inflows and reducing the present value of expected fixed costs.

The means to pull both these levers is the application of new technology to obtain more reliable profiles of an oilfield's value, better total oil recov-ery, and more efficient production facilities (fewer wells, lighter platforms). The next most sensitive lever, increased uncertainty and hence price volatil-ity, makes an option more attractive, but management cannot influence oil prices. At the less sensitive end of the spectrum, the option's duration should be managed to trade off potential improvements in cash inflow and outflow against the cost of holding the option and the risk of losing "dividends".

NPV analysis could allow for some of this potential through different scenarios. The danger, however, is that a classic net present value "go/no go", all-or-nothing decision would underestimate the value of expected cash inflows, which could result in a production facility incapable of handling higher-than-expected volume, as in the case of the Magnus Field. Net present value analysis would seriously undervalue volatility, accentuating the risk-averse behaviour already skewing forecasts and budgeting. Go/no go thinking also implicitly assumes (usually incorrectly) that the investment opportunity will be unaffected by competitor behaviour.

It should be clear by now that the lessons of real-options thinking apply as much to existing assets as they do to new areas of exploration and devel-opment, where they are much more often applied. Declining or exhausted oilfields are a case in point. Net present value analysis would probably suggest they be closed down. But keeping them running not only effectively defers new investment and saves the cost of removing redundant facilities (sometimes much higher than anticipated, as the enormously expensive Brent Spar incident two years ago showed)[2], it also keeps open the option of benefiting from the development of new technologies.

For instance, satellite unmanned gas platforms in the southern North Sea, extended-reach drilling (enabling wells to be bored into a reservoir tens of kilometres from a platform originally installed to service a nearby reservoir), and sub-sea templates that pump oil back to far-off platforms all make it possible to use processing capacity that would otherwise have become surplus as soon as the original reservoirs were exhausted. Such developments have greatly increased the option value of fields originally exploited with no thought of such possibilities.

In these circumstances, the importance of options thinking lies less in the way the present values of cash inflows and outflows are managed, and more in the recognition of the value of the option's duration. By exercising options to extend the life of existing infrastructure (thus driving down development costs), and by managing competitors' and its own incremental investments – variables that net present value ignores or oversimplifies – BP has managed to commercialize many small oilfields as its original giant fields have declined.

POWER MASTER-STROKE BY POWERGEN

In 1990, the UK government privatized the electricity generating industry. At a stroke, the stable market enjoyed by a state-owned monopoly was replaced by an unpredictable environment of fluctuating prices. A pool (or spot market) was established into which generators had to sell their electricity, and which priced electricity by the half-hour on the basis of bids from power stations. The new market is characterized by hour-to-hour and seasonal volatility – a nightmare for generators in a highly capital-intensive industry.

At the time, most generating stations were coal-fired baseload stations designed to generate more or less continuously. The variable nature of electricity demand and the availability of environmentally and economically attractive supplies of natural gas fuelled the "dash for gas": the development of combined-cycle gas turbine (CCGT) stations that could be switched on or off according to requirements, reaching full capacity without technical problems in 15 minutes. Most coal stations – PowerGen's among them – were forced out of baseload into periodic production, to which they were unsuited. Many were forced to close.

Net present value analysis of the dilemma faced by coal-fired stations would have suggested driving down costs (an insufficient measure, given the superior economics of CCGT); or hedging electricity output (which would have protected against the downside risk of losing market share but only at the price of eliminating the upside potential); or closing the plant to avoid investing against an uncertain cash inflow. Real-options thinking however, enabled PowerGen to exploit three variables ignored in net present value thinking – uncertainty, duration and dividend – to create a profitable business.

Price volatility meant that, for short periods, coal stations could earn large margins and would thus be worth life-extending investment, provided that PowerGen's operating staff rapidly developed the technological and

Table C3.1   Real-option valuation and strategy versus the net present value approach

Example	Net present value	Real-option valuation (reactive flexibility)	Real-option strategy (reactive and proactive flexibility)
BP: Maximizing the value of Andrew field	Sell/surrender licence blocks immediately	Still sell/surrender because oil price volatility does not increase value sufficiently	Increase present value of future cash inflows by maximizing recoverable reserves; reduce drilling and platform costs
PowerGen: Flexible operation of the power station	Shut coal-fired power stations immediately	Still shut most coal-fired power stations because they are unsuited to to on/off operation	Reduce exercise price by introducing flexible start/stop operation and transforming fixed costs into variable costs

operational flexibility to acquire two key capabilities (see Table C3.1):

1. The ability to switch coal plant on and off frequently. New operating skills such as managing the chemical balance in the boilers, in combination with limited investment such as the use of hardened chrome headers to prevent boilers cracking as tubes heat and cool, now enable some PowerGen stations to start up more than 200 times a year. Typical US coal-fired stations start up just eight to 10 times a year.

2. The ability to bid economically for marginal business by converting fixed costs into variable costs through the aggressive use of contractors.

Rather like BP, PowerGen raised its aspirations by benchmarking, by stretching its management to surpass world best practice, and by freeing business units and teams to find the best route forward. PowerGen ultimately enjoyed a double benefit, in fact, because unpredictable shutdowns of nuclear plants, combined with volatilities in supply and demand, have caused periodic shifts to coal production and an increase in prices.

NOTES

1. See "Unleashing the power of learning: An interview with British Petroleum's John Browne", *Harvard Business Review*, Sep–Oct 1997, for BP's own account of its value-creating strategy since 1992.
2. Shell sought to sink the redundant storage platform Brent Spar in mid-Atlantic, arousing a storm of protest.

5

Mergers, MNEs and Innovation
The Need for New Research Approaches

Christian Berggren

1. INTRODUCTION

Since the mid-1990s, a wave of merger has been sweeping through Europe and North America, affecting a wide range of sectors: banking, telecommunications, cars, pulp and paper, oil, and so on. Increasingly, these mergers are of the cross-border kind. According to UN estimates, cross-border mergers and acquisitions rose from the level of $86 billion a year in 1991 to $1.1 trillion in 1999 (United Nations, 2000). The record figure for 1999 represented a doubling of the previous year's figure, itself a record. Many of these deals have brought together firms of comparable size, with the result that the entity as a whole has roots in at least two countries. Examples include BP–Amoco, Astra–Zeneca, Daimler–Chrysler, Hoechst–Rhone Poulenc and Vodafone–Mannesmann. Recurrent merger waves have been part of economic life in Western economies since the end of the 19th century, and a rich literature of merger studies has emerged. In the financially oriented studies the focus is on economic outcomes, defined in various ways. In the management and organisation science field, the emphasis tends to be on post-merger implementation processes and problems such as culture clashes, competitive position games, communication challenges or learning potentials. In much of this management literature, the basic financial rationale and economic imperative justifying the merger is more or less taken for granted (see e.g. Haspeslagh & Jemison, 1991). The explicit or implicit agenda is to help managers manage the implementation process in a more effective way.

This article argues that the current merger phenomenon needs to be investigated in a fundamentally more critical way in management research. The purpose is first to problematise mergers – their economic rationale and behavioural motives, and their second-order effects on innovation and creativity. The aim is to contribute to a further debunking of deterministic notions about "economic imperatives". Second, an agenda for future merger research is proposed. This comprises two aspects, namely collaborative approaches to uncover the special-interest groups that drive the proposal to merge, and cross-disciplinary studies to investigate the long-term effects of mergers on creativity, projects and innovation in engineering.

Efficiency theory, which views mergers as effective instruments for reaping benefits of scale and scope, is still widely used as a basis for merger studies, sometimes being taken for granted without any qualifications (e.g. Seth, 1990). Efficiency theory lies at the heart of the prescriptive handbooks on merger strategies, and provides the ground for the public relations exercises that accompany merger announcements. The second section below thus offers a detailed review of the performance literature. A distinctive feature of the current merger wave is the prevalence of horizontal amalgamations, whereby firms in the same industry are combined. Compared to conglomerate structures these amalgamations are very difficult to dissolve; essentially they constitute irreversible processes. This highlights the importance of analysing motives and probable outcomes.

As is well known to the informed reader, most outcome studies present a bleak picture of financial post-merger performance. Much less attention is paid to the effects of mergers on innovative ability and engineering creativity. Studies of organisational learning and cognition tend to emphasise the positive potential of mergers for shared learning. One example is Leroy and Ramanantsoa (1997), which studied collaborative problem-solving workshops over an 8-month implementation period. In conclusion, these authors stress the importance of the merger implementation as a complex learning process, with "each firm being simultaneously a learner and a teacher", and advises managers to "improve the implementation process" by encouraging "learning between the merging firms" (pp. 889, 890). This interest in the opportunities of shared learning has been well received, but it tends to overlook the more long-term energy-absorbing processes of technological integration. Building on case studies of engineering management in merging companies, our third section highlights the specific difficulties of unifying product platforms in technology-intensive companies, the opportunity costs and the tendency to redirect R&D personnel from creative performance to engineering routines. With some important exceptions (Ridderstråle, 1996; Bresman & Birkinshaw, 1996) these difficulties are not captured by the literature on post-merger implementation problems, partly because of the very general orientation and the short-time focus, and partly because of the lack of interest in the interaction between organisation, behaviour and technology, or in the choice of firms where technology integration is not a critical issue.

Section 4 discusses the "merger enigma". Given the evidence that most mergers produce disappointing results, why is the phenomenon so persistent? This question is not new. After a brief review of previous studies of managerial merger motives, the article discusses recent explanations derived from game theory that purport to give managerial action a new type of "rational explanation". So far these approaches lack empirical support. The same seems to apply to one popular explanation in the business press of repeated merger behaviour, namely the assumption regarding an "M&A learning curve". The role of calculation asymmetries in the merger process – i.e. detailed pre-calculations at the time of the announcement, followed by a virtual absence of ex post calculations in the post-merger phase – is emphasised.

Section 5 develops an argument for an expanded agenda of merger studies, with the emphasis on two areas: (1) Merger motives and merger drivers, in particular the role of external financial promoters and the corporate finance industry. (2) Mergers and innovation. In this second area, two types of studies are suggested: micro-level studies of technology integration efforts and post-merger performance of previously innovative R&D units; and studies of industries in which contrasting logics and strategies obtain, so that economies of scale and size and economies of innovation and flexible networking exist side by side, or processes of "fusion" (mergers and acquisitions) occur alongside processes of "fission" (de-mergers and new-firm generation).

2. RESEARCH ON MERGER PERFORMANCE

"If merger incentives are taken into consideration at all, a group of firms is typically said to have incentives to merge *if* the profits of the merged entity in the new equilibrium is higher than the combined profits of the merging firms before the merger, this is the traditional criterion for merger incentives in the industrial organisation literature" (Horn and Persson, 1999, p. 2, our italics).

The problem that is not discussed here is: how do firms "know" that the combined profit will be higher? Maybe they think it will be, but what if they are wrong? Since the early 1970s a plethora of studies have tried to discover the actual financial consequences of mergers.

Three research approaches predominate:

- Stock market or event studies, i.e. studies focusing on the stock market reaction to merger announcements (the "event");

- accounting studies, i.e. studies of corporate performance as reflected in quarterly or annual reports, comparing pre-merger with post-merger performance, or comparing the performance of merging companies with a control sample of non-merging companies;

- interview and survey studies exploring the results of mergers and possible reasons for failures or successes.

Less frequently, there have also been attempts to explore the effects of mergers and acquisitions on other economic indicators, such as market share. Of the three main approaches – performance, market and interview studies – interview studies tend to be most positive. This might be a result of self-selection bias, as companies with a dismal post-merger performance would be reluctant to discuss this with external researchers. In these studies it may also be problematic to define "success" in rigorous terms.

2.1. The Disappointing Results of Stock Market and Accounting Studies

Bild (1998) provides an extensive overview of accounting and market studies from the 1920s to the mid-1990s. A cautious conclusion from his survey of performance studies, which cover a total of 2600 mergers, is that "companies engaging in merger activity do not earn a post-merger return that is different than the average of their industry, or any other chosen benchmark". If there is a tendency it is negative (Bild, 1998, p. 159). In a well-known overview, Scherer and Ross (1990) were more outspoken after finding that half the acquired businesses in a comprehensive sample of US manufacturing corporations had experienced "disastrous performance declines" after their mergers. "The picture that emerges is a pessimistic one: widespread failure, considerable mediocrity and only occasional success" (pp. 172, 173).

In evaluating market studies it is important to distinguish between effects on stock values for the acquirers and for the targets, and between the long- and short-term effects. If there is a positive effect on share prices at the time of a merger announcement, the gains accrue to the target's shareholders. Most acquisitions either have no value consequences or the consequences for the stockholders of the acquiring firms are negative. Several event studies comparing the stock market value of the involved firms, however, argue that the combined stock market gains are positive (Fridolfsson & Stennek 1999, p. 2). This result is greatly influenced by the length of the measurement period, normally a few weeks or days before and after the event. During this short period the stock market is heavily exposed to the orchestrated public relations efforts of the merger proponents – the top managers and their financial promoters and media channels. It takes longer for more critical information and analyses to make an impact on the discussion and evaluation. Unsurprisingly, the upward effect on share prices tends to be short-lived.

A recent case has been the much publicised Daimler–Chrysler merger. When this deal was announced, it was presented by Business Week as a "marriage in automotive heaven". Further, "if ever a merger had the potential for that elusive quality – synergy – this could be the one", and investors applauded by pushing Chrysler's shares up almost 20% after the announcement (Vlasic, Kerwin, & Woodruff, 1998). Since then, share prices and financial results have been on a long down-hill slide. This accords with other market studies that allow more time for measuring the stock performance of the acquiring firms. These studies have demonstrated a significant deterioration of the stock value over 1–3 years following the merger (Scherer & Ross, 1990, pp. 169, 170). It may be that while the capital market reaction at the time of the announcement reflects positive expectations that are supported by massive public relations exercises from the actors involved in the deal, disappointment follows as the proclaimed "synergies" fail to materialise. Rau and Vermaelen (1998) also found that merger firms tend to underperform on the stock market in the 3 years after the merger. Their explanation is that market and management both over-extrapolate from the past performance of successfully managed acquirers, so-called "glamour firms".

Most of these studies cover the merger waves of the 1960s and 1980s, while few scholarly investigations of the many horizontal M&As of the 1990s have been published up to now. However, reports from various consultants indicate that the problems of post-merger underperformance persist. According to a study by A.T. Kearner of 135 large-scale international mergers (1 billion dollar plus) between 1993 and 1996, 58% underperformed in terms of shareholder value 2 years after the merger. Moreover, the costs of failed mergers were higher than the gains of successful deals (Hedberg, 1998). A similar result was obtained in an interview study made by an international consultant firm in 1999 (KPMG 1999).

2.2. Mergers and Market Share – Adding to the Bleak Picture

Studies of mergers and market share are less common but tend to support the pessimistic conclusions of most accounting studies. In a study of mergers in the 1950s and 1960s it was found that the market share of acquired business lines deteriorated significantly relative to control samples of non-merging businesses, in the case of both conglomerate and horizontal mergers (Mueller, 1985). In an analysis of the pharmaceutical industry, changes in the market share of merging companies between 1993 and 1997 were compared with companies that were mainly growing organically. All the companies involved in major mergers – Smithkline/Beecham, Bristol&Myers/Squibb, American Home/American Cyanamid, Roche/Syntex, Glaxo/Wellcome, Pharmacia/Upjohn, Hoechst Roussel/Marion Merrel Dow – had lost market shares (AFV 1999). The "organic growers", from Pfizer to Astra, had all expanded their market shares during the same period. More recently, however, several firms in this group have also joined the merger camp.

Incidentally, the risk of losing market share was a major reason why the management of the Swedish truck producer Scania so vigorously opposed Volvo's take-over attempt in 1999–2000. Scania was finally salvaged by the veto of the European competition authorities. A study of the European heavy truck market in the period 1975–1997, cited by Scania managers, demonstrated that when going it alone the Swedish truck makers had enjoyed very respectable growth in market share. Volvo expanded its market share in Europe from 10.2% to 15.2%, and Scania increased its share from 8.8% to 15.1%, a 70% expansion of market share due entirely to organic growth. By contrast, several of the merging competitors suffered a disastrous decline. RVI, an amalgamation of Berlier, Saviem and Dodge UK saw its share fall from 13.7% to 11.5%, whereas Iveco, a combination of Enasa, FIAT-OM, Ford UK, UNIC, Magirus, Seddon–Atkinson and Astra, dropped from 19.2%

to 11.2%, in an implosion of market share. The great exception to this pattern of unsuccessful mergers was the German heavy truck specialist MAN, which leveraged the acquisitions of Buessing and Steyr to double its market share during the studied period (Scania 1999, p. 5).

Spurred by the keen interest of the Federal Reserve in the US, mergers in the banking industry have received the most attention. Larsson (1997) summarises the results of 174 studies. Taken together these fail to support any efficiency arguments. There is no clear positive correlation between unit cost and volume, and big banks are on average no more efficient than smaller banks (the cost curve may be U-shaped, implying that macro and micro banks are the most inefficient). The same applies to the economy-of-scope argument, such that big full-service banks are no more successful than smaller niche banks. In spite of this negative historical track record, bank mergers have been on the increase for several years.

2.3. The Difficult Trade-off Between Cost-cutting and Revenue-enhancement

One recent interview study (Capron, 1999) provides interesting insights as to why the synergies that are so often invoked at the time of the deal, are so difficult to realise. The study is based on a comprehensive survey of 200 firms. Cost-cutting, asset divestiture, and streamlining are kept separate from revenue-enhancing measures involving various forms of resource redeployment. The cross-effect between these two categories are also explored. Further, measures aimed at the acquiring firms and the target firms are analytically separated. The study found that post-merger actions to rationalise the acquirers' assets are effective, but rare. Rather, most such action is directed towards divesting the assets of the target companies. However, such measures have either a negative or at least no significant impact on cost savings. Moreover, they tend to damage the revenue-enhancing resources and capabilities of the target firm. "Overall, these results show the difficulties in capturing benefits of post-acquisition divestiture actions and support the limits . . . with respect to the effectiveness of acquisitions as a means of rationalising assets" (Capron, 1999, p. 1007).

Regarding revenue-enhancing measures, resources from the target firm may be productively redeployed, but in this case there is also a negative effect on total acquisition performance. If, on the other hand, resources from the acquiring firm are redeployed to enhance capabilities, the effects tend to be unambiguously positive. However, this is not the most common route taken in the post-merger process. In sum, this study draws attention to the important problems of asymmetries and interaction effects, that the target firm "is very likely to bear the burden of post-acquisition asset divestiture", and that cost-cutting activities often interfere with and damage long-term capabilities. The author comments: "Cost-based synergies, which have commonly been the focus of attention, are not easily achieved and may require more substantive changes in operating the business than those suggested by the dominant approach based on cost cutting and downsizing gains" (Capron, 1999, pp. 1009, 1010).

Thus, irrespective of research approach, be it stock market studies, accounting studies or interview studies, the majority of empirical investigations give no grounds for enthusiasm about mergers. If there are any discernible results at all, these tend to be disappointing. Studies of post-merger market shares confirm this: more often than not, merging companies suffer from declining market shares, sometimes even a veritable market implosion. And because of promises made to the stock market and the expectations it consequently maintains, the acquiring firms tend to focus on cost-cutting measures to the detriment of future revenue-enhancing capabilities. As will be shown in the next section, this is particularly problematic when it comes to the management of product technologies and product platforms.

3. MICRO-MERGER SNAFUS: THE UNDERESTIMATED PROBLEM OF INTEGRATING TECHNOLOGIES

The announcement of mergers in manufacturing industries is regularly accompanied by calculations to demonstrate the huge potential savings in production and purchasing costs. If the amalgamation results in a substantial increase in market share it may be possible for the new entity to put powerful pressure on suppliers to reduce their *prices*. A reduction of actual *costs*, however, requires the integration of idiosyncratic technical solutions into common technical platforms. This may be feasible in a relatively short time in fast-moving industries with short product lives, as in the ICT-sector (Cisco for instance stands out as a prominent example, or at least appeared to do so before the stock market tumble early in 2001). It is much more difficult and time-consuming, however, in other types of manufacturing or engineering sectors. In such cases there is seldom a simple set of objective parameters that can be used to select the superior design, be it a power transformer or a diesel engine. Instead there are dozens of relevant parameters relating to performance, cost, manufacturability, serviceability, customer preferences, user behaviour, etc. Moreover, engineers tend to have strong feelings about their designs, very different from the detached approach of financial analysts. The route to "integrated designs" is lined with long-drawn-out negotiations, tension, conflicts and compromises. And at the end, there is no guarantee that the best solution has been chosen. This process, which tends to be far more protracted than top management ever envisaged, is not captured adequately by general survey studies: longitudinal, in-depth, case studies are necessary. This is a time-consuming approach and therefore rather a rare one.

3.1. Protracted Technical Integration Problems at ABB

A much publicised case of international M&A in the 1990s concerned the electrotechnical firm ABB, the result of a merger between Swiss BBC and Swedish ASEA, and of subsequent acquisitions in the US. Numerous business journal articles and books have presented the new "global firm" as a resounding success; almost all of them based on interviews with top management (see e.g. Heimer & Barham, 1998). However, two of ABB's many business areas, Automation and Power Transformers, have been subjected to more thorough studies of the problems of integrating different technologies. In one of these the present author took part together with an international group (Berggren, 1996, 1999; Bélanger, Berggren, Björkman, & Köhler, 1999), while two researchers from Stockholm Business School were involved in the other (Bresman & Birkinshaw, 1996). Since such studies are not very common, the results will be presented in some detail below.

The first case is about product integration in the business area automation. When ASEA and BBC merged there were suddenly two competing systems in the industrial automation field, ASEA's Master and BBC's ProControl. Which one was to survive? The rivalry between the two systems and their proponents led to tough arguments. When management decided to cease development of ProControl there "was blood on the floor" according to one participant (Berggren, 1999, p. 239). In 1990, ABB acquired Combustion Engineering in the US including Taylor Instruments whose control and supervision system for industrial processes enjoyed a higher market share in the chemical industry. ABB Automation decided to keep both systems but to merge them successively in future product generations, and eventually to market one system only world-wide. A huge international project was set up consisting of 20 subprojects. The intention was to launch a fully integrated system within 3 years, but in 1996, 6 years after the start of the integration project, there were still big differences. One reason was the installed base of the existing systems. This was an important asset for the company, since customers rarely switch to a new system supplier. However, it also represented a major obstacle to the development of a unified platform, since new product releases need to be compatible "backwards", i.e. with all the existing installations.

Another reason for the difficulty in integrating the systems was the multi-site development structure, a result of growth through mergers and acquisitions. At the US site, for example, there was limited interest in eliminating all the specific features of the local system in favour of an international platform, since this could pose a threat to their own future (Berggren, 1999, pp. 239, 240). In ABB's business area Power Transformers the problem of technological fragmentation was even more daunting. After all the mergers and acquisitions in the late 1980s and early 1990s, seven different product technologies were competing internally. A common product programme started in 1989 but proved to be much more complicated than envisaged. In 1996,

7 years after the start, a common product protocol was in place, but only 20% of the transformers delivered that year were produced in accordance with it (Björkman, 1999, p. 49).

3.2. The Soul of Established Machines – Competing Design Philosophies at Volvo and Scania

When Volvo Trucks announced its plan to take over Scania in 1999, Scania's CEO publicly expressed his worries about the amalgamated company's future market share, and as we have seen above he had good reasons for his worry. In a less public way, there was also widespread concern in Scania's product-development departments about problems to do with technological integration and standardisation. Volvo and Scania both build trucks for the heavy market segment. For financial analysts this means obvious cost synergies in consolidating product platforms and harmonising component designs. As the product engineers and process engineers who participated in a training programme run by the present author in 1999–2000 put it, the engineer's perspective is completely different. Despite external similarities, Volvo's and Scania's design philosophies are remarkably incompatible, as the way they design their six-cylinder diesel engines, the most expensive component in a heavy truck chassis, clearly illustrates. Whereas Volvo offers a "modern" design with overhead cam shafts and one solid cylinder head, Scania prefers a "conventional" approach with individual cylinder heads and no overhead cam shaft, motivated by reference to the low rotation speed of truck diesels compared to gasoline engines.

To the architects of mergers such differences may seem like a mundane technical issue, easily resolved on the basis of an analysis involving both parties. However, such an assumption is the root cause of many micro-merger problems. As Scania engineers have pointed out when interviewed, diesel engines can be evaluated on many criteria, such as manufacturing cost, life cycle-cost, reliability, power, emissions, fuel consumption, driving smoothness and convenience, serviceability, compatibility with auxiliary equipment, and so on. And just to add to the complexity, all these criteria can be assigned different weights. The choice of a particular design will affect not only suppliers and plant tooling, but also spare parts systems and thousands of service shops. Following a Volvo–Scania merger, a unified design would be necessary if the previously announced cost rationalisation were to be to achieved. But in the absence of simple agreed criteria, such design decisions can easily be disputed as being political. Whereas engineers in the pre-merger situation concentrated on doing their best to develop their own solutions and to let the market decide, the post-merger process is often affected by internal arguments between competing designs, resulting in a loss of tempo and customer focus. None of this is taken into account in the calculations of cost savings that are regularly presented when mergers are announced.

3.3. Opportunity Costs and the Diversion of Innovative Energy

The difficulty in integrating different technologies into a common platform not only means that the expected cost synergies take longer to realise than anticipated; there is also a substantial opportunity cost. Once the merger is legally finalised, then designers and product and process engineers tend to become absorbed for several years in questions of co-ordination and harmonisation instead of concentrating on innovation and the development of new products. Engineering is a discipline involving creative problemsolving, it is about creating and implementing new solutions. In an amalgamated company that is preoccupied with establishing "common platforms", this role changes. To realise the economies of scale that have justified the merger, engineers and project managers are obliged to prioritise standardisation and formalisation, i.e. to establish common systems, common design rules, common purchasing policies, etc. Those in creative positions tend to be transformed into implementers, standardisers or engineering bureaucrats. This change is resisted by many. Some leave, perhaps going over to competitors. Others continue to fight for their own solutions and ideas, which is one reason why the technological integration process is so time-consuming.

Another consequence of large-scale mergers is that innovative individuals and groups in design and development departments become surrounded by, and have to report to, various new organisational and hierarchical layers. This exhausts scarce human capacities, and strains or severs the crucial direct links between innovators, manufacturing experts and advanced users. A legendary innovator in engine technology, Per Gillbrand at Swedish Saab, came up against this sort of increase in organisational layers and managerial reporting requirements, after Saab was acquired by GM. Instead of focusing on the early introduction of advanced combustion and ignition technologies, exploiting the advantage of their own small-scale inter-disciplinary environment, Gillbrand and his colleagues had to waste much of their energy trying to persuade various committees in the central US development office with its 23,000 heavily departmentalised engineers. (Interview by the author, 10 January 2001.)

Innovative projects call for a strong culture and practice of crossfunctional and inter-disciplinary information exchange and problem-solving. In the mega-enterprises spawned by the cross-border mergers of the 1990s, hierarchical structures are reinforced in order to reap the hoped-for synergies and economies of scale. The global product managers or functional managers take precedence over cross-functional project management. This may promote the sale and refinement of existing products but erode the capacity for future innovation.

4. THE CONUNDRUM: PERFORMANCE SO POOR, DEALS SO MANY

"Perhaps merger booms and stock market trading are behavioral phenomena – human beings, like some animals, are more active when the weather is sunny" (Brealey & Myers, 1996, p. 942).

When mergers are being announced, favourite arguments advanced to support the deal concern cost synergies, cost-rationalisation, and elimination of overlap. It is also commonly argued that mergers are a way of correcting managerial failure, that is, inefficient managers are weeded out by an active market in corporate control. The evidence does not support the view that striving for greater efficiency is the main motivation for mergers. At the beginning of the 1990s, it was already being shown that target firms significantly outperformed comparable non-targets in terms of profitability (Scherer & Ross, 1990, p. 170). This pattern has been confirmed more recently in Franks and Meyer (1996), where it is demonstrated that firms subject to take-overs tend to have outperformed the market over the previous 5 years, thereby contradicting what the efficiency arguments predict. Support for the general "weeding-out" hypothesis is thus weak.

4.1. A Positive Merger Learning Curve?

In recent years, management research has shown a great interest in organisational learning. Transposed to the M&A field this suggests the assumption of an "acquisitions learning curve", and the notion that "the experienced acquirer" would be more successful than the less experienced. Empirical studies fail to find support for this assumption. Studies reported in Ravenscraft and Scherer (1987) found active acquirers to be less profitable than the US industry average, and less successful in terms of long-term stock performance. An explanation of this outcome in organisational behaviour terms would be that although executives ride the learning curve of acquisitive assessments and negotiations, the managerial ranks tend to become exhausted, and their commitment to be further eroded by every new acquisition or restructuring or restaffing exercise. In conversations with the author, professional investors have suggested a performance curve shaped like an inverted U. First, the acquirer experiences a positive learning curve as its executives learn to assess targets and to direct post-merger integration more effectively. After a series of successful acquisitions, however, top management tends to over-extend, trying to digest objects that are too large and to become less attentive to details, with the result that their merger performance starts to deteriorate. The evolution of Electrolux between the 1960s and the 1990s is cited as a case in point (L. Låftman, senior pension fund manager, interviewed by the author, 8 February 2001).

One reason for the survival of the claims regarding efficiency is the lack of follow-up studies, either within companies or in the business press.

Quantitative analyses of expected benefits are often used ex ante, but very seldom ex post. In an in-depth financial analyses of seven merger cases, it was found that very few companies conducted any post-audits of merger performance. And if they did do so, it was at the explicit request of the board. As one financial director put it: "Ex post evaluations are seldom made. Restructurings protect the management from evaluations" (quoted in Bild 1998, p. 95). The absence of follow-ups or critical scrutiny of track records is evident even in cases where relevant information is easily accessible from public sources, such as annual reports. In 1995, for example, ABB announced the merger of its traction division (trains and railway systems) with German AEG, owned by Daimler-Benz. At the press conference the CEO of ABB described a very positive future for the new entity, known as Adtranz. The expected synergy effects would quickly result in new orders and increased profitability, he said, and he was convinced that "we will improve earnings every year" (SvD, 1995). The same year the ABB traction division was still a profitable business, reporting earnings of USD 207 million. The next year the results of the amalgamated entity had slipped into the red (USD 2 million), and by 1997 its economic performance had gone from bad to worse (USD 111 million). In 1998 ABB sold the whole business. That very year the same CEO, but now in a different position, was espousing the virtues of merging the Swedish pharmaceutical company Astra with British Zeneca. This was an industry of which he had no experience, and yet he was never confronted by the grossly misleading ex ante calculations of the Adtranz merger, an industry of which he had 15 years experience. The corporate lack of interest in ex post calculations seems to be shored up, at least in small countries, by the media's deference for the grandiose executive merger promoters.

4.2. An Explanation Building on Game Theory

The conundrum of "performance so poor, deals so many" has not been resolved. So many studies have revealed the economic disappointments of mergers, and yet their numbers continue to increase. A survey of existing studies of merger motives (Trautwein, 1990) has suggested a list of possible explanations, such as the bounded rationality of decision processes, managerial self-interest and hopes of higher compensation and more power, and of "empire-building". Executive hubris is another hypothesis (Roll, 1986). Several studies support such explanations, but so far the empirical evidence seems to be limited and a bit dated. The World Investment Report (UN, 2000) asked basically the same question: why are there so many mergers, when the results are so discouraging? The short answer is that fear is a more powerful driver than greed (although on a personal management level the two appear together). A dubious deal is preferred to no deal at all.

Recently economists have sought to formulate a "rational" explanation along the same lines, using game theory to formalise the argument (Fridolfsson & Stennek, 1999, pp. 3–4). According to this theory of "pre-emptive or defensive merger motives", mergers are performance-reducing propositions for all the actors in an oligopolistic industry. But company A would rather take the initiative and merge with B, than wait for a merger between B and C and becoming an outsider: "Even if a merger reduces the profit flow compared to the initial situation, it may increase the profit flow compared to the relevant alternative – another merger. . . . In particular, the event studies can be interpreted to show that there exists an industry-wide anticipation of a merger and that the relevant information content of the merger announcement is which firms are insiders and which are outsiders" (Fridolfsson & Stennek, 1999, p. 3, 4, 17). This may sound plausible, but two questions remain. First, are "merger insiders" actually more successful than outsiders? So far, such a hypothesis is not supported by empirical evidence, showing that outsiders' stock value suffer, or that outsiders are less profitable than the merging insiders (Fridolfsson & Stennek, 1999, pp. 23, 24). Second, how and by whom is the "industry-wide anticipation of a merger" created and sustained? This leads us to the role of the financial promoters of mergers.

4.3. The Increasing Importance of the Corporate Finance Industry

Most merger studies focus on the motives of acquiring firms. A different approach is taken by studies specifically concerned with the role of match-makers and financial promoters. The conclusion drawn in studies of the first American merger waves has been summarised by Scherer and Ross (1990, p. 161): "the quest for promotional profits was the most important single motive for merger during the frenzied 1897–1899 and 1926–1929 periods". The hectic and dubious activities of financial match-makers rushing into the market for corporate control in the early 20th century, was also observed by the Swedish Commission of Anti-Trust Legislation in 1921 (Rydén, 1972).

In the 1960s the deal-makers seem to have played a less prominent role. But the 1980s witnessed explosive growth in the number of corporate finance firms and management strategy consultants, and their involvement in M&A businesses. "We were in the era of megabid mania. The City was awash with money. One was getting approaches from banks all over the world offering all sorts of propositions for any sort of deal that one could think" (Ernest Saunders, former CEO of Guinness, quoted in O'Shea & Madigan, 1997, p. 236). The prizes for participation in mega deals are difficult to resist. For example, in 1986 when Guinness took control of Distillers, the largest British corporate acquisition of the time, the transaction generated more than USD 250 million in fees to brokers, consultants, bankers and others (O'Shea & Madigan, 1997, p. 241).

In the late 1990s American firms were at the forefront of the merger wave in Europe, while the relative importance of German and other mainland European banks was declining. According to an estimate in Business Week

(1 November 1999), Goldman Sachs was involved in European mergers and acquisitions totalling 430.9 billion dollars during the first 10 months of 1999 alone. Morgan Stanley's European M&A business totalled deals of 421.3 billion dollars during the same period. These two firms were No. 1 and No. 2 in the market for mergers and acquisitions in Europe, outdistancing by far any local rivals. Corporate finance advisors and consultants are not neutral service providers. Since mergers present them with good opportunities for earning large commissions, they are active contributors to the making of new deals: "I would rather say that they/the investment banks/are accelerating corporate restructuring. It's their job to present analyses and proposals for transactions all the time" (Senior advisor at Morgan Stanley AFV 2000, p. 34).

Previous research has revealed the importance of managerial self-interest in driving mergers. However, apart from anecdotal evidence, there are very few studies of the role of "financial advisors" and deal-makers in the recent merger booms. Consulting firms are going through a phase of concentrations and mergers themselves, and many of them now constitute a key component of the current international business environment, alongside governments and international organisations. Moreover, in the case of the so-called "Big Five", a potential conflict of interest exists between the roles of these firms as advisors and auditors (Perks, 1993). More broadly, the issue is about the role of these special interests in the shaping of the M&A agenda. What part do the financial mediators and "advisors" play in shaping the "industry-wide anticipation of a merger", referred to above by Fridolfsson and Stennek (1999), as a precondition for merger moves which for all those involved will result in a lower level of performance relative to a no-merger development?

5. THE NEED FOR AN EXPANDED RESEARCH AGENDA TO INCLUDE DEAL-MAKERS AND THE IMPACT OF MERGERS ON INNOVATION

As this article has shown there is a rich literature on merger performance, as measured in a variety of ways. However, the new wave of international cross-border mergers starting in the 1990s calls for further study of the merger-making process, and specifically of the role of external financial promoters, deal-makers and consultants. The question of the extent to which the wave of mergers is driven by models and economic interests perpetuated by deal-makers is clearly an important one. Case studies are needed to investigate the role of financial advisors and consultants in selected processes from the initial steps in the drafting of a business case and its financial motivation, on to participation in negotiations and the setting up of financial arrangements, and finally to involvement in post-merger restructuring and integration. To achieve this, efforts would be necessary on the part of academics to team up with insiders, perhaps with executives who have recently retired.

Cross-disciplinary studies will be needed, involving students of financial economics, organisational behaviour and economic sociology.

Systematic efforts are also needed to explore the impact of mergers on technological development and innovation, within both firms and industries. The exploration of mergers and innovation at the level of the firm would benefit from case studies, involving researchers in organisational behaviour as well as engineering management. One line would be to look at efforts to harmonise technological platforms and design structures: the time required relative to the initial forecasts, departmental relations and friction, opportunity costs, and changes in the overall activities and orientation of the R&D staff in the merging firms. It would also be interesting to see how new-product development projects are affected by increasing organisational complexity and hierarchical reporting requirements – or perhaps in some cases how they escape from such things. It would be particularly important to study the kind of highly uncertain development projects that tend to depend on informal networks, cross-departmental problem-solving and project autonomy, all of which may be at risk after international mergers, which normally generate more complex management layers and more stringent requirements regarding formal progress reviews. It is also vital to identify particular innovative units or in-company networks, perhaps by checking earlier patents, to see whether they become surrounded and compartmentalised by additional organisational boundaries and intermediaries and – if so – to what extent. This applies to the problem of opportunity costs, and to the type of management, through trust or formal reviews. If innovative units lose their direct contact with process specialists or advanced customers, this will not only slow down their problem-solving but may even degrade their innovative abilities in general.

Longitudinal, in-depth case studies will be important to capture the effects of mergers on innovativeness and the orientation of the R&D staff in the firms. This is a difficult undertaking, however. The potential for bias that affects multi-firm interview studies is even greater in the context of in-depth case studies. Most insider stories are published by journalists, who provide a mass of imaginative details and outspoken opinions but tend to be highly partisan and lacking any comparative perspectives. A recent example of this was the all-American account of the Daimler–Chrysler merger in Vlasic and Stertz (2000). Academic case studies on the other hand tend to be cautious and restrained, refraining from interviewing dissidents and external critics and sometimes failing to clarify the role of the researchers concerned: are they investigators or dialogue partners for senior management? This was a highly controversial issue for the research team behind the ABB study "Being local world-wide", in which the present author was a key participant (Bélanger et al., 1999). In other cases it might be very difficult to get the stories released for publication. This has been the case for the planned publication "Acquisitions: the management of social drama" by John Hunt at London Business School, a well-known specialist in merger processes and co-author of Hunt, Lees, Grumbar, and Vivian (1987). The new book was to have been released by the Oxford University Press in 1998, but by 2000 no definite date had yet been settled, for reasons explained in a personal communication to the present author (16 February 2000): "We are having great problems getting the cases released. Of the 10 acquisitions we studied only one has so far been released. The problem, as you know, is that the 'real' story is very personal. It is this story we want to tell. It is not the story corporations want to read in public." Mergers are strategically important affairs, and reports of failures and stifled innovation will land squarely on the table of top management, sometimes affecting the share price, but almost certainly affecting the relationship of the researchers to management in the future.

As MacDonald and Hellgren (1994) have noted "most management researchers who interview in organisations crave access to the executive suite". This applies particularly to merger studies. The focus on the top levels exacerbates the problems of selectivity and subtle adaptation: "It is hard to question closely a manager who normally would not tolerate being questioned at all. It is much easier simply to accept what is said, . . . It is easier still, and much more conducive to reaping the benefits that flow from the satisfaction of those interviewed, to ask the questions managers wish to answer and to ask them in ways managers will find immediately acceptable. Thus, for example, a question on the role the manager has played in corporate success is much more acceptable than a question about his role in corporate failure" (MacDonald & Hellgren, 1994, pp. 13, 15). Corporate failures, however, abound in merger processes. One way out of the dilemma, albeit a time-consuming one, may be to go for lower levels of the organisation, which are anyway the most important for investigating the effects on innovation and development projects. A complementary approach that might help to counter the problems of publication could be to focus on project, rather than firm performance.

Another type of meso-oriented approach should also be explored, alongside the rich longitudinal case studies, in order to capture the effects of mergers on industrial dynamics and innovativeness. Such an approach would mean identifying industries within which companies pursuing international economies of scale come up against firms, or clusters of firms, which seek to exploit knowledge networks and innovation as their means of competition. The Swedish industry that embraces pharmaceutical and biotechnical companies, roughly defined, can represent such a case. For many years this industry was dominated by two domestic giants, Pharmacia and Astra. Both these firms experienced rapid growth based on original innovations, but increasingly they both changed orientation, first Pharmacia and then Astra, focussing instead on incremental product refinement and international scale. In the 1980s Pharmacia embarked on a series of mergers and acquisitions that ended in the cross-border merger with American Upjohn. In the Swedish debate this merger has been viewed as a particularly disastrous deal, followed by exorbitant implementation costs and repeated rounds of restructuring and relocation exercises (Frankelius, 1999). For a long time Astra professed its belief in organic growth, but in 1998 it joined forces with British Zeneca, a descendant of ICI. In the Pharmacia case corporate control was transferred to the US, and in the Astra case to London. The merger proponents saw this as a deterministic development due to the new economies of scale and the demands of a global presence, but the consequences at the local level were often demoralising.

However, in a highly unintentional process the Swedish pharmaceutical and biotechnical industry has been granted a new lease of life by a plethora of research-based start-ups, often stemming from university projects but managed by former employees of Astra or Pharmacia. Specialising in narrow niches, these firms tend to cluster in the Uppsala region – the "Cambridge" of Sweden and the previous headquarters of Pharmacia. Here they form close knowledge networks with academics and other dedicated firms (Thorén, 2000). The jury is still out as regards the long-term prospects for this breed of small-scale, research-intensive firms. From the perspective of industrial innovation this process of fission offers a challenging antidote to the large-scale processes of mergers and "fusion", which has been proclaimed for so long as the only way forward for a competitive pharmaceutical industry. A study of this or similar cases would include long-term growth in earnings and high-tech job creation, as well as specific company strategies for circumventing the problems of small scale and resource restrictions compared to the accumulated powers of international mega-companies.

6. SUMMARY AND CONCLUSION

Historically there have been several merger booms in the Western economies. In the US and in Sweden, the first three decades of the 20th century witnessed major waves of horizontal amalgamations, often with the explicit motive of creating dominant market positions. Tight anti-trust legislation in the US made this more difficult in the decades following the Great Depression. The merger booms in the 1960s and 1980s were consequently dominated by the conglomerate type of combination. Among the expressed motives for mergers in the waves of the 1960s and 1980s, financial risk reduction due to diversification and cross-industry technological synergies, figured prominently. During the 1980s there was a considerable relaxation of American antitrust legislation. Encouraged by this trend, the new boom of the late 1990s was once again characterised by horizontal mergers, involving firms in the same industry and the same principal market. In many industries this implied a renewed move towards consolidation and oligopoly. Compared to previous amalgamations, the scale and volume increased by an order of magnitude. This was accompanied by an ideology proclaiming the benefits of size and economies of scale despite recent advances in flexible manufacturing technologies and the increasing importance of customisation. While most of the mergers of the early 20th century and of the 1960s and 1980s remained domestic in nature, the mergers in the 1990s were predominantly of a cross-border character. The diffusion of international mergers was supported by a new "deal-making industry" of consultants, corporate lawyers, investment banks and corporate finance specialists. These bodies seemed to be driving the merger process in a manner somewhat reminiscent of the role of the financial promoters of the early 20th century, but in a decidedly more international and aggressive way.

This article opened with a review of studies of the historical performance of mergers, singling out three types of approach: stock market, accounting and interview studies. The content of this overview supported the observation in Bild (1998, p. 216): "It is striking that the three approaches have largely presented fairly similar, that is, mostly insignificant, results. Where any significant outcomes have been found, they have been reported to be predominantly negative." Available studies of the mergers of the 1990s did not deviate from this bleak picture. After marshalling the evidence for disappointing performance the article has delved more deeply into one specific reason for post-merger problems: namely the difficulties involved in integrating idiosyncratic corporate technologies into common product platforms. A related argument focused on the opportunity costs of mergers. By concentrating on cost synergies and streamlining, it has been argued, mergers in knowledge-intensive industries tend to distract and impede innovative energy. This development is aggravated by the tendency to redirect product and technology units towards standardisation and uniformity at the expense of innovation and experimentation.

After reviewing mergers from the perspective of performance and the effects on innovation, a conundrum was presented: why are there so many mergers when most of them perform so dismally? The "rational propositions" inspired by game theory that have recently been suggested were found to lack empirical support, and the need for a closer look at the industry of merger-makers has been emphasised. The problematic influence of these financial intermediaries was noted as early as the merger boom in the first decades of the 20th century, and again in the analyses of the notorious role played by Drexel Burnham Lambert and Kohlberg, Kravis and Roberts in the US merger boom of the 1980s (Stearns & Allan, 1996). The time is now due for further studies involving the co-operation of academic scholars with senior ex-insiders from business. Inter-disciplinary studies combining research in business and engineering management are necessary in order to investigate the "micro-merger" problems of integrating diverse technologies and, more broadly, to assess the complex impact of mergers on innovation.

In-depth studies in individual companies are important here, but need to be complemented by analyses of selected industries, in which very contradictory logics obtain, ranging from large-scale mergers or "fusions" to small-scale "fissions", i.e. spin-offs and new start-ups initiated or inspired by the former employees of big firms and their professional networks. In many industries, such as the car industry, the capital intensity of production or distribution systems erect steep barriers against new entrants, even when the mergers result in enormous inefficiencies. In other sectors, scientific and/or technical breakthroughs may succeed in demolishing previous barriers. A possible case in point could be the pharmaceutical/biotechnological sector, for example in Sweden. Here the persistent pursuit of size and scale on the part of the dominant firms ended in international mergers and relocations between 1995 and 1999. Since the late 1990s, however, this route has come up against a new industrial logic of networking and research-based entrepreneurial start-ups, frequently managed by veterans of the merging giants. Studies of such diverging logics within industries are important not only for the insights they will provide about factors supporting or impeding innovative processes, but even more importantly for any contribution they make to the deconstruction of the economic determinism, the arithmetic modelling and linear thinking that are so popular in the era of international mega-mergers.

REFERENCES

AFV. (1999). Den oundvikliga fusionen. *Affärsvärlden* ("*Business World*"), 1–2, January 13, 22–27.

AFV. (2000). Anders Ljung. Inte förvånande att Telia dröjde. *Affärsvärlden*, 24, June 15, 29–34.

Belanger, J., Berggren, C., Björkman, T., & Köhler, C. (Eds). (1999). *Being local world-wide. ABB and the challenge of global management.* Ithaca: Cornell University Press.

Berggren, C. (1996). Building a truly global organization? ABB and the problem of integrating a multi-domestic enterprise. *Scandinavian Journal of Management*, *12*(2), 123–137.

Berggren, C. (1999). In Belanger, et al. (Eds), Distributed development in a multinational, pp. 233–247.

Bild, M. (1998). *The valuation of take-overs.* Stockholm: Stockholm School of Economics.

Björkman, T. (1999). In Belanger, et al. (Eds), Lean management in practice, the headquarters perspective, pp. 36–60.

Brealey, R. A., & Myers, S. C. (1996). *Principles of corporate finance.* New York: McGraw-Hill.

Bresman, H., & Birkinshaw, J. (1996). *ABB and combustion engineering.* Stockholm: IIB.

Capron, L. (1999). The long-term performance of horizontal acquisitions. *Strategic Management Journal*, *20*, 987–1019.

Frankelius, P. (1999). *Pharmacia & Upjohn, erfarenherter från ett världsföretags utveckling.* Värnamo: Liber Ekonomi.

Franks, J., & Meyer, C. (1996). Do hostile takeovers improve performance? *Business Strategy Review*, *7*(4), 1–6.

Fridolfsson, S.-O., & Stennek, J. (1999). *Why mergers reduce profits and raise share prices.* Stockholm: IUI.

Haspeslagh, P. C., & Jemison, D. D. (1991). *Managing acquisitions: Creating value through corporate renewal.* New York: Free Press.

Hedberg, C. (1998). Många fusioner misslyckas. *Svenska Dagbladet*, December 14.

Heimer, C., & Barham, K. (1998). *ABB the dancing giant.* London: Financial Times/Pitman Publishing.

Horn, H., & Persson, L. (1999). *The equilibrium ownership of an international oligopoly.* London: Centre for Economic Policy Research.

Hunt, J., Lees, S., Grumbar, J. J., & Vivian, P. D. (1987). *Acquisitions: The human factor.* Oxford: Oxford University Press.

KPMG. (1999). *Unlocking shareholder value: The keys to success.* London: KPMG.

Larsson, C.-G. (1997). Bankfusioner – kan de löna sig? *Ekonomisk debatt, 25*(4), 229–239.

Leroy, F., & Ramanantsoa, B. (1997). The cognitive and behavioural dimensions of organisational learning in a merger: An empirical study. *Journal of Management Studies, 34*(6), 871–894.

MacDonald, S., & Hellgren, B. (1994). *The interview in management research.* Warwick Business School Working paper.

Mueller, D. C. (1985). Mergers and market share. *Review of Economics and Statistics, 67*(2), 259–267.

Perks, R. (1993). *Accounting and society.* London: Chapman & Hall.

O'Shea, J., & Madigan, C. (1997). *Dangerous company.* London: Nicholas Brealey Publishers.

Ravenscraft, D., & Scherer, F. (1987). *Mergers, sell-offs and economic efficiency.* Washington, DC: Brookings Institution.

Ridderstråle, J. (1996). *Global innovation. Managing international innovation projects at ABB and Electrolux.* Stockholm: IIB.

Roll, R. (1986). The Hubris hypothesis of corporate takeovers. *Journal of Business. Part I, 59*(2), 197–216.

Rydén, B. (1972). *Mergers in Swedish industry.* Stockholm: Almqvist & Wiksell.

Scania. (1999). *Scania inside*, No. 2, January 27.

Scherer, F. M., & Ross, D. (1990). *Industrial market structure and economic performance.* Boston: Houghton Mifflin Company.

Seth, A. (1990). Sources of value creation in acquisitions: An empirical investigation. *Strategic Management Journal, 11*, 431–446.

Stearns, L. B., & Allan, K. D. (1996). Economic behavior in institutional environments: The corporate merger wave of the 1980s. *American Sociological Review, 61*(4), 699–718.

SvD. (1995). ABB gör storaffär med Daimler-Benz. *Svenska Dagbladet*, March 17.

Thorén, M. (2000). Det våras i biotech valley. *Veckans affärer, 14*, 39–48.

Trautwein, F. (1990). Merger motives and merger prescriptions. *Strategic Management Journal, 11*(4), 283–295.

United Nations. (2000). *World investment report.* New York: UN.

Vlasic, B., & Stertz, B. A. (2000). *Taken for a ride.* New York: William Morrow & Company.

Vlasic, B., Kerwin, K., & Woodruff, D. (1998). Daimler & Chrysler: what the deal would mean. *Business Week*, May 18.

Reprinted from *Scandinavian Journal of Management*, Vol. 19, No. 2, Christian Berggren, "Mergers, MNES and Innovation: The Need for New Research Approaches", pp. 173–191. © 2003 with permission from Elsevier.

CASE STUDY 4

Why Most Cross-Border Deals End in Tears

Simon London

Hardly a week goes by without news of a company abandoning plans for foreign expansion and retreating to its home market. The latest example of this sorry breed is Scottish Power, the UK utility, which is selling for $9.4bn (£5.1bn) the US business it acquired for $10bn in 1999. A $1.7bn write-off will result.

The tale is so familiar, it begs the question of why companies make overseas acquisitions at all. Yet they do – and in increasing numbers. Cross-border merger and acquisition activity increased fivefold in the 1990s and, following a brief lull, it is making a strong comeback.

Cross-border deals amounted to $75bn in the first quarter, a threefold increase from last year, according to Dealogic, the research firm. Eye-catchers include Pernod Ricard's proposed $13bn acquisition of drinks rival Allied Domecq and IBM's $1.75bn sale of its personal computer business to Lenovo, China's biggest personal computer maker.

Academic findings suggest three legitimate reasons for buying foreign companies. One: such deals can be a quicker, easier way to enter an overseas market than starting from scratch. The acquiring company buys not only an ongoing business but also a brand familiar to customers in the target country. If trade barriers are in place, an acquisition may be the only way to gain access to a new market.

Two: international diversification can stabilise cash flows and make the acquiring company appear less risky to financial markets. This may again, in theory, result in a lower cost of capital. Whether this happens in practice is a moot point.

Three: expanding into overseas markets increases the scale on which companies can exploit intangible assets (such as expertise and business processes) and technology. These are the "synergies" that executives tout as justification for almost every deal.

These potential benefits help explain why foreign bidders pay more, on average, for companies than their domestic counterparts. The propensity of overseas buyers to pay a premium, known in corporate finance circles as "the cross-border effect", is well documented.

Jo Danbolt, lecturer in finance at Glasgow University, found that UK target company shareholders gain significantly more from cross-border than from domestic acquisitions. Foreign bidders offer better prices, and are also more likely to pay in cash.

So far, so good. There are sound reasons why companies might want to buy overseas and, in some cases, justifications for paying more than a domestic buyer. Yet research supports anecdotal evidence that most cross-border M&A ends in tears.

Sara Moeller, of the Cox School of Business at Southern Methodist University, and Frederik Schlingemann, of the University of Pittsburgh's Katz Graduate School of Business, studied 4,430 acquisitions by US companies from 1985 to 1995. They looked at both the initial stock market reaction to the deals and the longer-term operational performance of the acquirer. Their conclusion was unequivocal: "US acquirers experience significantly lower stock and operating performance for cross-border than for domestic transactions."

Remember that the track record of domestic M&A deals is hardly stellar. Most academic studies have found that, on average, acquisitions destroy value. In those instances where value is created, it usually flows to shareholders of the company being acquired. Professors Moeller and Schlingemann found that cross-border deals underperformed even this dismal benchmark.

Ervin Black, of Brigham Young University, and Thomas Carnes and Tomas Jandik, of the University of Arkansas, reach a similar conclusion. In a study of the long-term share price performance of 361 successful US bidders for foreign targets, they say: "It appears that in the majority of instances, expansion of US bidding firms through acquisition of foreign targets is a value-destroying activity."

So, while overseas acquisitions are justifiable on paper, in practice they usually fail. Bidders either find it difficult to value correctly the target company or they fail to capture synergies that were presumed to exist.

Differences in accounting standards can make it hard for the acquirer to understand the underlying performance of the target company. Even the best financial analyst will err if accurate balance sheet and cash flow data is not available.

"International accounting differences, whether they result in upward or downward biases in earnings, add noise to the reported earning number, making it more difficult to perform accurate financial analysis," argue Professors Black, Carnes and Jandik. In domestic transactions, bidders respond to such uncertainty by offering equity. This gives shareholders and managers in the target company an incentive to make sure that all the facts are on the table. In cross-border transactions, however, investors are often reluctant to accept foreign shares in payment. The acquiring company has no alternative but to offer cash.

Even if potential synergies are valued correctly, the acquirer still has to capture them. This can be difficult in countries where the institutional structure and the framework of laws and regulations place restrictions on the actions of management. As a result, US companies moving into Europe find it easier to cut costs in the UK than in Germany, where extensive consultations are required by law before jobs can be eliminated.

Indeed, Professors Moeller and Schlingemann found that US bidders fared worse when target companies were located in countries with restrictive capital markets. The only exception to this rule was the UK, where returns to US acquirers were poor, notwithstanding a shareholder- and manager-friendly climate.

Even if the institutional structure is benign, however, managers have to deal with differences in business culture and custom. Only when they are comfortable working in the new environment – a process that could take years – will the acquiring company find it possible fully to capture synergies.

With such a weight of evidence against cross-border M&As, why do companies continue to shop overseas for off-the-peg opportunities?

Agency conflicts may be partly to blame. From this view, the hunger of senior executives (agents) for power leads them to make decisions that are not in the best interests of shareholders (principals).

Overseas acquisitions offering the glamour of jetset dealmaking may be more attractive to self-aggrandising managers than domestic deals.

The puzzle is that cross-border M&A continues to boom in spite of strenuous efforts to minimise agency conflicts by better aligning the financial incentives of managers with the long-term interests of shareholders. It is clear that more research is required.

In the meantime, long-suffering Scottish Power shareholders can take solace from knowing that their plight is hardly unique.

Why do a cross-border merger?

1. It can be a quick way to enter a foreign market.

2. International diversification can stabilise cash flows and make the acquiring company appear less risky to financial markets.

3. It widens the opportunities to exploit a company's intangible assets – such as expertise and business processes.

Why not do a cross-border deal? Acquirers experience lower stock performance when completing a cross-border deal than they do when closing a domestic deal. This is, principally, because of two factors: one, it is difficult to value a foreign target company accurately; and two, it is difficult to realise the synergies that are presumed to exist.

REFERENCES

Jo Danbolt, Cross-Border Acquisitions into the UK: An Analysis of Target Company Returns (2003)

Ervin Black, Thomas Carnes and Tomas Jandik, The Long-Term Success of Cross-Border Mergers and Acquisitions (2003)

Sara Moeller and Frederik Schlingemann, Are Cross-Border Acquisitions Different from Domestic Acquisitions? Evidence on Stock and Operating Performance for US Acquirers (2002)

All available for download from www.SSRN.com

Section 3

Adding Value through Financing

SECTION OVERVIEW

Janette Rutterford

The last ten or twenty years have seen a radical shift in the approach to corporate finance. In the old days, corporate finance was somehow a given, with industry norms for debt-equity ratios, borrowing limits imposed by banks and little emphasis on adding value through financing. Managers concentrated on investment rather than financing decisions. This approach could be vindicated by the early research into the firm's capital structure and dividend policy by Franco Modigliani and Merton Miller. This showed that, in perfect markets, with no corporate taxes, neither dividend policy nor capital structure could be altered to add value to the firm.

However, once taxes were introduced, the irrelevance proposition broke down. The 1963 paper by Franco Modigliani and Merton Miller, which showed that, once corporate taxes were taken into account, capital structure *did* matter[1], can be blamed for the dramatic rise in leveraged buyouts[2] which we saw particularly in the 1980s and 1990s. In the late 1990s, companies reacted to the threat of leveraged buyouts by reorganising their own capital structures through share repurchases, using debt to buy back equity and increasing their leverage as a result. The twenty-first century has seen the rise of private equity funds and venture capital funds, both of which specialise in acquiring companies and, as part of their "value added", restructuring the capital structure to include more cost-effective debt.

Not all firms have followed the high leverage route. For example, Samsung, a large and quoted South Korean electronics firm, is striving to reduce its debt-equity ratio to zero. With a Modigliani and Miller approach, this would destroy rather than add value. There must be factors other than corporate taxes which explain the capital structure choices that firms make. One factor which appears relevant is bankruptcy risk – the higher the leverage, the higher the probability of bankruptcy. Above a certain level of debt, lenders will charge a premium which may wipe out its tax advantage. Also, not all firms pay taxes against which to offset their debt interest. New firms, or highly capital-intensive firms, may not be able to benefit from the "Modigliani and Miller" effect. Also, alternative models, such as "pecking order" theory, use agency theory, in particular the asymmetry of information built into the relationship between insider managers and outsider investors, to explain capital structure choice.

The optimal dividend policy literature had the same roots as that on optimal capital structure. For dividends, however, a puzzle appeared. Given that, in the US, where the theory was developed, there was until very recently double taxation of dividends, the puzzle was why companies would pay dividends at all. This was not the case for the UK, for example, where the imputation tax system in operation between 1973 and 1997 positively encouraged companies to pay dividends since non-taxpaying investors such as pension funds could claim tax relief direct from the government on any dividends paid.

However, the dividend policy literature, dominated as it has been by US authors and the US tax system, developed models similar to those developed for capital structure to explain the apparently irrational payment of dividends. Agency theory was again employed, in particular the role of dividends as signals by good managers to differentiate themselves from bad managers who would not have cash from which to pay dividends. It is only recently that US academics came to realise that firms were beginning to behave in accordance with Modigliani and Miller. Research carried out by Eugene Fama and Kenneth French, published in 2001,[3] showed that only a minority of US firms were paying dividends while the majority were not paying any at all.

In choosing articles for this section, I have had in mind that the literature on optimal capital structure and optimal dividend policy is probably the largest in the finance field. Since my PhD was in this area, I can still remember the piles of articles – two to three feet high – that I had to get through before I could write a literature survey. With this in mind, as an overview of where we are now in the optimal capital structure debate, I have chosen a recent article by Michael Barclay and Clifford Smith Jr., "The Capital Structure Puzzle: Another Look at the Evidence", which provides an up-to-date summary of the competing theories of optimal capital structure as well as the evidence to support them.

"Disappearing Dividends: Changing Firm Characteristics or Lower Propensity to Pay?", by Eugene Fama and Kenneth French, is a readable article on how and why US firms are no longer paying dividends. Indeed, when I was working as a consultant to a broking firm which valued equities in the stock market boom of the late 1990s, it was acknowledged by analysts that they disapproved of firms which paid dividends. It seemed to imply that they did not – as they should – have an excess of positive Net Present Value projects in which to invest. In fact, Fama and French find that it is the new firms with low profitability and high growth opportunities which do not pay dividends. Large stable firms tend to be both ones which pay dividends and which also do share repurchases. A striking exception to this rule is Microsoft, which paid no dividends at all until 2004, when it paid one so large that it had a major boosting effect on the US economy. Case Study 14, in the last section of this book, discusses Microsoft's dividend policy, as well as other financial strategy issues.

The third article in this section looks at share repurchases, a phenomenon which really took off in the 1990s. Companies restructured their balance sheets, using debt to buy back equity, and taking advantage of a lower Weighted Average Cost of Capital. The article, by Richard Dobbs and Werner Rehm, is called "The Value of Share Buybacks" and looks at reasons other than the Modigliani and Miller tax relief on interest rationale, including behavioural reasons, to explain why so many firms carry out share buybacks. Case Study 5, "Capital Ideas" by Keith Boyfield, looks at a particular industry, the utility sector, to show how capital structure decisions are no longer cast in stone and how private equity and other financial market participants are devoting time and energy to optimising capital structures.

Case Study 6, "Death of the Dividend?", by Adrian Wood, is an up-to-date survey of what European companies are doing with their dividends. This gives a broader perspective than just a US view, and shows that signaling still seems to be a major factor in the dividend decision.

Case Study 7, "Sciona: A Venture Capital Case Study", is a short case study which illustrates how, in practice, an outside financing agency, in this case a venture capital company, becomes involved over a number of different stages in a small company financing.

The remaining article and case study of this section are devoted to the topic of new equity issues or, using US terminology, Initial Public Offerings or IPOs. Here, we are concerned with how, when and why companies come to the equity markets for finance. The finance literature on IPOs is similar to that on M&A in the sense that there are numerous articles which analyse the pricing of new issues over different periods, types of company and on different stock markets. What is similar, too, is the consistency of results. While the M&A literature confirms that little or no value is added through M&A deals, the IPO literature is fairly unanimous on two issues.

The first is that IPOs are under-priced as far as the issuer is concerned in that, on average, shares stand at a higher price at the close of the first day of issue than the issue price. The implication for companies is that they receive less in funds than they could – referred to as "leaving money on the table". The implication for investors is that buying shares at an IPO and selling at the close of the first day of trading is a profitable undertaking for "stags" hunting the new issue premium.[4] Possible explanations for the "under-pricing" phenomenon are that the methods of issue are not optimal from the issuer point of view.

The second "new issue puzzle" is that investors buying at the close of day one – without the new issue premium – will do less well than will investors buying equivalent risk/sector "seasoned" equities. Possible explanations for this second phenomenon are that investors and analysts are irrational in the sense that they are over-optimistic when they buy new companies. New issues follow a cycle as do mergers and acquisitions. Thus, new issues occur at a time when shares are naturally expensive and may be over-priced as a result. It may also be that analysts are over-optimistic in their earnings fore-casts. There is evidence that analysts do ratchet down their forecasts during the five-year period after the IPO, becoming more realistic in their forecasts as time goes on.[5]

In this section of the book, we concentrate on the first phenomenon – the underpricing of new issues. Jay Ritter has produced a number of articles on this topic. The article included here, "Initial Public Offerings", is a chapter from a book, summarising the results so far and the possible reasons for the under-pricing. It is also worth visiting Jay Ritter's home page (http://bear.cba.ufl.edu/ritter) for further articles and up-to-date numbers on new issue premia.

Case Study 8 is a series of press cuttings dating from before, during and after the 2004 IPO for Google. This issue was not only interesting because of the difficulty in valuing such a young, high-growth company, but also because the IPO method used tried to get round some of the disadvantages outlined in the Ritter article. The third interesting point to note in the press cuttings is the changing value attributed to Google both in terms of its chang-ing share price and its potential. Note the dates of each of the articles and the value that Google had at the time. As far as analysts were concerned, no-one was quite clear whether Google was just another "dot com" boom and bust, or the exception that proved the rule. When you have finished reading the case, look up the Google share price. Who was right and who was wrong?

NOTES

1. F. Modigliani and M.H. Miller (1963) "Corporate Income Taxes and the Cost of Capital: A Correction", *American Economic Review*, Vol. 53, No. 3, pp. 433–43.
2. A leveraged buyout is the acquisition of a company usually by a private con-sortium using substantial amounts of debt, some of which might have "junk" status.
3. E.F. Fama and K.R. French (2001) "Disappearing Dividends: Changing Firm Characteristics or Lower Propensity to Pay?", *Journal of Financial Economics*, Vol. 60, No. 1, pp. 3–43.
4. The first mention of "stags" in new issues was during the railway share boom in England in the 1840s. See J. Rutterford (2005) "The Company Prospectus: Marketing shares on the London Stock Exchange, 1850 to 1940", presented at the *European Business History Association Conference*, Frankfurt, September.
5. For an interesting paper on the "New Issue Puzzle", read P. Dechow, A. Hutton, and R. Sloan (1997) "Solving the New Equity Puzzle", *Financial Times*, Mas-tering Finance Series, Summer.

6

The Capital Structure Puzzle
Another Look at the Evidence

Michael J. Barclay and Clifford W. Smith, Jr.

A perennial debate in corporate finance concerns the question of optimal capital structure: Given a level of total capital necessary to support a company's activities, is there a way of dividing up that capital into debt and equity that maximizes current firm value? And, if so, what are the critical factors in setting the leverage ratio for a given company?

Although corporate finance has been taught in business schools for almost a century, the academic finance profession has found it remarkably difficult to provide definitive answers to these questions – answers that can guide practicing corporate executives in making their financing decisions. Part of the difficulty stems from how the discipline of finance has evolved. For much of this century, both the teaching of finance and the supporting research were dominated by the case-study method. In effect, finance education was a glorified apprenticeship system designed to convey to students the accepted wisdom – often codified in the form of rules of thumb – of successful practitioners. Such rules of thumb may have been quite effective in a given set of circumstances, but as those circumstances change over time such rules tend to degenerate into dogma. An example was Eastman Kodak's long-standing decision to shun debt financing – a policy stemming from George Eastman's brush with insolvency at the turn of the century that was not reversed until the 1980s.

But this "anecdotal" approach to the study of finance is changing. In the past few decades, financial economists have worked to transform corporate finance into a more scientific undertaking, with a body of formal theories that can be tested by empirical studies of market and corporate behavior. The ultimate basis for judging the usefulness of a theory is, of course, its consistency with the facts – and thus its ability to predict actual behavior. But this brings us to the most important obstacle to developing a definitive theory of capital structure: namely, the difficulty of designing empirical tests that are powerful enough to distinguish among the competing theories.

What makes the capital structure debate especially intriguing is that the different theories represent such different, and in some ways almost diametrically opposed, decision-making processes. For example, some finance scholars have followed Miller and Modigliani by arguing that both capital

structure and dividend policy are largely "irrelevant" in the sense that they
have no significant, predictable effects on corporate market values. Another
school of thought holds that corporate financing choices reflect an attempt
by corporate managers to balance the tax shields of greater debt against the
increased probability and costs of financial distress, including those arising
from corporate underinvestment. But if too much debt can destroy value by
causing financial distress and underinvestment, others have argued that *too
little* debt – at least in large, mature companies – can lead to *over*investment
and low returns on capital.

Still others argue that corporate managers making financing decisions are
concerned primarily with the "signaling" effects of such decisions – for
example, the tendency of stock prices to fall significantly in response to
common stock offerings (which can make such offerings very expensive for
existing shareholders) and to rise in response to leverage-increasing recapi-
talizations. Building on this signaling argument, MIT professor Stewart
Myers has suggested that corporate capital structures are simply the cumulative result of individual financing decisions in which managers follow a
financial *pecking order* – one in which retained earnings are preferred to
outside financing, and debt is preferred to equity when outside funding is
required. According to Myers, corporate managers making financing decisions are not really thinking about an optimal capital structure – that is,
a long-run targeted debt-to-equity ratio they eventually want to achieve.
Instead, they simply take the "path of least resistance" and choose what then
appears to be the low-cost financing vehicle – generally debt – with little
thought about the future consequences of these choices.

In his 1984 speech to the American Finance Association in which he first
presented the pecking order theory, Professor Myers referred to this conflict
among the different theories as the "capital structure puzzle." As we already
suggested, the greatest barrier to progress in solving the puzzle has been the
difficulty of devising conclusive tests of the competing theories. Over 30
years ago, researchers in the *capital markets* branch of finance, with its focus
on portfolio theory and asset pricing, began to develop models in the form
of precise mathematical formulas that predict the values of traded financial
assets as a function of a handful of (mainly) observable variables. The predictions generated by such models, after continuous testing and refinement,
have turned out to be remarkably accurate and useful to practitioners. For
example, the Black-Scholes option pricing model – variations of which have
long been widely used on options exchanges – has enabled traders to calculate the value of traded options of all kinds as a function of just six variables
(all but one of which can be directly observed).

The key to financial economists' success in capital markets is this: Armed
with specific hypotheses, they have been able to develop sophisticated and
powerful empirical tests. The evidence from such tests has in turn allowed
theorists to increase the "realism" of their models to the point where they
have been used, and in some cases further refined, by practitioners. And while
no one would argue that all major asset pricing issues have been resolved,

the continuing interaction between theory and testing has yielded a richer understanding of risk-return tradeoffs than anyone might have imagined decades ago.

Empirical methods in corporate finance have lagged behind those in capital markets for several reasons. First, our models of capital structure decisions are less precise than asset pricing models. The major theories focus on the ways that capital structure choices are likely to affect firm value. But rather than being reducible, like the option pricing model, to a precise mathematical formula, the existing theories of capital structure provide at best qualitative or directional predictions. They generally identify major factors like taxes or bankruptcy costs that would lead to an association between particular firm characteristics and higher or lower leverage. For example, the tax-based theory of capital structure suggests that firms with more non-interest tax shields (like investment tax credits) should have less debt in their capital structures; but the theory does not tell us how much less.

Second, most of the competing theories of optimal capital structure are not mutually exclusive. Evidence consistent with one theory – say, the tax-based explanation – generally does not allow us to conclude that another factor – the value of debt in reducing overinvestment by mature companies – is unimportant. In fact, it seems clear that taxes, bankruptcy costs (including incentives for underinvestment), and information costs all play some role in determining a firm's optimal capital structure. With our current tests, it is generally not possible to reject one theory in favor of another.

Third, many of the variables that we think affect optimal capital structure are difficult to measure. For example, signaling theory suggests that the managers' "private" information about the company's prospects plays an important role in their financing choices. But, since there is no obvious way to identify when managers have such proprietary information, it is hard to test this proposition.

For all of these reasons and others, the state of the art in corporate finance is less developed than in asset pricing. Thus it is important for the academic community to continue to develop the theory to yield more precise predictions, and to devise more powerful empirical tests as well as better proxies for the key firm characteristics that are likely to drive corporate financing decisions.

In this paper, we offer our assessment of the current state of the academic finance profession's understanding of these issues and suggest some new directions for further exploration. We also offer in closing what we feel is a promising approach to reconciling the different theories of capital structure.

THE THEORIES[1]

Current explanations of corporate financial policy can be grouped into three broad categories: (1) taxes, (2) contracting costs, and (3) information costs. Before discussing these theories, it is important to keep in mind that they are not mutually exclusive and that each is likely to help us understand at least particular facets of corporate financing. Our aim is to determine the relative importance of the different theories and to identify those aspects of financial policy that each theory is most helpful in explaining.

Taxes

The basic corporate profits tax allows the deduction of interest payments but not dividends in the calculation of taxable income. For this reason, adding debt to a company's capital structure lowers its expected tax liability and increases its after-tax cash flow. If there were only a corporate profits tax and no individual taxes on corporate securities, the value of a levered firm would equal that of an identical all-equity firm plus the present value of its interest tax shields. That present value, which represents the contribution of debt financing to the market value of the firm, could be estimated simply by multiplying the company's marginal tax rate (34% plus state and local rates) times the principal amount of outstanding debt (assuming the firm expects to maintain its current debt level).

The problem with this analysis, however, is that it overstates the tax advantage of debt by considering only the corporate profits tax. Many investors who receive interest income must pay taxes on that income. But those same investors who receive equity income in the form of capital gains are taxed at a lower rate and can defer any tax by choosing not to realize those gains. Thus, although higher leverage lowers the firm's corporate taxes, it increases the taxes paid by investors. And, because investors care about their *after-tax* returns, they require compensation for these increased taxes in the form of higher yields on corporate debt – higher than the yields on, say, comparably risky tax-exempt municipal bonds.

The higher yields on corporate debt that reflect investors' taxes effectively reduce the tax advantage of debt over equity. In this sense, the company's shareholders ultimately bear all of the tax consequences of its operations, whether the company pays those taxes directly in the form of corporate income tax or indirectly in the form of higher required rates of return on the securities it sells. For this reason alone,[2] the tax advantage of corporate debt is almost certainly not 34 cents for every dollar of debt. Nor is it likely to be zero, however, and so a consistently profitable company that volunteers to pay more taxes by having substantial unused debt capacity is likely to be leaving considerable value on the table.

Contracting Costs

Conventional capital structure analysis holds that financial managers set leverage targets by balancing the tax benefits of higher leverage against the greater probability, and thus higher expected costs, of financial distress. In this view, the optimal capital structure is the one in which the next dollar of debt is expected to provide an additional tax subsidy that just offsets the resulting increase in expected costs of financial distress.

Costs of Financial Distress (or the Underinvestment Problem). Although the *direct* expenses associated with the administration of the bankruptcy process appear to be quite small relative to the market values of companies,[3] the *indirect* costs can be substantial. In thinking about optimal capital structure, the most important indirect costs are likely to be the reductions in firm value that result from cutbacks in promising investment that tend to be made when companies get into financial difficulty.

When a company files for bankruptcy, the bankruptcy judge effectively assumes control of corporate investment policy – and it's not hard to imagine circumstances in which judges do not maximize firm value. But even in conditions less extreme than bankruptcy, highly leveraged companies are more likely than their low-debt counterparts to pass up valuable investment opportunities, especially when faced with the prospect of default. In such cases, corporate managers are likely not only to postpone major capital projects, but to make cutbacks in R&D, maintenance, advertising, or training that end up reducing future profits.

This tendency of companies to underinvest when facing financial difficulty is accentuated by conflicts that can arise among the firm's different claimholders. To illustrate this conflict, consider what might happen to a high-growth company that had trouble servicing its debt. Since the value of such a firm will depend heavily on its ability to carry out its long-term investment plan, what the company needs is an infusion of equity. But there is a problem. As Stewart Myers pointed out in his classic 1977 paper entitled "Determinants of Corporate Borrowing,"[4] the investors who would be asked to provide the new equity in such cases recognize that much of the value created (or preserved) by their investment would go to restoring the creditors' position. In this situation, the cost of the new equity could be so high that managers acting on their shareholders' behalf might rationally forgo both the capital and the investment opportunities.

Myers referred to this as "the underinvestment problem." And, as he went on to argue, companies whose value consists primarily of intangible investment opportunities – or "growth options," as he called them – will choose low-debt capital structures because such firms are likely to suffer the greatest loss in value from this underinvestment problem. By contrast, mature companies with few profitable investment opportunities where most of their value reflects the cash flows from tangible "assets in place" incur lower expected costs associated with financial distress. Such mature companies, all else equal, should have significantly higher leverage ratios than high-growth firms.

The Benefits of Debt in Controlling Overinvestment. If too much debt financing can create an underinvestment problem for growth companies, too little debt can lead to an *over*investment problem in the case of mature companies. As Michael Jensen has argued,[5] large, mature public companies generate substantial "free cash flow" – that is, operating cash flow that cannot be profitably reinvested inside the firm. The natural inclination of corporate managers is to use such free cash flow to sustain growth at the expense of profitability, either by overinvesting in their core businesses or, perhaps worse, by diversifying through acquisition into unfamiliar ones.

Because both of these strategies tend to reduce value, companies that aim to maximize firm value must distribute their free cash flow to investors. Raising the dividend is one way of promising to distribute excess capital. But major substitutions of debt for equity (for example, in the form of leveraged stock repurchases) offer a more reliable solution because contractually obligated payments of interest and principal are more effective than discretionary dividend payments in squeezing out excess capital. Thus, in industries generating substantial cash flow but facing few growth opportunities, debt financing can add value simply by forcing managers to be more critical in evaluating capital spending plans.[6]

Information Costs

Corporate executives often have better information about the value of their companies than outside investors. Recognition of this information disparity between managers and investors has led to two distinct, but related theories of financing decisions – one known as "signaling," the other as the "pecking order."

Signaling. With better information about the value of their companies than outside investors, managers of undervalued firms would like to raise their share prices by communicating this information to the market. Unfortunately, this task is not as easy as it sounds; simply announcing that the companies are undervalued generally isn't enough. The challenge for managers is to find a *credible* signaling mechanism.

Economic theory suggests that information disclosed by an obviously biased source (like management, in this case) will be credible only if the costs of communicating falsely are large enough to constrain managers to reveal the truth. Increasing leverage has been suggested as one potentially effective signaling device. Debt contracts oblige the firm to make a fixed set of cash payments over the life of the loan; if these payments are missed, there are potentially serious consequences, including bankruptcy. Equity is more forgiving. Although stockholders also typically expect cash payouts, managers have more discretion over these payments and can cut or omit them in times of financial distress.

For this reason, adding more debt to the firm's capital structure can serve as a credible signal of higher future cash flows.[7] By committing the firm to make future interest payments to bondholders, managers communicate their confidence that the firm will have sufficient cash flows to meet these obligations.

Debt and equity also differ with respect to their sensitivity to changes in firm value. Since the promised payments to bondholders are fixed, and stockholders are entitled to the residual (or what's left over after the fixed payments), stock prices are much more sensitive than bond prices to any proprietary information about future prospects. If management is in possession of good news that has yet to be reflected in market prices, the release of such news will cause a larger increase in stock prices than in bond prices; and hence current stock prices (prior to release of the new information) will appear more undervalued to managers than current bond prices. For this reason, signaling theory suggests that managers of companies that believe their assets are undervalued will generally choose to issue debt – and to use equity only as a last resort.

To illustrate this with a simple example, let's suppose that the market price of a stock is $25.00. Investors understand that its "real" value – that is, the value they would assign if they had access to the same information as the firm's managers – might be as high as $27.00 or as low as $23.00; but given investors' information $25.00 is a fair price. Now let's suppose that the managers want to raise external funds and they could either sell equity or debt. If the managers think the stock is really worth only $23.00, selling shares for $25.00 would be attractive – especially if their compensation is tied to stock appreciation. But if the managers think the stock is really worth $27.00, equity would be expensive at $25.00 and debt would be more attractive.

Investors understand this – and so if the company announces an equity offer, investors reassess the current price in light of this new information. Since it is more likely that the stock is worth $23.00 than $27.00, the market price declines. Such a rapid adjustment in valuation associated with the announcement thus eliminates much of any potential gain from attempting to exploit the manager's superior information.

Consistent with this example, economists have documented that the market responds in systematically negative fashion to announcements of equity offerings, marking down the share prices of issuing firms by about 3% on average. By contrast, the average market reaction to new debt offerings is not significantly different from zero.[8] The important thing to recognize is that most companies issuing new equity – those that are undervalued as well as those that are overvalued – can expect a drop in stock prices when they announce the offering. For those firms that are fairly valued or undervalued prior to the announcement of the offering, this expected drop in value represents an economic dilution of the existing shareholders' interest. Throughout the rest of this paper, we refer to this dilution as part of the "information costs" of raising outside capital.

The Pecking Order. Signaling theory, then, says that financing decisions are based, at least in part, on management's perception of the "fairness" of the market's current valuation of the stock. Stated as simply as possible, the theory suggests that, in order to minimize the information costs of issuing securities, a company is more likely to issue debt than equity if the firm appears undervalued, and to issue stock rather than debt if the firm seems overvalued.

The pecking order theory takes this argument one step farther, suggesting that the information costs associated with issuing securities are so large that they dominate all other considerations. According to this theory, companies maximize value by systematically choosing to finance new investments with the "cheapest available" source of funds. Specifically, they prefer internally generated funds (retained earnings) to external funding and, if outside funds are necessary, they prefer debt to equity because of the lower information costs associated with debt issues. Companies issue equity only as a last resort, when their debt capacity has been exhausted.[9]

The pecking order theory would thus suggest that companies with few investment opportunities and substantial free cash flow will have low debt ratios – and that high-growth firms with lower operating cash flows will have high debt ratios. In this sense, the theory not only suggests that interest tax shields and the costs of financial distress are at most a second-order concern; the logic of the pecking order actually leads to a set of predictions that are *precisely the opposite* of those offered by the tax and contracting cost arguments presented above.

THE EVIDENCE

Having discussed the different theories for observed capital structure, we now review the available empirical evidence to assess the relative "explanatory power" of each.

Evidence on Contracting Costs

Leverage Ratios. Much of the previous evidence on capital structure supports the conclusion that there is an optimal capital structure and that firms make financing decisions and adjust their capital structures to move closer to this optimum. For example, a 1967 study by Eli Schwartz and Richard Aronson showed clear differences in the average debt to (book) asset ratios of companies in different industries, as well as a tendency for companies in the same industry to cluster around these averages.[10] Moreover, such industry debt ratios seem to align with R&D spending and other proxies for corporate growth opportunities that the theory suggests are likely to be important in determining an optimal capital structure. In a 1985 study, Michael Long and Ileen Malitz showed that the five most highly leveraged industries – cement, blast furnaces and steel, paper and allied products, textiles, and petroleum refining – were all mature and asset-intensive. At the other extreme, the five industries with the lowest debt ratios – cosmetics, drugs, photographic equipment, aircraft, and radio and TV receiving – were all growth industries with high advertising and R&D.[11]

Other studies have used "cross-sectional" regression techniques to test whether the theoretical determinants of an optimal capital structure actually affect financing decisions. For example, in their 1984 study, Michael Bradley, Greg Jarrell, and Han Kim found that the debt to (book) asset ratio was negatively related to both the volatility of annual operating earnings and to advertising and R&D expenses. Both of these findings are consistent with high costs of financial distress for growth companies, which tend to have more volatile earnings as well as higher spending on R&D.[12]

Several studies have also reported finding that the debt ratios of individual companies seem to revert toward optimal targets. For example, a 1982 study by Paul Marsh estimated a company's target ratio as the average ratio observed over the prior ten years. He then found that the probability that a firm issues equity is significantly higher if the firm is above its target debt ratio, and significantly lower if below the target.[13]

As described in a 1995 article in this journal, we (together with colleague Ross Watts) attempted to add to this body of empirical work on capital structure by examining a much larger sample of companies that we tracked for over three decades.[14] For some 6,700 companies covered by Compustat, we calculated "market" leverage ratios (measured as the book value of total debt divided by the book value of debt and preferred stock plus the *market* value of equity) over the period 1963–1993. Not surprisingly, we found considerable differences in leverage ratios, both across companies in any given year and, in some cases, for the same firm over time. Although the average leverage ratio for the 6700 companies over the 30-year period was 25%, one fourth of the cases had market leverage ratios that were higher than 37.5% and another one fourth had leverage ratios less than 10.3%.

To test the contracting cost theory described earlier in this paper, we attempted to determine the extent to which corporate leverage choices can be explained by differences in companies' investment opportunities. As suggested earlier, the contracting cost hypothesis predicts that the greater these investment opportunities (relative to the size of the company), the greater the potential underinvestment problem associated with debt financing and, hence, the lower the company's target leverage ratio. Conversely, the more limited a company's growth opportunities, the greater the potential overinvestment problem and, hence, the higher should be the company's leverage.

To test this prediction, we needed a measure of investment opportunities. Because stock prices reflect intangible assets such as growth opportunities but corporate balance sheets do not, we reasoned that the larger a company's "growth options" relative to its "assets in place," the higher on average will be its market value in relation to its book value. We accordingly used a company's market-to-book ratio as our proxy for its investment opportunity set.

The results of our regressions provide strong support for the contracting cost hypothesis. Companies with high market-to-book ratios had significantly lower leverage ratios than companies with low market-to-book ratios. (The t-statistic on the market-to-book ratio in the leverage regression was about 130.) To make these findings a little more concrete, our results suggest that, as one moves form companies at the bottom 10th percentile of market-to-book ratios (0.77) to the 90th percentile (2.59), the predicted leverage market ratio falls by 14.3 percentage points – which is a large fraction of the average ratio of 25%. (For further discussion of these results, see the box on the next page.)

Moreover, such a negative relation between corporate leverage and market-to-book ratios appears to hold outside the U.S. as well. In a 1995 study, Raghuram Rajan and Luigi Zingales examined capital structure using data from Japan, Germany, France, Italy, the U.K. and Canada, as well as the U.S. They found that, in each of these seven countries, leverage is lower for firms with higher market-to-book ratios and higher for firms with higher ratios of fixed assets to total assets.[15]

The above evidence on leverage ratios, it should be pointed out, is also generally consistent with the tax hypothesis in the following sense: The same low-growth companies that face low financial distress costs and high free-cash-flow benefits from heavy debt financing are also likely to have greater use for interest tax shields than high-growth companies. At the same time, the above evidence is inconsistent with the predictions of the pecking order theory – which, again, suggests that low-growth firms with high free cash flow will have relatively low debt ratios.

Debt Maturity and Priority. Like this article up to this point, most academic discussions of capital structure focus just on the leverage ratio. In so doing, they effectively assume that all debt financing is the same. In practice, of course, debt differs in several important respects, including maturity, covenant restrictions, security, convertibility and call provisions, and whether the debt is privately placed or held by widely dispersed public investors. Each of these features is potentially important in determining the extent to which debt financing can cause, or exacerbate, a potential under-investment problem. For example, debt-financed companies with more investment opportunities would prefer to have debt with shorter maturities (or at least with call provisions, to ensure greater financing flexibility), more convertibility provisions (which reduce the required coupon payments), less restrictive covenants, and a smaller group of private investors rather than public bondholders (which makes it easier to reorganize in the event of trouble). By recognizing this array of financing choices, we can broaden the scope of our examination and raise the potential power of our tests, while at the same time increasing the relevance of the analysis for managers who must choose the design of their debt securities.

As described in our 1996 article in this journal,[16] we designed an empirical test of the suggestion – offered by Stewart Myers in his 1977 article – that one way for companies with lots of growth options to control the under-investment problem is to issue debt with shorter maturities. The argument is basically this: A firm whose value consists mainly of growth opportunities could severely reduce its future financing and strategic flexibility – and in the process destroy much of its value – by issuing long-term debt. Not only

Box 6.1 Robustness of the evidence on contracting costs

A number of empirical tests of the contracting cost hypothesis have taken the form of a regression with market leverage (measured as the ratio of the book value of debt to the total market value of the firm) as the dependent variable and the corporate market-to-book ratio together with a few "control" variables as the independent variables. Because the market value of the firm appears on both the left and right hand sides of this regression (in the denominator of the leverage ratio and in the numerator of the market-to-book ratio), some researchers have questioned whether the strong negative relation between these variables really supports the theory or is simply the "artificial" result of large variations in stock prices.

To examine the robustness of these results, our 1995 study with Ross Watts used other proxies for the firms' investment opportunities (the independent variable) that do not rely on market values. For example, when we substituted a company's R&D and advertising as a percentage of sales for its market-to-book ratio, our results were consistent with the contracting cost hypothesis. The coefficients on both of our alternative proxies for the firm's investment opportunities had the correct sign, and the t-statistics, although lower than 130, were still impressive – about 65 in the R&D regression and 18 in the advertising regression.

In a more recent series of tests, we used two different proxies for leverage (the dependent variable): (1) the ratio of total debt to the *book* value of assets; and (2) the interest coverage ratio (EBIT over interest). On purely theoretical grounds, these regressions are expected to produce less significant results. Recall that the contracting cost hypothesis predicts that tangible "assets in place" provide good collateral for loans while intangible investment opportunities do not. If leverage is measured as the ratio of total debt to the book value of assets, we are really measuring the extent to which the firm has leveraged just its tangible (book) assets while essentially ignoring the intangible assets. For this reason, the theory predicts less variation in leverage when measured in relation to book assets than when measured in relation to total market value.

Nevertheless, when we re-estimated the leverage regression substituting book leverage as the dependent variable, the results again supported the contracting cost hypothesis. The regression coefficient on the market-to-book ratio in the book-leverage regression was smaller (with a somewhat lower t-statistic), as predicted. But the coefficient was still reliably negative, with a t-statistic greater than 45.

A similar problem arises with the coverage ratio. In this case, the benefits of intangible growth opportunities (in the form of higher expected future cash flow) are not reflected in current earnings when we use the coverage ratio as our proxy for leverage. Yet, even so the correlation coefficient was positive; that is to say, companies with higher market-to-book values tended to have significantly higher interest coverage ratios (the t-statistic exceeded 70).

would the interest rate have to be high to compensate lenders for their greater risk, but the burden of servicing the debt could cause the company to defer strategic investments if their operating cash flow turns down. By contrast, shorter-term debt, besides carrying lower interest rates in such cases, would also be less of a threat to future strategic investment because, as the firm's current investments begin to pay off, it will be able over time to raise capital on more favorable terms.[17]

When we tested this prediction (again using market-to-book as a measure of growth options), we found that growth companies tended to have significantly less debt with a maturity greater than three years than companies with limited investment opportunities. More specifically, our regressions suggest that moving from companies at the 10th to the 90th percentile of market-to-book ratios (that is from 0.77 to 2.59) reduces the ratio of long-term debt to total debt by 18 percentage points (a significant reduction, given our sample average ratio of 46%).

Moreover, we also found in the same study that the debt issued by growth firms is significantly more concentrated among high-priority classes. Consistent with our results indicating that firms with more growth options tend to have lower leverage ratios, we find that changing the market-to-book ratio from the 10th to the 90th percentile is associated with reductions in leasing of 89%, in secured debt of 71%, in ordinary debt of 78%, and in subordinated debt of almost 250%. Our explanation for this is as follows: When firms get into financial difficulty, complicated capital structures with claims of different priorities can generate serious conflicts among creditors, thus exacerbating the underinvestment problem described earlier. And because such conflicts and the resulting underinvestment have the greatest potential to destroy value in growth firms, those growth firms that do issue fixed claims are likely to choose mainly high-priority fixed claims.

The Evidence on Information Costs

Leverage. Signaling theory says that companies are more likely to issue debt than equity when they are undervalued because of the large information costs (in the form of dilution) associated with an equity offering. The pecking order model goes even farther, suggesting that the information costs associated with riskier securities are so large that most companies will not issue equity until they have completely exhausted their debt capacity. Neither the signaling nor the pecking order theory offers any clear prediction about what optimal capital structure would be for a given firm. The signaling theory seems to suggest that a firm's actual capital structure will be influenced by whether the company is perceived by management to be undervalued or overvalued. The pecking order model is more extreme; it implies that a company will not have a target capital structure, and that its leverage ratio will be determined by the gap between its operating cash flow and its investment requirements over time. Thus, the pecking order predicts that companies with consistently high profits or modest financing requirements are likely to have low debt ratios – mainly because they don't need outside capital. Less profitable companies, and those with large financing requirements, will end up with high leverage ratios because of managers' reluctance to issue equity.

A number of studies have provided support for the pecking order theory in the form of evidence of a strong negative relation between past profitability and leverage. That is, the lower are a company's profits and operating cash flows in a given year, the higher is its leverage ratio (measured either in terms of book or market values).[18] Moreover, in an article published in 1998, Stewart Myers and Lakshmi Shyam-Sunder added to this series of studies by showing that this relation explains more of the time-series variance of debt ratios than a simple target-adjustment model of capital structure that is consistent with the contracting cost hypothesis.[19]

Such findings have generally been interpreted as confirmation that managers do not set target leverage ratios – or at least do not work very hard to achieve them. But this is not the only interpretation that fits these data. Even if companies have target leverage ratios, there will be an *optimal deviation* from those targets – one that will depend on the transactions costs associated with adjusting back to the target relative to the costs of deviating from the target. To the extent there are fixed costs and scale economies in issuing securities, companies with capital structure targets – particularly smaller firms – will make infrequent adjustments and often will deliberately overshoot their targets. (And, as we argue in the closing section of this paper, a complete theory of capital structure must take account of these adjustment costs and how they affect expected deviations from the target.)

In our 1995 paper with Ross Watts, we attempted to devise our own test of how information costs affect corporate financing behavior. According to the signaling explanation, undervalued companies will have higher leverage than overvalued firms. One major challenge in testing this signaling argument is coming up with a reliable proxy for undervaluation that can be readily observed. In devising such a measure, we began with the assumption that corporate earnings follow a random walk, and that the best predictor of a company's next year's earnings is thus its current year's earnings. We then classified firms as undervalued in any given year in which their earnings (excluding extraordinary items and discontinued operation and adjusted for any changes in shares outstanding) increased in the following year. We designated as overvalued all firms whose ordinary earnings decreased in the next year.

Our regressions showed a very small (but statistically significant) positive relation between a company's leverage ratio and its unexpected earnings, thus suggesting that this undervaluation variable has a trivial effect on corporate capital structure. For example, moving from the 10th percentile of abnormal earnings in our sample (those firms whose earnings decreased by 12%) to the 90th percentile (those whose earnings increased by 13%) raised the predicted leverage ratio by only 0.5 percentage points. Moreover, in our 1996 study (which also uses Compustat data, although for a somewhat different time period), we again found a small relation between leverage and unexpected earnings. In this regression, however, the relation was *negative*.

Debt Maturity and Priority. Signaling theory implies that undervalued firms will have more short-term debt and more senior debt than overvalued firms because such instruments are less sensitive to the market's assessment of firm value and thus will be less undervalued when issued. The findings of our 1996 study are inconsistent with the predictions of the signaling hypothesis with respect to debt maturity. Companies whose earnings were about to increase the following year in fact issued less short-term debt and more long-term debt than firms whose earnings were about to decrease. And, whereas the theory predicts more senior debt for firms about to experience earnings increases, the ratio of senior debt to total debt is lower for overvalued than for undervalued firms.

In sum, the results of our tests of managers' use of financing choices to signal their superior information to the market are not robust, and the economic effect of any such signaling on corporate decision-making seems minimal.

According to the pecking order theory, the firm should issue as much of the security with the lowest information costs as it can. Only after this capacity is exhausted should it move on to issue a security with higher information costs. Thus, for example, firms should issue as much secured debt or capitalized leases as possible before issuing any unsecured debt, and they should exhaust their capacity for issuing short-term debt before issuing any long-term debt. But these predictions are clearly rejected by the data. For example, when we examined the capital structures of over 7,000 companies between 1980 and 1997 (representing almost 57,000 firm-year observations), we found that 23% of these observations had no secured debt, 54% had no capital leases, and 50% had no debt that was originally issued with less than one year to maturity.

To explain these more detailed aspects of capital structure, proponents of the pecking order theory must go outside their theory and argue that other costs and benefits determine these choices. But once you allow for these other costs and benefits to have a material impact on corporate financing choices, you are back in the more traditional domain of optimal capital structure theories.

The Evidence on Taxes

Theoretical models of optimal capital structure predict that firms with more taxable income and fewer non-debt tax shields should have higher leverage ratios. But the evidence on the relation between leverage ratios and tax-related variables is mixed at best. For example, studies that examine the effect of non-debt tax shields on companies' leverage ratios find that this effect is either insignificant, or that it enters with the wrong sign. That is, in contrast to the prediction of the tax hypothesis, these studies suggest that firms with more non-debt tax shields such as depreciation, net operating loss carryforwards and investment tax credits have, if anything, *more* not less debt in their capital structures.[20]

But before we conclude that taxes are unimportant in the capital structure decision, it is critical to recognize that the findings of these studies are hard to interpret because the tax variables are crude proxies for a company's effective marginal tax rate. In fact, these proxies are often correlated with other variables that influence the capital structure choice. For example, companies with investment tax credits, high levels of depreciation, and other non-debt tax shields also tend to have mainly tangible fixed assets. And, since fixed assets provide good collateral, the non-debt tax shields may in fact be a proxy not for limited tax benefits, but rather for low contracting costs associated with debt financing. The evidence from the studies just cited is generally consistent with this interpretation.

Similarly, firms with net operating loss carryforwards are often in financial distress; and, since equity values typically decline in such circumstances, financial distress itself causes leverage ratios to increase. Thus, again, it is not clear whether net operating losses proxy for low tax benefits of debt or for financial distress.

More recently, several authors have succeeded in detecting tax effects in financing decisions by focusing on incremental financing choices (that is, *changes* in the amount of debt or equity) rather than on the levels of debt and equity. For example, a 1990 study by Jeffrey Mackie-Mason examined registered security offerings by public U.S. corporations and found that firms were more likely to issue debt if they had a high marginal tax rate and to issue equity if they had a low tax rate.[21] In another attempt to avoid the difficulties with crude proxy variables, a 1996 study by John Graham used a sophisticated simulation method to provide a more accurate measure of companies' marginal tax rates.[22] Using such tax rates, Graham also found a positive association between changes in debt ratios and the firm's marginal tax rate.

On balance, then, the evidence appears to suggest that taxes play at least a modest role in corporate financing and capital structure decisions. Moreover, as mentioned earlier, the results of our tests of contracting costs reported above can also be interpreted as evidence in support of the tax explanation.

TOWARD A UNIFIED THEORY OF CORPORATE FINANCIAL POLICY

In addition to explaining the basic leverage (or debt vs. equity) decision, a useful theory of capital structure should also help explain other capital structure choices, such as debt maturity, priority, the use of callability and convertibility provisions, and the choice between public and private financing. As discussed above, the contracting-cost theory provides a unified framework for analyzing the entire range of capital structure choices while most other theories, such as the signaling and pecking order theories, are at best silent about – and more often inconsistent with – the empirical evidence on these issues.

We now take this argument one step further by suggesting that a productive capital structure theory should also help explain an even broader array of corporate financial policy choices, including dividend, compensation, hedging, and leasing policies. The empirical evidence suggests that companies choose coherent *packages* of these financial policies. For example, small high-growth firms tend to have not only low leverage ratios and simple capital structures (with predominantly short-maturity, senior bank debt), but also low dividend payouts as well as considerable stock-based incentive compensation for senior executives. By contrast, large mature companies tend to have high leverage, more long-term debt, more complicated capital structures with a broader range of debt priorities, higher dividends, and less incentive compensation (with greater reliance on earnings-based bonuses rather than stock-based compensation plans).[23] Thus, corporate financing, dividend, and compensation policies, besides being highly correlated with each other, all appear to be driven by the same fundamental firm characteristics: investment opportunities and (to a lesser extent) firm size. And this consistent pattern of corporate decision-making suggests that we now have the rudiments of a unified framework for explaining most, if not all, financial policy choices.

As mentioned earlier, proponents of the pecking order theory argue that the information costs associated with issuing new securities dominate all other costs in determining capital structure. But, as we also noted, the logic and predictions of the pecking order theory are at odds with, and thus incapable of explaining, most other financial policy choices. For example, in suggesting that firms will always use the cheapest source of funds, the model implies that companies will not simultaneously pay dividends and access external capital markets. But this prediction can, of course, be rejected simply by glancing at the business section of most daily newspapers. With the exception of a few extraordinarily successful high tech companies like Microsoft and Amgen, most large, publicly traded companies pay dividends while at the same time regularly rolling over existing debt with new public issues. And, as already discussed, although the pecking order predicts that mature firms that generate lots of free cash flow should eventually become all equity financed, they are among the most highly levered firms in our sample. Conversely, the pecking order theory implies that high-tech startup firms will have high leverage ratios because they often have negative free cash flow and incur the largest information costs when issuing equity. But, in fact, such firms are financed almost entirely with equity.

Thus, as we saw in the case of debt maturity and priority, proponents of the pecking order must go outside of their theory to explain corporate behavior at both ends of the corporate growth spectrum. In so doing, they implicitly limit the size and importance of information costs; they concede that, at least for the most mature and the highest-growth sectors, information costs are less important than other considerations in corporate financing decisions.

Integration of Stocks and Flows

Although the pecking order theory is incapable of explaining the full array of financial policy choices, this does not mean that information costs are unimportant in corporate decision-making. On the contrary, such costs will influence corporate financing choices and, along with other costs and benefits, must be part of a unified theory of corporate financial policy.

In our view, the key to reconciling the different theories – and thus to solving the capital structure puzzle – lies in achieving a better understanding of the relation between corporate financing *stocks* and *flows*. The theories of capital structure discussed in this paper generally focus either on the stocks (that is, on the levels of debt and equity in relation to the target) or on the flows (the decision of which security to issue at a particular time). For example, the primary focus of the contracting-cost theories has been leverage ratios, which are measures of the *stocks* of debt and equity. By contrast, information-based theories like the pecking order model generally focus on flows – for example, on the information costs associated with a new issue of debt or equity. But, since both stocks and flows are likely to play important roles in such decisions, neither of these theoretical approaches taken alone is likely to offer a reliable guide to optimal capital structure.

In developing a sensible approach to capital structure strategy, the CFO should start by thinking about the firm's target capital structure in terms of stock measures – that is, *a ratio of debt to total capital that can be expected to minimize taxes and contracting costs* (although information costs may also be given some consideration here). That target ratio should take into consideration factors such as the company's projected investment requirements; the level and stability of its operating cash flows; its tax status; the expected loss in value from being forced to defer investment because of financial distress; and the firm's ability to raise capital on short notice (without excessive dilution).

If the company is not currently at or near its optimal capital structure, the CFO should come up with a plan to achieve the target debt ratio. For example, if the firm has "too much" equity (or too much capital in general), it can increase leverage by borrowing (or using excess cash) to buy back shares – a possibility that the pecking order generally ignores. (And the fact that U.S. corporate stock repurchases have been growing at almost 30% per year for most of this decade is by itself perhaps the single most compelling piece of evidence that corporate managers *are* thinking in terms of optimal capital structure.) But, if the company needs more capital, then managers choosing between equity and various forms of debt must consider not only the benefits of moving toward the target, but also the associated adjustment costs. For example, a company with "too much" debt may choose to delay an equity offering – or issue convertibles or PERCS instead – in order to reduce the cost of issuing securities that it perceives to be undervalued.

As a more general principle, the CFO should adjust the firm's capital structure whenever the costs of adjustment – including information costs as well as out-of-pocket transactions costs – are less than the costs of deviating from the target. Based on the existing research, what can we say about such adjustment costs? The available evidence on the size and variation of such costs suggests that there is a material fixed component – one that again includes information costs as well as out-of-pocket costs.[24] And, since average adjustment costs fall with increases in transaction size, there are scale economies in issuing new securities that suggest that small firms, all else equal, are likely to deviate farther from their capital structure targets than larger companies.

Although the different kinds of external financing all exhibit scale economies, the structure of the costs varies among different types of securities. Equity issues have both the largest out-of-pocket transactions costs and the largest information costs. Long-term public debt issues, particularly for below-investment-grade companies, are less costly.[25] Short-term private debt or bank loans are the least costly. And, because CFOs are likely to weigh these adjustment costs against the expected benefits from moving closer to their leverage target, it is not surprising that seasoned equity offerings are rare events, that long-term debt issues are more common, and that private debt offerings or bank loans occur with almost predictable regularity. Moreover, because of such adjustment costs, most companies – particularly smaller firms – are also likely to spend considerable time away from their target capital structures. Other things equal, larger adjustment costs will lead to larger deviations from the target before the firm readjusts.

In sum, to make a sensible decision about capital structure, CFOs must understand both the costs associated with deviating from the target capital structure and the costs of adjusting back toward the target. The next major step forward in solving the capital structure puzzle is almost certain to involve a more formal weighing of these two sets of costs.

NOTES

1. This section draws on the discussion of capital structure theory in Michael J. Barclay, Clifford W. Smith, Jr. and Ross L. Watts "The Determinants of Corporate Leverage and Dividend Policies," *Journal of Applied Corporate Finance*, Vol. 7 No. 4 (Winter 1995).
2. The extent to which a company benefits from interest tax shields also depends on whether it has other tax shields. For example, holding all else equal, companies with more investment tax credits or tax loss carryforwards should have lower leverage ratios to reflect the lower value of their debt tax shields. See Harry DeAngelo and Ronald Masulis, "Optimal Capital Structure Under

Corporate and Personal Taxation," *Journal of Financial Economics*, Vol. 8 No. 1 (1980), pp. 3–29.

3. Perhaps the best evidence to date on the size of direct bankruptcy costs comes from Jerry Warner's study of 11 railroads that declared bankruptcy over the period 1930–1955. (Jerold B. Warner, "Bankruptcy Costs: Some Evidence," *Journal of Finance*, Vol. 32 (1977), pp. 337–347.) The study reported that out-of-pocket expenses associated with the administration of the bankruptcy process were quite small relative to the market value of the firm – less than 1% for the larger railroads in the sample. For smaller companies, it's true, direct bankruptcy costs are a considerably larger fraction of firm value (about five times larger in Warner's sample). Thus there are "scale economies" with respect to *direct* bankruptcy costs that imply that larger companies should have higher leverage ratios, all else equal, than smaller firms. But, even these higher estimates of direct bankruptcy costs, when weighted by the probability of getting into bankruptcy in the first place, produce *expected costs* that appear far too low to make them an important factor in corporate financing decisions.

4. Stewart C. Myers, "Determinants of Corporate Borrowing," *Journal of Financial Economics*, Vol. 5 (1977), pp. 147–175.

5. See Michael C. Jensen, "Agency Costs of Free Cash Flow, Corporate Finance, and Takeovers," *American Economic Review* 76 (1986), pp. 323–329.

6. More generally, the use of debt rather than equity reduces what economists call the agency costs of equity – loosely speaking, the reduction in firm value that arises from the separation of ownership from control in large, public companies with widely dispersed shareholders. In high-growth firms, the risk-sharing benefits of the corporate form are likely to outweigh these agency costs. But, in mature industries with limited capital requirements, heavy debt financing has the added benefit of facilitating the concentration of equity ownership. To illustrate this potential role of debt, assume that the new owner of an all-equity company with $100 million of assets discovers that the assets can support $90 million of debt. Reducing the firm's equity from $100 million to $10 million greatly increases the ability of small investor groups (including management) to control large asset holdings.

   The concentration of ownership made possible by leverage appears to have been a major part of the value gains achieved by the LBO movement of the '80s, and which has been resurrected in the 1990s. And, to the extent there are gains from having more concentrated ownership (and, again, these are likely to be greatest for mature industries with assets in place), companies should have higher leverage ratios.

7. Stephen Ross, "The Determinination of Financial Structure: The Incentive Signaling Approach," *Bell Journal of Economics*, Vol. 8 (1977), pp. 23–40.

8. More generally, the evidence suggests that leverage-increasing transactions are associated with positive stock price reactions while leverage-reducing transactions are associated with negative reactions. In reaction to large debt-for-stock exchanges, for example, stock prices go up by 14% on average. The market also reacts in a predictably negative way to *leverage-reducing* transactions, with

prices falling by 9.9% in response to common-for-debt exchanges and by 7.7% in preferred-for-debt exchanges. For a review of this evidence, see Clifford Smith, "Investment Banking and the Capital Acquisition Process," *Journal of Financial Economics*, Vol. 15 (1986), pp. 3–29.

9. See Stewart Myers, "The Capital Structure Puzzle," *Journal of Finance*, 39 (1984), pp. 575–592.

10. Eli Schwartz and J. Richard Aronson, "Some Surrogate Evidence in Support of Optimal Financial Structure," *Journal of Finance* Vol. 22 No. 1 (1967).

11. Michael Long and Ileen Malitz, "The Investment-Financing Nexus: Some Empirical Evidence," *Midland Corporate Finance Journal*, Vol. 3 No. 3 (1985).

12. Michael Bradley, Greg Jarrell, and E. Han Kim, "The Existence of an Optimal Capital Structure: Theory and Evidence," *Journal of Finance*, Vol. 39 No. 3 (1984).

13. Paul Marsh, "The Choice Between Equity and Debt," *Journal of Finance*, 37, (1982), pp. 121–144.

14. Barclay, Smith, and Watts (1995), cited above.

15. See Raghuram Rajan and Luigi Zingales, "What Do We Know About Capital Structure? Some Evidence From International Data," *Journal of Finance*, Vol. 50 No. 5 (1995). These relations are statistically significant for each country for the coefficient on growth options and for every country but France and Canada for the coefficient on assets in place.

16. Michael J. Barclay and Clifford W. Smith, Jr., "On Financial Architecture: Leverage, Maturity, and Priority," *Journal of Applied Corporate Finance*, Vol. 8 No. 4 (1996).

17. If the firm's debt matures before a company's growth options must be exercised, the investment distortions created by the debt are eliminated. Since these investment distortions are most severe, and most costly, for firms with significant growth options, high-growth firms should use more short-term debt.

18. See, for example, Carl Kester, "Capital and Ownership Structure: A Comparison of United States and Japanese Manufacturing Corporations," *Financial Management*, Vol. 15 (1986); Rajan and Zingales (1995); and Sheridan Titman and Roberto Wessels, "The Determinants of Capital Structure Choice," *Journal of Finance*, 43 (1988), pp. 1–19.

19. Lakshmi Shyam-Sunder and Stewart Myers, "Testing Static Tradeoff Against Pecking Order Models of Capital Structure," *Journal of Financial Economics*, Vol. 51 No. 2.

20. See, for example, Bradley, Jarrell, and Kim (1984); Titman and Wessels (1988); and Barclay, Smith, and Watts (1995), all of which are cited above.

21. Jeffrey Mackie-Mason, "Do Taxes Affect Corporate Financing Decisions?", *Journal of Finance*, 45 (1990), pp. 1471-1494.

22. John Graham, "Debt and the Marginal Tax Rate", *Journal of Financial Economics*, 41 (1996), pp. 41-73.

23. See Clifford W. Smith and Ross L. Watts, "The Investment Opportunity Set and Corporate Financing, Dividend and Compensation Policies," *Journal of Financial Economics*, 32 (1992), pp. 263-292.

24. See, for example, David Blackwell and David Kidwell, "An Investigation of Cost Differences Between Private Placements and Public Sales of Debt," *Journal of Financial Economics*, 22 (1988), pp. 253–278; and Clifford Smith, "Alternative Methods for Raising Capital: Rights vs. Underwritten Offerings," *Journal of Financial Economics*, 5 (1977), pp. 273–307.

25. See, Sudip Datta, Mai Iskandar-Datta, and Ajay Patel, "The Pricing of Debt IPOs," *Journal of Applied Corporate Finance*, Vol. 12 No. 1 (Spring 1999).

Reproduced from *Journal of Applied Corporate Finance*, Vol. 12 No. 1 (Spring 1999), pp. 8–20.

7

Disappearing Dividends
Changing Firm Characteristics or Lower
Propensity to Pay?

Eugene F. Fama and Kenneth R. French

The proportion of U.S. firms paying dividends drops sharply during the 1980s and 1990s. In 1973, the first year of complete data coverage on NYSE, AMEX, and NASDAQ firms, 52.8% of publicly traded firms (excluding utilities and financials) pay dividends. This proportion rises to 66.5% in 1978. It then falls rather relentlessly. In 1999, only 20.8% of firms pay dividends.

The decline after 1978 in the percent of firms paying dividends raises three questions: (i) What are the characteristics of dividend payers? (ii) Is the decline in the percent of payers due to a decline in the prevalence of these characteristics among publicly traded firms, or (iii) have firms with the characteristics typical of dividend payers become less likely to pay?

Three characteristics tend to affect the likelihood that a firm pays dividends: profitability, growth, and size. Larger firms and more profitable firms are more likely to pay dividends, and high-growth firms are less likely to do so. The decline after 1978 in the percent of firms paying dividends is due in part to an increasing number of small, publicly traded firms with low reported earnings and high growth. This tilt in the population of firms is driven by an explosion of newly listed firms, as well as by the changing nature of the new firms. Newly listed firms always tend to be small, with high asset growth rates and high market-to-book ratios. What changes after 1978 is their profitability. In 1973–1977, the earnings of new lists average a hefty 17.79% of book equity, versus 13.68% for all firms. The profitability of new lists falls throughout the next 20 years; their earnings average only 2.07% of book equity in 1993–1998, versus 11.26% for all firms.

This decline in profitability is accompanied by a decline in the percent of new lists that pay dividends. During 1973–1977, one-third of newly listed firms pay dividends. In 1999, only 3.7% of new lists pay dividends. The surge in and the changing nature of new lists produce a swelling group of small firms with low profitability but high growth rates that have never paid dividends.

It is perhaps obvious that investors have become more willing to hold the shares of small, relatively unprofitable growth companies. This group of firms is a big factor in the decline in the percent of firms paying dividends. But the resulting tilt of the publicly traded population toward such firms is only half of the story for the declining incidence of dividend payers. Our more striking finding is that firms in general have become less likely to pay dividends. This change, which we characterize as a lower propensity to pay, suggests that the perceived benefits of dividends have declined over time.

The lower propensity to pay is quite general. For example, the percent of payers among firms with positive earnings declines after 1978, but the percent of dividend payers among firms with negative earnings also declines. Small firms become much less likely to pay dividends after 1978, but there is also a lower incidence of dividend payers among large firms. High-growth firms become much less likely to pay dividends after 1978, but firms with fewer investment opportunities also show less inclination to pay dividends.

Share repurchases jump in the 1980s, and it is interesting to examine the role of repurchases in the declining incidence of dividend payments. It turns out that repurchases are mainly the province of dividend payers, so they leave the decline in the percent of payers largely unexplained. Instead, the primary effect of repurchases is to increase the already high payouts of cash dividend payers.

TIME TRENDS IN CASH DIVIDENDS

We begin by examining the incidence of dividend payers among NYSE, AMEX, and NASDAQ firms. We exclude utilities from the sample to avoid the criticism that their dividend decisions are a byproduct of regulation. We exclude financial firms because our data on the characteristics of dividend payers are from COMPUSTAT and COMPUSTAT's historical coverage of financial firms is spotty.

Figure 7.1 shows the total number of firms each year since 1926, as well as the number of payers and non-payers. These data are from the Center for

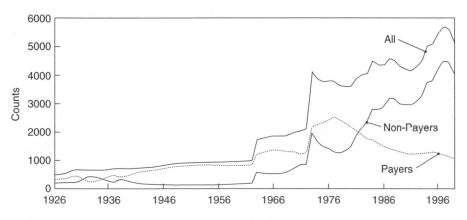

Figure 7.1 Number of firms in different dividend groups

Research in Security Prices (CRSP). Until mid-1962, CRSP covers only NYSE firms. The jumps in the total number of firms in 1963 and 1973 in Figure 7.1 are due to the addition of first AMEX and then NASDAQ firms. Swelling numbers of new listings cause the total number of firms to expand by about 40%, from 3,638 firms in 1978 to 5,113 in 1999, with a peak of 5,670 in 1997. New lists average 5.2% of listed firms (114 per year) during 1963–1977, versus 9.6% (436 per year) for 1978–1999.

Figure 7.2 shows that the proportion of firms paying dividends falls by half during the early years of the Great Depression, from 66.9% in 1930 to 33.6% in 1933, and then rises thereafter. In every year from 1943 to 1962, more than 82% of firms pay dividends. With the addition of AMEX firms in 1963, the proportion of dividend payers drops to 69.3%. The addition of NASDAQ firms in 1973 further lowers the proportion of payers to 52.8%, from 59.8% in 1972. The proportion of dividend payers rises to 66.5% in 1978, the peak for the post-1972 period of NYSE-AMEX-NASDAQ data coverage, and then declines sharply. In 1999, only 20.8% of firms pay dividends.

After 1977, more than 85% of new lists begin trading on NASDAQ, which might lead one to suspect that the declining incidence of dividend payers is a NASDAQ phenomenon. As Figure 7.3 shows, however, all three exchanges experience a declining incidence of dividends. The proportion of NYSE firms paying dividends drops from 88.6% in 1979 to 52.0% in 1999, a level not seen since the Great Depression. The proportions of AMEX and NASDAQ payers drop from their peaks of 63.4% and 54.1% in 1978 and 1977 to 16.9% and 8.6% in 1999. Thus, although it coincides with the explosion of NASDAQ new lists, the decline in the percent of firms paying dividends is not limited to NASDAQ.

Despite the fact that the total population of NYSE, AMEX, and NASDAQ firms grows by about 40%, the number of dividend payers shrinks by more than 50% from 1978 to 1999. There are 2,419 dividend payers in 1978 but

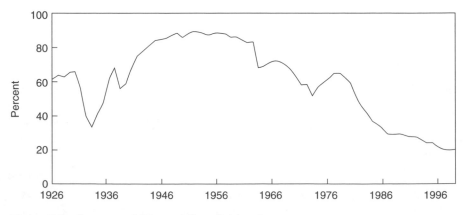

Figure 7.2   Percent of firms paying dividends

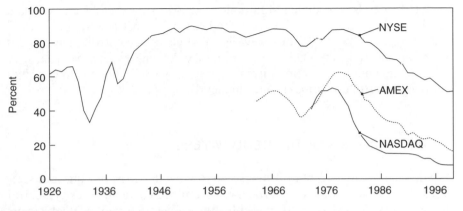

Figure 7.3 Percent of firms paying dividends

only 1,063 in 1999 (see Figure 7.1). The rate at which dividend payers disappear from the sample (due to dividend terminations, delistings, and mergers) rises from 6.8% per year for 1963–1977 to 9.8% for 1978–1999. Most of this increase is due to mergers. The rate at which dividend payers terminate dividends remains relatively steady at 4–5% per year, consistent with previous evidence that only distressed firms (with strongly negative earnings) terminate dividends.[1] Dividend payers also delist at a fairly constant rate (0.9% per year during 1978–1999 versus 0.8% for 1963–1977). In contrast, the rate at which dividend payers merge into other firms increases after 1977, from only 0.6% per year for 1927–1962 and 2.7% for 1963–1977, to 3.9% per year during 1978–1999.

Although mergers contribute to the decline in the *number* of dividend payers, they are not important in the decline in the *percent* of payers. During the 1978–1999 period, non-payers merge into other firms at about the same rate (3.8% per year) as payers (3.9% per year), so mergers have little net effect on the percent of firms paying dividends. Delistings have a bigger impact on the percent of firms paying, but not in the direction one might expect. Non-payers delist at a higher rate (6.3% per year for 1978–1999) than payers (0.9% per year). Thus, although delistings reduce the number of firms paying dividends, they actually increase the percent of firms paying.

In the end, the decline in both the total number of dividend payers and the proportion of firms paying dividends is driven mainly by the failure of new payers to replace those that are lost. Former payers (always a relatively small group) resume dividends at an average rate of 11.8% per year during 1963–1977; this rate falls to 6.2% per year for 1978–1999 and is only 2.5% in 1999. New lists surge after 1978, but the proportion paying dividends in the year of listing declines from 50.8% for 1963–1977 to 9.0% for 1978–1999. Only 3.7% of new lists pay dividends in 1999. And the non-paying new lists feed a swelling group of firms that never get around to paying dividends. The dividend initiation rate for firms that have never paid dividends drops from 7.1% per year for 1963–1977 to 1.8% for 1978–1999 and a tiny 0.7% for 1999. Thus, new lists that never become dividend payers are a big factor in the decline in the number of payers and, because they increase the number of sample firms, they play an even bigger role in reducing the proportion of firms paying dividends.

CHARACTERISTICS OF DIVIDEND PAYERS

The decline in the percent of firms paying dividends raises two questions: (i) Does the population of firms drift away from the characteristics typical of dividend payers or (ii) do firms with the characteristics typical of payers become less likely to pay? We use COMPUSTAT data to answer these questions. Although the COMPUSTAT data are available for only 1963–1998, they do cover the post-1972 NYSE-AMEX-NASDAQ period and the post-1978 period of most interest to us. Table 7.1 summarizes the data.

Profitability

Dividend payers typically have higher measured profitability than non-payers. For the full 1963–1998 period, the ratio of aggregate earnings before interest to aggregate assets averages 7.82% per year for dividend payers versus 5.37% for non-payers. Among non-payers, this ratio averages 6.11% per year for firms that have never paid dividends and only 4.54% per year for former dividend payers.

Earnings before interest represent the payoff on a firm's assets, but earnings available for common may be more relevant for the decision to pay dividends. The gap between the profitability of payers and non-payers is even wider when profitability is measured as aggregate common stock earnings over aggregate book equity. For 1963–1998, this measure averages 12.75% for dividend payers, versus 6.15% for non-payers. Among non-payers, the average is 7.94% for firms that have never paid dividends and only 3.18% for former payers.

Low profitability becomes more common in the second half of the 1963–1998 period. Before 1982, fewer than 10% of firms have negative earnings before interest, but at least 20% of firms do after 1984. In the last three years of our COMPUSTAT period, 1996–1998, negative earnings before interest afflicts more than 30% of firms.

Many of the firms that are unprofitable later in the sample period are new listings. Until 1978, more than 90% of new lists are profitable. Thereafter, the fraction with positive earnings falls. In 1998, only 51.5% of new lists have positive common stock earnings. Before 1982, new lists – even new lists that do not pay dividends – tend to be more profitable than all publicly

Table 7.1 Profitability, growth, and size data for different dividend groups and for new listings*

	1963–98	1963–77	1978–98	1978–82	1983–87	1988–92	1993–98
EARNINGS BEFORE INTEREST BUT AFTER TAXES/ASSETS (%)							
All Firms	7.59	7.84	7.41	9.02	8.04	6.45	6.35
Payers	7.82	7.98	7.72	9.13	8.37	6.64	6.88
Non-Payers	5.37	5.48	5.20	7.01	4.90	4.94	4.30
Never Paid	6.11	6.37	6.05	9.58	5.54	5.10	3.95
Former Payers	4.54	4.39	4.34	4.32	3.89	4.64	5.13
All New Lists	7.56	9.07	6.60	10.49	5.71	6.70	3.69
Payers	9.04	9.52	8.71	11.18	10.69	6.75	6.59
Non-Payers	6.97	8.38	6.10	10.60	4.97	6.19	3.00
COMMON STOCK EARNINGS/BOOK EQUITY (%)							
All Firms	12.04	12.58	11.60	14.36	11.37	9.62	11.26
Payers	12.75	12.85	12.67	14.60	12.07	10.46	13.41
Non-Payers	6.15	7.49	4.81	8.96	3.96	3.44	4.12
Never Paid	7.94	9.60	6.73	13.73	5.70	4.64	3.70
Former Payers	3.18	4.55	1.38	0.67	0.40	0.46	5.78
All New Lists	10.71	15.27	7.45	16.08	7.09	6.29	2.07
Payers	13.52	15.31	12.58	17.50	14.78	6.78	10.41
Non-Payers	9.88	15.48	5.90	15.76	5.25	4.75	0.27
RATE OF GROWTH IN ASSETS (%)							
All Firms	9.25	9.64	9.02	10.44	7.11	9.28	9.00
Payers	8.78	9.66	8.19	10.44	6.57	9.20	6.65
Non-Payers	11.62	9.93	12.78	10.32	12.43	9.62	17.67
Never Paid	16.50	14.02	18.29	17.35	18.20	13.80	22.82
Former Payers	4.67	4.70	5.09	2.85	3.33	3.42	7.61
All New Lists	23.29	18.69	26.48	30.15	28.79	16.04	31.71
Payers	13.42	14.38	11.96	17.54	14.93	6.50	12.50
Non-Payers	30.28	27.36	32.44	38.43	33.15	22.93	36.38
MARKET EQUITY/BOOK EQUITY							
All Firms	1.40	1.45	1.36	1.06	1.24	1.35	1.72
Payers	1.39	1.46	1.34	1.05	1.22	1.34	1.69
Non-Payers	1.42	1.29	1.49	1.25	1.42	1.42	1.86
Never Paid	1.64	1.47	1.76	1.52	1.65	1.65	2.13
Former Payers	1.10	1.06	1.13	0.94	1.07	1.12	1.34
All New Lists	1.76	1.70	1.86	1.81	1.61	1.68	2.09
Payers	1.51	1.62	1.47	1.32	1.46	1.39	1.55
Non-Payers	1.90	1.81	2.04	2.16	1.71	1.85	2.20
R&D/ASSETS (%)							
All Firms	1.67	1.02	2.10	1.66	2.36	2.17	2.27
Payers	1.61	1.03	2.01	1.62	2.30	2.05	2.09
Non-Payers	2.07	0.93	2.71	2.38	2.89	3.19	3.03
Never Paid	2.76	1.09	3.85	3.15	3.93	4.67	4.07
Former Payers	1.03	0.75	1.12	1.52	1.24	1.04	1.08
All New Lists	1.44	0.77	1.91	1.96	1.57	1.79	2.36
Payers	1.05	0.65	1.15	1.10	0.94	0.81	2.31
Non-Payers	1.70	0.93	2.32	2.62	1.86	2.42	2.23

Table 7.1 Continued

	1963–98	1963–77	1978–98	1978–82	1983–87	1988–92	1993–98
BOOK ASSETS ($MM)							
All Firms	577.06	323.68	773.72	544.63	584.55	877.91	977.27
Payers	1,389.18	448.45	2,040.48	838.59	1,345.67	2,452.04	3,343.61
Non-Payers	110.43	60.98	157.37	70.88	92.44	143.87	255.46
Never Paid	81.68	46.18	111.90	47.53	68.40	99.20	195.88
Former Payers	262.42	102.11	411.82	148.30	211.73	399.68	689.62
All New Lists	70.24	42.41	90.76	23.96	65.96	96.32	159.43
Payers	323.21	62.24	488.51	64.34	208.77	608.28	1,048.80
Non-Payers	52.98	29.48	70.54	15.69	55.76	63.66	130.62

* The table reports averages of annual estimates. The yearly ratios are the aggregate value of the numerator divided by the aggregate value of the denominator

traded firms. After 1982, the profitability of new lists falls. The deterioration occurs as the number of new lists explodes, and it is dramatic for the increasingly large group of new lists that do not pay dividends. By 1993–1998 (when there are 511 new lists per year and only 5.2% paid dividends), the common stock earnings of newly listed non-payers average only a mere 0.27% of book equity, versus 11.26% for all firms. All three exchanges contribute to the growth of unprofitable new lists. Among firms that began trading between 1978 and 1998, 10.7% of NYSE new lists, 29.0% of AMEX new lists, and 23.6% of NASDAQ new lists have negative common stock earnings. The low profitability of new lists later in the sample period is in line with previous research on the low post-issue profitability of IPOs.[2]

Growth

Like profitability, opportunities for growth differ between dividend payers and non-payers. Firms that have never paid dividends have the strongest growth. Table 7.1 shows they have much higher asset growth rates for 1963–1998 (16.50% per year) than dividend payers (8.78%) or former payers (4.67%). Because the market value of a firm's stock tends to reflect its growth opportunities, we also look at ratios of the aggregate market value of assets to the aggregate book value. The average market-to-book ratio is higher for firms that have never paid dividends (1.64) than for payers (1.39) or former payers (1.10). Higher R&D expenditures also tend to be associated with firms that have stronger growth opportunities, and R&D expenditures of firms that have never paid dividends are on average 2.76% of their assets, versus 1.61% for dividend payers and 1.03% for former payers. Thus, although firms that have never paid dividends are less profitable than payers, they seem to have more growth opportunities. In contrast, former payers are victims of a double whammy – low profitability and low growth.

Newly listed firms are again of interest. Dividend-paying new lists have higher asset growth rates during 1963–1998 (13.42% per year) than do all dividend payers (8.78%), and the 1963–1998 average growth rate for non-paying new lists – an extraordinary 30.28% per year – is almost twice as high as the 16.50% average growth rate for all firms that have never paid dividends.[3]

Firms that do not pay dividends are also big issuers of equity. During 1971–1998, the aggregate net stock issues of non-payers average 2.80% of the aggregate market value of their common stock, versus a trivial –0.05% for dividend payers. Dividend payers' share of gross stock issues drops from 90.4% for 1973–1977 to 35.8% for 1993–1998. Thus, firms that do not pay dividends currently account for almost two-thirds of the aggregate value of stock issues. This is not surprising, given that the non-payer group tilts increasingly toward growth firms with investment outlays greatly exceeding their earnings – the type of firm that would normally have significant financing needs.

Size

Dividend payers tend to be much larger than non-payers. During 1963–1977, the assets of payers average about seven times those of non-payers. In the non-payer group, former payers are about twice the size of firms that have never paid. In later years, as the number of firms grows and the number of payers declines, payers become even larger relative to non-payers. During 1993–1998, the assets of dividend payers average more than 13 times those of non-payers.

The aggregate earnings of dividend payers and non-payers provide more perspective on the relative size of these firms. Even during 1993–1998, when fewer than one-quarter of COMPUSTAT firms pay dividends, payers account for more than three-quarters of aggregate book and market values and all but 8.3% of aggregate earnings. The fact that dividend payers account for a large fraction of aggregate earnings (even at the end of the sample period) is, however, a bit misleading. Firms with negative earnings (mostly non-payers) become more common later in the sample period. As a result, dividend payers continue to account for a large fraction of aggregate earnings even though an increasing proportion of profitable firms, that in earlier times would have been dividend payers, are now non-payers.

Synopsis

In sum, three fundamentals – profitability, growth, and size – are factors in the decision to pay dividends. Dividend payers tend to be large, profitable firms with earnings on the order of investment outlays. Firms that have never paid dividends are smaller and they seem to be less profitable than dividend payers, but they have higher asset growth rates, higher market-to-book ratios, and higher R&D expenditures, and their investment outlays are much larger than their earnings. The salient characteristics of former dividend payers are low earnings and few investment opportunities.

Our findings on the characteristics of dividend payers and non-payers complement previous evidence that among dividend payers, larger and more profitable firms have higher payout ratios, and firms with higher growth have lower payouts.[4] And all of these results are consistent with a pecking-order model of financing in which firms are reluctant to issue risky securities, and with the role of dividends in controlling the agency costs of free cash flow.[5]

THE PROPENSITY TO PAY DIVIDENDS

The steady decline after 1978 in the percent of firms paying dividends is due in part to the surge in the number of newly listed firms with the timeworn characteristics – small size, low earnings, and strong growth opportunities – of firms that have typically never paid dividends. But this is not the whole story. Our more interesting finding is that, no matter what their characteristics, firms in general have become less likely to pay dividends.

If the decline in the percent of dividend payers were due entirely to the changing characteristics of firms, then firms with particular characteristics would be as likely to pay dividends now as in the past. But this is not the case. In 1978, 72.4% of firms with positive common stock earnings pay dividends. In 1998, 30.0% of profitable firms pay dividends, less than half the fraction for 1978. Similarly, the proportion of dividend payers among firms with earnings that exceed investment outlays falls from 68.4% in 1978 to 32.4% in 1998. These results suggest that dividends become less common among firms with the characteristics (positive earnings and lower growth) typical of dividend payers. But firms with investment outlays that exceed earnings also become less likely to pay; the proportion paying dividends drops from 68.6% in 1978 to 15.6% in 1998. And, although dividends have never been common among unprofitable firms, these firms also become less likely to pay dividends in the 1980s and 1990s. Before 1983, about 20% of firms with negative common stock earnings pay dividends. In 1998, only 7.2% of unprofitable firms do. In short, the evidence suggests that, whatever their characteristics, firms have become less likely to pay dividends.

It is worth dwelling a bit on these findings. The surge in unprofitable non-paying new lists causes the aggregate profitability of firms that do not pay dividends to fall in the 1980s and 1990s. But this decline in aggregate profitability hides the fact that an increasing fraction of firms with positive earnings – firms that in the past would typically have paid dividends – now choose not to pay. Similarly, for non-payers the spread of aggregate investment over aggregate earnings widens later in the sample period, again largely as a result of new lists. But an increasing fraction of firms with earnings that exceed investment – firms that in the past would typically have paid dividends – are now non-payers. In short, the surge in lower-profit, high-growth new lists causes the aggregate characteristics of non-payers to mask widespread evidence of a lower propensity to pay dividends.

To disentangle the effects of changing characteristics and changing propensity to pay on the percent of dividend payers, we use logit regressions to measure the probabilities that firms with given characteristics (size, profitability, and growth) pay dividends during 1963–1977, the 15-year period of COMPUSTAT coverage preceding the 1978 peak in the percent of dividend payers. We then apply the probabilities from the 1963–1977 base period to the sample firm characteristics observed in subsequent years to estimate the *expected* percent of dividend payers for each year after 1977. Since the probabilities associated with the various characteristics are fixed at their base period values, variation in the expected percent of payers after 1977 is due to the changing characteristics of sample firms. We then use the annual differences between the *expected* percent of payers (calculated using the base period probabilities) and the *actual* percent to measure the change in the propensity to pay dividends. (The details of the logit regression approach can be found in the longer version of our paper published in the *Journal of Financial Economics*.)

Table 7.2 shows the expected proportion of dividend payers obtained by applying the probabilities for 1963–1977 to the sample firm characteristics of subsequent years. For 1978, the expected proportion of payers is 66.9%. The actual proportion of dividend payers for 1963–1977 is 68.5%. Thus, roughly speaking, the characteristics of firms in 1978 are similar to those of the base period. The expected proportion of payers falls after 1978, reaching 52.1% in 1998. The 14.8 percentage point decline in the expected proportion of payers (from 68.5% to 52.1%) is an estimate of the effect of changing characteristics on the proportion of firms paying dividends. In other words, the decline in the *expected* proportion of dividend payers reflects the change in the population of publicly traded firms toward smaller, less profitable, higher-growth firms.

The difference between the actual percent of dividend payers for a given year of the 1978–1998 period and the expected percent measures changes in the propensity to pay dividends. For 1978–1980, the actual number of dividend payers is comparable to the expected number. The spread between the expected and actual percent widens thereafter. By 1998, when the base period probabilities predict that 52.1% of firms would pay dividends, only 21.3% actually do. The difference, 30.8 percentage points, between the expected and actual percents for 1998 is an estimate of the reduction in the percent of dividend payers due to a lower propensity to pay. In other words, of the total decline in the proportion of dividend payers between 1978 and 1998, roughly one-third (14.8 percentage points) is caused by the changing characteristics of publicly traded firms and two-thirds (30.8 percentage points) is caused by a reduced propensity to pay dividends.

Behavior of Dividend Payers versus Non-payers

Because there is inertia in dividend decisions, the likelihood that a dividend payer will continue to pay is higher than the likelihood that a non-payer with

Table 7.2 Estimates from logit regressions of the percent of firms expected to pay dividends each year (for all firms and grouped by dividend status)*

	All Firms			Payers			Former Payers			Never paid		
	Act	Exp	Exp–Act	Act	Exp	Exp–Act	Act	Exp	Exp–Act	Act	Exp	Exp–Act
1963–1977	68.5			97.3			13.0			9.1		
1978	68.5	66.9	−1.6	97.2	97.9	0.7	18.1	17.4	−0.7	11.3	11.3	0.0
1979	68.0	67.3	−0.7	97.7	98.0	0.3	18.4	18.2	−0.2	5.1	11.3	6.2
1980	65.0	67.9	2.9	96.4	97.6	1.2	13.8	15.3	1.5	4.2	9.7	5.5
1981	58.2	65.9	7.7	95.4	97.9	2.5	8.9	16.6	7.7	3.8	9.8	6.0
1982	53.7	62.5	8.8	95.7	96.6	0.9	6.9	14.5	7.6	3.2	8.7	5.5
1983	47.0	60.1	13.1	94.1	96.4	2.3	6.7	10.5	3.8	2.4	5.9	3.5
1984	43.0	58.9	15.9	96.3	97.1	0.8	10.5	13.9	3.4	3.1	7.9	4.8
1985	41.3	57.6	16.3	96.8	96.8	0.0	8.2	10.4	2.2	2.2	6.5	4.3
1986	36.3	54.1	17.8	94.8	95.5	0.7	6.1	8.4	2.3	2.2	5.6	3.4
1987	32.4	53.8	21.4	95.2	96.5	1.3	6.9	10.0	3.1	2.5	5.8	3.3
1988	32.6	55.4	22.8	95.5	97.1	1.6	8.4	9.7	1.3	3.8	6.7	2.9
1989	33.4	57.0	23.6	95.6	97.5	1.9	10.6	12.2	1.6	3.2	6.6	3.4
1990	32.8	57.9	25.1	95.3	97.2	1.9	6.2	10.5	4.3	2.6	7.1	4.5
1991	31.1	57.2	26.1	94.8	95.6	0.8	4.7	8.5	3.8	2.0	5.5	2.5
1992	29.6	55.7	26.1	94.8	95.8	1.0	7.8	9.0	1.2	2.5	5.1	2.6
1993	26.8	53.4	26.6	95.0	96.2	1.2	5.6	7.4	1.8	2.3	4.6	2.3
1994	25.6	53.3	27.7	95.3	97.2	1.9	6.6	8.8	2.2	2.1	5.5	3.4
1995	24.7	53.9	29.2	97.3	97.1	−0.2	5.9	9.9	4.0	1.6	5.1	3.5
1996	22.2	52.1	29.9	96.4	97.4	1.0	6.4	10.0	3.6	1.2	4.8	3.6
1997	21.1	51.2	30.1	95.0	96.6	1.6	3.0	8.6	5.6	1.2	4.7	3.5
1998	21.3	52.1	30.8	96.2	97.0	0.8	4.0	9.9	5.9	0.8	5.2	4.4
1978–1998				95.7	96.9	1.2	8.3	11.4	3.1	3.0	6.8	3.8

* The expected percents change through time due to changes in the characteristics of sample firms. The difference between the expected and actual percents measures the effect of changing propensity to pay. For dividend payers, the expected percent measures the percent of firms expected to continue paying dividends. For former payers, the expected percent is the percent of firms expected to resume dividends. For firms that have never paid dividends, the expected percent is the percent of firms expected to initiate dividends.

the same characteristics will initiate dividends. To examine how the effects of changing characteristics and changing propensity to pay differ between dividend payers and non-payers, we use separate 1963–1977 regressions for payers, former payers, and firms that have never paid to estimate the expected percents of payers in subsequent years. As shown in Table 7.2, the proportion of dividend payers expected to continue paying falls only a little, from 97.9% in 1978 to 97.0% in 1998. Thus, roughly speaking, the characteristics of dividend payers do not change much through time. Although our measure of lower propensity to pay – the difference between the expected and actual percent of payers – averages only a modest 1.2% per year, it is positive in all but one year of the 1978–1998 period. Moreover, this small decline in the propensity to pay has a nontrivial cumulative effect on the payer population: the annual spreads between expected and actual percents of payers for 1978–1998 cumulate to about 320 payers lost due to a lower propensity to pay.

Changing characteristics and lower propensity to pay have bigger effects on the dividend decisions of former payers. When the average coefficients of the 1963–77 regressions for former payers are applied to the former payer samples of later years, the expected proportion of those resuming dividends falls (due to changes in characteristics) from 17.4% in 1978 to 9.9% in 1998. Given their characteristics, the propensity of former payers to resume dividends is also lower after 1978; the difference between expected and actual percents resuming is positive after 1979, and the average difference for 1978–98 is 3.1 percentage points. In 1998, 9.9% of former payers are expected to resume, but only 4.0% (less than half the expected number) actually do.

Changing characteristics and lower propensity to pay also have strong separate effects on the dividend decisions of firms that have never paid dividends. Changes in characteristics cause the expected proportion of dividend initiators among firms that have never paid to fall from 11.3% in 1978 to 5.2% in 1998, a decline of more than half. The consistently positive differences between the expected and actual percents of initiators after 1978 then suggest that controlling for characteristics, firms that have never paid dividends become even less likely to initiate dividends. For 1978–1998, the difference averages 3.8 percentage points (6.8% expected versus 3.0% actual). Of the 5.2% that are expected to start paying dividends in 1998, only 0.8% (less than one-sixth the expected number) actually do – rather strong evidence of a declining propensity to initiate dividends.

Portfolio Approach to Explaining the Declining Incidence of Dividends

The logit regressions summarized in Table 7.2 assume a specific functional form to model the relation between a firm's characteristics and the probability that it pays dividends. If this functional form is misspecified, our inferences may be incorrect. To confirm our results, we use a more robust portfolio approach to estimate the base period relation between firm characteristics and the likelihood that a firm pays dividends. This approach allows the base period probabilities to vary with characteristics in an unrestricted way.

For each year from 1963 to 1977, we form 27 portfolios using independent sorts on profitability, growth, and size. We sort firms into three equal groups according to profitability (low, medium, and high) and three equal groups according to growth (low, medium, and high). Instead of forming equal groups by size, however, we use the 20th and 50th percentiles of market capitalization for NYSE firms to assign NYSE, AMEX, and NASDAQ firms to portfolios. This prevents the growing population of small NASDAQ firms from changing the meaning of small, medium, and large over the sample period. (The 20th and 50th NYSE percentiles lead to similar average numbers of firms in the medium and large groups, and many more in the small group.)

We estimate the base period probabilities that firms in each of the 27 portfolios pay dividends as the sum of the number of payers in a portfolio during the 15 years of 1963–77 divided by the sum of the number of firms in the portfolio. For example, if the portfolio of firms with medium profitability, high growth, and small size has an average of 250 firms and 100 dividend payers per year in 1963–1977, then the base period probability that a firm in that portfolio pays dividends is 40%. These base period probabilities are free of assumptions about the form of the relation between characteristics and the probability that a firm pays dividends (except, of course, that all firms in a portfolio are assigned the same probability). The total number of observations (firm-years) in the base period probability estimates is always at least 45, and it is 165 or greater for all but one portfolio. The base period probabilities vary across portfolios in a familiar way – larger firms and more profitable firms are more likely to pay dividends, and higher-growth firms are less likely to pay.

We form portfolios each year after 1977 using breakpoints designed to have the same economic meaning as those of the 1963–77 base period. For profitability and investment opportunities, we assume values after 1977 are comparable to the 1963–1977 values and use the average profitability and growth breakpoints from the base period. As a result, the number of firms in each portfolio varies according to changes in the distribution of these characteristics across firms. In contrast, the size breakpoints for each year are the 20th and 50th NYSE percentiles for that year, so the proportions of firms in the three size groups vary through time with the size and number of AMEX and NASDAQ firms relative to NYSE firms.

We use the actual proportion of dividend payers in a portfolio for 1963–1977 to estimate the expected percent of payers in that portfolio for each year after 1977. Since the expected percent of payers for each portfolio is fixed, the aggregate expected percent of dividend payers varies over time only because changes in the characteristics of firms alter the allocation of firms among the 27 portfolios. Any trend in the *expected* percent of payers after 1977 can thus be attributed to changing characteristics. The difference between the expected percent of payers for a year and the *actual* percent again measures the effect of changes in the propensity to pay dividends.

Using the portfolio approach lowers our estimate of the effect of changing characteristics on the decline in the percent of dividend payers. The expected proportion of payers falls by only 6.8 percentage points, from 65.1% in 1978 to 58.3% in 1998 (Table 7.3). Correspondingly, a greater share of the decline in the percent of payers is attributable to a lower propensity to pay. In 1978, the actual proportion of payers is 3.5 percentage points above the expected. After 1979, however, the expected percent exceeds the actual, and by increasing amounts. In 1998, 58.3% of firms are expected to pay dividends, but only 21.3% actually do. Thus, the end-of-sample shortfall in the proportion of dividend payers due to a lower propensity to pay is 37.0 percentage points.

What kinds of firms do not pay dividends in 1998 that would have paid in earlier years? The answer is – all kinds. Lower propensity to pay cuts across all size, profitability, and growth groups. Whatever their characteristics, most large firms pay dividends at the 1978 peak. The 1978 proportion

Table 7.3 Estimates from the portfolio approach of the percent of firms expected to pay dividends each year*

	Firms	Payers	Actual Percent	Expected Percent	Expected–Actual
1963–77	1,823	1,218	66.8		
1978	2,901	1,988	68.5	65.1	−3.5
1979	2,819	1,918	68.0	65.0	−3.0
1980	2,806	1,825	65.0	65.7	0.6
1981	2,917	1,698	58.2	64.4	6.1
1982	2,974	1,596	53.7	62.0	8.4
1983	3,127	1,470	47.0	61.2	14.2
1984	3,239	1,393	43.0	60.3	17.3
1985	3,196	1,319	41.3	59.3	18.0
1986	3,357	1,220	36.3	57.6	21.3
1987	3,587	1,162	32.4	57.3	24.9
1988	3,526	1,151	32.6	58.1	25.5
1989	3,429	1,144	33.4	58.7	25.3
1990	3,451	1,131	32.8	59.4	26.6
1991	3,582	1,115	31.1	59.4	28.3
1992	3,845	1,137	29.6	59.1	29.5
1993	4,265	1,143	26.8	57.4	30.6
1994	4,558	1,168	25.6	57.8	32.2
1995	4,768	1,177	24.7	58.4	33.7
1996	5,211	1,157	22.2	57.9	35.7
1997	5,278	1,113	21.1	57.3	36.2
1998	4,906	1,045	21.3	58.3	37.0

* This table presents the effects of changing characteristics and propensity to pay on the percent of firms paying dividends, estimated from 27 portfolios formed according to size, profitability, and growth. The expected percents change through time due to changes in the characteristics of sample firms. The difference between the expected and actual percents of payers measures the effect of changing propensity to pay.

of payers exceeds 85.0% in all nine large-firm portfolios, and it is above 92.0% in seven of the nine. But even among large firms, the propensity to pay declines sharply after 1978. The 1998 proportion of payers is below 80.0% for all nine large-firm portfolios, it is below 65.0% for five of the nine, and it is 40.6% or less for three large-firm portfolios.

The decline in the propensity to pay dividends is even greater among small firms. The 1978 proportion of dividend payers is less than 40.0% in only one of the nine small-firm portfolios and it is 52.0% or higher in seven. In contrast, the 1998 proportion of dividend payers exceeds 20.0% in only four small-firm portfolios. In the five small-firm portfolios with low profitability or high growth, dividend payers become an endangered species; the 1998 proportion of payers is 13.1% or less.

Finally, the propensity to pay declines substantially from 1978 to 1998 for firms with high growth. The large-firm portfolios provide striking examples. In 1978, 85.7%, 97.8%, and 92.4% of the firms in the three large-firm portfolios with high growth pay dividends. In 1998, only 28.4%, 40.6%, and 33.6% pay. It is clear that, like firms in the other portfolios, large rapidly growing firms no longer feel compelled to pay dividends.

SHARE REPURCHASES

Dividends have long been an enigma. Since they are taxed at a higher rate than capital gains, they are presumably less valuable than capital gains. The fact that many firms continue to pay dividends is then difficult to explain. The declining propensity to pay suggests that firms are responding to the tax disadvantage of dividends. The results in Table 7.4 are consistent with this view; share repurchases surge beginning in the mid-1980s. For 1973–1977 and 1978–1982, aggregate share repurchases average 3.37% and 5.12%, respectively, of aggregate common stock earnings. For 1983–1998, repurchases are 31.42% of earnings.[6]

For our purposes, however, repurchases turn out to be rather unimportant. In particular, because repurchases are primarily the province of dividend payers, they leave most of the decline in the percent of payers unexplained. Instead, repurchases primarily increase the already high cash payouts of dividend payers.

We first address a problem. Most researchers treat all share repurchases as non-cash dividends, but there are at least two important cases in which repurchases should not be viewed as a substitute for dividends: (i) repurchased stock is often reissued to employee stock ownership plans (ESOPs) or as executive stock options, and (ii) repurchased stock is often reissued to the acquired firm in a merger.[7] The annual change in treasury stock is a better measure of repurchases that qualify as non-cash dividends. Treasury stock captures the cumulative effects of stock repurchases and reissues, and it is not affected by new issues of stock (seasoned equity offerings). Treasury stock data are not available on COMPUSTAT before 1982, so our first

Table 7.4 Aggregate dividends, share repurchases, share issues, and changes in treasury stock as percents of aggregate earnings and market equity*

	1963–98	1983–98	1963–77	1978–98	1978–82	1983–87	1988–92	1993–98
AGGREGATE DIVIDENDS AS A PERCENT OF AGGREGATE COMMON STOCK EARNINGS								
All Firms	43.27	45.24	44.00	43.04	34.86	40.73	56.86	39.31
Payers	44.78	47.22	45.19	44.76	35.63	41.84	58.02	42.71
AGGREGATE DIVIDENDS AS A PERCENT OF AGGREGATE MARKET EQUITY								
All Firms	2.95	2.37	2.91	2.87	4.39	3.09	2.62	1.56
Payers	3.22	2.78	2.99	3.25	4.66	3.47	3.00	2.02

	1971–98	1983–98	1973–77	1978–98	1978–82	1983–87	1988–92	1993–98
AGGREGATE SHARE REPURCHASES, SHARE ISSUES, AND CHANGES IN TREASURY STOCK AS PERCENTS OF AGGREGATE COMMON STOCK EARNINGS FOR ALL FIRMS								
Repurchases	19.71	31.42	3.37	25.22	5.12	27.98	30.02	35.46
Issues	24.64	33.71	8.90	28.93	14.93	26.00	35.91	38.29
Net Repurchases	–4.93	–2.28	–5.54	–3.71	–9.80	1.98	–5.89	–2.83
Change in Treasury Stock		14.95				14.92	11.76	17.63
AGGREGATE CHANGE IN TREASURY STOCK AS A PERCENT OF AGGREGATE MARKET EQUITY								
All Firms		0.80				1.10	0.67	0.66
Payers		0.89				1.19	0.72	0.79
Non-Payers		0.28				0.36	0.27	0.23
Never Paid		0.24				0.25	0.30	0.18
Former Payers		0.52				0.91	0.17	0.49

* This table presents annual ratios calculated as the aggregate value of the numerator divided by the aggregate value of the denominator, averaged over the years in a period. Results are for all firms and, where indicated, for firms grouped according to dividend status. Data on share repurchases and share issues are not available until 1971. The change in treasury stock is not available until 1983.

measured change is for 1983. But the treasury stock data do cover the period of strong repurchase activity. (Some firms use the retirement method, rather than treasury stock, to account for repurchases; our aggregate changes in treasury stock include the net repurchases of these firms, measured for each firm as the difference between purchases and sales of stock, when the difference is positive, and zero otherwise.)

During 1983–1998, the annual change in treasury stock is 14.95% of earnings, and gross share repurchases are 31.42% of earnings. Cash dividends are 45.24% of common stock earnings, so if gross repurchases are treated as an additional payout of earnings, the total payout for 1983–1998 averages 76.66% of earnings. Substituting the more appropriate annual change in treasury stock drops the payout to (a still high) 60.19% of earnings.

Aggregate changes in treasury stock are substantial relative to aggregate earnings, but they fall far short of explaining the decline in the percent of dividend payers due to a lower propensity to pay. During 1983–1998, on average, only 14.5% of non-payers have positive changes in treasury stock. And the percent of such firms overstates the extent to which firms substitute repurchases for dividends.[8] In contrast, 33.4% of dividend payers have positive changes in treasury stock. The aggregate changes in treasury stock of dividend payers average 0.89% of their aggregate market equity (versus 0.28% for non-payers). Aggregate cash dividends average 2.78% of the aggregate market equity of dividend payers during 1983–1998. Thus, dividend payers use share repurchases rather than dividends for about 25% of their payouts to shareholders.

The cash dividend payout ratio of dividend payers shows no tendency to decline. The aggregate dividends of payers are 47.22% of their aggregate common stock earnings in 1983–1998 and 42.71% in 1993–1998, versus 45.19% in 1963–1977. We infer that the large share repurchases of 1983–1998 are mostly due to an increase in the desired payout ratios of dividend payers, who are nonetheless reluctant to increase their cash dividends.

Finally, even during the 1993–1998 period, when dividend payers are only 23.6% of COMPUSTAT firms, they account for 91.7% of common stock earnings. It is thus not surprising that the aggregate payout ratio (the ratio of aggregate dividends to aggregate common stock earnings) for all firms is basically the same as the ratio for dividend payers – and likewise shows no tendency to decline over time. In fact, the aggregate payout ratio for all firms actually increases from 33.95% in 1973–1977, when 64.3% of firms pay dividends, to 39.31% in 1993–1998, when only 23.6% of firms pay dividends.[9]

We emphasize, however, that the aggregate payout ratio says nothing about the propensity of firms to pay dividends. As noted earlier, the surge in unprofitable, non-paying new lists in the 1980s and 1990s keeps the aggregate profits of non-payers low even though the non-payer group includes an increasing fraction of firms with positive earnings – firms that in the past would have paid dividends. As a result, the aggregate payout ratio for all firms masks widespread evidence of a lower propensity to pay dividends among individual firms of all types.

CONCLUSIONS

From a post-1972 peak of 66.5% in 1978, the proportion of dividend payers among NYSE, AMEX, and NASDAQ firms falls to 20.8% in 1999. The decline in the incidence of dividend payers is in part due to an increasing tilt of publicly traded firms toward the characteristics – small size, low earnings, and high growth – of firms that typically have never paid dividends. This change in the nature of publicly traded firms is driven by a surge in new listings after 1978 and by the changing nature of new lists, producing a swelling group of small firms with low profitability but high growth that have never paid dividends.

But the change in the characteristics of publicly traded firms only partially explains the declining incidence of dividend payers. Our more interesting result is that, whatever their characteristics, firms have simply become less likely to pay dividends.

The evidence that firms have become less likely to pay dividends, even after controlling for characteristics, suggests that the perceived benefits of dividends have declined through time. Some (but surely not all) of the reasons for this may be lower transactions costs for selling stocks (due in part to the increased use of open-end mutual funds), more sophisticated corporate governance techniques (reducing the reliance on dividends as a means of corporate discipline), and larger holdings of stock options by managers who prefer capital gains to dividends.

NOTES

1. H. DeAngelo and L. DeAngelo, "Dividend Policy and Financial Distress: An Empirical Examination of Troubled NYSE Firms," *Journal of Finance*, Vol. 45, 1990, pp. 1415–1431; H. DeAngelo, L. DeAngelo, and D. Skinner, "Dividends and Losses," *Journal of Finance*, Vol. 47, 1992, pp. 1837–1863.
2. B. Jain and O. Kini, "The Post-Issue Operating Performance of IPO Firms," *Journal of Finance*, Vol. 49, 1994, pp. 1699–1726; W. Mikkelson, M. Partch, and K. Shah, "Ownership and Operating Performance of Companies That Go Public," *Journal of Financial Economics*, Vol. 44, 1997, pp. 281–307.
3. The profitability advantage of dividend payers over firms that have never paid dividends is probably exaggerated, however, for three reasons: (i) If investments take time to reach full profitability, profitability (measured by accounting earnings as a percent of assets) is understated for growing firms. And firms that have never paid dividends grow faster than dividend payers. (ii) When R&D is a multiperiod asset, mandatory expensing of R&D causes earnings and assets to be understated. If R&D is growing, profitability is therefore understated. R&D as a percent of assets is higher for firms that have never paid dividends than for dividend payers, and this differential increases over time, from 0.32% in 1973–1977 to 1.98% in 1993–1998. (iii) Since firms that have never paid dividends grow faster, their assets are on average younger than those of dividend

payers. Inflation is then likely to cause us to overstate the profitability advantage of dividend payers relative to firms that have never paid.

4. See our unpublished working paper entitled "Testing Tradeoff and Pecking Order Predictions About Dividends and Debt," Sloan School of Management, MIT, Cambridge, MA (1999).

5. The pecking order model is developed by S. Myers and N. Majluf in "Corporate Financing and Investment Decisions When Firms Have Information the Investors Do Not Have", *Journal of Financial Economics*, Vol. 13, 1984, pp. 187–221, and by S. Myers in "The Capital Structure Puzzle," *Journal of Finance*, Vol. 39, 1984, pp. 575–592; see also elsewhere in this issue. The agency costs of free cash flow are addressed in M. Jensen, "Agency Costs of Free Cash Flow, Corporate Finance, and Takeovers," *American Economic Review*, Vol. 76, 1986, pp. 323–329.

6. In their paper entitled "Cash Distributions to Shareholders," *Journal of Economic Perspectives*, Vol. 3, 1989, pp. 129–149, L. Bagwell and J. Shoven argue that the increase in repurchases indicates that firms have learned to substitute repurchases for dividends in order to generate lower-taxed capital gains for stockholders. But subsequent tests of this hypothesis produce mixed results; see DeAngelo, DeAngelo, and Skinner (2000), cited earlier; M. Jagannathan, C. Stephens, and M. Weisbach, "Financial Flexibility and the Choice Between Dividends and Stock Repurchases," *Journal of Financial Economics*, Vol. 57, 2000, pp. 355–384; and G. Grullon and R. Michaely, "Dividends, Share Repurchases, and the Substitution Hypothesis," unpublished manuscript, Cornell University, Ithaca, NY (2000).

7. In their article entitled "Dividend Policy," in *Handbooks in Operations Research and Management Science: Finance*, edited by R. Jarrow, V. Maksimovic, and W. Ziemba (Amsterdam: North-Holland, 1995, pp. 793–838), F. Allen and R. Michaely show that the surge in repurchases after 1983 lines up with a surge in mergers.

8. Consider a firm that repurchases shares in one fiscal year and reissues them as part of an ESOP, executive compensation plan, or merger in the next. Because the repurchase and reissue are spread across two fiscal years, they cause a positive change in treasury stock in the first year and a negative change in the second. Although the repurchase just accommodates a reissue, a simple count of firms with positive changes in treasury stock misclassifies the repurchase as a substitute for a cash dividend. On average, 6.9% of non-payers have negative changes in treasury stock during 1983–1998. The results for 1993–1998 are similar; 14.5% of non-payers have positive changes in treasury stock and 6.6% have negative changes.

9. This is consistent with the results in A. Dunsby, "Share Repurchases, Dividends, and Corporate Distribution Policy," Ph.D. thesis, The Wharton School, University of Pennsylvania, Philadelphia, PA (1995).

Reproduced from *Journal of Applied Corporate Finance*, Vol. 14 No. 1 (Spring 2001), pp. 67–79.

8

The Value of Share Buybacks

Richard Dobbs and Werner Rehm

Share buybacks are all the rage. In 2004 companies announced plans to repurchase $230 billion in stock – more than double the volume of the previous year. During the first three months of this year, buyback announcements exceeded $50 billion.[1] And with large global corporations holding $1.6 trillion in cash, all signs indicate that buybacks and other forms of payouts will accelerate.[2]

In general, markets have applauded such moves, making buybacks an alluring substitute if improvements in operational performance are elusive. Yet while the increases in earnings per share that many buybacks deliver help managers hit EPS-based compensation targets, boosting EPS in this way doesn't signify an increase in underlying performance or value. Moreover, a company's fixation on buybacks might come at the cost of investments in its long-term health.

A closer inspection of the market's response to buybacks illustrates these risks, since some companies' share price declined – or didn't respond at all. For example, Dell's announcement earlier this year that it would increase its buyback program by an additional $10 billion didn't slow the decline of its share price, which had begun to slide because of worries about operating results.

Buybacks aren't without value. It is crucial, however, for managers and directors to understand their real effects when deciding to return cash to shareholders or to pursue other investment options. A buyback's impact on share price comes from changes in a company's capital structure and, more critically, from the signals a buyback sends. Investors are generally relieved to learn that companies don't intend to do something wasteful – such as make an unwise acquisition or a poor capital expenditure – with the excess cash.

EPS MAY BE UP, BUT INTRINSIC VALUE REMAINS FLAT

Many market participants and executives believe that since a repurchase reduces the number of outstanding shares, thus increasing EPS, it also raises a company's share price. As one respected Wall Street analyst commented in a recent report, "Share buybacks . . . improve EPS, return on equity, return on capital employed, economic profit, and fundamental intrinsic value." At first glance, this argument seems to make sense: the same earnings divided by fewer shares results in a higher EPS and so a higher share price. But this belief is wrong.

Consider a hypothetical example that illustrates how transferring cash to shareholders creates no fundamental value (setting aside for now a buyback's impact on corporate taxes), because any increase in EPS is offset by a reduction in the P/E ratio. The company's operations earn €94 million annually and are worth €1.3 billion.[3] It has €200 million in cash, on which it earns interest of €6 million (Figure 8.1). What happens if the company decides to use all its excess cash to repurchase its stock – in this case, a total of 13.3 million shares?[4]

Since the company's operations don't change, its return on operating capital is the same after the buyback. But the equity is now worth only €1.3 billion – exactly the value of the operations, since there is no cash left. The company's earnings fall as a result of losing the interest income, but its EPS rises because the number of shares has fallen more than earnings have. The share price remains the same, however, as the total company value has fallen in line with the number of shares. Therefore, the P/E ratio, whose inputs are intrinsic value and EPS, drops to 13.8, from 15. The impact is similar if the company increases debt to buy back more shares.

Why does the P/E ratio decline? In effect, the buyback deconsolidates the company into two distinct entities: an operating company and one that holds cash. The former has a P/E of 13.8; the latter, 33.3.[5] The P/E ratio of 15 rep-

Share buyback, hypothetical example[1]						
	Before	**After**			**Before**	**After**
Balance sheet			**Income statement**			
Cash, € million	200	0	Earnings before interest,		94	94
Operating assets, € million	580	580	taxes (EBIT), € million			
			Interest, € million		6	0
Total assets, € million	780	580	**Net income**, € million		**100**	**94**
Equity, € million	780	580				
Value			Shares outstanding, million	100.0	86.7	
Value of operations, € million	1,300	1,300	Share price, €		15.00	15.00
Cash, € million	200	0	Earnings per share [EPS], €		1.00	1.08
Total equity value, € million	1,500	1,300	P/E		15.0	13.8
			Return on invested capital (ROIC)[2]		**16%**	**16%**

[1]Excludes corporate taxes; assumes cost of equity = 10%, cost of debt = 3%, growth = 5%.
[2]Posttax EBIT ÷ operating capital.

Figure 8.1   No fundamental value from buyback

resents a weighted average of the two. Once the excess cash is paid out, the P/E will go down to that of the operating company, since the other entity has ceased to exist. Thus the change of EPS and P/E is a purely mechanical effect that is not linked to fundamental value creation.

TAXES SHIELD VALUE FROM LEVERAGE

When corporate taxes *are* part of the equation, the company's value does increase as a result of share buybacks – albeit by a small amount – because its cost of capital falls from having less cash or greater debt. The cost of capital is lower when a company uses some debt for financing, because interest payments are tax deductible while dividends are not. Holding excess cash raises the cost of capital: since interest income is taxable, a company that maintains large cash reserves puts investors at a disadvantage. In general, having too much cash on hand penalizes a company by increasing its cost of financing.

The share price increase from a buyback in theory results purely from the tax benefits of a company's new capital structure rather than from any underlying operational improvement. In the example, the company incurs a value penalty of €18 million from additional taxes on the income of its cash reserves.[6] A buyback removes this tax penalty and so results in a 1.4 percent rise in the share price. In this case, repurchasing more than 13 percent of the shares results in an increase of less than 2 percent. A similar boost occurs when a company takes on more debt to buy back shares (Figure 8.2).

We can estimate the impact on share prices from this tax effect (Figure 8.3), but historical and recent buyback announcements typically result in a much bigger rise in share price than this analysis indicates. Research from both academics and practitioners consistently finds that companies initiating small repurchase programs see an average increase in their share price of 2 to 3 percent on the day of the announcement; those that undertake larger buybacks, involving around 15 percent or more of the shares, see prices increase by some 16 percent, on average.[7] Other, more subtle reasons explain this larger positive reaction to share buybacks.

SENDING SIGNALS

The market responds to announcements of buybacks because they offer new information, often called a signal, about a company's future and hence its share price.

One well-known positive signal in a buyback is that management seems to believe that the stock is undervalued. Executives can enhance this effect by personally purchasing significant numbers of shares, since market participants see them as de facto insiders with privileged information about future earnings and growth prospects. A second positive signal is management's

Share buyback, hypothetical example[1]

Balance sheet	Before	After	Income statement	Before	After
Cash, € million	200	0	Earnings before interest, taxes (EBIT), € million	134	134
Operating assets, € million	580	580	Interest, € million	6	0
Total assets, € million	780	580			
Equity, € million	780	580	Earnings before taxes, € million	140	134
Value			Tax, € million	−42	−40
Value of operations, € million	1,300	1,300	**Net income, € million**	98	94
Cash, € million	200	0			
Tax penalty of cash, € million	−18	0	Shares outstanding, million	100	86.5
Total equity value, € million	**1,482**	**1,300**	Share price, €	14.80	15.0
			Earnings per share [EPS], €	0.98	1.09
			P/E	15.1	13.8
			Return on invested capital (ROIC)[2]	**16%**	**16%**

[1]Assumes cost of equity = 10%, cost of debt = 3%, growth = 5%; assumes no growth in excess cash, posttax interest streams discounted at cost of equity.
[2]Posttax EBIT ÷ operating capital.

Figure 8.2 The tax benefit

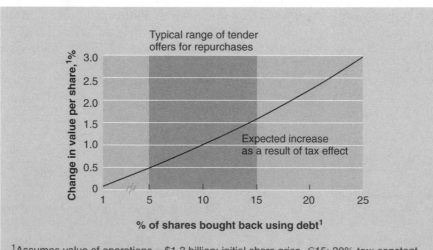

[1]Assumes value of operations = $1.3 billion; initial share price, €15; 30% tax; constant debt; tax shields discounted with unlevered cost of equity; no excess cash.

Figure 8.3 Expected tax impact of buyback

confidence that the company doesn't need the cash to cover future commitments such as interest payments and capital expenditures.

But there is a third, *negative*, signal with a buyback: that the management team sees few investment opportunities ahead, suggesting to investors that they could do better by putting their money elsewhere. Some managers are reluctant to launch buyback programs for this reason, but the capital market's mostly positive reaction to such announcements indicates that this signal isn't an issue in most cases. In fact, the strength of the market's reaction implies that shareholders often realize that a company has more cash than it can invest long before its management does.

Therefore, the overall positive response to a buyback may well result from investors being *relieved* that managers aren't going to spend a company's cash on inadvisable mergers and acquisitions or on projects with a negative net present value. In many cases, a company seems to be undervalued just before it announces a buyback, reflecting an uncertainty among investors about what management will do with excess funds.

Such shareholder skepticism would be well founded. In many industries, management teams have historically allocated cash reserves poorly. The oil industry since 1964 is one example (Figure 8.4): a huge price umbrella for much of this period, courtesy of the Organization of Petroleum Exporting Countries (OPEC), provided oil companies with relatively high margins. Nevertheless, for almost three decades the spread between ROIC and cost of

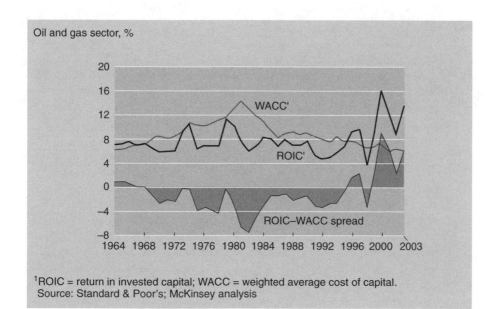

[1]ROIC = return in invested capital; WACC = weighted average cost of capital.
Source: Standard & Poor's; McKinsey analysis

Figure 8.4 Poor returns on capital

capital for the industry as a whole was negative. Convinced that on a sustained basis the petroleum industry could not deliver a balanced source of income, many companies committed their excess cash to what turned out to be value-destroying acquisitions or other diversification strategies. For example, in the 1970s, Mobil bought retailer Montgomery Ward; Atlantic Richfield purchased Anaconda, a metal and mining company; and Exxon bought a majority stake in Vydec, a company specializing in office automation. All of these cash (or mostly cash) acquisitions resulted in significant losses.

With cash levels at an all-time high and mergers on the increase, managers risk repeating past behaviors. Clearly, for cash-rich industries with insufficient investment opportunities, a critical task for boards will be forcing management to pay out the excess cash sooner rather than later. But by allowing management compensation to be linked to EPS, boards run the risk of promoting the short-term effects of buybacks instead of managing the long-term health of the company. Similarly, value-minded executives in industries where good investment opportunities are still available must resist the pressure to buy back shares in order to reach EPS targets.

In most cases, buybacks create value because they help improve tax efficiency and prevent managers from investing in the wrong assets or pursuing unwise acquisitions. Only when boards and executives understand the difference between fundamental value creation through improved performance and the purely mechanical effects of a buyback program on EPS will they put share repurchases to work creating value.

NOTES

1. McKinsey analysis.
2. US listed companies (excluding financial institutions) valued at more than $1 billion have a total of $1 trillion in cash – nearly 9 percent of their market capitalization. Non-US companies with American Depositary Receipts on US exchanges have about $600 billion in cash and cash equivalents, a solid 12 percent of their market capitalization.
3. Based on a discounted-cash-flow valuation with 5 percent growth.
4. At €15 a share. The calculation assumes the shares are bought back at the current value.
5. A cash value of €200 million divided by €6 million of interest income.
6. Assuming $200 million in cash, a 3 percent interest rate, and a 30 percent tax rate, discounted at the cost of equity of 10 percent. See also Tim Koller, Marc Goedhart, and David Wessels, *Valuation: Measuring and Managing the Value of Companies*, fourth edition, Hoboken, New Jersey: John Wiley & Sons, 2005 (book information available online), for a discussion of using the cost of equity for discounting instead of the cost of debt. This calculation assumes that the amount of cash doesn't grow and that it is held in perpetuity.

7. Robert Comment and Gregg A. Jarrell, "The relative signaling power of Dutch-auction and fixed-price self-tender offers and open-market share repurchases," *Journal of Finance*, 1991, Volume 46, Number 4, pp. 1243–71; and Theo Vermaelen, "Common stock repurchases and market signaling: An empirical study," *Journal of Financial Economics*, 1981, Volume 9, Number 2, pp. 138–83.

CASE STUDY 5

Capital Ideas

Keith Boyfield

Goldman Sachs employs some impressive people. Bill Young, a managing director within the bank's Financing Group, is one of them. He gave a thought-provoking presentation recently on the scramble for international capital at Oxera's conference on the future of infrastructure regulation.

The event drew a large and distinguished audience. Young's insights into the current health of the world's capital markets struck at the heart of many utilities' funding dilemmas. He posed a crucial question: what is the competitive return a utility must offer to attract the large amounts of capital required to invest in developing its infrastructure asset base over the next 20 years?

Young emphasised that given the large capital investment needed, the regulator must provide returns that are adequate to compete. The European Investment Bank estimates that €180 billion of investment in infrastructure assets is required over the next five years. And the competition is getting tougher, particularly with airport operators and toll road managers across Europe seeking to raise substantial sums of capital.

In fact, a wide range of commercial concerns need to raise considerable money to renew or develop their infrastructure asset base. Having said that, if the capital structure is balanced correctly between debt and equity, tremendous value can be created for both debt and equity holders. A good example is Autostrade, which manages 3,400 km of motorways in Italy, the most extensive high-speed road network in Europe.

Over the past two years, Autostrade recapitalised its balance sheet and ultimately issued €6.5 billion in bonds. That is a lot of money. But as Young points out, the offer proved an extremely attractive investment opportunity for many insurance companies and pension funds on the look out for low risk securities that could be relied on to pay a stable return. Since its recapitalisation, Autostrade's share price has doubled. And all of this despite the fact that Autostrade has a €9.5 billion investment programme to complete between 2004 and 2010.

Large concerns that generate reliable cash-flows – typified by the likes of Autostrade – may well prove more attractive to investors than the more modest regulated returns offered by companies in the water and electricity sector. If these businesses are to attract the vast sums of capital they require, then regulators need to recognise that they must be allowed to pay a competitive return to their investors. In practice, this translates into longer regulatory review periods rather than the current five-year review process, clarity on levels of returns and capital base, and the opportunity for companies to keep some of the benefits of outperformance. These attributes combine to reduce risk and make an investment attractive.

As privatised utilities become increasingly skilled at driving down costs and identifying operational efficiencies, one of the most promising ways of delivering value to share-holders is to devise more efficient capital structures to fund their capital requirements. This is where the correct mix of debt and equity instruments can prove extremely attractive.

"Debt capital is relatively inexpensive, both in sterling and euro markets," observes Young. "In addition to credit spreads remaining near historic lows, interest remains tax deductible, which is very attractive. Also, properly apportioned debt capital can help a company's share price, as we have seen in the recent case of Autostrade."

The international capital markets are seeing a blurring in the traditional distinction between debt and equity securities. Many investors in subordinated or mezzanine debt are the same investors who invest in equity. Rather than ask the regulators to define precise debt and equity targets, regulated utilities might find a more efficient mix of these hybrid securities, thereby lowering the cost of capital. Since the investors are primarily the same group of individuals, the incentives created for management should remain the same.

Another potential source of capital is the thriving private equity sector. As regulation tightens on publicly quoted companies, financial institutions are allocating a higher proportion of their capital to private equity funds, such as Apax, Blackstone Capital and the Carlyle Group, where regulatory requirements are less intrusive.

What is more, over the past 12 months, banks have been prepared to lend far more debt to private equity houses in frenetic competition for leveraged buy-out financing mandates. In this context, mezzanine debt can be important, since it enables a further tranche of debt to be raised. It also has priority ahead of equity in the event of bankruptcy.

Figures released by Standard & Poor's reveal that the number of deals with total debt over five times Ebitda (earnings before interest, depreciation and amortisation) surged to 35 percent in 2004, compared with 23.3 percent in 2003 and 16 percent in 2002. Indeed, when PIK (payment in kind) debt is included, debt multiples have soared as high as eight times Ebitda in some recent acquisitions.

In contrast to the US, however, private equity houses have tended to shun utility assets in Europe. This is because the returns offered tend to fall below the target rates of return set by private equity funds, which generally promise to pay their limited partners (investors) a return of 20 percent or more.

Private equity funds often lose out in competitive auctions to a new power in utility finance, the specialised infrastructure investment vehicles, typified by Macquarie Bank's Infrastructure & Specialised Funds Division. On a global basis, Macquarie manages €12 billion in infrastructure equity. Over the past decade it has invested in toll roads, airports, water, rail, power and telecoms assets. Last year it launched a European Infrastructure Fund specifically to invest in the more developed European economies.

The bank is looking for sustainable and predictable cashflows over the long term. It has already made four high-profile investments. In the UK it owns a stake in South East Water and it has announced a substantial stake in the consortium that recently acquired Welsh and West gas distribution network for £1.1 billion. However, its other two investments reflect the international breadth of the fund. Macquarie has taken a substantial stake in the dedicated rail link between Arlanda airport and Stockholm's city centre, and it also owns 70 percent of the company operating Brussels International airport.

Specialised infrastructure funds such as Macquarie's generally seek to target equity returns in the teens as opposed to the 20 percent plus levels required by traditional private equity players. Consequently, they can often outbid private equity houses for the available opportunities. This is exemplified by the experience of CVC, a private equity house that successfully acquired electricity transmission assets from Spain's Iberdrola, but then lost out to a consortium of institutional investors on the Northumbrian Water sale in 2003.

Iain Smedley, an executive director with Morgan Stanley and a rising star on the utility scene, is optimistic about the prospects for utility financing. In his view there is "a large quantity of capital from a range of sources focused on the European utility sector". He points out that "in addition to private equity investors like CVC and KKR, key sources of equity capital now include specialist infrastructure funds, such as ABN Amro and Macquarie Bank's funds, as well as pension funds making direct investments, such as Ontario Teachers and Borealis, and special situation hedge fund investors like Perry Capital. These providers of capital have a sophisticated understanding of the sector and regulatory issues, and how to optimise the capital structure. They are frequently willing to invest all across the capital structure – equity, mezzanine, preference shares and conventional debt".

Significantly, a clutch of financial players were among the key bidders when National Grid Transco put its local gas distribution networks on the auction block last year. Indeed, the winning bidders included Macquarie Bank, a consortium comprising Canadian pension funds Ontario Teachers and Borealis alongside Scottish and Southern Energy, and Hong Kong based utility CKI.

This auction demonstrated "real competition between financial and industry buyers for these assets – the process reflected the strength of interest from financial parties of all kinds, and their willingness to take on the operational and regulatory risks of a new business model", says Smedley.

Smedley believes there are relatively few opportunities to invest in utilities that pay an attractive return. But when they come up for sale, they attract a lot of interest. As evidence Smedley cites the recent sale of Mid Kent Water, which was sold to Australia's Hastings/Westpac for a premium of more than 25 percent on its regulatory capital value after a hotly contested auction.

As far as funding requirements are concerned, the key message for managers running regulated utilities must be to continue to bear down on costs while at the same time exploring the potential to build on innovative new financial strategies. This should enable them to establish an optimal capital structure and deliver greater value to the owners of the business. And the message for policy-makers is that regulatory structures need to provide a framework of stability and attractive returns on capital to attract private funds to make the necessary investments in infrastructure assets.

Reproduced from *Utility Week* (29 April 2005), by permission of Keith Boyfield.

CASE STUDY 6

Death of the Dividend?

Adrian Wood

AIMS, OBJECTIVES AND THEORETICAL SETTING

Our aim was to investigate whether or not European companies are changing the way they return cash to their shareholders. Traditionally, European firms have distributed cash via the payment of a stream of dividends. We wanted to see if that was changing and, specifically, if dividends were losing ground in favour of share repurchase programmes.

The survey didn't aim to investigate when companies distribute cash to shareholders – which should only happen if they have truly excess capital and no positive net-present-value (NPV) projects to invest in. We were only interested in the distribution technique, i.e., dividends versus share buy-backs.

Of course, classic corporate finance theory maintains that, when a company does decide to return cash to shareholders, how it does so is irrelevant (under assumptions of efficient capital markets and the absence of transaction costs). Investors are no better or worse off if the company pays a dividend or carries out a share buyback. For evidence of this, consider the following:

A company has 100 m shares, each worth E1, giving a market capitalisation of E100 m. The company also has E10 m of excess cash to give back to shareholders. The company can either pay a dividend or carry out a share buy-back:

a) If it pays the E10 m of cash as a dividend – equal to a dividend of E0.1 per share – then after the distribution has taken place, the market capitalisation of the firm drops to E90 m. The company still has 100 m shares outstanding, but each share is now only worth E0.9. Investors are left holding E0.1 of cash and a share worth E0.9, giving a total of E1. (Investors are no better or worse off after the cash distribution has taken place.)

b) If a firm instead chooses to buy back shares, then it pays no cash dividend. Instead, it uses the E10 m to repurchase 10 m shares and cancels them, causing its market capitalisation to drop to E90 m. There are now only 90 m shares, each still worth E1. (Investors are no better or worse off after the cash distribution has taken place.)

We hoped our survey would show whether or not such theory tells the whole picture behind corporate dividend and distribution policy.

METHODOLOGY

The study period for the survey ran from 1993 to 2000. We chose this period for one reason in particular: in 1993, share buy-back programmes were unfeasible in many European countries thanks to onerous tax regulations and corporate laws that banned them outright. However, by 2000, almost all countries in Europe had changed their taxes and their laws so that share repurchases were possible. For example, in Finland, it wasn't until September 1997 that share repurchases became legal. We thus hoped to capture how such changes would impact on corporate dividend and distribution policy.

In all, our survey included 127 companies taken from among Europe's 500 largest firms (by market capitalisation). By choosing such large companies, we aimed to avoid young, fast growing companies (with plenty of positive NPV projects) which tend to pay out less cash to their shareholders than mature companies do.

We also wanted a broad geographic spread in order to be sure to include companies from different tax regimes and with diverse investor bases. In the end we included companies from ten countries, with the biggest constituents being the UK (23%), Germany (21%), and France (20%). The smallest exposure was Austria, with just three companies included.

Additional considerations for inclusion in the sample were that the company must have kept the same dates for its financial year over the course of the study period, it must have published earnings figures dating back to 1992 and it must have been floated since then too.

Thomson Financial provided much of the data for the survey. However, share buy-back data was gathered directly from corporate investor relations departments.

RESULTS: DIMINISHING DIVIDEND SIGNALLING POWER

Traditionally, one of the main functions of dividends has been their "signaling power", whereby investors can gauge the health of a company by its ability to continue to pay out a constant stream of cash. As such, in the past, companies have been reluctant to cut their dividend, even if they wanted to reinvest the profits within the business, for fear that the stockmarkets will read the dividend cut as a sign of weakness.

Our research confirms that such behaviour is still very much in evidence today. Figure C6.1 shows how very few companies ever cut their dividend, and when they do it is usually a drastic cut.

Nonetheless, while companies appear to cling religiously to the belief that they must maintain a steady dividend, investors, on the other hand, seem to be focusing less on dividends – perhaps because standards of financial disclosure and corporate governance have improved so much in recent years. Instead, shareholders appear to take much more notice of a company's earnings than its dividends. Indeed, earnings often appear to lag share price as

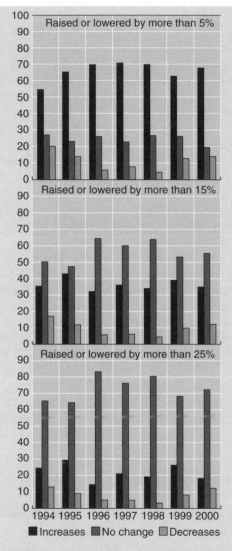

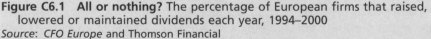

Figure C6.1   All or nothing? The percentage of European firms that raised,
    lowered or maintained dividends each year, 1994–2000
Source: *CFO Europe* and Thomson Financial

investors respond to earnings announcements even before a company's actual
figures are quantified or broadcast to the market. Consider the case of British
Airways, as shown in Figure C6.2, where the company's share price clearly
tracks its earnings, and not its dividends.

It all suggests that dividends may slowly be losing their significance as a
barometer of future corporate performance. And British Airways is by no
means alone. If you plot similar graphs for the five biggest sectors in our
survey, then similar patterns emerge, as Figure C6.3 shows.

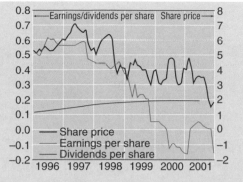

Figure C6.2   Crash Landing. At British Airways, share price has tracked earnings, not dividends.
Source: corporateinformation.com

And the trend is further repeated when analysed for the entire 127 companies in our survey. As Figure C6.4 indicates, in 1993, the correlation between changes in share price and changes in dividends was extremely strong, supporting the notion that dividends did indeed possess signaling power. By 2000, however, stock prices were more highly correlated to reported earnings than to dividends.

It appears earnings become particularly significant in determining share prices when earnings fall significantly. Under these conditions some corporations attempt to create the illusion of "business as usual" by sustaining last period's nominal dividend per share. This established dividend obligation can potentially amount to a figure larger than the current earnings per share. Under these circumstances investors are no longer fooled and punish the share price accordingly, suggesting dividends no longer offer such a smoke-screen to corporate performance.

RESULTS: GREATER RELIANCE ON BUYBACK SCHEMES

Despite the fact that most companies in Europe stick steadfastly to paying dividends, our survey shows that they are also starting to use share buybacks too. In fact, buybacks are growing in importance at the expense of traditional dividends.

As Table C6.1 shows, while the percentage of net earnings returned to shareholders each year has barely changed between 1993 and 2000 – at around 55% – the amount of cash returned via buybacks has grown significantly. In 1993, no cash was returned through stock repurchases, while in 2000, 15% of all cash returned to investors came via buybacks.

Why are share buybacks becoming a more important part of distribution policy in corporate Europe? There are several possible explanations:

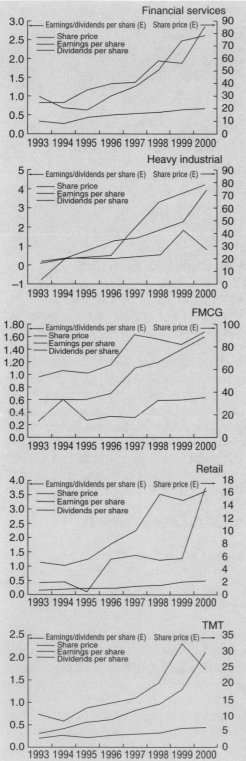

Figure C6.3   Earnings rule.
Dividends are losing their significance as a barometer of corporate performance.
Source: *CFO Europe* and Thomson Financial

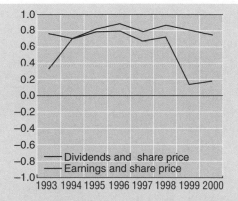

Figure C6.4 Is "dividend signalling" dead? The correlation between earnings and share price, and between dividends and share price.*
* Correlation: a score of +1 means the variables are perfectly positively correlated. A score of –1 implies that the variables move in opposite directions.
Source: *CFO Europe* and Thomson Financial

a) Flexibility for companies: When a company starts paying a regular dividend, it becomes like a contract and it's hard to persuade investors to let a company reduce it. Buybacks are more flexible and give a company more scope to decide when is the best time to return cash to shareholders. With share buybacks, a highly cash-generative company can return cash to investors whenever it is excess, but decide to retain it whenever it identifies good investment opportunities.

b) Flexibility for investors: Whereas dividends force all shareholders to participate in a cash distribution – and so also force them to incur tax – buybacks let investors choose when to take part. Those who want cash now, or to take a tax hit today, can sell some of their shares to create "home-made" dividends. Those who don't can hang on to their stock.

c) Tax: Dividends give investors an income, whereas share repurchases give them capital gains. In many countries, capital gains tax is lower than income tax, which makes repurchases more efficient than dividends as a way of returning cash. In Germany, for example, investors who hold a share for longer than one year are exempt from capital gains tax, whereas all dividend payments incur income tax. If the majority of a company's investors incur lower capital gains tax than income tax then it makes sense for a company to reduce its dividend and return more cash via buybacks.

d) Transaction costs: In addition to the increased managerial and investor flexibility, buy backs can also lead to a reduction in transaction costs – both for the company and its shareholders. As a repurchase equates to little more than a "buy" order for a broker, many of the costs of a dividend payment are not incurred. And investors aren't forced to incur the costs of handling their dividend payments.

e) Signalling Power: For those CFOs who still believe traditional dividends can serve a valuable signaling role, why shouldn't buybacks carry an

Table C6.1 Buyback bonanza. While there are no clear trends in the proportion of earnings returned to investors, buybacks have increased in significance as a means of distribution

	1993	1994	1995	1996	1997	1998	1999	2000
Overall payout ratio* (%)	54.16	75.48	48.48	47.53	44.88	82.36	66.36	57.29
Overall payout cover** (times)	1.85	1.32	2.06	2.10	2.23	1.21	1.51	1.75
Proportion of cash returned via buybacks (% of overall payout)	0	0	0.03	1.52	0.29	11.04	9.76	15.14

* Overall payout ratio = the total value of the cash returned to investors via regular dividends, special dividends and share buybacks, all divided by net income ** Overall payout cover = how many times net income covers the total value of the cash returned to investors via regular dividends, special dividends and buybacks.
Source: CFOEurope and Thomson Financial

equally potent message? This idea is intuitive as an announcement of a buy back scheme inevitably increases latent demand and signals management's confidence in the future performance of the stock or that the stock is currently selling at or near the lower end of its trading range.

The results of *CFO Europe's* survey suggest that CFOs are increasingly taking these factors into consideration. Not that any companies in the survey have abandoned their dividend entirely in favour of buybacks. That could be for historical reasons – it's difficult to get rid of a dividend that investors have come to rely on. It could also be that the tax preferences of investors are very varied, with some preferring income, and others preferring capital gains, leading CFOs to set a distribution policy that is made up of both income (dividends) and capital gains (share buybacks).

RESULTS: THE CASE OF INTEL

Intel, the $33.7 billion (E38.4 billion) US-based computer chip manufacturer, is an example of a large corporation that has moved a long way towards distributing cash via buybacks rather than dividends. Between the start of 1994 and the end of 2000, Intel paid out $1.6 billion in dividends. But over the same period, it returned almost 14 times as much cash ($21.8 billion) by repurchasing its shares and cancelling them, as Table C6.2 shows.

Intel has adopted a policy of continually paying only a token dividend, possibly because the US Inland Revenue Service wouldn't stand for a company disguising its dividend entirely as buybacks in an attempt to enable investors to circumvent income tax.

This low annual dividend aids both managers and investors. Managers, by paying such a low dividend, are furnished with flexibility to adjust the overall payout ratio in light of current earnings and future growth potential without wild swings in share price. This is demonstrated by the fact that Intel's payout

Table C6.2 Intelligent distribution? How Intel has returned cash to its shareholders ($m)

	1995	1996	1997	1998	1999	2000
Net Income	3,566	5,157	6,945	6,068	7,314	10,535
Cash Dividends	116	148	180	217	366	470
Dividend Payout Ratio	3.2%	2.8%	2.5%	3.5%	5.0%	4.4%
Dividend Cover	30.7	34.8	38.5	27.9	19.9	22.4
Share Re-purchases	1,034	1,302	3,372	6,785	4,612	4,007
Overall Payout Ratio	32.2%	28.1%	51.1%	115.3%	68.0%	42.5%
Overall Payout Cover	3.1	3.5	1.9	0.8	1.4	2.3
% of payout from buybacks	89.9%	89.7%	94.9%	96.9%	92.6%	89.5%

Source: Intel and *CFOEurope*

ratios have oscillated wildly – between 28% and 115% – over the past six years during a period of steadily increasing earnings and almost constant dividends. Investors also receive greater flexibility as they can choose when to receive their payoff to best suit their particular circumstances. Figure C6.5 further depicts Intel's circumstances and the market's reaction to them, again reinforcing the reduced effect of dividends on share price.

RESULTS: GREATER PRESSURE FROM SHAREHOLDERS TO CONDUCT BUYBACKS

The benefits of buyback schemes have not gone unnoticed by investors who have increasingly voted to let company managers undertake share repurchases. (See Table C6.3.) It would appear also that this sentiment has been

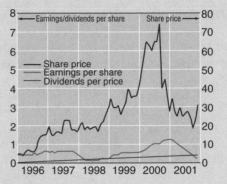

Figure C6.5   In the chips. Intel's share price bears no relation to its dividend payments.
Source: corporateinformation.com

Table C6.3   The greenlight. The number of companies with shareholder approval to buy back shares, and the number that have completed a repurchase (%)

	1993	1994	1995	1996	1997	1998	1999	2000	2001
Companies with shareholder approval to buy back shares (%)	3.9	4.7	6.3	17.3	18.9	25.2	43.3	62.2	80.3
Companies doing a buy-back (% of all firms in survey)	0	0.8	1.6	7.1	10.2	15	21.3	35.4	N/A
Proportion of companies acting on their buy-back approval (%)	0	17	25.4	41	54	59.5	49.2	57	N/A

Source: *CFOEurope* and Thomson Financial

heeded by Europe's largest companies as the percentage of companies acting on their buy back approval has risen consistently over recent years.

In light of such dependable shareholder approval of buyback schemes, it appears management may often have sought approval with little or no intention of acting on it. Instead managerial motivation may have been driven by the luxury of having an additional distribution avenue should market conditions alter significantly, investment opportunities run dry or merely because competitors had similar approvals in place.

Today however, either due to shareholder weariness of such managerial procrastination or due to greater corporate acceptance of the benefits of buyback schemes, companies are more likely than not to act on their buyback approval. Indeed the proportion of companies implementing repurchase programmes once approval is in place has been steadily growing.

CAVEATS

Several legimate arguments could be made to water down some of our conclusions

a) The changes in legislation enabling buybacks have only been implemented recently. It is feasible, therefore, that the rapid acceptance – and completion – of buybacks has been fuelled more by one off restructuring of corporate balance sheets than by the desire to fundamentally alter the way in which companies return cash to their shareholders.

b) The study period for this research was a period of significant economic growth and healthy corporate profits. Under such conditions managers may have a greater requirement for the flexibility offered by share repurchase schemes. Under this proposition, the trend towards greater buyback activity depicted in this survey may not continue uniformly into the future but instead adopt a cyclical pattern. It is then possible that, as the current economic uncertainty lingers and a potential recession sets in, our findings are reversed and traditional dividends make a resurgence at the expense of the newly implemented re-purchase programmes.

c) As suggested in this paper, one of the most attractive attributes of buybacks is flexibility. This flexibility, however, may not last forever. If the current trend for buybacks to grow in importance does indeed continue, investors may begin to expect buybacks in the same way that their predecessors expected dividends. Such an eventuality would suggest that eventually buybacks may adopt a similar signaling power to that previously enjoyed by traditional dividends. This implies that any buyback reduction would signal poor recent corporate performance and reduced future potential, leading to a lower share price.

A CFO Europe Research Report (2001).

Sciona: A Venture Capital Case Study

Colin Bond

SCIONA

Sciona is a bio-technology company working in the area of genetic personalisation. This field of work involves creating products and services tailored to an individual's genetic makeup.

Sciona researches and develops DNA screens for common gene variants that affect an individual's response to food, medication and the environment. These genetic screens serve as the basis for providing personalised advice to consumers. They can also help companies to customise personal care and nutrition products.

Sciona's geneticists, molecular biologists and dieticians work with universities and commercial companies to identify sets, or "panels", of genes that influence vital health areas, such as cardiovascular health, as well as genes that affect certain aspects of performance and well-being.

Sciona has an efficient and scalable ability to collect DNA samples and analyse the DNA for specific gene variants. The resultant information is used to generate personalised advice concerning lifestyle choices and consumer product selection. A key component of Sciona's service is its report-generation engine based on the latest information technology. It converts the scientific data into consumer-friendly reports of great practical value.

THE FUNDING HISTORY

Sciona was initially funded in 2000 by "seed money" totalling £1.5m, predominantly from a high wealth individual ("angel") investor together with a number of smaller contributions from other private investors.

In 2002 "first round funding" totalling £3m was obtained from two UK venture capital companies – Prelude Trust (who were the lead investor) and Abbey National Treasury Services. This investment "round" followed the successful merger of Sciona and Genostic Pharma – the latter being a Cambridge-based company which held a UK patent on a system of screens for personalised genetic medicines (known as genostics).

Over fifty venture capital companies in the UK and Europe were contacted in the process of securing "first round funding". Two of the fifty reached the "due diligence" stage before deciding not to invest in the company.

At this time Sciona also entered into a strategic partnership with Genaissance Pharmaceuticals, a US-based and NASDAQ-quoted company. Genaissance agreed to license its HAP™ technology to Sciona for use in the development and marketing of consumer products. The multi-year agreement gave Genaissance the right to support Sciona's pharmacogenomic research and customer genotyping. In exchange Genaissance obtained a 30% fully-diluted equity position in Sciona.

In September 2004, "second round funding" totalling $4.1m was raised to develop further products and markets for genetic personalisation of nutrition and personal care advice and products. Burrill & Company and Prelude Trust led the "round", which also included the investors BASF Venture Capital and DSM Venturing. The "round" was interesting as it included venture capital from two traditional European chemical companies. The funding also accompanied a shift in the company's marketing focus, research and operations to the US market.

THE VENTURE CAPITAL COMPANIES

Burrill & Company is a life sciences merchant bank, focused exclusively on companies involved in biotechnology, pharmaceuticals, diagnostics, human healthcare and related medical technologies, wellness and nutraceuticals, agricultural technologies and industrial biotechnology. Burrill & Company has over $500m under management in its family of venture capital funds, and has one of the premier strategic advisory and partnering practices in the life sciences.

Prelude Trust is an investment trust, launched in 1997, with the unique objective to seek significant capital appreciation over the long-term, primarily through venture capital investment in unquoted high-growth technology and life science based businesses.

BASF Venture Capital was established in 2001 as a wholly-owned subsidiary of BASF Future Business. This German-based company participates in start-up businesses by providing venture capital to open up new growth potentials. In doing so, it focuses on companies with innovative business models and technologies in which chemistry is an important key to success. Investment is channelled towards companies that can demonstrate successful applications for their product developments as well as market demand. BASF also supports these companies with its expertise.

DSM Venturing is part of the DSM Venturing and Business Development business group. It is an active investor in several venture capital funds and start-up companies in DSM's strategic growth fields of food ingredients, pharmaceutical intermediates and performance materials.

SCIONA'S OBSERVATIONS OF THE VENTURE CAPITAL EXPERIENCE

Sciona's experience with raising funds from the venture capital market provided the following observations.

1. What are the Venture Capital Companies Looking for?

Sciona's experience demonstrated that the venture capitalists look at both the quality and originality of a company's business plan. This not only involves assessing whether the company's products are commercially viable but also whether the management team has sufficient expertise and credibility to make the business plans succeed. The venture capitalists also like to assess the significance and worth of the intellectual property held. Finally, they need to feel comfortable that investing in a company fits well with their existing investments.

2. Issues Arising during the Funding

Sciona found that, although there are a large number of venture capitalists, there are only a few that are able to invest in businesses like Sciona due to its specialist nature. The venture capitalists themselves need the necessary skills and experience to assess the business risks. This is particularly so at the "first round" stage of funding when the business has a very limited track record.

Sciona also learnt of some more general issues that arise from raising venture capital funds.

The funding process – particularly the "first round" stage – normally results in significant covenants being placed on the company that is raising money. These limit management freedom and may also place constraints on "angel" investors. Such covenants may include:

- Board representation requirements.
- Restrictions on recruitment and capital expenditure.
- The requirement to provide regular financial statements and monthly management reports.

Additionally, the valuation of the company, particularly at the "first round" stage, may be extremely disappointing for the management and the initial "angel" investors.

3. The Search for Venture Capital

Sciona also experienced some more general issues relating to the search venture capital.

Firstly, the process is a major and time consuming management commitment. Much time becomes involved in writing and giving presentations to prospective investors and the results from applications to the venture capitalists often yield poor results. The rejection rate is very high.

Secondly, scarce "seed" money may be used in the search for a venture capital partner.

Consequently, rather than send in "cold" applications to the venture capitalists, it is much better to obtain an introduction to the relevant representatives of these investors through a business contact or friend.

9

Initial Public Offerings

Jay R. Ritter

1. INTRODUCTION

An initial public offering (IPO) occurs when a security is sold to the general public for the first time, with the expectation that a liquid market will develop. Although an IPO can be of any debt or equity security, this article will focus on equity issues by operating companies.

Most companies start out by raising equity capital from a small number of investors, with no liquid market existing if these investors wish to sell their stock. If a company prospers and needs additional equity capital, at some point the firm generally finds it desirable to "go public" by selling stock to a large number of diversified investors. Once the stock is publicly traded, this enhanced liquidity allows the company to raise capital on more favorable terms than if it had to compensate investors for the lack of liquidity associated with a privately-held company. Existing shareholders can sell their shares in open-market transactions. With these benefits, however, come costs. In particular, there are certain ongoing costs associated with the need to supply information on a regular basis to investors and regulators for publicly-traded firms. Furthermore, there are substantial one-time costs associated with initial public offerings that can be categorized as direct and indirect costs. The direct costs include the legal, auditing, and underwriting fees. The indirect costs are the management time and effort devoted to conducting the offering, and the dilution associated with selling shares at an offering price that is, on average, below the price prevailing in the market shortly after the IPO. These direct and indirect costs affect the cost of capital for firms going public.

Firms going public, especially young growth firms, face a market that is subject to sharp swings in valuations. The fact that the issuing firm is subject to the whims of the market makes the IPO process a high-stress period for entrepreneurs.

Because initial public offerings involve the sale of securities in closely-held firms in which some of the existing shareholders may possess non-public information, some of the classic problems caused by asymmetric information may be present. In addition to the adverse selection problems that can arise when firms have a choice of when and if to go public, a further problem is that the underlying value of the firm is affected by the actions that the managers can undertake. This moral hazard problem must also be dealt with by the market. This article describes some of the mechanisms that are used in practice to overcome the problems created by information asymmetries. In addition, evidence is presented on three patterns associated with IPOs: (i) new issues underpricing, (ii) cycles in the extent of underpricing, and (iii) long-run underperformance. Various theories that have been advanced to explain these patterns are also discussed.

While this chapter focuses on operating companies going public, the IPOs of closed-end funds and real estate investment trusts (REITs) are also briefly discussed. A closed-end fund raises money from investors, which is then invested in other financial securities. The closed-end fund shares then trade in the public market.

The structure of the remainder of this chapter is as follows. First, the mechanics of going public and the valuation of IPOs are discussed. Second, evidence regarding the three empirical patterns mentioned above is presented. Third, an analysis of the costs and benefits of going public is presented in the context of the life cycle of a firm, from founding to its eventual ability to self-finance. This includes a short analysis of venture capital. The costs of going public and explanations for new issues underpricing are then discussed.

2. VALUING IPOs

2.1. The Mechanics of Going Public

In the United States, Securities and Exchange Commission (S.E.C.) clearance is needed to sell securities to the public. The regulations are based upon the Securities Act of 1933, but in practice much case law and professional judgment applies. The S.E.C. is explicitly concerned with full disclosure of material information, and does not attempt to determine whether a security is fairly priced or not. Many state securities regulators in the past attempted to ascertain whether a security is fairly priced (the "blue sky" laws) before allowing investors to purchase an issue, but the National Securities Markets Improvement Act of 1996 has given blanket approval for all IPOs that list on the American Stock Exchange (Amex), New York Stock Exchange (NYSE), or the National Market System (NMS) of Nasdaq.

In preparation for going public, a company must supply audited financial statements. The level of detail that is required depends upon the size of the company, the amount of money being raised, and the age of the company. The required disclosures are contained in S.E.C. Regulations S-K or S-B (covering the necessary descriptions of the company's business) and Regulation S-X (covering the necessary financial statements). For large offerings, Registration of Form S-1 is required, but Form SB-2 can be used by companies with less than $25 million in revenues. Form SB-2 registrations allow the use of financial statements prepared in accordance with generally accepted accounting principles, whereas Form S-1 registrations require that certain details specified in Regulation S-X be followed. The smallest offerings, raising less than $5 million, may register under Regulation A, which has the least stringent disclosure requirements. Disclosure requirements differ for certain industries (such as banking) that are subject to other regulations, and for other industries with a history of abuses (such as oil & gas, and mining stocks).

In going public, an issuing firm will typically sell 20–40% of its stock to the public. The issuer will hire investment bankers to assist in pricing the offering and marketing the stock. In cooperation with outside counsel, the investment banker will also conduct a due diligence investigation of the firm, write the prospectus, and file the necessary documents with the S.E.C. For young companies, most or all of the shares being sold are typically newly-issued (primary shares), with the proceeds going to the company. With older companies going public, it is common that many of the shares being sold come from existing stockholders (secondary shares).

Since, as discussed in section 7.3 below, investment bankers rarely compete for business on the basis of offering lower underwriting discounts (or gross spreads), an issuer will generally choose a lead underwriter on the basis of its experience, especially with IPOs in the same industry. Having a well-respected analyst who will supply research reports on the firm in the years ahead is a major consideration. The investment bankers with large market shares of IPOs include, in addition to large investment banking firms such as Merrill Lynch and Goldman Sachs, five firms that specialize in IPOs: BT Alex. Brown, Hambrecht & Quist, BancAmerica Robertson Stephens, Nationsbank Montgomery, and Friedman, Billings, Ramsey Group.

After the preliminary prospectus (or "red herring," since on the front page certain warnings are required to be printed in red) is issued, the company management and investment bankers conduct a marketing campaign for the stock. Regulations limit what can be said in this marketing campaign. This marketing effort includes a "road show" to major cities, in which presentations are made before groups of prospective institutional buyers as well as in one-on-one discussions with important IPO buyers, such as mutual funds. If the offering is sufficiently large and has an international tranche, the road show may include presentations in London and Asia.

2.2. Valuing IPOs

In principal, valuing IPOs is no different from valuing other stocks. The common approaches of discounted cash flow (DCF) analysis and comparable firms analysis can be used. In practice, because many IPOs are of young growth firms in high technology industries, historical accounting information is of limited use in projecting future profits or cash flows. Thus, a preliminary valuation may rely heavily on how the market is valuing comparable firms. In some cases, publicly-traded firms in the same line of business are easy to find. In other cases, it may be difficult to find publicly-traded "pure plays" to use for valuation purposes.

The final valuation of the firm going public typically occurs at a pricing meeting the morning a firm is expected to receive S.E.C. clearance to go public. This pricing meeting is described below in section 7.1 concerning bookbuilding. Because the IPO market is especially sensitive to changes in market conditions, and because it takes at least several months to complete the process of going public, going public is a high-stress event for entrepreneurs. Numerous cases have occurred where a firm was expecting to raise tens of millions of dollars, only to withdraw the deal at the last moment due to factors outside of its control.

Because most companies prefer an offer price of between $10.00 and $20.00 per share, firms frequently conduct a stock split or reverse stock split to get into the target price range. Stocks with a price below $5.00 per share are subject to the provisions of the Securities Enforcement Remedies and Penny Stock Reform Act of 1990, aimed at reducing fraud and abuse in the penny stock market.

3. NEW ISSUES UNDERPRICING

3.1. In General

The best-known pattern associated with the process of going public is the frequent incidence of large initial returns (the price change measured from the offering price to the market price on the first trading day) accruing to investors in IPOs of common stock. Numerous studies document the phenomenon, showing that the distribution of initial returns is highly skewed, with a positive mean and a median near zero. In the U.S., the mean initial return is about 15 percent.

The new issue underpricing phenomenon exists in every nation with a stock market, although the amount of underpricing varies from country to country. (In this article, the term "new issue" is used to refer to unseasoned security offerings, although the term is frequently applied to seasoned (previously traded) security offerings as well. Furthermore, we focus on IPOs of equity securities, even though many security offerings involve fixed-income securities.) Table 9.1 gives a summary of the equally-weighted average initial returns on IPOs in a number of countries around the world. The incredibly high average initial return in China is for "A" share IPOs, which are restricted to Chinese residents.

Table 9.2 reports the equally weighted average initial return in the U.S., by year, from 1960–1996. The numbers from 1960–84 include best efforts offerings and penny stocks. The numbers from 1985–1996 include only firm commitment offerings. The 1960–1984 average initial returns are higher and more volatile than if only firm commitment offerings were included.

Table 9.1 Average initial returns for 33 countries

Country	Author(s) of article(s)	Sample size	Time period	Average initial return
Australia	Lee, Taylor & Walter	266	1976–89	11.9%
Austria	Aussenegg	67	1964–96	6.5%
Belgium	Rogiers, Manigart & Ooghe	28	1984–90	10.1%
Brazil	Aggarwal, Leal & Hernandez	62	1979–90	78.5%
Canada	Jog & Riding; Jog & Srivastava	258	1971–92	5.4%
Chile	Aggarwal, Leal & Hernandez	19	1982–90	16.3%
China	Datar and Mao	226	1990–96	388.0%
Denmark	Bisgard	32	1989–97	7.7%
Finland	Keloharju	85	1984–92	9.6%
France	Husson & Jacquillat; Leleux & Muzyka; Paliard & Belletante	187	1983–92	4.2%
Germany	Ljungqvist	170	1978–92	10.9%
Greece	Kazantzis and Levis	79	1987–91	48.5%
Hong Kong	McGuinness; Zhao and Wu	334	1980–96	15.9%
India	Krishnamurti and Kumar	98	1992–93	35.3%
Israel	Kandel, Sarig & Wohl	28	1993–94	4.5%
Italy	Cherubini & Ratti	75	1985–91	27.1%
Japan	Fukuda; Dawson & Hiraki; Hebner & Hiraki; Pettway & Kaneko; Hamao, Packer, & Ritter	975	1970–96	24.0%
Korea	Dhatt, Kim & Lim	347	1980–90	78.1%
Malaysia	Isa	132	1980–91	80.3%
Mexico	Aggarwal, Leal & Hernandez	37	1987–90	33.0%
Netherlands	Wessels; Eijgenhuijsen & Buijs	72	1982–91	7.2%
New Zealand	Vos & Cheung	149	1979–91	28.8%
Norway	Emilsen, Pedersen & Saettern	68	1984–96	12.5%
Portugal	Alpalhao	62	1986–87	54.4%
Singapore	Lee, Taylor & Walter	128	1973–92	31.4%
Spain	Rahnema, Fernandez & Martinez	71	1985–90	35.0%
Sweden	Rydqvist	251	1980–94	34.1%
Switzerland	Kunz & Aggarwal	42	1983–89	35.8%
Taiwan	Chen	168	1971–90	45.0%
Thailand	Wethyavivorn & Koo-smith	32	1988–89	58.1%
Turkey	Kiymaz	138	1990–95	13.6%
United Kingdom	Dimson; Levis	2,133	1959–90	12.0%
United States	Ibbotson, Sindelar & Ritter	13,308	1960–96	15.8%

Sources: See references listed in the bibliography to this article and in Loughran, Ritter, and Rydqvist (1994). This is an updated version of their Table 1

   While on average there are positive initial returns on IPOs, there is a wide variation on individual issues. Figure 9.1 shows the distribution of first day returns for IPOs from 1990–1996. One in eleven IPOs has a negative initial return, and one in six closes on the first day at the offer price. One in a hundred doubles on the first day.

Table 9.2 Number of U.S. offerings, average initial return, and gross proceeds of initial public offerings in 1960–96

Year	Number of offerings	Average initial return, %	Gross proceeds, $ millions
1960	269	17.8	553
1961	435	34.1	1,243
1962	298	−1.6	431
1963	83	3.9	246
1964	97	5.3	380
1965	146	12.7	409
1966	85	7.1	275
1967	100	37.7	641
1968	368	55.9	1,205
1969	780	12.5	2,605
1970	358	−0.7	780
1971	391	21.2	1,655
1972	562	7.5	2,724
1973	105	−17.8	330
1974	9	−7.0	51
1975	14	−1.9	264
1976	34	2.9	237
1977	40	21.0	151
1978	42	25.7	247
1979	103	24.6	429
1980	259	49.4	1,404
1981	438	16.8	3,200
1982	198	20.3	1,334
1983	848	20.8	13,168
1984	516	11.5	3,932
1985	507	12.4	10,450
1986	953	10.0	19,260
1987	630	10.4	16,380
1988	435	9.8	5,750
1989	371	12.6	6,068
1990	276	14.5	4,519
1991	367	14.7	16,420
1992	509	12.5	23,990
1993	707	15.2	41,524
1994	564	13.4	29,200
1995	566	20.5	39,030
1996	845	17.0	42,150
1960–69	2,661	21.2	7,988
1970–79	1,658	9.0	6,868
1980–89	5,155	15.3	80,946
1990–96	3,834	15.6	196,833
TOTAL	13,308	15.8	292,635

Source: This is an updated version of Table 1 of Ibbotson, Sindelar, and Ritter (1994)

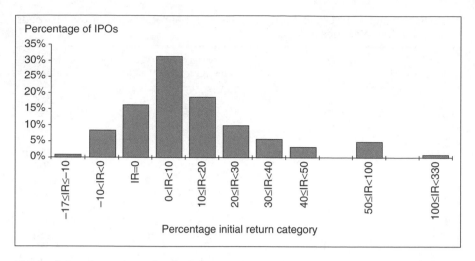

Percentage of IPOs

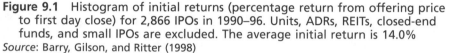

Percentage initial return category

Figure 9.1   Histogram of initial returns (percentage return from offering price
to first day close) for 2,866 IPOs in 1990–96. Units, ADRs, REITs, closed-end
funds, and small IPOs are excluded. The average initial return is 14.0%
Source: Barry, Gilson, and Ritter (1998)

3.2. Reasons for New Issues Underpricing

A number of reasons have been advanced for the new issues underpricing
phenomenon, with different theories focusing on various aspects of the relations between investors, issuers, and the investment bankers taking the firms
public. In general, these theories are not mutually exclusive. Furthermore, a
given reason can be more important for some IPOs than for others.

3.2.a   The Winner's Curse Hypothesis

An important rationale for the underpricing of IPOs is the "winner's curse"
explanation. Since a more or less fixed number of shares are sold at a fixed
offering price, rationing will result if demand is unexpectedly strong.
Rationing in itself does not lead to underpricing, but if some investors are at
an informational disadvantage relative to others, some investors will be worse
off. If some investors are more likely to attempt to buy shares when an issue
is underpriced, then the amount of excess demand will be higher when there
is more underpricing. Other investors will be allocated only a fraction of the
most desirable new issues, while they are allocated most of the least desirable new issues. They face a winner's curse: if they get all of the shares which
they ask for, it is because the informed investors don't want the shares. Faced
with this adverse selection problem, the less informed investors will only
submit purchase orders if, on average, IPOs are underpriced sufficiently to
compensate them for the bias in the allocation of new issues.

Numerous studies have attempted to test the winner's curse model, both for the U.S. and other countries. While the evidence is consistent with there being a winner's curse, other explanations of the new issues underpricing phenomenon exist.

3.2.b The Market Feedback Hypothesis

Where bookbuilding is used, investment bankers may underprice IPOs to induce regular investors to reveal information during the pre-selling period, which can then be used to assist in pricing the issue. In order to induce regular investors to truthfully reveal their valuations, the investment banker compensates investors through underpricing. Furthermore, in order to induce truthful revelation for a given IPO, the investment banker must underprice issues for which favorable information is revealed by more than those for which unfavorable information is revealed. This leads to a prediction that there will only be a partial adjustment of the offer price from that contained in the preliminary prospectus to that in the final prospectus. In other words, those IPOs for which the offer price is revised upwards will be *more* underpriced than those for which the offer price is revised downwards. This pattern is in fact present in the data, as shown in Table 9.3.

3.2.c The Bandwagon Hypothesis

The IPO market may be subject to bandwagon effects. If potential investors pay attention not only to their own information about a new issue, but also to whether other investors are purchasing, bandwagon effects may develop. If an investor sees that no one else wants to buy, he or she may decide not to buy even when there is favorable information. To prevent this from happening, an issuer may want to underprice an issue to induce the first few potential investors to buy, and induce a bandwagon, or cascade, in which all subsequent investors want to buy irrespective of their own information.

Table 9.3 IPOs in 1990–96 with proceeds = $5 million, excluding units and ADRs

| | | Offer price relative to the file price range | | |
	All	OP < Low	Lo = OP = Hi	OP > High
Average initial return	13.99%	3.54%	11.99%	30.22%
Standard deviation	21.06%	8.92%	17.97%	27.12%
Percent positive	75%	53%	76%	95%
Number of IPOs	2,861	708	1,511	642

Source: Barry, Gilson, and Ritter (1998). The sample of 2,861 IPOs is less than in Figure 9.1 because five IPOs with missing file price ranges are deleted

An interesting implication of the market feedback explanation, in conjunction with bandwagons, is that positively-sloped demand curves can result. In the market feedback hypothesis, the offering price is adjusted upwards if regular investors indicate positive information. Other investors, knowing that this will only be a partial adjustment, correctly infer that these offerings will be underpriced. These other investors will consequently want to purchase additional shares, resulting in a positively sloped demand curve. The flip side is also true: because investors realize that a cut in the offering price indicates weak demand from other investors, cutting the offer price might actually scare away potential investors. And if the price is cut too much, investors might start to wonder why the firm is so desperate for cash. Thus, an issuer faced with weak demand may find that cutting the offer price won't work, and its only alternative is to postpone the offering, and hope that market conditions improve.

3.2.d The Investment Banker's Monopsony Power Hypothesis

Another explanation for the new issues underpricing phenomenon argues that investment bankers take advantage of their superior knowledge of market conditions to underprice offerings, which permits them to expend less marketing effort and ingratiate themselves with buy-side clients. While there is undoubtedly some truth to this, especially with less sophisticated issuers, when investment banking firms go public, they underprice themselves by as much as other IPOs of similar size. Investment bankers have been successful at convincing clients and regulatory agencies, including the Office of Thrift Supervision (in the case of mutual savings bank conversions), that underpricing is normal for IPOs.

3.2.e The Lawsuit Avoidance Hypothesis

Since the Securities Act of 1933 makes all participants in the offer who sign the prospectus liable for any material omissions, one way of reducing the frequency and severity of future lawsuits is to underprice. Underpricing the IPO seems to be a very costly way of reducing the probability of a future lawsuit. Furthermore, other countries in which securities class actions are unknown, such as Finland, have just as much underpricing as in the U.S.

3.2.f The Signalling Hypothesis

Underpriced new issues "leave a good taste" with investors, allowing the firms and insiders to sell future offerings at a higher price than would otherwise be the case. This reputation argument has been formalized in several signaling models. In these models, issuing firms have private information about whether they have high or low values. They follow a dynamic issue strategy, in which the IPO will be followed by a seasoned offering. Various empirical studies, however, find that the hypothesized relation between initial returns and subsequent seasoned new issues is not present, casting doubt on the importance of signaling as a reason for underpricing.

3.2.g The Ownership Dispersion Hypothesis

Issuing firms may intentionally underprice their shares in order to generate excess demand and so be able to have a large number of small shareholders. This dispersed ownership will both increase the liquidity of the market for the stock, and make it more difficult for outsiders to challenge management.

3.2.h Summary of Explanations of New Issues Underpricing

All of the above explanations for new issues underpricing involve rational strategies by buyers. Several other explanations involving irrational strategies by investors have been proposed. These irrational strategies will be discussed under the heading of the long-run performance of IPOs, for any model implying that investors are willing to overpay at the time of the IPO also implies that there will be poor long-run performance.

Many of the above explanations for the underpricing phenomenon can be criticized on the grounds of either the extreme assumptions that are made or the unnecessarily convoluted stories involved. On the other hand, most of the explanations have some element of truth to them. Furthermore, the underpricing phenomenon has persisted for decades with no signs of its imminent demise.

3.3. Why Don't Issuers Get Upset About Leaving Money on the Table?

The dollar amount of underpricing per share, multiplied by the number of shares offered, is referred to as the amount of money "left on the table." An extreme example is Netscape's August 1995 IPO, in which (including the international tranche and overallotment options), 5.75 million shares were sold at $28.00 per share. The first-day market price closed at $58.25, leaving $174 million on the table. If the same number of shares could have been sold at $58.25 per share instead of $28.00, the issuing firm's pre-issue shareholders would have been better off by $174 million (before investment banker fees). Instead, the wealth of those who were allocated shares at the offer price increased by this amount. Yet, amazingly, Netscape's pre-issue shareholders weren't visibly upset by this transfer of wealth from their pockets. Why not?

The reason probably lies in the "partial adjustment phenomenon," illustrated in Table 9.3. The highest initial returns, and therefore the most amount of money left on the table, tend to be associated with issues where the offer price has been revised upwards from the file price range. Furthermore, frequently the number of shares are revised in the same direction as the price. To use the extreme example of Netscape, the preliminary prospectus contained an offer price range of $12–14 per share, for 3,500,000 shares (not including a 15% overallotment option). Thus, just a few weeks before the offering, the company was expecting to raise about $50 million. Instead, it raised $161 million before fees. So the bad news that a lot of money was left on the table arrived at the same time that the good news of high proceeds and a high market price arrived. Because a lot of money is left on the table almost exclusively when it is packaged with good news, issuers rarely complain. And the investment banker will always be willing to argue that the price jump was due to a successful job of marketing the issue by the investment banker.

4. "HOT ISSUE" MARKETS

A second pattern is that cycles exist in both the volume and the average initial returns of IPOs. This is illustrated for 1977–1996 in Figures 9.2 and 9.3.

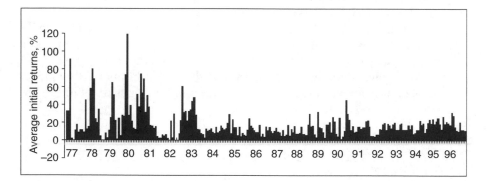

Figure 9.2   Average initial returns by month for S.E.C.-registered IPOs in the U.S. during 1977–96
Source: Ibbotson, Sindelar, and Ritter (1994), as updated

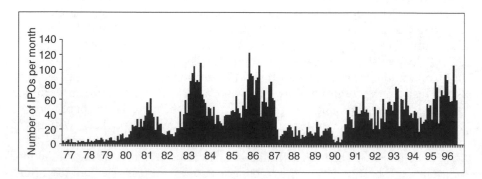

Figure 9.3   The number of IPOs by month in the U.S. during 1977–96, excluding closed-end fund IPOs
Source: Ibbotson, Sindelar, and Ritter (1994), as updated

Inspection of these figures shows that high initial returns tend to be followed by rising IPO volume. The periods of high average initial returns and rising volume are known as "hot issue" markets. The volume of IPOs, both in the U.S. and other countries, shows a strong tendency to be high following periods of high stock market returns, when stocks are selling at a premium to book value. Rational explanations for the existence of hot issue markets are difficult to come by.

Hot issue markets exist in other countries as well as the U.S. For example, there was a hot issue market in the United Kingdom between the "Big Bang" (the end of fixed commission rates) in October 1986 and the crash a year later. In South Korea, there was a hot issue market in 1988 that coincided with a major bull market.

5. LONG-RUN PERFORMANCE

5.1. Evidence on Long-Run Performance

The third pattern associated with IPOs is the poor stock price performance of IPOs in the long run. Measured from the market price at the end of the first day of trading, Figure 9.4 shows that companies going public during 1970–1993 produced an average return of just 7.9 percent per year for the

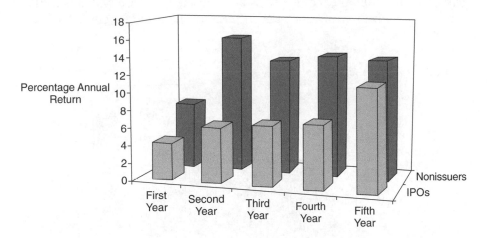

Figure 9.4 Average annual returns for the five years after the offering date for 5,821 IPOs in the U.S. from 1970–93, and for nonissuing firms that are bought and sold on the same dates as the IPOs. Nonissuing firms are matched on market capitalization, have been listed on the CRSP tapes for at least five years, and have not issued equity in a general cash offer during the prior five years. The returns (dividends plus capital gains) exclude the first-day returns. Returns for IPOs from 1992–93 are measured through Dec. 31, 1996

Source: Loughran and Ritter (1995), as updated

five years after the offering, using the first closing market price as the purchase price. A control group of nonissuing firms, matched by market capitalization, produced average annual returns of 13.1 percent. Thus, IPOs underperform by 5.2 percent per year in the five years after going public.

It should be noted that most firms going public have relatively high market-to-book ratios, and most are "small-cap" stocks. Small growth stocks in general have very low returns, and if IPOs are compared with nonissuers that are chosen on the basis of market-to-book ratios, as well as size, the underperformance is less than when the nonissuers are chosen on the basis of size alone.

The low returns in the aftermarket for IPOs partly reflect the pattern that IPO volume is high near market peaks when market-to-book ratios are high. The underperformance is concentrated among firms that went public in the heavy-volume years, and for younger firms. Indeed, for more established firms going public, and for those that went public in the light-volume years of the mid- and late-1970s, there is no long-run underperformance. IPOs that are not associated with venture capital financing, and those not associated with high-quality investment bankers, also tend to do especially poorly. Older firms going public, including "reverse LBOs," do not seem to be subject to long-run abnormal performance. Reverse LBOs are companies going public that previously had been involved in a leveraged buyout.

Figure 9.4 treats all IPOs equally, whether the market capitalization was $20 million, with no institutional buyers, or $120 million, with institutions participating. In Figure 9.5, the IPOs are restricted to those with a post-IPO market capitalization of at least $50 million. The average return for these

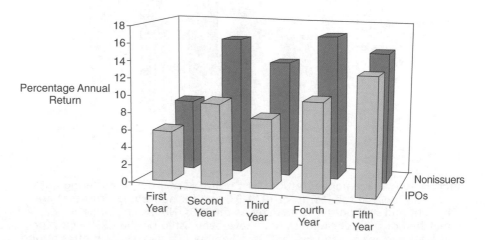

Figure 9.5 Same as Figure 9.4, but restricted to firms with a post-issue market capitalization of greater than $50 million (expressed in terms of 1996 purchasing power). Approximately half of all IPOs (lower in the 1970s, higher in the 1990s) meet this criterion

IPOs was 10.1 percent per year, compared to 13.8 percent per year for their matching firms. Thus, the larger IPOs underperform by 3.7 percent per year in the five years after going public. Smaller IPOs do much worse.

The earnings per share of companies going public typically grows rapidly in the years prior to going public, but then actually declines in the first few years after the IPO. During the first two quarters after going public, firms rarely have negative earnings surprises.

The international evidence on the long-run performance of IPOs is summarized in Table 9.4. Total abnormal performance is calculated as 100% minus the ratio of the average three-year buy-and-hold gross return divided by the average three-year buy-and-hold gross return on the benchmark. Thus, the total abnormal return of -20% for the U.S. can be interpreted as meaning that buying a portfolio of IPOs would have left an investor with 20% less wealth three years later than if the money had been invested in nonissuing firms instead.

The long-run underperformance of IPOs is not limited to operating companies going public. Investors in a closed-end fund IPO pay a premium over net asset value (the market value of the securities that the fund holds), because commissions equal about 7 percent of the offering price. Thus every $10.00 invested at the offering price buys only $9.30 of net asset value. Given that closed-end funds typically sell at about a 10 percent discount to net asset value, it is difficult to explain why investors are willing to purchase the shares

Table 9.4 International evidence on long-run IPO overpricing

Country	Author(s)	Number of IPOs	Issuing years	Total abnormal return
Australia	Lee, Taylor & Walter	266	1976–89	−46.5%
Austria	Aussenegg	57	1965–93	−27.3%
Brazil	Aggarwal, Leal & Hernandez	62	1980–90	−47.0%
Canada	Jog and Srivistava	216	1972–93	−17.9%
Chile	Aggarwal, Leal & Hernandez	28	1982–90	−23.7%
Finland	Keloharju	79	1984–89	−21.1%
Germany	Ljungqvist	145	1970–90	−12.1%
Japan	Cai & Wei	172	1971–90	−27.0%
Korea	Kim, Krinsky & Lee	99	1985–88	+2.0%
Singapore	Hin & Mahmood	45	1976–84	−9.2%
Sweden	Loughran, Ritter & Rydqvist	162	1980–90	+1.2%
U.K.	Levis	712	1980–88	−8.1%
U.S.	Loughran & Ritter	4,753	1970–90	−20.0%

Notes: Total abnormal returns are measured as $100 \cdot [(1 + R_{ipo,T})/(1 + R_{m,T})] - 100$, where $R_{ipo,T}$ is the average total return (where a 50% return is measured as 0.5) on the IPOs from the market price shortly after trading commences until the earlier of the delisting date or 3 years; $R_{m,T}$ is the average of either the market return or matching-firm returns over the same interval
Source: This is an updated version of Table 7 in Loughran, Ritter, and Rydqvist (1994). The Canadian numbers have been supplied by Vijay Jog of Carleton University

at a premium in the IPO. On average, it takes only about six months for closed-end funds to move from their 7 percent premium to a 10 percent discount. Perhaps it is no surprise that practitioners say that "closed-end funds are sold, not bought." Almost all closed-end fund shares are sold to individuals, rather than more sophisticated institutional investors, at the time of the IPO. Furthermore, new issues of closed-end funds are highly cyclical.

REITs are similar to closed-end funds, but they invest in property and mortgage-related securities. REIT shares used to be overwhelmingly purchased by individual investors, as are closed-end funds. With the explosion of REIT offerings in the 1990s, they now comprise a substantial portion of the Russell 2000 index, and many institutional investors now hold REITs. In the 1970s and 1980s, REITs underperformed in the first six months after their IPO, but the pattern has been less clear in the 1990s.

Three theories have been proposed to explain the phenomena of the long-run underperformance of IPOs.

5.2. The Divergence of Opinion Hypothesis

One argument is that investors who are most optimistic about an IPO will be the buyers. If there is a great deal of uncertainty about the value of an IPO the valuations of optimistic investors will be much higher than those of pessimistic investors. As time goes on and more information becomes available, the divergence of opinion between optimistic and pessimistic investors will narrow, and consequently, the market price will drop.

5.3. The Impresario Hypothesis

The "impresario" hypothesis argues that the market for IPOs is subject to fads and that IPOs are underpriced by investment bankers (the impresarios) to create the appearance of excess demand, just as the promoter of a rock concert attempts to make it an "event." This hypothesis predicts that companies with the highest initial returns should have the lowest subsequent returns. There is some evidence of this in the long run, but in the first six months, momentum effects seem to dominate. One survey of individual investors in IPOs found that only 26 percent of the respondents did any fundamental analysis of the relation between the offer price and the firm's underlying value.

5.4. The Windows of Opportunity Hypothesis

If there are periods when investors are especially optimistic about the growth potential of companies going public, the large cycles in volume may represent a response by firms attempting to "time" their IPOs to take advantage of these swings in investor sentiment. Of course, due to normal business cycle activity, one would expect to see some variation through time in the volume of IPOs. The large swings in volume displayed in Figure 9.3, however, seem difficult to explain as merely normal business cycle activity.

The windows of opportunity hypothesis predicts that firms going public in high volume periods are more likely to be overvalued than other IPOs. This has the testable implication that the high-volume periods should be associated with the lowest long-run returns. This pattern indeed exists.

6. GOING PUBLIC AS A STAGE IN THE LIFE CYCLE OF A FIRM'S EXTERNAL FINANCING

6.1. Financing of Startups

Most startup companies seeking external financing do not immediately utilize the public capital markets, but instead raise capital from private sources. Because young firms frequently have much of their value represented by intangibles such as growth opportunities, rather than assets in place, outside investors face a difficult job of valuing them. Usually, the value of these opportunities is dependent upon the actions taken by the entrepreneur (the moral hazard problem). Self-selection in terms of which firms seek external financing may also create an adverse selection problem for potential investors.

The source of capital for an entrepreneur that is least subject to problems caused by information asymmetries is self-financing: entrepreneurs contribute their own money. With limited resources, however, the ability to grow rapidly will be constrained if external sources of capital are not used. Because of the discipline imposed by social networks, friends and relatives might be the next source of capital. If a firm approaches potential external investors for financing when the entrepreneur and closely associated individuals have not invested a substantial fraction of their own assets in the venture, suspicions will be aroused. Only when these sources have been tapped will non-affiliated sources of capital become readily available. Even then, the ability to disclose proprietary information to potential investors encourages the use of private financing, either from banks, "angels," or venture capitalists. Angel financing is the term used for capital provided by wealthy individuals who aren't part of formal venture capital organizations.

6.2. Venture Capital

In the U.S., a venture capital industry exists to assist in the financing of private firms in their early stages of growth. Venture capitalists typically specialize by industry, size, or region, developing a network of contacts that can assist them in evaluating potential investment opportunities, and allowing the investments to live up to their potential. Adverse selection and moral hazard considerations are of paramount importance in deciding which deals to finance, and how to structure the deals.

Typically, venture capitalists do not make passive financial investments in young firms. Instead, they typically insist on board membership, and provide advice. This advice-giving role is one of the reasons for industry specialization. Thus, the returns to the venture capitalist are partly a return on capital, and partly a return on the other services provided. Of course, there can be disagreements between entrepreneurs and their financiers, for the interests of the various parties will not be identical. Venture capitalists typically provide capital in stages, with further commitments contingent upon performance up to that time.

While there are advantages to raising capital from a small number of investors who actively monitor the firm and to whom proprietary information can be disclosed, there are disadvantages as well. As long as the firm is private, any equity investment is illiquid, and investors will have to be compensated both for the lack of liquidity and the lack of diversification associated with a blockholding. Furthermore, conflicts between entrepreneurs and venture capitalists may arise. As a firm becomes larger, these disadvantages may come to outweigh the advantages of private financing. This is the point in the life cycle of a firm's financing at which it is optimal to go public, even though there are substantial costs associated with "outside" equity.

6.3. Mechanisms to Distinguish Among Firms

Among those firms that do go public, if investors are unable to fully distinguish the high-value firms from low-value firms, wealth transfers will result. The extent of these wealth transfers is dependent upon the dispersion of values among firms that are being pooled together. This encourages firms to go public when other high value firms go public, and may partly account for the cycles in the volume of IPOs that are observed. At each point in time, however, the high-value firms have incentives to differentiate themselves, in order to raise capital on more favorable terms. A number of mechanisms are employed in practice to accomplish this.

In practice, sophisticated investors do look at whether major shareholders are selling some of their stock in the IPO. Furthermore, insiders frequently agree to retain any stock not sold at the time of the IPO for a specified length of time, known as the lock-up period. This lock-up period is mandated by law to be at least 90 days in the U.S., but frequently insiders agree to a longer time period (usually 180 days). Investors are willing to pay more for a firm where the insiders have agreed to retain their shares for a long period of time for two reasons: i) any negative information being withheld is likely to be divulged before the shares can be sold, reducing the benefit of withholding the information, and ii) as long as the insiders retain large shareholdings, their incentives will be more closely aligned with those of outside equityholders.

Another relevant variable is the structure of compensation contracts: entrepreneurs who are willing to accept low base salaries and who have large amounts of company stock have their incentives more closely aligned with outside equityholders than entrepreneurs who demand large amounts of non-contingent compensation. Relevant corporate governance issues that affect firm valuation include the size and composition of the board of directors, and whether there are antitakeover provisions.

Since most theories of new issue underpricing imply that firms with greater uncertainty about the value per share will be underpriced more, issuing firms have incentives to reduce the amount of uncertainty. One method by which an issuer may reduce the degree of information asymmetry surrounding its initial public offering is to hire agents (auditors and underwriters) who, because they have reputation capital at stake, will have the incentive to certify that the offer price is consistent with inside information. The need to have repeat business gives underwriters a role that issuing firms cannot credibly duplicate. Consistent with this (but not with market efficiency), the long-run returns on IPOs underwritten by less prestigious investment bankers are low.

6.4. Investor Relations After Going Public

The market prince of a stock after going public is primarily determined by market conditions and the operating performance of the company. But there is also a role for an active investor relations program, and, everything else the same, the more analysts who follow the stock, the more potential buyers there will be. Thus, in choosing an underwriter, an important consideration for an issuing firm is that the underwriter has a well-respected analyst following the industry, who can be counted on to produce bullish research reports. These bullish research reports are especially important for creating demand when insiders are selling shares in the open market.

7. CONTRACTUAL FORMS AND THE GOING PUBLIC PROCESS

In the U.S., firms issuing stock use either a firm commitment or best efforts contract. With a firm commitment contract, a preliminary prospectus is issued containing a preliminary offering price range. After the issuing firm and its investment banker have conducted a marketing campaign and acquired information about investors' willingness to purchase the issue, a final offering price is set. The final prospectus is then issued, and when the S.E.C. clears the offering, the IPO goes "effective". The investment banker must sell all of the shares in the issue at a price no higher than the offering price once this has been set.

With a best efforts contract, the issuing firm and its investment banker agree on an offer price as well as a minimum and maximum number of shares to be sold. A "selling period" then commences, during which the investment banker makes its "best efforts" to sell the shares to investors. If the minimum number of shares are not sold at the offer price within a specified period of time, usually 90 days, the offer is withdrawn and all investors' monies are refunded from an escrow account, with the issuing firm receiving no money. Best efforts offerings are used almost exclusively by smaller, more speculative, issuers. Essentially all IPOs raising more than $10 million use firm commitment contracts.

7.1. Bookbuilding

Firm commitment offerings in the U.S. use "book-building." During and immediately after the road show period, the lead investment banker canvasses potential buyers and records who is interested in buying how much at what price. In other words, a demand curve is constructed. The offering is then priced based upon this information. In contrast, in many countries (and in the U.S. with best efforts offerings), the number of shares to be sold and the offer price are set before information about the state of demand is collected. The international evidence summarized in Table 9.1 shows that countries using fixed price offerings typically have more underpricing than in countries using book-building procedures. This evidence is summarized in Figure 9.6.

Partly because it results in more accurate pricing than if the offer price is set too early, many countries have moved in recent years to book-building, at least in the case of large offerings. Denmark, Finland, and Japan are among these countries.

Book-building is not without its critics, however. Book-building typically results in some offerings being underpriced, with investment bankers allegedly allocating a disproportionate number of shares in hot issues to their favored clients. There is, however, a desirable aspect to this favoritism. One reason, as explained earlier in section 3.2.b with regard to the market feedback hypothesis, is that IPOs are underpriced as a way of giving something back to regular investors who assist an investment banker in getting more accurate pricing. If regular investors can be favored by getting more shares in hot deals, they don't have to be favored by underpricing as much as otherwise would be required. A dark side to the favoritism in allocation surfaced in 1997 with a *Wall Street Journal* article, and subsequent S.E.C. investigation, alleging that underwriters competed for IPO business partly by allocating shares in hot deals to some venture capitalists and executives of private companies that were likely candidates to go public. This practice, called spinning, is intended to influence the choice of underwriter.

Classification of selling mechanisms:

		Determination of the Offer Price	
		Before Information Acquisition	After Information Acquisition
Allocation of Shares	Discretionary	Fixed price	Book-building Placing (UK)
	Non-discretionary	Offer for sale (UK)	Auctions

Average initial returns (averaged across countries):

		Determination of the Offer Price	
		Before Information Acquisition	After Information Acquisition
Allocation of Shares	Discretionary	37%	12%
	Non-discretionary	27%	9%

Figure 9.6 Selling mechanisms classified on the basis of how shares are allocated and when the offer price is determined (top), and average initial returns by category (bottom).
Source: Based upon Loughran, Ritter, and Rydqvist (1994).

7.2. Overallotment Options and Stabilization

When taking a firm public using a firm commitment contract, the investment bankers will typically presell more than 100% of the shares offered. Almost all IPOs include an overallotment option, in which the issuing firm or selling shareholders give the investment banker the right to sell up to 15% more shares than guaranteed. The overallotment option is also called the Green Shoe option, since the first offering to include one was the February 1963 offering of the Green Shoe Manufacturing Company. If the investment bankers expect aftermarket demand to be hot, they will typically presell 115% of the issue, with the expectation that they will exercise the overallotment option. If they expect aftermarket demand to be weak, they will typically presell 135% of the offering, with the shares above the overallotment option representing a naked short position in the stock. The advantage of pre-selling extra shares is that if many shares are "flipped," that is, immediately sold in the aftermarket by investors who had been allocated shares, the investment banker can buy them back and retire the shares, just as if they had never been issued in the first place.

While it is generally illegal to manipulate a stock price, manipulation is permitted directly after a securities offering. Investment bankers have legal authority to post a "stabilizing" bid, at or below the offer price, at which they stand ready to buy shares once trading has commenced. The existence of this floor price allows investors to get out of an offer before the price declines, and may also head off a larger price drop if no stabilization occurred. Stabilizing a stock is also referred to as supporting the stock.

Why would an underwriter allocate extra shares (the extra 35%) to investors when it expects to buy them back, rather than just allocate fewer shares in the first place? One possibility is that some investors are willing to buy and hold the stock if they can get shares at the offer price when these same investors wouldn't be willing to buy these same shares at the same price in the market, once trading commences. Thus, the inclination to hold the stock may be stronger if more shares are allocated initially. Another reason may be that favored clients of the investment banker are more likely to sell back their shares, and offering price support is a way of favoring some clients over others. Yet a third reason is that by offering price support, the investment banker is telling investors that there are fewer incentives to overprice a deal, and this reassures investors who would otherwise not be willing to buy at the offer price.

For IPOs that are stabilized, on average the price drops by about 4% during the subsequent month (say, from a $10 offer price to $9 5/8). For the roughly two-thirds of issues that aren't stabilized, there is a slight uptrend in price during the month after the issue. When all IPOs are grouped together, the downtrend for stabilized issues and the uptrend for other IPOs tend to cancel out. Thus, there is little in the way of abnormal performance, on average, in the months after an IPO's first day of trading. For IPOs that increase on the first day, there tends to be positive momentum during the following six months. This is especially true when there is relatively little flipping by institutions on the first day.

7.3. The Costs of Going Public

There are a number of direct and indirect costs of going public. One of the direct costs is the compensation paid to underwriters. There are substantial economies of scale in underwriting costs. In spite of these economies of scale, the majority of IPOs raising between $20 million and $80 million have gross spreads of exactly 7.0%. Table 9.5 reports the direct and indirect costs of going public for IPOs from 1990–1994. The indirect cost that is included is the new issues underpricing cost; management time and effort isn't included.

Table 9.5 Direct and indirect costs, in percent, of equity IPOs, 1990–94

Proceeds[1] ($ millions)	Gross spreads[2]	Other expenses[3]	Total direct costs[4]	Average initial return[5]	Average direct and indirect costs[6]	Number of IPOs	Interquartile range of spread
2–9.99	9.05%	7.91%	16.96%	16.36%	25.16%	337	8.0–10.0%
10–19.99	7.24%	4.39%	11.63%	9.65%	18.15%	389	7.00–7.14%
20–39.99	7.01%	2.69%	9.70%	12.48%	18.18%	533	7.00–7.00%
40–59.99	6.96%	1.76%	8.72%	13.65%	17.95%	215	7.00–7.00%
60–79.99	6.74%	1.46%	8.20%	11.31%	16.35%	79	6.55–7.00%
80–99.99	6.47%	1.44%	7.91%	8.91%	14.14%	51	6.21–6.85%
100–199	6.03%	1.03%	7.06%	7.16%	12.78%	106	5.72–6.47%
200–499	5.67%	0.86%	6.53%	5.70%	11.10%	47	5.29–5.86%
500–up	5.21%	0.51%	5.72%	7.53%	10.36%	10	5.00–5.37%
Total	7.31%	3.69%	11.00%	12.05%	18.69%	1767	7.00–7.05%

Source: Lee, Lochhead, Ritter, and Zhao (1996)

Notes: There are 1,767 domestic operating company IPOs in the sample. Unit offerings are excluded. The first four columns express costs as a percentage of the offer price, and the fifth column expresses costs as a percentage of the market price.
[1] Total proceeds raised in the United States, excluding proceeds from the exercise of overallotment options.
[2] Gross spreads as a percentage of proceeds (including management fee, underwriting fee, and selling concession).
[3] Other direct expenses as a percentage of total proceeds (including registration fee and printing, legal, and auditing costs).
[4] Total direct costs as a percentage of total proceeds (the average total direct costs are the sum of average gross spreads and average other direct expenses).
[5] Initial return = 100% * [(first closing market price–offering price)/offering price].
[6] Total direct and indirect costs = $(d + e)/(1 + e/100)$, where d is the percentage total direct costs, and e is the percentage initial return. Computed for each issue individually (excluding firms with other expenses or initial returns missing), and then averaged.

The National Association of Securities Dealers (NASD) sets limits on underwriter compensation. One way that underwriters may overcome the limits on direct compensation set by the NASD and state regulators is to include warrants to purchase additional shares as part of the compensation of the investment banker. Underwriter warrants tend to be associated with smaller and riskier issues and low-quality underwriters. Since Table 9.5 does not include underwriter warrants as a cost of going public, their inclusion would boost the average costs associated with smaller offerings. In other words, Table 9.5 understates the economies of scale that exist.

7.4. Direct Public Offerings

Beginning in the mid-1990s, a growing number of small companies have gone public without using an investment banker in what have come to be called direct public offerings (DPOs). According to one count, 190 companies attempted to raise $273 million during 1996 using direct public offerings. Some of these have been consumer product companies (i.e., microbreweries) where the target shareholders have been customers of a company's product. An advantage for an issuing firm of a direct public offering is the possibility of reduced costs. Investors must be wary, however, of the lack of a third party (i.e., underwriter) putting its reputation on the line, especially as regards due diligence and valuation.

8. SUMMARY

Companies going public, especially young companies, face a market that is subject to sharp swings in valuations. Pricing deals can be difficult, even in stable market conditions, because insiders presumably have more information than potential outside investors. To deal with these potential problems, market participants and regulators insist on the disclosure of material information.

Three patterns have been documented for IPOs in the U.S. and many countries: i) new issues underpricing, ii) cycles in volume and the extent of underpricing, and iii) long-run underperformance. In some respects, the poor performance of IPOs in the long run makes the new issues underpricing phenomenon even more of a puzzle.

The U.S. IPO market is enormous in comparison with that of most countries. The contrast with continental Europe is especially noteworthy. Part of the difference is undoubtedly cultural: the willingness of U.S. employees to work for young, unstable companies makes it easier to start a firm. Venture capitalists are willing to finance these firms, knowing that an active IPO market will allow them to cash out if the startup firm succeeds. Because of the immense number of U.S. IPOs, a large infrastructure has developed to create and fund young companies, especially in the high technology sector.

In addition to liquid labor markets, the large volume of IPOs in the U.S. can be partly attributable to a legal system that protects, albeit imperfectly, minority investors. Yet another factor may be the willingness of U.S. investors to, on average, overpay for IPOs. There is evidence that in the choice between an additional round of venture capital financing and going public, firms have some success at choosing periods when the public market is willing to pay the highest valuations. As a result, when the IPO market is most buoyant, investors frequently receive low long-run returns.

SUGGESTED READING

Affleck-Graves, J., S. Hegde, and R. Miller (1996) Conditional price trends in the aftermarket for initial public offerings. *Financial Management* 25, 25–40.

Aggarwal, R., and P. Rivoli (1990) Fads in the initial public offering market? *Financial Management* 22, 42–53.

Alexander, J. C. (1993) The lawsuit avoidance theory of why initial public offerings are underpriced. *UCLA Law Review* 41, 17–71.

Aussenegg, Wolfgang (1997) Short and Long-run performance of Initial Public Offerings in the Austrian Stock Market. Unpublished Vienna University of Technology working paper.

Baron, D. (1982) A model of the demand for investment banking advising and distribution services for new issues. *Journal of Finance* 37, 955–976.

Barry, C. (1989) Initial public offerings underpricing: The issuer's view – A comment. *Journal of Finance* 44, 1099–1103.

Barry, C., and R. Jennings (1993) The opening price performance of initial public offerings of common stock. *Financial Management* 22, 54–63.

Barry, C., C. Muscarella, J. Peavy, and M. Vetsuypens (1990) The role of venture capital in the creation of public companies: Evidence from the going public process. *Journal of Financial Economics* 27, 447–471.

Barry, C., R. Gilson, and J. R. Ritter (1998) Initial public offerings and fraud on the market. Unpublished TCU, Stanford, and University of Florida working paper.

Beatty, R. P., and J. R. Ritter (1986) Investment banking, reputation, and the underpricing of initial public offerings. *Journal of Financial Economics* 15, 213–232.

Beatty, R. P., and I. Welch (1996) Issuer expenses and legal liability in initial public offerings. *Journal of Law and Economics* 39, 545–602.

Benveniste, L., and P. Spindt (1989) How investment bankers determine the offer price and allocation of new issues. *Journal of Financial Economics* 24, 343–361.

Benveniste, L., and W. Wilhelm (1990) A comparative analysis of IPO proceeds under alternative regulatory environments. *Journal of Financial Economics* 28, 173–207.

Benveniste, L., and W. Wilhelm (1997) Initial public offerings: Going by the book. *Journal of Applied Corporate Finance* 10, 98–108.

Bisgard, S. (1997) Danish initial public offerings, unpublished Copenhagen Business School masters thesis.

Booth, J., and L. Chua (1995) Ownership dispersion, costly information, and IPO underpricing. *Journal of Financial Economics* 41, 291–310.

Bray, A., and P. Gompers (1997) Myth or reality? The long-run underperformance of initial public offerings: Evidence from venture and nonventure capital-backed companies. *Journal of Finance* 52, 1791–1821.

Brennan, M., and J. Franks (1995) Underpricing, ownership and control in initial public offerings of equity securities in the U.K. *Journal of Financial Economics* 45, 391–413.

Cai, J., and K. C. Wei (1997) The investment and operating performance of Japanese IPO firms. *Pacific-Basin Finance Journal* 5, 389–417.

Carter, R., R. Dark, and A. Singh (1997) Underwriter reputation, initial returns, and the long-run performance of IPO stocks. *Journal of Finance* 53, 289–311.

Chemmanur, T. J., and P. Fulghieri (1994) Investment banker reputation, information production, and financial intermediation. *Journal of Finance* 49, 57–79.

Chowdhry, B., and V. Nanda (1996) Stabilization, syndication, and pricing of IPOs. *Journal of Financial and Quantitative Analysis* 31, 25–42.

Chowdhry, B., and A. Sherman (1996) The winner's curse and international methods of allocating initial public offerings. *Pacific-Basin Finance Journal* 4, 15–30.

Datar, V., and Mao (1997) Initial public offerings in China: Why is underpricing so severe? Working paper, Seattle University.

Drake, P. D., and M. R. Vetsuypens (1993) IPO underpricing: Insurance against legal liability? *Financial Management* 22, 64–73.

Dunbar, C. (1995) The use of warrants as underwriter compensation in initial public offerings. *Journal of Financial Economics* 38, 59–78.

Garfinkel, J. (1993) IPO underpricing, insider selling and subsequent equity offerings: Is underpricing a signal of quality? *Financial Management* 22, 74–83.

Grinblatt, M., and C. Y. Hwang (1989) Signalling and the pricing of new issues. *Journal of Finance* 44, 393–420.

Hamao, Y., F. Packer, and J. R. Ritter (1998) Institutional affiliation and the role of venture capital: Evidence from Initial Public Offerings in Japan, Unpublished Columbia University working paper.

Hanley, K. W. (1993) Underpricing of initial public offerings and the partial adjustment phenomenon. *Journal of Financial Economics* 34, 231–250.

Hanley, K. W., and J. R. Ritter (1992) Going public. *The New Palgrave Dictionary of Money and Finance*. London: MacMillan.

Hebner, K. J., and T. Hiraki (1993) Japanese initial public offerings. *Restructuring Japan's Financial Markets*. Edited by I. Walter and T. Hiraki. Homewood, IL: Business One/Irwin.

Ibbotson, R. G. (1975) Price performance of common stock new issues. *Journal of Financial Economics* 2, 235–272.

Ibbotson, R. G., and J. F. Jaffe (1975) "Hot issue" markets. *Journal of Finance* 30, 1027–1042.

Ibbotson, R. G., and J. R. Ritter (1995) Initial Public Offerings. Chapter 30 of *North-Holland Handbooks in Operations Research and Management Science, Vol. 9: Finance*. Edited by R. Jarrow, V. Maksimovic, and W. Ziemba.

Ibbotson, R. G., J. Sindelar, and J. Ritter (1994) The market's problems with the pricing of initial public offerings. *Journal of Applied Corporate Finance* 7, 66–74.

Jain, B., and O. Kini (1994) The post-issue operating performance of IPO firms. *Journal of Finance* 49, 1699–1726.

James, C. (1992) Relationship specific assets and the pricing of underwriter services. *Journal of Finance* 47, 1865–1885.

James, C., and P. Wier (1990) Borrowing relationships, intermediation, and the costs of issuing public securities. *Journal of Financial Economics* 28, 149–171.

Jegadeesh, N., M. Weinstein, and I. Welch (1993) An empirical investigation of IPO returns and subsequent equity offerings. *Journal of Financial Economics* 34, 153–175.

Jenkinson, T., and A. Ljungqvist (1996) *Going Public: The Theory and Evidence on How Companies Raise Equity Finance.* Oxford: Clarendon Press.

Jog, V. M., and A. Srivastava (1994) Underpricing of Canadian initial public offerings 1971–1992 – An update. *FINECO* 4, 81–89.

Kazantzis, C., and M. Levis (1995) Price support and initial public offerings: Evidence from the Athens Stock Exchange. *Research in International Business and Finance* 12, JAI Press.

Keloharju, M. (1993) The winner's curse, legal liability, and the long-run price performance of initial public offerings in Finland. *Journal of Financial Economics* 34, 251–277.

Kim, M., and J. Ritter (1997) Valuing IPOs, unpublished University of Florida working paper.

Kiymaz, H. (1997) Turkish IPO underpricing in the short and long run. Unpublished Bilkent University working paper.

Krigman, L., W. Shaw, and K. Womack (1997) The persistence of IPO mispricing and the predictive power of flipping, unpublished Dartmouth College working paper.

Krishnamurti, C., and P. Kumar (1994) The initial listing performance of Indian IPOs. Unpublished Indian Institute of Science working paper, Bangalore.

Lee, I., S. Lochhead, J. Ritter, and Q. Zhao (1996) The costs of raising capital. *Journal of Financial Research* 19, 59–74.

Lee, P., S. Taylor, and T. Walter (1996) Australian IPO underpricing in the short and long run. *Journal of Banking and Finance* 20, 1189–1210.

Leland, H., and D. Pyle (1977) Informational asymmetries, financial structure and financial intermediation. *Journal of Finance* 32, 371–387.

Lerner, Josh (1994) Venture capitalists and the decision to go public. *Journal of Financial Economics* 35, 293–316.

Levis, M. (1993) The long-run performance of initial public offerings: The UK experience 1980–88. *Financial Management* 22, 28–41.

Ling, D., and M. Ryngaert (1997) Valuation uncertainty, institutional involvement, and the underpricing of IPOs: The case of REITs. *Journal of Financial Economics* 43, 433–456.

Ljungqvist, A. P. (1997) Pricing initial public offerings: Further evidence from Germany. *European Economic Review* 41, 1309–1320.

Logue, D. (1973) On the pricing of unseasoned equity issues: 1965–69. *Journal of Financial and Quantitative Analysis* 8, 91–103.

Loughran, T. (1993) NYSE vs NASDAQ returns: Market microstructure or the poor performance of IPOs? *Journal of Financial Economics* 33, 241–260.

Loughran, T., and J. R. Ritter (1995) The new issues puzzle. *Journal of Finance* 50, 23–51.

Loughran, T., J. R. Ritter, and K. Rydqvist (1994) Initial public offerings: International insights. *Pacific-Basin Finance Journal* 2, 165–199.

Michaely, R., and W. Shaw (1994) The pricing of initial public offerings: Tests of adverse selection and signaling theories. *Review of Financial Studies* 7, 279–317.

Miller, E. (1977) Risk, uncertainty, and divergence of opinion. *Journal of Finance* 32, 1151–1168.

Miller, R., and F. Reilly (1987) An examination of mispricing, returns, and uncertainty for initial public offerings. *Financial Management* 16, 33–38.

Muscarella, C., and M. Vetsuypens (1989) A simple test of Baron's model of IPO underpricing. *Journal of Financial Economics* 24, 125–135.

Pagano, M., F. Panetta, and L. Zingales (1998) Why do firms go public? An empirical analysis. *Journal of Finance*, forthcoming.

Rajan, R., and H. Servaes (1997) Analyst following of initial public offerings. *Journal of Finance* 52, 507–529.

Ritter, J. R. (1984a) The "hot issue" market of 1980. *Journal of Business* 57, 215–240.

Ritter, J. R. (1984b) Signaling and the valuation of unseasoned new issues: A comment. *Journal of Finance* 39, 1231–1237.

Ritter, J. R. (1987) The costs of going public. *Journal of Financial Economics* 19, 269–281.

Ritter, J. R. (1991) The long-run performance of initial public offerings, *Journal of Finance* 46, 3–27.

Rock, K. (1986) Why new issues are underpriced. *Journal of Financial Economics* 15, 187–212.

Sahlman, W. (1988) Aspects of financial contracting in venture capital. *Journal of Applied Corporate Finance* 1, 23–36.

Schneider, C., J. Manko, and R. Kant (1996) Going public: practice, procedures and consequences. This is an updated reprint of a 1981 *Villanova Law Review* article, available from Bowne Financial Printers of Tampa, Florida.

Schultz, P. (1993) Unit initial public offerings: A form of staged financing. *Journal of Financial Economics* 34, 199–229.

Shiller, R. J. (1990) Speculative prices and popular models. *Journal of Economic Perspectives* 4, 55–65.

Siconolfi, M. (1997) Underwriters set aside IPO stock for officials of potential customers. *Wall Street Journal* November 12, A1.

Simon, C. (1989) The effect of the 1933 securities act on investor information and the performance of new issues. *American Economic Review* 79, 295–318.

Smith, C. (1986) Investment banking and the capital acquisition process. *Journal of Financial Economics* 15, 3–29.

Uttal, B. (1986) Inside the deal that made Bill Gates $350,000,000. *Fortune* (July 21), 343–361.

Welch, I. (1991) An empirical examination of models of contract choice in initial public offerings. *Journal of Financial and Quantitative Analysis* 26, 497–518.

Welch, I. (1992) Sequential sales, learning, and cascades. *Journal of Finance* 47, 695–732.

Zeune, Gary D. (1997) *Going Public: What the CFO Needs to Know.* Forthcoming from the AICPA.

Reproduced from *Contemporary Finance Digest*, Vol. 2 No.1 (Spring 1998), pp. 5–30.

Google Press Cuttings

(A) ARE YOU ABOUT TO GET GOOGLED?

Tony Glover

It has been one of the canniest image-building exercises ever. From a standing start less than six years ago, the name Google has risen to stand alongside Coke and Ford as a giant among American brands. The search-engine company, which this weekend is distributing shares to investors who have signed up to its initial public offering (IPO), has become synonymous with being the coolest, fastest, most reliable place to find information on the web.

But all is not well in the land of Google. The IPO process has been bungled: many big institutions who have been left out of the process by the bizarre auction method being used to allocate shares are angry at the way it is being floated. They accuse its founders of wanting too much money and they claim it has an unproven business model.

The behaviour of the two, young nerdish founders in the run-up to the bid has bordered on the farcical. Late last week they were under fire for possibly leaking information – not to a leading financial newspaper or a broker, but to a girlie magazine.

Many fear the IPO harks back to the worst years of dot.com excesses. "You've been googled" looks likely to enter the business world's phrasebook, as a saying for investors being persuaded to buy something risky that they don't really want.

There have been many signs that the IPO has not been going as well as the founders had hoped, although the press releases will undoubtedly claim otherwise. Traffic to the internet site where investors had to register for Google's IPO of stock has been lower than anticipated in the run-up to the Thursday evening deadline for registration to the Dutch auction-style share sale.

Online bookmakers were last week receiving bets suggesting that people expect the share price to drop when trading in the stock begins, supporting the view of most institutions that Google may have set its initial price too high.

Silicon Valley tends to favour positive-sounding buzzwords like "empowerment" over old-fashioned pejorative terms such as "greed". But, with an initial target price range of $108 (£59.40, E89.04) to $132 a share, Google founders Larry Page and Sergey Brin are valuing their company at a huge 170 times last year's earnings. By valuing their search engine company at between $29bn and $35bn, Google's founders and early investors stand to become overnight billionaires.

The future is less assured for new investors in the stock. Analysts warn that Google's IPO is playing in a very different market today than it was last year, when Page and Brin first announced their IPO plans.

The company now faces heavyweight competition from new rivals including mighty Microsoft. Worse, Google's own business model is being overshadowed by lawsuits and industry reports of companies mischievously manipulating Google's advertising charges.

The behaviour of the founders in the run-up to the bid has also raised eyebrows. An interview with Page and Brin published last week in Playboy magazine cast a cloud over the IPO by potentially breaking US "quiet period", rules which forbid company executives from releasing price sensitive information in the run-up to a share offering. Earlier meetings with potential investors left many potential investors frustrated at the lack of key financial information.

In addition, the world that Google will be trading in is likely to change dramatically over the next few years. Although the search engine company is a different proposition to the failed dot.coms of five years ago, generating revenues of $1.5bn last year, roughly 95% is from online advertising, and the company's business is still far from mature. Search engines are still in their infancy and the internet itself is about to undergo a revolution that may make many of today's business models redundant within a year. Microsoft and Yahoo are developing software designed to surpass Google's current search engine.

Microsoft is also a key player in the video and audio revolution that is about to transform the internet from a text and picture-based medium to a kind of interactive TV and film library. This transformation is being made possible by the global rollout of broadband internet connections. Data speeds fast enough to receive live video streaming are fast becoming standard in fixed-line internet connections with wireless connections using technologies such as wi-fi and wi-max catching up.

Google could rightly argue that the expansion of the internet represents a vast revenue opportunity. The theory is that by buying into Google at the dawn of the internet's new age, investors are getting into the next Microsoft on the ground floor. But the trouble is, Microsoft itself, with tens of billions in ready cash, has its own plans to become the next giant of the broadband internet age. It has already signed software deals with service providers such as British Telecom as well as with the world's leading electronics manufacturers. Rival Yahoo also has an advantage over Google because of its large, loyal customer base of e-mail users.

As a small start-up and as a private company, Google was able to run through the legs of global corporations like Microsoft and establish a reputation for irreverence and humour. Its propensity to add seasonal features such as snow to the tops of the brightly coloured lettering of its distinctive logo bears testimony to its founders' youthful exuberance, as do the extensive recreational facilities of its sprawing Googleplex offices.

But as a listed company with a market value of around $30bn, Google will be thrust into the adult corporate world of quarterly reporting and share-price fluctuations. Its founders argue that, by selling direct to small investors, the company will retain an independence not shared by blue-chip

rivals who must take the views of their big institutional investors into account
. . .

   Because of the unique way in which Page and Brin have decided to bring
their company to market, these challenges could have a disproportionate
effect on Google's share price. Google is more vulnerable to shifting market
sentiment than it might have been had it pursued a more traditional strategy.
Most major IPOs are done in close collaboration with major stockbrokers
who place the bulk of the shares with a small number of financial institutions. This enables the brokers to set the share price accurately in advance
of the offering. Page and Brin eschewed this method because they wanted to
retain independent control of corporate strategy after the IPO and because
they believed they could raise more cash by auctioning Google shares over
the internet.

   Some of the annoyance at the process of the IPO is undoubtedly down to
sour grapes and lost fees. Wall Street has largely been excluded from
Google's IPO process and, at a time when investment banking revenues are
low, the bankers fear they are missing out on the hottest deal of the year.

   Yet it is hard to dismiss claims that the hyping of the share offering is
obscuring real worries about the IPO, in the wake of market uncertainty and
the series of corporate blunders. Google has been one of the darlings of the
recent dot.com revival.

   Those who invest in Google must hope that they haven't "been googled"
and set to become victims of the hubris and overblown expectations that have
characterised many companies in the technology sector over the past few
years.

(B) IGNORE WALL ST'S WHINING – GOOGLE'S IPO WORKED

James Surowiecki

When Google went public yesterday, it immediately became one of the most
highly valued companies in the world. Sergey Brin and Larry Page, its co-
founders, are now billionaires (at least on paper). And the company raised
an immense pile of cash that will stand it in very good stead as it faces an
increasingly competitive future. You might think, then, that Google's initial
public offering was a success. But that is far from the message from Wall
Street and much of the financial press. They prefer words such as "debacle"
and "amateur hour" to describe Google's performance. On this view, Google
looks like a runner staggering across the finish line, out of breath and gasping
for water.

   The obvious reason for describing Google this way is that the company
had to cut the price of its share offer and reduce the number of shares that
would be sold. Wall Street has interpreted this as evidence that Google's decision to circumvent the traditional IPO process – going directly to investors
with a "Dutch auction" instead of allowing an investment bank to underwrite

its shares – was a terrible mistake. Had the company just given itself over to the Street's warm embrace, everything would have turned out fine.

This is undoubtedly a comforting story for investment bankers to tell themselves as they cling to their lucrative sinecures. But that is bunk. In the first place, Google's valuation is, by any standard, a quite healthy one. When the company first announced it was planning to go public, most estimated that the company would end up with a market cap of $15bn (£8.2bn) to $25bn. When trading started yesterday, it was worth $27bn. The company did have to mark down its price from the initial range it had suggested back in April, but that was almost entirely the result of the recent minor meltdown in technology shares.

If Google's unorthodox method of going public has had any impact on the company's stock price, it is only because it forced Wall Street into a con-certed whispering campaign designed to sabotage the IPO. It is hardly a coin-cidence that after Google directly challenged Wall Street's stranglehold on the capital-raising process, it suddenly went from being among the most-loved companies in America to among the most criticised. Much of the bad-mouthing we heard before the IPO came from money managers looking to talk down the company's price so that they could get a better bargain. One of the more laughable aspects of the whole Google circus has been false sanc-timony about "valuation" from money managers who happily bought Cisco when its market capitalisation was $400bn and from Wall Street investment banks that bid internet stocks up to billion-dollar market caps. We can be forgiven for thinking that something other than devotion to the principles of Warren Buffett is at work.

As self-serving as most of these attacks on Google have been, even more dismaying have been the criticisms levied against the Dutch-auction method. Because a Dutch auction in effect allows investors to set the IPO price col-lectively it makes it unlikely that a company's stock price will soar soon after it goes public. This is an entirely good thing, since the higher the price at which a company goes public, the more money it will raise. But in the looking-glass world in which Google has found itself, the absence of that big first-day "pop" has been labelled a problem, proof that the company is "greedy" and that the whole IPO has been just a greed-fest.

This is a sign of how much of our thinking about markets is deeply con-fused. The stock market is, at least in part, a mechanism for allocating capital (and during an IPO, that is exactly what it is). The better it does that job, the better the economy as a whole will be. What that entails is getting prices roughly right. A big first-day pop is a sign that the opening price was wrong, not a sign that it was right. As for Google's supposed greediness, it is doing precisely what it is supposed to be doing: maximising the value it gets for selling off part of the company. Because it used the Dutch auction, it knows it is getting what people were really willing to pay, instead of what a coterie of investment bankers thought their friends and cronies should have to pay.

Google's IPO was hardly perfect. But it looks positively brilliant compared with the way Wall Street takes companies public. That route is rife with conflicts of interest and gives investment banks a clear incentive to hold down the opening price – essentially taking money from a company and distributing it to the investment bank's clients and customers.

Wall Street can spin this however it wants. But Google went public without underwriting from a major investment bank, without handing out favours to well-connected executives and without dictating a price in the manner of Soviet central planners. Because it did, it now has hundreds of millions of dollars that it would not otherwise have had. By any standard, this was one IPO that worked.

(C) GOOGLE'S EARNINGS MORE THAN DOUBLE 1ST QUARTERLY RESULTS AS PUBLIC FIRM STRONG

Robert Weisman

Web search provider Google Inc., posting its first financial results as a public company, yesterday said its third-quarter earnings and revenues both more than doubled from a year ago on the strength of an online advertising boom that continues to gather steam.

Google's shares jumped $8.89, or 6.33 percent, to $149.38 in Nasdaq trading yesterday in anticipation of the earnings report, which was released after the market closed. In after-hours trading, Google's shares continued racing ahead, reaching a high of $162.15. The company, based in Mountain View, Calif., priced its stock at $85 a share on Aug. 19, raising $1.67 billion in an auction-style initial public offering that had riveted the attention of the investment community throughout the summer.

Because company executives have broken with technology industry practice by refusing to offer guidance about their financial outlook, investors had looked to yesterday's report to help them gauge the value of a stock that has behaved like a dot-com era highflier over the past two months while the overall market has been weak.

The results did not disappoint. Google's earnings of $52 million, or 19 cents a share, were up from $20.4 million, or 8 cents a share, in the July-to-September period last year. And without one-time charges to cover its stock-based compensation and the settlement of a patent dispute with rival Yahoo Inc., Google said it would have earned 70 cents a share. That beat the consensus estimate of 56 cents a share from securities analysts polled by the Thomson Financial research firm.

Google executives, in a conference call with analysts, said the company is continuing to ride the wave of Internet advertising, which it distributes next to its search results and next to content on third-party partner sites. "Online advertising is becoming a larger and larger percentage of global advertising spending," noted Larry Page, Google cofounder and president for products. Google's own sites accounted for 51 percent of its advertising revenue for the three months ending Sept. 30, with its partner sites accounting for 48 percent.

The company reported overall third-quarter revenue of $805.9 million, up from $393.9 million for the same period a year ago.

While the company's top managers discussed a range of new initiatives, from the launch of a desktop search feature to the opening of a European headquarters in Dublin, they stopped short of unveiling the kind of integrated strategy some Google watchers were anticipating.

"Until such time as they know what the whole house is going to look like, they're not going to reveal the blueprint," suggested David M. Garrity, a technology analyst for Caris & Co. in New York, who said Google's valuation may be justified not simply by Internet advertising but by a larger computing strategy. "Right now they're still in the process of expanding into their potential end point, which is replacing Microsoft. I think their intention is to take our computing experience and make it more Web-centric rather than personal computer-centric."

Google faces stiff competition from Microsoft and Yahoo, which have beefed up their search initiatives this year.

While noting the strength of Google's business, Scott Kessler, a Standard & Poor's equity analyst, said he was concerned about the run-up of its share price. "A lot of people see that these shares are being bought regardless of valuation," he said. "But once there's a chink in the armor, people will sell the shares without reservation."

(D) HOW HIGH CAN GOOGLE FLY?

Verne Kopytoff

The popular Internet search engine has defied gravity since the company's high-profile initial public offering less than six months ago.

Google's stock has soared 140 percent, closing Wednesday at $205.96, up $14.06 on the heels of a stellar fourth quarter. The rise has been so dramatic that the company, once run out of a Stanford University dorm room, now has a market capitalization of $56.3 billion, larger than eBay and Yahoo individually and larger than General Motors and Ford Motor Co. combined.

Several analysts are predicting even bigger success for Google's stock over the next year. However, the forecasts raise comparisons to the Internet bubble, when some analysts made stratospheric projections about companies that ultimately foundered.

Whatever the case, Google has consistently defied naysayers. The legions of investors who stood on the sidelines for the company's IPO, believing the stock at $85 was an impending train wreck, have missed out on a big potential payday.

"The company has certainly been able to drive revenues at a better rate than we thought possible," said David Garrity, an analyst for Caris & Co. who increased his price target on Google Wednesday to $300.

Other analysts issued reports Wednesday that were almost as positive. John Tinker of Think Equity Partners placed a target of $290 on Google's shares in a report titled "Search On." Mark Mahaney of American Technology Research upped his target to $275 in a note titled "The Michael Jordan of the Nets."

Garrity denied any return to the overexuberance of the late 1990s, saying: "Back then, these were companies that were hemorrhaging cash, these were people who were blowing half their annual ad budgets on a 30-second Super Bowl ad, and holding parties that cost way too much."

Indeed, Google is unlike its predecessors. For the fourth quarter, the company reported a profit of $204.1 million on $1.03 billion in revenue.

Google, based in Mountain View, makes its money by running ads alongside its search results and on partner Web sites. Each time a visitor clicks on an ad, the advertiser pays a fee.

Using Wall Street's favorite stock yardstick, the price-to-earnings ratio, Google's shares are pricey. Based on Wednesday's closing price, Google's price-to-earnings ratio for 2004 was 142.8 versus 26.2 for the Nasdaq 100, 69.2 for eBay and 61.7 for Yahoo.

But analysts expect Google's valuation to become more reasonable in the future because of its rapid growth. For 2005, analysts forecast the company's price-to-earnings ratio will be 53.34 versus 51.44 for eBay and 67.95 for Yahoo.

However, Pete Sealey, an adjunct professor of marketing at UC Berkeley, is skeptical of Google's ability to sustain the climb. He said that the frenzy hasn't reached the proportions of 1999, but that hype is nevertheless a factor in the rise.

"If I were advising someone in my family or investing money for my kid's college education, would I put my money in Google?" Sealey said. "No."

There's too much risk, he added. Yahoo and Microsoft's MSN could ultimately steal market share and hurt Google's financial prospects, he said.

Don MacAskill, who bought five Google shares in its initial public offering, said that he is happy with the stock's performance and has no plans to sell. He bought in for the long term because of the way the company is run and its unconventional policies such as refusing to give financial forecasts in defiance of Wall Street tradition.

MacAskill, who is chief executive of Smugmug, an online photo storage service in Mountain View, said that many investors in eBay's IPO sold their shares quickly, missing out on that company's subsequent meteoric ascension.

"For me, the decision to sell would be more based on the behavior of the company in terms of its approach in hiring and taking care of its employees than actual financial numbers," MacAskill said.

(E) BOWLING FOR GOOGLE

Paul R. La Monica

Is Google on its way to hitting a perfect bowling score, a $300 stock price, in the near future? At Tuesday's closing price of $256, it's less than 20 percent away.

Shares of the leading search engine have been on a tear, shooting up 25 percent since the company reported much better than expected sales and earnings for the first quarter, thanks to a booming market for online advertising.

During the past month, Google has also released several new features – including a desktop search function for businesses and a test version of a personalized home page tool – that should help the company remain competitive against rivals Yahoo! and Microsoft.

Most recently, speculatoin that Google will soon be added to the S&P 500 index has helped propel the stock higher.

So is it possible that Google could continue climbing? Is $300 in the bag and should we be talking about Google hitting $350 or higher?

Investors Still Feel Lucky

Crazy as it may sound, Google could still have a lot more upside. Sure, the stock price looks frothy on an absolute basis. Few companies have prices in the triple digits, let alone, approaching $300.

But Google has maintained that it would not split its stock to make the shares more affordable for the average investor. Clearly, that hasn't hindered the stock's performance.

In fact, data from Vickers Stock Research suggests that Google's surge has been fueled by retail investors, not big mutual funds. According to Vickers, only 35 percent of Google's shares are held by institutional investors while 73 percent of Yahoo!'s shares are owned by mutual funds and other money managers.

So what's more important for investors to look at is not the dollar amount of Google's stock price but what Google's valuation is relative to its peers. And on that basis, Google still looks reasonably attractive, if not exactly cheap.

Shares trade at 50 times 2005 earnings estimates and 39 times 2006 projections. Yahoo!, on the other hand, trades at 64 times 2005 profit forecasts and has a P/E of 50 times 2006 estimates.

Steve Weinstein, an analyst with Pacific Crest Securities, said that Google's fundamentals could justify a $330 stock price. At that level, Google would trade at a multiple in line with Yahoo!

If anything, Google looks to be the company that deserves the premium right now. It has reported stronger gains in sales and earnings than Yahoo!

lately since Google has more exposure to the online advertising market, specifically ads tied to key word search results, than Yahoo!

"In the short-term, Google could grow faster than Yahoo!, as it has over the past few quarters," said Marianne Wolk, an analyst with Susquehanna Financial Group.

To that end, earnings estimates for Google have risen at a meteoric pace.

Three months ago, analysts expected Google's earnings to come in at $3.94 a share this year. Now the consensus estimate is $5.14 a share, an increase of 30 percent. Likewise, estimates for 2006 have surged nearly 30 percent in the past three months, from $5.14 a share to current projections of $6.56 a share.

By way of comparison, estimates for Yahoo! have increased by about 10 percent for 2005 and 2006 during the past three months.

Searching for the S&P 500

The S&P 500 speculation is also worth keeping an eye on. I wrote last year about why I thought Google probably would be added to the index sometime in 2005.

At the time, the only major knock against Google was that less than half of its outstanding shares were available to the public. One of Standard & Poor's criteria for adding a stock to the index is that a company's float, or available share, must be at least 50 percent of the total shares.

That's no longer an issue. According to Vickers, the float now accounts for nearly two-thirds of shares outstanding. And if Google does get added to the S&P, many institutions that run index funds would have to buy the stock.

"We view the possible inclusion of Google in the S&P as a potential positive catalyst due to the relatively low institutional ownership as compared to Yahoo! and eBay," wrote David Edwards, an analyst with American Technology Research in a recent report.

Since going public last August, Google has faced a lot of skepticism (from me included) and has defied all the critics.

Fears about how the stock could take a hit following a deluge of new shares hitting the market after IPO lock-up periods expired were for naught.

Worries about a slowdown in Internet ad spending proved temporary.

And the valuation, while rich, never seems to have gotten ahead of itself because the stock has simply moved higher as earnings estimates for Google have increased.

So as long as online ad spending doesn't take a sudden sharp turn downward, it's hard to imagine Google's stock losing serious ground.

"Internet advertising is in its infancy. The long-term prospects for Google are quite strong," said Wolk.

(F) GOOGLE'S RISING SHARE PRICE IS COLD COMFORT FOR INVESTORS

Stephen Schurr

Google's stock briefly reached $300 last week, a stratospheric rise from its $85 offer price less than a year ago. The good news for Google investors is that the stock's valuation has not approached the insane, untenable levels touched five years ago by the likes of Cisco, Oracle, Yahoo and JDS Uniphase.

The bad news: Google's valuations can be justified only in the best of all possible worlds, and even then, returns may be decidedly less than investors expect.

Before 2000, no stock market had seen companies with market capitalisations in tens of billions carrying price-to-earnings multiples near 100. It is also worth noting that none of the above companies trade anywhere near their bubble-level prices. On current estimates, Google, whose market cap is $82bn, sports a price-to-earnings multiple of 56.

"While we're not where we were five years ago, Google is still extremely high," said Jeremy Siegel, finance professor at Wharton and author of The Future for Investors.

The online search engine is expected to increase its earnings by 33 per cent a year for the next three to five years – no small feat, even for a growth company of epic proportions such as Google. If it achieves that growth, and the stock hits returns of 10 per cent a year for those five years, Google's p/e will be a high but reasonable 22 after five years.

In this sanguine scenario, Google continues its rapid growth, stockholders get 10 per cent a year and the stock is reasonably valued.

But are Google's risk-friendly investors comfortable with accepting huge potential downside risk for 10 per cent a year?

The fact that Google compares favourably with 2000's burst bubble is cold comfort. "Right now," said Fred Hickey, writer for the High-Tech Strategist newsletter, "Google is the mania." He notes that most of Google's earnings rise stems not from internet growth, which is slowing, but from price rises for the word-search-based advertisements it sells.

Of all the lessons of the tech bubble, two best apply to Google. First, in technology, no moat can protect you from competition. Second, earnings growth based on pricing power almost inevitably erodes due to competition. Arguably the only company that has been able to defy these lessons is Microsoft, which also presents a threat to Google.

The risk associated with Google's stock may have been best summed up by Steve Ballmer, Microsoft chief executive. In an interview with Computer Reseller News, Mr Ballmer was asked why he did not just buy Google.

He said: "There's not something there I want to buy. I'm not saying it's not a good company. It's a very expensive company. Do you actually believe there's not enough innovation in search that somebody's not going to challenge them? It's the easiest application in the world to switch."

Section 4

Adding Value through Risk Management

SECTION OVERVIEW

Martin Upton

When I joined the treasury of a major UK financial services company in 1987 there were no risk managers in the division. The treasury was staffed by the dealers in the "front office" and a small "back office" team. The division employed only one primitive computer system. This provided a valuation of the holdings of government securities, which constituted only a small proportion of the total assets held in the company's investment portfolio.

At the end of trading each day the front office staff helped out the back office team by manually updating portfolio records and valuations. A PC-based valuation model was introduced a few months after I joined, albeit programmed by one of the dealers!

The world had changed seventeen years later when I left the company. The treasury division then had a large risk management department (known as the "middle office") with staff numbers matching those in the front office. The division also had its own legal and compliance team. Strict segregation of duties applied: front office staff were denied free access to the middle and back offices by the introduction of key card systems. The front office reciprocated by similarly controlling access to the dealing room by the middle and back office staff. Remuneration levels for middle office staff were rising to match those of the dealers. Extensive use of treasury computer systems was made to ensure correct market valuations and compliance with the risk management controls on market, operational and credit risks. The Financial Services Authority had a regular dialogue with the division and periodically visited to assess the technical competence of treasury management and the soundness of the control infrastructure. In the wake of these developments – that matched those elsewhere in the financial services industry – it was not uncommon to hear dealers and brokers comment that treasury divisions had been taken over by the risk managers.

Looking back at the emergence of the culture of risk management it is tempting to ascribe it as a reaction to the series of high profile treasury calamities of the past twenty years. In 1991, activities by UK local authorities in derivatives were deemed unlawful (and hence unenforceable) after a protracted legal case that made it all the way to the House of Lords. The judgement triggered a plethora of litigation as parties to the voided derivative contracts sought financial restitution.

Seven years on came the demise of Barings Bank as a result of losses on derivatives trading incurred in its Singapore subsidiary. The speed of the collapse of Barings staggered the financial markets: as one former senior employee remarked, "on the Friday before it happened we were arranging international loans; on the following Monday the milkman was refusing to deliver to us"!

The fall-out from the collapse of Barings probably helped to encourage changes to banking supervision – with the Government moving this from the Bank of England to the newly formed Financial Services Authority in 2000. Additionally the collapse spawned extensive guidance from regulators and professional bodies about risk management practices and standards. Fundamentally, though, the lesson from Barings was a simple one – front and back office activities need to be segregated to ensure that dealers cannot conceal their trading positions. Indeed inadequate segregation of responsibilities was also at the heart of the huge trading losses incurred by the Allied Irish Bank's US subsidiary Allfirst in 2002. One of the articles in this section looks at this episode in detail.

The collapse of the US energy company Enron in 2001 also showed that there were major lessons in risk management to be learnt. Enron did employ risk managers and extensive risk management systems. The problem appears to have been that senior management did not sufficiently empower the risk managers to rein in the company's trading activities. Again the demise of Enron and subsequently WorldCom prompted legislation in the US in the form of the Sarbanes-Oxley Act of 2002 requiring, *inter alia*, closer understanding and stewardship of company financial risks by senior management.

The above are only a sample of the recent episodes of organisations failing in the task of risk management. These have been very influential in the direction and pace of the growth of risk management around the globe. In all probability, though, this evolution in risk management would have happened without them. One reason to believe this is that the growing globalisation and the associated increase in the complexity of the financial activities of organisations, particularly in their treasury transactions, has necessitated a more considered and fully resourced approach to risk management. For example, at the company for whom I worked the move from being a solely sterling-based operation to a multi-currency treasury necessitated measuring and managing foreign exchange (FX) exposure. A second factor supporting the evolution of risk management has been the development of computer systems – and the capacity of these to be built to produce bespoke solutions for organisations. These now provide the means of applying active risk management and the monitoring of controls in a live environment without inhibiting the pace of trading activities in the front office.

The articles selected for this section are intended to provide coverage of the main financial risks facing organisations – interest rate, foreign exchange, contingency, operational, refinancing and credit risk – and analysis of how risk management techniques can be employed to manage them.

Foreign exchange risk – the exposure to potential losses from changes in exchange rates – is well understood and is a financial risk for many organisations. The impact of "operating" (or, as also termed, "economic") exposure is less well understood. The article by Donald Lessard and John Lightstone, "Operating Exposure", examines this subject and helps us understand that this is a further – and in many ways more complicated – facet to foreign exchange risk than that arising through "transaction" and "translation" exposures.

The article by Sharon Burke, "Currency Exchange Trading and Rogue Trader John Rusnak", details the foreign exchange transactions that resulted in losses of US$691 m by Allied Irish Bank's US subsidiary Allfirst in 2002. The article is more than just a catalogue of bad – and false – FX transactions and options trades: it should be compulsory reading for anyone managing or auditing a treasury function. The article documents the operational weaknesses in Allfirst's treasury department that provided the fertile environment for a "rogue trader". The flawed FX trades that led to the losses could not have happened within a well controlled treasury. Read the article and see if you agree with me.

We then move on to look at the current favourite "tool" of risk managers worldwide: "Value at Risk" or "VaR". The article by Christopher Culp, Merton Miller and Andrea Neves, "Value at Risk: Uses and Abuses", provides not only a lucid explanation of VaR methodology but also a critique of its usefulness for managing interest rate and other risks. The article assesses how well the technique would have helped avoid the financial calamities (or "derivatives disasters" as the authors call them) that befell Procter & Gamble, Barings, Metallgesellschaft and Orange County.

The next article, "Learning to Live with Fixed Rate Mortgages", is my own contribution, and looks at interest rate risk management in practice by studying the evolving approach to hedging mortgage products in the UK financial services industry. In addition to examining the use of various hedging instruments, like swaps and options, the article demonstrates an evolutionary approach to risk management where methods of hedging are refined in the wake of growing experience about customer activity. Hedging efficiently here involves second-guessing customer behaviour – a difficult task since such behaviour is often financially irrational!

We then move on to examine *the* growth area in risk management since the 1990s: credit derivatives. "Credit Derivatives" by John Kiff and Ron Morrow provides a succinct and intelligible examination of this complex subject and identifies the advantages and disadvantages of these risk management tools.

EXCHANGE RATE ENVIRONMENT

To understand the impact of exchange rates on operating profit, we need to understand both the long- and short-term behaviour of exchange rates.

The exchange rate environment is characterised by a long-term tendency for changes in the nominal US dollar/foreign currency exchange rate to be approximately equal to the difference between the rates of inflation in the price of traded goods in the US and the foreign country.[1] If the inflation rate in the US is 4 per cent greater than the Japanese inflation rate during the year, the Yen will tend to strengthen approximately 4 per cent against the dollar. This long-term relationship between exchange rates and price levels – usually called purchasing power parity (PPP) – implies that changes in competitiveness between countries, which would otherwise arise because of unequal rates of inflation, tend to be offset by corresponding changes in the exchange rate between the two countries. However, in the short-term of six months to several years, exchange rates are extremely volatile and have a major impact on the relative competitiveness of companies selling into the same market but sourcing from different countries.

This change in relative competitiveness in the short term is the result of changes in the nominal exchange rate which are not offset by the difference in inflation rates in the two countries. If the Yen strengthens 4 per cent against the US dollar and the Japanese inflation rate is 1 per cent, a US exporter into a Japanese market served primarily by Japanese producers would see his dollar price increase by 5 per cent. However, if the inflation rate in the US is 4 per cent, which is 3 per cent higher than the inflation rate in Japan, the operating margin of the US producer will only increase by one percentage point. This example (and other examples developed later in more detail) show that the change in relative competitiveness does not depend on changes in the *nominal* exchange rate – the number of Yen we obtain for each US dollar – but on changes in the *real* exchange rate, which are changes in the nominal exchange rate from which are subtracted the difference in inflation rates in the two countries.[2] In the case of our US exporter into Japan, the change in the nominal exchange rate is 4 per cent but the change in the real exchange rate (which flows through to operating profit) is only 1 per cent.

Changes in real exchange rates reflect deviations from purchasing power parity, so that the cumulative change in the real exchange rate tends to be smaller than that of the nominal exchange rate over a long period of time. In the short term of six months to several years, both nominal and real exchange rates are volatile, with implications for the profitability of the company. This volatility of real exchange rates in the time-frame of six months to several years gives rise to an exaggerated variability in operating margin.

UNDERSTANDING OPERATING EXPOSURE

The traditional analysis of currency exposure (Figure 10.1) emphasises contractual items on the company's balance sheet, such as debt, payables and

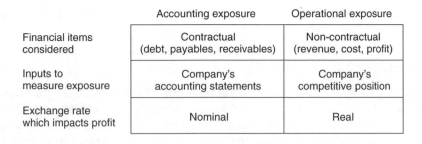

	Accounting exposure	Operational exposure
Financial items considered	Contractual (debt, payables, receivables)	Non-contractual (revenue, cost, profit)
Inputs to measure exposure	Company's accounting statements	Company's competitive position
Exchange rate which impacts profit	Nominal	Real

Figure 10.1   Currency exposure

receivables, which are denominated in a foreign currency and whose US dollar value is affected by changes in the nominal exchange rate. The company may enter into forward contracts to cover this contractual exposure. A traditional analysis recognises two types of impacts on the profits of the company, which arise from translation of outstanding contractual items as of year-end and transactions involving contractual items closed out during the year. The information required to define this contractual or accounting exposure is obtained from the accounting statements of the company. Under the US accounts standard FASB 52, physical assets also enter into the calculation of translation gains and losses. However, in general these translation gains or losses will bear little or no relationship to the operating exposure of the company.

In economic terms, these contractual items are properly identified as exposed to changes in exchange rates. Our problem lies in the fact that, in many cases, this contractual exposure captures only a small part of the total impact of exchange rates on the company, which should properly include the effect of changes in real exchange rates on non-contractual items, such as revenues, costs and operating profit. If a company covers its contractual exposure, it may be increasing its total exposure because of the operating exposure component of total exposure which has not been separately identified. The operating exposure and contractual exposure of the company may have different origins, so that in many cases the two exposures will indeed have opposite significance.

Both contractual exposure and operating exposure must be taken into account by the company, so that the two approaches are complementary and not mutually exclusive. Unfortunately, the difference in emphasis in considering each type of exposure tends to introduce a sense of defensiveness in practitioners who have historically only managed contractual exposure. A balanced perspective is not helped by the fact that the effects of changes in nominal exchange rates are separately identified in the income statement but the effects of changes in real exchange rates on revenues and costs are not similarly recognised.

The effects of changes in exchange rates on operating profits can be separated into margin effects and volume effects. We shall illustrate each kind of effect by a series of examples based on composites of companies studied.

Example 1

Economy Motors is a US manufacturer of small cars, that purchases inputs in the US and sells exclusively in the domestic market and has no foreign debt. From a traditional point of view, Economy Motors has no exposure to changes in exchange rates: in fact, however, the operating profit of Economy Motors is exposed to changes in the real yen/US dollar exchange rate.

Economy Motors competes in the US small car market with Japanese manufacturers which are the market leaders. The Japanese companies take into account their yen costs in setting a dollar price in the US. The competitive position of Economy Motors is shown in Figure 10.2. In some base year when the yen and the dollar are at parity, the dollar costs of Economy Motors are assumed to be equal to the dollar equivalent costs of its Japanese competitors and Economy Motors enjoys a normal operating profit margin.[3] In some later year, if the yen strengthens in line with PPP, to offset a higher inflation rate in the US than in Japan, there is no change in the competitive position of Economy Motors. The increase in the dollar equivalent costs of the Japanese companies from Japanese inflation plus the effect of the yen appreciation is equal to the increase in the costs of Economy Motors from US inflation. In this case,

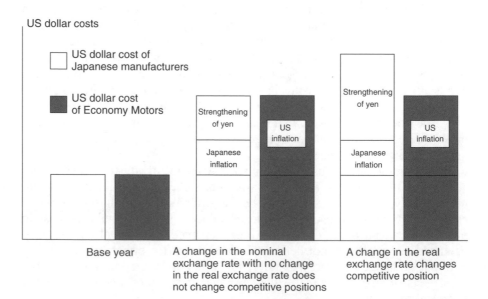

Figure 10.2   The competitive position of Economy Motors

the nominal exchange rate has changed with no change in the real exchange rate and there is no change in the competitive position of Economy Motors. However, if the yen strengthens relative to the dollar by a greater amount than required by PPP, the dollar equivalent costs of the Japanese companies will be greater than the costs of Economy Motors and there will be a strengthening in the competitive position of Economy Motors relative to its Japanese Competition.

This example illustrates several characteristics of operating exposure:

- Operating exposure bears no necessary relationship to accounting or contractual exposure.

- Operating exposure is determined by the structure of the markets in which the company and its competitors source inputs and sell products. The measurement of operating exposure must accordingly take into account the nature of the company and its competition. The measurement of accounting exposure has traditionally looked to the company alone.

- Operating exposure is not necessarily associated with the country in which goods are sold or inputs sourced. Economy Motors, for example, is a US manufacturer selling in the US market and has a significant yen exposure.

- Operating exposure is not necessarily associated with the currency in which prices are quoted.

- Operating profit varies with changes in the real exchange rate. The nominal exchange rate may change without any change in the real exchange rates and with no effect on operating profit. Conversely, the nominal exchange rate may remain constant while the real exchange rate is changing and impacting operating profit.

The importance of the details of market structure in determining operating exposure is easily seen in Examples 2 and 3.

Example 2

Specialty Chemicals (Canada) Limited is the Canadian subsidiary of a US company which distributes chemicals produced in the US by its parent. As a distribution subsidiary with few fixed assets, it has little debt. It quotes prices in Canadian dollars. When the Canadian dollar weakens relative to the US dollar, there is a decline in the US dollar value of its Canadian dollar receivables and, from an accounting viewpoint, Specialty Chemicals is exposed because of these receivables.

When we look beyond the accounting treatment, we recognise that when the Canadian dollar weakens, the cost of Specialty Chemicals will increase in Canadian dollars. This raises a number of questions:

- Does Specialty Chemicals have a Canadian dollar operating exposure?
- Should Specialty Chemicals construct a Canadian manufacturing plant to match revenues and costs?
- Should the company issue Canadian dollar debt, so that if the Canadian dollar weakens, there will be a reduced US dollar value of its repayments?

We cannot answer these questions by looking at Specialty Chemicals alone; we have to examine the structure of the marketplace in which it sells its products. We find that Specialty Chemicals and all its competitors import products from the US, with no significant production in Canada. Any increase in Canadian dollar costs will be felt equally by all companies, without any change in their relative competitive position, and will be reflected very quickly in an increased price. The responsiveness in price offsets the cost responsiveness so that there is no operating exposure except in the very short term. Issuing Canadian dollar debt or building a plant in Canada will introduce a new operating exposure where there was no operating exposure previously.

Operating exposure often differs substantially among companies which at first glance appear similar but where the companies sell into markets which have a different structure. For example, Home Products (Canada) Limited, like the previous case, is also a Canadian subsidiary of a US company which purchases product from its US parent. However, the competitors of Home Products (Canada) Limited have manufacturing facilities in Canada and have the major share of the Canadian market. If the Canadian dollar weakens in real terms, the Canadian dollar costs of Home Products will increase without any associated increase in price. There is a cost responsiveness without any offsetting price responsiveness, so that Home Products has a Canadian dollar/US dollar operating exposure.

Changes in the real Canadian dollar/US dollar exchange rate will affect a Canadian exporter into the US with a small share of the American market in opposite ways to Home Products. When the Canadian dollar weakens in real terms, there will be a decline in the profits of Home Products but an increase in the profits of the Canadian exporter.

Home Products can reduce this exposure by building a plant in Canada or entering into a financial hedge which offsets the effect of the change in the real exchange rate. Alternatively, if Home Products increases its share of the Canadian market to become the market leader, it may be able to raise prices to offset some or all of the increased Canadian dollar costs caused by a weakening Canadian dollar and thereby reduce its operating exposure.

Figure 10.3 illustrates the effect of various combinations of cost responsiveness and price responsiveness on the magnitude of the resulting operating exposure.

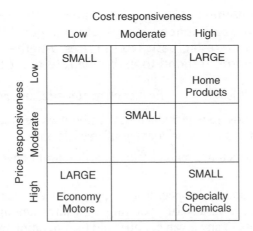

Figure 10.3 Operating exposure matrix

Example 3

The same analysis can be applied to the more realistic but also more complex case of companies that compete globally rather than in specific national markets. Consider the case of International Instrumentation, a US company that sells precision measurement instruments throughout the world and is the market leader in its industry. Its prices are approximately uniform across countries, as product requirements do not vary from country to country and transhipment costs are small relative to the value of the product.

Demand is insensitive to price, as its products represent a small fraction of the total costs of its customers. Nevertheless, prices and margins are not allowed to be so high that other firms possessing the relevant technologies would be encouraged to enter the market. International Instrumentation will set its prices with a view toward its costs and the costs of actual and potential competitors. If most of its potential competitors are also based in the US, its prices in dollars will be relatively independent of exchange rates. If International Instrumentation is attempting to discourage potential competitors which are located in other countries, it will set lower dollar prices in periods of relative dollar strength.

Example 4

Contrast the above example with Earthworm Tractors, a US-based manufacturer of heavy construction equipment. Its prices vary somewhat across countries because of variations in product specifications and substantial shipping costs, but it nevertheless faces substantial global competition. However, in contrast to International Instrumentation, it faces two major competitors: Germany and Japan. The cost positions of the three firms are such that exchange rate changes shift cost and price leadership and, as a result, basic world prices, whether measured in US dollars, yen, or euros, respond to exchange rate changes.

These examples illustrate some further characteristics of operating exposure:

- Operating exposure is introduced by differences between competitors in sourcing or technology or country of manufacture.

- Companies which are market leaders will tend to have a reduced operating exposure.

- Operating exposure is specific to a particular business. A company is likely to have a variety of operating exposures among its subsidiaries doing business in any given country and the operating exposures of these business units must be evaluated separately. This is in contrast to a standard accounting treatment which aggregates the exposure of the various businesses in a company.

- It will generally be possible to identify two companies which have opposite operating exposures with respect to the same real exchange rate.

So far we have focused on the impact of changes in the real exchange rate on operating margin. In some cases, changes in real exchange rates will have their most important impact on volume.

Example 5

United Kingdom Airways is a UK-based charter airline which sells airline transportation and package tours to the US. When sterling weakens relative to the US dollar in real terms, there were fewer UK travellers to the US. As travel cost is only about 30 per cent of the total cost of a vacation, there is little that a seller of travel services can do to offset the increasing cost of a trip to the US.

Laker Airways had a similar operating exposure. Laker was a UK-based company whose marketing seems to have been primarily directed to UK travellers. With a marketing strategy which was more evenly balanced between travel originating in the US and the UK, changes in the real exchange rate would have had relatively little effect on the demand for total air travel between the two countries. Fewer British tourists would visit the US when the US is relatively expensive from a British perspective but this would be offset by more US travellers to Britain. Laker transported an increasing number of British tourists until 1980. This was to a large extent the result of a sterling strengthening beyond its parity with the dollar, with the implication that eventually sterling would again weaken to regain parity. However, in 1980, Laker financed new aircraft purchases in US dollars, in effect doubling its exposure to the subsequent weakness in the pound.

In summary, several factors contribute to the nature and severity of the company's competitive exposure. There include the degree of cross-border market integration, the extent of global competition, the extent to which the cost structure of the industry is variable versus fixed, and the extent to which the industry is characterised by lead competitors with differing costs. Figure 10.4 illustrates the competitive exposure of various companies combining the degree of currency mismatch in costs and the relative importance of variable versus fixed costs.

Turning to actual examples, Airbus is a company with an extreme competitive exposure. It sells its product in international markets in direct competition with Boeing, although almost all its costs are in European currencies. The market is almost completely integrated and the variable cost component of aircraft manufacturing is substantial. Caterpillar is another company that has a similar high degree of competitive exposure, because the market for its products is highly integrated and it faces in most of those markets a key competitor, Komatsu, which has a very different cost structure.

At the other extreme lie some pharmaceutical companies such as Merck. Here, market integration across national boundaries is low as national regulation serves as an effective barrier to transhipment. Also, the variable cost component of producing products is low, and substantial advertising and distribution costs are incurred in the country of sale. Another company with relatively low competitive exposure is McDonald's, which receives franchise fees as a percentage of sales from its operations in various countries. These fees are effectively denominated in local currency as relatively few people cross the Atlantic to arbitrage the "Big Mac" and there is little cross-border

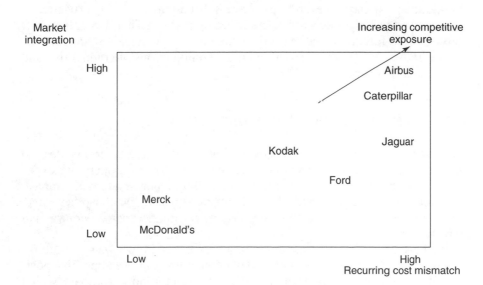

Figure 10.4 Determinants of competitive exposure

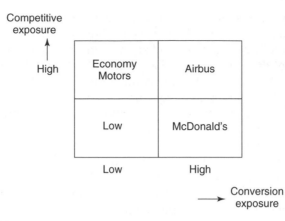

Figure 10.5   Components of operational exposure

integration of markets and most variable costs are incurred in the country of sale.

Jaguar[4] is an example of a company with a moderately high competitive exposure, as it has a variable cost mismatch as great as that of Airbus or Caterpillar, but a somewhat lesser degree of market integration between Europe and the US because of the greater differentiation of its product and its ability to control distribution channels. Nevertheless, even though Jaguar is a unique product, its pricing in the US cannot differ substantially from the pricing of other luxury cars. Companies like Kodak and DEC also fit into this middle category.

Companies such as Merck and McDonald's, which have low levels of competitive exposure, nevertheless have substantial operating exposure to exchange rate changes because of the conversion effect. Their US dollar profitability from foreign operations will change in time with real exchange rates. Figure 10.5 shows companies with various combinations of competitive and conversion exposures.

MEASURING OPERATING EXPOSURE

Contractual or accounting exposure is readily identified with any desired degree of precision from accounting statements. However, operating exposure cannot be directly estimated from accounting records, and will not have the precision of an estimate of contractual exposure. On the other hand, the operating exposure of a company may be far greater than its contractual exposure.

We have been able to estimate operating exposure in two ways, a bottom-up estimate, which relies on a detailed understanding of the competitive position of the various businesses of the company and a top-down estimate, which is derived from an analysis of the historical profitability of the company.

Bottom-up Estimates

A bottom-up measurement of operating exposure requires an understanding of:

- the structure of the markets in which the company and its competitors source inputs and sell their products; and
- the degree of flexibility of the company and its competitors in changing markets, product mix, sourcing and technology.

We have been successful in obtaining this information in a structured dialogue with operating management. Most managers have the information to answer these questions but lack the analytical framework to use this information, and usually the treasury group will have the responsibility of coordinating the process of measuring operating exposure. For many companies this represents a closer involvement of the treasury group with operations and an enlarged treasury responsibility. This involvement of the treasury function in operating considerations reflects the fact that the impact of exchange rates on the profitability of the company is in some sense a financial effect, to a large extent outside the business control of the company, and yet it corresponds to a very important aspect of the external competitive environment.

This exposure audit with operating management will typically include the following types of questions:

- Who are actual and potential major competitors in various markets?
- Who are low cost producers?
- Who are price leaders?
- What has happened in the past to profit margins when real exchange rates have become overvalued and undervalued?
- What is the flexibility of the company to shift production to countries with undervalued currencies?

These questions are usually well received by operating management, because an understanding of the operating exposure of a company can be used directly to improve operating decisions and it is critical to measure management performance after taking into account exchange rate effects. In Example 1, Economy Motors is likely to be more successful in increasing market share during a period of weakness in the dollar, when its Japanese competitors are seeing decreasing yen equivalent prices, if management has previously anticipated this set of circumstances in contingency planning. There is also less conflict in the management of operating exposure between the welfare of a partly owned foreign subsidiary and its parent whereas these conflicts are often present in the management of contractual exposure.

Top-down Estimates

The bottom-up process of dialogue with operating management is likely to be time-consuming and costly. We have also developed top-down analytical techniques to estimate operating exposure at the company level or at the level of individual business units. This analysis can be performed quickly. We have found that it is an effective method of communicating the operating exposure of the company to senior management, in particular when the exposure of the company arises from import competition in the domestic market.

The top-down estimate is derived from an analytical comparison of the historical profitability of the company with the changes in profitability expected on the basis of changes in real exchange rates assuming that the competitive position of the company is constant during the period of the comparison and that the company has not undergone major structural changes at the level of aggregation under review.

The effect of changes in real exchange rates on the profitability of the company will be determined by the volatility in exchange rates and the fraction of revenues exposed. The top-down analysis identifies both the principal exchange rates to which the company is exposed and the fraction of revenues exposed.

If the exporter has some market power in the overseas marketplace, the exposure will be limited to some fraction of his total revenue and there will be less volatility in mark-up and operating profit. Similarly, the exposure of Economy Motors (Example 1) is limited to some fraction of its revenues which corresponds to the power of Japanese importers in the US marketplace. However, in general, the volatility in earnings may be a cause of financial distress to the company. In an environment where there is not a good understanding of the exchange rate cause of this volatility, management decisions will often not take advantage of the underlying business opportunity.

The top-down estimates of operating exposure have identified many companies where a large part of the variability in the profits of the company results from exposure to real exchange rate effects, in some cases with only a small fraction of the revenues exposed. In the absence of an analytical framework to demonstrate these operating exposure effects, there is a tendency for them not to be fully recognised by management, whose culture in many cases will want to attribute the success of the company to the performance of its operating management.

NOTES

1. The exact relation is that $\dot{S}_{12} = (\dot{P}_1 - \dot{P}_2)/(1 + \dot{P}_2)$. where $\dot{S}_{12}$ is the fractional change in the spot exchange rate (currency 1/currency 2) and $\dot{P}_1$ and $\dot{P}_2$ are the annual inflation rates in country 1 and country 2.

2. More exactly, the fractional change in the real exchange rate is $\dot{S}_{12} - [(\dot{P}_1 - \dot{P}_2)/(1 + \dot{P}_2)]$.
3. The argument can be extended to the case when the US dollar costs of Economy Motors in the base year bear their normal relationship (but are not necessarily equal) to the US dollar equivalent costs of its Japanese competitors.
4. Jaguar's parent company is Ford. The commentary on p. 242 and the depiction of the competitive exposure of Jaguar and Ford in Figure 10.4 relate to the circumstances of the companies *prior* to the acquisition of Jagnar by Ford in 1989.

11

Currency Exchange Trading and Rogue Trader John Rusnak

Sharon Burke

INTRODUCTION

In 1993, a foreign currency trader, John Rusnak, was hired by Allfirst bank in Maryland. John Rusnak was hired to bring profits to Allfirst via proprietary foreign exchange trading. Prior to Rusnak's arrival, foreign exchange trading at the bank was limited to assisting bank customers in hedging against currency risk. Allfirst performed this service for companies that were dealing with overseas trades.

This decision would eventually incur a $691 million loss for Allied Irish Bank, the owner of Allfirst bank. The story of this loss involves foreign exchange trading, bank organization, organizational politics, inadequate accounting controls and more. This article will include a review of foreign currency trading concepts, the strategies that Rusnak employed to trade and to cover his losses and the findings of the subsequent investigation by Eugene Ludwig.

CURRENCY MARKETS

The foreign currency market is virtual. That is, there is no one central physical location that is the foreign currency market. It exists in the dealing rooms of various central banks, large international banks, and some large corporations. The dealing rooms are connected via telephone, computer and fax. Some countries co-locate their dealing rooms in one centre. The Eurocurrency market is one example of where borrowing and lending of currency takes place. Interest rates for the various currencies are also set in this market.[1]

Trading on the foreign exchange market (FOREX) establishes rates of exchange for currency. Exchange rates are constantly fluctuating on the FOREX market. As demand rises and falls for particular currencies, their exchange rates adjust accordingly. Instantaneous rate quotes are available from information services like Reuters. A rate of exchange for currencies is the ratio at which one currency is exchanged for another.[2]

The following are examples of currency rates from the Wall Street Journal on April 16, 2003:[3]

FX summary	Prior US close	6:45 ET
USD/JPY	120.16	120.29
EUR/USD	1.0815	1.0843
USD/CAD	1.4485	1.4474

This shows the closing exchange rates from the foreign exchange market. For example, the USD/JPY value is the exchange rate for US dollars to yen, that is, 120.16 yen per one US dollar. The US dollar is the base currency in this case, as it is one unit of a US dollar per an amount of yen.

The foreign exchange market has no regulation, no restrictions or overseeing board. Should there be a world monetary crisis in this market; there is no mechanism to stop trading.[4] The Federal Reserve Bank of New York publishes guidelines for foreign exchange trading. In their "Guidelines for Foreign Exchange Trading", they outline 50 best practices for trading on the FOREX market.[5] This document is not legally binding or regulatory in nature.

EXCHANGE CONTRACTS

The actual exchange of currencies is governed by contracts between the buyer and seller of the currencies. There are a variety of contract options available to investors. Rusnak focused on spot and forward contracts in his trading.

SPOT EXCHANGE

The spot exchange is the simplest contract. A spot exchange contract identifies two parties, the currency they are buying or selling and the currency they expect to receive in exchange. The currencies are exchanged at the prevailing spot rate at the time of the contract. The spot rate is constantly fluctuating. When a spot exchange is agreed upon, the contract is defined to be executed immediately. In reality, a series of confirmations occurs between the two parties. Documentation is sent and received from both parties detailing the exchange rate agreed upon and the amounts of currency involved. The funds actually move between banks two days after the spot transaction is agreed upon.[6]

FORWARD EXCHANGE

The forward exchange contract is similar to the spot exchange; however, the time period of the contract is longer. These contracts use a forward exchange rate that differs from the spot rate. The difference between the forward rate and the spot rate reflects the difference in interest rates between the two currencies. This prevents an opportunity for arbitrage. If the rates did not differ, there would be a profit difference in the currencies. That is, investing in one currency for a year and then selling it should be the same profit or loss as setting up a forward contract at the forward rate one year in the future. If investing in one currency was more profitable than investing in the other, there would exist an opportunity for arbitrage.[7] Forward exchange contracts are settled at a specified date in the future. The parties exchange funds on this date. Forward contracts are typically custom written between the counterparty and the bank, or between banks.

CURRENCY FUTURES AND SWAP TRANSACTIONS

Currency futures are standardized forward contracts. The amounts of currency, time to expiry, and exchange rates are standardized. The standardized expiry times are specific dates in March, June, September, and December. These futures are traded on the Chicago Mercantile Exchange (CME). Futures give the buyer the ability to set up a contract to exchange currency in the future. This contract can be purchased on an exchange, rather than custom negotiated with a bank like a forward contract.[8]

A currency swap is an agreement to two exchanges in currency, one a spot and one a forward. An immediate spot exchange is executed, followed later by a reverse exchange. The two exchanges occur at different exchange rates. It is the difference in the two exchange rates that determines the swap price.[9]

OPTIONS

A currency option gives the holder the right, but not the obligation, either to buy (call) from the option writer, or to sell (put) to the option writer, a stated quantity of one currency in exchange for another at a fixed rate of exchange, called the strike price. The options can be American, which allows an option to be exercised until a fixed day, called the day of expiry, or European, which allows exercise only on the day of expiry, not before. The option holder pays a premium to the option writer for the option. The option differs from other currency contracts in that the holder has a choice, or option, of whether they will exercise it or not. If exchange rates are more favorable than the rate guaranteed by the option when the holder needs to exchange currency, they can choose to exchange the currency on the spot exchange rather than use the option. They lose only the option premium. Options allow holders to limit their risk of exposure to adverse changes in the exchange rates.

CURRENCY HEDGING

It is common for currency options to be used to hedge cash positions. For example, if Company A is buying stereos from Japan, they will make an agreement to pay Company B for the stereo equipment in yen. The spot rate at the time of the deal is 119Y to the US dollar. Suppose that the stereos are selling for $100.00 each or ¥11,900 a piece. The company is purchasing 100 stereos. They need to provide ¥1,190,000 to the seller. If the stereos were purchased today, they would cost the company $10,000. The company would exchange $10,000 for ¥1,190,000.

This deal will be transacted in three months. In three months, currency rates will change. If the US dollar falls against the yen, for example, the spot rate for yen in exchange for US dollars may be ¥100 to the dollar. In that case, in order to provide ¥1,190,000 to the seller of the stereos, the company must exchange $11,900. The deal costs an extra $1,900. However, if the yen falls against the US dollar, the spot rate might become ¥130 per US dollar. In that case, the ¥1,190,000 needed to close the deal will cost $9,154. The company has saved $846.

Companies are not typically in the business of gambling with their profits on deals. It is in their best interest to lock in an exchange rate they can count on. They are motivated to insure that their profits are as expected. Two ways they might do this are to enter forward contracts or to buy options. Company A could choose to enter into a forward contract with a bank. They would settle on a forward rate that was acceptable to both parties. The contract would settle in three months when the delivery was due. The forward contract is a binding contract and they must make the exchange.

The company could also assess the interest rates available in the US and in the Eurocurrency market. They could either invest $10,000 in the US for 3 months, or exchange $10,000 into yen and invest the ¥1,190,000 for 3 months.

Company A could also use options to reduce their exposure to currency fluctuation. The company will need yen to pay for the stereos. They could purchase a call option to exchange ¥1,190,000 with an expiry date of 3 months. They would select an exchange rate that would be acceptable but not too expensive. They might choose to buy a slightly out-of-the-money call option to cover them if the currency exchange rate falls. If it stays the same or rises, they will exchange at the spot exchange rate at the time the payment is due.

TRADING STRATEGY OF JOHN RUSNAK

The foreign currency market is the market that John Rusnak gambled and lost in. He used spot transactions, forward transactions and options to amass losses of $691 million. Rusnak had been employed in foreign currency trading beginning in 1986 at Fidelity Bank in Philadelphia. He worked at Chemical Bank in New York from 1988 to 1993. In 1993, he was looking for a new position. Coincidentally, David Cronin, the Treasurer of Allfirst Bank in Maryland was looking for a new foreign currency trader. Cronin was originally from Ireland. He had come to the U.S. to represent the interests of Allied Irish Bank when they had purchased Allfirst. Allfirst was formerly known as First National Bank of Maryland.

Rusnak proposed a trading strategy that sounded new and inventive. He told Cronin, ". . . he could consistently make more money by running a large option book hedged in the cash markets, buying options when they were cheap and selling them when they were expensive."[10] The Ludwig Report, a report commissioned by AIB to determine the extent of Rusnak's fraud, states that "Mr. Rusnak promoted himself as a trader who used options to engage in a form of arbitrage, attempting to take advantage of price discrepancies between currency options and currency forwards." In order to execute this strategy, Rusnak would have had to buy options ". . . when they were cheap relative to cash (when the implied volatility of the option was lower than its normal range) and sell them when they were expensive (when the implied volatility is higher than normal)."

In his trading, Rusnak did not achieve these lofty goals. Rusnak executed simple directional trades on the spot and forward markets. He mostly traded in yen and euro. Occasionally, he would use complex options.[11] Rusnak placed large sum one-way bets that the yen would increase in value against the US dollar. Specifically, he bought yen for future delivery, probably with forward contracts. As the yen declined, he could not go back on the forward contracts as they are binding, and was forced to take his losses. He did not hedge these bets with options contracts.

Rusnak's core trading belief was that the yen was going to rise against the US dollar. His strategy throughout all his trading was to place bets in this direction. It is interesting to note what was happening with the yen during the time period Rusnak was trading. From 1990 to 1995, the yen appreciated. From mid-1995 to 1997, the yen was depreciating against the dollar. In April of 1997, the exchange rate was around 125 yen to the US dollar. The Asian market crisis followed soon after causing further problems for the yen.[12] As the yen depreciated, Rusnak began to have great problems with his one-sided trading.

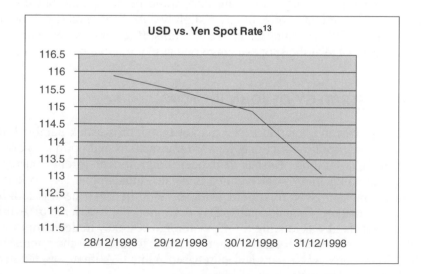

At the end of 1997, Rusnak had lost $29.1 million by his wrong bets in trading. The jargon of gambling suits his activities well. After his losing bets and heavy losses, Rusnak embarked on a path to cover up those losses. Instead of taking responsibility and reporting his losses immediately, he decided to hide them, buy himself some time and see if he could win back the money he had lost. He used many complicated schemes to hide his losses. They included falsification of documents, misuse of office technology and fraudulent entries in accounting systems.

BOGUS OPTIONS

The first technique Rusnak used to hide his losses was to enter bogus options in the banking system. The purpose of these fake options was two-fold. The options appeared to hedge his directional trades. They also gave him a way to hide the losses with a bogus asset. At the end of his trading day, when Rusnak was entering his daily trades in the bank system, he would enter two false trades. He would enter two options that would offset each other. The options had the same premium in identical currencies. They were for the same amounts of currencies and used the same strike price. The expiry dates on the options were different.

For example, Rusnak would enter a put option "sold" by Allfirst to a party in Tokyo. The option would allow the Japanese bank to sell yen at a certain strike price. This option would expire on the day it was written. He would also enter a call option written by the Japanese bank to buy yen at the same strike price as the other option. This option would expire months in the future. The put option would disappear off the books the next day, removing that liability from the bank's records. The call option would stay on the books as a valuable asset that covered his losses.[14]

It was important to have the premiums of the two options exactly cancel each other out. If the options had not canceled out to zero, there would have been a payment due to either Allfirst or to the counterparty in Tokyo. All payments were required to go through the treasury department's back office. Keeping the premiums the same meant there was no net payment and thus no requirement for the back office to be involved in payment. Anyone who really looked at the options would have questioned the fact that the two options had different expiry dates but the same premium. That did not make sense. Also, the put option was a deep-in-the-money option. The holder of the option would make a profit by exercising it. The option went off the books in one day unexercised. That was unusual and did not make sense.[15] It is probable that the call option was also deep-in-the-money.[16] There were several of these options that the bank had "paid" high premiums for. The high premium indicates they were probably deep-in-the-money options. Their high value was necessary to cover the high losses that Rusnak was incurring. The fake option trades were written in the opposite direction of the losing bets he placed. This made it appear to Allfirst that he had offset his losses.[17]

FALSIFIED DOCUMENTS

The bogus options solved one problem, covering the losses; however, they created another problem. The back office was responsible for confirming all trades. The foreign exchange operation at Allfirst was operating on a shoe-string compared to what a large bank would have in place. Typically a true foreign exchange operation has research departments, dealing rooms, computer programs that automatically confirmed trades and a more sophisticated set-up. Allfirst was using telephone and fax to execute and confirm trades.

Rusnak knew that the back office was going to need to confirm his trades. He used his PC to create false trade confirmation documentation. His PC was discovered to have a directory called "fake docs". This directory contained logos and stationery from various banks in Tokyo and Singapore. Rusnak used these files to construct fake confirmation documents on his computer. He was able to convince the back office to accept these documents from him, rather than confirming the trades themselves as required.[18] Eventually, Rusnak was able to convince the back office to not confirm the trades at all. He was able to argue that since the trades netted to zero, they did not need to be confirmed. This argument was probably acceptable given that confirming Asian trades with their system would have required night-time phone calls. Some in the company say that it was a senior management decision to not confirm Asian counter party trades that netted to zero. The Ludwig report indicates that no evidence of this management decision could be found.[19]

PRIME BROKERAGE ACCOUNTS

In 1999, with $41.5 million lost, Rusnak turned to prime brokerage accounts. He needed to increase the size of his trades so he could catch up on his losses. Prime brokerage accounts are typically used by high profile traders. They are very often used by hedge funds.[20] The prime brokerage accounts provided Rusnak with net settlements. Daily spot transactions were rolled into one forward transaction to be settled at a future date with the prime broker. This accomplished several things for Rusnak. Having all the daily spot transactions rolled into one net settlement meant that the back office could not track his daily trades as effectively. It was a means of obscuring what he was really doing.

Rusnak was able to expand the scale and scope of his trading to large volume high value currency trades.[21] He needed to be able to do this to win back the large amounts of money that he was losing. Rusnak was able to convince David Cronin, the Allfirst Treasurer, that the prime brokerage accounts were a sound idea. He sold them as a way of growing Allfirst's foreign exchange operation. He also said that using the prime brokerage accounts would relieve the back office of the extra work they needed to do on his behalf. His false concern for the back office is quite interesting in light of how often he was at odds with that department over his trading practices. Rusnak used the prime brokerage accounts as another opportunity to enter fictitious trades. He could enter fictitious trades with the brokerage banks to further manipulate the bank's records. He would reverse these transactions by month end before the monthly settlement was done.[22]

The prime brokerage accounts allowed Rusnak to use a type of foreign exchange contract called a "historical rate rollover." This type of contract was invented to assist companies in handling delayed shipments from foreign companies. It is a method to extend a currency contract in the event that a settlement of the contract would create a loss for the contract holder. For a purchaser of goods, when the goods are delayed, it can be convenient to extend a contract and wait to exchange funds until the time payment is required.

However, for a trader, these types of contracts allow losses to be rolled forward. If the trader's contract is due to be settled, and settlement would not be in his favour, he can delay settlement and keep the original rate of the contract. The New York Times reports "The rollover buys time for a trader who hopes that the currency rates will change in his favour in the future. The risk, of course, is that the losses will deepen . . ."[23] For Rusnak, this was certainly the case. The historical rate rollover is warned against in the Federal Reserve Bank of NY standard of conduct:

> "Accommodation of customer requests for off-market transactions (OMTs) or historical rate rollovers (HRROs) should be selective, restricted, and well documented, and should not be allowed if the sole intent is to hide a loss or extend a profit or loss position. Counterparties should also show that a requested HRRO is matched by a real commercial flow."[24]

The Federal Reserve had been warning against the HRROs since 1991. The use of historical rate rollovers by Rusnak should have alerted his trading partners that something was suspicious.[25]

VALUE AT RISK CALCULATIONS

Rusnak avoided detection by manipulating the bank's Value at Risk (VaR) calculations. Value at Risk can be calculated using the Monte Carlo simulation technique. One thousand hypothetical exchange rate fluctuations are generated. Those rate fluctuations are applied to the trader's portfolio. The tenth worst outcome produced may be used as the bank's Value at Risk.

The VaR is the main check used on traders to make sure they are not losing more than the bank can afford to lose. A VaR limit is the largest amount of money the bank is prepared to lose if there are adverse trading conditions. For Rusnak, the VaR limit was $1.5 million. As of the end of 1999, Rusnak had lost $90 million. He had clearly found a way around this check.

A trader is responsible for calculating and monitoring their own VaR. The VaR is also independently calculated by treasury risk control as a check on the trader. The bogus options discussed earlier made Rusnak's open forward positions look as if they were hedged. This improved his VaR as it made his portfolio seem less risky. The fictitious prime brokerage account transactions he was entering also obscured his true VaR. He was able to convince the risk control group to accept a spreadsheet of his open currency positions from him with no confirmation. He altered the values in this spreadsheet to make his open positions seem less than they were. And since the risk control group did not confirm these values, he got away with this technique.

Rusnak was able to take advantage of technology and cost cutting measures to obscure his stop-loss limit. The stop-loss limit was an amount of loss, after which, Rusnak's trading would have been shut down for the month. Rusnak could not afford to lose any time in trying to win his losses back. He had to find a way around the stop-loss limit because he was regularly exceeding it. Rusnak found that he could manipulate the currency exchange rates used by the bank to produce calculations that made it look like he had not exceeded his stop-loss limit. Again, he was able to provide his own spreadsheet with the exchange rate values. These exchange rates were supposed to be independently confirmed by the risk management office of Allfirst's treasury.[26]

Rusnak had convinced the computer operations department to download exchange rate data from Reuters onto his PC. He claimed he needed to have these rates downloaded to his system so he could monitor his VaR. From his PC, a spreadsheet was then forwarded to the systems in the treasury front and back offices. All of the bank's foreign exchange rates were passing through Rusnak's hand before being fed into the computer system. This was a serious breach of the integrity of the bank's systems. One of the reasons this happened was that the bank did not want to pay $10,000 for an additional feed from Reuters for the back office.[27] This additional feed would have enabled the back office to independently confirm exchange rates and check Rusnak's calculations.

SALE OF OPTIONS

By the end of 2000, Rusnak had lost $300 million. He was getting pressure from his superiors to reduce his use of the company's balance sheet. The balance sheet of a company lists their assets, liabilities and stock holder's equity at a given time. It shows the resources the company has available to it for operating activities and investment.[28] David Cronin was taking notice of the large amount of the balance sheet Rusnak was using. Foreign exchange trading revenue was $13.6 million. The net trading income, however, was only $1.1 million. Rusnak was using more of the balance sheet but getting less in return. Cronin asked Rusnak to reduce his use of the balance sheet.

Rusnak needed large amounts of cash to continue his gamble to win back the money he had lost. Having his balance sheet usage restricted was somewhat of a blow. To get around this restriction and continue his quest to win back his losses, he came up with a plan. He would sell deep-in-the-money options at high premiums to finance his trading. The options he sold had deep-in-the-money strike prices. The strike prices were so deep, it was extremely likely that the options would be exercised. They were European options that expired in a year and a day. They were essentially loans from the counterparties to Allfirst.

As an example, in February 2001, Rusnak made an agreement with Citibank. For a premium of $125 million, Rusnak wrote a put that gave Citibank the right to sell yen at a strike rate of 77.37 yen to the US dollar. The exchange rate at the time was 116 yen to the US dollar. The US dollar would have to fall 35% for the option to go unexercised. The option was effectively a high interest loan. The loan payment would come due as a lump sum with interest when Rusnak had to buy the yen that Citibank wanted to sell in one year's time. Rusnak had found another way to buy the time. However, it created a liability that was sitting on Allfirst's books. Rusnak entered a bogus deal with Citibank that made it appear that Allfirst had repurchased the option.[29] Rusnak repeated this process with Bank of America, Deutsche Bank, Bank of New York and Merrill Lynch.[30] The options he sold totalled over $300 million raising his total losses to $691 million, when the yen depreciated further.

LOSSES REVEALED

Rusnak avoided an amazing number of situations where he could have been caught. He avoided detection over a period of five years. In my research I found 12 separate occasions where his activities were questioned by the back office, the risk management department at Allfirst, the SEC, and the CEO of Allied Irish Bank. Rusnak was able to avoid detection on all occasions.

A particularly involved scheme occurred during an audit conducted at Allfirst during the five year time period of the fraud. Rusnak was asked to confirm an Asian trade that was bogus. He set up a fax account at Mailboxes etc. in Manhattan under the name David Russell. He gave the fax id code of that account to the auditors. The auditors faxed a confirmation request to that fax id. Rusnak then called the Mailbox etc. store, posed as David Russell and had them fax a return confirmation.

At one point, the bank gave Rusnak Travel Bloomberg software so that he could trade from home and while on vacation. This was a direct violation of U.S. law. U.S. law requires that traders take 10 consecutive days off from trading every year.[31] This is specifically so someone else takes over their duties and fraud can be discovered.

Finally in December 2001, Rusnak's luck began to run out. A back office supervisor happened to look over the shoulder of an employee and saw that there were two trade documents from Asian trades that Rusnak executed that did not have attached confirmations as required.[32] The supervisor discussed with the employee that all trades had to have confirmations. The employee believed that any Asian trades that netted to zero did not need to be confirmed. The supervisor requested that the employee get the trades confirmed. In late January, the supervisor again found that Asian trades that netted to zero were still not being confirmed. The back office had become lax and given up after years of losing battles over concerns with Rusnak's trading. Unfortunately, they were not getting the backing they needed to do their job. The back office employee did not bother to seek confirmations.

Around this time, David Cronin, the Allfirst treasurer, noticed that Rusnak's use of the balance sheet had spiked up to $200 million in January. Cronin had directed that it stay under $150 million. Also, Cronin discovered that the foreign exchange trading volume for the bank had been at $25 billion for the month of December. He decided to shut down Rusnak's trading positions for a month. Meanwhile, the back office requested Rusnak's help in obtaining confirmations for the Asian trades. Rusnak was able to stall for time and offered to get the confirmations himself. He resurrected his fake documents file and created false trade confirmations on his computer. When the trade confirmations were provided, the back office supervisor noticed that they looked suspicious.[33]

For the next week, Rusnak stalled. There was a day or two where the bank thought that he had disappeared. It later turned out that he had been conferring with his family, a lawyer and finally the FBI. He essentially turned himself in and cooperated. His most important task at that time was convincing the FBI that he had not embezzled the money, that he did not have it hidden anywhere. It had all been lost on the foreign exchange market. Rusnak had acted alone. He was charged with seven counts of bank fraud and entering false entries in bank records.[34] He pleaded guilty and was sentenced to $7\frac{1}{2}$ years in prison and a $1 million fine.[35]

THE LUDWIG REPORT

Shortly after Rusnak's fraud was discovered, the Allied Irish Bank (AIB) Board of Directors authorized an investigation by Eugene Ludwig of Promontory Financial Group LLC of Washington DC. Eugene Ludwig had been Comptroller of the Currency from 1993 to 1998 under President Bill Clinton.[36] He had a strong background in bank regulation. The Board needed to bring in an impartial party to investigate. They needed to restore the confidence of their shareholders.

When the news of Rusnak's fraud was reported, shares of AIB fell from €13.62 to €11.36 on the first day. AIB had been the largest capitalized company on the Dublin Stock Exchange with a capitalization of €12 billion.[37] In one day it fell to €10 billion, losing AIB €2 billion in capitalization. AIB had been about to announce a profit of €1.4 billion ($1 billion) for 2001. The discovery of Rusnak's fraud reduced this to €612 million ($426 million).[38] There were interviews in the media at the time with Nick Leeson, the trader whose losses had caused the fall of Barings Bank. Although there were many similarities to the two stories, AIB, unlike Barings, was able to absorb the loss.

Eugene Ludwig's team investigated Allfirst and Rusnak's fraud beginning on February 8, 2002. They published their report on March 12, 2002. The Ludwig team discovered what Rusnak had done to conceal his losses. They determined that he had worked alone. They identified the following failings in control at Allfirst and AIB that taken altogether, allowed Rusnak to commit fraud[39]:

- "The failure of the back office to attempt to confirm bogus options with Asian counterparties."

- "The failure of the middle and back offices to obtain foreign exchange rates from an independent source."

- "In 1999, an internal audit of treasury operations took no samples of Rusnak's transactions to see if they had been properly confirmed."

- "In 2000, the internal audit sampled only one trade of Mr. Rusnak's to check if it was properly confirmed."

In addition to these failures of control, the bank missed opportunities by ignoring problems raised by the back office. Employees in the back office raised issues ranging from problems confirming trades to warnings that there was a possibility that Rusnak could be manipulating foreign exchange rates. But Rusnak had been showing a yearly profit for five years straight. He became untouchable in organizational politics because he appeared to be so good. The back office staff eventually gave up raising flags on his trading practices as they were continually shot down by management.[40] With executive backing, the back office could have performed a very valuable function and assisted with detecting Rusnak's fraud.

Rusnak's supervisors were not experienced in foreign exchange trading. They did not adequately supervise his activities. A knowledgeable supervisor would have seen that the deep-in-the-money bogus options expiring on the same day they were purchased were odd. The sheer size of Rusnak's positions warranted closer scrutiny. No one was monitoring Rusnak's daily profit and loss (P&L) figures. They were not reconciled against the general ledger.[41] If this step had been taken, questions would have arisen as to why his daily P&L swung so widely from profit to loss and back.

There were many who had an opportunity to be aware of the size of Rusnak's positions. In 1999, a risk assessment auditor questioned the size of Rusnak's over limits. Citibank contacted AIB's Group Treasurer to confirm

that AIB could cover a net settlement of $1 billion on Rusnak's prime bro-
kerage account. The SEC 10k filings of Allfirst showed the size of Rusnak's
positions. Credit limits were exceeded by Rusnak. There was a trader that
worked with Rusnak who could have noticed the size of his positions and
questioned it but didn't.[42] The traders at the prime brokerage accounts also
knew his positions. All traders should be aware of the foreign exchange
trading guidelines. These guidelines outline suspicious trading activity. For
example, the use of historical rate rollovers (HRRO) expressly states that
HRROs should not be used to cover losses.[43] Those who were watching the
forex market came to recognize Rusnak's trades.[44] There were many who
knew or could have guessed the size of his positions and raised an alarm.

Following are some highlights of the Ludwig Report findings on what contributed to the fraud:

- "The architecture of Allfirst's trading activity was flawed." They had one
  lone trader trying to essentially implement a hedge fund. He had none
  of the "specialized knowledge, scale, diversification and specialized
  expertise" that his competitors had.

- Senior management in Baltimore and Dublin did not focus sufficient
  attention on the Allfirst trading operation.

- Rusnak knew the banking systems well from his experience at Chemical Bank so he was able to circumvent their controls.

- Treasury management weaknesses at Allfirst also contributed to the environment that allowed Rusnak's fraud to occur. The Allfirst Treasurer had
  a dual reporting structure. David Cronin reported into Allfirst through a
  variety of different managers. He also reported into AIB. The CEO of
  Allfirst thought AIB was managing Cronin and vice versa. Therefore, the
  treasury operation was not managed as thoroughly as it should have
  been.

- Senior management at both Allfirst and AIB thought their control structures and auditing were more robust than they actually were. The risk
  reporting processes needed to be more robust. The risk management
  team needed to be more proactive in finding problems rather than dealing
  with what was presented to them.[45]

The Ludwig Report provides great detail into what happened at Allfirst
and the various areas of laxity, weakness and fault that contributed to
Rusnak's activities. The most significant were the failures in technology, the
disorganization and the auditing and monitoring failures.

TECHNOLOGY

As the Ludwig report highlights, Allfirst was running a foreign exchange
trading operation without the full backup needed to sustain the levels of
trading Rusnak was involved in. Banks that trade in the volume Rusnak

was trading in typically have a large support staff. There are individuals backing up the trader by doing market research. Traders are working in groups where it is more difficult to commit fraud. In particular, many larger trading organizations use the Crossmar Matching System to confirm trades. This system can confirm trades in effect instantaneously. Instead of using this state of the art computing system, Allfirst was using a system of telephone and fax communication.

The system suited a small state bank that traded occasionally to assist its clients when they needed a currency hedge. It was inadequate for the volume and size of the positions Rusnak was taking. The inadequate system left openings for John Rusnak to fake fax communications and create fake confirmation letters. It is of interest to note that Allfirst felt the Crossmar matching system was too expensive to implement for only two foreign exchange traders.[46]

A glaring technology and design lapse was the use of Rusnak's spreadsheet to feed exchange rates from Reuters to the bank's system. The treasury operations department allowed Rusnak to have the only feed from Reuters for exchange rates. The operations department designed an information system that included an employee's personal computer. This is a serious breach of good system design practices. It was a security hole. Rusnak was able to insert himself into the bank's information system and change data.

ACCOUNTING PRACTICES

The lack of audits and inadequacy of audits, the failure to review profit and loss, the practices of not confirming trades, not independently confirming exchange rates and not checking VaR independently with independent data allowed Rusnak to get away with fraud. Many of the techniques that Rusnak used were in direct violation of the Guidelines for Foreign Exchange Trading. In particular, trades are expressly recommended to be confirmed as soon as possible.[47] The practices that Rusnak used would not have been effective if regular audits were conducted, if data used for calculations was independently verified and if trade confirmations had been made. Also, if the risk management departments had strong executive backing, they could have been much more effective.

CONCLUSION

John Rusnak did act alone. He had no direct accomplices. However, there were many indirect accomplices. All those who did not report what they saw, allowed him to talk them out of doing their jobs, and trusted the status quo rather than ask questions to get to the truth assisted Rusnak. Allfirst experienced problems that many corporations have. They had organizational political conditions influencing decisions. The fact that Allfirst was owned by a foreign company introduced some additional complexity in politics. Decision making in corporations can be based on budgets at the expense of other important considerations. Some decisions are made by looking at short term cost, rather than long term considerations. Employees don't always follow the standards set by their company. And supervisors can be too busy to enforce the standards. How a corporation and the people in it address these challenges is the differentiator between failure and long term success.

Albert Einstein is quoted as saying "insanity is doing the same thing and expecting different results." Rusnak was a person who got himself in trouble and then kept using the same methods to get himself out of trouble. He kept placing the same types of bets hoping for the same outcome: that the dollar would fall against the yen. He had full responsibility for his actions. The corporation had responsibility also. AIB and Allfirst allowed an environment where he could commit his fraudulent actions.

In the case of AIB and Allfirst, the suggestions of the Ludwig Report were implemented. The company hopefully learned quite a bit from the analysis and suggestions in the report.

NOTES

1. Brian Coyle, *Foreign Exchange Markets* (Chicago: Glenlake Publishing Company, Ltd, 2000) 3.
2. J. Monville Harris Jr. PhD, International Finance (Barron's Educational Series 1992) 9.
3. *Interbank Foreign Exchange Rates*, table (WallStreet Journal) Apr. 16, 2003.
4. Andrew J. Kreiger, *The Money Bazaar: Inside the Trillion-Dollar World of Currency Trading* (New York: Times Books, 1992) 21–22.
5. Foreign Exchange Committee. The Federal Reserve Bank of NY, *Guidelines for Foreign Exchange Trading Activities* (New York: Foreign Exchange Committee, October, 2002) 3.
6. Brian Coyle, *Foreign Exchange Markets* 16.
7. Brian Coyle, *Foreign Exchange Markets* 63.
8. Brian Coyle, *Currency Futures* 15, 25.
9. Brian Coyle, *Foreign Exchange Markets* 101–102.
10. Siobhán Creaton and Conor O'Clery, *Panic at the Bank: How John Rusnak lost AIB $691,000,000* (Dublin: Gill & Macmillan, 2002) 69, 73.
11. Promontory Financial Group and Wachtell, Lipton, Rosen, & Katz. *Report to the Boards of Directors of Allied Irish Banks, P.L.C., Allfirst Financial Inc., and Allfirst Bank concerning Currency Trading Losses.* (Mar. 12, 2002) 7, 9–10.

12. Robert Soloman, *Money on the Move – The Revolution in International Finance since 1980* (Princeton: Princeton University Press, 1999) 134.
13. http://www.federalreserve.gov/releases/H10/hist/dat96_ja.txt
14. Siobhán Creaton and Conor O'Clery, 78.
15. Promontory Financial Group, 10.
16. Siobhán Creaton and Conor O'Clery, 78.
17. Jonathan Fuerbringer, "Bank Report says Trader Had Bold Plot.", *New York Times* 15 Mar. 2002, C9.
18. Siobhán Creaton and Conor O'Clery, 77, 78.
19. Promontory Financial Group, 15.
20. Siobhán Creaton and Conor O'Clery, 83.
21. Promontory Financial Group, 12.
22. Siobhán Creaton and Conor O'Clery, 84.
23. Jonathan Fuerbringer, "Arcane Rollover System Let Trader Hide Losses," C-3.
24. Foreign Exchange Committee, 7.
25. Jonathan Fuerbringer, "Arcane Rollover System Let Trader Hide Losses," C-3.
26. Siobhán Creaton and Conor O'Clery, 86, 87, 102.
27. Promontory Financial Group, 16.
28. Thomas P. Edmonds, ed. and Francis M. McNair, Edward E. Milam, Philip R. Olds, Cindy D. Edmonds, Nancy W. Schneider, Claire N. Sawyer. *Fundamental Finance Accounting Concepts*. (McGraw Hill 2003) 61.
29. Siobhán Creaton and Conor O'Clery, 97–99.
30. Jonathan Fuerbringer, "Former Trader indicted on Bank Fraud Charges" *New York Times* 6 June, 2002, C-5.
31. Siobhán Creaton and Conor O'Clery, 90–91.
32. Siobhán Creaton and Conor O'Clery, 108.
33. Siobhán Creaton and Conor O'Clery, 107–109.
34. Jonathan Fuerbringer, "Former Trader Indicted on Bank Fraud charges", C-5.
35. Jonathan Fuerbringer, "Ex-Currency Trader Sentenced to Seven and a half years," *New York Times* 18 Jan. 2003, C-14.
36. Siobhán Creaton and Conor O'Clery, 15.
37. Siobhán Creaton and Conor O'Clery, 24.
38. AIBgroup, Annual Reports and Accounts 2001 for the Year ended 31 December, 2001 (Dublin: 2002) 4, 13.
39. Promontory Financial Group, 15–19.
40. Siobhán Creaton and Conor O'Clery, 91.
41. Promontory Financial Group, 19–20.
42. Promontory Financial Group, 22–25.
43. Foreign Exchange Committee, 7.
44. Siobhán Creaton and Conor O'Clery, 93.
45. Promontory Financial Group, 31–38.
46. Siobhán Creaton and Conor O'Clery, 80.
47. Foreign Exchange Committee, 24.

REFERENCES

AIBgroup. *Annual Reports and Accounts 2001 for the Year ended 31 December, 2001* Dublin. *http://www.aib.ie.*

Coyle, Brian. *Currency Futures*. Chicago: Glenlake Publishing Company, Ltd, 2000.

Coyle, Brian. *Foreign Exchange Markets*. Chicago: Glenlake Publishing Company, Ltd, 2000.

Coyle, Brian. *Hedging Currency Exposures*. Chicago: Glenlake Publishing Company, Ltd, 2000.

Creaton, Siobhán and O'Clery, Conor. *Panic at the Bank: How John Rusnak lost AIB $691,000,000*. Dublin: Gill & Macmillan, 2002.

Edmonds, Thomas P., ed., Francis M. McNair, Edward E. Milam, Philip R. Olds, Cindy D. Edmonds, Nancy W. Schneider, Claire N. Sawyer. *Fundamental Finance Accounting Concepts*. McGraw Hill 2003.

"Ex-Currency Trader Sentenced to Seven and a half years" *New York Times* 18 Jan. 2003, C-14.

Foreign Exchange Committee. The Federal Reserve Bank of NY. *Guidelines for Foreign Exchange Trading Activities*. October, 2002 *http://www.newyorkfed.org/fxc.*

Fuerbringer, Jonathan. "Arcane Rollover System Let Trader Hide Losses" *New York Times* 19 Feb. 2002, C-3.

Fuerbringer, Jonathan. "Bank Report says Trader Had Bold Plot." *New York Times* 15 Mar. 2002, C9.

Fuerbringer, Jonathan. "Former Trader Indicted on Bank Fraud Charges" *New York Times* 6 June, 2002, C-5.

Harris, J. Monville, Jr. PhD. *International Finance*. Barron's Educational Series. 1992.

Interbank Foreign Exchange Rates. Table. *Wall Street Journal*, Apr. 16, 2003.

Kreiger, Andrew J. *The Money Bazaar: Inside the Trillion-Dollar World of Currency Trading* with Edward Claflin. New York: Times Books, 1992.

Promontory Financial Group and Wachtell, Lipton, Rosen, & Katz. *Report to the Boards of Directors of Allied Irish Banks, P.L.C., Allfirst Financial Inc., and Allfirst Bank concerning Currency Trading Losses*. Mar. 12, 2002 *http://www.aib.ie.*

Soloman, Robert. *Money on the Move – The Revolution in International Finance since 1980*. Princeton: Princeton University Press, 1999.

Sutton, William. *Trading in Currency Options*. New York: New York Institute of Finance, 1988.

http://www.ft.com Financial Times. London.

Reproduced by permission from Sharon Burke, "Currency Exchange Trading and Rogue Trader John Rusnak", edited by Klaus Volpert, *Concept*, Vol. 25 (Spring 2004), Villanova University. Retrieved on 10th October 2005 from http://www.publications.villanova.edu/concept/2004.html. Edited by Martin Upton.

12

Value at Risk
Uses and Abuses

Christopher L. Culp, Merton H. Miller and Andrea M. P. Neves

Value at risk ("VAR") is now viewed by many as indispensable ammunition in any serious corporate risk manager's arsenal. VAR is a method of measuring the financial risk of an asset, portfolio, or exposure over some specified period of time. Its attraction stems from its ease of interpretation as a summary measure of risk and consistent treatment of risk across different financial instruments and business activities. VAR is often used as an approximation of the "maximum reasonable loss" a company can expect to realize from all its financial exposures.

VAR has received widespread accolades from industry and regulators alike.[1] Numerous organizations have found that the practical uses and benefits of VAR make it a valuable decision support tool in a comprehensive risk management process. Despite its many uses, however, VAR – like any statistical aggregate – is subject to the risk of misinterpretation and misapplication. Indeed, most problems with VAR seem to arise from what a firm *does* with a VAR measure rather than from the actual computation of the number.

Why a company manages risk affects *how* a company should manage – and, hence, should measure – its risk.[2] In that connection, we examine the four "great derivatives disasters" of 1993–1995 – Procter & Gamble, Barings, Orange County, and Metallgesellschaft – and evaluate how *ex ante* VAR measurements likely would have affected those situations. We conclude that VAR would have been of only limited value in averting those disasters and, indeed, actually might have been *misleading* in some of them.

WHAT IS VAR?

Value at risk is a summary statistic that quantifies the exposure of an asset or portfolio to market risk, or the risk that a position declines in value with adverse market price changes.[3] Measuring risk using VAR allows managers to make statements like the following: "We do not expect losses to exceed $1 million on more than 1 out of the next 20 days."[4]

To arrive at a VAR measure for a given portfolio, a firm must generate a probability distribution of possible changes in the value of some portfolio

over a specific time or "risk horizon" – e.g., one day.[5] The value at risk of
the portfolio is the dollar loss corresponding to some pre-defined probability level – usually 5% or less – as defined by the left-hand tail of the distribution. Alternatively, VAR is the dollar loss that is expected to occur no more
than 5% of the time over the defined risk horizon. Figure 12.1, for example,
depicts a one-day VAR of $10X at the 5% probability level.

The Development of VAR

VAR emerged first in the trading community.[6] The original goal of VAR was
to systematize the measurement of an active trading firm's risk exposures
across its dealing portfolios. Before VAR, most commercial trading houses
measured and controlled risk on a desk-by-desk basis with little attention to
firm-wide exposures. VAR made it possible for dealers to use risk measures
that could be compared and aggregated across trading areas as a means of
monitoring and limiting their consolidated financial risks.

VAR received its first public endorsement in July 1993, when a group representing the swap dealer community recommended the adoption of VAR by
all active dealers.[7] In that report, the Global Derivatives Study Group of The
Group of Thirty urged dealers to "use a *consistent measure* to calculate daily
the market risk of their derivatives positions and compare it to market risk
limits. Market risk is best measured as 'value at risk' using *probability analysis* based upon a common confidence interval (*e.g.*, two standard deviations)
and *time horizon* (*e.g.*, a one-day exposure). [emphasis added]"[8]

The italicized phrases in The Group of Thirty recommendation draw
attention to several specific features of VAR that account for its wide-spread
popularity among trading firms. One feature of VAR is its *consistent*
measurement of financial risk. By expressing risk using a "possible dollar
loss" metric, VAR makes possible direct comparisons of risk across differ-

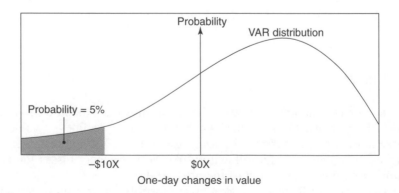

Figure 12.1

ent business lines and distinct financial products such as interest rate and currency swaps.

In addition to consistency, VAR also is *probability-based*. With whatever degree of confidence a firm wants to specify, VAR enables the firm to associate a specific loss with that level of confidence. Consequently, VAR measures can be interpreted as forward-looking approximations of potential market risk.

A third feature of VAR is its reliance on a *common time horizon* called the risk horizon. A one-day risk horizon at, say, the 5% probability level tells the firm, strictly speaking, that it can expect to lose no more than, say, $10X on the next day with 95% confidence. Firms often go on to assume that the 5% confidence level means they stand to lose more than $10X on no more than five days out of 100, an inference that is true only if strong assumptions are made about the stability of the underlying probability distribution.[9]

The choice of this risk horizon is based on various motivating factors. These may include the timing of employee performance evaluations, key decision-making events (*e.g.*, asset purchases), major reporting events (*e.g.*, board meetings and required disclosures), regulatory examinations, tax assessments, external quality assessments, and the like.

Implementing VAR

To estimate the value at risk of a portfolio, possible future values of that portfolio must be generated, yielding a distribution – called the "VAR distribution" – like that we saw in Figure 12.1. Once the VAR distribution is created for the chosen risk horizon, the VAR itself is just a number on the curve – *viz.*, the change in the value of the portfolio leaving the specified amount of probability in the left-hand tail.

Creating a VAR distribution for a particular portfolio and a given risk horizon can be viewed as a two-step process.[10] In the first step, the price or return distributions for each individual security or asset in the portfolio are generated. These distributions represent possible value changes in all the component assets over the risk horizon.[11] Next, the individual distributions somehow must be aggregated into a portfolio distribution using appropriate measures of correlation.[12] The resulting portfolio distribution then serves as the basis for the VAR summary measure.

An important assumption in almost all VAR calculations is that the portfolio whose risk is being evaluated *does not change* over the risk horizon. This assumption of no turnover was not a major issue when VAR first arrived on the scene at derivatives dealers. They were focused on one- or two-day – sometimes *intra*-day – risk horizons and thus found VAR both easy to implement and relatively realistic. But when it comes to generalizing VAR to a longer time horizon, the assumption of no portfolio changes becomes problematic. What does it mean, after all, to evaluate the *one-year* VAR of a portfolio using only the portfolio's contents *today* if the turnover in the portfolio is 20–30% per day?

Methods for generating both the individual asset risk distributions and the portfolio risk distribution range from the simplistic to the indecipherably complex. Because our goal in this paper is not to evaluate all these mechanical methods of VAR measurement, readers are referred elsewhere for explanations of the nuts and bolts of VAR computation.[13] Several common methods of VAR calculation are summarized in the Appendix.

Uses of VAR

The purpose of any risk measurement system and summary risk statistic is to facilitate risk reporting and control decisions. Accordingly, dealers quickly began to rely on VAR measures in their broader risk management activities. The simplicity of VAR measurement greatly facilitated dealers' reporting of risks to senior managers and directors. The popularity of VAR owes much to Dennis Weatherstone, former chairman of JP Morgan & Co., Inc., who demanded to know the total market risk exposure of JP Morgan at 4:15pm every day. Weatherstone's request was met with a daily VAR report.

VAR also proved useful in dealers' risk *control* efforts.[14] Commercial banks, for example, used VAR measures to quantify current trading exposures and compare them to established counterparty risk limits. In addition, VAR provided traders with information useful in formulating hedging policies and evaluating the effects of particular transactions on net portfolio risk. For managers, VAR became popular as a means of analyzing the performance of traders for compensation purposes and for allocating reserves or capital across business lines on a risk-adjusted basis.

Uses of VAR by Non-Dealers. Since its original development as a risk management tool for active trading firms, VAR has spread outside the dealer community. VAR now is used regularly by non-financial corporations, pension plans and mutual funds, clearing organizations, brokers and futures commission merchants, and insurers. These organizations find VAR just as useful as trading firms, albeit for different reasons.

Some benefits of VAR for non-dealers relate more to the exposure monitoring facilitated by VAR measurement than to the risk measurement task itself. For example, a pension plan with funds managed by external investment advisors may use VAR for policing its external managers. Similarly, brokers and account merchants can use VAR to assess collateral requirements for customers.

VAR AND CORPORATE RISK MANAGEMENT OBJECTIVES

Firms managing risks may be either *value risk managers* or *cash flow risk managers*.[15] A value risk manager is concerned with the firm's total value at a particular point in time. This concern may arise from a desire to avoid bankruptcy, mitigate problems associated with informational asymmetries, or reduce expected tax liabilities.[16] A cash flow risk manager, by contrast, uses risk management to reduce cash flow volatility and thereby increase debt capacity.[17] Value risk managers thus typically manage the risks of a *stock of assets*, whereas cash flow risk managers manage the risks of a *flow of funds*. A risk measure that is appropriate for one type of firm may not be appropriate for others.

Value Risk Managers and VAR-Based Risk Controls

As the term *value* at risk implies, organizations for which VAR is best suited are those for which *value* risk management is the goal. VAR, after all, is intended to summarize the risk of a stock of assets over a particular risk horizon. Those likely to realize the most benefits from VAR thus include clearing houses, securities settlement agents,[18] and swap dealers. These organizations have in common a concern with the value of their exposures over a well-defined period of time *and* a wish to limit and control those exposures. In addition, the relatively short risk horizons of these enterprises imply that VAR measurement can be accomplished reliably and with minimal concern about changing portfolio composition over the risk horizon.

Many value risk managers have risks arising mainly from *agency* transactions. Organizations like financial clearinghouses, for example, are exposed to risk arising from intermediation services rather than the risks of proprietary position taking. VAR can assist such firms in monitoring their customer credit exposures, in setting position and exposure limits, and in determining and enforcing margin and collateral requirements.

Total vs. Selective Risk Management

Most financial distress-driven explanations of corporate risk management, whether value or cash flow risk, center on a firm's *total risk*.[19] If so, such firms should be indifferent to the *composition* of their total risks. *Any* risk thus is a candidate for risk reduction.

Selective risk managers, by contrast, deliberately choose to manage some risks and not others. Specifically, they seek to manage their exposures to risks in which they have no comparative informational advantage – for the usual financial ruin reasons – while actively exposing themselves, at least to a point, to risks in which they *do* have perceived superior information.[20]

For firms managing total risk, the principal benefit of VAR is facilitating explicit risk control decisions, such as setting and enforcing exposure limits. For firms that selectively manage risk, by contrast, VAR is useful largely for diagnostic monitoring *or* for controlling risk in areas where the firm perceives no comparative informational advantage. An airline, for example, might find VAR helpful in assessing its exposure to jet fuel prices; but for the airline to use VAR to analyze the risk that seats on its aircraft are not all sold makes little sense.

Consider also a hedge fund manager who invests in foreign equity because the risk/return profile of that asset class is desirable. To avoid exposure to the exchange rate risk, the fund could engage an "over-lay manager" to hedge the currency risk of the position. Using VAR on the *whole position* lumps together two separate and distinct sources of risk – the currency risk and the foreign equity price risk. And *reporting* that total VAR without a corresponding expected return could have disastrous consequences. Using VAR to ensure that the currency hedge is accomplishing its intended aims, by contrast, might be perfectly legitimate.

VAR AND THE GREAT DERIVATIVES DISASTERS

Despite its many benefits to certain firms, VAR is not a panacea. Even when VAR is calculated appropriately, VAR *in isolation* will do little to keep a firm's risk exposures in line with the firm's chosen risk tolerances. Without a well-developed risk management infrastructure – policies and procedures, systems, and well-defined senior management responsibilities – VAR will deliver little, if any, benefits. In addition, VAR may not always help a firm accomplish its particular risk management objectives, as we shall see.

To illustrate some of the pitfalls of using VAR, we examine the four "great derivatives disasters" of 1993–1995: Procter & Gamble, Orange County, Barings, and Metallgesellschaft.[21] Proponents of VAR often claim that many of these disasters would have been averted had VAR measurement systems been in place. We think otherwise.[22]

Procter & Gamble

During 1993, Procter & Gamble ("P&G") undertook derivatives transactions with Bankers Trust that resulted in over $150 million in losses.[23] Those losses traced essentially to P&G's writing of a put option on interest rates to Bankers Trust. Writers of put options suffer losses, of course, whenever the underlying security declines in price, which in this instance meant whenever interest rates rose. And rise they did in the summer and autumn of 1993.

The put option actually was only one component of the whole deal. The deal, with a notional principal of $200 million, was a fixed-for-floating rate swap in which Bankers Trust offered P&G 10 years of floating-rate financing at 75 basis points below the commercial paper rate in exchange for the put and fixed interest payments of 5.3% annually. That huge financing advantage of 75 basis points apparently was too much for P&G's treasurer to resist, particularly because the put was well out-of-the-money when the deal was struck in May 1993. But the low financing rate, of course, was just premium collected for writing the put. When the put went in-the-money for Bankers Trust, what once seemed like a good deal to P&G ended up costing millions of dollars.

VAR would have helped P&G, *if* P&G also had in place an adequate risk management infrastructure – which apparently it did not. Most obviously, senior managers at P&G would have been unlikely to have approved the original swap deal if its exposure had been subject to a VAR calculation. But that presupposes a lot.

Although VAR would have helped P&G's senior management measure its exposure to the speculative punt by its treasurer, much more would have been needed to stop the treasurer from taking the interest rate bet. The first requirement would have been a system for measuring the risk of the swaps *on a transactional basis*. But VAR was never intended for use on single transactions.[24] On the contrary, the whole appeal of the concept initially was its capacity to aggregate risk *across* transactions and exposures. To examine the risk of an individual transaction, the *change* in portfolio VAR that would occur with the addition of that new transaction should be analyzed. But that still requires first calculating the total VAR.[25] So, for P&G to have looked at the risk of its swaps in a VAR context, its entire treasury area would have needed a VAR measurement capability.

Implementing VAR for P&G's entire treasury function might *seem* to have been a good idea *anyway*. Why not, after all, perform a comprehensive VAR analysis on the whole treasury area and get transactional VAR assessment capabilities as an added bonus? For some firms, that *is* a good idea. But for other firms, it is not. Many non-financial corporations like P&G, after all, typically undertake risk management in their corporate treasury functions for *cash flow* management reasons.[26] VAR is a *value* risk measure, not a cash flow risk measure. For P&G to examine value at risk for its *whole* treasury operation, therefore, presumes that P&G was a *value* risk manager, and that may not have been the case. Even had VAR been in place at P&G, moreover, the assumption that P&G's senior managers would have been *monitoring* and *controlling* the VARs of individual swap transactions is not a foregone conclusion.

Barings

Barings PLC failed in February 1995 when rogue trader Nick Leeson's bets on the Japanese stock market went sour and turned into over $1 billion in trading losses.[27,28] To be sure, VAR would have led Barings senior management to shut down Leeson's trading operation in time to save the firm – *if they knew about it*. If P&G's sin was a lack of internal management and control over its treasurer, then Barings was guilty of an even more cardinal sin. The top officers of Barings lost control over the trading operation *not* because no VAR measurement system was in place, but because they let the same individual making the trades also serve as the recorder of those trades – violating one of the most elementary principles of good management.

The more interesting question emerging from Barings is why top management seems to have taken so long to recognize that a rogue trader was at work. For that purpose, a fully functioning VAR system would certainly have helped. Increasingly, companies in the financial risk-taking business use VAR as a monitoring tool for detecting unauthorized increases in positions.[29] Usually, this is intended for *customer* credit risk management by firms like futures commission merchants. In the case of Barings, however, such account monitoring would have enabled management to spot Leeson's run-up in positions in his so-called "arbitrage" and "error" accounts.

VAR measurements at Barings, on the other hand, would have been impossible to implement, given the deficiencies in the *overall* information technology ("IT") systems in place at the firm. At any point in time, Barings' top managers knew only what Leeson was telling them. If Barings' systems were incapable of reconciling the position build-up in Leeson's accounts with the huge wire transfers being made by London to support Leeson's trading in Singapore, no VAR measure would have included a complete picture of Leeson's positions. And without that, no warning flag would have been raised.

Orange County

The Orange County Investment Pool ("OCIP") filed bankruptcy in December 1994 after reporting a drop in its market value of $1.5 billion. For many years, Orange County maintained the OCIP as the equivalent of a money market fund for the benefit of school boards, road building authorities, and other local government bodies in its territory. These local agencies deposited their tax and other collections when they came in and paid for their own wage and other bills when the need arose. The Pool paid them interest on their deposits – handsomely, in fact. Between 1989 and 1994, the OCIP paid its depositors 400 basis points more than they would have earned on the corporate Pool maintained by the State of California – roughly $750 million over the period.[30]

Most of the OCIP's investments involved leveraged purchases of intermediate-term securities and structured notes financed with "reverse repos" and other short-term borrowings. Contrary to conventional wisdom, the Pool was making its profits *not* from "speculation on falling interest rates" but rather from an investment play on the *slope* of the yield curve.[31] When the Federal Reserve started to raise interest rates in 1994, the intermediate-term securities declined in value and OCIP's short-term borrowing costs rose.

Despite the widespread belief that the leverage policy led to the fund's insolvency and bankruptcy filing, Miller and Ross, after examining the OCIP's investment strategy, cash position, and net asset value at the time of the filing, have shown that the OCIP was *not* insolvent. Miller and Ross estimate that the $20 billion in total assets on deposit in the fund had a positive net worth of about $6 billion. Nor was the fund in an illiquid cash situation. OCIP had over $600 million of cash on hand and was generating further cash at a rate of more than $30 million a month.[32] Even the reported $1.5 billion "loss" would have been completely recovered within a year – a loss that was realized only because Orange County's bankruptcy lawyers forced the liquidation of the securities.[33]

Jorion has taken issue with Miller and Ross's analysis of OCIP, arguing that VAR would have called the OCIP investment program into question long before the $1.5 billion loss was incurred.[34] Using several different VAR calculation methods, Jorion concludes that OCIP's one-year VAR at the end of 1994 was about $1 billion at the 5% confidence level. Under the usual VAR interpretation, this would have told OCIP to expect a loss in excess of $1 billion in one out of the next 20 years.

Even assuming Jorion's VAR number is accurate, however, his interpretation of the VAR measure was unlikely to have been the OCIP's interpretation – at least not *ex ante* when it could have mattered. The VAR measure in isolation, after all, takes no account of the *upside* returns OCIP was receiving as compensation for that downside risk. Remember that OCIP was pursuing a very deliberate yield curve, net cost-of-carry strategy, designed to generate high expected cash returns. That strategy had risks, to be sure, but those risks seem to have been clear to OCIP treasurer Robert Citron – and, for that matter, to the people of Orange County who re-elected Citron treasurer in preference to an opposing candidate who was criticizing the investment strategy.[35]

Had Orange County been using VAR, however, it almost certainly *would* have terminated its investment program upon seeing the $1 billion risk estimate. The reason probably would *not* have been the actual informativeness of the VAR number, but rather the fear of a public outcry at the number. Imagine the public reaction if the OCIP announced one day that it expected to lose more than $1 billion over the next year in one time out of 20. But that reaction would have far less to do with the actual risk information conveyed by the VAR number than with the lack of any corresponding expected profits reported *with* the risk number. Just consider, after all, what the public reaction would have been if the OCIP publicly announced that it would *gain* more than $1 billion over the next year in one time out of 20![36]

This example highlights a major abuse of VAR – an abuse that has nothing to do with the meaning of the value at risk number but instead traces to the presentation of the information that number conveys. Especially for institutional investors, a major pitfall of VAR is to highlight large potential losses over long time horizons *without conveying any information about the corresponding expected return*. The lesson from Orange County to would-be VAR users thus is an important one – for organizations whose mission is *to take some risks*, VAR measures of risks are meaningful *only* when interpreted alongside estimates of corresponding potential *gains*.

Metallgesellschaft

MG Refining & Marketing, Inc. ("MGRM"), a U.S. subsidiary of Metallgesellschaft AG, reported $1.3 billion in losses by year-end 1993 from its oil trading activities. MGRM's oil derivatives were part of a marketing program under which it offered long-term customers firm price guarantees for up to 10 years on gasoline, heating oil, and diesel fuel purchased from MGRM.[37] The firm hedged its resulting exposure to spot price increases with short-term futures contracts to a considerable extent. After several consecutive months of *falling* prices in the autumn of 1993, however, MGRM's German parent reacted to the substantial margin calls on the losing futures positions by liquidating the hedge, thereby turning a paper loss into a very real one.[38]

Most of the arguments over MGRM – in press accounts, in the many law suits the case engendered, and in the academic literature – have focused on whether MGRM was "speculating" or "hedging." The answer, of course, is that like all other merchant firms, they were doing both. They were definitely speculating on the oil "basis" – inter-regional, intertemporal, and inter-product *differences* in prices of crude, heating oil, and gasoline. That was the *business they were in.*[39] The firm had expertise and informational advantages far beyond those of its customers or of casual observers playing the oil futures market. What MGRM did not have, of course, was any special expertise about the level and direction of oil prices generally. Here, rather than take a corporate "view" on the direction of oil prices, like the misguided one the treasurer of P&G took on interest rates, MGRM chose to hedge its exposure to oil price *levels*.

Subsequent academic controversy surrounding the case has mainly been not whether MGRM was hedging, but whether they were *over*-hedging – whether the firm could have achieved the same degree of insulation from price level changes with a lower commitment from MGRM's ultimate owner-creditor Deutsche Bank.[40] The answer is that the day-to-day cash-flow volatility of the program *could* have been reduced by any number of cash flow variance-reducing hedge ratios.[41] But the cost of chopping off some cash drains when prices fell was that of losing the corresponding cash inflows when prices spiked up.[42]

Conceptually, of course, MGRM could have used VAR analysis to measure its possible financial risk. But why would they have wanted to do so? The combined marketing/hedging program, after all, was *hedged* against changes in the *level* of oil prices. The only significant risks to which MGRM's program was subject thus were basis and rollover risks – again, the risk that MGRM was *in the business of taking.*[43]

A much bigger problem at MGRM than the change in the *value* of its program was the large negative *cash flows* on the futures hedge that would have been offset by eventual gains in the future on the fixed-price customer contracts. Although MGRM's former management claims it had access to adequate funding from Deutsche Bank (the firm's leading creditor and stock holder), perhaps some benefit might have been achieved by more rigorous cash flow simulations. But even granting that, VAR would have told MGRM very little about its *cash flows* at risk. As we have already emphasized, VAR is a *value*-based risk measure.

For firms like MGRM engaged in *authorized* risk-taking – like Orange County and unlike Leeson/Barings – the primary benefit of VAR really is just as an internal "diagnostic monitoring" tool. To that end, estimating the VAR of MGRM's basis trading activities *would* have told senior managers and directors at its parent what the basis risks were that MGRM actually was taking. But remember, MGRM's parent appears to have been fully aware of the risks MGRM's traders were taking *even without a VAR number*. In that sense, even the monitoring benefits of VAR for a proprietary trading operation would not have changed MGRM's fate.[44]

ALTERNATIVES TO VAR

VAR certainly is not the *only* way a firm can systematically measure its financial risk. As noted, its appeal is mainly its conceptual simplicity and its consistency across financial products and activities. In cases where VAR may *not* be appropriate as a measure of risk, however, other alternatives *are* available.

Cash Flow Risk

Firms concerned *not* with the value of a stock of assets and liabilities over a specific time horizon but with the volatility of a *flow of funds* often are better off eschewing VAR altogether in favor of a measure of cash flow volatility. Possible cash requirements over a *sequence* of future dates, for example, can be simulated. The resulting distributions of cash flows then enable the firm to control its exposure to cash flow risk more directly.[45] Firms worried about cash flow risk for preserving or increasing their debt capacities thus might engage in hedging, whereas firms concerned purely about liquidity shortfalls might use such cash flow stress tests to arrange appropriate standby funding.

Abnormal Returns and Risk-Based Capital Allocation

Stulz suggests managing risk-taking activities using abnormal returns – *i.e.*, returns in excess of the risk free rate – as a measure of the expected profitability of certain activities. Selective risk management then can be accomplished by allocating capital on a risk-adjusted basis and limiting capital at risk accordingly. To measure the risk-adjusted capital allocation, he suggests using the cost of new equity issued to finance the particular activity.[46]

On the positive side, Stulz's suggestion does not penalize selective risk managers for exploiting perceived informational advantages, whereas VAR does. The problem with Stulz's idea, however, lies in any company's capacity actually to implement such a risk management process. More properly, the difficulty lies in the actual estimation of the firm's equity cost of capital. And in any event, under M&M proposition three, all sources of capital are equivalent on a risk-adjusted basis. The source of capital for financing a particular project thus should not affect the decision to undertake that project. Stulz's reliance on equity only is thus inappropriate.

Shortfall Risk

VAR need not be calculated by assuming variance is a complete measure of "risk," but in practice this often *is* how VAR is calculated. (*See* the Appendix.) This assumption can be problematic when measuring exposures in markets characterized by non-normal (*i.e.*, non-Gaussian) distributions – *e.g.*, return distributions that are skewed or have fat tails. If so, as explained in the Appendix, a solution is to generate the VAR distribution in a manner that does *not* presuppose variance is an adequate measure of risk. Alternatively, other summary risk measures can be calculated.

For some organizations, asymmetric distributions pose a problem that VAR on its own *cannot* address, no matter how it is calculated. Consider again the OCIP example, in which the one-year VAR implied a $1 billion loss in one year out of 20. With a symmetric portfolio distribution, that would also imply a $1 billion gain in one year out of 20. But suppose OCIP's investment program had a *positively skewed* return distribution. Then, the $1 billion loss in one year out of 20 might be comparable to, say, a $5 billion gain in one year of 20.

One of the problems with interpreting VAR thus is interpreting the confidence level – *viz.*, 5% or one year in 20. Some organizations may consider it more useful *not* to examine the loss associated with a chosen probability level but rather to examine the risk associated with a *given loss* – the so-called "doomsday" return below which a portfolio must *never* fall. Pension plans, endowments, and some hedge funds, for example, are concerned primarily with the possibility of a "shortfall" of assets below liabilities that would necessitate a contribution from the plan sponsor.

Shortfall risk measures are alternatives to VAR that allow a risk manager to define a specific target value below which the organization's assets must *never* fall and they measure risk accordingly. Two popular measures of shortfall risk are below-target probability ("BTP") and below-target risk ("BTR").[47]

The advantage of BTR, in particular, over VAR is that it penalizes large shortfalls more than small ones.[48] BTR is still subject to the same misinterpretation as VAR when it is reported without a corresponding indication of possible *gains*. VAR, however, relies on a somewhat arbitrary choice of a "probability level" that can be changed to exaggerate or to de-emphasize risk measures. BTR, by contrast, is based on a real target – *e.g.*, a pension actuarial contribution threshold – and thus reveals information about risk that can be much more usefully weighed against expected returns than a VAR measure.[49]

CONCLUSION

By facilitating the consistent measurement of risk across distinct assets and activities, VAR allows firms to monitor, report, and control their risks in a manner that efficiently relates risk control to desired and actual economic exposures. At the same time, reliance on VAR can result in serious problems when improperly used. Would-be users of VAR are thus advised to consider the following three pieces of advice:

First, VAR is useful only to certain firms and only in particular circumstances. Specifically, VAR is a tool for firms engaged in *total value* risk management, where the consolidated values of exposures across a variety of activities are at issue. Dangerous misinterpretations of the risk facing a firm can result when VAR is wrongly applied in situations where total value risk management is *not* the objective, such as at firms concerned with *cash flow* risk rather than value risk.

Second, VAR should be applied very carefully to firms selectively managing their risks. When an organization deliberately takes certain risks as a part of its primary business, VAR can serve at best as a diagnostic monitoring tool for those risks. When VAR is analyzed and reported in such situations with no estimates of corresponding expected profits, the information conveyed by the VAR estimate can be extremely misleading.

Finally, as all the great derivatives disasters illustrate, no form of risk measurement – including VAR – is a substitute for good management. Risk management as a process encompasses much more than just risk measurement. Although judicious risk measurement can prove very useful to certain firms, it is quite pointless without a well-developed organizational infrastructure and IT system capable of supporting the complex and dynamic process of risk taking and risk control.

NOTES

The authors thank Kamaryn Tanner for her previous work with us on this subject.

1. *See, for example*, Global Derivatives Study Group, *Derivatives: Practices and Principles* (Washington, D.C.: July 1993), and Board of Governors of the Federal Reserve System, *SR Letter 93–69* (1993). Most recently, the Securities and Exchange Commission began to require risk disclosures by all public companies. One approved format for these mandatory financial risk disclosures is VAR. For a critical assessment of the SEC's risk disclosure rule, *see* Merton

H. Miller and Christopher L. Culp, "The SEC's Costly Disclosure Rules," *Wall Street Journal* (June 22, 1996).

2. This presupposes, of course, that "risk management" is consistent with value-maximizing behavior by the firm. For the purpose of this paper, we do not consider whether firms *should be* managing their risks. For a discussion of that issue, *see* Christopher L. Culp and Merton H. Miller, "Hedging in the Theory of Corporate Finance: A Reply to Our Critics," *Journal of Applied Corporate Finance*, Vol. 8, No. 1 (Spring 1995): 121–127, and René M. Stulz, "Rethinking Risk Management," *Journal of Applied Corporate Finance*, Vol. 9, No. 3 (Fall 1996): 8–24.

3. More recently, VAR has been suggested as a framework for measuring credit risk, as well. To keep our discussion focused, we examine only the applications of VAR to market risk measurement.

4. For a general description of VAR, *see* Philippe Jorion, *Value at Risk* (Chicago: Irwin Professional Publishing, 1997).

5. The risk horizon is chosen exogenously by the firm engaging in the VAR calculation.

6. An early precursor of VAR was SPAN™ – Standard Portfolio Analysis of Risk – developed by the Chicago Mercantile Exchange for setting futures margins. Now widely used by virtually all futures exchanges, SPAN is a non-parametric, simulation-based "worst case" measure of risk. As will be seen, VAR, by contrast, rests on well-defined probability distributions.

7. This was followed quickly by a similar endorsement from the International Swaps and Derivatives Association. *See* Jorion, cited previously.

8. Global Derivatives Study Group, cited previously.

9. This interpretation assumes that asset price changes are what the technicians call "iid," independently and identically distributed – *i.e.*, that price changes are drawn from essentially the same distribution every day.

10. In practice, VAR is not often implemented in a clean two-step manner, but discussing it in this way simplifies our discussion – without any loss of generality.

11. Especially with instruments whose payoffs are non-linear, a better approach is to generate distributions for the underlying "risk factors" that affect an asset rather than focus on the changes in the values of the assets themselves. To generate the value change distribution of an option on a stock, for example, one might first generate changes in the stock price and its volatility and *then* compute associated option price changes rather than generating option price changes "directly." For a discussion, *see* Michael S. Gamze and Ronald S. Rolighed, "VAR: What's Wrong With This Picture?" unpublished manuscript, Federal Reserve Bank of Chicago (1997).

12. If a risk manager is interested in the risk of a particular financial instrument, the appropriate risk measure to analyze is *not* the VAR of that instrument. Portfolio effects still must be considered. The relevant measure of risk is the *marginal risk* of that instrument in the portfolio being evaluated. *See* Mark Garman, "Improving on VAR," *Risk* Vol. 9, No. 5 (1996): 61–63.

13. *See, for example*, Jorion, cited previously, Rod A. Beckström and Alyce R. Campbell, "Value-at-Risk (VAR): Theoretical Foundations," in *An Introduction to VAR*, Rod Beckström and Alyce Campbell, eds (Palo Alto, Ca.: CAATS Software, Inc., 1995), and James V. Jordan and Robert J. Mackay, "Assessing Value at Risk for Equity Portfolios: Implementing Alternative Techniques," in *Derivatives Handbook*, Robert J. Schwartz and Clifford W. Smith, Jr., eds (New York: John Wiley & Sons, Inc., 1997).

14. *See* Rod A. Beckström and Alyce R. Campbell, "The Future of Firm-Wide Risk Management," in *An Introduction to VAR*, Rod Beckström and Alyce Campbell, eds (Palo Alto, Ca.: CAATS Software, Inc., 1995).

15. For a general discussion of the traditional corporate motivations for risk management, *see* David Fite and Paul Pfleider, "Should Firms Use Derivatives to Manage Risk?" in *Risk Management: Problems & Solutions*, William H. Beaver and George Parker, eds (New York: McGraw-Hill, Inc., 1995).

16. *See, for example*, Clifford Smith and René Stulz, "The Determinants of Firms' Hedging Policies," *Journal of Financial and Quantitative Analysis*, Vol. 20 (1985): 391–405.

17. *See, for example*, Kenneth Froot, David Scharfstein, and Jeremy Stein, "Risk Management: Coordinating Corporate Investment and Financing Policies," *Journal of Finance* Vol. 48 (1993): 1629–1658.

18. *See* Christopher L. Culp and Andrea M.P. Neves, "Risk Management by Securities Settlement Agents," *Journal of Applied Corporate Finance* Vol. 10, No. 3 (Fall 1997): 96–103.

19. *See, for example*, Smith and Stulz, cited previously, and Froot, Scharfstein, and Stein, cited previously.

20. *See* Culp and Miller (Spring 1995), cited previously, and Stulz, cited previously.

21. In truth, Procter & Gamble was the only one of these disasters actually *caused* by derivatives. *See* Merton H. Miller, "The Great Derivatives Disasters: What Really Went Wrong and How to Keep it from Happening to You," speech presented to JP Morgan & Co. (Frankfurt, June 24, 1997) and chapter two in Merton H. Miller, *Merton Miller on Derivatives* (New York: John Wiley & Sons, Inc., 1997).

22. The details of all these cases are complex. We thus refer readers elsewhere for discussions of the actual events that took place and limit our discussion here only to basic background. *See, for example*, Stephen Figlewski, "How to Lose Money in Derivatives," *Journal of Derivatives* Vol. 2, No. 2 (Winter 1994): 75–82.

23. *See, for example*, Figlewski, cited previously, and Michael S. Gamze and Karen McCann, "A Simplified Approach to Valuing an Option on a Leveraged Spread: The Bankers Trust, Procter & Gamble Example," *Derivatives Quarterly* Vol. 1, No. 4 (Summer 1995): 44–53.

24. Recently, some have advocated that derivatives dealers should evaluate the VAR of specific transactions *from the perspective of their counterparties* in order to determine counterparty suitability. Without knowing the rest of the

counterparty's risk exposures, however, the VAR estimate would be meaningless. Even with full knowledge of the counterparty's total portfolio, the VAR number still might be of no use in determining suitability for reasons to become clear later.

25. *See* Garman, cited previously.

26. *See, for example*, Judy C. Lewent and A. John Kearney, "Identifying, Measuring, and Hedging Currency Risk at Merck," *Journal of Applied Corporate Finance* Vol. 2, No. 4 (Winter 1990): 19–28, and Deana R. Nance, Clifford W. Smith, and Charles W. Smithson, "On the Determinants of Corporate Hedging," *Journal of Finance* Vol. 48, No. 1 (1993): 267–284.

27. *See, for example*, Hans R. Stoll, "Lost Barings: A Tale in Three Parts Concluding with a Lesson," *Journal of Derivatives* Vol. 3, No. 1 (Fall 1995): 109–115, and Anatoli Kuprianov, "Derivatives Debacles: Case Studies of Large Losses in Derivatives Markets," in *Derivatives Handbook: Risk Management and Control*, Robert J. Schwartz and Clifford W. Smith, Jr., eds. (New York: John Wiley & Sons, Inc., 1997).

28. Our reference to rogue traders is not intended to suggest, of course, that rogue traders are only found in connection with derivatives. Rogue traders have caused the banks of this world far more damage from failed real estate (and copper) deals than from derivatives.

29. *See* Christopher Culp, Kamaryn Tanner, and Ron Mensink, "Risks, Returns and Retirement," *Risk* Vol. 10, No. 10 (October 1997): 63–69.

30. Miller, cited previously.

31. When the term structure is upward sloping, borrowing in short-term markets to leverage longer-term government securities generates positive cash carry. A surge in inflation or interest rates, of course, could reverse the term structure and turn the carry negative. That is the real risk the treasurer was taking. But it was not much of a risk. Since the days of Jimmy Carter in the late 1970s, the U.S. term structure has never been downward sloping and nobody in December 1994 thought it was likely to be so in the foreseeable future.

32. Merton H. Miller and David J. Ross, "The Orange County Bankruptcy and its Aftermath: Some New Evidence," *Journal of Derivatives*, Vol. 4, No. 4 (Summer 1997): 51–60.

33. Readers may wonder why, then, Orange County did declare bankruptcy. That story is complicated, but a hint might be found in the payment of $50 million in special legal fees to the attorneys that sued Merrill Lynch for $1.5 billion for selling OCIP the securities that lost money. In short, *lots* of people gained from OCIP's bankruptcy, even though OCIP was not actually bankrupt. *See* Miller, cited previously, and Miller and Ross, cited previously.

34. Philippe Jorion, "Lessons From the Orange County Bankruptcy," *Journal of Derivatives* Vol. 4, No. 4 (Summer 1997): 61–66.

35. Miller and Ross, cited previously.

36. Only for the purpose of this example, we obviously have assumed symmetry in the VAR distribution.

37. A detailed analysis of the program can be found in Christopher L. Culp and Merton H. Miller, "Metallgesellschaft and the Economics of Synthetic Storage," *Journal of Applied Corporate Finance* Vol. 7, No. 4 (Winter 1995): 62–76.

38. For an analysis of the losses incurred by MGRM – as well as why they were incurred – *see* Christopher L. Culp and Merton H. Miller, "Auditing the Auditors,' *Risk* Vol. 8, No. 4 (1995): 36–39.

39. Culp and Miller (Winter 1995, Spring 1995), cited previously, explain this in detail.

40. *See* Franklin R. Edwards and Michael S. Canter, "The Collapse of Metallgesellschaft: Unhedgeable Risks, Poor Hedging Strategy, or Just Bad Luck?," *Journal of Applied Corporate Finance* Vol. 8, No. 1 (Spring 1995): 86–105.

41. *See, for example*, Froot, Scharfstein, and Stein, cited previously.

42. A number of other reasons also explain MGRM's reluctance to adopt anything smaller than a "one-for-one stack-and-roll" hedge. *See* Culp and Miller (Winter 1995, Spring 1995).

43. The claim that MGRM was in the business of trading the basis has been disputed by managers of MGRM's parent and creditors. Nevertheless, the marketing materials of MGRM – on which the parent firm signed off – suggests otherwise. *See* Culp and Miller (Spring 1995), cited previously.

44. Like P&G and Barings, what happened at MGRM was, in the end, a *management* failure rather than a *risk management* failure. For details on how management failed in the MGRM case, *see* Culp and Miller (Winter 1995, Spring 1995). For a redacted version of the story, *see* Christopher L. Culp and Merton H. Miller, "Blame Mismanagement, Not Speculation, for Metall's Woes," *Wall Street Journal Europe* (April 25, 1995).

45. *See* Stulz, cited previously.

46. *See* Stulz, cited previously.

47. See Culp, Tanner, and Mensink, cited previously. For a complete mathematic discussion of these concepts, *see* Kamaryn T. Tanner, "An Asymmetric distribution Model for Portfolio Optimization," manuscript, Graduate School of Business, The University of Chicago (1997).

48. BTP accomplishes a similar objective but does *not* weight large deviations below the target more heavily than small ones.

49. *See* Culp, Tanner, and Mensink, cited previously, for a more involved treatment of shortfall risk as compared to VAR.

APPENDIX: CALCULATING VAR

To calculate a VAR statistic is easy *once you have generated the probability distribution for future values of the portfolio*. Creating that VAR distribution, on the other hand, can be quite hard, and the methods available range from the banal to the utterly arcane. This appendix reviews a few of those methods.

Variance-Based Approaches

By far the easiest way to create the VAR distribution used in calculating the actual VAR statistic is just to *assume* that distribution is normal (*i.e.*, Gaussian). Mean and variance are "sufficient statistics" to fully characterize a normal distribution. Consequently, knowing the variance of an asset whose return is normally distributed is all that is needed to summarize the risk of that asset.

Using return variances and covariances as inputs, VAR thus can be calculated in a fairly straightforward way.[1] First consider a single asset. If returns on that asset are normally distributed, the 5th percentile VAR is always 1.65 standard deviations below the mean return. So, the variance is a sufficient measure of risk to compute the VAR on that asset – just subtract 1.65 times the standard deviation from the mean. The risk horizon for such a VAR estimate corresponds to the frequency used to compute the input variance.

Now consider two assets. In that case, the VAR of the portfolio of two assets can be computed in a similar manner using the variances of the two assets' returns. These variance-based risk measures then are combined using the correlation of the two assets' returns. The result is a VAR estimate for the portfolio.

The simplicity of the variance-based approach to VAR calculations lies in the assumption of normality. By *assuming* that returns on all financial instruments are normally distributed, the risk manager eliminates the need to come up with a VAR distribution using complicated modeling techniques. All that *really* must be done is to come up with the appropriate variances and correlations.

At the same time, however, by assuming normality, the risk manager has greatly limited the VAR estimate. Normal distributions, after all, are symmetric. Any potential for skewness or fat tails in asset returns thus is totally ignored in the variance-only approach.

In addition to sacrificing the possibility that asset returns may *not* be normally distributed, the variance-only approach to calculating VAR also relies on the critical assumption that asset returns are totally independent across increments of time. A multi-period VAR can be calculated only by calculating a single-period VAR from the available data and then extrapolating the multi-day risk estimate. For example, suppose variances and correlations are available for historical returns measured at the *daily* frequency. To get from a one-day VAR to a T-day VAR – where T is the risk horizon of interest – the variance-only approach requires that the one-day VAR is multiplied by the square root of T.

For return variances and correlations measured at the monthly frequency or lower, this assumption may not be terribly implausible. For daily variances and correlations, however, serial independence is a very strong and usually an unrealistic assumption in most markets. The problem is less severe for short risk horizons, of course. So, using a one-day VAR as the basis for a five-day VAR might be acceptable, whereas a one-day VAR would be highly problematic in most markets.

Computing Volatility Inputs

Despite its unrealistic assumptions, simple variance-based VAR calculations are probably the dominant application of the VAR measure today. The approach is especially popular for corporate end users of derivatives, principally because the necessary software is cheap and easy to use.

All variance-based VAR measures, however, are not alike. The sources of inputs used to calculate VAR in this manner can differ widely. The next several subsections summarize several popular methods for determining these variances.[2] Note that these methods are *only* methods of computing *variances* on single assets. Correlations still must be determined to convert the VARs of individual assets into portfolio VARs.

Moving Average Volatility. One of the simplest approaches to calculating variance for use in a variance-based VAR calculating involves estimating a historical moving average of volatility. To get a moving average estimate of variance, the average is taken over a rolling window of historical volatility data. For example, given a 20-day rolling window,[3] the daily variance used for one-day VAR calculations would be the average daily variance over the most recent 20 days. To calculate this, many assume a zero mean daily return and then just average the squared returns for the last 20 trading days. On the next day, a new return becomes available for the volatility calculation. To maintain a 20-day measurement window, the first observation is dropped off and the average is recomputed as the basis of the next day's VAR estimate.

More formally, denote the daily return from time $t - 1$ to time t as r_t. Assuming a zero mean daily return, the moving average volatility over a window or the last D days is calculated as follows:

$$v_t^2 = \left[\frac{1}{D}\right]\sum_{i=0}^{D-1} r_{t-i}^2$$

where v_t is the daily volatility estimate used as the VAR input on day t.

Because moving-average volatility is calculated using equal weights for all observations in the historical time series, the calculations are very simple. The result, however, is a smoothing effect that causes sharp changes in volatility to appear as plateaus over longer periods of time, failing to capture dramatic changes in volatility.

Risk Metrics. To facilitate one-day VAR calculations and extrapolated risk measures for longer risk horizons, JP Morgan – in association with Reuters – began making available their RiskMetrics[TM] data sets. This data includes historical variances and covariances on a variety of simple assets – sometimes called "primitive securities."[4] Most other assets have cash flows that can be "mapped" into these simpler RiskMetrics™ assets for VAR calculation purposes.[5]

In the RiskMetrics data set, daily variances and correlations are computed using an "exponentially weighted moving average." Unlike the simple moving-average volatility estimate, an exponentially weighted moving average allows the most recent observations to be more influential in the calculation than observations further in the past. This has the advantage of capturing shocks in the market better than the simple moving average and thus is often regarded as producing a better volatility for variance-based VAR than the equal-weighted moving average alternative.

Conditional Variance Models. Another approach for estimating the variance input to VAR calculations involves the use of "conditional variance" time series methods. The first conditional variance model was developed by Engle in 1982 and is known as the autoregressive conditional heteroskedasticity ("ARCH") model.[6] ARCH combines an autoregressive process with a moving average estimation method so that variance still is calculated in the rolling window manner used for moving averages.

Since its introduction, ARCH has evolved into a variety of other conditional variance models, such as Generalized ARCH ("GARCH"), Integrated GARCH ("IGARCH"), and exponential GARCH ("EGARCH"). Numerous applications of these models have led practitioners to believe that these estimation techniques provide better estimates of (time-series) volatility than simpler methods.

For a GARCH(1,1) model, the variance of an asset's return at time t is presumed to have the following structure:

$$v_t^2 = a_0 + a_1 r_{t-1}^2 + a_2 v_{t-1}^2$$

The conditional variance model thus incorporates a *recursive* moving average term. In the special case where $a_0 = 0$ and $a_1 + a_2 = 1$, the GARCH(1,1) model reduces *exactly* to the exponentially weighted moving average formulation for volatility.[7]

Using volatilities from a GARCH model as inputs in a variance-based VAR calculation does not circumvent the statistical inference problem of presumed normality. By incorporating additional information into the volatility measure, however, more of the actual time series properties of the underlying asset return can be incorporated into the VAR estimate than if a simple average volatility is used.

Implied Volatility. All of the above methods of computing volatilities for variance-based VAR calculations are based on historical data. For more of a forward-looking measure of volatility, option-implied volatilities sometimes can be used to calculate VAR.

The implied volatility of an option is defined as the *expected future volatility* of the underlying asset over the remaining life of the option. Many studies have concluded that measures of option-implied volatility are, indeed, the *best* predictor of future volatility.[8] Unlike time series measures of volatility that are entirely backward-looking, option implied volatility is "backed-out" of actual option prices – which, in turn, are based on actual transactions and expectations of market participants – and thus is inherently forward-looking.

Any option-implied volatility estimate is dependent on the particular option pricing model used to derive the implied volatility. Given an observed market price for an option *and* a presumed pricing model, the implied volatility can be determined numerically. This variance may then be used in a VAR calculation for the asset underlying the option.

Non-Variance VAR Calculation Methods

Despite the simplicity of most variance-based VAR measurement methods, many practitioners prefer to avoid the restrictive assumptions underlying that approach – *viz.*, symmetric return distributions that are independent and stable over time. To avoid these assumptions, a risk manager must actually generate a full distribution of possible future portfolio values – a distribution that is neither necessarily normal nor symmetric.[9]

Historical simulation is perhaps the easiest alternative to variance-based VAR. This approach generates VAR distributions merely by "re-arranging" historical data – *viz.*, re-sampling time series data on the relevant asset prices or returns. This can be about as easy *computationally* as variance-based VAR, and it does *not* presuppose that everything in the world is normally distributed. Nevertheless, the approach is highly dependent on the availability of potentially massive amounts of historical data. In addition, the VAR resulting from a historical simulation is totally sample dependent.

More advanced approaches to VAR calculation usually involve some type of forward-looking simulation model, such as Monte Carlo. Implementing simulation methods typically is computationally intensive, expensive, and heavily dependent on personnel resources. For that reason, simulation has remained largely limited to active trading firms and institutional investors. Nevertheless, simulation does enable users to depart from the RiskMetrics normality assumptions about underlying asset returns without forcing them to rely on a single historical data sample. Simulation also eliminates the need to assume independence in returns over time – *viz.*, VAR calculations are no longer restricted to one-day estimates that must be extrapolated over the total risk horizon.

NOTES

1. A useful example of this methodology is presented in Anthony Saunders, "Market Risk," *The Financier* Vol. 2, No. 5 (December 1995).
2. For more methods, *see* Jorion (1997), cited previously.
3. The length of the window is chosen by the risk manager doing the VAR calculation.

4. Jorion (1997), cited previously.
5. For a detailed explanation of this approach, *see* JP Morgan/Reuters, *Risk Metrics – Technical Document*, 4th ed. (1996).
6. Robert Engle, "Autoregressive Conditional Heteroskedasticity with Estimates of the Variance of United Kingdom Inflation," *Econometrica* Vol. 50 (1982): 391–407.
7. *See* Jorion (1997), cited previously.
8. *See, for example*, Phillipe Jorion, "Predicting Volatility in the Foreign Exchange Market," *Journal of Finance*, Vol. 50 (1995): 507–528.
9. Variance-based approaches avoid the problem of generating a new distribution by *assuming* that distribution.

Reproduced from Joel Stern and Donald Chew, eds, *The Revolution in Corporate Finance*, Fourth Edition (2003), pp. 416–29.

13

Learning to Live with Fixed Rate Mortgages
An Evolutionary Approach to Risk Management

Martin Upton

BACKGROUND

Until the late 1980s fixed rate mortgages were a rarity in the United Kingdom. In the current world of personal financial services, though, they have now become a commonplace offering from the mortgage lending industry. In recent years they have accounted for a third of new mortgage lending with the bulk of the business being in shorter term products with rates fixed for one to five years.

In a highly competitive market the rates offered have afforded the lenders narrow margins over the cost of borrowing. Yet despite this competitive environment the fixed rate mortgage market has attracted interest and criticism from politicians and other observers culminating in the Miles Report on "The UK Mortgage Market: Taking a Longer-Term View" published in April 2004.

This article explains the development of the fixed rate mortgage market in the UK, the risk management and margin implications for the lenders, the potential future development of the market in the wake of the introduction of CAT standards for mortgages and the publication of the Miles Report, and the issues for mortgage lenders arising from the application from 2005 of International Financial Reporting Standards (IFRS).

THE MORTGAGE WORLD BEFORE FIXED RATES

Until the late 1990s the vast majority of mortgage lending was undertaken by the building societies – mutual organisations owned by their savers and mortgagors. Until 1984 a cartel led by the major building societies and operated through their trade association, the Building Societies Association (BSA), set the levels for mortgage and savings rates, effectively guaranteeing their net interest margin. These rates were known as "administered" rates

– meaning that the rates were set by the societies themselves rather than in accordance with an official or reference rate. Changes to rate levels were agreed by the cartel, normally only after changes to UK official rates. Whilst some variability around the cartel rates was applied by societies – for example to adjust the rate charged for larger loans – the business environment was essentially non-competitive in price terms. In so far as there was competition it was confined to fighting for market share via advertising and through the presence of branches in the high streets. The liberalisation of financial services in the 1980s ended these practices and heralded a competitive multi-product mortgage market in the UK.

Virtually all mortgage lending until the late 1980s was on an ("administered") variable rate basis. Fixed and capped rate lending was conspicuous by its absence. Why was this?

The answer is that, with the majority of building society funding coming in the form of variable rate retail deposits, there was also little structural incentive to offer fixed rate mortgages. Until the mid-1980s there was also no wide scale availability of hedging products like interest rate swaps for institutions to manage the risks of offering fixed rate mortgages. Indeed, until the Building Societies Act of 1986 came into effect societies had, in any case, very limited powers to enter into derivative transactions. Societies additionally had to await the publication of Statutory Instrument (SI 1988 No. 1344), which advised on the hedging contracts they were permitted to use, and the Building Societies Commission's Prudential Note (1988/5) on "Balance Sheet Mismatch and Hedging" prior to developing their use of derivatives. In such circumstances it was hardly surprising that fixed rate offerings were not a feature of the mortgage market.

THE EMERGENCE OF FIXED RATE MORTGAGES

The development of the fixed rate mortgage market from the late 1980s can be ascribed to a number of concurrent developments.

Firstly, and most importantly, the 1986 Building Societies Act together with SI 1988 1344 gave the sector the power to use derivatives for hedging purposes. The wording, in Section 23 of the Act, was not the most helpful since it required each new transaction in derivatives by a society to be:

> . . . for the purpose of reducing the risk of loss arising from changes in interest rates, currency rates or other factors of a prescribed description which affect its business. (Building Societies Act 1986 23(1))

At the very least societies had to initiate audit trails to prove compliance with this rule. Failure to provide such a link to "loss reduction" would have meant that the use of the derivative was *"ultra vires"* – outside the powers of a building society.

With fixed rate mortgages, it was in any case relatively easy for societies to prove (with or without legal opinions) that entering into an interest rate swap to convert the fixed rate flows from a fixed rate mortgage asset to variable rate flows to match the variable rate funding that supported the mortgage loan was a manifest process of risk reduction. Consequently the terms of the 1986 Act did not inhibit the emergence of fixed rate products in the late 1980s.

Section 23 was, in any case, amended by Section 9A of the 1997 Building Societies Act. Derivatives could still only be used for risk management purposes (and not for trading) but a "safe harbour" was allowed whereby failure to achieve risk reduction did not make the contract entered into *ultra vires*. This amendment was designed to give comfort to the financial counterparties to derivatives transactions with building societies. Societies were no longer at risk of entering into unenforceable derivatives contracts through failure to comply with Section 23 of the 1986 Act. The comfort this provided to the industry and financial counterparts was material particularly in the wake of the House of Lords' judgement in 1991 on the use of derivatives by UK local authorities which declared such contracts entered into by the authorities *ultra vires* and, hence, unenforceable.

Secondly, the growth of commercial banks' activity in the mortgage market impacted on the scale of fixed rate lending. With no legal restrictions on their use of derivatives and with more fixed rate liabilities on their balance sheets, the banks had greater flexibility to engage in fixed rate lending than building societies. This meant that the building society industry had to follow or lose market share.

The growth in the banks' fixed rate mortgage market share was, in any case, subsequently inflated in the mid-1990s by the decision of five major building societies (Halifax, Alliance & Leicester, Woolwich, Bradford & Bingley and Northern Rock) to follow the lead of Abbey National in 1989 and convert to banking status. This led to a sharp reduction in the size of the building society sector and its share of the mortgage market. The shift in sectoral share was accentuated by Halifax's merger with Leeds Permanent Building Society in 1995, two years prior to conversion to banking status; by the acquisition of Cheltenham & Gloucester Building Society by Lloyds TSB in 1995; by the acquisition of National & Provincial Building Society by Abbey National in 1995; and by the acquisition of Bristol & West Building Society by the Bank of Ireland in 1997.

Thirdly, the particular interest rate characteristics of late 1980s and early 1990s – high nominal (and real) interest rates and an inverted yield curve – provided an opportunity to market fixed rate mortgages successfully. With the standard variable rate for mortgages rising above 15% per annum, borrowers were keen to seek out products which mitigated this punitive rate for borrowing. The inverted yield curve meant that fixed rate products, priced by reference to the interest rate swap rates for the same fixed rate term, could be offered at a lower rate than variable rate mortgages. In 1990, some five-year fixed rate mortgages were offered at rates 3% per annum lower than standard variable rate alternatives. Unsurprisingly mortgagors were keen for fixed rate products which immediately offered a material reduction in their borrowing costs.

Witnessing this development, it certainly appeared that the key driver of the emergence of the fixed rate market was the consumer. The preceding fifteen years had seen significant volatility in UK rates and three periods when variable mortgage rates were higher than 14% per annum. Consequently products which provided cost certainty were easy to sell – particularly for those whose mortgage costs represented a high proportion of household expenditure. If you could also secure (at least temporarily) a cut in cost by switching from variable to fixed rate – as indeed you could in the early 1990s – then the appetite for fixed rate mortgage products was reinforced. Once the lenders had seen the market potential, the product offerings became – and have since remained – profuse. The extent of the competition has placed downward pressure on the pricing of fixed rate mortgages, thereby further helping to sustain the attractions of the product to borrowers.

The margins secured on fixed rate mortgages have normally been lower than on standard variable rate business. The lenders have, though, been reluctant to step back from fixed rate lending, partly because of a fear of reducing their share of new lending – always an important performance indicator for lenders. Primarily, though, lenders see the tight margins on fixed

Table 13.1   Interest rates 1988–1992

Year	Average base rates (%)
1988	10.3
1989	13.9
1990	14.8
1991	11.5
1992	9.4

Source: www.houseweb.co.uk/house/market/irfig.html
(accessed 20 July 2005)

Table 13.2   Fixed rate lending 1993–2004

Year	Fixed rate lending as % of total lending
1993	45
1994	42
1995	23
1996	17
1997	35
1998	50
1999	36
2000	29
2001	27
2002	23
2003	36
2004	29

Source: www.cml.org.uk/servlet/dycon/zt-cml/cml/
live/en/cml/xls_sml_Table-PR3.xls (accessed 20 July 2005)

rate lending as a price that has to be paid to get customers through the door, at which point other products can be sold to them – including further mortgage products when the initial fixed rate deal matures.

Since 1992 the volume of fixed rate lending has ranged between 17% and a peak of 50% of new lending, the share being largely driven by the relative levels of fixed rate and variable rate mortgages – the lower the fixed rates relative to variable, the higher the fixed rate share of the total market.

RISK MANAGEMENT ISSUES

Selling fixed rate mortgages gives rise to a number of risk management issues for lenders.

An important initial point to make, though, is that in the UK market the fixed rate period normally only applies to the first few years of the full term of the mortgage. For example, mortgagors may enter into a mortgage repayable over twenty-five years with the mortgage rate fixed initially usually for a term of up to five years. At the end of this fixed rate term, the mortgage typically reverts to a variable rate unless the mortgagor opts for a new fixed rate term (or indeed another mortgage product, e.g. a capped rate mortgage). The hedging requirement for the lender therefore relates to the initial term only and not the full potential term of the mortgage.

Interest Rate Risk: Hedging to Variable Rate

When it is necessary to hedge fixed rate mortgages, the basic mechanism is to use a simple interest rate swap, with the lender paying fixed rate for the term of the fixed rate mortgage and receiving the variable rate – typically three month libor (see Figure 13.1). The net result is that lenders end up with an asset yielding a fixed margin (the difference between the swap and mortgage rates) over Libor. Standard practice is to hedge the entire tranche size which is being offered although some providers have used an amortisation schedule reflecting the fact that, subject to interest rate movements, some prepayment of fixed rate mortgages occurs prior to the end of the fixed rate term.

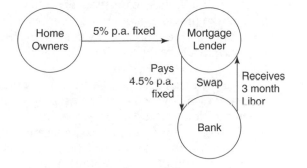

Figure 13.1   Typical fixed rate mortgage swap

To reflect the time at which a customer draws down on a mortgage commitment (particularly if a house move is involved) it is sound practice to arrange for a forward start for the swap (typically three months forward). Whilst this makes for sound risk management, it does mean that the mortgage lender is signaling to the swap market makers which way round they are at the point of quotation and indeed the exact structure may identify the name of the mortgage lender to the swap market. In mitigation of the risk this poses to obtaining a fair price is the huge liquidity in the sterling interest rate swap market and the large number of banks prepared to quote on tight bid-to-offer spreads.

One observation which may be made is why mortgage lenders do not make more use of the "internal" hedges available to them by the simultaneous offering of fixed rate savings bonds to their customers. Clearly putting a, say, two-year bond against a two-year fixed rate mortgage product eliminates the need to use the derivatives market to hedge either. The reality is, though, that the market for fixed rate mortgages is, and always has been, huge relative to that for fixed rate bond products. There is a particularly limited appetite for fixed rate bonds with a term of more than two years, reducing further the scope for internal hedges of longer term fixed rate mortgage products. The reasons for the lack of appetite for fixed rate bonds are unclear but may be related to the requirement with most products for the investor to pay a financial penalty for access to the funds invested ahead of the maturity term.

One alternative "set off" against the fixed rate mortgage applied by several lenders in the 1990s was to reduce the holdings of gilt-edged stocks in their liquidity investment portfolios, switching the funds realised into variable rate products. This eliminated the need to swap fixed rate mortgages since the lenders effectively had one set of fixed rate assets (gilts) replaced by another (fixed rate mortgages), leaving the balance sheet interest rate risk position largely unchanged. The sheer scale of fixed rate mortgage business during the early 1990s meant, however, that this hedging option became exhausted for many lenders.

The one-sidedness of the use of the swap market to hedge mortgages results in another problem – that of the credit exposure. Mortgage lenders find that their swap portfolios are dominated by swaps where the fixed rate is being paid. If interest rates fall, these exposures grow in market value (or replacement cost) to the swap provider and on this "marked to market" basis the swap provider's exposure to the mortgage lender rises. This has created situations where swap providers have declared themselves full on their credit limit to mortgage lenders.

The extent of the impact on exposure can be shown as follows: suppose a bank has £1bn (notional) of five-year swaps outstanding with a mortgage lender. If the contracted rates match market rates, the NPV of this exposure is zero. The bank would, however, mark some exposure against the credit line for the mortgage lender to allow for risk of future rate movements – perhaps of the order of 5% of the notional principal (£50m). If rates fall by 2% per annum, however, the value of the contracts to the bank rises by the NPV of

2% per annum for five years on £1bn (notional). This amounts to £87m if yields are 5% per annum, raising the total exposure against the mortgage lender to £137m – since £50m would still be added to allow for further rate movements. At such exposure levels the bank's credit division may stop further new business being written with that mortgage lender.

Scope to mitigate this position does now exist through the growth in swap collateralisation arrangements whereby the swap provider is provided with either cash or bond collateral from the mortgage lender to reduce the outstanding net credit exposure and open up the credit line again for further derivatives business. The continued development of the credit derivatives market could also provide a further avenue for swap providers to reduce their exposure to counterparties.

Basis Risk and Impact on the Net Interest Margin

The usual hedge for fixed rate mortgages does leave lenders with a basis risk issue. Variable rate flows are linked to Libor and not (usually) base rates. Three-month Libor rates can be higher or lower than base rates particularly during periods when movements in base rates are anticipated by the markets. It is not uncommon to see Libor *circa* 20–25 bps above or below base rates under such circumstances. Why does this matter?

The hedge of a fixed rate mortgage converts the fixed rate asset to variable rate to match to variable rate funding. For many mortgage lenders – particularly the building societies – funding is in the form of retail flows where rate movements are largely related in timing and size to base rate movements. Few lenders have an appetite to alter these "administered" rates without the "cover" of a base rate move given the fear of adverse coverage in the media. The upshot is that in times of falling rates Libor falls below base rate often for a sustained period and the synthetic earnings from a swapped fixed rate mortgage asset fall. This reduction in earnings cannot be recouped since the cost of funding cannot be reduced until the expected base rate rise materialises.

Whilst the issue may appear to be a minor risk to the mortgage lender the reality is that the cost can sometimes be material. If 30% of all mortgage assets are on fixed rate the full year impact of Libor consistently 25 bps below base rate is a reduction in the net interest margin of 8 bps. This represents a *circa* 6% drop in net interest income for an average building society (given that the interest margin for societies ranges between 120 bps and 160 bps). The percentage reduction is, however, less for the banking sector where margins are significantly wider. This is due to the fact that banks, unlike the mutual building societies, need additional profits to fund their dividend payments to shareholders.

Mitigation of this basis risk can be achieved by using the market for base rate swaps – either by swapping to base rate instead of Libor in the first instance or arranging Libor to base rate swaps. There are, though, two problems with this: firstly the base rate swap market is not huge and has limited

Table 13.3   Base rates and average three-month Libor 2001–2004

Year	Base rates (%)	Average three-month Libor (%)	General trend for interest rates during year
2000	6.12	6.19	Up
2001	5.12	5.04	Down
2002	4.00	4.06	Mixed
2003	3.68	3.74	Up
2004	4.40	4.47	Up

Source: *www.houseweb.co.uk/house/market/irfig.html* (accessed 20 July 2005); *www.econstats.com/r/rlib_am10.htm* (accessed 20 July 2005)

liquidity since swap providers have difficulty covering the positions that arise through putting such swaps onto their books. Secondly, if Libor rates are, or are expected to fall, below base rates the market will reflect this in the swap price (e.g. 3 month Libor received against base rate less 10 bps paid) with the result that the loss arising from the basis risk is, at least in part, crystallised through this swap arrangement.

The consequence is that in most cases lenders carry this basis risk and accept (or hope) that in complete interest cycles the losses when rates are falling (and Libor rates are below base rates) are offset – as Table 13.3 implies – when rates start their upward path (with Libor rates rising above the prevailing base rates).

Sales and Hedging Mismatches: "Attrition Rates" and "Balloons"

Lenders are exposed to interest rate risk whilst fixed rate mortgage products are being sold if, as is usually the case, the swap is arranged ahead of product sales. This risk materialises particularly if rates move sharply higher or lower immediately after the swap is arranged.

If rates move lower, the risk is that the mortgage products do not sell in sufficient quantities to match the swap size, with potential customers either holding back in anticipation of lower fixed rate products or defecting to those lenders who are offering a lower fixed rate (hedged by a lower swap rate). Lenders have two options if this happens: they can either lower the price of the mortgage product or withdraw the product and cancel the unwanted element of the swap. Both measures though effectively incur a cost either through a reduction in mortgage earnings or through the cancellation fee on a swap which has moved into loss in market value. Mitigation of this risk can be achieved through a number of techniques. Firstly, during times of volatile rates (particularly when they are falling) swap sizes can be kept lower than normal to ensure that there is less risk of large unsold tranches of fixed rate products. This approach is often unwelcome in the marketing departments and amongst sales staff who prefer to have some longevity in the sales period of products. Frequent repricing of products also incurs higher marketing costs. A second alternative requires the detailed analysis of sales records by the risk management divisions of lenders. By looking at past experiences of sales volumes and "attrition rates" (where commitments to borrow do not turn into actual mortgage assets as customers do not take up their mortgage option), the likely mortgage sales and drawdowns for a particular product can be estimated. Although not an exact science it can mitigate the worst of the risks arising from selling fixed rate products during a period of volatile market rates. A third hedging option is to buy the swaption (an option on a swap) rather than entering into the swap itself. The maximum downside to this transaction would be the cost of the swaption – potentially significantly lower than the write-off costs of a cancelled swap. If product sales materialise and the strike price is "in the money", the swaption can be exercised in whole or part to match the actual mortgage assets taken onto the balance sheet. The downside of this hedging technique is, though, the cost of the option which will also become more expensive during those volatile periods for market rates (which is just when such protection from potential losses may be needed). The fixed rate mortgage market is, as noted earlier, very competitive and any additional risk protection costs may make a product unattractive to potential customers. Finally, attrition rates can be reduced if a commitment fee is paid by customers on securing (but before drawing down) the fixed rate mortgage. Although discouraged by the introduction of CAT standards for mortgages (see below), the payment of such an upfront fee can help prevent mortgage sales from failing to turn into mortgage assets.

A reverse set of problems arises if rates rise sharply after a product has been launched and prior to when it is withdrawn. In such circumstances customers advised by the media or their financial intermediary or even branch staff move in great numbers into fixed rate products with the risk that a "balloon" in sales occurs in the period immediately before a product is withdrawn (to be replaced by higher priced alternatives). The result can be that the swap size is exceeded by the product sales and the excess can now only be hedged at the prevailing market rate for the swap. This risk is reinforced by the fact that the attrition rate typically moves close to zero during an upward rate cycle. Containment of this risk can again be helped by good record keeping and risk management systems which can estimate just how large the "balloon" might be under these market conditions. The better alternative is to have effective reporting systems (to provide an up-to-date record of actual sales) and fast closedown procedures to withdraw products at short notice. The problem with the latter approach is that it may expose a culture conflict within the mortgage lender: the treasury division will want to see sales stop before a "balloon" gets oversized whilst the sales-driven branches (and intermediaries) who inevitably will want to be seen to be doing the best for their customers will be anxious to carry on selling even whilst the shutters are coming down on a product. Sales of products after their closing date are certainly not unheard of! Such issues represent excellent examples of the operational risks that exist within financial services firms.

Prepayment Risks

In the aftermath of sterling's suspension from the membership of the ERM in September 1992, UK interest rates fell sharply. Given that monetary policy no longer had to be set to ensure sterling's compliance with the designated exchange rate band (DM2.78 "floor" to DM3.12 "cap" around the DM2.95 mid-point) interest rates were able to fall to stimulate what was, in 1992, an economy in recession with the housing market experiencing falling prices in many areas of the country.

This sharp reduction in long and short term rates gave lenders of fixed rate mortgages their first material experience of prepayment risk. Borrowers who had taken out fixed rate mortgages – particularly the longer term fixes of five years and beyond – found that it was financially attractive to prepay the mortgage, even if this incurred prepayment costs, and refinance at the prevailing lower rates. Growing encouragement to take the refinancing route came from the financial intermediaries in the mortgage market who clearly saw increasing turnover on the mortgage market as enhancing their fee income. The intermediaries were able to advise the less sophisticated mortgagors how to add the prepayment penalties on redemption of the original mortgage to the new mortgage at the prevailing lower rate. Given how far rates had fallen the mortgagors still achieved a financial saving – which by implication meant that the lenders were losing money through this refinancing activity.

The standard protection to this interest rate risk applied by mortgage lenders was typically a flat rate prepayment charge of three or six months' interest (based on the original fixed rate). This clearly made prepayments unattractive if rates only moved slightly lower over the term of the mortgage but was insufficient to provide a defence against the quantum fall in rates that occurred both between 1991 and 1994 and between 1999 and 2003.

Table 13.4 Base rates and five-year gilt-edged stock yields 1991–1995

Date	Base rates (%)	Five-year UK Government bond yields (%)
June 1991	11.5	10.41
June 1992	10.0	9.12
June 1993	6.0	7.01
June 1994	5.25	8.22
June 1995	6.75	7.79

Sources: www.houseweb.co.uk/house/market/irfig.html (accessed 20 July 2005); www.statistics.gov.uk/statbase/Expodata/Spreadsheet/D4084.xls (accessed 20 July 2005); Annual Abstract of Statistics (1998) Table 17.14, p. 349

For example a 12.5% per annum five-year fixed rate mortgage taken out 1991 and then refinanced at 8% per annum in 1993, with a penalty of six months' interest paid by the mortgagor, would have resulted in the lender losing (in undiscounted terms): 3 years × 4.5% of interest less the 0.5 years × 12.5% penalty payment received: a total (pre-tax) loss of 7.25% of the principal sum.

Figure 13.2 depicts the degree of protection provided by repayment penalties of six months and three months on a five-year fixed rate mortgage at 6% per annum. In both cases, the breakeven line for the mortgagor to pay the penalty and refinance for the residual period of the five years is depicted. The breakeven points assume there are no other costs incurred on refinancing: since in reality some costs are likely to be incurred, the actual "breakeven" interest rate may be a little lower than those shown. The figure demonstrates that the greatest vulnerability to prepayment risk occurs if rates fall sharply soon after a fixed rate mortgage has been drawn down by the mortgagor.

Realisation of the risks arising from prepayment made some mortgage lenders review their risk assessments and policy. Aided by growing dossiers on prepayment activity under different interest conditions, risk managers were able to forecast with some accuracy the volumes of fixed rate mortgages that would be prepaid. The assessment was not a simple economic matter as most borrowers would need to see sufficient financial daylight between prepaying/refinancing and staying with their existing mortgage deal before taking action. This reflects a mixture of customer inertia and the peripheral financial costs of moving a mortgage (legal fees, etc.). Elsewhere,

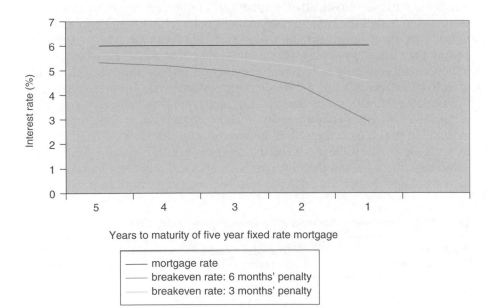

Figure 13.2   Refinancing a five-year fixed rate mortgage

though, prepayments do result from personal as opposed to financial circumstances (e.g. marriage breakdown) and these factors have to be factored into the analysis. Building on the assumptions of the potential cost under differing economic conditions it is possible to consider the policy alternatives for covering the exposure to prepayment risk not hedged by prepayment penalties. Table 13.5 provides an example of prepayment propensity rates applied by one mortgage lender in the UK.

Where exposure is deemed to be material and potential, the policy that can be adopted is to buy options cover. This can take various forms. "Bermudan" options give the mortgage lender the right to receive the fixed rate originally paid to hedge the relevant mortgage tranche for the residual term of the fixed rate period. To exercise this option the lender pays an exercise fee amounting to the value of the prepayment penalties due from the borrower on prepayment of the fixed rate mortgage. Clearly it only makes financial sense for the lender to exercise these options if rates had fallen to the point beyond that amount covered by the prepayment penalty. To reflect the fact that prepayment activity occurs at a rate over a period of time (i.e. it is not instantaneous for all cases where it makes sense for the borrower to refinance) the options should ideally be exercisable regularly (e.g. each month) enabling this hedging cover to track the actual pace of prepayment. These options do have some particular issues: firstly, such tailored options are only offered by a handful of market makers and consequently tend to be expensive – thereby pushing up the overall cost of hedging. Additionally, their esoteric nature makes them difficult to value (a matter compounded by their illiquidity). An alternative is to buy standard interest rate floors (which pay out to the buyer automatically if market rates fall below the strike rate of the contract) to hedge the "tail" of prepayment risk. Whilst such options do not provide an exact hedge for the risk – particularly as the returns from the contract are linked to money market rates and not to the levels of swap rates which would primarily influence prepayment activity – they are sufficiently effective to cover most of the residual interest rate risks on prepayment.

For some lenders protection against prepayment is achieved simply by requiring borrowers to pay a penalty linked to market rates. This "marking to market" of penalties extinguishes the interest rate risks arising from prepayment. Its downside is the impact on the company's profile with the public, with some customers finding that this approach either leaves them locked in to a high fixed rate deal or forced to pay a large penalty to exit from it.

Table 13.5 Example of forecast prepayment propensity rate

Breakeven rate less prevailing rate (%)	Minimum expected prepayment (%)	Maximum expected prepayment (%)
0%	12.5%	25%
1%	25%	50%
2%	50%	100%

Policy towards prepayments in the UK varies starkly with that overseas – and particularly with the United States. Here mortgages are placed into pools, securitised and sold to investment funds. The mortgagors normally pay *no* penalties if they prepay one loan and move to another – which clearly invites them to do just that in a falling rate environment. The costs of prepayment are also not borne by the mortgage lenders as can be the case in the UK. The costs fall instead on the investment funds which find that the mortgage-backed securities they have bought "pay down" more quickly than expected (due to the prepayment of the underlying mortgages) leaving them to reinvest in new securities. These new investments, will, of course, be at lower yields in the falling rate environment which has generated the prepayment activity!

CAT Standards

In 2000, as part of the move by the Government and the FSA to move towards the regulation of the mortgage market, CAT ("Cost", "Access", "Terms") standards were introduced to the mortgage market.

For fixed rate mortgages the CAT standard includes:

1. A maximum reservation fee of £150.

2. A maximum prepayment penalty of 1% for each remaining year of the fixed rate mortgage, reducing monthly.

3. No prepayment penalties after the end of the fixed rate period.

4. No prepayment penalty if the mortgagor moves house and stays with the same lender.

Potentially these restrictions on the size of the reservation fee and on prepayment charges expose lenders to more interest rate risk by increasing the risk of mortgage commitments not turning into mortgage drawdowns and by increasing the likelihood of prepayment activity at the lenders' expense.

The alternative would be to hedge the enlarged risks by the increased use of options, although this would either impact on the headline rate of the mortgage or on the net margin achieved by the lender.

The outcome, though, has been softened by the decision to make the standards for mortgages voluntary. Consequently, even customer-orientated lenders like the Nationwide Building Society have felt able, after a period, to dispense with the CAT standards. Future mortgage regulation could, however, revisit these issues and make standards mandatory.

The Miles Report

A further recent development to the fixed rate market came with the report by Professor David Miles on "The UK Mortgage Market: Taking a

Longer-Term View". This report had been commissioned by the Treasury and was published in April 2004.

One of the particular areas of focus was why long term fixed rate mortgages were largely nonexistent in the UK market compared with their prevalence in the USA and their existence in certain parts of Europe (e.g. Denmark).

The reality of the fixed rate market, as the report highlighted, is that it is dominated by one-, two- and three-year fixed rate deals. These can be priced lower than longer term deals for two reasons: firstly the UK yield curve since 1992 has predominantly been positive so the swap rate to hedge a 10-year or 25-year fixed rate deal is higher than for a shorter term product. Secondly the risks associated with selling longer term fixed rate products are enhanced both in circumstances where products do not sell and in the case of prepayment. A hedge on an unsold tranche of a 25-year mortgage product is much more costly to unwind than, say, an equivalent two-year product for the same adverse move in the yield curve. Hedging these risks inevitably puts upward pressure on the rate sought by lenders on long term fixes and, thereby, discourages customer appetite. The situation is not the same where lenders securitise the mortgages sold and sell the resultant mortgage backed securities to investors – a practice, as noted above, which is the norm in the United States. Here the bond investors take the prepayment risk and so there is no need for the lenders to hedge it. The result is that the rates on the long term fixed rate mortgages are therefore not inflated by hedging costs thus making the products more attractive to the public.

One further factor skews demand to the short term products. Lenders make assumptions when setting the fixed rate about the likelihood both of cross sales of insurance and other products to the mortgagor and of the chance that at the end of the fixed rate period borrowers will move to the lenders' standard variable rate product.

The earnings coming from these two sources can then be considered when deciding how keenly to price the rate on the fixed rate mortgage. For longer term products these enhanced earnings will be further away (in the case of conversion to the standard variable rate) or the subsidisation effect of the cross sales will have to be spread over a higher number of years when setting the fixed rate on the mortgage.

The upshot is that the ability to price very keenly to attract demand is magnified for short term fixtures with the inevitability that this is where the customers gravitate to. The reality of the past decade is that the key driver when it comes to choosing first fixed over variable rate, and then between the alternative fixed rate products, is the "headline" rate – and the lowest rates have normally been seen in the very short term fixed rate mortgages. Indeed this pattern of behaviour by borrowers was commented on in the Miles Report which noted that borrowers attach enormous weight to the level of initial monthly payments when choosing between mortgage products.

IFRS and Fixed Rate Mortgages

From 1 January 2005, International Financial Reporting Standards (IFRS) were adopted by the member states of the European Union and a number of other countries globally. With common accounting standards being applied, the intended results include both greater transparency of company activities and an improved capability to make comparisons between companies.

This has impacted upon the mortgage lenders through one of the new standards – International Accounting Standard 39 (IAS) 39. This requires all derivatives contracts to be "marked to market" and for them to be reported at fair value on the balance sheet. This clearly has implications for mortgage lenders who, as has been explained, use interest rate swaps in huge volumes to hedge their fixed rate products.

The original proposals raised the prospect of the swaps and other derivatives that support fixed rate lending being revalued without a similar treatment for the mortgages they were hedging. This could have resulted in large movements in profitability being recorded since changes to interest rates would have caused the consequent profits or losses on the derivatives portfolio being taken to the profit & loss account without the offsetting movement in the valuation of the underlying fixed rate mortgages.

In recognition of the issues which this would cause, the finalised treatment of hedged items under IAS 39 allows for the application of "hedge accounting" where assets and liabilities are linked to derivatives contracts. The mortgage lenders must either demonstrate a clear and specific link between a mortgage asset and the derivative hedging it ("mini-hedge") or must demonstrate, to a satisfactory degree of proximity, the general linkage of derivatives positions hedging a portfolio of assets ("maxi-hedge"). With the latter there may not be an exact, product-by-product, linkage between fixed rate mortgages and the derivatives hedging them. There needs, however, to be a close degree of relatedness (i.e. in the size and maturity of the mortgages and the linked derivatives) to obtain approval for hedge accounting treatment by the auditors.

The application of hedge accounting eliminates the risk of large swings in profitability arising from the revaluation of hedging transactions. It also reflects the true position that if the derivatives positions have fallen in value it is because the fixed rate mortgages they are hedging have risen in value and *vice versa*. Whilst providing a solution, the realities of hedge accounting have proved challenging for the mortgage lenders, particularly as a large volume of hedged products were sold well before the notion of "hedge accounting" for them was proposed. The larger lenders, who have typically hedged fixed rate products on a portfolio, rather than a product-by-product basis, have found the requirement to link derivatives to the underlying assets challenging – a problem that has been reinforced by the fact that the outstanding balances on fixed rate products do move lower during the fixed rate period due to capital repayments and prepayments.

The use of hedge accounting for fixed rate products does provide a rational assessment of the fair value of hedged mortgage assets. It does, however, place an onus on the mortgage lenders to maintain rigorous standards of documentation about the ongoing linkage of fixed rate mortgages to their supporting derivatives positions.

CONCLUSIONS

Analysing the development and growth of the fixed rate mortgage market leads to a number of observations about the risk management issues they generate for lenders.

Firstly, fixed rate mortgages reveal the potential for a culture clash within lending institutions. Customer-facing staff, particularly if business volumes are a key performance measure, will be motivated to sell products beyond the amount hedged by the treasury department. The consequence is that such "excess" sales volumes may result in financial losses being incurred.

Secondly, the structuring of products and the sales process risk ignoring (and thereby not pricing in properly) the embedded optionality effectively sold to the customer.

Where a customer commits to a mortgage for the payment of a small upfront fee, the lender has in effect sold them a cut price option. If interest rates move lower, the customer will be incentivised not to take up the option to drawdown that mortgage but to shift to a new, lower priced alternative.

Thirdly, the hedging of prepayment risk by the use of fixed penalty payments on redemption (e.g. six-months' interest) provides sufficient cover to lenders during periods of low interest volatility. These cannot provide sufficient protection to the lender when there are quantum moves in rates of the sort experienced by the UK in the 1990s. The exposed "tail" of prepayment risk is indeed an excellent example of the consequences of an embedded option sold (usually without charge) to the customer.

Fourthly, the impact on the profitability of lenders is likely to be adverse and the lower is likely to be the net interest margin, the greater the proportion of fixed rate products in the mortgage portfolio. Fixed rate mortgages are priced keenly and the growth of the market has diminished the size of the "back books" of the mortgage lenders – the stable holdings of mortgages on standard variable rates which normally generate the highest interest margins for lenders. Aided by the mortgage intermediaries becoming increasingly attuned to methods for maximising the turnover of mortgage deals – to their advantage in terms of fee generation from new sales – customers have slowly become more financially sophisticated and less loyal to a particular lender. The result is that increasingly customers move from one keenly priced product to another and the impact over time is to deflate the average margin of a mortgage portfolio.

But although customer behaviour has become more financially astute of late, the reality is that many borrowers still have a less than full appreciation of interest rate risk. The take-up of the products with the lowest rate, regardless of the term of the fixture and seemingly without any assessment of future rates, has been a feature of customer behaviour. The evidence of prepayment activity falling well short of that justified by the economics (to the relief of lenders!) has further supported the view that a significant proportion of customers are still not financially adept.

THE FUTURE

Fixed rate mortgages are here to stay. The likelihood is that, despite any market developments which emanate from the final Miles Report, the focus of demand for fixed rate mortgages will remain in shorter term products. Indeed this product area has in recent years become the battleground where lenders have fought most aggressively for market share.

When mortgage lenders first offered fixed rate products it was seen by some as simply adding a product line to their mortgage offerings. Fifteen years on from the birth of the fixed rate era, the proliferation of products and the keenly priced terms on which they are written are threatening to reduce the profitability of the UK mortgage lenders whilst continuing to present challenging risk management issues to their treasury teams.

REFERENCES

Building Societies Act 1986 (Chapter 53). HMSO.
Building Societies Act 1997 (Chapter 32). The Stationary Office.
"Balance Sheet Mismatch and Hedging" Prudential Note 1988/5: Building Societies Commission.
CAT Standards for Mortgages
http://www.hmtreasury.gov.uk/documents/financial_services/mortgages/fin_mort_catstand.cfm (accessed 8 December 2005).
Miles, D. 2004. "The UK Mortgage Market: Taking a Longer-term View: Final Report and Recommendations." The Stationary Office.

14

Credit Derivatives

John Kiff and Ron Morrow

Credit derivatives are swap, forward, and option contracts that transfer risk and return from one counterparty to another without actually transferring the ownership of the underlying assets. Similar products have been around for centuries and include letters of credit, government export credit and mortgage guarantees, private sector bond reinsurance, and spread locks.[1] Credit derivatives differ from their predecessors because they are traded separately from the underlying assets; in contrast, the earlier products were contracts between an issuer and a guarantor. Credit derivatives are an ideal tool for lenders who want to reduce their exposure to a particular borrower but find themselves unwilling (say, for tax- or cost-related reasons) to sell outright their claims on that borrower.

TYPES OF CREDIT DERIVATIVES

The three major types of credit derivatives are default swaps, total-rate-of-return swaps, and credit-spread put options. These transactions can all be structured as derivatives contracts embedded in a more traditional on-balance-sheet structure, such as a credit-linked note.

Default swaps transfer the potential loss on a "reference asset" that can result from specific credit "events" such as default, bankruptcy, insolvency, and credit-rating downgrades. Marketable bonds are the most popular form of reference asset because of their price transparency. While bank loans have the potential to become the dominant form of reference asset (because of their sheer quantity), this is impeded by the fact that loans are more heterogeneous and illiquid than bonds.[2]

Default swaps involve a "protection buyer," who pays a periodic or upfront fee to a "protection seller" in exchange for a contingent payment if there is a credit event (Figure 14.1a). Some default swaps are based on a basket of assets and pay out on a first-to-default basis, whereby the contract terminates and pays out if any of the assets in the basket are in default. Default swaps are the largest component of the global credit derivatives market.[3]

Total-rate-of-return swaps (TRORSs) transfer the returns and risks on an underlying reference asset from one party to another. TRORSs involve a "total-return buyer," who pays a periodic fee to a "total-return seller" and

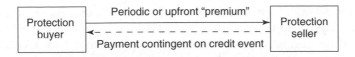

Figure 14.1a A default swap

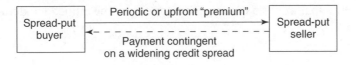

Figure 14.1b A total-rate-of-return swap

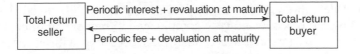

Figure 14.1c A credit-spread put option

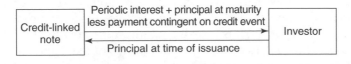

Figure 14.1d A credit-linked note

receives the total economic performance of the underlying reference asset in return. "Total return" includes all interest payments on the reference asset plus an amount based on the change in the asset's market value. If the price goes up, the total-return buyer gets an amount equal to the appreciation of the value, and if the price declines, the buyer pays an amount equal to the depreciation in value (Figure 14.1b). If a credit event occurs prior to maturity, the TRORS usually terminates, and a price settlement is made immediately.[4]

Credit-spread put option contracts isolate and capture devaluations in a reference asset that are independent of shifts in the general yield curve. Essentially, they are default swaps that stipulate spread widening as an "event" (Figure 14.1c). The spread is usually calculated as the yield differential between the reference bond and an interest rate swap of the same maturity.[5] Unlike default or total-rate-of-return swaps, counterparties do not have to define the specific credit event – the payout occurs regardless of the reasons for the credit-spread movement. Spread puts usually involve the "put buyer" paying an upfront fee to a "put seller" in exchange for a contingent payment if the spread widens beyond a pre-agreed threshold level.

The advantage of the spread put's detachment from defined credit events became particularly apparent during the periods of turmoil in Asian, Latin American, and eastern European financial markets during the late 1990s, where spreads widened dramatically in the absence of any "event" as defined in typical default-swap documentation. However, credit-spread derivatives can be difficult to hedge and very complicated to model and price, and most investors and hedgers can accomplish their objective with cheaper default swaps (Bowler and Tierney 1999).

Credit-linked notes are securities that effectively embed default swaps within a traditional fixed-income structure. In return for a principal payment when the contract is made, they typically pay periodic interest plus, at maturity, the principal minus a contingent payment on the embedded default swap (Figure 14.1d).

MARKET SIZE AND MAJOR PARTICIPANTS

The credit derivatives market is still relatively small compared with other, more mature, derivatives markets (e.g., derivatives markets for interest rates and currencies). However, it is growing rapidly, reflecting the fact that credit derivatives have proven to be a very useful means of managing the relatively large and growing volumes of credit risk that global markets deal with on a daily basis.[6,7]

Several observers have suggested that global markets are faced with much larger exposures to credit risk than to interest rate or currency risk. They therefore suggest that the credit derivatives market has virtually unlimited growth potential. This enthusiastic assessment, however, overlooks a number of practical difficulties. First, the documentation underlying these transactions can be quite complex and lengthy, and the interpretation of credit-event clauses (i.e., determining whether or not a contingent payout has been triggered) can be difficult. Second, the market for these derivatives is not perceived to be very liquid (with infrequent trading in specific credits) or transparent (given the over-the-counter structure of the market and the relatively small number of market-makers who actively quote and disseminate prices). In addition, credit risk will always be a less standardized and more complex "commodity" than interest rate and currency risks (whose homogeneity has helped propel the growth of other derivatives markets). Finally, a number of market participants have suggested that regulatory capital charges on credit derivative positions, particularly when they are being used in a hedging context, make credit derivatives a prohibitively expensive hedging tool (Box 14.1).

Box 14.1   The Regulatory Landscape

Banking supervisors have been supportive of the credit derivatives market within the confines of their interpretations of the current BIS regulatory capital framework known as Basel 1. Broadly speaking, the regulatory treatment of credit derivatives depends on whether the position is "uncovered" or hedges an existing position. The regulatory capital charge on an uncovered position is generally the same as the charge on an equivalent cash position in the reference asset. For example, the sale or purchase of protection on a corporate bond that draws an 8 per cent capital charge, would also draw an 8 per cent charge.[1]

The capital charge on an existing position that is hedged with an offsetting credit derivative can be reduced to the charge associated with the counterparty, if the counterparty is more creditworthy than the issuer of the reference asset (within the BIS credit-risk framework). For example, if a corporate bond held in the banking book (on which the capital charge is 8 per cent) is offset by a matching credit derivative with an OECD bank (on which a 1.6 per cent charge applies), the capital charge on the bond is reduced to 1.6 per cent. Essentially, the credit risk of a properly matched position is deemed to relate primarily to the potential for default by the derivative counterparty.[2]

A number of market participants have suggested that the counterparty-risk charges on positions that are deemed to be matched are too high. They argue that the purchaser of protection will face a loss only if the reference asset and the seller of the protection default simultaneously. As a result, they believe that historical default correlations should be used to recognize this "added" level of protection. However, given that default correlations have proven to be quite unstable over time, banking supervisors remain justifiably skeptical about the extent to which these correlations could be used to reduce capital charges on matched positions.

1. The regulatory rules discussed in this note relate primarily to "banking-book" positions. Buy-and-hold positions are held in the banking book, and positions that are held for potentially short-term horizons and marked to market are held in the "trading book." However, the thrust of the rules is the same for both banking-book and trading-book positions. For more detail on Canadian regulatory rules, see Office of the Superintendent of Financial Institutions (OSFI) (1999).
2. To obtain relief from regulatory capital by using a credit derivative hedge, the transaction must meet certain criteria for effectiveness and permanence. For Canadian practitioners, these criteria are detailed in the OSFI (1999) regulatory rules.

However, a number of developments facilitated the growth of this market. For example, in 1999, the International Swaps and Derivatives Association (ISDA) introduced new, streamlined default-swap documentation. The launches of two Internet trading platforms for credit derivatives (CreditTrade – *http://www.credittrade.com* and Creditex – *http://www.creditex.com*) helped bring some much-needed transparency to the credit derivatives market.[8] The European Credit Swap Index was launched in March 2000 by J.P. Morgan, tracking default-swap premiums on about 100 European corporations. Finally, in April 2000, Standard and Poors launched a series of U.S. corporate credit-spread indexes that could be used as the basis for a more generic and useful style of credit-spread put option.

Commercial banks account for over half the trading activity in the market for credit derivatives. Trading is concentrated among a small number of institutions, which is not unusual for derivatives.[9] Anecdotal evidence suggests that market activity is concentrated in, and about evenly split between, London and New York. Insurance companies and securities dealers account for most of the remaining activity, insurance companies being particularly active sellers of protection.

Anecdotal evidence also suggests that Canadian banks have been slower to embrace credit derivatives than their international counterparts. Reasons cited for the slow emergence of credit derivatives in Canada include the Canadian banks' access to cost-effective funding through their retail deposit base, as well as their ability to achieve a broad diversification of credit risk internally through their national branch networks. However, competition from global financial institutions may put pressure on Canadian banks to increase their activity in credit derivatives markets to allow them to offer similar services to their clients.

Most credit derivative transactions are written on non-sovereign reference entities. According to the British Bankers' Association (2000), transactions written against sovereign reference entities comprised only 20 per cent of the market at the end of 1999, with corporate and bank assets comprising 55 per cent and 24 per cent, respectively.

HOW CREDIT DERIVATIVES ARE USED

Credit-line management and "regulatory arbitrage" are two of the most important applications of credit derivatives motivating market participants to purchase protection against credit risk. Funding arbitrage and product restructuring are important factors that motivate market participants to sell protection against credit risk.

Credit-line management is particularly relevant for dealing with situations where a bank is over-concentrated in loans to companies in specific sectors of the economy, for example, because it has a comparative advantage in originating loans in those sectors. While concentration risk can be mitigated by other means (such as selling loans in the secondary market or originating loans in non-traditional sectors), there are advantages to using credit derivatives for this purpose. To begin with, loan sales can potentially damage valuable client relationships (i.e., clients may resent the fact that their bank is reducing its exposure to them, seeing this as a signal that the bank has diminished faith in their creditworthiness). Second, the origination of loans in non-traditional sectors can expose the bank to new risks. Credit derivatives can help banks to diversify their loan portfolios more cost-effectively, without damaging client relationships.

Credit derivatives can also be used for regulatory arbitrage, which is motivated by the one-size-fits-all capital charge structure imposed by national regulators according to the rules set out in the Bank for International Settlements "Capital Accord" (BIS 1988). Most bank loans, for example, require that 8 per cent of a loan's book value be charged against capital. In contrast, many of the larger banks use internal credit-risk models that indicate a wide range of applicable capital charges based on borrowers' creditworthiness. These banks thus have an incentive to off-load credit-risk exposure on those loans for which the internally generated capital charge is lower than the 8 per cent regulatory requirement (i.e., to divest themselves of relatively "low-risk" loans that would otherwise dilute the bank's return on capital).[10] Figure 14.2 shows a bank's gain from such arbitrage in the triangle labelled "perceived excess charge."

Credit derivatives can be used to facilitate a type of funding arbitrage in which low-funding-cost banks "rent" some of their comparative advantage to high-funding-cost investors (such as hedge funds and securities firms) in return for credit-risk mitigation. For example, Figure 14.3 shows a situation in which a bank buys a risky bond that pays 6.00 per cent (1), funds it at 5.00 per cent (2) and enters into the pay side of a total-rate-of-return swap with a dealer (who faces a higher funding rate of 5.25 per cent). The dealer receives the 6.00 per cent total rate of return on the bond (3) and, in return,

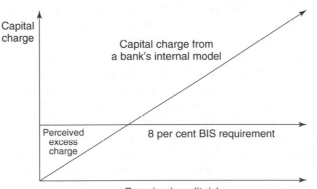

Figure 14.2 Hypothetical capital requirements as a percentage of book value

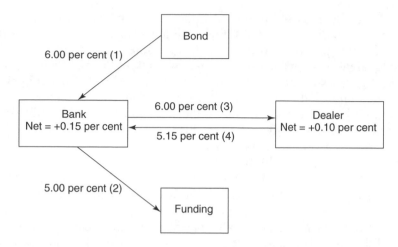

Figure 14.3 An example of funding arbitrage using a total-rate-of-return swap

Figure 14.4 Rate of return to a dealer not using a credit derivative

pays 5.15 per cent to the bank (4). The bank improves its risk profile and earns 0.15 per cent (since it borrowed at only 5.00 per cent and is effectively lending the dealer funds at 5.15 per cent), but now has counterparty exposure to the dealer. The dealer earns a net 0.85 per cent rate of return on its risky bond position, which is 0.10 per cent higher than if it had conducted the transaction on its own (see Figure 14.4, in which the dealer purchases the risky bond (5) and funds itself at 5.25 per cent (6)), but now has counterparty exposure to the bank. In essence, the bank could charge the dealer a lending rate anywhere between 5.00 per cent and 5.25 per cent, leaving both counterparties better off. In practice, the incremental revenue that both the bank and dealer receive must compensate them for the added counterparty credit risk they bear by undertaking this transaction. Box 14.2 generalizes some of these ideas and applies them to default swaps.

On the product-structuring side, credit derivatives facilitate the creation of risk/return profiles that may be either too expensive or impossible to achieve in cash markets.[11] For example, suppose that an investor wishes to purchase a 5-year bond issued by the Government of Brazil and denominated in euros. If no such asset exists, the investor could purchase a 5-year bond issued by the Republic of Germany and denominated in euros. Simultaneously, the investor would sell 5-year default protection on the Government

Box 14.2 Some Basic Pricing Economics for Credit Derivatives

The pricing of a credit derivative is closely tied to funding costs. The total-rate-of-return swap is an obvious case, being not much more than a synthetic financing transaction or lease. Hence, the periodic fee on total-rate-of-return swaps should be below the rate at which the total-return buyer can fund the reference asset. Since the total-return seller is effectively selling the underlying asset, the swap fee should be above the rate at which the seller can invest funds.

Pricing a default swap is more complex because its economic performance is tied to specific credit events. However, if it is assumed that the terms of the default swap cover all "events" that would affect the total rate of return on the underlying reference asset, a protection sale can be viewed as being equivalent to a fully funded long position in the reference asset. Hence, the premium should be closely related to the spread between the expected total rate of return on the reference asset and the funding cost.

The wider the gap between the buyer's marginal funding cost and the seller's marginal reinvestment rate, the greater should be the incentive to trade credit derivatives. The ideal counterparties would therefore be high-cost funders (like hedge funds) and highly rated banks with easy access to low-cost funding. Note that the incremental revenue associated with these transactions must sufficiently compensate both counterparties for the additional counterparty credit risk that they must bear.

of Brazil. By entering into these transactions, the investor will receive regular coupon payments on the German bonds *plus* a periodic fee for the default protection it has sold to its credit derivative counterparty. In exchange for this periodic fee, the investor will face a loss (i.e., be forced to make a payment to its credit derivative counterparty) if Brazil were to default on its debt. The profile of net risk and return for these transactions is very similar to a 5-year, euro-denominated bond issued by Brazil (in which investors would receive a slight premium vis-à-vis the German government bonds but face a loss if Brazil were to default on its debt).[12]

Potential Risks Associated with Credit Derivatives

Credit derivatives offer many benefits. If used inappropriately, however, they can exacerbate some of the risks that market participants regularly face. Moreover, the use of credit derivatives can potentially distort existing risk-monitoring and risk-management incentives.

While regulatory arbitrage may lead to a more appropriate allocation of capital (premised on the assumption that the flat capital charges outlined in the 1988 BIS Capital Accord may not be optimal), there is a risk that this activity can lead to an increase in banks' risk profiles. This is because banks engaged in regulatory arbitrage are effectively off-loading low-risk assets and retaining higher-risk assets (in a manner consistent with their own internal risk-assessment models). The net impact of this activity (i.e., the extent to which banks are left with too much or too little capital) depends on how well banks' models reflect the true risks of the aggregate loan portfolio, compared with the flat 8 per cent BIS charge.

More specifically, if individual banks' specialized models of risk and required capital are more accurate than the regulators' simpler model, then such arbitrage can allow banks to obtain a better risk-return trade-off with no adverse systemic consequences. The Basel Committee on Banking Supervision has proposed a new capital-adequacy framework, Basel 2 (which will replace the 1988 BIS Capital Accord) from 2007. This should reduce the incentives for regulatory arbitrage. The proposed framework moves away from the current generic capital charges and towards charges based on the ratings assigned by external credit-rating agencies. Such charges could range from 1.6 per cent for top-rated credits to 12.0 per cent for bottom-rated credits. This framework may also allow banks to use their own risk-assessment models to compute capital charges.[13]

Another potential downside of credit derivatives, particularly with respect to credit derivatives on bank loans, concerns loan-monitoring incentives. For any given loan, the originating bank is usually in the best position to monitor the ongoing creditworthiness of the borrower. The bank's incentive to perform this monitoring function will, however, be significantly reduced if the bank subsequently purchases credit protection on this loan via a credit derivative. Whereas loan sales and securitizations are structured so that monitoring incentives are retained by the originator, credit derivatives typically are not.[14] If, however, the term to maturity of the credit derivative is shorter than the term to maturity of the loan, monitoring incentives might be maintained because the originating bank retains the risk of late default.[15] Also, a bank that shirks its monitoring responsibilities could suffer reputational damage that would make it costly to transact in this market. At the same time, it is worth noting that, in some cases, monitoring and collection services can be transferred to third parties that specialize in such activities.

However, mitigating some of these risks on a systemic level is the fact that credit derivative transactions could potentially increase total banking system capitalization. For example, in a typical bank-to-bank transaction, the protection buyer reduces its capital charge from 8 per cent to 1.6 per cent, while the protection seller's charge goes from zero to 8 per cent (see Box 1). Hence, in this example, the system-wide capitalization is actually higher by 1.6 per cent of the notional value of the transaction than it was before the transaction. Only if the protection seller is an OECD government or a fully guaranteed agency of an OECD government will there be a reduction in system-wide capitalization (by 6.4 per cent of the transaction).[16] Unfortunately, it is very difficult, based on available data, to determine the net impact on the total capitalization of the banking system.

Scott-Quinn and Walmsley (1998) discuss a number of other potential downsides to the development of the credit derivatives market. They point out that this market could complicate the resolution of a potential default situation, resulting in smaller and delayed recoveries, which could, in turn, distort the default data that risk managers might used to check pricing and measure risk exposure.[17] For example, there could be a temptation, in the middle of a restructuring negotiation, for a protected bank to play "hardball" and trigger a default swap payout, especially if the protection was about to expire.

Thus, despite the certain advantages associated with credit derivatives, there is a risk that these transactions could distort existing risk-monitoring and risk-management incentives. Generally speaking, however, credit derivatives should enhance the liquidity and efficiency of markets for risky products by facilitating risk transfer and unbundling (i.e., by allowing market participants to separate and transparently price and trade credit risk). Credit derivatives may also improve the price-discovery process for credit risk by facilitating the trading of such risks for which cash markets are illiquid or are distorted by various technical factors.

NOTES

1. Letters of credit and bond reinsurance are very similar. In both instances, an issuer pays a bank (in the case of a letter of credit) or a reinsurance company (in the case of bond insurance) to cover or guarantee debt repayments on a particular issue or issuance program. Spread locks are contracts that guarantee the ability to enter into an interest rate swap at a predetermined rate above some benchmark rate.

2. Armstrong (1997) discusses recent trends in Canadian banking, particularly in the area of securitization.

3. Surveys by the British Bankers' Association (2000) and Hargreaves (2000) both concluded that default swaps were the largest single component of the credit derivatives market at the end of 1999 (based on the outstanding principal amounts of underlying reference assets).

4. Some contracts allow for optional physical delivery of the reference asset or a pre-agreed substitute asset.

5. Yield spreads are often calculated against government bonds, but such spreads implicitly measure a combination of credit risk and liquidity preference (see Miville and Bernier 1999). Calculating the spread against the swap curve more effectively isolates changes to the perceptions of credit risk. See Fleming (2000) for a U.S. perspective on the government bond versus swap curve "benchmark" issue.

6. The steady decline in the overall relative size of the government bond market from 62.1 per cent of the world bond market in 1990 to 54.3 per cent at the end of 1999 (Basta et al. 2000) has increased the credit-risk profile of outstanding global debt.

7. According to the U.S. Office of the Comptroller of the Currency (OCC), the outstanding notional amount of credit derivatives reported by U.S. commercial banks almost doubled from the end of 1998 (US$144 billion) to the end of 1999 (US$287 billion).

8. Both CreditTrade and Creditex are backed by major market participants. CreditTrade features major involvement from The Chase Manhattan Bank and Prebon Yamane (a leading over-the-counter financial market broker). Creditex's backers include J.P. Morgan, Deutsche Bank, Bank of Montreal, and Canadian Imperial Bank of Commerce.

9. In terms of concentration of business, the OCC estimates that five banks accounted for 95 per cent of the total notional outstanding credit derivatives contracts reported by U.S. commercial banks at the end of 1999, with Morgan Guaranty Trust accounting for 57 per cent and Citibank for 14 per cent. By comparison, the OCC reported that five banks accounted for 91 per cent of outstanding interest rate and currency swaps. The British Bankers' Association (2000) survey found that banks and securities houses were both the largest buyers of protection (with an 81 per cent market share) and the largest sellers of protection (with a 63 per cent market share) at the end of 1999.

10. For example, consider a bank that wishes to off-load its exposure on a loan made to a AA-rated corporation (such loans face a capital charge of 8 per cent). The bank purchases protection on the AA-rated corporation from a lower-rated OECD-regulated bank (all OECD-regulated banks draw a 1.6 per cent charge, regardless of their credit rating). This transaction will improve the bank's return on capital as long as the return on the "freed-up" capital (by moving to a 1.6 per cent capital charge from an 8 per cent capital charge) exceeds the fee charged by the commercial bank. Some regulators – including Canada's Office of the Superintendent of Financial Institutions (OSFI) – have, however, limited the extent to which banks can engage in these activities by insisting that the protection seller must have a credit rating at least as high as that of the reference asset in order for the purchase of protection to be recognized. In the above example, then, the OECD-regulated bank selling protection would need to have at least a AA credit rating for regulators to recognize the hedging benefits of a protection purchase.

11. Das (1998) provides a complete list of potential structuring and investment applications.

12. The default risk on the German bond position is assumed to be trivial and has been ignored in this example, but one could mitigate even this risk by purchasing protection against a German government default.

13. The proposal was published in June 1999. The cut-off date for comments from interested parties was 31 March 2000, but no implementation date has been set.

14. Gorton and Pennacchi (1995) suggest that, in the case of loan sales, originating banks either retain a fraction of all loans sold or provide buyers with some sort of implicit guarantee. Securitizations often involve credit enhancements by which the originating bank retains some degree of credit risk.

15. See Duffee and Zhou (1999) for a more theoretical discussion of this point and other aspects of the economics of the credit derivatives market.

16. OSFI (1995) assigns a zero charge to obligations of OECD governments and their fully guaranteed agencies, and to obligations of Canadian provincial and territorial governments. On the other hand, insurance companies and other private entities draw a full 8 per cent charge. Hence, protection purchased from such entities provides no capital relief, leaving banking-system capitalization unchanged.

17. Distorted default data would be a particular problem for those who use structural models to manage credit risk. Structural models measure credit risk as a function of estimated default probabilities and post-default recovery rates, so distortions in default data would make back-testing almost meaningless. Nandi (1998) provides a concise summary of various valuation models for default-risky securities.

REFERENCES

Armstrong, J. 1997. "The Changing Business Activities of Banks in Canada." *Bank of Canada Review* (Spring): 11–38.

Bank for International Settlements. 1988. *International Convergence of Capital Measurement and Capital Standards.* Basel Committee on Banking Regulations and Supervisory Practices (July).

———. 1999. *A New Capital Adequacy Framework.* Basel Committee on Banking Supervision (June).

———. 2000. *The Global OTC Derivatives Market at End-December 1999* (May). www.bis.org/publ/otc_hy000s.pdf

Basta, K., G. Bales, T. Sowanick, C. Molinas, and T. Vera. 2000. "Size and Structure of the World Bond Market: 2000." Merrill Lynch & Co.

Bowler, T. and J. Tierney. 1999. "Credit Derivatives and Structured Credit." *Deutsche Bank Research* (May).

British Bankers' Association. 2000. *BBA Credit Derivatives Report 1999/2000.*

Das, S. 1998. *Credit Derivatives: Trading & Management of Credit & Default Risk.* John Wiley & Sons.

Duffee, G.R. and C. Zhou. 1999. *Credit Derivatives in Banking: Useful Tools for Managing Risk?* Working Paper No. 289. Research Program in Finance, Hass School of Business, University of California, Berkeley.

Fleming, M.J. 2000. "The Benchmark U.S. Treasury Market: Recent Performance and Possible Alternatives." *Federal Reserve Bank of New York Economic Policy Review* (April): 129 45.

Gorton, G. and G. Pennacchi. 1995. "Banks and Loan Sales: Marketing Nonmarketable Assets." *Journal of Monetary Economics* (June): 389–411.

Hargreaves, T. 2000. "Default Swaps Drive Growth." *Risk* 13 (March): S2–S3.

Miville, M. and A. Bernier. 1999. "The Corporate Bond Market in Canada." *Bank of Canada Review* (Autumn): 3–8.

Nandi, S. 1998. "Valuation Models for Default-Risky Securities: An Overview." *Federal Reserve Bank of Atlanta Economic Review* 83 (Fourth Quarter): 22–35.

Office of the Superintendent of Financial Institutions. 1995. *Guideline A – Part 1: Capital Adequacy Requirements* (October).

———. 1999. *Credit Derivative Capital Treatment – Interim Appendix to Guideline A – Parts I and II* (November).

Scott-Quinn, B. and J. Walmsley. 1998. *The Impact of Credit Derivatives on Securities Markets.* Zurich: International Securities Market Association.

Smithson, C. and G. Hayt. 1999. "Credit Derivatives Go From Strength to Strength." *Risk* 12 (December): 54–55.

United States Office of the Comptroller of the Currency. 2000. *OCC Bank Derivatives Report: Fourth Quarter 1999* (March).

CASE STUDY 9

Journey to Junk

Jenny Wiggins

Owning General Motors' bonds in recent years must have seemed to some like being a passenger in a car speeding down a mountain road. From a position close to the peak of creditworthiness, the largest US carmaker has seen its credit rating career towards the precipice that separates the best-rated, investment grade companies from their junk-rated counterparts.

Now, the edge of the cliff appears to some to be drawing closer. Over the past few weeks, bonds issued by GM and General Motors Acceptance Corp – its finance subsidiary, which issues the vast bulk of the car company's overall debt – have fallen sharply in value. Investors have become increasingly convinced that Standard & Poor's, one of the three leading credit ratings agencies, is moving closer to lowering GM's ratings to junk.

Such a downgrade would be a striking confirmation of the problems at a company whose fortunes have traditionally been regarded by investors as closely intertwined with those of the wider US economy. But just as important would be the potential reaction in US debt markets. If GM loses its investment-grade rating some holders of its bonds will be forced to sell them – and it is the extent of any market upheaval this could cause that has been unnerving many.

In 2002, the downgrade to junk of more than $30bn of debt issued by WorldCom, the telecommunications company that went bankrupt, was one of the factors contributing to a sharp widening in yield spreads. With GM and GMAC having a combined $51bn of debt tracked by Lehman's Credit Index, some market observers are worried that the downgrade of billions of dollars of their debt to junk could cause similar havoc.

"It's unlikely that the market could absorb such a large issuer," says Craig Hutson, analyst at Gimme Credit, an independent bond research firm. "If it does happen, it would be a monumental event." Freshly fallen GM and GMAC debt would comprise almost 10 per cent of the US junk bond market, according to analysts at UBS.

Worries would be exacerbated if Ford – another US carmaker whose bonds have also been trading at levels more associated with junk – also eventually loses its investment grade credit rating, though this is not seen as imminent. Like GM, it has a rating one notch above junk. "It was like Chinese water torture," says a portfolio manager at one large bond fund, describing the state of the bond markets in 2002. "The fear is that $95bn of debt [GM and Ford] will go through this."

There is a contrary view, however. Other market observers believe that a downgrade of GM has been so well telegraphed that if and when it finally happens, the markets will manage it well. The belief is based on a series of adjustments being made by participants – agencies, investors and others – to make sure that the impact will be minimised.

If GM does take the plunge to junk, in other words, most market players may yet emerge unscathed.

Fears that a downgrade is on the way increased this month after GM reported poor February sales figures and announced production cutbacks, which will hurt its earnings. Already in January S&P had warned that it was becoming increasingly worried about GM's ability to improve its competitiveness. It hinted it was considering changing its "stable" outlook on GM's and GMAC's ratings to "negative".

In the early 1990s GM held a relatively high AA- credit rating from S&P. But as the company's fortunes have waned, with increasing competition from foreign manufacturers and rising pension costs, ratings for it and GMAC have drifted steadily lower. Today, GM and GMAC are assigned a BBB-rating from S&P – the lowest possible rating they can hold and still be considered investment grade.

Moody's, S&P's main rival, also warned in February that GM faced "increasing challenges" and changed its outlook to negative for both GM and GMAC. However Moody's ratings are higher than S&P's, at two and three notches above junk status for GM and GMAC respectively. Fitch, the third-largest credit rating agency, also has GM and GMAC two notches above junk. That means S&P's movements are the ones being most closely watched.

The line that separates investment-grade companies from non-investment grade companies is more than just an arbitrary difference of letters (BBB-versus BB+, in the case of S&P). The opinions of ratings agencies are enshrined in federal securities laws, limiting the kinds of debt that investment funds can buy. When an agency drops a rating on a company's corporate bonds from investment-grade status some investors have to get rid of the bonds, sparking forced selling.

GMAC's bonds are widely held by big US and European investment firms including Pimco, Fidelity and Allianz Dresdner Asset Management. Pimco is the largest US holder of GMAC bonds with a face value of some $901m, according to Lipper, a company that provides research on equity and bond funds.

While some junk bond fund managers may want to buy GM's debt if it is downgraded, they are under no obligation to do so. So-called "fallen angels" – companies that lose their investment-grade ratings – are typically unpopular with junk bond managers because their debt issues generally have weaker covenants (financial arrangements that protect the lender's interests) than bonds originally issued with junk ratings. If there are no immediate buyers for the debt the price of GM's bonds could fall sharply until it hits a level at which it becomes attractive to distressed debt investors.

"Even though [a downgrade] is anticipated, you could have a somewhat unruly market in GM paper," says Martin Fridson, chief executive of independent high-yield research firm Fridson-Vision.

Credit rating agencies move slowly, however, and this has advantages for both GM and investors: it allows them to prepare for a possible ratings downgrade.

Some credit analysts compare the rating agencies' tactics to the hints that the US Federal Reserve drops before it changes its closely watched Federal funds interest rate. "It's like the Fed funds," says Kingman Penniman, president of KDP Investment Advisors, an independent corporate bond research firm. "They tell you everything that happens before it happens so when it happens there's a rally." Mr Penniman is among those who believe that a downgrade of GM would not be a tremendous financial event for the market.

One of the beneficiaries of the agencies' slow and steady approach has been GM itself. Because it is GMAC's unsecured debt that is at risk of a downgrade to junk, the company has been cutting back the amount of unsecured debt it issues while increasing the amount of asset-backed securities and retail bonds it sells. "We have fundamentally changed the way we approach the credit markets," says Eric Feldstein, chairman of GMAC.

Some 65 per cent of GMAC's funding was sourced from the unsecured market in 2001, compared with only 32 per cent in 2004. About 33 per cent of GMAC's funding last year came from selling asset-backed securities, while 22 per cent was achieved through selling bonds to retail investors (see Figure C9.2).

Combined, GM's and GMAC's total debt outstanding at the end of 2004 was about $301bn, including some $268.7bn issued by GMAC.

GMAC is also considering insulating parts of its business from the main company so that, even if GMAC's rating falls, its profitable business segments will retain a higher rating. Mr Feldstein says GMAC may restructure its residential mortgage operations – one of the key businesses within its finance operations, accounting for $1.1bn out of an overall $2.9bn in profits last year – into a new holding company that would have its own credit rating.

GMAC says it has already received assurances from rating agencies that the new company would command a higher rating than GM or GMAC.

Rating agencies say they are frequently contacted by investment bankers trying to find ways to restructure GMAC in order to secure a higher overall rating for the business.

Scott Sprinzen, motor analyst at S&P in charge of GM's credit rating, said the agency was often shown ideas. "If it ever came to pass that we look at lowering the credit rating you can be sure that will get a lot of attention," he says.

One possibility raised by financial analysts is a mirror of the structure used by Italy's Fiat Auto, which is rated as junk. It sold a controlling stake in Fidis, its finance arm, to a group of banks – thus securing Fidis a higher rating. But GM has dismissed such ideas and analysts admit that relinquishing control is a last resort for the carmaker, as the finance arm provides essential support to its network of dealerships.

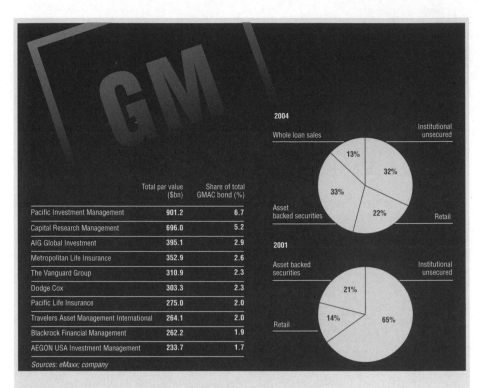

Figure C9.1   Top 10 holders of GMAC bonds
Figure C9.2   GMAC US funding mix
GM has reduced its reliance on expensive unsecured debt by utilising lower-
cost secured funding

Meanwhile, investors also have been preparing for a downgrade by getting rid of carmakers' bonds and buying the debt of other investment-grade companies – one of the factors contributing to record tight credit spreads as demand for non-motor industry paper has outstripped supply. In February, investment grade credit spreads hit their tightest levels since May 1998, according to Lehman.

"People have pared down auto exposure dramatically and have reallocated to other sectors," says Mary Rooney, head of credit strategy at Merrill Lynch, adding that most investors appear to be well positioned for a potential downgrade of the carmakers.

In the junk bond market, some investors have been preparing for a possible influx of carmakers' debt by starting to track so-called "constrained" indices, which limit the weighting of any one debt issuer. These indices prevent investors from being too exposed to a single issuer – such as WorldCom, which composed nearly 4 per cent of Merrill Lynch's global high-yield index before its default in 2002. Merrill subsequently introduced a constrained US high-yield index, putting a 2 per cent cap on any one name in the index.

Other market participants have also been taking action to minimise potential market disruption. One is Lehman Brothers, whose indices are the most widely tracked in the bond markets, with the vast majority of bond fund managers benchmarking their performance against them.

Traditionally, Lehman has used only ratings from Moody's and S&P, meaning that if one of these two agencies downgraded a company to junk, it would automatically fall out of Lehman's investment-grade index. But in January Lehman decided to start including ratings from Fitch.

That means that if S&P does strip GM of its investment grade rating but other agencies do not, GM will stay in the index and fund managers will not necessarily be forced to sell. Lehman's move follows similar action by Merrill Lynch, which included Fitch in its bond indices last year.

Lehman's change relieved fund managers, encouraging some investors to buy back GM bonds amid expectations that GM will stay in the investment grade index for some time to come. "Everyone breathed a sigh of relief," says Stephen Peacher, chief investment officer, corporates and emerging markets, at Putnam Investments.

It remains to be seen whether the careful approach taken by the ratings agencies as well as the steps taken by investors and the investment banks will allow a downgrade of GM debt to be absorbed by the markets without disruption. But one other factor that would support a smooth transition to junk status is that GM's problems are considered company-specific.

In 2002, revelations of fraud and accounting misdemeanours at many US companies created enormous volatility in the corporate bond market because investors did not know which company would be next to succumb to scandal. But GM's problems, which are related to its cost structure and loss of market share, are not considered leading indicators of potential problems at companies in other sectors.

"GM's problems are not viewed as systemic risk," says Ms Rooney at Merrill Lynch. "In 2002, there were systemic issues related to corporate governance and fraud, and over-leveraged balance sheets."

This would mean that, even if investors sold GM's bonds heavily following a downgrade, contagion selling throughout the bond markets would not be likely.

Some market observers liken the demise of GM's creditworthiness to that of AT&T, which once held a top-notch AAA credit rating and was considered the pricing benchmark for the corporate bond markets. AT&T, the telecoms company that had some $10bn of corporate debt outstanding, slipped to junk status last year but bond markets barely stirred.

"AT&T was a pricing benchmark in the bond market for a long time," says Mr Fridson, "But there was not much in the way of repercussions."

That gives some hope to those who believe that, even if GM is on a journey to junk status, the heartstopping ride may yet get most passengers home safely.

CASE STUDY 10

Who Rates the Raters?

STARTING in 1909, a dense book from John Moody would thud on to subscribers' desks in America, following days or even weeks in the post. The annual railroad-bond ratings were out. America's fledgling debt markets moved accordingly.

Moody's business still thrives almost a century later. Credit ratings – assessments of the likelihood that an issuer will default on the interest or principal due on its bonds – now shoot through the market at internet speed and cover bond issues of all kinds. Whether a company has the highest possible AAA rating or a BBB- plays an important part in determining the rate at which it can borrow. In America only a bold or foolish company, municipality, state or even school district would try to issue debt without first getting a rating from Moody's, Standard & Poor's (S&P), its chief rival, or Fitch, a French-owned upstart that has become the world's third-biggest rating agency (see Figure C10.1).

The leading ratings firms have lucrative franchises and face only limited competition in a business that, thanks to the growth of global capital markets, has greatly expanded. These days, S&P, for example, rates $30 trillion of debt, representing nearly 750,000 securities issued by more than 40,000 borrowers. All three big raters are highly profitable, with Moody's enjoying the highest operating margin – of more than 50% of revenues.

Credit ratings have been embraced by financial markets because they mostly do what agencies claim they do – accurately predict the likelihood of defaults. The agencies' overall long-term record is a good one (see Table C10.1).

But they have also faced heavy criticism in recent years, for missing the crises at firms such as Enron, WorldCom and Parmalat. These errors, the agencies' growing importance, the lack of competition among them and the absence of outside scrutiny are beginning to make some people nervous. This month regulators in America, the biggest market for ratings, called for more oversight of the agencies.

As debt markets have expanded, ratings have been built into financial arrangements of all kinds. Mutual funds and government-run pension funds often restrict their investments to certain grades of bonds, typically excluding those rated as "junk". The Basel 2 accords on bank-capital requirements, concocted by the world's central bankers and due to take effect in 2007, require regulators to use ratings in assessing banks' sturdiness. More controversially, during the era of corporate scandals it emerged that many banks had build so-called "ratings triggers" into their loan agreements. There meant that, if something happened to lower the borrower's creditworthiness to a specified level, the loans could be called in. Several high-profile cases, notably Vivendi in France, were trapped in liquidity crises as a result.

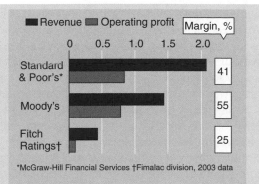

Figure C10.1 Smooth operators: Credit-rating agencies, 2004, $bn
*McGraw-Hill Financial Services. †Fimalac division, 2003 data. *Source*: Company reports.

Table C10.1 Good grades Cumulative average corporate default rates*
1981–2004 %

Rating	1 year	5 years	10 years	15 years
AAA	0.00	0.10	0.45	0.61
AA	0.01	0.30	0.85	1.35
A	0.04	0.61	1.94	2.98
BBB	0.29	2.99	6.10	8.72
BB	1.20	11.25	19.20	22.59
B	5.71	25.40	33.75	38.63
CCC/C	28.83	50.85	56.45	59.44
Investment grade	0.11	1.20	2.71	3.92
Speculative grade	4.91	20.22	28.25	32.42
All rated	1.64	7.08	10.45	12.51

Source: Standard & Poor's
* By years after initial rating

The agencies' power raises questions about their role and methods that have not been fully answered. Critics argue that the business is riddled with conflicts of interest because the raters are paid for their work by the bond issuers, rather than by investors who actually use the ratings (a change from old railroad-bond days). In addition, the big agencies are trying to grow consulting businesses that advise on matters which could affect their ratings, done by the same big agencies. This seems, at least on the face of it, a potential source of conflicts of interest.

S&P launched its "Risk Solutions" business in 2000, aimed mainly at helping banks meet Basel 2 requirements. Vickie Tillman, head of ratings at S&P, insists that "there is no relationship between that business and the ratings business; no mixture of personnel." Moody's "Rating Assessment Service" offering does mix personnel – the company views it as an extension of assigning ratings – but Raymond McDaniel, Moody's president, says he does not expect this business's contribution to rise above 1% of annual revenues. Consulting units (Fitch has one too) compete head-on with investment banks, almost all of which have highly profitable teams that advise corporate clients on how to manage their finances in order to impress the raters.

Others in the industry are dubious about this development. "Firewalls are really good until it gets really hot," says Glenn Reynolds of CreditSights, an independent credit-research firm. "It is an absolute parallel to what the auditors went through" when they tried to expand from auditing to consulting.

Indeed, the conflicts inherent in the agencies' business model have raised fears that the rating industry might be asking for regulatory trouble. The agencies are, says Mr Reynolds, "the most powerful force in the capital markets that is devoid of any meaningful regulation." Sure enough, this month in America, William Donaldson, chairman of the Securities and Exchange Commission (SEC) told a Senate committee that Congress should allow him to regulate the industry.

That prospect alarms the big agencies, which are stoutly defending their role and business practices and would prefer a voluntary code of conduct. They have begun by explaining more to outsiders, including journalists, how they work and what methods they use to set ratings. Critics have charged that many ratings are assigned almost arbitrarily. The agencies, of course, argue that they are impeccably thorough.

STEP BY STEP

When a company or government wants to issue debt, it usually calls a rating agency (or three, to boost credibility). Analysts then spend weeks, sometimes months, poring over data and interviewing company management. The team reports back to a committee of senior ratings staff. The committee formally decides the rating, although it usually follows the lead analyst's recommendation. If the issuer objects to the conclusion, some agencies allow it to veto the release of the initial rating. (When a new issuer has only one rating, the market may assume that a second rating is "hidden" in this way.)

Ratings are re-evaluated annually unless something happens that merits further attention. They change for many reasons – merger prospects, revenue shortfalls, regulatory changes and so on. Issuers retain the right of appeal if they feel wronged, although unlike an initial rating they cannot elect to "hide" subsequent ratings. The agencies say they will hear an appeal when the issuer provides new information or shows that their analysis is faulty, but they actively discourage sour grapes appeals.

But can an agency objectively assess a company that is paying its bills? Rating agencies argue that they manage this difficulty by barring analysts from involvement in fee negotiations. Further, say the raters, any individual issuer contributes only a tiny proportion of the rating agency's revenues, though some companies such as General Motors (GM) and General Electric would seem to carry more weight because they issue masses of debt. In this context, notes Ms Tillman, the fact that a recent study by a lobby group found one-third of issuers to be unhappy with their ratings is reassuring evidence that the potential conflict is, in fact, well managed.[1]

The "issuer pays" conflict is more worrying when it comes to the rating agencies' efforts to acquire new business. Sometimes agencies issue a rating even when the issuer has not requested it and has no intention of paying for it. The agency must then rely on public information to decide the rating. In other words, if the firm paid up, the rating might be more accurate.

Targeted companies despise such practices, which Mr Reynolds of CreditSights describes as "the equivalent of extortion". Carne Curgenven of Brit Insurance, a specialist insurer, has gone through this experience with his company's syndicate at Lloyd's, London's insurance market. Moody's has been rating the financial strength of the syndicate for years (S&P started more recently) without payment or agreement from Brit. Moody's methodology in particular, he says, caused him concern. But when he contacted Moody's, the response was that nothing could be done while the syndicate was not interacting: in other words, payment would open doors. Moody's says its methodology is "robust", and that "a more accurate analysis is not contingent on payment."

Rating agencies defend unsolicited ratings in two ways. First, they say that such ratings are designed to broaden their own understanding of the market. "If we want to be competing with S&P and Moody's, it's really bad if an investor phones us up and says 'I saw your opinion on Ford, it was interesting, what do you think about BMW?' And we say, "Actually, we don't cover them'," says Paul Taylor, managing director of Fitch.

Second, the agencies argue that unsolicited ratings are the only way for new ratings competitors to get a foothold. This seems somewhat disingenuous coming from the likes of S&P, which hastens to add that "way less than 1%" of its ratings are unsolicited. Moody's says it discontinued unsolicited ratings five years ago owing to widespread misunderstanding of the practice, though it continues to analyse a small number of companies (it will not say exactly how many) whose initial unsolicited ratings pre-date 2000.

Fitch probably does the most unsolicited rating – up to 5% of its portfolio. But it emphasises that it will accept information from a firm's managers even if it is not paying for a rating. Should the fact that a rating is unsolicited be disclosed to the market? Logic and practice say it should. S&P has only recently clarified its policy and now flags all unsolicited ratings: Fitch and Moody's also provide such flags.

Although critics generally accept the long-term validity of ratings, there has been vociferous criticism of the agencies' short-term performance. They conspicuously failed to predict the sudden collapses at Enron and WorldCom, which were rated investment-grade until the last minute. They were also slow to realise that senior managers at Vivendi were exploiting the agencies' traditional reluctance to force an issuer to make public highly sensitive internal financial information. In Vivendi's case, among other factors, hidden information about inter-company loans almost brought the company down.

WE'RE NOT WATCHDOGS

The agencies respond, reasonably, that they cannot be expected to spot frauds based on audited numbers or an intent to deceive them. But why, asks Frank Partnoy of the University of San Diego's law school, were the big agencies maintaining investment-grade ratings on Enron's debt when the bad news was mostly out and its share price had slumped to $3?

Similarly, how could S&P, Moody's and Fitch have been so oblivious to Asia's gathering financial problems in the mid-1990s (only to catch up with repeated downgrades once the problems were widely known)? And why do the agencies now keep ratings for GM and Ford just above investment grade, when the markets trade their bonds at spreads equivalent to junk status? The implication in all of these cases is that the agencies are reluctant to face the broader consequences of their decisions. By moving slowly, they avoid the accusation that their actions might lead to financial turmoil of one kind or another.

Rating agencies argue that speed is not their job – only accuracy. They are simply issuing a long-term opinion about creditworthiness and not trying to move the markets, or ride the ups and downs of the business cycle. "Investors don't want volatility from credit-rating agencies," says Mr Taylor. The agencies point out that they signal their intentions to the market ahead of a downgrade, typically by putting an issuer on "watch" status. But investors say that market prices are a better short-term indicator of trouble.

Big investment managers, equipped with their own bond-research teams, can profit nicely if they think the market has mispriced bonds in response to ratings decisions. "When the raters do something strange and spreads move significantly, we hope to take advantage of that," says one. Enron's collapse, for example, proved a fantastic buying opportunity because the agencies, fearful of more scandal, slashed corporate-bond ratings. "A lot of companies' bonds traded at 50 to 55 cents on the dollar, but they weren't going under," says Mark Kiesel, a strategist at PIMCO, a fixed-income manager.

UNDER-RATED?

Perhaps the biggest shadow hanging over the ratings industry is its perceived lack of competition. The business functions as an oligopoly. Upstarts have a hard time breaking in because it takes years, even decades, to build a sufficient reputation. "It is difficult for a rating agency to pop up because you need a 20-year track record," says one asset manager. Fitch is an unusual case because it was formed from several established agencies. Mr Reynolds thinks this could happen again with, say, Indian, Japanese and European agencies coming together. Private-equity funds, he says, could help pull something together. Others in the industry think more sector-specific rating agencies will emerge.

Ironically, the only power which America's SEC really has over rating agencies is to designate which ones are acceptable – and for three decades that has effectively impeded competition. Plenty of pension funds and other investors stipulate that their bond investments must have a rating from a "Nationally Recognised Statistical Rating Organisation", the SEC's designation. Some states have laws that specify S&P and Moody's. The fact that the SEC recently designated two more agencies as "nationally recognised" is misleading. S&P and Moody's still dominate the market, there and worldwide. The industry remains a duopoly or, at best, an oligopoly in important new areas such as structured finance (i.e., repackaged pools of assets).

One result is that there is little price competition between agencies. When asked how Moody's sets prices, Mr McDaniel explains that it decides annually after assessing how much value its services add. "We do not base our prices on someone saying 'We're going to get a cheaper deal down the street'," he says.

Fitch has been gaining ground as the third force in the business. In January it was admitted to the Lehman Brother's bond index, so its ratings now matter for all bonds included in that index. Following a similar move last year by Merrill Lynch, this was seen as an important stamp of approval. "Three is a big difference from just two," says one asset manager.

Still, Fitch admits that it has not really prospered by stealing business from S&P and Moody's, but rather by expanding the use of ratings. "We've benefited greatly from companies going for more than two ratings," particularly in America, says Mr Taylor. S&P and Moody's, he adds, are "so powerful that a company would be incredibly reluctant to drop their rating."

In fact there are plenty of thriving local rating agencies, especially in continental Europe and Japan. European companies have traditionally held information close, and some have resented the idea of being assessed by a big American firm. But resistance has weakened. Mr McDaniel characterises Europe as a "very good growth opportunity" for Moody's, in particular for ratings for complex structured financings.

Large credit markets exist in China and India, where local rating agencies are springing up (S&P is in talks to increase its stake in one of India's biggest agencies). Other developing markets are also opening up, as firms there shift away from a traditional reliance on bank loans towards funding debt in the capital markets.

But for big international issuers of debt there is little choice, especially since they will often want a rating from at least two agencies. Regulators are waking up to the problem. This month the SEC recognised AM Best, which specialises in the insurance industry, as a nationally acceptable rating agency (Dominion Bond Rating Service, a Canadian firm, is the fifth officially sanctioned rater.) Still, for many bond investors the imprint of S&P or Moody's will drive decisions for a long time to come. The system works, but, as one asset manager says, "You probably wouldn't invent" it to serve today's financial markets.

A NATURAL OLIGOPOLY

Is there room for a fourth or fifth global agency? One might emerge, but there might also be a natural limit to how many can thrive. Issuers content to have three ratings on their debt, might not unreasonably balk at paying for a fourth. Indeed, real competition to the established rating agencies could come from other quarters. Plenty of small firms assess credit and, unlike the agencies, make buy and sell recommendations as well. These firms charge subscribers rather than issuers, so pension funds and other investment managers that lack the resources to monitor the bond market themselves could hire one of these outfits. "The market is requiring more intensive coverage," says Kingman Penniman, who runs a research firm called KDP.

But the rise of independents, as well as the growing importance of other predictors of default such as credit-default swaps and other financial derivatives, are unlikely to slow down the expansion of the rating agencies' reach as financial markets continue to grow around the world. The agencies are now so woven into the fabric of the investment community that, barring a huge scandal, any changes are likely to be slow and incremental. Nevertheless, regulators have a reasonable case for gaining the power to monitor them a bit more closely. They should also encourage, as much as they can, more competition between the agencies – above all to avoid any transformational scandals like those which have already hit auditors and investment banks.

NOTE

1. The study can be found at: http://www.afponline.org/pub/pr/pr_20041018_cra.html

Reproduced from *The Economist* (26 March 2005), pp. 91–3.

Section 5

Measuring Performance

SECTION OVERVIEW

Janette Rutterford

As I mentioned in the Introduction, one of the changes affecting organisations, whether privately owned or public sector, has been the increased emphasis on performance measurement. The UK 1980s privatisation of the major utilities has led to traditional monopolies being run by private sector firms, subject to regulators imposing both financial and operating performance targets. For example, hospitals, prisons, train companies, all have their operating performance measured and this performance, relative to pre-set benchmarks and published as league tables, affects their revenues. Late trains mean that the train operating companies incur fines. Schools failing to achieve the requisite numbers of A level passes receive less funding. And so on. One example of the introduction of financial performance into the public sector is the introduction of Best Value for local authorities through the Local Authorities Act of 1999. This required English local authorities, from April 2000, to implement the 4Cs: *consult* about the level and method of providing services, *compare* its performance with other authorities and past performance, *challenge* the status quo of its provision and assess the *competitiveness* of its service provision in comparison with other authorities and the private sector.[1]

The UK privatisation programme was accompanied by the modernising of public sector accounting. Instead of the traditional cash-based accounting systems, with annual budgets, the public sector has now switched to accrual accounting, in line with the private sector. At the same time, assets owned by the government were valued and, if the return being achieved was under the required rate of return, these assets – such as shipyards, soldiers' homes, unused public buildings – were sold to the private sector.

Also, in the UK, new public sector projects such as hospitals, prisons and schools are no longer automatically funded, owned and managed by the public sector. Any new projects have to be assessed both under conventional public ownership, using a government imposed required real rate of return, *and* under private ownership, owned and possibly run by the private sector, providing services for the public sector in return for an annual charge. At the end of the life of the project, ownership may or may not return to the public sector, depending on the terms of what is known as the Public Private Partnership contract. Such partnerships raise interesting issues to do with risk transfer, which are exacerbated by the long lives of some of the projects. Again, the private sector is judged in such projects according to predetermined performance measures, which, if not met, incur financial penalties. The private sector funding of these projects has also meant a new approach to the capital structure decision – instead of projects being 100% debt funded by government, these projects now have a number of types of debt finance, with a small element of equity. The relatively higher overall cost of capital is deemed to be compensated for by more efficient management and hence lower overall cost cash flows.

This has been not just a British phenomenon, but a global one. Other countries, from Malaysia to Germany, from Eastern Europe to Australia, from Japan to Russia, have implemented privatisation programmes and private sector funding of public sector projects. This has meant imposing financial performance measures on organisations previously measured according to outputs, or not measured at all.

In the private sector, there has also been change. The traditional demarcation between finance and accounting is being removed. The situation where accounting was based on historic cost, and where management accounts bore little relation to financial market values is changing. As well as using discounted cash flow concepts for *ex ante* project appraisal, discounted cash flow and market values are also being used for *ex post* performance measurement. Examples of such measures have included Economic Value Added (EVA®) and cash flow return on investment (CFROI). Management compensation is now commonly linked to financial market performance and not just to accounting measures such as earnings growth. In this way, it is believed, management will act in such a way as to maximise shareholder value, rather than just trying to beat accounting measures based on, for example, historic cost. The use of options to remunerate executives was an attempt to ensure that managers behaved in a way which would enhance shareholder value. The disadvantages, though, of executive options are brought out in Case Study 14, an interview with Microsoft's CFO. It is difficult to motivate managers in a bear market when half of them are sitting on realised gains from their options and the other half on options with no intrinsic value. What is certain, though, is that the performance measurement system by which managers are judged affects the way that managers behave. Behavioural finance, again!

Another major change in the private sector is in financial reporting and the link with financial values. There has been pressure from the two major accounting bodies, the FASB in the US and the IASB in Europe and beyond, to move towards market values in financial accounts, away from historic costs. The aim here is to help the investor or stakeholder to get a better estimate of the value of the firm and of its true risk. So, for example, accounting rules for goodwill, for pension liabilities and for derivatives now require current rather than historic estimates of value to be taken into consideration. Executive options, previously off-balance sheet, now have to be expensed. Such changes are affecting companies across the world. Today, the FASB in the US and the IASB in Europe dominate the financial reporting of major companies. To be taken seriously, wherever a company is based, managers have to produce financial statements according to one or other of the two major bodies. However, as financial reporting requirements change, the less scrupulous managers take steps to enhance accounting performance rather than true performance. The more emphasis that the financial markets place on earnings, for example, the more pressure there is on managers to deliver the expected performance. This has led to some unpleasant surprises when apparently high-performing companies such as Enron turn out to have feet of clay.

The article by Gilbert Gélard, "What can be Expected from Accounting Standards?", looks at the impact of the introduction of common accounting standards, those of the International Accounting Standards Board, for all listed companies in the European Union. The change is relatively limited for UK companies, since the UK financial reporting body has had a major influence on the contents of the IASB accounting standards. The change is quite dramatic for French and German companies, which, apart from multinationals, have not hitherto felt the need to produce accounts which are of great relevance to stakeholders, in particular investors, preferring to conform to the law and concentrate on tax minimisation rather than profit maximisation. The change is even greater for companies based in Eastern Europe; such companies have had to switch, in a period of under ten years, from communist forms of accounting to an emphasis on reporting for investors.

Case Study 11, "Queens Moat Houses plc", gives an example of creative accounting. Although a relatively old example, it is a classic of its kind. The case consists simply of an extract from the 1992 Annual Report and Accounts of Queens Moat, a UK company which used a number of accounting methods to appear more profitable than it actually was. The 1992 accounts show how, by creative accounting, a 1991 *loss* of £56 million appeared as a *profit* of £90 million. These numbers pale into insignificance when we look at companies such as Enron, Royal Ahold, Parmalat and WorldCom. But what is interesting is that, despite the example of Queens Moat and others in the 1990s, and despite the increasingly stringent requirements of the financial reporting bodies, company collapses of greater magnitude could happen in the most sophisticated stock markets in the world. In the next section, in Case Study 15, the example of Parmalat will be looked at in greater depth.

Case Study 12 is an article by Keith Boyfield, "Learn by Numbers", on the impact of the switch to international accounting standards from January 2005 on utility companies. The main point that he makes is that even stock market analysts, used to studying such companies closely, had difficulty with the changes which led to quite different earnings and balance sheet values. Some companies had to spend substantial amounts of effort in trying to explain the impact of the changes in terms of what were real changes and what were merely accounting changes. In a few years' time, researchers will be able to estimate how investors valued the accounting changes and whether they were able to separate real and accounting movements.

The Economist article, "A Star to Sail By?", looks at financial performance measures, such as financial ratios and Economic Value Added, and the balanced scorecard approach, which uses both financial and non-financial numbers, as means of assessing organisational performance. The aim of all such measures is to make sure that managers take decisions which are optimal for the shareholder, that is, to make sure that they add value to the firm. However, each financial performance measurement system will have flaws and will lead to perhaps non-optimal behaviour. For example, if short-term remuneration depends on a particular measure, managers will attempt to maximise this, perhaps at the expense of long-term performance. Similarly, if there is too much concentration on financial performance measures, customer satisfaction may suffer. This article gives a good overview of a number of financial performance measurement systems. The following articles go into more depth on each one.

For example, "EVA Implementation, Market Over-Reaction, and the Theory of Low-Hanging Fruit", by Barbara Lougee, Ashok Natajaran and James Wallace, not only has an interesting title, it also looks at the impact – perhaps unexpected – of introducing a particular kind of financial performance measurement system, in this case, Economic Value Added. Economic Value Added measures the difference between the return on capital employed (operating profit after tax) and the cost of capital (WACC) – all multiplied by the capital employed. Such a measure will be high for firms which make high profits, use limited capital employed or have a low WACC and in theory forces managers to concentrate on adding value through both investment and financing, at both the divisional and group level. The authors of the article look at a sample of over 70 firms which introduced EVA® as a performance measurement scheme, linked to manager remuneration, and analysed the impact on the financial markets and on manager behaviour. What is interesting is that markets initially reacted extremely positively to the introduction of EVA® in a firm – which seems to show that just announcing a change can have perhaps more impact than the change itself. Also, manager behaviour changed. Not surprisingly, managers were keen to sell divisions or subsidiaries which did not earn a return on capital employed equal to the WACC. They also reduced their WACC by such financial restructuring as share repurchases. It is worth thinking back as you read the article to the economic environment at the time that EVA® programmes were being introduced. Interest rates fell throughout the 1990s, having a windfall benefit on WACC and on EVA®. Would managers introduce such incentive schemes in an era of rising interest rates?

"Transforming the Balanced Scorecard from Performance Measurement to Strategic Management: Part I" is an article by the authors of the balanced scorecard approach, Robert Kaplan and David Norton. This article is essentially an update and expansion of their initial article in 1992[2] which proposed the use of a wider set of performance measures, both financial and non-financial. This is specifically designed to avoid the pitfalls which can arise when purely financial goals are set. The authors also propose that the measures chosen should be specifically linked to the firm's strategic objectives, a point on which they elaborate in this more recent article. Part II of this article[3] gives case study examples of the balanced scorecard approach in practice.

Such ideas are also relevant to the public sector. As I have already mentioned, the UK has introduced a number of changes to performance measurement in the public sector, in particular the switch from cash to accrual accounting. These were masterminded by Sir Andrew Likierman, the author of the last article in this section, "Performance Indicators: 20 Early Lessons from Managerial Use". In the article, Sir Andrew gives a first-hand analysis of the successes and problems which arose from using a wide range of performance measures and indicators in a number of UK public sector organisations.

NOTES

1. For further information on this local authority (municipality) programme, consult the website of the Local and Regional Government Research Unit, Cardiff University, www.cardiff.ac.uk/research/lgru.
2. R. Kaplan and D. Norton (1992) "The Balanced Scorecard – Measures that Drive Performance", *Harvard Business Review*, 70 (1), pp. 71–80.
3. R. Kaplan and D. Norton (2001) "Transforming the Balanced Scorecard from Performance Measurement to Strategic Management: Part II", *Accounting Horizons*, 15 (2), pp. 147–60.

15

What can be Expected from Accounting Standards?

Gilbert Gélard

At a time when the issues surrounding accounting standards in Europe and worldwide grow in importance in a way unknown before now, it is worth questioning why our leaders and governments are suddenly interested in a subject matter that has been somewhat despised until now. Even the President of the French Republic has expressed his anxieties that certain accounting standards would lead to an excessive "financialization" of the economy. The debate may soon turn to politics or even party politics, which does not encourage serenity. Behind this new word, one can see looming the idea that the economy is too much the servant of the markets, which are whimsical, irrational, too volatile. They favour short-termism and work as a disincentive to long-term, stable investment etc. There is a long list of arguments, more often used when markets are falling than when they are rising. Not all these arguments are without merit, though.

General de Gaulle is said to have once declared: "the policies of France are not dictated by the market". That may have been true. However, it is on that market that the French state at present sells its holdings in its state-owned enterprises. This is also where it borrows, and its financial soundness is then scrutinized like that of any borrower.

True, the ups and downs of the markets in recent years are not commonly perceived as having been dictated by a pattern of rational behaviour. As any theory, that of efficient markets, on which globalization is based, does not in all cases appear to match the facts. However, a theory should only be abandoned for a better one which does not yet appear to be available.

If an efficient market is one that reacts in an optimal way to all the information available to it, one can see that the key to efficiency is in the provision of relevant information to that market. The hard core of this information is financial accounting information. A public company must present financial statements enabling investors to make the most rational choices possible.

The European Union has realized that a single financial market cannot work without a single accounting language. But what is true of Europe, as a region of the world, is also true worldwide. Markets operate around the clock and the only thing that is beyond our reach is to suppress time differences. It is therefore essential that this single language be adequate to the task.

1. TARGETING THE USER

The problem is that financial and accounting information works within a series of constraints, and one has to accept that trade-offs are necessary between conflicting objectives: readability versus completeness; general principles versus detailed rules; short term versus long term; belated precision versus rapid estimate; transparency versus confidentiality; past versus future. Financial statements cannot cater for the needs of everyone. Financial reporting by listed companies must target its public, i.e. define a particular type of external user, for whom periodic financial statements are the main, if not unique, source of verified financial information concerning the enterprise.

This hypothetical user, the "average prudent investor", cannot be an accounting illiterate. He (she) must be able to understand the financial statements, including all accompanying disclosures. Brevity will often conflict with completeness; clear and elegant communication with wealth of information. Certain market participants, professional analysts and the press often make it worse by an excess of simplification in focusing on certain key figures and ratios that soon get the status of "sacred cows": above all, net income, but also the debt/equity ratio or gearing, various other ratios and of course turnover or sales. However, none of these figures is any more than a mere accounting convention. Although such conventions are mostly rational and reasonable, they are also formulaic and simplifying. The resulting information content is poor and may be misleading. The widespread over-use of *p/e* ratios is typical of the problem of this low quality information.

2. THE TYRANNY OF NET INCOME AND RATIOS

Analysts using financial statements know that the net income of a period is a very partial indicator; it should be used with utmost care, analysed and completed by many other accounting indicators. Accounting indicators themselves are only a small part of the data that an analyst uses to rate a security. Yet facts are stubborn: net income remains the key figure, and as a consequence it is the one most submitted to stress when it comes to writing standards or to modifying the standards applicable to it. A recent illustration of this is the debate about the IASB project on "Performance Reporting". Resistance to change is, in such a case, rooted in fear of the unknown, a psychological factor, rather than on sound technical grounds.

In addition, this is also the ratio that managements are most tempted to manipulate through a contrived or sometimes plainly dishonest application of existing rules. When this is not practicable or when the net income figure is far too bad to be embellished, the enterprise will focus on some type of "income before deducting certain expenses", such as EBITDA, going sometimes so far as trying to ridicule the importance of net income and the relevance of the applicable standards.

The other recognized key figures – (1) debt–equity ratios, (2) the distinction between liabilities and equity, and (3) turnover or sales – are submitted to almost as much pressure as net income. The first two nourish a financial engineering industry, one goal of which is to help entities circumvent the spirit of accounting standards. This also fuels the debate between principle-based and rule-based standard-setting. For the third one, the occurrence of recent scandals about a measure that was thought to be so straightforward shows that neither the standard setter, nor the auditors and market authorities can take anything for granted.

In such highly sensitive areas, the accounting standard setter must be particularly convincing. Any technical change also has cultural and political dimensions. Nowhere has the tension been so great as on the debate on stock options awarded to employees. In this area, it is very clear that the refusal to consider the value of these options as expenses to be deducted from net income is not rational. It is based, however, on the quasi-sacred character of net income and of its perceived (and to an extent real) impact on the value of shares. If one simply follows the sequence of accounting entries when a company grants stock options, the equity, including the net income of the period, is unchanged by the granting of stock options, as the value of the option credited to equity is offset by an equal decrease of the profit of the period. From this point of view, the accounting is as "harmless" as it can be. But the Sacred Cow cannot be touched. Therefore, any bad reason will be used to try to discredit the only sound accounting conceivable, and any shameless lobbying will be used.

3. THE CULTURAL DEBATE ON VOLATILITY

The "financialization" of the economy is a fact of life for listed multinational companies and the CAC 40 French companies have a substantial proportion of foreign shareholders. This is a form of "relocation" of capital which has some similarities with the "relocation" of employment. They are the two sides of the same coin called globalization. When a government tries to favour a national champion in a transnational merger, it had better understand that it cannot control permanently either of these two "relocations".

Any linkage between this economic mutation and the (more or less extended) use of market values or fair values in the financial statements would be confusing two different things. It is perfectly true that measuring assets and liabilities at fair value instead of historical cost increases the volatility of income and equity, but it is equally true that it portrays the entity in a more faithful way.

The combination of historical cost and of the principle of realization would be prudent, some say. What is clear is that it allows the management of net income in such a way that it progresses smoothly, but often this involves artificial or contrived transactions and lack of transparency. It can

conceal real volatility that the market should be aware of if a correct allocation of resources is to be achieved.

The debate between historical cost and fair value will continue, but in the
meantime the real question is to assess whether volatility in accounting results
has a significant, measurable and lasting impact on volatility in share prices.
This is far from being proved. In the atypical period of the New Economy
bubble, the most volatile shares were those of companies which did not even
prepare financial statements, but only published dreams of fairy-tale future
sales. In more settled periods and for better established companies, when a
company presents two sets of accounts, say one at historical cost (continental European or Japanese) and another more "volatile" (US GAAP), the share
price is the same on both markets. The markets are not blind.

Even if a correlation was proved, a fundamental debate would remain
open: is volatility good or bad, is there a good volatility and a bad one? That
is another story.

The task of the global accounting standard setter, who is only one part of
the chain that ideally leads to good financial reports, is very complex. It must
work in serenity, while being attentive to the considerable social and economic impact of its work, which is all the greater in a complex world without
boundaries. One cannot expect simplistic nor immediate solutions to issues
that become increasingly complex. An effort of persuasion and education at
all levels is required. It cannot be achieved by the standard setter alone.

The guiding lines for its actions should be relevance and transparency.
Market players should be treated like adults who will understand that the
more transparent they are, the better they serve their stakeholders. Financial
reporting for a global market is still in its infancy. The standard setter should
not detract from its recognized framework. It must itself be transparent.
Calling a spade a spade has certain virtues.

Reproduced from *Accounting in Europe*, Vol. 1 (2004), pp. 17–20.

CASE STUDY 11

Queens Moat Houses plc

The following text is extracted from the Notes to the Accounts for the year to 31 December 1992 of Queens Moat Houses plc.

PRIOR YEAR ADJUSTMENTS AND RECLASSIFICATIONS

Following an investigation into the affairs of the group, including a review of the group's accounting policies and the treatment of certain transactions in prior years, the current directors have concluded that the accounts for 1992 and future years would be unlikely to give a true and fair view of the group's results and financial position if such policies and treatments continued to be adopted. Accordingly, certain changes have been made which, in the opinion of the current directors, ensure that the accounts are prepared in accordance with best practice and give a fairer presentation of the group's results and financial position. In order to ensure comparability, the 1991 accounts have been restated to reflect these changes. In addition, certain profit and loss account and balance sheet items have been reclassified. Further details of the prior year adjustments and reclassifications are set out below together with a summary of their effects on the accounts as at 31 December 1991 and for the year then ended.

Prior Year Adjustments

(a) Licence Fees

Previously, licence fees receivable from hotel operations not directly managed by the group were included in income in full at the commencement of the period of the licence and the turnover and net operating costs of such operations were included in group turnover and net operating costs. These policies have been changed and licence fees are now recognised on a straight line basis over the period of the licence. Furthermore, in view of the fact that the group's only contractual entitlement in respect of such operations is the receipt of a licence fee, the turnover and net operating costs of these operations are no longer recognised in the group's profit and loss account.

(b) Hotel Sale and Leaseback Transactions

Previously, sale and leaseback transactions which the group entered into with respect to certain UK hotel properties were accounted for as sales and operating leases, with the sales proceeds and profit on sale included in group

337

turnover and operating profit respectively. In view of the nature of the leases, the current directors consider that they should, more appropriately, be accounted for as finance leases. Accordingly, this treatment has been changed and sale and leaseback transactions of this type are now accounted for as finance leases and the sales proceeds and profit on sale are no longer recognised in the accounts. The accounts have been restated accordingly.

(c) Office Properties Held under Finance Leases

As at 31 December 1991, the group held certain office properties under finance leases in connection with which there were outstanding liabilities amounting to £12.1 million. The properties were included in stocks as properties held for development at their cost of £12.1 million and the outstanding liabilities of £12.1 million were netted off in arriving at the total amount disclosed for stocks. The current directors consider that the nature of these properties was such that it was inappropriate to include them in stocks and that they should have been included in tangible fixed assets at their market value, which has subsequently been determined by the group's independent property advisers at £6.5 million and that the outstanding finance lease obligations of £12.1 million should have been included in creditors and not netted against stocks. The accounts have been restated for these and certain other related adjustments.

(d) Depreciation and Repairs and Maintenance Expenditure

Previously, certain tangible fixed assets comprising fixtures, fittings, plant and equipment were revalued annually and not depreciated. In addition, certain expenditure in respect of hotel repairs and maintenance was capitalised in tangible fixed assets. These policies have been changed, and all fixtures, fittings, plant and equipment, other than certain integral fixed plant, are now depreciated on a straight line basis over periods of four to fifteen years and expenditure in respect of hotel repairs and maintenance is now charged to the profit and loss account when incurred.

(e) Acquisition of Globana

During 1991, the company acquired the remaining 51% interest in the Globana (France) group of companies ("Globana"). As part of the overall transaction the company received a fee of £10.3 million in respect of the cancellation of the management contract under which it previously managed the hotels owned or leased by Globana. This fee was included in the group's turnover in 1991. The current directors consider that the fee was part of a series of transactions which resulted in the acquisition of the remaining 51% of Globana and, accordingly, that it should have been treated as a reduction in the purchase price and not as income to the group. The accounts have been restated accordingly.

(f) Rationalisation Costs

Previously, rationalisation costs incurred in connection with the acquisition of new hotels, comprising principally wages, replacements, stationery and advertising for a period of six months following acquisition, were capitalised as part of the cost of acquisition. This policy has been changed and all such costs are now charged to the profit and loss account when incurred.

(g) Loan Finance Costs

Previously, certain loan finance costs incurred in connection with the acquisition, construction or redevelopment of hotel properties were capitalised in fixed assets. This policy has been changed and all such loan finance costs are now charged to the profit and loss account when incurred.

(h) Deferred Revenue Expenditure

Previously, expenditure incurred in the creation and marketing of new projects was deferred and charged to the profit and loss account over a five year period, commencing when income was first derived. This policy has been changed and all such expenditure is now charged to the profit and loss account when incurred.

(i) Acquisition of the Ashford Group

Shares issued by the company as consideration for the acquisition of Ashford Group Holdings Limited ("Ashford Group") in September 1989 were recorded in both the company's accounts and the group accounts at their nominal value and no share premium or merger reserve was created. As a result, in the consolidated accounts the consideration was not recorded at its fair value, the effect of which was to reduce the amount of goodwill arising on the acquisition. Adjustments have now been made to record the consideration at its fair value by creating additional share premium in both the company's accounts and the consolidated accounts and to increase the amount of goodwill written off to the consolidated profit and loss account. Furthermore, no accrual was made as at 31 December 1991 for deferred consideration payable in respect of the acquisition of the Ashford Group. Such deferred consideration was dependent on the profits of the companies of the Ashford Group for the year then ended, and the current directors consider that an accrual should have been made. The accounts have been restated accordingly.

(j) Profit on Disposals of Fixed Assets

Previously, profits and losses arising on the disposal of fixed assets carried at valuation were included in the profit and loss account based on the difference between the sales proceeds and depreciated historical cost. In accordance with the requirements of FRS 3 this policy has been changed and such profits and losses are now included based on the difference between the sales proceeds and net carrying amount, whether at valuation or at depreciated historical cost.

(k) Exchange Rates

Previously, the results of overseas subsidiary undertakings were translated into pounds sterling at the rates ruling at the balance sheet date. This policy has changed and such results are now translated at the average rates of exchange for the year.

(l) Sale and Repurchase of Land

During 1991, the group disposed of an interest in land which was subsequently repurchased under an option entered into at the time of the sale contract. The current directors consider that the nature of the agreement was such that a realised profit should not have been recognised and that, rather, the sale proceeds should have been treated as a short term loan. The accounts have been restated accordingly.

(m) Bonuses Capitalized

During 1991, a bonus paid to an executive director of the company was capitalised as part of the cost of the company's investment in a subsidiary undertaking which was acquired from the director in March 1988. In view of the nature of the bonus arrangements, this treatment has been changed and all such bonuses are now charged to the profit and loss account.

(n) Other Changes

Certain other changes have been made in order that the accounts are prepared on a more prudent basis. These include: the accrual of holiday pay, the reversal of an adjustment to goodwill written off in prior years which was released to profit and loss account in 1991 and the deferral of part of the profit recognised on a sale and leaseback transaction where the sale was at above market value.

Reclassifications

(a) Stocks

Certain stocks held by hotels as at 31 December 1991, which were previously included in tangible fixed assets or debtors, have been reclassified to stocks.

(b) Non-hotel Properties

Certain non-hotel properties, including the group's head office, which were included in stocks as properties held for development as at 31 December 1991, have been reclassified to tangible fixed assets.

(c) Telephone Revenue

Previously, both revenue and expenditure arising from the use of telephones by guests in the group's United Kingdom hotels were included in net operating costs. This has been changed and the revenues arising in this regard are now included in turnover and the related expenditure remains in net operating costs.

(d) Deferred Tax Write Back

During 1991, £1.7 million was credited to operating costs, being the write back of certain deferred tax provisions no longer required. This amount has now been reclassified to taxation in the profit and loss account.

(e) Finance Lease Creditors

Finance lease creditors amounting to £30.5 million, which were included in other creditors as at 31 December 1991, have been reclassified to bank and other borrowings as obligations under finance leases.

Company Balance Sheet

Certain of the above prior year adjustments and reclassifications, principally those relating to the acquisition of Globana, the acquisition of the Ashford Group and bonuses capitalised, also affect the accounts of the company. In addition, certain loan finance costs and deferred revenue expenditure were previously capitalised into the cost of the company's investment in subsidiary undertakings. Adjustments have been made to restate the accounts of the company for the year ended 31 December 1991 on a basis consistent with the revised accounting policies and treatments adopted by the group in the 1992 accounts. Furthermore, as at 31 December 1991, the balance sheet of the company included cash at bank and in hand amounting to £36.8 million which the current directors consider should have been included in the accounts of certain subsidiary undertakings; accordingly, adjustments have now been made to include such amounts in group balances.

A summary of the effects of the above prior year adjustments and reclassifications on consolidated net assets and on the consolidated profit and loss on ordinary activities before taxation for the year ended 31 December 1991 is set out in Table C11.1.

Table C11.1

		Net assets (£m)	Profit/(loss) on ordinary activities before taxation (£m)
As previously reported		1,297.9	90.4
(a)	Licence fees	(48.6)	(13.5)
(b)	Hotel sale and leaseback transactions	(33.3)	(9.8)
(c)	Office properties held under finance leases	(7.9)	(8.5)
(d)	Depreciation and repairs and maintenance expenditure	(2.5)	(50.9)
(e)	Acquisition of Globana	–	(10.3)
(f)	Rationalisation costs	3.0	(5.9)
(g)	Loan finance costs	(0.5)	(14.6)
(h)	Deferred revenue expenditure	(5.2)	(1.4)
(i)	Acquisition of the Ashford Group	(5.0)	–
(j)	Profit on disposals of fixed assets	–	(24.2)
(k)	Exchange rates	–	1.5
(l)	Sale and repurchase of land	(0.2)	(0.3)
(m)	Bonuses capitalised	(1.2)	(1.2)
(n)	Other changes	(3.9)	(7.6)
		(105.3)	(146.7)
As restated		1,192.6	(56.3)

CASE STUDY 12

Learn by Numbers

Keith Boyfield

As a topic, international accounting standards are not necessarily guaranteed to send a shiver of excitement down people's spines. But this indifference may soon change because UK public companies have been required – as from 1 January 2005 – to comply with International Financial Reporting Standards (IFRS).

The new accounting standards are likely to have a profound effect on the way in which utilities state their financial results. As this involves money along with a potential volatility in share prices, investors are likely to give it their rapt attention. Yet it is important to highlight the fact that the implications of IFRS will vary between utilities depending on their business activities.

Why introduce IFRS? In part, like Sarbanes-Oxley, it is a reaction to the succession of corporate scandals that have surfaced in recent years. Regulators believe that the more rigorous rules established under IFRS will curb potential fraudsters, limit any damage that might be associated with maverick management methods and allow companies less flexibility to manage how they present their financing activities.

Experience suggests, nonetheless, that fraudsters will always be with us and IFRS may simply encourage some managers to cut corners in new and innovative ways. But overall, the utilities sector across Europe has a good record when it comes to observing accounting standards.

Another of the key goals linked to IFRS is the desire to enable investors to compare in a more accurate and transparent manner the operational and financial performance of companies across Europe, particularly where these companies operate in the same sector. Furthermore, IFRS is closer to US GAAP than the old national accounting standards, making transatlantic comparisons easier, too. As the utilities sector in the European Union continues to consolidate, this objective is close to the hearts of institutional investors.

IFRS introduces a host of changes – which is good news for accountants – but relatively few will fundamentally change the stated profits or assets of most utilities.

One of the most important new standards for the utilities sector as a whole is the new "financial instruments" standard (IAS 39), which will require companies to "mark to market" many commodity contracts. To mark to market is to calculate the value of a financial instrument at current market rates. Furthermore, any changes in marked-to-market (MTM) values may need to be stated in the profit and loss account, which could trigger considerable earnings volatility. This is because the whole change in value for a long-term contract will flow through the earnings statement every year.

Commenting on this likely trend, Iain Smedley, an executive director with Morgan Stanley's investment banking division based in London, says: "The market will tend to look at 'pre volatility' numbers when assessing financial performance and multiples such as price/earnings ratios."

"At the same time, the greater disclosure of details required under IFRS may well throw up a raft of interesting facts – including issues relating to pension funding, financial leases and commodity contracts. This could well have a significant impact on share price, or at the very least highlight areas on which investors should focus."

There is still some uncertainty about exactly what commodity and derivative contract structures count as "hedges", and can therefore be termed "IFRS friendly", because they are unlikely to cause earnings volatility. Inflation risk hedging is particularly significant to regulated water and electricity networks companies, where both the regulatory base of the assets and the revenues earned from those assets are indexed to inflation. In the interests of optimal risk management, a clutch of utilities have sought to issue inflation-linked financing or achieve the same risk management goal using derivatives.

But a note of caution should be sounded. The interpretation of IFRS in these areas is as yet unclear, so many accountants are reluctant to support the use of derivatives to hedge against inflation risks. "Companies must avoid the paradoxical trap of being exposed to real economic risks just because they are trying to follow an 'accounting safe' approach," says Smedley.

James Leigh, an energy and utilities partner at Deloitte makes a similar point: "As the complex IAS 39 rules become better understood by energy and utilities companies, the areas of debate become narrower and arguably more marginal. While these areas are important, companies also need to focus on explaining the impact of new standards to their investors and, in particular, how their trading and hedging strategies drive their commodity accounting. However, this debate should not be limited to IAS 39, as a number of energy and utilities companies will also suffer the erosion of net assets from changes to pension, deferred tax and possibly fixed asset accounting. Nobody in the energy and utilities sector finds the introduction of IFRS easy."

Sir Roy Gardner, chief executive of Centrica, reckons there are four specific areas linked to the introduction of IFRS that are particularly relevant to his company. First are "mark-to-market energy contracts that are not for own use or do not qualify as hedges under IAS 39". In his review for the latest financial year, he noted that the "form and timing of IAS 39 is still uncertain". Alas, there is still some uncertainty almost 12 months later.

Second, he pointed out there was a need to "confirm a final, industry treatment for Petroleum Revenue Tax [PRT]". In this context, "there is uncertainty over whether PRT should be treated as income tax or a production cost which impacts the method of calculation".

Third, Gardner notes that IFRS will demand that companies record any pension deficit, net of deferred tax, on the balance sheet under the IAS 19 rule. This standard has been the subject of technical revision but the latest position appears to be that companies will be able to use the FRS 17 model as well as what is referred to in jargon as the corridor method, with actuarial adjustments recognised in equity.

Fourth, IFRS will require publicly quoted companies to subject goodwill to an annual impairment test rather than an amortisation charge, as happened previously.

In a recent presentation to investors, Phil Bentley, Centrica's group finance director, observed that: "It is important to note that IFRS has no impact on our business strategy, nor on the cash flows generated by the business, and it does not change the underlying drivers of value of Centrica's business model." Indeed, Bentley argues that cash generation will continue to be one of the key performance measures for the company. In a separate presentation to investors, Simon Lowth, Scottish Power's director of finance and strategy, has made precisely the same point.

No doubt both are trying to impress experienced analysts such as Catherina Saponar, now of Bank of Montreal. For her part, Saponar points out that "cash flow remains one of the most important measures for utility companies". Indeed, she adds, "IFRS may lead to an ever increased focus on cash-based measures".

Bentley recognises that the commodity mark-to-market requirement is particularly significant for Centrica's business (in comparison, say, with a company like National Grid Transco). Specifically, Bentley acknowledges, "the requirement to mark to market more of our commodity transactions requires the initial recognition of unrealised profits and losses and introduces volatility in the Group's reported profits".

The adoption of the new IFRS rules will have an even more profound impact on the future financial results reported by National Grid Transco. In overall terms, the new accounting standards are expected to lead to an increase in operating profit, pre-tax profit and earning per share. Yet the treatment of net assets is likely to lead to a lower figure.

Table C12.1 illustrates the impact that the adoption of IFRS would have had on National Grid Transco's consolidated profit and loss account and net assets for the year ended 31 March 2004.

Table C12.1 The effect of IFRS on National Grid Transco's results (2004)

	Under IFRS	Under UK GAAP	Change	Change (%)
Underlying operating profit (£m)	2,763	2,213	+550	+25
Underlying pre-tax profit (£m)	1,935	1,391	+544	+39
Underlying earnings per share (pence)	46	33.9	+12.1	+36
Statutory operating profit (£m)	2,476	1,837	+639	+35
Pre-tax statutory operating profit (£m)	1,874	1,337	+537	+40
Statutory earnings per share (pence)	47	35	+12	+34
Net assets @ 31/3/04 (£m)	1,104	1,271	−257	−20

One of the drivers behind IFRS is the extensive use of fair value accounting. But this has proved a controversial initiative because this can lead to a host of practical difficulties, most notably the increased volatility that goes hand in hand with such accounting techniques.

BAA, the airport operator that runs Heathrow, Gatwick and Stansted, has decided to stop issuing quarterly results because the company feels it is impractical to revalue its £8.6 billion property portfolio so often. It is the first major publicly quoted company to adopt such a strategy, specifically to avoid IFRS reporting standards, but not necessarily the last. What is particularly significant is that BAA only opted to make this move after extensive consultation with its major institutional shareholders.

From an investor's point of view, some of the more sophisticated institutions and fund managers may use the new IFRS accounting standards as a hook on which to conduct speculative activity in the hope of significant share movement. For the most part, such wholesale investors will take IFRS in their stride. But individual investors, some of whom may have acquired their shareholdings at the time of privatisation, may find the new accountancy standards confusing.

Probably the best advice for such investors is to consult company websites – most utilities have been at pains to explain the practical implications of the new IFRS rules. And it would pay individual investors to examine the detailed research prepared by equity analysts on this topic. Again, some of this can be downloaded free of charge from a number of financial websites.

One final point is worth mentioning. Charlie McCreevy, Ireland's former finance minister and now Commissioner for the internal market in the European Commission, is taking a close interest in the implementation of IFRS standards. If investors have any complaints about the impact of these new rules, he would be a good person to contact. After all, he is a chartered accountant by profession, so at least he should be able to understand the numbers.

Reproduced from *Utility Week* (17 June 2005), by permission of Keith Boyfield.

16

A Star to Sail By?

The Economist

Were Siemens an American firm, the news that it is making the creation of value for its shareholders its top priority would be loudly applauded. But in Germany, where fans of "stakeholder capitalism" argue that their interests should be balanced with those of employees, suppliers and customers, its decision to become the first firm to adopt a measure of shareholder value known as economic value added (EVA) will provoke jeers as well as cheers.

Karl-Hermann Baumann, Siemens's chief financial officer, says that the trains-to-telecoms giant, which will switch to EVA in October, is now convinced that focusing on shareholder value is the best way to ensure its long-term prosperity. A growing number of other companies in Europe, Asia and Latin America, have reached the same conclusion – and are turning to consultants offering "performance metrics" to measure how much value is being created (or destroyed). Measures such as EVA are already well established in America, where a growing number of Wall Street stockpickers, not to mention many large companies, including Coca-Cola, Monsanto and Procter & Gamble, swear by them.

Inevitably the measures are also a big business for consultants. Stern Stewart, the New York firm that developed EVA, is the leader of the pack. But in recent years it has faced competition from the Boston Consulting Group (BCG), Braxton Associates, McKinsey and others. Many consultancies produce league tables of value added and go to increasingly absurd lengths to protect their particular "brand". As well as registering EVA as a trademark in several countries, Stern Stewart has also registered the term "EVAngelist".

Such hype is reminiscent of another management fad that swept the world and cost thousands of people their jobs – business process re-engineering. The argument about the effectiveness of re-engineering (motto: "don't automate, obliterate") still rages. On balance, it now seems that most of the firms that applied it became more efficient; but it is also clear that it was hopelessly oversold, and that it is much more use to some types of firm, or business people doing some types of thing, than it is to others. In other words, it is a useful tool, not a complete answer. Much the same seems to be true of EVA and its rivals.

ALPHABET SOUP

The notion behind the yardsticks is simple: a company creates value only if the return on its capital is greater than the opportunity cost of it, or the rate that investors could earn by investing in other securities with the same risk. Far from novel, this is one of the oldest nostrums in business. Companies have long used "hurdle" rates of return to judge individual investment projects. The new measures extend this practice to an entire business. "It's a very basic concept that big companies simply forgot over time," says Marcel Telles, the boss of Brahma, a Brazilian drinks firm that is an EVA addict.

EVA seeks to jog managers' memories by deducting from a firm's net operating profit a charge for the amount of capital it employs. If the result is positive, then the firm created value over the period in question; if the EVA is negative, it was a "value destroyer". Providing a company knows how much capital its operating units use, it can work out their EVA too. For example, if a division's capital is $100m and its cost of capital is 10%, its target rate of return will be $10m. If it earns $50m, then its EVA will be $40m. Although EVA sums involve tweaking published accounts (see Example 1 on next page), the principle is easy enough to grasp.

Other measures involve trickier calculations. A popular one is "cash flow return on investment" (CFROI), which is promoted by both BCG and HOLT Value Associates, a Chicago firm that advises fund managers and firms on questions of valuation. This is a return-on-investment measure that is adjusted to take account of the distortions that can be caused by inflation, different asset ages and lives, and different depreciation methods. Unlike EVA, which is based on adjusted accounting profit and is therefore a near-cash measure, CFROI compares a firm's cash flows with the inflation-adjusted capital used to produce them.

The problem with EVA and CFROI is that they are backward-looking measures, which tell managers nothing about how their current strategies are likely to affect the future value of their companies. So Stern Stewart has come up with a measure of overall corporate value, market value added (MVA), which takes the total capital of a firm, including equity, loans and retained earnings, and deducts this from the value of its share capital and debt. Not to be outdone, BCG has come up with a rival measure, total shareholder return (TSR), which is the change in a firm's market capitalisation over a one-year period plus dividends paid out to shareholders, expressed as a percentage of its initial value.

As well as looking at historical performance, these measures capture the market's estimates of firms' growth prospects. Stern Stewart says that there is a close correlation between EVA and MVA – if managers improve EVA, the company's MVA is highly likely to improve too. Other firms claim that their backward-looking and forward-looking measures are even more closely correlated.

Example 1   The EVA brew

Although economic value added may sound simple in theory, it can be tricky to apply in practice. Stern Stewart advises clients to make anything up to 164 changes to their accounts. The following example (see Table 16.1) shows how the same consultancy works out the 1996 EVA of South African Breweries (SAB), a company that owns hotels and shops, as well as being one of the world's biggest brewers.

First, Stern Stewart calculates SAB's "economic capital" (1). This is its equity and debt, plus adjustments for items such as cumulative goodwill associated with acquisitions. Accounting rules treat goodwill as an expense charged against profits, but Stern Stewart says that goodwill and other things such as R&D are capital investments that should produce returns in future.

Next, Stern Stewart works out how much SAB's assets earned after tax in 1996 (2). Then it calculates the company's cost of capital. The cost of its debt is simply the average interest rate that the company pays. But what about its cost of equity? To calculate this, Stern Stewart uses the capital asset pricing model, which holds that a firm's cost of equity consists of a risk-free rate of return for a stockmarket plus a risk premium that reflects how volatile its share price has been relative to that market.

Table 16.1   EVAluating

South African Breweries	1996, rand, m
1. Economic capital = shareholders' equity	5,799
+ goodwill written off	1,521
+ capitalised cumulative unusual loss	930
+ deferred tax	405
+ minority interests	2,352
+ total debt	4,415
	15,422
2. Net operating profit after tax (NOPAT) = operating profit	3,406
+ interest expense	689
− unusual gain	68
− taxes	978
	3,049
3. Weighted average cost of capital (WACC)	
cost of equity	20.4%
cost of debt	10.7%
WACC =	17.5%
4. EVA = NOPAT − (capital × WACC)	
= 3,049 − (15,422 × 17.5%)	= 305 m

Source: Stern Stewart

Applied to SAB, this produces a cost of equity of 20.4%. Because SAB has more equity than debt, its weighted cost of capital is 17.5% (3).

Lastly, Stern Stewart multiplies this percentage figure by SAB's capital employed to produce a capital charge, which is then deducted from the company's profit figure. The result shows that SAB had a positive EVA of 350m rand ($81m) last year (4). Its shareholders no doubt raised their glasses to that.

CASH IS FACT, PROFIT IS OPINION

How well do these different measures perform? They are undoubtedly superior to traditional yardsticks of corporate performance, such as return on capital employed and earnings per share, which rely on accounting figures. The defect of accounting figures is that they can easily be manipulated. For example, by extending the depreciation life of assets (which improves earnings per share) or using operating leases to keep assets off a balance sheet (which boosts return on capital), firms can disguise their true financial health at the flick of a pen. Such "creative" accounting explains why changes in, say, earnings per share explain very little of the changes in firms' price-earnings ratios, a traditional gauge of corporate value.

Because they focus on cash flow, which is harder to manipulate, the new measures provide a more reliable picture of firms' performance. They also make it easier to compare them across borders. Looking at national accounts creates a severe apples-and-oranges problem, because depreciation, brand valuations and other issues are treated differently by different accounting regimes. A classic example of this was provided by Daimler-Benz, which in 1993 became the first German firm to list its stock in New York. Under German rules, it reported a $372m profit; under tougher American ones, its loss was $1.1 billion.

Little wonder that financial analysts are scrutinising the new yardsticks carefully. HOLT has signed up more than 200 fund-management firms as subscribers to its CFROI-based forecasting model, including several in Japan. And a growing number of investment banks, such as Goldman Sachs and Credit Suisse First Boston (CSFB), are using EVA to analyse equities.

Stern Stewart and other consultants claim that their metrics can be useful early warning signals. For instance, anybody monitoring IBM's EVA would have seen it decline consistently between 1984 and 1989 (see Figure 16.1). In 1988 it turned negative (i.e., IBM was destroying value), even though the firm's net profit rose. However, the metric also did not predict Big Blue's turnaround in 1994.

VALUE FOR MONEY?

Although EVA, CFROI and other metrics are useful as pure performance measures, consultants say they can be far more than that. Used as corporate-

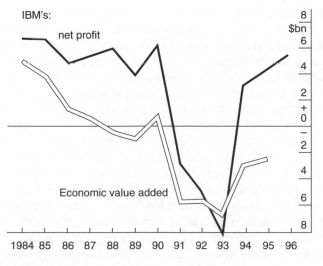

Figure 16.1 Early warning
Source: Stern Stewart

governance tools, they can persuade managers tempted to build huge empires at shareholders' expense to put the interest of owners first.

Firms that have taken the plunge by tying executives' share options and/or bonuses to improvements in EVA claim that such "value-based management" strategies have had a big impact. Harnischfeger Industries, an acquisitive Milwaukee company that makes mining equipment, paper-making machinery and overhead cranes, is one of EVA's converts. When it adopted the technique in 1993, the company was destroying some $100m of wealth a year, largely because the managers in its operations rarely thought about the cost of the capital they consumed. To make matters worse, they often exaggerated the likely returns from proposed acquisitions, forcing head office to scrutinise every deal closely. "We were the policemen," says Francis Corby, the firm's head of finance.

Now, with EVA-related bonuses at stake, both operating managers and financial ones are on the same wavelength, because nobody wants to make an acquisition whose returns will be smaller than the company's 12% cost of capital. In June Harnischfeger withdrew from a takeover battle for Giddings & Lewis, America's biggest machine-tool company, after the rival bidder, Germany's Thyssen, upped the stakes. With managers also slashing inventories abroad, helping to reduce capital employed by $300m since 1993, the company turned EVA positive last year, two years earlier than the target date it had set itself.

Another way for managers to boost the new measures (and thus their bonuses) is to reduce the cost of the capital they use. Often this means reducing a firm's equity capital, because equity is often more expensive than debt. Since 1995 Brazil's Brahma has retired some $1 billion-worth of equity via a series of buybacks.

Altogether more than 300 firms worldwide have adopted EVA-based systems – which puts this method ahead of its rivals. Stern Stewart's longer track record is one reason. Brahma's Mr Telles likens choosing a metrics adviser to choosing a surgeon: "You want someone who has done a lot of operations." But EVA's biggest selling point is its relative simplicity. Rival measures, such as CFROI, are harder to explain to managers.

This simplicity, argue its rivals, comes at a cost. In a pamphlet last October, Eric Olsen of BCG argue that EVA discourages executives from making big investments because the upfront capital charge for them immediately depresses EVA. He also noted that the easiest way to boost the measure in the short run was to "milk" a business by slashing capital spending. Unchecked, this could cause a fatal spiral of under-investment. "In five years you might not have a business left," says Alistair Cox, group strategy director of Blue Circle Industries, a British manufacturer of building materials that prefers measures based on total shareholder returns.

Stern Stewart, which admits that EVA could restrict growth if used too simply, advises clients to spread out part of the capital charge associated with big projects over their expected pay-back period. And it suggests that firms allow some of a bonus awarded for beating EVA targets in one year to be clawed back if future goals are missed. In Harnischfeger's case, growth has not been a problem: sales have more than doubled since it introduced the technique.

How different are the competing products? The top-ten lists produced by the various consultancies do indeed turn up different winners and losers (see Tables 16.2–16.4). But that is largely because of the different time periods and samples chosen by the different consultancies. (HOLT, which uses CFROI analysis, ranks firms on a particularly complicated scale linked to the present cash value of their future investments.) Monsanto and other compa-

Table 16.2 Top ten US companies*, by market value added, 1995

	$bn
Coca-Cola	87.8
General Electric	80.8
Merck & Co	63.4
Philip Morris	51.6
Microsoft	44.9
Johnson & Johnson	42.5
AT&T	40.2
Procter & Gamble	40.0
Exxon	39.0
Wal-Mart	36.0

* Industrial and non-financial
Source: Stern Stewart

Table 16.3 Top ten US* companies by "HOLT % future",[†] June 30th 1997

	% future
Coca-Cola	80.12
Merck & Co	67.31
Johnson & Johnson	64.93
Procter & Gamble	63.33
General Electric	59.89
3M	54.29
Hewlett-Packard	48.78
Philip Morris	42.48
Allied Signal	41.10
Wal-Mart	40.56

* Non-financial companies in Dow Jones industrial average, excludes AT&T
[†] % of total market value attributed to future investments
Source: HOLT Value Associates

Table 16.4 Top ten US companies* by TSR[†], 1991–96 average

	%
3Com	92.0
Tellabs	83.6
EMC	73.9
Cisco Systems	72.7
Oracle	66.9
Dell Computer	65.6
Intel	61.1
Andrew Corp.	60.1
Citicorp	60.0
Micron Technology	59.9

* In S&P 500
[†] Total shareholder return
Source: The Boston Consulting Group

nies that have carefully compared EVA, CFROI and other measures say that they mostly do not turn up wildly different results. The bigger question is whether performance metrics, as a whole, carry any dangers.

In many parts of Europe and Asia, it is hard to see what harm a little bit of concentration on value can do. Siemens, where Mr Baumann admits that several of the firm's divisions currently have negative EVAs, is a case in point. In Asia, firms that have been growing, such as Singapore's SNP and Indonesia's Bakrie & Brothers, are now using similar yardsticks to re-examine their mix of businesses.

As a way of measuring things rather than reorganising them, EVA and the other tools are helpful. But there are still weaknesses. Inevitably, performance measures are a bit more useful in some industries than others. It is harder (though clearly not impossible) to find ways to calculate ratios in industries where many of the assets are intangible items such as brand names or marketing brains. Consultants have to make the similar guesstimates about the value of, say, a newspaper title to those which normal accountants are increasingly being asked to make.

Yet Stern Stewart insists that its approach works as well with service-sector companies as with manufacturing ones: it cites the example of Equifax, a credit-scoring company based in Atlanta which started using EVA in 1992 – and has saved a small fortune by selling off property and rejigging the way it collects its own debts. However, even Stern Stewart admits that two sorts of companies are not well suited to EVA-style analysis: financial institutions (which must set aside capital for regulatory reasons) and very young companies, where most of the revenue calculations would have to be guesswork.

There is a wider criticism to be made. In a recent exchange in *Fortune* magazine, Gary Hamel, a respected management writer, pointed out that the efficient use of capital is not the be-all and end-all for successful companies. Strategy and innovation, he says, count for more. It is indeed hard to imagine EVA having told Bill Gates anything useful when he started Microsoft, or when he decided to embrace the Internet last year. A stock analyst who bets on a company because he thinks the chairman is a genius may do better than the one looking for a positive CFROI.

Already, some companies are introducing yet another technique – "balanced scorecards". These try to mitigate the drawbacks of making purely numerical estimates of a firm's performance. Originally developed by David Norton, a consultant, and Robert Kaplan, an accounting professor at Harvard Business School, these models combine financial scores with measures of less tangible assets such as customer satisfaction and loyalty, and a firm's ability to nurture the skills of its employees.

The metrics merchants think that such an approach is wrong-headed. A profusion of different measures can cause more problems than they solve. It helps to have a clear focus. But then the balanced scorecard – no less than EVA – is just another form of corporate thermometer. As Siemens would concede, it is useful to know just how sick you are; but what matters is whether you get better.

17

EVA Implementation, Market Over-Reaction and the Theory of Low-Hanging Fruit

Barbara Lougee, Ashok Natarajan and James S. Wallace

One often hears the expression that a picture is worth a thousand words. This may be especially true when attempting to describe mathematical relationships. In such situations, charts, like pictures, are able to convey the hypothetical thousand words. Sometimes, however, a thousand words only takes one to the middle chapter of a longer story. In such cases, the reader (or viewer of the picture) could be led astray in thinking the picture is complete.

In an effort to sell their products in an efficient manner, marketers may justifiably resort to using time and space saving devices such as charts to convey their message. This appears to be the case with regard to recent advertisements that appeared in the Harvard Business Review.[1] Stern Stewart and Company used charts in a series of advertisements to demonstrate a claimed relationship between a firm's stock price and the announcement of the firm adopting EVA. The advertisements had titles such as "Every Company Is in Business to Create Value. EVA Makes It Happen" and "Forget EPS, ROE, and ROI. EVA Is What Drives Stock Prices." A pair of charts representing two of the featured companies, reproduced in Figure 17.1, documents a phenomenal stock price surge following the announcement of the firm's EVA adoption.

A fitting title to this story may be the "Tale of Two Firms." It seems the charts only went to the middle chapters for this tale. As the following charts in Figure 17.2 demonstrate, these two companies experienced much different stock price performance the following two years.

By completing the next few chapters, i.e., years, we can see, at least in these examples, the mere act of announcing EVA adoption is not always sufficient to insure continual superior stock performance. At first glance it may appear that these two charts reveal vastly different stories. This may not be the case if we consider additional information. The advertisements really are making two claims. The one implied by the charts is that simply announcing EVA adoption leads to surging stock prices. As we see for these two firms, this was initially the case. The second claim being made explicitly is that EVA drives stock prices. For these two firms, during the period shown,

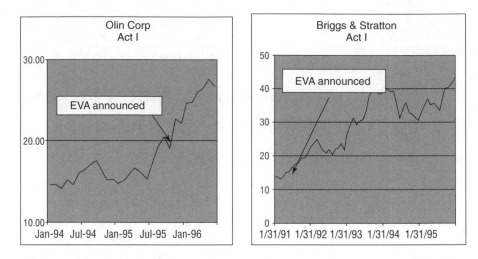

Figure 17.1

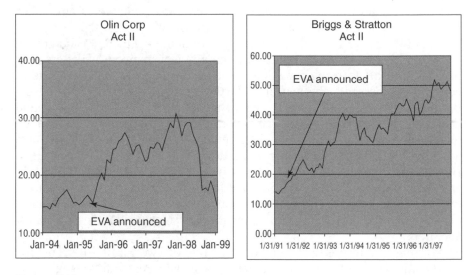

Figure 17.2

this claim appears to have some validity. Olin averaged a negative $132M EVA for the couple of years prior to EVA adoption. This improved to an average negative $25M EVA for the implementation year and the year following implementation. Olin, however, was not able to maintain the improvement. EVA slipped to an average negative $55M over the last couple of years on the chart, corresponding to the ending drop in stock price. Briggs & Stratton's EVA, in contrast, continued to improve throughout the period shown, from an average −$41M prior to adoption, to −$20M in the period shortly after implementation, to an average positive $24M the last couple of years shown.[2]

Of course these are just two of many firms that have adopted EVA. In this paper we study over seventy firms that have contracted with Stern Stewart to implement EVA, examining several items. First, we wish to see if the market reacts positively, on average, to the announcement of the EVA adoption as demonstrated with the two firms above. Second, we examine subsequent stock performance several years later. Also related to the EVA adoption, we examine several management actions that have been hypothesized to be associated with residual income-based measures (e.g., investing decisions, share repurchases, asset utilization). Finally, we examine changes in the overall firm's calculated EVA from prior to EVA adoption, through the initial implementation period, to several years later.

We find, similar to stock price reaction in the above charts, firms experience superior stock price performance in the two-year period beginning with the adoption of EVA. On average, firms reported positive market-adjusted returns of over 7% in the two-year period including the year of announcement and the following year. During the next three-year period, however, the firms, on average, reported negative market-adjusted returns of approximately 6.5%. In other words, the previous gains were virtually all given back. This stock performance is consistent with our findings for calculated EVA. While still negative, the firms' average EVA improved nearly 40% in the period following EVA adoption compared to the prior couple of years. EVA did continue to improve during the period a few years later, however the improvement declined from nearly 40% to under 9%. These results, taken together, suggest that the market over-reacted to the initial EVA adoption. The data is suggestive that the market anticipated large performance gains, and further anticipated that these gains would persist. When the performance improvement declined, the market adjusted its valuations of these firms downward. Our findings are consistent with the firms initially experiencing large EVA improvements from "picking the low hanging fruit." Suggestive evidence appears in such characteristics as firm dispositions following EVA adoptions. Dispositions (e.g., disposing of low return assets) increased over 50% in the two-year period following EVA implementation and then increased only an additional 9% the following two-year period. An obvious explanation is that the firm first identifies the actions that will have the biggest effect on EVA (i.e., the low-hanging fruit) and performs these actions first. It becomes increasingly more difficult to identify such fruitful actions, and hence improvements in EVA decline. Interestingly, the market did not appear to anticipate this phenomenon.

The remainder of the paper is organized as follows. In the next section we review some of the related literature. Next we describe both our sample selection procedure and our research design. The results are presented in the following section. We provide some concluding remarks in the final section.

LITERATURE REVIEW

Much of the early research examining the EVA concept has looked at its correlation with security returns, usually in relation to some measure of GAAP
earnings (e.g., Biddle, Bowen & Wallace [1997], Chen and Dodd [1997]).
These studies generally find that while a positive association exists between
EVA and stock returns, traditional earnings does a relatively better job of
explaining returns.

While the studies of correlations with current stock prices are interesting,
they may cloud a more important question. Does the adoption of EVA
provide internal incentives that lead to a better performing firm? This is
nicely articulated in the Merrill Lynch studies that find earnings do matter.
"EVA is indeed an important analytical tool for corporate managers as are
all tools that focus on returns in excess of capital requirements. However,
there is nothing in these results that supports the contention that earnings are
irrelevant. This work suggests that EVA techniques by themselves will
probably be no more effective in enhancing shareholder value than will other
management techniques if the EVA process does not ultimately drive earnings and earnings growth" (Bernstein 1998, p. 6). Another researcher points
out the possibility that too much attention is being placed on correlations
with stock returns when that is probably not what is of interest to managers.
Robert Kleiman, a professor who has studied EVA and shareholder value
states, "When companies consider making EVA their primary performance
criterion, they are searching for more than just a better financial metric. They
are seeking a better way to motivate value-adding behavior throughout
the organization" (Kleiman 1999, p. 80). This concern has led several
researchers to question whether EVA and EVA-like management systems,
when adopted by firms, lead to internal changes within the firm.

EVA, unlike accounting earnings, includes a charge for all capital, including equity financing. This should theoretically lead to a greater capital awareness among managers and affect behavior accordingly. Wallace (1997) is one
of the first to study how EVA-type incentives affect internal decision-making.
Wallace looks at a group of 40 firms that adopt an economic profit metric
(including, but not limited to EVA) and compares certain operating, investing, and financing behavior of these firms before and after the metric adoption. Wallace compares these findings with a group of similar firms that
continues to use traditional accounting metrics, such as EPS, in their incentive compensation contracts.

Wallace hypothesizes that the increased capital awareness associated with
EVA measures will alter managers' behavior through investing, operating,
and financing decisions. Specifically, he reasons that managers will become
more selective in new investment since they will now face a capital charge
based on a more comprehensive (and higher) cost of capital and capital base.
He also reasons that managers, faced with a capital charge on all capital
employed, will become more willing to dispose of under-performing assets.
These assets, however, under traditional measures may appear profitable

without an associated capital charge. Wallace finds that the firms adopting economic profit measures are significantly more willing to dispose of assets and, although they still increase new investment after the adoption, they do so at a significantly lower pace relative to the matched control sample of firms.

Wallace next looks at how the firms manage assets in place. He finds that assets turnover, defined as sales divided by average total assets, increases significantly following adoption, relative to the control firms. Wallace further reasons that the capital charge provides incentive to return capital to shareholders that, under prior incentives, may have been kept in low return forms. Wallace finds that share repurchases for the adopting firms significantly increase relative to the control firms, suggesting this is a preferred method over dividends to return capital. Finally, Wallace reports that residual income for the adopting firms increases relative to the control firms. He concludes that the incentive effects of these newly adopted metrics prove to be powerful. In other words, the firms get what they choose to measure and reward.

Balachandran (2001) extends Wallace (2001)'s examination of the investing decision by partitioning EVA adopters based on the performance measure they had previously employed. Balachandran hypothesizes that firms that previously used an earnings-based measure are addressing an over-investment problem and that switching to an EVA-based measure will result in a decrease in investment and an increase in cash distributed to shareholders. In contrast, the author hypothesizes that firms that previously used ROI-based measures are addressing an under-investment problem and that switching to an EVA-based measure will result in an increase in investment and a decrease in cash distributed to shareholders. Balachandran finds significant results consistent with his predictions for firms switching from earnings-based measures, but insignificant results for the other partition of firms. Balachandran also reports that residual income significantly increased for both groups of firms from the period prior to the switch.

These studies represent a good first step toward learning whether adopting EVA-like measures provide increased shareholder value since these studies provide evidence of the incentive effects of EVA. While the research indicates that managers alter behavior when adopting economic profit measures, and that these changes may be consistent with shareholder value enhancement, the primary focus of these studies is not to investigate the impact on the firms' future performance of this behavior. Some recent studies have begun to fill this void.

Kleiman (1999) examines stock price performance of 71 firms that have adopted EVA as their economic profit measure and matches each of his 71 EVA firms to a single control firm based on industry classification and firm size. For an additional comparison, the author also matches each EVA firm to the median peer in the same four-digit SIC (instead of matching on only the single closest firm based on size).

Using market returns as a measure of firm performance, Kleiman finds the EVA firms to significantly outperform each control group. The

EVA firms, on average have a 7.8 percent larger return over the three-year period following EVA adoption than do their industry and size matched control firm. The results are more pronounced, 28.8 percent over the three-year post-adoption period, when the comparison is made with median peer firms.

Hogan and Lewis (2000) find contrary evidence on the future performance of firms adopting economic profit plans. The authors examine 65 firms adopting a more general definition of economic profit (which includes EVA) and compare these firms to control firms matched on industry, size, and pre-event performance. Hogan and Lewis document significant improvements in operating performance for their sample firms in the four-year period following adoption. The authors also find, however, that the sample of control firms show no significant difference in operating performance to economic profit adopting firms. They conclude that economic profit plans are no better than traditional plans that provide a blend of earnings-based bonuses and stock-based compensation.

We extend the prior literature by examining both internal firm performance and external market reactions over an extended examination period subsequent to EVA adoption. Further, we partition the subsequent period in order to compare initial performance gains with subsequent period gains along with the associated market reactions in each period to the firm's performance in that period.

SAMPLE SELECTION

Our sample consists of 74 firms that not only adopted an EVA financial management system, but also contracted with Stern Stewart and Co. for the implementation. We deleted any firms that did not have the required financial and market data on Compustat and CRSP in order to do our empirical testing. The EVA adoption date was obtained directly from Stern Stewart. Table 17.1, Panel A contains a listing of the sample firms along with their primary SIC classification and their EVA adoption date. Panel B of Table 17.1 provides a breakdown of the SIC classifications. We compared this distribution to that of the S&P 500 (not shown) and found a great deal of similarity. The EVA sample had a larger representation in the 3000 SIC (36% to 27%) and a smaller representation in the 6000 SIC (4% to 16%), when grouped by 1 digit SIC. For the two samples, all other 1 digit SIC categories were within 2% of each other.

Panel B of Table 17.1 provides a distribution of the EVA adoptions by year of adoption. The earliest implementation took place in 1983, however only 14 (19%) of the adoptions occur prior to 1994. Nearly half of the adoptions took place in the three-year period from 1994 through 1996. A slight fall-off of implementations is noted following 1996. This is consistent with Balachandran (2001) who notes a similar decrease in the frequency of adoptions and suggests that there may be some degree of market saturation.

Table 17.1 EVA adopters

Panel A: Sample Firms

Company Name	Primary SIC[1]	Month of Adoption[2]
Adaptive Broadband Corp.	3663	10/97
ADC Telecommunications Inc.	3661	8/95
Alexander & Baldwin Inc.	4400	7/94
Allied Holdings Inc.	4213	3/96
Alltrista Corp.	3080	1/94
Armstrong Holdings Inc.	3089	1/94
Ball Corp.	3411	8/91
Bard (C. R.) Inc.	3841	2/96
Bausch & Lomb Inc.	2834	8/96
Becton Dickinson & Co.	3841	10/95
Best Buy Co. Inc.	5731	1/98
Boise Cascade Corp.	5110	10/94
Boise Cascade Office Products Corp.	5110	5/95
Bowater Inc.	2621	1/96
Briggs & Stratton	3510	1/90
Calmot Co.	1400	1/95
Case Corp.	3523	12/96
CDI Corp.	7363	1/94
Centura Banks Inc.	6022	3/94
Cilcorp Inc.	4931	8/89
Coca-Cola Co.	2080	7/83
Columbus McKinnon Corp.	3530	4/97
Cox Communications	4841	1/98
Crane Co.	3490	7/90
Donnelley (R. R.) & Sons Co.	3750	11/94
Dun & Bradstreet Corp.	7320	4/97
Equifax Inc.	7320	6/92
Federal-Mogul Corp.	3714	5/97
Fleming Companies Inc.	5141	2/94
Furon Co.	3050	9/92
GC Companies Inc.	7830	4/96
Georgia-Pacific Group	2600	4/94
Grainger (W. W.) Inc.	5000	7/89
Guidant Corp.	3841	1/95
Harnischfeger Corp.	3532	7/92
Hershey Foods Corp.	2060	9/96
Insteel Industries	3310	3/93
International Multifoods Corp.	5140	4/97
Johnson Outdoors Inc.	5090	2/96
Kansas City Power & Light	4911	7/95
KLLM Transport Services Inc.	4213	3/96
Knape & Vogt Manufacturing Co.	2540	10/96
Lilly (Eli) & Co.	3834	6/94
Manitowoc Co.	3585	3/93
Material Sciences Corp.	3470	9/97
Midamerican Energy Holdings	4991	10/97
Millennium Chemicals Inc.	2810	10/96
Miller (Herman) Inc.	2520	3/96
Monsanto Co.	2870	4/95
Montana Power Co.	4931	2/97
Noble Drilling Corp.	1381	7/97
Olin Corp.	3350	2/95
Penney (J. C.) Co.	5310	10/97
Perkinelmer Inc.	3826	8/94
Pharmacia Corp.	2834	2/95
Polaroid Corp.	3861	8/96
Premark International Inc.	3580	9/92

Table 17.1 Continued

Panel A: Sample Firms

Company Name	Primary SIC[1]	Month of Adoption[2]
Pulte Homes Inc.	1531	11/95
Quaker Oats Co.	2040	11/90
Rubbermaid Inc.	3089	1/95
Ryder System Inc.	7510	3/96
Safety-Kleen Corp	4955	5/96
Shaw Industries Inc.	2273	3/98
Silicon Valley Bankshares	6022	6/95
Sprint Fon Group	4813	10/94
SPX Corp.	3490	10/95
Standard Motors Products	3690	6/97
Tenet Healthcare Corp.	8062	4/96
Toys R Us Inc.	5945	9/97
Tupperware Corp.	3089	6/96
Vulcan Materials Co.	1400	1/94
Webster Financial Corp. Waterbury	6035	10/96
Wellman Inc.	2820	7/89
Whirlpool Corp	3630	1/94

Panel B: Industry distribution

Panel C: Adoption year distribution

SIC Code	# of Firms	% of Sample	Adoption Year	# of Firms	% of Sample
1300	1	1.3%	1983	1	1.3%
1400	2	2.7%	1989	3	4.1%
1500	1	1.3%	1990	3	4.1%
2000	3	4.1%	1991	1	1.3%
2200	1	1.3%	1992	4	5.4%
2500	2	2.7%	1993	2	2.7%
2600	2	2.7%	1994	14	18.9%
2700	1	1.3%	1995	13	17.6%
2800	6	8.1%	1996	18	24.3%
3000	5	6.8%	1997	12	16.2%
3300	2	2.7%	1998	3	4.1%
3400	4	5.4%			
3500	6	8.1%	Total	74	
3600	4	5.4%			
3700	1	1.3%			
3800	5	6.8%			
4200	2	2.7%			
4400	1	1.3%			
4800	2	2.7%			
4900	5	6.8%			
5000	2	2.7%			
5100	4	5.4%			
5300	1	1.3%			
5700	1	1.3%			
5900	1	1.3%			
6000	3	4.1%			
7300	3	4.1%			
7500	1	1.3%			
7800	1	1.3%			
8000	1	1.3%			
Total	74				

[1] Primary SIC is obtained from Compustat
[2] Adoption date represents the date the firm started their EVA implementation per Stern Stewart

RESEARCH METHODOLOGY

Our tests of EVA performance drivers, EVA performance, and the corresponding market reactions are based on the timeline appearing in Figure 17.3.

The letter A in Figure 17.3 represents the implementation date. This date occurs somewhere during year 0. As shown, the two years prior to year 0, years −2 and −1, represent the period prior to EVA adoption. The year in which implementation begins, year 0, and the subsequent year, year 1, represent the initial-implementation period. This period will be compared to both the pre-adoption period and the subsequent post-implementation period, years 2, 3, and 4.

Tests of EVA drivers and performance are conducted by first calculating the average level of each metric in each of the three periods. Each firm serves as its own control in these tests.[3] This avoids some questionable matches resulting from the formulaic approaches used in prior studies.[4] Using the firm as its own control, (i.e., comparing firm characteristics over time) is consistent with typical EVA-based performance plans. Performance is typically based on period-to-period improvements, not on levels relative to comparable firms (Young and O'Byrne [2001]).

RESULTS

First we study changes within firms surrounding the decision to adopt EVA. Our hypotheses are motivated by the claimed incentive effects associated with the increased focus on the capital charge embedded within the EVA computation. We examine seven variables, labeled as EVA drivers, each of which is also tested in Wallace (1997).

The first two variables are associated with investing decisions. Because there is likely a greater incentive to avoid excess invested capital under an EVA performance metric (unless that capital provides higher returns than the

Figure 17.3

imputed cost of capital), it is reasonable to assume that firms will dispose of poorly performing assets to avoid the associated capital charge. In addition, firms will likely be more selective in newer investment because of the heightened concern for the associated capital charge. This leads to our first two hypotheses, stated in the null form.

(H1)   There will be no effect on disposition of assets following the adoption of an EVA-based financial management system.

(H2)   There will be no effect on new investment following the adoption of an EVA-based financial management system.

The results of our study are reported in Table 17.2. We report a significant increase in dispositions of assets during the implementation period relative to the prior period, however this level of increased dispositions does not continue into the post-implementation period. This finding is not surprising since firms will likely first target the worse performing assets where they will receive the largest savings. Once this "low-hanging fruit" is gone, it becomes more difficult to find areas that can provide the same level of EVA improvement and therefore it is natural to see a lessening of dispositions.

Unlike Wallace (1997), we find a slight, though significant, increase in new investment, both in the implementation and the post-implementation periods. Some critics of EVA claim EVA is biased against growth and encourages managers to milk a business through under-investment (Olsen 1996). Stern Stewart counter that the EVA framework encourages investment as long as the projects yield positive NPV. They further claim that their implementation of EVA compensation, with such items as three-year rolling bonus banks, mitigates any short-term gaming of the system (Leander 1997). John Sheily, President and Chief Operating Officer of the EVA firm Briggs & Stratton, shares this attitude. After being accused of missing opportunities to expand because of their EVA system, Sheily responds, "The assertion that Briggs and Stratton is 'dieting its way down to the core' is silly. We have made extensive capital investments in new products and facilities in the last few years. And we will continue to make significant capital investments" (Sheily [1997]).[5] Our results support the view that EVA firms may be more selective in their investment choice, but they do not appear to be "dieting their way down to the core."

Our next hypothesis involves whether the firm returns capital to the shareholders in order to avoid a capital charge on excess accumulated capital. Wallace (1997) noted that firms appear to favor share repurchases over dividends because of the "sticky" nature of dividends. Hypothesis (H3), stated in the null form follows.

(H3)   There will be no effect on share repurchases following the adoption of an EVA-based financial management system.

We find that share repurchases significantly increase during the implementation period. This increase is likely associated with the corresponding

Table 17.2 Changes in EVA drivers associated with the adoption of EVA[1] (T-values in parentheses)[12]

	Pre-Implement[9]	Implement[10]	Post-Implement[11]	Implement – Pre-Implement	Post-Implement – Implement
Dispositions[2]	0.000012	0.000018	0.000019	0.000006 (1.456)*	0.000001 (0.306)
New Investment[3]	0.000205	0.000208	0.000224	0.000003 (0.064)	0.000016 (0.225)
RPS[4]	0.48	0.78	0.69	0.30 (1.974)**	−0.09 (−0.703)
Asset Turnover[5]	1.45	1.44	1.40	−0.01 (−0.142)	−0.04 (−1.457)*
Inventory Turnover[6]	8.90	10.82	11.35	1.92 (1.506)*	0.53 (0.737)
A/R Turnover[7]	10.79	10.50	10.09	−0.29 (−0.544)	−0.41 (−0.759)
A/P Turnover[8]	14.79	13.10	10.96	−1.69 (−1.868)**	−2.14 (−2.307)**

[1] EVA drivers are defined as operating, investing, or financing decisions managers can make to drive changes in EVA
[2] Dispositions are defined as sales of property plant and equipment reported on the Statement of cash flow divided by beginning period total assets. This number is then deflated by beginning period assets
[3] New Investment is defined as the sum of acquisitions and capital expenditures reported on the Statement of cash flow divided by beginning period total assets. This number is then deflated by beginning period assets
[4] RPS is defined as the dollar value of shares repurchased reported on the Statement of cash flow divided by the number of shares outstanding
[5] Asset Turnover is defined as net sales divided by average capital invested. Average capital invested is reported by Compustat and represents the firm's invested capital as adjusted by a standardized set of EVA adjustments
[6] Inventory Turnover is defined as the sum of cost of goods sold and the change in the LIFO reserve divided by the sum of average inventory and the LIFO reserve
[7] A/R Turnover is defined as net sales divided by average accounts receivable
[8] A/P Turnover defined as cost of goods sold divided by average accounts payable
[9] Pre-implement is the two-year period prior to the start of the firm's fiscal year in which EVA implementation begun
[10] Implement is the two-year period beginning with the start of the firm's fiscal year in which EVA implementation began
[11] Post-implement is the two-year period following the implement period
[12] t-values are for the test that the abnormal return is zero.
* Significant at the 10% level using a one-tailed test
** Significant at the 5% level using a one-tailed test

significant increase in asset dispositions during this period. We also report an insignificant decrease in repurchases the following period.

The next four hypotheses are all associated with capital utilization. In addition to paying out free cash flows, EVA is also increased by using existing assets more intensively. We examine asset turnover, defined as sales divided by average capital employed, inventory turnover defined as cost of goods sold divided by average inventory,[6] accounts receivable turnover defined as sales divided by average accounts receivable, and accounts payable turnover defined as cost of goods sold divided by average accounts payable. The incentives associated with EVA's focus on capital would lead one to expect improvement in capital utilization (i.e., an increase in asset turnover, inventory turnover, and accounts receivable turnover, and a decrease in accounts payable turnover). Hypotheses (H4)–(H7), stated in the null form, follow.

(H4)   There will be no effect on asset turnover following the adoption of an EVA-based financial management system.

(H5)   There will be no effect on inventory turnover following the adoption of an EVA-based financial management system.

(H6)   There will be no effect on accounts receivable turnover following the adoption of an EVA-based financial management system.

(H7)   There will be no effect on accounts payable turnover following the adoption of an EVA-based financial management system.

We report significant increases in inventory turnover and significant decreases in accounts payable turnover in the initial implementation period. Only accounts payable turnover continues to be significant in the following period. Surprisingly, and in contrast to Wallace (1997), asset turnover is lower following EVA implementation, although insignificantly so during the implementation period.

Our next hypothesis involves how EVA performance changes following the firms' EVA adoptions. If the incentives implied by an EVA financial management system are effective, one would expect the behavior changes to translate into improvements in firm performance. Hypothesis (H8), stated in the null form, follows:

(H8)   There will be no effect on firm performance following the adoption of an EVA-based financial management system.

Table 17.3 reports our findings on how firm performance, measured in terms of EVA, changes following the firms' EVA adoptions. Perhaps not sur-

Table 17.3 Firm performance (in $millions) for the periods surrounding EVA implementation. T-values in parentheses

	Pre-Implement	Implement	Post-Implement	Implement – Pre-Implement	Post-Implement – Implement
EVA[1]	$–60.5	$–37.9	$–34.5	$22.6 (1.426)*	$3.4 (0.120)
Earnings[2]	$95.1	$143.9	$146.5	$48.9 (2.632)***	$2.6 (0.111)

[1] EVA is Economic Value Added as reported in Compustat
[2] Earnings are earnings before extraordinary items (Data item 18 in Compustat)
See Table 17.2 for other definitions
* Significant at the 10% level using a one-tailed test
*** Significant at the 1% level using a one-tailed test

prisingly, EVA was on average negative for the sample firms prior to their decision to adopt EVA. Again, this follows the common wisdom that one is more apt to fix something that appears broken. While still negative, on average the firms improve EVA by nearly 40% during the implementation period. We hypothesize that this large increase in EVA helps account for the previously discussed increase in the firms' abnormal returns for the same period. We also hypothesize that this initial increase in EVA may be the result of "picking the low-hanging fruit" (e.g., selling non-performing assets).

Quite telling is the computed EVA for the following period. While still improving, the improvement is only 15% of the prior period's improvement. We again hypothesize this diminished improvement in performance likely accounts for the negative abnormal returns previously discussed for the post-implementation period. The market may have initially over-reacted to the anticipated improvements in performance with a corresponding overvaluation of the firm's stock. When the continued improvements fail to materialize, the market revalues the firm's stock. These results are also consistent with the low-hanging fruit theory whereas it becomes increasingly more difficult to sustain improvement.

While EVA incentives are designed in motivate behavior leading to improved EVA performance, the stated ultimate goal of such plans is increased shareholder value. Therefore, to test this final linkage, we investigate how the market reacts to the firm's decision to adopt and implement an EVA-based financial system. This leads to our hypothesis (H9), again stated in null form.

(H9)   There will be no effect on stock returns following the adoption of an EVA-based financial management system.

The results of our tests appear in Table 17.4. We first compute the pre-adoption abnormal returns.[7] On average, the sample firms under-perform the market by a cumulative 2.6% during this two-year period. While not significant, this is consistent with the common notion that firms generally do not fix something that is not broken.

Table 17.4 Cumulative abnormal stock price reaction to the firm's EVA adoption announcement[1]

	Pre-Implement	Implement	Post-Implement	Implement − Pre-Implement	Post-Implement − Implement
Return	−2.6%	7.1%	−6.5%	9.7%	−13.6%
t-value	−0.87	1.20	−2.00**	1.36*	−2.06**

[1] Annual abnormal returns are computed by subtracting the annual return from the CRSP value-weighted index from the firm's buy and hold annual return. Cumulative abnormal returns are computed by summing annual abnormal returns
See Table 17.2 for other definitions
* Significant at the 10% level using a one-tailed test
** Significant at the 5% level using a one-tailed test

We next compute abnormal returns during the implementation period. During this two-year period the sample firms outperformed the market by a cumulative 7.1%. Although not to the degree implied by the Stern Stewart advertisements, this is consistent with the marketing hype that stock returns increase following the announcement of an EVA adoption.

Finally, we compute abnormal returns during the post-implementation period. During this three-year period the sample firms, on average, under-perform the market by a cumulative 6.5%. In other words, nearly all the "gains" of the prior period are given back. This evidence is suggestive that the market initially overvalues the sample firms around the time EVA adoption is announced, and later corrects the valuations after assessing the firms' subsequent performance.

The results presented in Tables 17.2–4 are designed to address the related questions of whether the firms' appear to be picking the low-hanging fruit, whether this helps explain their initial performance improvements, and whether the market appears to fail to anticipate this behavior and overreacts to EVA adoptions. We next address a different assertion that also appears in the Stern Stewart advertisements, namely that EVA drives stock prices. Hypothesis (H10), stated in the null form, relates to this assertion.

(H10)   There will be no association between EVA performance and the firm's stock returns.

Table 17.5 reports our results. The first regression shows that, as claimed, there is a significantly positive association between market-adjusted returns and EVA improvement. This result occurs even after controlling for indus-try and size effects and changes over time.[8]

We next substituted traditional GAAP earnings for EVA in our test and find an even higher positive association between earnings and returns than between EVA and returns. In other words, EVA may appear to drive stock prices as stated in the advertisements, but that does not mean one should "forget earnings." These results are consistent with prior research that has found a similar relative ranking among performance measures for informa-tion content (e.g., Biddle, et al. 1997).

SENSITIVITY

In order to test the robustness of our results we partitioned the sample firms into early and late EVA adopters. Early adopters are defined as firms that began implementation prior to 1994 and late adopters are those firms that began their EVA implementations in 1994 or subsequent years. We first com-puted EVA improvements for each firm from pre-adoption through post-implementation periods. We then compared these findings with market reactions in each corresponding period.

A rather interesting pattern emerges from this partition. While we find EVA improvement for both early and late adopters from the pre-adoption

Table 17.5 Regressions of abnormal stock price returns on firm performance and control variables. T-values in parentheses

	Dependent Variable	
	Market-adjusted Returns	Market-adjusted Returns
Intercept	19.420	16.442
	(1.45)*	(1.31)
Change in EVA	1.005	
	(2.87)***	
Change in Earnings		1.410
		(4.29)***
Industry Control[1]	0.001	0.003
	(0.07)	(0.23)
Year Control[2]	−0.010	−0.008
	(−1.47)*	(−1.32)*
Size Control[3]	0.030	0.023
	(1.88)**	(1.55)*
R^2	0.018	0.034
F-Value	3.31***	5.68***
N	498	537

[1] Industry control is the 1-digit SIC of the firm
[2] Year control is the year the firm adopts EVA
[3] Size control is the log of beginning period total assets
*** Significant at the 1% level using a one-tailed test
** Significant at the 5% level using a one-tailed test
* Significant at the 10% level using a one-tailed test
See Tables 17.2 and 17.4 for other definitions

period to the initial implementation period, the improvement all but disappears for the late adopters in the post-implementation period. This suggests these later adopters may see EVA as a quick fix solution. This is further supported by the abnormal returns of each group of firms. The earlier adopters, in contrast to common thought, experienced positive abnormal returns in the period prior to adoption. These positive abnormal returns increased in the initial implementation period, and continue positive, though at a lower rate, in the post-implementation period. The later adopters experienced negative abnormal returns prior to adoption. This is more in line with the expectation that firms seek to fix what is broken. Corresponding to their EVA performance improvements in the initial implementation period these late adopters experienced positive abnormal returns. The abnormal returns turned negative for these firms in the post-implementation period corresponding to the failure to deliver continued EVA improvements.

SUMMARY

Stern Stewart has advertised EVA as the metric needed to drive stock price. Charts have been used to illustrate how a firm's stock price skyrockets following the announcement of a decision to adopt EVA. We test these claims by studying over seventy of Stern Stewart's EVA clients to see how their performance changes over time, from pre-EVA adoption, through initial implementation, and beyond. We then examine how the market reacts to the firms over the corresponding periods.

We find that, on average, the firms that chose to retain Stern Stewart to help them implement EVA were under-performers prior to adoption. This is reflected in both their low EVA and negative abnormal returns. On average the sample firms did quite well after their initial implementation relative to how they performed in the prior period. This is reflected in a nearly 40%, on average, increase in EVA and a corresponding average abnormal return in excess of 7%. The evidence suggests, however, that this rapid improvement was the result of doing the easier things first. In other words, the firms went after the low-hanging fruit. Once this fruit is picked, it becomes progressively more difficult to sustain the EVA improvement. We note that in the period following the initial EVA implementation the firms' improvements decline. We also note that the market appears to have expected the large improvements to continue. On average, the firms experienced negative abnormal returns of approximately 6.5% in this later period, virtually giving back the previous gains. This suggests that the market initially over-reacted to the EVA adoptions, over-valuing the firms based on overly optimistic expectations of future improvements, and later revalued the firms downward when those improvements failed to materialize.

NOTES

1. See *Harvard Business Review*, July 8, 1996 and September 10, 1996.
2. While an association is noted between EVA improvement and stock price performance, this does not prove EVA drives stock prices. We later compare EVA and traditional earnings with stock price performance and find a higher association between earning and stock price than between EVA and stock price.
3. Prior research is marked with inconsistency in the area of firm controls. Wallace (1997) matches sample firms to individual control firms based on industry classification and size. Kleiman (1999) also compares sample firms to a single control firm based on a match of industry and size, but the author further compares sample firms to the median peer firm within the same industry. Hogan and Lewis (2000) extend the matching procedure by utilizing a three characteristic match, including pre-event performance. Balachandran (2001) notes the inherent problems with these matching procedures and instead uses each firm as its own control.
4. Balachandran (2001) notes a matching based on industry and size would match Caterpillar with Compaq.
5. O'Byrne (1999) investigates this issue and provides a theoretical discussion of the conflict between shareholder value and economic profit caused by straight line depreciation and the more severe conflict between shareholder value and

economic profit created by acquisition resulting from historical cost accounting. O'Byrne demonstrates how this conflict can be resolved through negative economic depreciation. This type of depreciation allows lesser charges in early years and more depreciation taken in the later years in order to match the cash flows of the asset. O'Byrne reports that only one EVA firm he is aware of uses such a method. He goes on to provide examples of how firms deal with the conflict. He finds many firms use "ad hoc" methods to mitigate the conflict between shareholder value and economic profit. In some cases, however, the conflict proves so extreme as to cause the firm to abandon EVA as a performance measure.

6. Inventory is calculated as Compustat^{TM} data item D3, inventory, plus data item D240, LIFO reserve. Cost of goods sold is adjusted by the annual change in the LIFO reserve. Data item D240 is included in order to place all firms on a common FIFO basis.

7. Abnormal returns are computed by subtracting the annual return from the CRSP value-weighted index from the firm's buy and hold annual return. Cumulative abnormal returns are computed by summing annual abnormal returns. We also compute abnormal returns by substituting the S&P 500 index for the CRSP value-weighted index with similar findings.

8. Industry and size controls are included to mitigate the effect of not matching the sample firms against control firms based on industry and size, two measures used in prior research. We previously discussed our justification for using each firm as its own control. A year variable is included to mitigate the possible effects of any time clustering in our sample. We further address this issue under sensitivity analysis.

REFERENCES

Balachandran, S. 2001. Over-investment and Under-investment in Firms that Implement Residual Income-based Compensation, Working paper, Columbia University.

Bernstein, R. 1998. *Quantitative Viewpoint: an Analysis of EVA – Part II*, Merrill Lynch & Co. Global Securities & Economics Group, Quantitative & Equity Derivative Research Department. Pp. 1 7.

Biddle, G., R. Bowen, and J. Wallace. 1997. Does EVA beat earnings? Evidence on association with stock returns and firm values. *Journal of Accounting and Economics* 24, pp. 301–336.

Chen, S., and J. Dodd. 1997. Economic value added: An empirical examination of a new corporate performance measure. *Journal of Managerial Issues*. Pp. 318–333.

Hogan, C., and C. Lewis. 2000. The long-run performance of firms adopting compensation plans based on economic profits. Working paper, Vanderbilt University.

Kleiman, R. 1999. Some new evidence on EVA companies. *Journal of Applied Corporate Finance* 12, pp. 80–91.

Leander, T. 1997. EVA and Growth. *EVAngelist* 1, pp. 10–11.

O'Byrne, S. 1999. Does value based management discourage investment in intangibles? Working paper.

Olsen, E. E. 1996. Economic Value Added. *Perspectives*. Boston Consulting Group. Boston, Massachusetts.

Sheily, J. 1997. Wanton EVA: Briggs & Stratton's John Shiely sets the record straight. *EVAngelist* 1, pp. 8–9.

Stern Stewart. 1997. EVA and Growth. *EVAngelist* 1, pp. 10–11.

Stewart III, G. B. 1994. EVA: Fact or fantasy? *Journal of Applied Corporate Finance* 7, pp. 71–84.

Wallace, J. 1997. Adopting residual income-based compensation plans: Do you get what you pay for? *Journal of Accounting and Economics* 24, pp. 275–300.

Young, S., and S. O'Byrne. 2001. *EVA and Value-Based Management: A Practical Guide to Implementation*. McGraw Hill.

18

Transforming the Balanced Scorecard from Performance Measurement to Strategic Management: Part I

Robert S. Kaplan and David P. Norton

Several years ago we introduced the Balanced Scorecard (Kaplan and Norton 1992). We began with the premise that an exclusive reliance on financial measures in a management system is insufficient. Financial measures are lag indicators that report on the outcomes from past actions. Exclusive reliance on financial indicators could promote behavior that sacrifices long-term value creation for short-term performance (Porter 1992; AICPA 1994). The Balanced Scorecard approach retains measures of financial performance – the lagging outcome indicators – but supplements these with measures on the drivers, the lead indicators, of future financial performance.

THE BALANCED SCORECARD EMERGES

The limitations of managing solely with financial measures, however, have been known for decades.[1] What is different now? Why has the Balanced Scorecard concept been so widely adopted by manufacturing and service companies, nonprofit organizations, and government entities around the world since its introduction in 1992?

First, previous systems that incorporated nonfinancial measurements used *ad hoc* collections of such measures, more like checklists of measures for managers to keep track of and improve than a comprehensive system of linked measurements. The Balanced Scorecard emphasizes the linkage of measurement to strategy (Kaplan and Norton 1993) and the cause-and-effect linkages that describe the hypotheses of the strategy (Kaplan and Norton 1996b). The tighter connection between the measurement system and strategy elevates the role for nonfinancial measures from an operational checklist to a comprehensive system for strategy implementation (Kaplan and Norton 1996a).

Second, the Balanced Scorecard reflects the changing nature of technology and competitive advantage in the latter decades of the 20th century. In the industrial-age competition of the 19th and much of the 20th centuries, companies achieved competitive advantage from their investment in and management of tangible assets such as inventory, property, plant, and equipment (Chandler 1990). In an economy dominated by tangible assets, financial measurements were adequate to record investments on companies' balance sheets. Income statements could also capture the expenses associated with the use of these tangible assets to produce revenues and profits. But by the end of the 20th century, intangible assets became the major source for competitive advantage. In 1982, tangible book values represented 62 percent of industrial organizations' market values; ten years later, the ratio had plummeted to 38 percent (Blair 1995). By the end of the 20th century, the book value of tangible assets accounted for less than 20 percent of companies' market values (Webber 2000, quoting research by Baruch Lev).

Clearly, strategies for creating value shifted from managing tangible assets to knowledge-based strategies that create and deploy an organization's intangible assets. These include customer relationships, innovative products and services, high-quality and responsive operating processes, skills and knowledge of the workforce, the information technology that supports the work force and links the firm to its customers and suppliers, and the organizational climate that encourages innovation, problem-solving, and improvement. But companies were unable to adequately measure their intangible assets (Johnson and Kaplan 1987, 201–202). Anecdotal data from management publications indicated that many companies could not implement their new strategies in this environment (Kiechel 1982; Charan and Colvin 1999). They could not manage what they could not describe or measure.

INTANGIBLE ASSETS: VALUATION VS. VALUE CREATION

Some call for accountants to make an organization's intangible assets more visible to managers and investors by placing them on a company's balance sheet. But several factors prevent valid valuation of intangible assets on balance sheets.

First, the value from intangible assets is indirect. Assets such as knowledge and technology seldom have a direct impact on revenue and profit. Improvements in intangible assets affect financial outcomes through chains of cause-and-effect relationships involving two or three intermediate stages (Huselid 1995; Becker and Huselid 1998). For example, consider the linkages in the service management profit chain (Heskett et al. 1994):

- investments in employee training lead to improvements in service quality
- better service quality leads to higher customer satisfaction
- higher customer satisfaction leads to increased customer loyalty
- increased customer loyalty generates increased revenues and margins.

Financial outcomes are separated causally and temporally from improving employees' capabilities. The complex linkages make it difficult, if not impossible, to place a financial value on an asset such as workforce capabilities or employee morale, much less to measure period-to-period changes in that financial value.

Second, the value from intangible assets depends on organizational context and strategy. This value cannot be separated from the organizational processes that transform intangibles into customer and financial outcomes. The balance sheet is a linear, additive model. It records each class of asset separately and calculates the total by adding up each asset's recorded value. The value created from investing in individual intangible assets, however, is neither linear nor additive.

Senior investment bankers in a firm such as Goldman Sachs are immensely valuable because of their knowledge about complex financial products and their capabilities for managing relationships and developing trust with sophisticated customers. People with the same knowledge, experience, and capabilities, however, are nearly worthless to a financial services company such as etrade.com that emphasizes operational efficiency, low cost, and technology-based trading. The value of an intangible asset depends critically on the context – the organization, the strategy, and other complementary assets – in which the intangible asset is deployed.

Intangible assets seldom have value by themselves.[2] Generally, they must be bundled with other intangible and tangible assets to create value. For example, a new growth-oriented sales strategy could require new knowledge about customers, new training for sales employees, new databases, new information systems, a new organization structure, and a new incentive compensation program. Investing in just one of these capabilities, or in all of them but one, could cause the new sales strategy to fail. The value does not reside in any individual intangible asset. It arises from creating the entire set of assets along with a strategy that links them together. The value-creation process is multiplicative, not additive.

THE BALANCED SCORECARD SUPPLEMENTS CONVENTIONAL FINANCIAL REPORTING

Companies' balance sheets report separately on tangible assets, such as raw material, land, and equipment, based on their historic cost – the traditional financial accounting method. This was adequate for industrial-age companies, which succeeded by combining and transforming their tangible resources into products whose value exceeded their acquisition and production costs. Financial accounting conventions relating to depreciation and cost of goods sold enabled an income statement to measure how much value was created beyond the costs incurred to acquire and transform tangible assets into finished products and services.

Some argue that companies should follow the same cost-based convention for their intangible assets – capitalize and subsequently amortize the expenditures on training employees, conducting research and development, purchasing and developing databases, and advertising that creates brand awareness. But such costs are poor approximations of the realizable value created by investing in these intangible assets. Intangible assets can create value for organizations, but that does not imply that they have separable market values. Many internal and linked organizational processes, such as design, delivery, and service, are required to transform the potential value of intangible assets into products and services that have tangible value.

We introduced the Balanced Scorecard to provide a new framework for describing value-creating strategies that link intangible and tangible assets. The scorecard does not attempt to "value" an organization's intangible assets, but it does measure these assets in units other than currency. The Balanced Scorecard describes how intangible assets get mobilized and combined with intangible and tangible assets to create differentiating customer-value propositions and superior financial outcomes.

STRATEGY MAPS

Since introducing the Balanced Scorecard in 1992, we have helped over 200 executive teams design their scorecard programs. Initially we started with a clean sheet of paper, asking, "what is the strategy," and allowed the strategy and the Balanced Scorecard to emerge from interviews and discussions with the senior executives. The scorecard provided a framework for organizing strategic objectives into the four perspectives displayed in Figure 18.1:

1. *Financial* – the strategy for growth, profitability, and risk viewed from the perspective of the shareholder.

2. *Customer* – the strategy for creating value and differentiation from the perspective of the customer.

3. *Internal Business Processes* – the strategic priorities for various business processes that create customer and shareholder satisfaction.

4. *Learning and Growth* – the priorities to create a climate that supports organizational change, innovation, and growth.

From this initial base of experience, we subsequently developed a general framework for describing and implementing strategy that we believe can be as useful as the traditional framework of income statement, balance sheet, and statement of cash flows for financial planning and reporting. The new framework, which we call a "Strategy Map," is a logical and comprehensive architecture for describing strategy, as illustrated in Figure 18.2. A strategy map specifies the critical elements and their linkages for an organization's strategy.

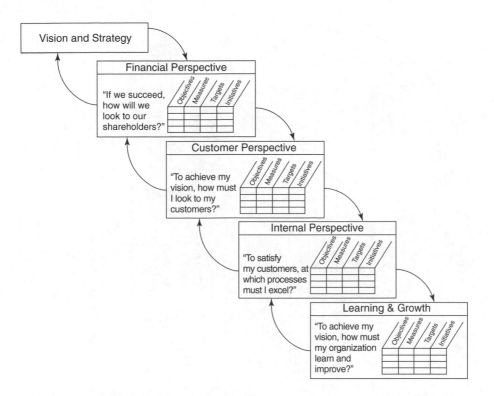

Figure 18.1 The Balanced Scorecard defines a strategy's cause-and-effect relationships

- Objectives for growth and productivity to enhance shareholder value.

- Market and account share, acquisition, and retention of targeted customers where profitable growth will occur.

- Value propositions that would lead customers to do more higher-margin business with the company.

- Innovation and excellence in products, services, and processes that deliver the value proposition to targeted customer segments, promote operational improvements, and meet community expectations and regulatory requirements.

- Investments required in people and systems to generate and sustain growth.

By translating their strategy into the logical architecture of a strategy map and Balanced Scorecard, organizations create a common and understandable point of reference for all organizational units and employees.

Organizations build strategy maps from the top down, starting with the destination and then charting the routes that lead there. Corporate executives first review their mission statement, why their company exists, and core

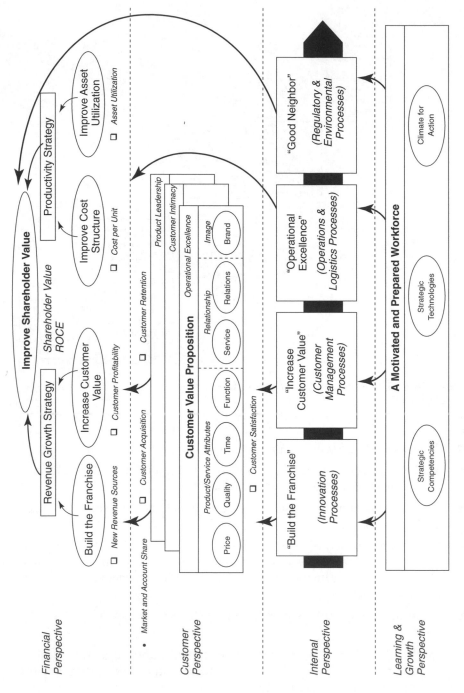

Figure 18.2 The Balanced Scorecard strategy map

values, what their company believes in. From that information, they develop their strategic vision, what their company wants to become. This vision creates a clear picture of the company's overall goal, which could be to become a top-quartile performer. The strategy identifies the path intended to reach that destination.

Financial Perspective

The typical destination for profit-seeking enterprises is a significant increase in shareholder value (we will discuss the modifications for nonprofit and government organizations later in the paper). Companies increase economic value through two basic approaches – *revenue growth* and *productivity*.[3] A revenue growth strategy generally has two components: build the franchise with revenue from new markets, new products, and new customers; and increase sales to existing customers by deepening relationships with them, including cross-selling multiple products and services, and offering complete solutions. A productivity strategy also generally has two components: improve the cost structure by lowering direct and indirect expenses; and utilize assets more efficiently by reducing the working and fixed capital needed to support a given level of business.

Customer Perspective

The core of any business strategy is the *customer-value proposition*, which describes the unique mix of product, price, service, relationship, and image that a company offers. It defines how the organization differentiates itself from competitors to attract, retain, and deepen relationships with targeted customers. The value proposition is crucial because it helps an organization connect its internal processes to improved outcomes with its customers.

Companies differentiate their value proposition by selecting among *operational excellence* (for example, McDonald's and Dell Computer), *customer intimacy* (Home Depot and IBM in the 1960s and 1970s), and *product leadership* (Intel and Sony) (Treacy and Wiersema 1997, 31–45). Sustainable strategies are based on excelling at one of the three while maintaining threshold standards with the other two. After identifying its value propositions, a company knows which classes and types of customers to target.

Specifically, companies that pursue a strategy of operational excellence need to excel at competitive pricing, product quality, product selection, lead time, and on-time delivery. For customer intimacy, an organization must stress the quality of its relationships with customers, including exceptional service, and the completeness and suitability of the solutions it offers individual customers. Companies that pursue a product-leadership strategy must concentrate on the functionality, features, and performance of their products and services.

The customer perspective also identifies the intended outcomes from delivering a differentiated value proposition. These would include market share in targeted customer segments, account share with targeted customer, acquisition and retention of customers in the targeted segments, and customer profitability.[4]

Internal Process Perspective

Once an organization has a clear picture of its customer and financial perspectives, it can determine the means by which it will achieve the differentiated value proposition for customers and the productivity improvements for the financial objectives. The internal business perspective captures these critical organizational activities, which fall into four high-level processes:

1. *Build the franchise* by spurring innovation to develop new products and services and to penetrate new markets and customer segments.

2. *Increase customer value* by expanding and deepening relationships with existing customers.

3. *Achieve operational excellence* by improving supply-chain management, internal processes, asset utilization, resource-capacity management, and other processes.

4. *Become a good corporate citizen* by establishing effective relationships with external stakeholders.

Many companies that espouse a strategy calling for innovation or for developing value-adding customer relationships mistakenly choose to measure their internal business processes by focusing only on the cost and quality of their operations. These companies have a complete disconnect between their strategy and how they measure it. Not surprisingly, organizations encounter great difficulty implementing growth strategies when their primary internal measurements emphasize process improvements, not innovation or enhanced customer relationships.

The financial benefits from improvements to the different business processes typically occur in stages. Cost savings from increase in *operational efficiencies* and process improvements deliver short-term benefits. Revenue growth from enhancing *customer relationships* accrues in the intermediate term. Increased *innovation* generally produces long-term revenue and margin improvements. Thus, a complete strategy should generate returns from all three high-level internal processes.

Learning and Growth Perspective

The final region of a strategy map is the learning and growth perspective, which is the foundation of any strategy. In the learning and growth perspective, managers define the employee capabilities and skills, technology, and corporate climate needed to support a strategy. These objectives enable a company to align its human resources and information technology with the strategic requirements from its critical internal business processes, differentiated value proposition, and customer relationships. After addressing the learning and growth perspective, companies have a complete strategy map with linkages across the four major perspectives.

Strategy maps, beyond providing a common framework for describing and building strategies, also are powerful diagnostic tools, capable of detecting flaws in organizations' Balanced Scorecards. For example, Figure 18.3 shows the strategy map for the Revenue Growth theme of Mobil North America Marketing & Refining. When senior management compared the scorecards being used by its business units to this template, it found one unit with no objective or measure for dealers, an omission immediately obvious from looking at its strategy map. Had this unit discovered how to bypass dealers and sell gasoline directly to end-use consumers? Were dealer relationships

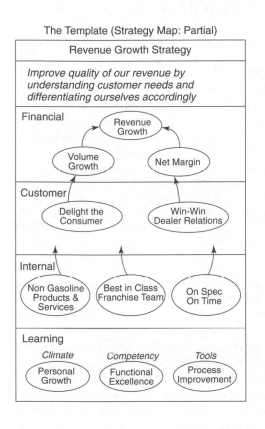

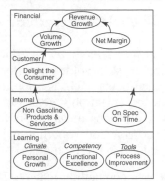

Figure 18.3 Mobil uses reverse engineering of a strategy map as a strategy diagnostic

no longer strategic for this unit? The business unit shown in the lower right corner of Figure 18.3 did not mention quality on its scorecard. Again, had this unit already achieved six sigma quality levels so quality was no longer a strategic priority? Mobil's executive team used its divisional strategy map to identify and remedy gaps in the strategies being implemented at lower levels of the organization.

STAKEHOLDER AND KEY PERFORMANCE INDICATOR SCORECARDS

Many organizations claim to have a Balanced Scorecard because they use a mixture of financial and nonfinancial measures. Such measurement systems are certainly more "balanced" than ones that use financial measures alone. Yet, the assumptions and philosophies underlying these scorecards are quite different from those underlying the strategy scorecards and maps described above. We observe two other scorecard types frequently used in practice: the *stakeholder scorecard* and the *key performance indicator scorecard*.

Stakeholder Scorecards

The *stakeholder scorecard* identifies the major constituents of the organization – shareholders, customers, and employees – and frequently other constituents such as suppliers and the community. The scorecard defines the organization's goals for these different constituents, or stakeholders, and develops an appropriate scorecard of measures and targets for them (Atkinson and Waterhouse 1997). For example, Sears built its initial scorecard around three themes:

- "a compelling place to shop"
- "a compelling place to work"
- "a compelling place to invest"

Citicorp used a similar structure for its initial scorecard – "a good place to work, to bank, and to invest." AT&T developed an elaborate internal measurement system based on financial value-added, customer value-added, and people value-added.

All these companies built their measurements around their three dominant constituents – customers, shareholders, and employees – emphasizing satisfaction measures for customers and employees, to ensure that these constituents felt well served by the company. In this sense, they were apparently *balanced*. Comparing these scorecards to the strategy map template in Figure 18.2 we can easily detect what is missing from such scorecards: no objectives or measures for *how* these balanced goals are to be achieved. A vision describes a desired outcome; a strategy, however, must describe *how* the outcome will be achieved, how employees, customers, and shareholders will be satisfied. Thus, a stakeholder scorecard is not adequate to describe the strategy of an organization and, therefore, is not an adequate foundation on which to build a management system.

Missing from the stakeholder card are the drivers to achieve the goals. Such drivers include an explicit value proposition such as innovation that generates new products and services or enhanced customer management processes, the deployment of technology, and the specific skills and competencies of employees required to implement the strategy. In a well-constructed *strategy scorecard*, the value proposition in the customer perspective, all the processes in the internal perspective, and the learning and growth perspective components of the scorecard define the "how" that is as fundamental to strategy as the outcomes that the strategy is expected to achieve.

Stakeholder scorecards are often a first step on the road to a strategy scorecard. But as organizations begin to work with stakeholder cards, they inevitably confront the question of "how." This leads to the next level of strategic thinking and scorecard design. Both Sears and Citicorp quickly moved beyond their stakeholder scorecards, developing an insightful set of internal process objectives to complete the description of their strategy and, ultimately, achieving a strategy Balanced Scorecard. The stakeholder scorecard can also be useful in organizations that do not have internal synergies across business units. Since each business has a different set of internal drivers, this "corporate" scorecard need only focus on the desired outcomes for the corporation's constituencies, including the community and suppliers. Each business unit then defines how it will achieve those goals with its business unit strategy scorecard and strategy map.

Key Performance Indicator Scorecards

Key Performance Indicator (KPI) scorecards are also common. The total quality management approach and variants such as the Malcolm Baldrige and European Foundation for Quality Management (EFQM) awards generate many measures to monitor internal processes. When migrating to a "Balanced Scorecard," organizations often build on the base already established by classifying their existing measurements into the four BSC categories. KPI scorecards also emerge when the organization's information technology group, which likes to put the company database at the heart of any change program, triggers the scorecard design. Consulting organizations that sell and install large systems, especially so-called executive information systems, also offer KPI scorecards.

As a simple example of a KPI scorecard, a financial service organization articulated the 4Ps for its "balanced scorecard:"

1. Profits
2. Portfolio (size of loan volume)

3. Process (percent processes ISO certified)

4. People (meeting diversity goals in hiring)

Although this scorecard is more balanced than one using financial measures alone, comparing the 4P measures to a strategy map like that in Figure 18.2 reveals the major gaps in the measurement set. The company has no customer measures and only a single internal-process measure, which focuses on an initiative not an outcome. This KPI scorecard has no role for information technology (strange for a financial service organization), no linkages from the internal measure (ISO process certification) to a customer-value proposition or to a customer outcome, and no linkage from the learning and growth measure (diverse work force) to improving an internal process, a customer outcome, or a financial outcome.

KPI scorecards are most helpful for departments and teams when a strategic program already exists at a higher level. In this way, the diverse indicators enable individuals and teams to define what they must do well to contribute to higher level goals. Unless, however, the link to strategy is clearly established, the KPI scorecard will lead to local but not global or strategic improvements.

Balanced Scorecards should not just be collections of financial and non-financial measures, organized into three to five perspectives. The best Balanced Scorecards reflect the strategy of the organization. A good test is whether you can understand the strategy by looking only at the scorecard and its strategy map. Many organizations fail this test, especially those that create stakeholder scorecards or key performance indicator scorecards.

Strategy scorecards along with their graphical representations on strategy maps provide a logical and comprehensive way to describe strategy. They communicate clearly the organization's desired outcomes and its hypotheses about how these outcomes can be achieved. For example, *if* we improve on-time delivery, *then* customer satisfaction will improve; *if* customer satisfaction improves, *then* customers will purchase more. The scorecards enable all organizational units and employees to understand the strategy and identify how they can contribute by becoming aligned to the strategy.

APPLYING THE BSC TO NONPROFITS AND GOVERNMENT ORGANIZATIONS

During the past five years, the Balanced Scorecard has also been applied by nonprofit and government organizations (NPGOs). One of the barriers to applying the scorecard to these sectors is the considerable difficulty NPGOs have in clearly defining their strategy. We reviewed "strategy" documents of more than 50 pages. Most of the documents, once the mission and vision are articulated, consist of lists of programs and initiatives, not the outcomes the organization is trying to achieve. These organizations must understand Porter's (1996, 77) admonition that strategy is not only what the organization intends to do, but also what it decides *not* to do, a message that is particularly relevant for NPGOs.

Most of the initial scorecards of NPGOs feature an operational excellence strategy. The organizations take their current mission as a given and try to do their work more efficiently – at lower cost, with fewer defects, and faster. Often the project builds off of a recently introduced quality initiative that emphasizes process improvements. It is unusual to find nonprofit organizations focusing on a strategy that can be thought of as product leadership or customer intimacy. As a consequence, their scorecards tend to be closer to the KPI scorecards than true strategy scorecards.

The City of Charlotte, North Carolina, however, followed a customer-based strategy by selecting an interrelated set of strategic themes to create distinct value for its citizens (Kaplan 1998). United Way of Southeastern New England also articulated a customer (donor) intimacy strategy (Kaplan and Kaplan 1996). Other nonprofits – the May Institute and New Profit Inc. – selected a clear product-leadership position (Kaplan and Elias 1999). The May Institute uses partnerships with universities and researchers to deliver the best behavioral and rehabilitation care delivery. New Profit Inc. introduces a new selection, monitoring, and governing process unique among nonprofit organizations. Montefiore Hospital uses a combination of product leadership in its centers of excellence, and excellent customer relationships – through its new patient-oriented care centers – to build market share in its local area (Kaplan 2001). These examples demonstrate that NPGOs can be strategic and build competitive advantage in ways other than pure operational excellence. But it takes vision and leadership to move from continuous improvement of existing processes to thinking strategically about which processes and activities are most important for fulfilling the organization's mission.

Modifying the Architecture of the Balanced Scorecard

Most NPGOs had difficulty with the original architecture of the Balanced Scorecard that placed the financial perspective at the top of the hierarchy. Given that achieving financial success is not the primary objective for most of these organizations, many rearrange the scorecard to place customers or constituents at the top of the hierarchy.

In a private-sector transaction, the customer plays two distinct roles – paying for the service and receiving the service – that are so complementary most people don't even think about them separately. But in a nonprofit organization, donors provide the financial resources – they pay for the service – while another group, the constituents, receives the service. Who is the customer – the one paying or the one receiving? Rather than have to make such a Solomonic decision, organizations place both the donor perspective and the recipient perspective, in parallel, at the top of their Balanced Scorecards. They develop objectives for both donors and recipients, and then identify the internal processes that deliver desired value propositions for both groups of "customers."

In fact, nonprofit and government agencies should consider placing an over-arching objective at the top of their scorecard that represents their long-term objective such as a reduction in poverty or illiteracy, or improvements in the environment. Then the objectives within the scorecard can be oriented toward improving such a high-level objective. High-level financial measures provide private sector companies with an accountability measure to their owners, the shareholders. For a nonprofit or government agency, however, the financial measures are not the relevant indicators of whether the agency is delivering on its mission. The agency's mission should be featured and measured at the highest level of its scorecard. Placing an over-arching objective on the BSC for a nonprofit or government agency communicates clearly the long-term mission of the organization as portrayed in Figure 18.4.

Even the financial and customer objectives, however, may need to be re-examined for governmental organizations. Take the case of regulatory and enforcement agencies that monitor and punish violations of environmental, safety, and health regulations. These agencies, which detect transgressions,

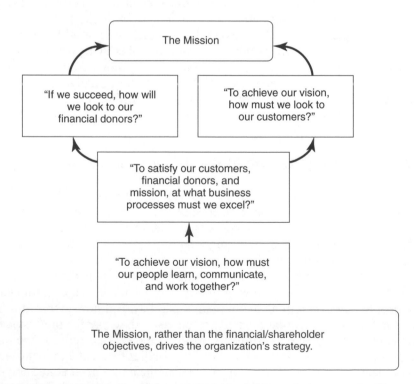

Figure 18.4 Adapting the Balanced Scorecard framework to nonprofit organizations

and fine or arrest those who violate the laws and regulations, cannot look to their "immediate customers" for satisfaction and loyalty measures. Clearly not; the true "customers" for such organizations are the citizens at large who benefit from effective but not harsh or idiosyncratic enforcement of laws and regulations. Figure 18.5 shows a modified framework in which a government agency has three high-level perspectives:

1. *Cost Incurred*: This perspective emphasizes the importance of operational efficiency. The measured cost should include both the expenses of the agency and the social cost it imposes on citizens and other organizations through its operations. For example, an environmental agency imposes remediation costs on private-sector organizations. These are part of the costs of having the agency carry out its mission. The agency should minimize the direct and social costs required to achieve the benefits called for by its mission.

2. *Value Created*: This perspective identifies the benefits being created by the agency to citizens and is the most problematic and difficult to measure. It is usually difficult to financially quantify the benefits from improved education, reduced pollution, better health, less congestion, and safer neighborhoods. But the balanced scorecard still enables organizations to identify the outputs, if not the outcomes, from its activities, and to measure these outputs. Surrogates for value created could include percentage of students acquiring specific skills and knowledge; density of pollutants in water, air, or land, improved morbidity and mortality in

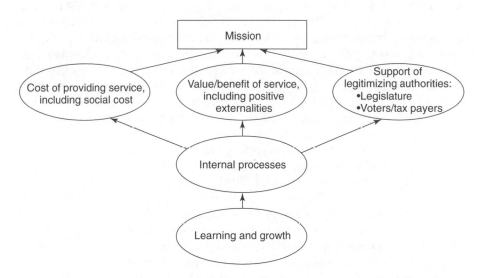

Figure 18.5 The Financial/customer objectives for public sector agencies may require three different perspectives
Professor Dutch Leonard, Kennedy School of Government, Harvard University, collaborated to develop this diagram

targeted populations; crime rates and perception of public safety; and transportation times. In general, public-sector organizations may find they use more output than outcome measures. The citizens and their representatives – elected officials and legislators – will eventually make the judgments about the benefits from these outputs vs. their costs.

3. *Legitimizing Support*: An important "customer" for any government agency will be its "donor," the organization – typically the legislature – that provides the funding for the agency. In order to assure continued funding for its activities, the agency must strive to meet the objectives of its funding source – the legislature and, ultimately, citizens and taxpayers.

After defining these three high-level perspectives, a public-sector agency can identify its objectives for internal processes, learning, and growth that enable objectives in the three high-level perspectives to be achieved.

BEYOND MEASUREMENT TO MANAGEMENT

Originally, we thought the Balanced Scorecard was about performance measurement (Kaplan and Norton 1992). Once organizations developed their basic system for measuring strategy, however, we quickly learned that *measurement* has consequences far beyond reporting on the past. Measurement creates focus for the future. The measures chosen by managers communicate important messages to all organizational units and employees. To take full advantage of this power, companies soon integrated their new measures into a *management system*. Thus the Balanced Scorecard concept evolved from a performance measurement system to become the organizing framework, the operating system, for a new strategic management system (Kaplan and Norton 1996c, Part II). The academic literature, rooted in the original performance measurement aspects of the scorecard, focuses on the BSC as a measurement system (Ittner et al. 1997; Ittner and Larcker 1998; Banker et al. 2000; Lipe and Salterio 2000) but has yet to examine its role as a management system.

Using this new strategic management system, we observed several organizations achieving performance breakthroughs within two to three years of implementation (Kaplan and Norton 2001a, 4–6, 17–22). The magnitude of the results achieved by the early adopters reveals the power of the Balanced Scorecard management system to focus the entire organization on strategy. The speed with which the new strategies deliver results indicates that the companies' successes are not due to a major new product or service launch, major new capital investments, or even the development of new intangible or "intellectual" assets. The companies, of course, develop new products and services, and invest in both hard, tangible assets, as well as softer, intangible assets. But they cannot benefit much in two years from such investments. To achieve their breakthrough performance, the companies capitalize on capabilities and assets – both tangible and intangible – that already exist within their organizations.[5] The companies' new strategies and the Balanced Scorecard unleash the capabilities and assets previously hidden (or frozen) within the old organization. In effect, the Balanced Scorecard provides the "recipe" that enables ingredients already existing in the organization to be combined for long-term value creation.

Part II of our commentary on the Balanced Scorecard (Kaplan and Norton 2001b) will describe how organizations use Balanced Scorecards and strategy maps to accomplish comprehensive and integrated transformations. These organizations redefine their relationships with customers, reengineer fundamental business processes, reskill the work force, and deploy new technology infrastructures. A new culture emerges, centered not on traditional functional silos, but on the team effort required to implement the strategy. By clearly defining the strategy, communicating it consistently, and linking it to the drivers of change, a performance-based culture emerges to link everyone and every unit to the unique features of the strategy. The simple act of describing strategy via strategy maps and scorecards makes a major contribution to the success of the transformation program.

NOTES

1. For example, General Electric attempted a system of nonfinancial measurements in the 1950s (Greenwood 1974), and the French developed the Tableaux de Bord decades ago (Lebas 1994, Epstein and Manzoni 1998).
2. Brand names, which can be sold, are an exception.
3. Shareholder value can also be increased through managing the right-hand side of the balance sheet, such as by repurchasing shares and choosing the low-cost mix among debt and equity instruments to lower the cost of capital. In this paper, we focus only on improved management of the organization's assets (tangible and intangible).
4. Measurement of customer profitability (Kaplan and Cooper 1998, 181–201) provides one of the connections between the Balanced Scorecard and activity-based costing.
5. These observations indicate why attempts to "value" individual intangible assets almost surely is a quixotic search. The companies achieved breakthrough performance with essentially the same people, services, and technology that previously delivered dismal performance. The value creation came not from any individual asset – tangible or intangible. It came from the coherent combination and alignment of existing organizational resources.

REFERENCES

American Institute of Certified Public Accountants (AICPA), Special Committee on Financial Reporting. 1994. *Improving Business Reporting – A Customer*

Focus: Meeting the Information Needs of Investors and Creditors. New York, NY: AICPA.

Atkinson, A. A., and J. H. Waterhouse. 1997. A stakeholder approach to strategic performance measurement. *Sloan Management Review* (Spring): 25–37.

Banker, R., G. Potter, and D. Srinivasan. 2000. An empirical investigation of an incentive plan that includes nonfinancial performance measures. *The Accounting Review* (January): 65–92.

Becker, B., and M. Huselid. 1998. High performance work systems and firm performance: A synthesis of research and managerial implications. In *Research in Personnel and Human Resources Management*, 53–101. Greenwich, CT: JAI Press.

Blair, M. B. 1995. *Ownership and Control: Rethinking Corporate Governance for the Twenty-First Century.* Washington, D.C.: Brookings Institution.

Chandler, A. D. 1990. *Scale and Scope. The Dynamics of Industrial Capitalism.* Cambridge, MA: Harvard University Press.

Charan, R., and G. Colvin. 1999. Why CEOs fail. *Fortune* (June 21): Vol. 189, issue 12: 68–78.

Epstein, M., and J. F. Manzoni. 1998. Implementing corporate strategy: From Tableaux de Bord to Balanced Scorecards. *European Management Journal* (April): 190–203.

Greenwood, R. G. 1974. *Managerial Decentralization: A Study of the General Electric Philosophy.* Lexington, MA: D.C. Heath.

Heskett, J., T. Jones, G. Loveman, E. Sasser, and L. Schlesinger. 1994. Putting the service profit chain to work. *Harvard Business Review* (March–April): 164–174.

Huselid, M. A. 1995. The impact of human resource management practices on turnover, productivity, and corporate financial performance. *Academy of Management Journal.* Vol. 38, issue 3: 635–672.

Ittner, C., D. Larcker, and M. Meyer. 1997. Performance, compensation, and the Balanced Scorecard. Working paper, University of Pennsylvania.

———, D. Larcker, and M. Rajan. 1997. The choice of performance measures in annual bonus contracts. *The Accounting Review* (April). Vol. 10: 231–255.

———, and D. Larcker. 1998. Innovations in performance measurement: Trends and research implications. *Journal of Management Accounting Research*: 205–238.

Johnson, H. T., and R. S. Kaplan. 1987. *Relevance Lost: The Rise and Fall of Management Accounting.* Boston, MA: Harvard Business School Press.

Kaplan, R. S., and D. P. Norton. 1992. The Balanced Scorecard. Measures that drive performance. *Harvard Business Review* (January–February): 71–79.

———, and ———. 1993. Putting the Balanced Scorecard to work. *Harvard Business Review* (September–October): 134–147.

———, and E. L. Kaplan. 1996. United Way of Southeastern New England. Harvard Business School Case 197–036. Boston, MA.

———, and D. P. Norton. 1996a. Using the Balanced Scorecard as a strategic management system. *Harvard Business Review* (January–February): 75–85.

———, and ———. 1996b. Linking the Balanced Scorecard to strategy. *California Management Review* (Fall): 53–79.

———, and ———. 1996c. *The Balanced Scorecard: Translating Strategy Into Action.* Boston, MA: Harvard Business School Publishing.

——. 1998. City of Charlotte (A). Harvard Business School Case 199–036. Boston, MA.

——, and R. Cooper. 1998. *Cost and Effect: Using Integrated Cost Systems to Drive Profitability and Performance.* Boston, MA: Harvard Business School Press.

——, and J. Elias. 1999. New Profit, Inc.: Governing the nonprofit enterprise. Harvard Business School Case 100–052. Boston, MA.

——. 2001. Montefiore Medical Center. Harvard Business School Case 101–067. Boston, MA.

——, and D. P. Norton. 2000. Having trouble with your strategy? Then map it. *Harvard Business Review* (September–October): 167–176.

——, and ——. 2001a. *The Strategy-Focused Organization: How Balanced Scorecard Companies Thrive in the New Business Environment.* Boston, MA: Harvard Business School Press.

——, and ——. 2001b. Transforming the Balanced Scorecard from performance measurement to strategic management, Part II. *Accounting Horizons.* (forthcoming).

Kiechel, W. 1982. Corporate strategists under fire. *Fortune* (December 27): 38.

Lebas, M. 1994. Managerial accounting in France: Overview of past tradition and current practice. *European Accounting Review* 3 (3): 471–487.

Lipe, M., and S. Salterio. 2000. The Balanced Scorecard: Judgmental effects of common and unique performance measures. *The Accounting Review* (July): 283–298.

Porter, M. E. 1992. Capital disadvantage: America's failing capital investment system. *Harvard Business Review* (September–October). Vol. 70, issue 5: 65–82.

——. 1996. What is strategy? *Harvard Business Review* (November–December).

Treacy, F., and M. Wierserma. 1997. *The Wisdom of Market Leaders.* New York, NY: Perseus Books.

Webber, A. M. 2000. New math for a new economy. *Fast Company* (January–February).

19

Performance Indicators
20 Early Lessons from Managerial Use

Andrew Likierman

As the use of performance indicators has spread throughout the UK public sector, academic writing has tended to focus on the implications and consequences. The concerns of practitioners, on the other hand, have often been centred on the technical qualities of the indicators and the costs of implementation and operation. Much less has so far been publicly discussed about the application of indicators and their effect, or what officials and managers have learned so far about devising, implementing and using them.

The early lessons outlined below are based on discussions and written feedback from over 500 middle- and senior-grade managers from all parts of the public sector. The text is illustrated by quotations from some of the written responses to requests for comments on the list, which has been tested and refined in the light of comments and suggestions from 20 groups of officials and managers over the same period. Problems of confidentiality (and potential embarrassment) mean that only some of the quotations and examples are attributed to organizations. In other cases the sector is identified, but not the organization.

A number of caveats are necessary in interpreting the list:

■ First, it is intended only to be indicative and the examples to be illustrative. There has been no attempt to seek a systematic sample of organizations across the public sector and the focus has been on the non-traded part.

■ Second, the general categories used to divide the 20 lessons into four groups (concept, preparation, implementation and use) are for convenience only. The boundaries are not definitive, or even easy to draw, and some of the lessons could fit into more than one category.

■ Third, the focus is on managerial use. Other, wider, issues such as public accountability, equity and the allocation of funding are not covered, although the lessons from use may have implications for some of these.

■ Finally, the position is changing all the time as experience is gained. So the list has to be seen as reflecting a situation in transition and one which will have to be updated in the light of developments. This last point is intended to be more than a managerial cliché, since what may be of interest is that, even taking account of the diversity of the public sector, it is the elements listed below and not others that have been seen by the managers as having priority.

The list has also been tested on groups of private sector managers. Apart from the few elements, such as accountability, which are specific to the public sector, the vast majority of the lessons were seen to apply to private sector organizations, although there was a different emphasis on which were seen as the most important.

CONCEPT

1. Include All Elements Integral to What is Being Measured

As performance indicators have been introduced, the phrase: "What gets measured, gets done" has been increasingly heard, often with concern about the implications for what is not measured. This puts the onus on those who devise the measures to ensure that they are appropriately comprehensive. There are certainly some who are reasonably satisfied. A Chief Probation Officer judged that his report to the Probation Committee was "'good enough' to give ourselves a broad indication as to the key outcomes we are seeking" and an official in the Department of Social Security extended the principle to individuals in emphasizing that individual objectives "should be linked to job purpose and should involve all the key areas for which a jobholder is accountable and which are within his/her control".

The problems in this area arise when there are elements of the task which are not included in the list of measures. Thus in the Prison Service, one of the goals [*sic*] is "helping prisoners prepare for their return to the community". But the 1993/94 Business Plan acknowledges that the key performance indicator – the proportion of prisoners held in establishments where prisoners have the opportunity to exceed the minimum visiting requirements – measures only one aspect of the Service's performance in achieving the goal. More generally, unless the set of indicators chosen covers all elements essential to completing the task, there will be a danger that "What gets measured, gets done" will backfire and that performance will be skewed towards what is being measured. The Chief Executive of a central government agency commented: "An important factor in setting targets, we have found, is that the whole of resource in a particular area should be covered by targets. If an area is not so covered, there is scope for performance to be manipulated by misallocating costs to areas where no penalty is incurred to the advantage of the area where performance is measured". This is particularly important when some aspects of an organization's operations, including quality, are difficult to measure. A civil servant noted that "A management unit may cover not only policy work, but also routine administration of settled policies, which may be more readily susceptible to targets. There is a danger that the targets may mislead both the staff inside and managers outside the unit to accord greater importance to the routine work".

2. Choose a Number Appropriate to the Organization and Its Diversity

The appropriate number of indicators will be particular to the organization and its aims. It will also need to take account of the diversity of its operations. As a Health Department official observed, ". . . some parts of the Department's work are more susceptible to the use of performance indicators than others". For some organizations, many indicators will be required, for others few. Too many will make it difficult to focus what is important, too few will distort action. The dangers of the latter have been exhibited to the point of parody many times – as in the preoccupation of the command economies of the former Soviet Union with output, regardless of quality or demand. Nearer home was the notorious case of a member of the Kent Constabulary who encouraged those charged with some offences to confess to others which they had not committed in order to "improve" the clear-up rate. Certainly the Audit Commission, in consulting on Citizen's Charter indicators, recognized the principle of the need to reconcile enough indicators to provide a reflection of sufficient diversity with few enough so that the "big picture" did not get lost.

However, the concerns expressed by those contributing to this study were almost entirely on the dangers of excessive numbers. The need for sampling was emphasized by a senior health executive worried about "the massive public sector tendency to try to measure everything all of the time" and the same sentiments were echoed by a central government agency ("performance indicators should not spawn their own cottage industry of forms and monitoring returns"); by a probation officer ("One of my fears is that we now have so much information being made available that we are unable to use most of it"); and by a local authority ("There is a tendency to have too many indicators . . . This tendency needs to be resisted, otherwise the indicators lose their impact and value"). From another part of the Health Service came a specific reason for parsimony: "The fewer there are, the better, as this makes them easier to promote and explain".

3. Provide Adequate Safeguards for "Soft" Indicators, Particularly Quality

The difficulties of measuring certain aspects of an organization's operations mean that there is a tendency for the more easily measurable to push out what is not. By extension, within what is more easily measurable, the tendency is for financial to push out non-financial indicators. Quality has proved notably difficult for organizations to measure, and great care needs to be taken to give it proper weight. A central government department emphasized the need to set and assess quality standards "against agreed competence frameworks. This reduces subjectivity in areas where mechanically measurable criteria are absent". However, an official in one of the armed services commented gloomily: "We are trying to develop the more difficult 'quality' PIs and are not yet in a position to offer any up for general consumption. It is possible we will never be, as the differences between organizations and the nature of services provided by them will profoundly influence their design and use of PIs".

Quality measures may well take more time than others to develop. Social Services in Enfield have a three-year programme for implementing quality assurance, and an example of successfully completed implementation is Down and Lisburn Health and Social Services. They have developed a system of multidisciplinary quality standards for multidisciplinary staff teams. The method in the service for people over 75 was to ask key groups (including the clients) for the valued features of service and to convert these into quality standards. Process, measurement technique and required records were linked to each standard. The system has been extended to services including child health and personal social services for children aged 0 to 5. Still in the middle of the process is the Central Office of Information, which is replacing quality measures based on timeliness of delivery and conformity with specification ("both of which have been problematical") by a new indicator based on customer satisfaction. Peer review is also increasingly in evidence as a means of measuring quality. For example this has now become an essential element of the Higher Education Funding Council's periodic reviews of universities.

4. Take Account of Accountability and Politics

Since public bodies operate in a political context, care needs to be taken that the indicators reflect political constraints and pressures. The balance here is between adequate accountability and recognition of the pressures of political life. "Data can be misused, particularly by the media" was the comment of a senior manager of a National Health Service (NHS) Trust. A consultant within public health medicine dismissed targets for perinatal and infant mortality as "a classic example of performance indicators . . . which have been included for political reasons only". The public impact of league tables in sectors such as education and local government has given rise to particular concern, and caution is also common across Whitehall about the activities of parliamentary select committees, notably the Public Accounts Committee. Whitehall departments enjoying good relationships with "their" select committees felt themselves to be in a better position to avoid misunderstandings than those where relationships were distant. On the other hand, there can be political gains from the adoption of measures. Home Office proposals for key performance indicators for the probation service pointed out: "you will remember that the Audit Commission has commented that a robust system of performance indicators could make a major contribution to enhancing the credibility of the probation service".

PREPARATION

5. Devise Them with People on the Ground, Who Must Feel Ownership

"Attitudes change depending on whether you are calling for PIs or you feel they are being imposed on you" commented the finance office of a quango, and a senior executive of a central government agency emphasized that: "Agreeing performance indicators is a negotiating process in the broadest sense. If this is ignored it will lead to poor commitment and sense of ownership", and went on "People must understand what is expected of them, and how this was decided. They must be allowed to contribute to the decision-making process". The Director of Social Services of the London Borough of Hackney emphasized that in involving staff further and further down the organization: "the process of getting them involved and thinking in terms of monitoring and evaluating is, I think, as important as the final document itself". A regional health authority is "currently negotiating with General Managers of DHAs and FHSAs a shared view of what is effective, appropriate and reasonable . . . agreement by General Managers is considered necessary in order to secure co-operation and a sense of ownership".

It will almost always be difficult for those who are not involved in an operation to understand the potential pitfalls of implementing a new system of using indicators, and in a number of cases middle managements have effectively sabotaged imposed systems by not pointing out the pitfalls of implementation. In others, they have helped to ensure that systems are successful by closely working with those charged with implementation. In the case of the City of Sheffield, the Director of the Arts and Museums Department pointed to the case of two theatres where the move was "from grant aid as a simple annual ritual to action with clearly designated outputs . . . they themselves have come up with a list of nine policy areas, to which they will be applying quantitative measures, and which will form the basis of a service level agreement between the theatres and the City Council". For local government more generally, the finding of Palmer in this issue that a high proportion of indicators have been introduced as a result of internal management proposals bodes well for success, at least in this aspect of implementation.

6. Build in Counters to Short-term Focus

Since many indicators are set on an annual cycle, the effect of first introducing them may well be to alter the time-scale of managerial effort to a shorter term and to focus on achievement of success on a year-by-year basis. The Operations Director of the Transport Research Laboratory suggested that, as an alternative to targets which are unrealistically long term, this may not necessarily be bad in itself. However, many organizations require a long-term perspective, and this needs to be recognized in the nature of, and time-scales set for, the indicators chosen. Remaining in the transport field, short-term performance measured by the number of miles of road built may show an improvement if resources are diverted from maintenance. But, if this results in existing roads having to be expensively rebuilt because the lack of maintenance means that they can no longer be patched up, the short-term improvement will be at a considerable cost. The link can be revealed by road-condition indicators, which can be juxtaposed to measures of additions to the road stock.

7. Ensure that They Fairly Reflect the Efforts of Managers

Unless managers' efforts are fairly reflected in the indicators, they will be seen at best as not relevant, at worst as unfair and/or potentially distorting to the managerial process. This may mean thinking about indicators as apply-ing in different ways. Thus the Central Statistical Office (CSO) noted that some performance measures successfully motivated the generality of staff by creating a sense of achievement and improvement or by directing attention to the public image. Other measures had more impact on senior managers by highlighting policy issues.

Staffordshire's Chief Probation Office commented on one of the major dif-ficulties in identifying true indicators of performance: "we are not necessarily measuring the performance of our organization, but more the decisions of sentencers within the criminal justice system". Imprecision in the measures chosen may be an indication that there is a problem. As a civil servant pointed out: "Some objectives may be almost entirely within the control of the unit, and others lying outside its control would not be chosen for performance indi-cators. But many objectives lie in between . . . it is not easy to find a formula which fairly reflects the efforts of the unit without sliding into the subjectivity of 'trying to achieve', 'seeking to influence', or 'facilitating others to . . .'".

8. Find a Means to Cope with Uncontrollable Items and Perceived Injustices

Linked to the previous lesson, whatever the organization, there will be events which are outside the control of managers. The way the indicators are oper-ated needs to combine the technical requirements of control with credibility to managers in recognizing the impact of such events. One way of accom-modating the problem is to make the measures more sophisticated. The Employment Service (ES) at first had performance targets which did not take account of labour market conditions. "More recently", as a section head explained, "placing indicators have been formulated so as to be immune from external factors outside ES control. The headline unemployed placing target is based on an assumed level of vacancies; if actual vacancies differ from this assumption, the level of placings achieved can be viewed in context". Another way of coping with uncertainty is to recognize that revisions of targets may be essential in the light of experience.

If neither of the above is possible, as Lessons 17 and 18 below indicate, the essential element in maintaining the integrity of the indicators is to ensure that the results are not misused. As a senior officer of Copeland Borough Council put it: "We have encouraged managers not to regard indicators as necessarily reflecting their own performance. While in some cases they do, in many others there are outside influences which, at least in the short term, are outside their control. We do not want to discourage the monitoring of service standards because some of the factors are partly or completely outside the short term control of the manager."

9. Use the Experience of Other Organizations or Other Parts of the Organization

"We have pushed for equalization of performance within the Area and as a result the worst performing offices have generally come up to the standard of the best" (Area Director, Benefits Agency). "The need to secure effectiveness and efficiency in the contracting process (for purchaser/provider contracts) has led to sharing with General managers a summary of all Health Authority performance in this area" (regional health authority). "We have made significant changes in the light of our experience and that of others, particularly other local authorities" (local authority). These examples of using comparisons do not appear to be as routine as would be desirable in the public sector. Many organizations have devised and used indicators with very little reference to others within the same sector, or even within other parts of the same organization and the tendency to reinvent wheels seems to be common in public sector performance measurement. Experience on the appropriate type of indicators, or their use, may well be available elsewhere, including from comparable organizations in other countries. (Indeed, they may even be available within the UK – a central government department found comparisons between England and Wales, Scotland and Northern Ireland worthwhile in at least raising issues of the reasons for differences.) Even if no comparable organizations are available, the process of finding the reasons why no lessons can be learned has often been useful.

10. Establish Realistic Levels of Attainment Before the First Targets Are Set

If an indicator has not been used before, it is likely to be very difficult to know what level to set. Careful preparatory work is necessary to see whether a level can be found so that the indicators themselves are not brought into disrepute by being shown to be unattainable or untesting. Many managers feel very strongly on this issue and the words "realistic" and "achievable" occur again and again. "One or two targets which are impossible or too easy to achieve could undermine the whole system" observes the manual of Tonbridge and Malling Borough Council, and from a civil servant: "Successful performance measurement is based on setting realistic and measurable objectives which are clearly linked to the business objectives of the organization and against which assessable success criteria can be established at the outset". If it is not possible to find a realistic level, a trial period or periods should be used to allow the appropriate levels to be established.

IMPLEMENTATION

11. Recognize that New Indicators Need Time to Develop and May Need Revision in the Light of Experience

As with any new managerial tool, performance indicators need time to develop. Even with careful preparation, it will take time to discover if there are flaws and unintended side-effects from the way the indicators have been constructed. Thus the Inspectorate of Constabulary started to develop indicators in 1983, and the matrix of 456 indicators first used to make comparisons has been progressively refined. Revisions to central government agency framework documents also indicate the value of the learning process and in local government a district council official commented that "our prime aim is to continuously develop the criteria for success". In part, revision may also be due to outside circumstances – "What we do and how we measure it is constantly changing" noted a central government agency. The British Airports Authority, when in the public sector, measured passenger service quality with two indicators, one of which was written complaints per 100,000 passengers. The two were seen to be unsatisfactory (for example, negative comments alone are not a good basis for inferring levels of quality), and, over the years, a sophisticated questionnaire procedure has been instituted.

12. Link Them to Existing Systems

For a variety of reasons, including caution about whether they will be effective and the difficulties of integrating them into existing information and control procedures, indicators have often been introduced into organizations in parallel to existing systems. The result has been costly in time and money and has engendered resentment among managers who have seen the new indicators as an unwelcome (and not necessarily useful) addition to their existing burdens. Early experience of performance indicators in the Health Service was blighted by their apparent irrelevance to many managers. By contrast, one local authority has linked the city council charter to annual service plans and also intends to tie it into the Citizen's Charter. In another, "performance service contracts are now the norm for our managers and in some areas . . . are used for all staff. This enables us to build PIs into the fabric of the organization and, to coin the hackneyed phrase, the way we do things round here". Three examples from very different parts of the public sector are those in Brignall's article on Solihull MBC[1]; the Lord Chancellor's Department, which has integrated circuit objectives into the planning and budgeting processes; and Liverpool's Maritime Housing Association, which has linked individual targets as part of a comprehensive review of the staff structure to the business plan.

13. They Must Be Easily Understandable by Those Whose Performance is Being Measured

In order to ensure that the indicators are trusted, the basis on which they are compiled, as well as the message from the outcomes, needs to be understood so that discussion about any action which needs to be taken is well-informed. The Employment Service Office for Scotland emphasized that "good communications to all levels is an important element in the preparation and implementation of performance indicators", and the area director of a central government agency wrote: "we are conscious of the need to make those measures that bit more . . . credible with staff and managers".

Over-complex indicators can distance those who need to take action from the indicators. A local authority manager complained that "the Arts Council and the Regional Arts Boards have spent a considerable amount of time attempting to develop performance indicators, many of which, in my opinion, are over-complex". In the case of another local authority, review of the annual service plan after a year showed that "some lessons are clear – terminology needs to be clearly understood . . .".

14. While Proxies May Be Necessary, They Must Be Chosen Cautiously

Since the outcomes of many public sector activities cannot be easily measured, proxy indicators will be necessary. But unless they are chosen with care, the proxies can distort the decision-making process by emphasizing an inappropriate outcome. As a Health Department official pointed out: "Within the Health Service, while we are always looking for outcome measures, what we have tend to be proxies for them, in some cases process measures, in others output measures – and we need to be very careful to be clear what is being measured and the extent to which it can bear further interpretation". In a similar vein, an official of the Management Executive of the NHS in Scotland indicated the importance of moving from measurement of processes towards "whether patients are healthier as a result of (NHS) interventions and whether they are being dealt with in a way they are entitled to expect". For the Driver and Vehicle Licensing Agency, speed of response and turnaround time were taken as proxies for quality. But, as the Executive Director, Operations noted, market research has indicated that speed is not regarded as the main requirement by customers and new performance measures are being devised. Even after careful review, the final result may still not be wholly satisfactory. The Director of Education for the London Borough of Croydon pointed out that "they are often the outcome of much painstaking failure to find something better". Finally, it is worth noting an imaginative use of proxies by the Customs and Excise. While drug seizures make the headlines, and the value of drugs prevented from entering the country is monitored, both are acknowledged to be unrelated to the total flow. So the street price is taken as one of the proxies of success.

15. The Period of Introduction Should Be Used to Reassess Internal and External Relationships

The introduction of performance indicators can be used, and may require, changes in an organization's internal and external relationships. For example: "The performance targets introduced when the CSO became an Executive Agency", explained the Head of the Policy Secretariat, "have had a profound positive effect on the way we view our customers and the way they view us. Most revealing of all was the difficulty our customers had in specifying what level of performance they really wanted of us". Internal reassessment of existing procedures should be welcomed as a manifestation of the fact that the measures are proving their worth. The Chief Executive of Hertfordshire County Council observed that "without other management changes, for example financial devolution, the performance indicator culture will not flourish . . . PIs would merely bob along the top of the organization making the occasional appearance on the agenda of management teams".

USE

16. The Data on Which the Results are Based Must Be Trusted

"Yes, but are the figures right?" is a constant refrain from those who take performance indicators seriously, or need to do so because their own performance is being measured. "The reliability of available data is a considerable factor in the preparation of performance indicators" commented an official of the Department of the Environment's Property Holdings Finance Division. "We need to be careful in the interpretation of data, particularly where there are a small number of samples" wrote an NHS Trust's personnel director, adding, in response to criticism for having too many trained district nurses at a certain grade, "It is questionable whether the use of this tool in order to prepare league tables of providers' performance is valuable since so much of the data is unreliable". A Chief Probation Officer indicated that some of the data "is quite unreliable since main grade staff have yet to cotton on to the importance of filling in the forms necessary to make this information available". Without data which is not only accurate, but trusted to be so, many of the potential benefits from introducing performance indicators may be dissipated.

17. Use the Results as Guidance, not Answers. Recognize that Interpretation is the Key to Action

The appropriate managerial response to performance measurement results is a basis for discussion among managers with a view to taking action. Results cannot, on their own, provide "definitive" evidence of success or failure and should be used to raise questions, not to provide answers. ". . . it is the dialogue that arises from review that is the important message" was the advice of the Chief Executive of Arun District Council. In the case of Birmingham Social Services, questions led to a review of objectives after it was found that nursery occupancy could range from 30% to 90%. Analysis of the reasons for the range showed that the nurseries were also providing other services and that these in part depended on "the objectives and professional leadership of local managers". By defining objectives more clearly, there was a 15% increase in occupancy levels, despite staffing shortages. Above all, according to the Assistant Director of Social Services, the discussion about the objectives of day nurseries refocussed the tasks and "finally led to a clear definition of a community day nursery and family centre". More generally, the Audit Commission has long used the technique of publishing profiles of performance of specific activities as a means of encouraging discussion of the reasons for differences between organizations.

The results should always be accompanied by a commentary so that the figures can be analysed and put in context. For example one local authority includes the minimum requirement of "An overview of the quarter . . . which is a brief summary of the main points of note . . . accompanied by some short text picking out the main points to note about the indicators and indicating action being taken". Another, Bracknell Forest Borough Council, has comments in the reports by chief officers where appropriate, as when the improvement in turnround of building control applications was realistically explained by "the better relationship of workload to resources that now exists compared with the peak of the 1980s' boom". Without a commentary there is considerable danger that the figures will be misused or at least misunderstood, as when, after great efforts were made in one police force to respond to a dramatic increase in car crime, further analysis through the matrix of indicators referred to in Lesson 11 revealed Volkswagen badge stealing as the main reason for the increase.

18. Acknowledge the Importance of Feedback. Follow-up Gives Credibility; No Feedback Means Atrophy; Negative-only Feedback Encourages Game-playing

The level of outside or senior managerial attention to the results indicates how performance indicators are regarded and gives powerful messages to all those involved in preparing and using them. Figures on submission rates in higher education may once have been regarded as "academic" but are now of enormous importance to universities since they affect future allocations of studentships. A central government department noted that for one of their sections "the sensible setting of targets, and senior management's clear interest in their setting and monitoring, has enhanced the section's motivation". In a central government agency the board holds quarterly performance dialogues with each regional director in preparation for a discussion with the Minister about the results.

Silence in response to results is likely to mean that the figures come to be regarded as irrelevant by those whose performance is being measured. Continued silence will mean that little trouble is taken to fix realistic target levels or respond to the results. Thus when senior officials in a government department who filled in regular annual reviews found that no action or feedback was forthcoming, first less attention was given to the results and then little importance was given to the levels of target set each year. The North East Thames Regional Health Authority, on the other hand, emphasized the importance not only of the information, but of getting it in on time "We have initiated a system of penalty points for lateness and incompleteness of routine returns".

If the only reaction of senior management is to emphasize the aspects of results involving failure, the message to those whose performance is being measured will swiftly be that great care is necessary to ensure that targets are set at a level that can be achieved. There is also the danger that considerable time will be spent in making sure that the figures "look right", regardless of the underlying performance, with elaborate alibis to protect those involved. A common criticism among those subject to scrutiny by the Public Accounts Committee is that the Committee has inhibited the development of a more managerial climate by not recognizing the greater element of risk involved in the changing nature of public organizations and by continuing to focus on mistakes, rather than a balance between successes and failures.

19. Trade-offs and Complex Interactions Must Be Recognized; Not all Indicators Should Carry Equal Weight

Emphasis on one aspect of performance will almost inevitably have effects on other aspects. The use of performance indicators needs to accommodate such effects and the accompanying trade-offs. Failure to do so can result in the performance measurement system as a whole being by-passed or dis-credited. For example the Employment Service "expresses three placing targets as percentages of the headline unemployed placing target. One con-sequence of this is that better than expected performance on the headline target can result in under achievement of the percentage subsidiary targets. This slightly paradoxical relationship needs to be clearly understood by man-agers in order to optimise their ability to meet all the targets and not just the headline target. Similar trade-offs exist between ES' benefit-related targets. Striving to pay people promptly may have consequences for the accuracy with which payments are made . . . To concentrate single-mindedly on one indicator runs the risk of failing to achieve the other; this may represent less success than narrowly failing to achieve both". Another agency commented on the indicators that "their real strength lies in their overall effect which is particularly important given the highly interrelated nature of our work". A third agency recognized the element of trade-off in ensuring that not all indi-cators can or should carry the same weight and altered the number of indi-cators after finding that the weighting towards one activity "sent the wrong messages round the organization". A Ministry of Defence official counselled the importance of careful interpretation: "Apply PIs to those activities that are carrying out the most important operations and not necessarily those where it is easiest to notch up a big score".

20. Results Must Be User-friendly and at Appropriate Levels of Aggregation and Response Time

Managers unable to understand the results of performance indicators will not be able to take appropriate action. What is done need not be very sophisti-cated, as indicated by a local authority's comment, "Emphasis has been placed on good presentation, particularly the appropriate use of graphs and tables etc., so as to make information as easy to assimilate as possible". The results also need to be presented at the right level of detail – not too aggre-gated to mask important trends, or too disaggregated for the manager to be overwhelmed with a mass of detail.

Since indicators may be relevant to different time-scales, the timing of results needs to reflect time-scales for decision. "One of the biggest criti-cisms levelled at the Health Service Indicators over the years have been that by the time they are disseminated to the service the information is out of date and the world has moved on" commented an official. And a central government agency admitted that a yearly, national survey of customer satisfaction was "fairly useless" because action was not possible as result – response times were too long to be meaningful, and disaggregation below national level was not possible.

The results for some indicators will need to be reviewed each month, for others the time-scale may be a year. North West Thames Regional Health Authority quotes quarterly immunization uptake rates as the relevant timescale. For some, highly specific time-periods are relevant, for example at particular points during a contract. The London Docklands Development corporation has established a system that focuses on the elements of project management – input, time and output. Assuming that counters to short-term focus have been built in, this lesson reinforces the importance of identifying the appropriate time-scales for the indicators chosen. The managerial response to the results should also reflect the appropriate time-scales.

CONCLUSION

Consideration of the early lessons outlined above should help organizations to use performance indicators to better effect. They will not guarantee success, but failure to take them into account could mean not only a waste of managerial time and cash resources but also, potentially more serious, a distortion of managerial action. It could also mean a wasted opportunity for the use of a valuable managerial tool.

NOTE

1. See S. Brignall, "Performance Measurement and Change in Local Government: A General Case and a Childcare Application", *Public Policy and Management* (Oct–Dec 1995).

"Performance Indicators: 20 Early Lessons from Managerial Use", by Andrew Likierman reprinted with permission from *Public Money and Management*, Oct–Dec. Copyright 1993 CIPFA.

Section 6

Governance and Ethics

SECTION OVERVIEW

Janette Rutterford

In this, the last section of *Financial Strategy*, we attempt to take a step back from the issues of adding value or measuring performance, and ask some more general questions, including: Is shareholder value maximisation the right goal? How can shareholder value be reconciled with the problems of using managers as agents for shareholders? And, what about other stake-holders such as employees and pensioners? Have they been forgotten at the expense of manager and shareholder greed? What role should ethics play in corporate governance? And, what is the best system of corporate gover-nance? We also try to link a number of the themes discussed in earlier sec-tions of the book.

These issues have become all the more urgent with the large number of company collapses from the last stock market boom. Commentators have begun to ask whether managers simply forgot to be ethical in their pursuit of gain for themselves or for their shareholders. And yet, the shareholder emphasis had already been brought into question by Will Hutton in his book, *The State We're In*, published as early as 1995. The stock market boom of the late 1990s had appeared to prove him wrong.

The US has perhaps suffered the greatest shock, with the apparent sophis-tication of accounting rules, of regulation and of investment analysts not being sufficiently on the ball to spot creative accounting or, indeed, fraud. The first article in this section, "It's Time to Rebalance the Scorecard", by James Higgins and David Currie, discusses possible reasons for the failure of corporate ethics in the US in the context of performance measurement. The authors look at a sample of firms using the balanced scorecard approach and find that about 90 per cent of these do not use social responsibility mea-sures of any kind. They argue that social responsibility and stakeholder con-siderations should be explicitly made part of the measurement of managerial performance.

The second article in this section is "Stakeholder Capitalism", an extract from Will Hutton's book, *The State We're In*. This book had a major impact on corporate governance thinking when it appeared, challenging the domination of the shareholder maximisation approach and arguing that the continental European version, which considered stakeholders such as employees, pensioners, the local community, lenders, government as well as shareholders, had much to offer. And yet, by the end of the twentieth century, the continental European model had apparently lost the battle to rampant capitalism. German companies such as Siemens introduced management incentive schemes linked to shareholder value, DaimlerChrysler threatened to close factories down unless workers worked longer hours for the same pay, and other companies such as Vivendi Universal in France made acquisition after acquisition in a bid to enhance shareholder wealth – as well as enrich the CEO, Jean Marie Messier.

Case Study 13 is an article published in 2005 in *The Economist*, which argues that, despite the stock market boom and bust in the years between the publication of Will Hutton's book and the publication of this article, stakeholder capitalism was essentially dead and buried and that, despite its flaws, the Anglo-American model of corporate governance was far superior. See if you agree.

"Controversy Incorporated", by David Cogman and Jeremy Oppenheim, looks at the role of ethics in corporate governance. It essentially argues, rather after the event, that ethics is in the end good for the firm and good for shareholders. In a sense, it is a reversion to the dividend policy and signaling literature. Firms can signal via their ethical stance that they are better than their competitors; this will give them access to cheaper cost finance and, in the end, achieve the desired goal of enhancing shareholder wealth.

Case Study 14 is a revealing interview with the CFO of Microsoft by Bertil Chappuis and Tim Koller. The discussion ranges over a number of topics, from the pitfalls of executive compensation using share options, to the role of dividends as a signaling mechanism, to the role of corporate ethics and the ever more complex role of the CFO and the finance division.

Case Study 15 is a detailed case study of Parmalat, an Italian dairy products company which entered bankruptcy protection in 2003 after acknowledging that $3.95 billion supposedly on deposit with a bank did not exist. It was subsequently discovered that Parmalat had debts totalling $14 billion, eight times higher than previously thought. In 2005, Calistro Tanzi, the firm's founder, with 15 others, went on trial in Italy charged with false accounting, market rigging and misleading Italy's financial markets regulator. Parmalat, a world leader in its field, had apparently complied with the Preda Code, the Italian code of corporate governance, and yet managed to hide accounting fraud for more than a decade. Creative accounting, and downright fraud, were hidden from stakeholders, and the governance bodies, until it was too late. An interesting cross-cultural case study.

The final case study, Case Study 16, touches on another issue which throws up cultural differences and conflicting objectives. Corporate pension funds in the Anglo-American-Dutch world have tended to be funded, with employees on retirement being paid pensions linked to salary. Investment risk has been borne by the firm and hence by the shareholders. In the boom years of the 1990s, with pension funds benefiting from high equity values, firms were able to reduce their pension contributions, enhancing earnings figures and hence shareholder value. In the bear market of the 2000s, the opposite is true, with the added problem of new accounting rules requiring greater disclosure of pension liabilities and actuaries requiring market values rather than historic cost values to be used. These combined changes have led companies to incur on- or off-balance sheet net pension liabilities, sometimes out of all proportion to the size of their business assets and liabilities. The interesting question here is who should bear the investment risk? Many companies are switching to defined contribution schemes, where employees take the investment risk, at the same time taking the opportunity to reduce their share of pension contributions. The pie is being divided differently between existing pensioners, who are doing well, future pensioners, likely to do worse, and companies which will suffer for years to come with the already accumulated liabilities. The case study, an article from the *Financial Times* by Lucy Warwick-Ching, raises a few of these unresolved issues.

20

It's Time to Rebalance
the Scorecard

James M. Higgins and David M. Currie

The headlines have been frequent and the allegations of misdeeds numerous. Major corporations and their senior managers have violated shareholder and societal trust. Sometimes they have even violated the law. These companies brought a whole new meaning to the term "creative accounting," and when cooking the books failed to provide enough cash for their purposes, some firms and their senior managers just flat-out lied about how well they were performing, what their sources of revenues were, and how expenses were incurred. Senior managers in a few firms even misappropriated corporate funds for their own personal uses, thereby supporting a lavish lifestyle at the expense of shareholders. Some corporate boards loaned their senior managers outrageously large amounts of money, then turned around and forgave these loans when stock prices plunged. There are instances of senior managers selling stock on the basis of negative insider information about the firm's future at the same time they were telling their employees, stock analysts, and investors that the company was financially healthy.

The names of the more prominent of the corporations associated with some or all of these misdeeds are familiar: Enron, Tyco, WorldCom, Qwest, and Adelphia Communications, to name a few. But other firms engaged in some of these same practices in a lesser fashion: Xerox, Lucent Technologies, Peregrine, AOL, and Bristol-Myers, for example, all had questionable accounting practices. And let's not forget that at least one major accounting firm failed to derail the runaway train at Enron even though the firm was aware of Enron's questionable accounting practices. Alas, Arthur Andersen paid the ultimate price since, for all practical purposes, it exists no more. The new managers of at least one of these firms, Adelphia Communications, sued its accounting firm, Deloitte Touche Tohmatsu. These managers charge, among other things, that Deloitte knew about the accounting irregularities but failed to inform the board of directors.

Enron, Tyco, Adelphia Communications, and WorldCom have all filed for bankruptcy protection. Qwest may have to follow suit after its financial statements were recently significantly restated, and it apparently hedged on future earnings. Political pundits who believe in the market as the correction mechanism for business can point to these bankruptcies as evidence that the market works. Investors with bankrupted 401K accounts would probably not disagree with that statement but would argue that more controls should be in place to protect the innocent. The thousands of employees who lost their jobs and their pensions as a result of these shenanigans would certainly echo similar sentiments.

Additional firms were directly affected by, and even helped cause, this financial-performance-at-all-costs scenario. Financial institutions failed to maintain control over interactions between their investment banking and research divisions. For example, at Merrill Lynch, analysts hyped stocks to investors while privately unloading these stocks. And in a somewhat different version of this theme, at Citigroup hot initial public offerings (IPOs) were allocated to clients who had borrowed heavily from Citigroup.

So what has been done to improve the way business does business?

THE CORRECTIVE ACTIONS TAKEN SO FAR

Several corrective actions have already taken place, with more on the horizon:

- The federal government has successfully prosecuted several senior corporate managers for their roles in these offenses, but only one CEO from among the most offending firms has been prosecuted.

- The federal government has also settled on an agreement for the separation between the investment banking divisions and the stock research departments of banks and brokerage houses.

- To that end, Citigroup CEO and Chairman Sandy Weill has done just that for his firm's beleaguered Salomon Smith Barney division, dropping the Salomon name from the division title as well.

- Merrill Lynch agreed to pay $100 million for settling charges regarding hyping stocks that were trashed internally.

- Major senior managers have been replaced at Enron, Tyco, WorldCom, Qwest, and Adelphia Communications.

- Numerous organizations not involved in any of these shenanigans have voluntarily made corporate governance changes. At many firms CEOs are personally required to certify their firms' financial results.

- At AutoZone Inc., senior managers will not sign off on division financials until division managers have certified the financial results for their divisions.

- The chairman of the Securities & Exchange Commission resigned amid charges of lack of disclosure of information pertinent to one of his appointees.

- Both public and private officials have begun to examine the value and risks of deregulation.

- Congress passed the Sarbanes–Oxley Act, which mandated a sweeping overhaul of corporate securities law.

Despite all of these well-intentioned improvements in the operating rules for businesses, these improvements are necessary but not sufficient; they fail to focus on the bottom-line motivations of the individual.

To understand why these actions are not enough, we need to examine the principal causes of the unethical and illegal behaviors that have shaken the foundation of business these past couple of years.

SOME CAUSES OF SUCH BEHAVIORS

When one examines the causes of such behaviors, it becomes evident that several key factors played a role – the business climate of that time, human nature, the societal climate, the competitiveness of the global business environment, and the nature of competitive organizations. Let's take a look at each of these factors in turn.

The Business Climate

The business climate within which these misdeeds and crimes occurred is reminiscent of the climate that characterized the roaring '20s – a booming economy buoyed by inflated stock prices. A euphoria existed that defied rational explanation, at least on a historical perspective. Judged by their actions, many investors, analysts, and top corporate managers apparently believed that this boom period would never end. So what if historically price to earnings ratios had been pegged at 12 to 1? "This was a new paradigm," cried the boom's proponents. Acceptable P/E ratios soon became 16 to 1 and then 18 to 1. Finally, businesses, investors, and society became comfortable with P/E ratios in the 30s and 40s, numbers comparable to those of the Japanese market during the investment bubble of the 1990s. And in this new paradigm, companies didn't have to pay dividends to increase stock price levels; the upward momentum of stock prices was sufficient to justify investment. Momentum investing replaced technical analysis and the more conservative fundamental analysis. The era of irrational exuberance was at hand.

Coupled with this new enthusiasm, and perhaps fomenting it, was the trend toward deregulation following the collapse of the Soviet Union. Capitalism became the remaining viable economic philosophy, which seemed to relieve markets from their responsibility for prudence. Industries such as telecommunications, airlines, meatpacking, energy, and banking were freed from regulation or supervision. The disadvantage of abandoning supervision and regulation is that it places greater reliance on managers to act responsibly and represent society in their decision making. The unfortunate fact is that not all managers behave in a socially responsible manner.

Human Nature

The causes of such behaviors included more than just the business climate, however. Another major cause was human nature. People have always wanted more. They want to achieve more. They want to have more. They want more power. Barring rules and regulations that prohibit certain behaviors, and often even in the face of such rules and regulations, some people will take whatever actions are necessary to achieve and have more. Often these behaviors violate the shareholder and public trust. They may be illegal, unethical, or immoral.

The Societal Climate

And then there's the societal climate. A lot has been written about this climate, and much of the anecdotal evidence suggests that the moral and ethical standards acceptable in our society have slipped a notch or two in the past few years. What used to be clearly "right and wrong" is at least a shade of gray now. Ethics involving "acceptable" industry or societal practices don't carry the same moral clout as morally right and wrong behaviors. And even what is right and wrong has changed. Society has become permissive. Religion, whether you personally practice it or not, does provide society with a set of moral standards. As the practice of organized religion has declined, by most measures so has our nation's morality.

The Competitive Global Environment

There is also the competitive global environment to consider. Firms based in the United States finally began to awaken to the competitiveness of foreign firms in the 1970s. Most dramatically, Japanese firms were proving to be wily and efficient competitors in virtually every market they entered. U.S.-based firms responded slowly at first, but competitiveness accelerated as it became obvious that long-term economic survival was the issue in automobiles, steel, and electronics. Being globally competitive has brought U.S. firms a sense of urgency – either they must become competitive or they will be forced out of the industry. Now, Chinese, Southeast Asian, and European firms all vie with U.S.-based firms for their share of the global marketplace. Firms from these countries often have a different set of ethical standards, further compounding an already difficult environment for U.S. firms.

The Nature of Competitive Organizations

The competitive organization is driven toward the achievement of a vision, a mission, and related strategic objectives. To achieve these purposes, the competitive organization utilizes performance-management systems. Most of these systems derive strategic objectives from the vision and mission of the organization. Strategic objectives are heavily influenced by the values of top management and the values of the organization's culture. Once determined, strategic objectives are then parceled down through the organization by means of the performance-management system.

During the late 1990s, irrational exuberance drove not only the stock market but also the companies listed on the major stock exchanges. Inside many firms the pressure to raise stock prices became excessive. The higher the stock price achieved, the higher the target stock price set by management. Greed had raised its ugly head. Top management decreed that the stock price had to go up regardless of corporate and competitive fundamentals. Long-term strategy was planning a quarter ahead in far too many organizations. Before long, irrational exuberance led to irrational performance expectations.

Sometimes when objectives must be met regardless of how excessive they are, top management behavior becomes irrational, unethical, or even illegal. To achieve objectives they have set, and in order not to disappoint Wall Street and have it lower the stock price, some executives cook the books. This happened at America Online (AOL) where financial performance results were inflated in order to keep the stock price high before the merger with Time Warner.[1] This also happened at Bristol-Myers.[2]

Sometimes when unobtainable objectives must be achieved, lower-level employee behavior may also become irrational, unethical, or illegal. The pressure to increase bottom-line results becomes unbearable. The performance-management system is used as a whip rather than as a performance-management tool. Some employees feel compelled to lie and cheat in order to keep their jobs. They say to themselves, "You want these objectives met? I'll meet them in a way that gets you off my back. I'll do whatever it takes." This clearly happened at Lucent Technologies, where lower-level managers and staff reported inventory movements as sales in order to meet unobtainable financial performance objectives.[3]

If you examine the illegal and unethical behaviors that have taken place, and if you examine some of the corporate violations of the law and of ethical standards that have occurred in the last few years, you find that much slips through the corporate control system. What is fundamental to solving this type of situation is for the organization to make a serious commitment to issues beyond the financial performance of the organization.

Some responsibility for the focus of U.S. corporations on short-term financial results falls on the shoulders of U.S. business schools. Since the 1950s, U.S. business schools have modeled the firm on returns to stockholders, and the goal of maximizing stockholder wealth has become embedded in the curricula of business schools and the psyche of corporate managers. Analytical techniques were developed to assess the firm's performance according to the financial criteria deemed most relevant to investors. Because of the triumph of the capitalist system, it was easy to fall into the trap that financial performance was the only way to evaluate an organization's success.

WHAT GETS MEASURED GETS DONE – ENTER THE BALANCED SCORECARD

It's a truism that "what gets measured gets done."

Robert S. Kaplan and David P. Norton first introduced the balanced score-card concept to business with an article in the Harvard Business Review in 1992.[4] The underlying concept of the balanced scorecard is that financial measures are too narrowly focused and that additional measures of organi-zational performance are necessary in order to drive the future performance of the firm. Kaplan and Norton suggested four cornerstone measurement per-spectives. Typically, several specific objectives are identified for each of these perspectives:

1. Financial – How do we look to shareholders?

2. Internal Business – What must we excel at?

3. Innovation and Learning – Can we continue to improve and create value?
    (Later changed to Growth and Learning)

4. Customer – How do customers see us?

Subsequent to publication of this article, Kaplan and Norton changed the title for perspective number 3, Innovation and Learning, to Growth and Learn-ing. More important, they have focused their writings and their consulting practice on the role of the scorecard in successful strategy execution rather than on its role as a performance-measurement system. Obviously it is both, and any good performance-management system should be both.

Kaplan and Norton are to be applauded for their introduction of a multiple-criteria strategy execution/performance-management system. A number of other corporate scorecards also exist, and several firms offer con-sulting assistance in developing and implementing these scorecards in an effort to help organizations successfully execute strategy. But the collective emphasis of scorecards is still primarily on translating strategy into financial performance. These scorecards do nothing to translate financial performance into performance of the corporation at a broader level than just the interests of stockholders and corporate management. Corporate scorecards are badly in need of rebalancing.

REBALANCING THE SCORECARD

Business serves at the pleasure of society. The historical role of business has largely been to provide goods and services for the marketplace. But there has been a growing feeling in our society over the past several decades that while businesses are providing those goods and services, they should also be good corporate citizens. The corporate scorecard needs to be expanded to include the broader issues with which businesses must cope, and for which they are responsible.

Legally, businesses are held accountable by society for providing equal opportunity in employment, their treatment of the physical environment, and obeying a host of laws that govern the conduct of business, for example, those governing contracts, relationships with unions, occupational health and safety, and mergers and acquisitions. Other issues that business has been asked to address by various constituencies include employee development and outplacement, plant closures and their impacts on the economic area, relationships with government, economic growth, education, urban renewal and development, support for culture and the arts, the development of an internal environment that supports diversity, and provision for employee health care.

If indeed "What gets measured gets done" is true, then it is no wonder that businesses have found themselves overly focusing on the financial aspects of the firm, because financial performance and its creators are what gets measured. Put another way, "If it's not on my performance appraisal, why should I care about it?" Many years ago, motivational speaker Larry Wilson stressed the importance of evaluating what you want done. His penetrating observation was, "People respect what you inspect, not what you expect."

Society expects business to be socially responsible. But expectations are not enough. Business respects what is inspected. What gets measured gets done. A firm sets objectives to move forward to achieve its vision and strategy. If solely financially related issues become part of objectives, then that's what is measured. The individual is no different. He or she respects what is inspected. People respect what they are accountable for. It's true that some businesses and some individuals will do what is expected without inspection. Yet given the complex set of demands that confront businesses and individuals, and given so little time to achieve all that is demanded, the tendency is to work on those things that count – for the organization's future well-being, or for one's personal performance appraisal and the rewards and power that ensue.

Kathleen Black, while publisher of *USA Today*, was once asked why Gannett Newspapers had been so successful in providing upward mobility opportunities for women and ethnic minorities. Her reply was that "The CEO (Allen Neuharth) made it happen." She went on to explain that Neuharth had made recruitment and promotion of all minorities an objective for all managers' performance reports. He tied bonuses and other rewards to success at this objective just as he did to more operationally oriented objectives. What got measured got done at Gannett.[5]

THE REBALANCING ACT

U.S.-based businesses operate within domestic and global environments. The complexities of these environments are enormous. The demands in various segments of these environments are often overwhelming. Business's first social responsibility is and must always be to make a profit. Beyond that effort lie many other equally important social responsibilities, and responsibilities of other sorts.

We propose that at a minimum a social responsibility performance perspective become part of the business scorecard. Some specific areas for which objectives should be set include the following:

- Satisfying all legal and ethical requirements for the conduct of the business, including

  1. Reporting performance results in an ethical and legal manner
  2. Ensuring responsible treatment of the external environment
  3. Providing equal opportunity employment
  4. Satisfying occupational health and safety requirements
  5. Meeting other relevant legal requirements

- Providing a climate supportive of diversity

- Providing financial performance information in a manner that is understandable and meaningful for the investor, and without any misleading approaches to accounting

- Committing to the communities within which the firms operate

- Committing support to nonprofit organizations

- Other local issues; for example, philanthropic actions

From Strategy and Responsibility to the Bottom Line

As with the traditional balanced scorecard, the rebalanced scorecard strategy execution and performance-management system would be concerned with parceling strategic objectives to each and every individual in the firm. Furthermore, each individual would have a set of social responsibility objectives that reflected an organization's performance commitment to society.

Additional Possible Perspectives

An additional perspective for a rebalanced scorecard is the Employee perspective. The balanced scorecard treats employees as an asset in the Growth and Learning perspective, but this new perspective would go past that level of thought and be concerned with the employee as a human being, not as an asset for manipulation. Considerations for objectives here might include employee satisfaction with leadership, employee experiences with equitable treatment, the impact of internal politics, and employee appraisal of their managers. We aren't the first to suggest that scorecards need rebalancing, but clearly now more than ever circumstances call for this action.

WHAT ARE CORPORATIONS CURRENTLY DOING TO INCLUDE SOCIAL RESPONSIBILITY ISSUES ON THEIR SCORECARD?

A review of the literature turned up one study that was reported in the past four years that related closely to the concerns expressed in this article. This study, by Best Practices LLC,[6] found that of 38 companies in their survey that used the balanced scorecard approach, most used only the four standard scorecard perspectives noted earlier, although several firms used an employee-oriented measurement area (for example, concern for employees or managing employees). None of these firms used a social responsibility perspective.[7] We then undertook two data-gathering efforts on our own. The first examined self-reported scorecard perspectives taken from articles written by authors from within scorecard participant companies over the past four years. Twenty companies were found and examined. The second was a combination telephone and email survey of 80 firms known to use the balanced scorecard. Twenty usable responses resulted. One company overlapped our study and the Best Practices study.

Taking our two groups of firms together for a total sample size of 40 firms, we found that

- 29 firms reported having Financial objectives
- 29 firms reported having Customer objectives
- 37 firms reported having Internal Business objectives
- 20 firms reported having Growth and Business objectives
- 15 firms reported having Responsibility to Employees objectives
- 4 reported having Responsibility to Society objectives
- 2 reported having Other types of objectives

Our research indicates that about 90 percent of the companies that use a scorecard approach for the execution of strategy do not use social responsibility measurements of any kind, and ethics in particular, as focal points of such efforts. This was a slight improvement over the research results uncovered by Best Practices LLC.

IMPLICATIONS AND CONCLUSIONS

The implications of this exploratory study have the potential to be substantial in helping explain why firms are not behaving in ways that are more beneficial to society. If what's measured is what gets done, and ethical behavior is not being measured, then we should not be surprised that ethical behavior is lacking. If it's not on someone's performance appraisal, he or she is not immediately motivated to perform such a task. Certainly, morality and values play major roles in influencing this process, but if a firm is not focused on, and is not holding its employees accountable for this desired behavior, then we can't expect employees to place as much emphasis on this behavior as they should. Notwithstanding the role that other social responsibility awareness and response programs might have – for example, training in ethics, diversity management, or environmental awareness – it is a question of focus, and the opportunity to execute what is being focused on.

All firms use some type of objective-setting system. The scorecard methodology is just one, but an ever more common one. If firms want to succeed in ethical and social performance, then these critical areas must be included in the process that links strategy to individual performance. Those who create and supervise the development and usage of performance management and strategy execution systems must be ever vigilant to ensure that what gets measured includes more than just financially oriented perspectives.

NOTES

1. Peter Thal Larsen and Christopher Grimes, "AOL's Admission Risks Further Lawsuits," *Financial Times* (October 25, 2002), p. 1.
2. Christopher Bowe, "Bristol-Myers to Restate $2bn in Sales," *Financial Times* (October 25, 2002), p. 15.
3. Dennis K. Berman and Rebecca Blumenstein, "Phone Numbers, Behind Lucent's Woes: All-Out Revenue Goal and Pressure to Meet It," *Wall Street Journal* (March 29, 2001), pp. A1, A8.
4. Robert S. Kaplan and David P. Norton, "The Balanced Scorecard – Measures That Drive Performance," *Harvard Business Review*, January–February 1992, 71–79.
5. Kathleen Black in an address to the Academy of Management at its annual meeting, Washington, DC, August 14, 1989.
6. Best Practices LLC, as reported at BenchmarkingReports.com 9/18/02 and 9/05/02. The study was actually performed in 1996.
7. Telephone call with consultant at Best Practices LLC, on September 30, 2003.

21

Stakeholder Capitalism

Will Hutton

Keynes famously called for the socialisation of investment at the end of his *General Theory*, and many critics of the British financial system have echoed that call. But the task is a more subtle one, if the object of the exercise is to keep the merits of private ownership while reshaping the way it works. Thus the great challenge of the twentieth century, after the experience of both state socialism and of unfettered free markets, is to create a new financial architecture in which private decisions produce a less degenerate capitalism. The triple requirement is to broaden the area of stake-holding in companies and institutions, so creating a greater bias to longterm commitment from owners; to extend the supply of cheap, longterm debt; and to decentralise decision-making. The financial system, in short, needs to be comprehensively republicanised.

The first breach would be made by establishing a republican-style central bank which understood that its role was to recast the financial system as a servant of business rather than as its master. Financial freedom would no longer be taken as axiomatically good but as a privilege which has to be earned, and which carries obligations. As matters stand the current Bank of England is a permanent obstacle to financial reform: a precondition for any wider reconstruction of the financial system is a transformation of its constitution, mission and values.

The Bank's structure would match the new federal structure of the state. As the country began to be organised politically around its constituent regions, nations and cities, there would be a framework of regional public banks reporting to the Central Bank, whose chief executives would be appointed by the elected parliaments of the appropriate region. They would sit on the governing board of the Bank, replacing the current Court (which is staffed by placemen of the rentier state) and deliberate over monetary policy and the wider reform of the financial system. The extent to which the Bank had the final word over interest rates or the extent to which it fell to the Chancellor of the Exchequer could be decided after the new arrangements had bedded down for at least one complete economic cycle and the character of the Bank became clearer. If it became a social partner in the republican sense, running monetary policy impartially with a democratic awareness of the trade-offs between lost output and lower inflation, the presumption would be that it would gain independence along US lines. With new constitutional arrangements there would, finally, be a way of ensuring its democratic accountability.

In its conduct of monetary policy the Bank would be armed with a more complete array of financial instruments than short-term interest rates. Instead of conceding the financial institutions' argument that their balance sheets are their own concern and that the only legitimate tool of policy is the price of money, the Bank would have the power to influence directly the structure and profitability of banking business in pursuit of its wider public objectives. It would, for example, reintroduce reserve requirements to support its interest rate policy, and it would follow the Bundesbank and the Federal Reserve by regulating the markets in a wider public interest than that defined by the markets themselves.

One of the Bank's chief preoccupations would be to lower the cost of capital in Britain – the combination of servicing of bank debt and share-holders' funds – and to lengthen the payback periods that companies set for their investment projects. This is the core of the British supply-side problem and the single most important explanation for indifferent levels of invest-ment. British companies need to borrow more long-term debt and lower their target rates of return from new investment. The Bank's objective, along with a reformed Treasury, must be to construct a financial system in which this can take place; the first time the British authorities will have played such a role since the Industrial Revolution.

In order for companies to borrow more, the banks have to lend funds that companies can afford to service. In the same way that purchasing a house on a three-year mortgage with a 20 per cent interest rate would mean that fewer houses would be bought, so very few companies can sustain high investment with three-year paybacks and 20 per cent nominal returns. The first task, then, is to change the conditions that give British clearing banks their short-term, anti-industrial lending policies.

But for the banks to lend longer term, they themselves need less demand-ing financial criteria because long-term loans are less profitable for them than short-term revolving credits. They need to have their own cost of capital lowered; they need access to long-term deposits; and they need better credit assessment techniques, with incentives to develop closer relationships with their industrial customers in order better to judge the viability of their invest-ment proposals.

Britain should copy other industrialised countries and create a public agency that will act as a financial intermediary collecting longer term deposits and channelling them to lending institutions. The Japanese use their post office network to collect long-term savings, and their great public invest-ment banks then lend directly or in partnership with Japan's commercial banks. The US has deployed their federal housing finance intermediaries, "Fannie Mae" (Federal National Mortgage Association) and "Freddie Mac" (Federal Home Loan Mortgage Corporation), to encourage direct and indi-rect long-term finance for home purchase and new home construction; while Germany has its *Kreditanstalt für Wiederaufbau* (the KfW or Bank for Reconstruction) which makes long-term loans in partnership with the commercial banks and a network of regional development banks. The UK has nothing.[1]

What it could have are regional banks collecting long-term deposits to recycle to clearing banks and other specialist lending institutions, like a housing bank to cater for housing associations, local authorities and the construction industry. A new benchmark for long-term bank lending would be established as more long-term bank loans were made. A specialist bank lending to small and medium-sized companies could support the same drive. In order to encourage long-term lending, the reformed Central Bank could offer assistance on favourable terms in the money markets to all longterm lenders – public and commercial banks alike. This would reassure them about the liquidity risk they were running.

But the banks are not charities and to entrench this new attitude the target rate of return on their own capital will have to be lowered. The Germans have two key mechanisms. First they exploit the stakeholder culture engendered by co-operative capitalism to lower the cost of capital for all enterprises, banks included. Shares are tokens of a long-term relationship rather than a trading asset, so that dividend payments can be lower and payback periods lengthened. Second, public banks at both state and regional level are constrained in their dividend distributions; profits build up as reserves and balance sheets are strengthened which gives a stable platform from which to lend long-term at keen rates of interest.

The combination is a potent one. Borrowers' loan packages, a mix of public and private loans, are cheaper because the private and public banks themselves need to earn lower financial returns. Nor do the commercial banks complain about this "subsidised" finance, as their counterparts in Britain might be expected to do. As they are themselves shareholders in the borrowing companies, they benefit from the impact that cheaper loan finance has on the borrowers' trading prospects.

To lower the cost of capital, British banks and their customers need more patient, committed shareholders and less of a hunger for dividends. The entire system could then move into a virtuous circle in which more long-term bank lending was validated by improved economic performance resulting from higher investment. Lowering the cost of capital would also allow the banks to invest more in internal systems for information gathering and credit assessment; these are expensive and time consuming, but would help the banks avoid the lending mistakes they made in the 1980s boom. If, at the same time, they could share in the success of the companies in which they invested the rewards for lending would be higher.

One immediate move would be to insist that banks take equity stakes in enterprises, and that banks which did not do so would rank lower in claims on firms' assets than stakeholding banks. The banks' legal capacity to take a "floating charge" on all of a company's assets should be abolished; this makes companies the prisoners of a single bank loan, prevents them from borrowing heavily to finance investment and encourages banks to look for property collateral to support their lending rather than offering finance for specific projects. It worsens the present disastrous arm's-length arrangements. A proper system of loan guarantees, run by a public institution, should be set up, allowing small firms in particular to borrow more aggressively. If these measures were combined with a legal requirement to regionalise the operations of the clearing banks, they would add up to a novel and important contribution to the creation of a British *Mittelstand* sector. Britain's small and medium-sized companies are damaged most by their inability to sustain high levels of long-term debt.

Perhaps, in the short run, bank dividends should be regulated and banks encouraged to build up cheaper internal reserves of capital. Banks will complain bitterly about any infringement of their "freedom", but since the state is required to bail them out if they get into financial difficulties and to carry the wider social costs of their anti-industrial lending policies, such an initiative would create a proper symmetry of obligations.

The most important factor in reducing the cost of capital for banks and business generally is shareholder commitment. This should be fostered by exploiting the proposed new system of corporate governance and the role of non-executive directors, for banks and business alike. Groups of core institutional shareholders might be formed who would be represented on company and bank boards by non-executive directors with their own, information-gathering secretariats. Voting rights might be limited only to those shareholders who are represented on company boards, thus legally linking ownership with obligations to commitment. It might even be useful to split the functions of the supervisory and executive boards, as in Germany, with representatives of the core voting shareholders joining the supervisory board. They would engage in an ongoing dialogue with management about business strategy, with share options and bonuses only exercisable after a specified minimum period – say ten years' service – and with tax incentives for those who exercised options later. The current incentives for paper entrepreneurship, unlocking so-called shareholder value by asset manipulation and so boosting executives' share options, would be reduced. There would be a penal short-term capital gains tax for shareholders who took early profits, tapering to near zero for long-term shareholders. This would encourage shareholders to value future returns more highly than they do and so help companies to extend their payback periods.

This would only work if takeovers were made harder to mount. The tightening of lax accounting standards, setting new upper limits for advisers' fees (in particular removing their tax-deductibility) and allowing firms a "public-interest" defence against hostile takeovers would all help. In addition the current obligation for any single shareholder to make a full bid if more than 30 per cent of the company is owned could be dropped. Large single shareholders can be sources of much needed stability. Although current doctrine is that effective stewardship of company assets requires the fear of takeover, this militates against the construction of long-term relationships within the company. Much of the so-called "shareholder value" that is "unlocked" by takeover amounts to no more than unravelling co-operative and committed relationships, which are priced above market-clearing levels, and reorganising them in a strictly price-mediated relationship. This lowers the company's variable costs which, taken together with the accountants' treatment of the financing costs of takeover, appears to make the acquisition profitable. But accounting fiddles are no route to industrial success, as Britain has discovered.

The approach to takeovers highlights another aspect of a properly constitutional democratic state – the role of audit. Without impartially prepared accounts that follow a transparent set of rules, the balance sheets and profits of firms are the playthings of private boards and their accountants. In their increasing anxiety to win business, accountants have been willing to bend accounting conventions to meet the short-term requirements of boards – so that accounts no longer offer a proper measure of company worth, failing to allow comparison of performance over time or with other firms. Corporate taxation becomes the quixotic result of whatever accounting standards are adopted, allowing boards in effect to choose their level of taxation. Audit needs to be regulated in the public interest, and auditors licensed like banks before they can go into business.

In the search for fees and commissions, investment and merchant banks have become ever more imaginative in their invention of financial assets that can be bought and sold, ranging from the sale of company bank debt to instruments that protect against future share price movements – with the Bank of England indulging the whole exercise as evidence of financial innovation. But this makes the system increasingly unstable, without increasing investment and innovation in the real economy. The system must be forced to exercise greater prudence and the financial institutions' balance sheets must be more strictly monitored. A balance needs to be struck between market contracts that protect against risk, and marketisation that destabilises long-term relationships between finance and industry.

The emergence of giant financial institutions, in particular pension funds, and their growing desire to hold company equity, paying dividends, has been one of the biggest motors of short-termism. Government and company bonds, of course, pay fixed rates of interest. Equity has offered a measure of protection against inflation, with profits and dividends tending to rise at least in line with inflation; but it has also been attractive because dividends have risen significantly in real term. As a result pension funds hold 85 per cent of their assets in company shares, bringing their total holdings of shares of 40 per cent of the value quoted on the London Stock Exchange.

Dividends are meant to fluctuate with profits but pension funds, with their long-term liabilities to their pensioners, cannot afford such fluctuation. For them, dividends need to be as secure as fixed-interest investments with the extra bonus that they always rise – and companies are now yoked to this demand from their principal shareholders with all the adverse consequences. Pension funds and insurance companies have become classic absentee landlords, exerting power without responsibility and making exacting demands upon companies without recognising their reciprocal obligation as owners.

Some funds have begun to exercise responsibilities, questioning some of the more outrageous executive pay deals, but typically the British savings institution is a supine accomplice of the board – happy to go along with corporate strategy as long as the financial returns are high. Their power to affect the course of whole industries is extraordinary. For example, Mercury Asset Management, one of the largest City investment managers, settled the fate of London Weekend Television in its fight for independence from Granada and so set in train the spate of takeovers and mergers in the independent TV sector. Should one person in one investment management group have such power? Should the sole criterion for such decisions be the maximisation of short-term value for the funds which he or she manages? Although the funds will resist the limitations on their freedom that new proposals on takeovers and their participation in corporate governance would imply, in fact they need to be relieved of such awesome responsibilities – or at least be forced to treat them as would properly informed shareholders rather than institutional rentiers.

However, the power of pension funds and institutional saving has not grown in a vacuum; it is the direct consequence, as we have seen, of the explosion of home-ownership and the private provision for old age, with the state progressively abdicating its responsibilities in the name of "choice" and "self-reliance". Pension fund contributions, the underlying fund and the final payment are all free of tax. The private has been privileged at least in part because of Britain's weaknesses in providing a solid state pension. That would demand a binding contract between the generations, but in Britain such contracts are expressed through Parliament whose guiding principle is that it cannot bind successors – a principle faithfully followed when the Conservatives carelessly debauched the SERPS scheme. Any inter-generational contract cannot be trusted – and the same is true for the provision of social housing.

As a result people have exploited tax privileges and protected themselves with private and occupational pensions, while even those for whom home-ownership is unsuitable have been forced to join the stampede into owner occupation, increasingly financed with an endowment insurance policy to pay off the mortgage. The consequence has been a flood of institutional savings, an acute demand for dividends and the foreshortening of investment time-horizons. These savings, if the wider financial system had been reformed to accommodate their new power and demands, could have been and still can be a fruitful source of finance for investment. Instead they have become destabilising.

NOTE

1. Only the Agricultural Mortgage Corporation continues to play a public part, albeit small.

The State of Denial We're In

The Economist

TEN YEARS ON, WILL HUTTON IS STANDING BY HIS BESTSELLING CRITIQUE OF BRITISH CAPITALISM

"Did I get it wrong?" It takes a brave pundit to ask that question. So Will Hutton deserves credit for challenging himself and readers of his column in *The Observer* newspaper on January 9th to re-examine his bestselling critique of British capitalism, and try to decide whether it has stood the test of time. Much has changed, in Britain and elsewhere, since *The State We're In* was published in January 1995 – and much of the change has been different from what Mr Hutton expected. Yet after (no doubt) many long hours of soul-searching, Mr Hutton has found that he is as convinced as ever of his "core analysis".

In essence, this analysis was that the increasingly market-oriented British model of capitalism was in trouble. It needed to be reformed in ways that, taking the best bits from the alternative models of capitalism, would reduce the power of short-termist shareholders and strengthen that of other "stakeholders" in companies, including workers and the state.

In 1995, British voters were preparing to bring to an end nearly two decades of Conservative Party rule. Their faith in the party's economic competence had been shattered by a deep recession, a series of corporate scandals and Britain's forced exit from Europe's exchange-rate mechanism, a forerunner of the euro. Mr Hutton's book caught the mood perfectly, especially among educated metropolitan sorts who had long hated the free-market rhetoric and reforms of the Thatcher and Major governments. Even the then opposition leader, Tony Blair, was impressed by the book – albeit only, as Mr Hutton notes ruefully, "for 10 days" after giving a speech based on it. Mr Hutton, in his own words, "changed from being another economics writer to someone the *Daily Telegraph* described as the most dangerous man in Britain". He profited, not just from huge book sales, but also by becoming (for four years) editor of *The Observer*.

In the event, the past ten years have been the best decade for British capitalism since (at least) the 1950s, when Harold Macmillan, the then prime minister, famously declared that the British had "never had it so good". GDP has grown each year, unemployment and inflation have been consistently low, incomes have risen – even at the bottom. And whereas in 1995 it was hard to think of one big British firm that was truly world class, today Vodafone, Tesco and BP lead a long and growing list.

The success of British capitalism is all the more striking when you consider the fate of the rival models of capitalism to which Mr Hutton unfavourably compared it. Japan was on course to become the world's biggest economy in 2005, he argued, thanks to its model based on the long-term co-operative relationships between its firms, banks, customers and workers, as well as the leadership given to business by the government. Alas, the Japanese economy has stagnated for most of the past decade. The state's role in the economy has come to be seen as largely negative. The *keiretsu* families of firms that tied together banks, firms and suppliers are loosening. Lifetime employment guarantees are disappearing. Above all, Japan's banking system – which Mr Hutton enthused about as he bashed British banks – has in effect gone bust and become a huge drag on business.

MODEL MISBEHAVIOUR

Mr Hutton was equally keen on Germany's consensus-based model of capitalism, with its long-term-focused banks and representation for workers on company boards. Germany's economy, too, has struggled ever since. Its banks are troubled, though not as much as Japan's, and are reducing their shareholdings in corporate Germany. The consensus between German bosses and workers is fast breaking down, as the bosses increasingly envy the freedom to manage enjoyed by their British counterparts.

Although it shares many of the short-termist stockmarket features of British capitalism, Mr Hutton was also more impressed by America's model of capitalism. Yet while the American economy has done even better than Britain's during the past decade, it has done so while exhibiting even more extreme short-termist behaviour than Britain's. This was exemplified by the stockmarket bubble – far bigger in America than elsewhere – and its aftermath. The short-termism of America and Britain may not actually be a good thing – Mr Hutton was right, and ahead of the game, to argue for better auditing and for institutional investors such as pension funds to devote more effort to corporate governance. But America's and Britain's relative success may indicate that financial short-termism is, on balance, less of a liability than a form of capitalism that is inflexible when faced with economic change (such as Germany's and Japan's), whether because of government rules or private arrangements.

Mr Hutton attributes the surprising (to him) success of British capitalism to two main factors. First, the efforts of the Labour government since 1997 to ease social tensions that might otherwise have impeded economic progress. This was surely never as big a risk as he feared. Second, that globalisation offered many parts of the British economy (notably in the service sector) opportunities that "could not be seen in 1994". Well, maybe. But it seems odd of Mr Hutton to gloss over the fact that positioning Britain to benefit from globalisation was an explicit goal of those he criticised in *The State We're In*: advocates of the market-based reforms initiated by the Conservatives and (later) maintained, despite Mr Hutton's urgings, by Labour.

Will the British and American models of capitalism continue to outperform their German and Japanese counterparts in the coming decade? Will a new model triumph: Chinese capitalism, perhaps? What reforms to different models of capitalism might alter the outcome? While sticking to his core analysis, Mr Hutton has come to realise that "modern capitalism is an ever moving target: trying to understand it, and then making a compelling case for reform, is bloody difficult." Quite so.

22

Controversy Incorporated

David Cogman and Jeremy M. Oppenheim

Milton Friedman once famously said that "the business of business is business."[1] Today, however, the search for growth increasingly takes companies into controversial areas in which the rules of the game can't be stated so neatly. Companies developing new high-growth opportunities in fields from technology to education to economic development must often navigate highly public ethical and social concerns and overcome restraints far more subtle than those encountered in standard business practice or law. Increasing numbers of large corporations thus find themselves caught between two seemingly contradictory goals: satisfying the investor's expectations for progressive earnings growth and the consumer's growing demand for social responsibility.

Companies have become more socially responsible primarily because apparent irresponsibility can carry a high price (see Box 22.1). Although many companies now spend significant sums of money to comply with their own codes of ethical conduct, most view these expenditures only as an essential cost of doing business, not as an investment that will provide a return. For some of these companies, however, this spending may well be a source of growth, since many of today's most exciting opportunities lie in controversial areas such as gene therapy, the private provision of pensions, and products and services targeted at low-income consumers in poor countries. These opportunities are large and mostly untapped, and many companies want to open them up. But people are often suspicious of any private-sector interest in contentious areas of this kind, and public debate rages over how they should be developed, if at all.

Corporations have to be recognized as socially responsible simply to gain access to these debates. To influence the outcome, however, it will be necessary to do more than just check boxes on a corporate-responsibility scorecard; unless companies can understand, engage with, and respond to the interests of all parties that have an interest in a contentious business opportunity, they are unlikely to win a society's permission to explore it. Without that permission, they will never convert the opportunity into a sustainable and profitable market.

> **Box 22.1   A force to be reckoned with**
>
> Two decades ago, the activists who demanded that companies practice a higher standard of social responsibility were scattered throughout a disparate collection of organizations, each focused, for the most part, on a single issue. No longer. Today's lobbyists are a well-coordinated and effective force. And they have teeth. In a recent poll of about 25,000 people in 23 countries, 60 percent of the respondents said they judged a company on its social record, 40 percent took a negative view of companies they felt were not socially responsible, and 90 percent wanted companies to focus on more than just profitability.[1]
>
> Meanwhile, the activist lobby has learned how to form unlikely alliances across the political spectrum – with people ranging from conservative protectionists to Left-wing trade unionists – and to mobilize public opinion on emotional issues through the skillful use of the mass media. Many multinational companies have learned from experience how effective these tactics can be. In particular, extractive industries such as petroleum have come under relentless pressure from environmental activists: Shell lost considerable market share in Germany in 1995 after activists persuaded consumers that its proposed disposal of the Brent Spar oil platform, in the North Sea, would harm the environment. Even though the UK government and independent scientists had endorsed the company's proposal as the one that would cause the least damage, motorists boycotted Shell's service stations, and some were vandalized by activists.
>
> These days, moreover, it isn't just consumers who are clamoring for change; shareholders too are making their voices heard. Prominent pension funds have begun to question companies on social issues, and socially responsible investing, though still a relatively small-scale phenomenon, is growing rapidly. In the United States, the assets of what are called ethical funds grew from $682 billion in 1995 to $2.16 trillion in 1999, and they now make up approximately 13 percent of investments under management in the United States, which is up from 9 percent in 1997. It is no wonder that so many corporations are beginning to take their social responsibilities seriously.
>
> 1.   From the 1999 Millennium Poll, conducted by Environics, the Prince of Wales International Business Leaders Forum, and The Conference Board.

CONTENTIOUS ATTRACTIONS

Ethical considerations might appear to clash with emerging business opportunities primarily in four areas: the exploitation of new technologies, the movement of activities from the public to the private sector, entry into the

Table 22.1 Where principles and profits clash

Estimated size of selected contentious markets, 2001

		United States		India[1]	
Area	Activities	Annual value, $ billion	Share of GDP, percent	Annual value, $ billion	Share of GDP, percent
Exploiting new technologies	Biotechnology (addressable markets)				
	• Human therapeutics	115	1	5	1
	• Agricultural products	30	0	1	0
Moving from public to private sector	Primary/secondary education	369	4	6	1
	Tertiary education	164	2	7	2
	Publicly funded health care	603	6	4	1
	Infrastructure	395	4	33	7
	Social insurance[2]	722	7	2	0
Entering developing markets[3]	Production outsourcing	93	1	0	0
	Exports to developing countries	206	2	13	3
	Imports from developing countries	295	3	14	3
Exploring legally contestable markets	Gambling	64[4]	1	N/A[5]	N/A[5]

[1] Calculated using 2001 GDP at average 2001 exchange rate
[2] Includes all government outlays on income security programs, other social security programs, and veterans' benefits and services
[3] US figures calculated using average percentage of GDP by activity, 1993–97 (inflated to 2001 GDP)
[4] Contains some revenues from nongambling amusement businesses
[5] Gambling is illegal in India
Source: ABN AMRO; Ninth Five-Year Plan. Ministry of Finance, Government of India; *Statistical Abstract of the United States, 2000*. US Census Bureau, US Agency for international Development (USAID); World Bank

world's developing markets, and the exploration of such legally contestable markets as gambling (Table 22.1).

Exploiting New Technologies

In recent decades, promising new developments, notably in biotechnology and information technology, have frequently been accompanied by debates about ethics. Take biotechnology: R&D into human therapies based on it is growing almost twice as quickly as R&D into conventional pharmaceuticals

– and leading to 40 percent of all new products. By the end of this decade, biotechnology is expected to generate revenues of around $34 billion (equivalent to 15 percent of today's total drug market) from health care and $25 billion from agrochemicals. And though existing biotechnology applications can compete for only 2 percent of today's $1.2 trillion market in industrial chemicals, this proportion is projected to rise to almost a third by the end of the decade, when the total market will be worth an estimated $1.6 trillion.

Yet there is concern about the moral legitimacy of the genetic research on which biotechnology depends. Consider the case of deCODE Genetics, a company in Iceland that has used a genealogical database of the country's population – one of the world's most genetically homogeneous – to conduct research into the inherited causes of common diseases. So far, the company has found links between at least 40 of them and 350 genes. The legislation that gave deCODE access to this data required Icelanders to opt out if they didn't want their records examined. Critics of the study claimed that this legislation violated the human rights of the Icelanders, especially since it didn't require the company to tell participants exactly how the data would be used. Ignoring such concerns may not only lead to further argument but also limit the ability of biotech companies to carry out valuable and much-needed research.

Moving from the Public to the Private Sector

Governments the world over increasingly use private-sector companies to provide public services such as education, health care, pensions, and transport. While this approach may improve efficiency and raise standards of service, it also generates criticism of the profits that private providers can earn, particularly for services, such as welfare benefits and housing, that affect the poorer segments of society.

Public education in the United States provides an example. The country spends more than $350 billion of public funds on primary and secondary education, which is widely thought to have fallen behind public education in other developed countries. Privatizing the provision of education is a possible solution. At present, only 4 percent of the spending goes to schools run for profit by private companies, but that proportion is expected to grow by 13 percent a year. At the end of the present decade, around 10 percent of all primary and secondary schools will probably be under for-profit management, suggesting a market worth almost $80 billion.

Nonetheless, the battle for privatized education run by companies seeking to make a profit is far from won. Business executives attempting to enter the debate – such as venture capitalist John Doerr and the convicted financier-turned-philanthropist Michael Milken – have met with suspicion and, often, outright hostility. Companies operating in this field face a continual battle to prove to skeptical teachers, parents, and administrators that a for-profit company can and will act in the best interest of students. This skepticism won't go away overnight.

Entering Developing Markets

Developing countries offer attractive opportunities both as markets and as sources of raw materials and productive capacity. But interest groups frequently criticize corporations active in these regions for failing to meet the environmental, labor, competitive, and marketing standards required of them at home.

Take health care in India, which illustrates both the scale of the opportunities in the emerging world and the ethical quandaries that accompany them. India's population will surpass China's in the near future. Even now, India is a popular location for the manufacture of drugs used in developed markets, but the country itself has health care expenditures of only $23 a head, of which $7 goes to drugs. The United States, the members of the European Union, and Japan spend, on average, more than 100 times that amount on health care per capita, and 50 times more on drugs.

The common causes of death in India – such as infection and perinatal problems – can be treated easily and cheaply. But most people there are so poor that it is difficult for companies to ask them to pay for medical help without seeming exploitative. Since 1991, the World Bank has supported projects in six Indian states to improve access to better health care, especially for the poor, in part by helping state-run health care providers outsource more of their services to the private sector. But this approach has attracted criticism from local activists opposed to the idea that local people should have to pay anything at all for health care.[2]

Exploring Legally Contestable Markets

Social norms define what each society considers legal, but they can change quickly: activities that once were against the law – such as euthanasia and the possession of cannabis (marijuana) – are now accepted in several European states. Black markets in illegal activities are often sizable, so sudden changes in the law can create substantial legitimate markets overnight. A black market in human trafficking, for example, has been created by tough immigration restrictions in Europe, but as its need for labor increases, they may be relaxed, thus opening up an opportunity for legitimate organizations seeking to place human resources.

Similarly, gambling, viewed in some times and places as a source of corruption, is increasingly seen as a legitimate form of entertainment; indeed, in several unlikely localities, including conservative states in the southern United States, it has proved to be an effective source of jobs and tax revenue.

As gambling has become more respectable, large corporations, including several household names, have entered the business. During the 1990s, the industry more than doubled in size, and it is currently worth more than $60 billion.

EARNING THE RIGHT TO OPERATE PROFITABLY

Not all companies will want to commercialize contentious activities. But those that do need, first, to persuade everyone involved that a private company has the moral right to undertake the activity in question and, second, to establish a profit norm acceptable to all stakeholders, including investors. Winning both battles can be difficult, and companies will have to adopt different tactics for each activity and geographical market. Yet some common principles can help those companies engage sensitively and proactively in such debates.

Take a Long-Term View of Market Design

Economic theory declares that a well-functioning market respects the property rights of its participants, matches consumers with producers at efficient prices, minimizes transaction costs, and ensures that contracts are enforced. In most private-sector markets – for instance, those for cement and crude oil – well-established laws, regulations, and practices ensure these conditions. But in contentious markets, such as the one for gene therapy, some or all of this infrastructure doesn't exist, so it must be developed by participants and regulators.[3]

Private companies entering these markets therefore need to decide how they should be structured. How will value be created? How will it be shared? How will risks be allocated? What regulatory or contractual rules must be put in place? Companies may naturally be tempted to lobby for a structure – opaque, with limited price discovery, high barriers to entry, and an inefficient allocation of risk – that favors their interests over those of other participants. Would that approach serve a company's best long-term interests? Probably not; over time, its inherent unfairness would most likely prompt governments and activists to intervene. Greedy participants may risk losing markets altogether.

Consider the contrast between the privatized markets for energy and rail transport in the United Kingdom. In the decade following the privatization of electricity supply, a substantial fall in the unit cost of energy benefited both consumers and producers. In part, this achievement was the result of a thoughtful market design, which separated supply and distribution through a pooling system, and of a strong regulatory framework. Together, these arrangements managed supply and demand efficiently over the medium term.

Compare that positive experience with the fate of the United Kingdom's privatized rail industry, in which relationships among stakeholders were structured poorly. The result was a public outcry over the declining standard of service and a widespread perception in the mass media that some of the new rail enterprises were extracting "excessive" profits. Safety problems and cost overruns attracted a storm of negative publicity; amid battles with regulators and politicians, the infrastructure company, Railtrack, went into bankruptcy and was returned to government control. Had the market structure been more carefully designed at the outset, the cost of Railtrack's collapse might have been avoided, and British consumers might now be enjoying a higher standard of rail travel.

Learn to Work With – Not Around – Stakeholders

To propose an acceptable structure for any market, companies must understand the needs of its other participants, some of whom may distrust the private sector profoundly. In these circumstances, companies often try to neutralize their opponents with gifts and grand gestures, which can appear to be cynical and often backfire. The winning way may be counterintuitive: view the opposition not as a threat but as a source of information about the other market participants' needs and concerns. With that information in hand, companies can develop business models that address them.

One example is Cargill's initial entry into the market for sunflower seeds in India. Starting in the early 1990s, this activity generated bitter political opposition, and Cargill offices in that country were set on fire twice. The company's response was to teach Indian farmers how to improve their crop yields. As a result, the productivity of the local farmers increased by more than 50 percent. Once Cargill had provided them with a palpable economic benefit, they understood that the company aspired to be their partner rather than their exploiter.[4]

This collaborative strategy stands in stark contrast to Monsanto's effort to create markets for genetically modified seeds. The company was bitterly opposed by farmers in developing countries who feared becoming dependent on a single supplier of expensive seed. Instead of accommodating these concerns, Monsanto responded with an effort to publicize scientific evidence about the benefits of genetically modified seeds, but few of the farmers believed that the scientists supporting the company's claims were truly independent. Arguably, Monsanto lost the opportunity by pressing its claim too hard, too soon. Buffeted by a steady backlash in developing and developed markets alike, the company lost almost half of its market capitalization in the year to September 1999, and a few months later it was acquired.

Understand Your Social Assets

If large numbers of people are convinced that a company's core operations harm society, changing that negative perception by spending more money on corporate-responsibility programs can be an uphill struggle. However, many companies – even those with flawed reputations – already contribute a great deal to society through their day-to-day activities; they just don't get any credit. Identifying and publicizing these inherent social assets could help such companies build trust among stakeholders.

Take McDonald's. Although the company makes large, well-publicized social investments in fields as diverse as animal welfare, conservation, education, and health care, it is still, to its critics, the archetype of global corporate exploitation. Yet McDonald's is also a company that introduces many young people to new skills and gives them the first job of their careers. It could claim that as one of the world's largest employers of unskilled youth, it contributes enormous social value just by doing business as usual. If this value were more widely appreciated, it might even help McDonald's enter markets more controversial than fast food.

Other companies also have largely untapped social assets. Although (or perhaps because) the oil majors are the number-one enemy of environmental groups such as Greenpeace, these companies now have unrivaled expertise in minimizing the ecological impact of industrial operations. This asset is evidence of responsible commerce that can also help a company decide which markets to enter. Opponents of moves to legalize cannabis, for example, fear that the tobacco giants would ruthlessly exploit the opportunity to sell it over the counter. This may be a battle the tobacco companies can never win, however. A more likely candidate to distribute the drug, if and when it becomes legal, could be suppliers of over-the-counter pharmaceuticals, whose business already depends on a guaranteed commitment to responsible health care.

Rethink Leadership and Governance

Forward-looking companies, sensitive to the new ground rules of controversial business areas, are opening up to – rather than fighting – their opponents. Corporations, such as those in oil and pharmaceuticals, that have years of experience collaborating with governments have a head start in training employees to work in contentious areas: these companies also regularly expose managers to a range of critical opinion by assigning them to work with nongovernmental organizations and by taking part in conferences.

In some cases, such companies even seek out critics to learn from them: the leading UK environmental activist Jonathon Porritt, for instance, speaks at and advises on training programs for BP executives. Indeed, such relationships can even work in both directions, for BP's chief executive serves on the board of Conservation International, a global conservation group. This kind of "cross-pollination" not only gives companies insights into the concerns of the not-for-profit sector but also gives not-for-profits accurate information about the companies they deal with. The free exchange of information makes the two sides better able to reach acceptable compromises on questions such as the way the oil majors might exploit reserves in virgin territory.

Finally, to involve consumers and communities, ventures in contentious markets usually require governance structures independent of the corporate parents.[5] Bolder companies may even experiment with new forms of governance that try to combine the strengths of the corporation with the social awareness of the not-for-profits – an approach that has already been used by a growing number of community-development financial institutions providing capital to businesses in disadvantaged areas that conventional banks can't or won't serve.[6] One example is Bridges Community Ventures, a UK venture fund founded by the venture capital firms Apax and 3i and by entrepreneur Tom Singh and financed by leading private-sector investors and the UK government. Bridges is a for-profit entity but invests solely in underdeveloped areas in England to stimulate growth and create jobs.

Companies willing and able to address the social concerns surrounding contentious markets will find that, in many cases, the rewards are more than worthwhile. Moreover, the participation of companies that know how to tackle such issues sensitively and effectively should improve the chances of addressing some of the world's most intractable problems. And it is increasingly difficult to imagine how such complex, large-scale tasks can be taken on without the private sector's involvement.

NOTES

1. Milton Friedman, "The social responsibility of business is to increase its profits," *New York Times Magazine*, September 13, 1970.
2. See the World Wide Web sites of Global Action, Corpwatch, and the World Bank.
3. For an analysis of the problems of market design, see John McMillan, *Reinventing the Bazaar: The Natural History of Markets*, New York: Norton, 2002.
4. For an account of these developments, see Stuart L. Hart and C. K. Prahalad, *Strategies for the Bottom of the Pyramid: Creating Sustainable Development*, July 2000.
5. See Rajat Dhawan, Chris Dorian, Rajat Gupta, and Sasi K. Sunkara, "Connecting the unconnected," *The McKinsey Quarterly*, 2001 Number 4 special edition: Emerging markets, pp. 61–70; and Amie Batson and Matthias M. Bekier, "Vaccines where they're needed," *The McKinsey Quarterly*, 2001 Number 4 special edition: Emerging markets, pp. 103–12.
6. For more details, see the UK Social Investment Forum report *Community Development Finance Institutions: A New Financial Instrument for Social, Economic, and Physical Renewal*, February 2002.

An Interview with Microsoft's CFO

Bertil E. Chappuis and Timothy M. Koller

When Microsoft announced, in July 2004, that it would tap its legendary cash reserves to return some $60 billion to shareholders, analysts immediately began scrambling to understand what the move might say about the software giant's strategy, its growth prospects, and the maturation of the entire high-technology sector.

For John Connors, Microsoft's chief financial officer, however, the decision to pay a onetime special dividend amounting to about $30 billion and to buy back as much as $30 billion of the company's own shares over the next four years was merely the latest in a series of financial moves that have positioned it at the cutting edge of financial innovation in the high-tech industry. In 2002 Connors helped reconfigure Microsoft's financial-reporting processes around seven clearly defined business units, each with its own CFO and profit-and-loss statement, to offer investors a greater degree of organizational stability and transparency. The following year, the company surprised many people by announcing that it would stop compensating employees with stock options and would instead issue stock awards.

Connors believes that this combination of initiatives has helped build a stronger value culture at Microsoft while permitting management to focus on performance in the company's increasingly diverse business lines. In an interview at Microsoft's headquarters, in Redmond, Washington, he talked with McKinsey's Bertil Chappuis and Tim Koller about the thinking behind Microsoft's finance moves, the company's plans for growth, and the role of finance in the next era at Microsoft.

The Quarterly: The first dividends for Microsoft come out in December. What was the strategic rationale for how much cash Microsoft holds onto, disburses in dividends, and applies to share buybacks?

John Connors: The first thing was to keep enough cash on hand to give us flexibility to manage things like a severe short-term economic dislocation or investment opportunities. We haven't publicly said how much cash that will be, but it's probably fair to assume that, after the upcoming distribution, we will still have around $25 billion to $40 billion on hand.

Even holding that much back, we still have a lot of money to distribute. We also had a number of constituencies pushing us to do different things with it: growth investors wanted a very large-scale buyback; income-oriented investors were clamoring for an increase in the regular dividend; and some investors just wanted all the money back so that they could decide what to do with it. Of course, we also had our employees, who now have stock awards as well as options from our legacy program.

We concluded we had enough cash to do something substantial on all fronts, but we decided against a huge buyback. Not only would that have disappointed the investors who simply wanted the cash but it would also have been a monumental undertaking. Our analysis also showed that if we had committed ourselves to a $60 billion share buyback, we could have ended up purchasing 5 to 8 percent of our stock every day that the Nasdaq allows us to buy our own shares for the next three years, and some of that inevitably would have been uneconomic. So we decided to take that $60 billion and use roughly half of it for a special onetime dividend, with the rest committed to a multiyear buyback. That's a pretty significant percentage of the enterprise value, and a fairly decent percentage of the shares.

We believe that this strategy will reward all of our investors. It will also increase growth in profits and cash flow, which are what drive our valuation and our return to shareholders.

The Quarterly: Any rules of thumb about how much cash companies need to remain flexible?

John Connors: We have a relatively unique model, in that our business is not capital-intensive. What drove our approach is that Bill [Gates] and Steve [Ballmer] and the board are pretty conservative. We don't want to be in the position where we have to make decisions because of the balance sheet. And while we don't anticipate that we would ever have a year with expenses but no revenue, we'll probably keep at least one year of operating expenses and cost of goods sold in cash on hand – that's around $20 billion in cash and short-term investments.

We also want to have enough for acquisitions. We have made a series of acquisitions, some of them for cash. And while most of them have been fairly small, we also want to be able to make some game-changing investments if we so choose. Any large acquisition would likely be a combination of cash and equity.

The Quarterly: The high-tech industry is seriously underleveraged. Are we seeing the beginning of a fundamental change in capital structure? Do you think the industry will take on more debt over the next couple of years in order to increase returns on equity?

John Connors: I don't think we have seen any large-scale move in that direction yet, primarily because tech companies still have high P/Es relative to most other industries. The growth rate assumption priced into tech companies' stock is that tech will continue to grow faster than other industries, although the differences in growth assumptions between tech and other industries have begun to narrow.

The real question would be whether the market starts assessing technology companies the way it measures companies in other industries. For startups, the last thing in the world a company like Google is worried about right

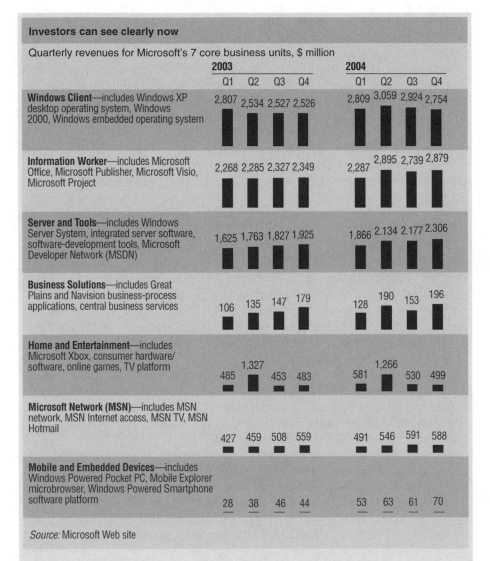

Investors can see clearly now

Quarterly revenues for Microsoft's 7 core business units, $ million

	2003				2004			
	Q1	Q2	Q3	Q4	Q1	Q2	Q3	Q4
Windows Client—includes Windows XP desktop operating system, Windows 2000, Windows embedded operating system	2,807	2,534	2,527	2,526	2,809	3,059	2,924	2,754
Information Worker—includes Microsoft Office, Microsoft Publisher, Microsoft Visio, Microsoft Project	2,268	2,285	2,327	2,349	2,287	2,895	2,739	2,879
Server and Tools—includes Windows Server System, integrated server software, software-development tools, Microsoft Developer Network (MSDN)	1,625	1,763	1,827	1,925	1,866	2.134	2.177	2.306
Business Solutions—includes Great Plains and Navision business-process applications, central business services	106	135	147	179	128	190	153	196
Home and Entertainment—includes Microsoft Xbox, consumer hardware/ software, online games, TV platform	485	1,327	453	483	581	1,266	530	499
Microsoft Network (MSN)—includes MSN network, MSN Internet access, MSN TV, MSN Hotmail	427	459	508	559	491	546	591	588
Mobile and Embedded Devices—includes Windows Powered Pocket PC, Mobile Explorer microbrowser, Windows Powered Smartphone software platform	28	38	46	44	53	63	61	70

Source: Microsoft Web site

now is whether or not it should have debt. While there will continue to be great start-up home runs, I don't see why the Wall Street analysis of midsize and large tech companies would be different from that of companies in other industries five or ten years from now. So if the market starts to measure technology in terms of returns on equity, capital, and assets, you will probably see more financial engineering of technology companies to bring them in line with companies in other industries.

The Quarterly: It has been a couple of years since Microsoft reorganized its financial reporting along business-unit lines. What has the impact been and has it lived up to expectations?

John Connors: One of the most positive outcomes is the transparency the reorganization created. Prior to 2000, Microsoft was viewed largely as a two-product company or a desktop company with phenomenal success in Windows and Office. But in the mid-1990s, we had expanded into gaming and mobile devices and into business applications for small to midsize companies. By 2001 people were not really certain which businesses we were involved in. Today the outside world can easily see Microsoft's business units and how well they are doing against their competitors. Now investors can answer the following questions every quarter: How is our Home and Entertainment Division competing against Sony? MSN against Yahoo! and Google? Our server and tools business against IBM and Oracle? How are we competing with Nokia in mobile devices? Investors can also easily track the performance of Windows and Office as well as the company's growth beyond those two products.

The P&L focus also forced some improvements in resource allocation. One of the big challenges we faced in 2001 was that, because of the company's orientation toward long-term investment, our research and development efforts had created a broad range of new products that often outpaced our capacity to sell and support them. Complicated products like the BizTalk server created a great opportunity to automate many business processes, but in order for our customers to earn the best returns on the purchase of our products they also needed specialist salespeople who understood the supply chain, data warehouses, and financial flows. In some rapidly growing categories, we also lacked a coherent worldwide brand proposition for certain unique products, compared with our brand proposition for the company as a whole. In the end, we had to decide what areas required continued investment – and what areas did not.

As the bubble collapsed and technology spending slowed, it became very clear that we could not continue to invest at the same levels. Today we all know how much money we have to invest, and we all have to agree on how much will go into R&D, sales, marketing, and tactical initiatives.

The restructuring also forced a degree of organizational stability and continuity. Historically, Microsoft had a major reorganization once a year that coincided with our budgeting in the spring. This process worked very well when we were smaller, had fewer units in fewer geographies, and weren't invested in so many segments. But as the company got larger and more complicated, we heard from customers and partners that Microsoft was hard to keep track of. So once we organized around these seven business groups and reported along those lines, customers and partners believed we were serious about them.

The Quarterly: Did anything about the move surprise you?

John Connors: It was surprising how many people within the company didn't really understand how intensely analysts, investors, and the press would follow each of these seven businesses. A lot of our businesses had flown under the radar, and while we would talk about their long-term opportunities in a way that investors appreciated, after a while they also wanted to see how those investments were performing. Now there's a quarterly score-card that reports – both relatively and absolutely – how we are doing.

Second, it was surprising how difficult it was to synchronize what we called the "rhythm of the business" between our field organization and the business groups. Traditionally, our field, or geographic, organizations could move both people and marketing around to take advantage of opportunities and to adjust to changing market conditions. While the P&Ls of our field organizations still matter today, and they still have a revenue quota, the busi-ness groups now have the ultimate financial accountability and make the final resource allocation decisions. The field is secondary in authority. That was a big shift, and if you look at companies that have had collapses in financial performance, it often has to do with the shifting of financial reporting from product to geography or vice versa. So we took a relatively measured step over a two-year period.

The Quarterly: What about the impact of the restructuring on the finance function specifically?

John Connors: It has allowed us to push much harder on performance because the finance folks in those groups report solid line into the business, dotted line back to the finance function in the center of the company. And it's much easier now for the center of the company to push on financial performance.

It's also helpful that this model can easily accommodate growth. When we want to do a deal, it's very clear that the CFO and the business-unit leader are on point for that deal. If we want to add new businesses, we have a model that will scale.

Last, the restructuring has allowed us to talk about the role of finance in the next generation of Microsoft, which is quite different from its traditional role.

The Quarterly: How will finance at Microsoft differ in the next generation?

John Connors: When we restructured, we decided very early on to designate as CFO the lead finance person in each of our seven businesses. This model is fundamentally different from the one Microsoft had in the past.

Historically, the top position outside the center of the company was a con-troller, whose role was to control and measure. But today the finance func-tion must do more. For example, if you look at the incredible diversity of the company now – the number of businesses, the different models, and the economics of some of the new businesses – Microsoft today requires much stronger strategy and business-development functions. Business units like MSN and Home and Entertainment are entering into multibillion-dollar con-tracts and alliances over long periods of time. Our mobile-devices business requires a very different alliance model with handset carriers and telecom operators than any we have had. Add the requirements of the Sarbanes-Oxley legislation and you find that the control and risk-modeling function has to be at a much higher level than it was three or four years ago.

In practical terms, that means we have a greater number of senior business leaders in finance than we had prior to 2002. Of 125 corporate vice presidents, for example, 9 are now from finance, whereas before there would have been 2 or 3. And corporate-finance leaders at that level also have different requirements: they have to be able to nurture other great business leaders, who then move into marketing, services, and sales, and they have to be articulate spokespeople for the company at technology conferences and industry events.

The Quarterly: What's the most value-added role a CFO can play in a high-tech company?

John Connors: We are in an era today when technology isn't really different from any other industry. In the 1990s it was just growing a heck of a lot faster than GDP. In the late 1990s the dot-com and telecom meltdown made it pretty clear that such growth had been part of a bubble. It's unrealistic to expect that an industry this large will grow substantially faster than GDP.

So a technology company's CFO must be good at both top- and bottom-line growth. The skills that a CFO has at Wal-Mart or GE or Johnson & Johnson are much closer to what will be expected at technology companies now.

Technology also resembles other industries in that its consolidation focuses mostly on cost synergies rather than growth synergies. At least in the near term, Sarbanes-Oxley requires CFOs of companies in every industry to spend a significant amount of time on how a company's ethical or business-integrity tone emanates across the organization. How does its internal-control structure operate? How does its disclosure-control process operate? And is it being really, really clear with investors in its SEC filings and press releases? Sarbanes-Oxley tends to make CFOs focus on similar tasks regardless of the industry.

The Quarterly: Speaking of Sarbanes-Oxley, what are the costs versus the benefits when it comes to implementing Section 404, for example?[1]

John Connors: Publicly traded US companies have historically had a premium on the equity side and a discount on the debt side relative to other markets because of the value of transparency and trust that investors had in US markets. That trust and transparency got violated, and we all have to bear the cost of earning it back. Microsoft accepts that.

Of course, there are negatives in Sarbanes-Oxley. For example, there isn't much guidance on what is material for public-company financial statements – not in the legislation itself or in the regulations or rules yet – nor is there any case law defining this. There are far too many areas where companies could take a reasonable risk with good business judgment but still be subject to litigation.

Yet there are real benefits to Sarbanes-Oxley. In our case, we knew what our key controls were, we knew what our materiality threshold was, we had tight budgeting and close processes and strong internal and external audits, but we didn't document everything in the way that Sarbanes-Oxley legislation requires. So we have done a complete business-process map of every transaction flow that affects the financials. In so doing, we have improved our revenue and procurement processes, and we can use controls to run the company in a more disciplined way. So we have gotten real business value out of all that process documentation.

Sarbanes-Oxley also really forces you to evaluate the policies that are in place and whether they make sense. One of its requirements is that if a company has a written management policy, people are expected to follow it – whether or not it has a financial impact. For example, how much can people discount contracts?

Even if a company can record that contract exactly right from a GAAP[2] perspective and the financials are correct, are people following the discount policy? At Microsoft, we have taken a really fresh and invigorating look at our management policy.

The Quarterly: Apart from the accounting issues, what was behind the decision to give employees restricted stock rather than options? What effect has the decision had?

John Connors: The options program was originally designed to give employees enough money for retirement or a vacation home or to pay for their kids' education – goals that usually take 15 or 20 or 25 years to achieve. Yet because of the stock performance, people were making enough money to send 3,000 kids to college or build 30 vacation homes. Then the bubble burst, our stock declined by half, and roughly half our employees had loads of money but were sitting in the same offices and doing the same jobs as the other half, who would likely earn nothing from their options.

It was the worst of all possible worlds. At the same time, we were diluting the heck out of shareholders, who were telling us loud and clear that we should rethink the long-term value proposition of our options program. Of course, shareholders hadn't paid much attention to that dilution when it was outstripped by growth, but when growth lags behind and expectations change, that dilution looks a lot different.

In the end, we wanted a program that aligned employee and shareholder interests over the long term. So we came up with the stock award program, and we were very clear with employees about how many shares they would get, how the stock would have to perform for them to be worse off, and how the program would work over a multiyear period.

The reaction has been pretty positive, and I think we have a good model. We will have been wrong if Microsoft really outperforms the market and the market performs extraordinarily well over the next seven years – then a number of employees would have been better off with options. That was a bet we were willing to make. If you look at the market in the 14 months since we made the announcement, and the predictions of most market prognosticators, the bet is pretty good so far.

The Quarterly: Having tackled such an ambitious agenda in your tenure, what challenges are next for you?

John Connors: The big challenge is probably institutionalizing the finance function and the finance 2.0 model we have been developing. And I feel the company is in a good place right now; if I got hit by a bus, got fired, or decided not to work here anymore, someone could step in and he or she would be really successful. That's important to me because I will have worked here for 16 years in January, and I believe people should leave a job in better condition than it was when they started.

Second, while it's essential to be viewed as a leader in investor relations, treasury, tax, and corporate reporting, it's also rewarding to be viewed as a leader in creating great finance talent. Keith Sherin from GE was here last week, and that corporation is just a machine for producing great talent. In the Puget Sound area alone, the CFO at Amazon is from GE; the CFO at Washington Mutual is from GE. The company takes good people and makes them great, and its ability to export these business leaders is phenomenal.

I'm happy to say that we have also had some success along these lines. In the past six months, two of our business-unit CFOs have left for CFO positions at other corporations. It's tough to lose good people, but what a great thing it is for people who are five or six years into their careers here to be able to say, "I can become a CFO – either at Microsoft or somewhere else. I can be a business leader."

And, on a personal note, I'd like to figure out how to have more time for my wife and our four kids so that I don't wake up someday and find that my kids are off to college and I'm too old to climb Mount Rainier again.

NOTES

1. Section 404 of the Sarbanes-Oxley Act of 2002 requires all public companies to give the Securities and Exchange Commission (SEC) an annual assessment of the effectiveness of their internal controls. In addition, the independent auditors of a corporation are required to review its management's internal-control processes with the same scrutiny as its financial statements.
2. Generally accepted accounting principles.

Corporate Governance Failures: To What Extent is Parmalat a Particularly Italian Case?

Andrea Melis

INTRODUCTION

The Parmalat situation started out as a fairly standard – although sizeable – accounting fraud. The Parmalat group, a world leader in the dairy food business, collapsed and entered bankruptcy protection in December 2003 after acknowledging massive holes in its financial statements. Billions of euros seem to have gone missing from the company's accounts. This dramatic collapse has led to the questioning of the soundness of accounting and financial reporting standards as well as of the Italian corporate governance system.

Some of the Anglophone business media (e.g. Heller, 2003; Mulligan and Munchau, 2003; Lyman, 2004) have been labelling the Parmalat case as a particularly Italian scandal, suggesting that a case such as Parmalat is country-specific and more likely to happen in Italy than elsewhere. This is not surprising as Italy is also widely represented as a bad example in the existing international academic literature on corporate governance (e.g. La Porta *et al*., 1997; Macey, 1998; Johnson *et al*., 2000). It has been argued that its reputation for corporate governance is "sufficiently bad" to let international authors on this topic "feel confident in awarding bad marks without serious field research". Institutions of Italian corporate governance have been "translated in black and white, and some have not been translated at all" (Stanghellini, 1999, p. 4).

The main purpose of this paper is to examine the Parmalat case in order to understand to what extent it may be considered a particularly Italian scandal, which might imply that international scholars and policy makers could disregard the corporate governance problems that emerged at Parmalat as country-specific, or whether it is a case that fits into a global corporate governance argument.

The main accounting and corporate governance issues related to the case will be examined and discussed. The paper will focus on the supply side of information (i.e. internal governance agents, senior management and external auditors). The role of the information demand-side agents (i.e. institutional and private investors, information analysers such as financial analysts and rating agencies, etc.) is out of the scope of the paper since those agents are not country-related factors. Legal aspects of the case will be not be discussed since prosecutors are still investigating these issues.

It has been argued (see Melis and Melis, 2004) that the Parmalat case is not due to a failure of generally accepted accounting principles. Although financial misreporting is the most evident issue, the Parmalat case is basically a false accounting story due to corporate governance failures.

Nevertheless, the question that it raises is how it was possible. Why did the corporate governance system not make senior managers accountable for their action and, if not prevent, stop their action well before the company's collapse?

Therefore, the main characteristics of Parmalat's corporate governance structure will be examined in order to understand why false accounting was possible and remained concealed for over a decade.

In the next sections the paper will investigate which monitoring mechanisms failed, and to what extent these failures are due to weaknesses specific to the Italian corporate governance system, or if in fact they fit into the global corporate governance issues. Hence the paper will compare and contrast the main characteristics of Parmalat's corporate governance system with the corporate governance system that prevails among Italian listed companies as well as with the recommendations of the Italian code of best practice, in terms of ownership, control and monitoring structures.

OWNERSHIP AND CONTROL STRUCTURES: PARMALAT VS ITALY

The ownership and control structure of Italian listed companies is characterised by a high level of concentration (see Table C15.1), and by the presence of a limited number of shareholders, linked by either family ties or

Table C15.1   Ownership and control structure of listed companies

	1996	1997	1998	1999	2000	2001	2002	2003
Type of control (1)								
Majority control	66.8	48.1	32.3	55.0	51.4	49.7	46.0	40.2
Working control	12.2	12.4	21.7	16.7	18.5	22.5	28.4	25.5
Under shareholders' agreement	4.8	6.3	7.4	10.8	9.6	11.4	10.2	15.3
No controlling shareholder(s)	16.2	33.2	38.6	17.5	20.5	16.4	15.4	19.0
Total	100	100	100	100	100	100	100	100
Concentration (2)								
Largest shareholder	50.4	38.7	33.8	44.2	44.0	42.2	40.7	33.5
Other major shareholders	10.7	8.4	9.7	8.2	9.4	9.2	8.0	11.6
Market	38.9	52.2	56.5	47.6	46.6	48.6	51.2	54.9
Total	100	100	100	100	100	100	100	100

Source: Elaborated from C.O.N.S.O.B. (2003, 2004). Data updated at December 2003. (1) Percentage ratio of the market share value of the ordinary share capital of the companies subject to each type of control to the market value of the ordinary share capital of all the companies listed at the Italian Stock Exchange. (2) As a percentage of the market value of the ordinary share capital of all the companies listed at the Italian Stock Exchange

agreements of a contractual nature (i.e. shareholders' agreements), who are willing and able to wield power over the corporation.

Parmalat was a complex group of companies controlled by a strong block-holder (the Tanzi family) through a pyramidal device.[1] From this viewpoint, it seems a very Italian case. Despite ownership disclosure rules, the structure of the group is not easy to trace, especially at an international level. This is not unusual among large Italian groups (Melis, 1999), but it is also a common problem among continental European groups (Becht, 1997). In these groups a holding company controls (directly or indirectly) the majority of voting rights of the companies which belong to the group. Its ultimate control is held by a single entrepreneur, or a family (as in the Parmalat case), or a coalition.

In fact, Parmalat S.p.A. represented the core milk and dairy food business of the Parmalat group, and controlled 67 other companies directly (as at 31 December 2002), and many others indirectly (Parmalat S.p.A., 2002). It was an unlisted company controlled by Parmalat Finanziaria with 89.18 per cent of its voting share capital. The remaining 10.82 per cent of the shares were owned by Dalmata S.r.l., an unlisted financial company which was fully controlled by Parmalat Finanziaria.

Parmalat Finanziaria was listed on the Milan stock exchange market. Its main shareholder (as at 30 June 2003) was represented by Coloniale S.p.A., which owned 50.02 per cent of the company voting share capital: 49.16 per cent was held directly, while 0.86 per cent was controlled indirectly through the Luxembourg-based Newport S.A. Two institutional investors (Lansdowne Partners Limited Partnership and Hermes Focus Asset Management Europe Limited), which owned 2.06 per cent and 2.2 per cent respectively, were the major minority shareholders.

Coloniale S.p.A., the holding company of the group, was under the control of the Tanzi family, through some Luxembourg-based companies. Therefore, the Tanzi family was the ultimate shareholder controlling Parmalat Finanziaria and the whole Parmalat group.

A simplified structure of the group will be shown, displaying only the links that are more relevant to the purpose of the paper (see Figure C15.1).

Shleifer and Vishny (1986) argued that large shareholders have adequate incentives to exercise monitoring. Empirical evidence (e.g. Becht, 1997; Molteni, 1997; Melis, 1999) shows that the Italian prevailing control structure is characterised by the presence of an active shareholder (the blockholder) who is willing and able to monitor the senior management effectively.

This type of ownership and control structure allegedly reduces the classical agency problem between senior management and shareholders: senior managers who pursue their own self-interest at the expense of shareholders will be displaced by the controlling shareholder. Nevertheless, the agency problem is only shifted towards the relationship between different types of shareholders: the controlling shareholder and minority shareholders (La Porta et al., 2000; Melis, 1999, 2000). If the main corporate governance issue in the USA is "strong managers, weak owners" (Roe, 1994), the key

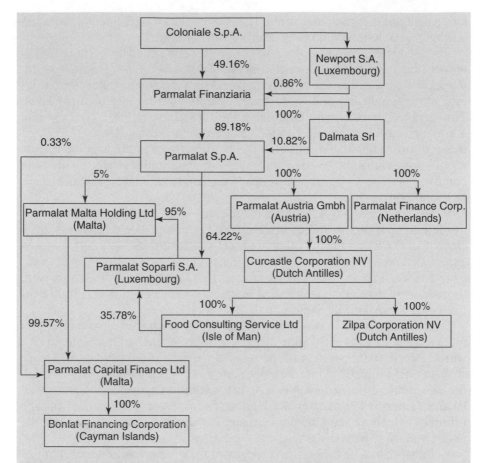

Figure C15.1 Parmalat's ownership structure: a simplified version

corporate governance problem in Italy is about "weak managers, strong blockholders and unprotected minority shareholders" (Melis, 2000, p. 351).

Blockholders may use their power to pursue their interests at the expense of minority shareholders, by diverting corporate resources from the corporation to themselves, either legally or illegally (Johnson *et al.*, 2000). This is what happened in the Parmalat case: Tanzi acknowledged to Italian authorities that Parmalat funnelled about Euro 500 million[2] to companies owned by the Tanzi family, especially to Parmatour. The latter was not a subsidiary of Parmalat. It was an unlisted company owned by Nuova Holding, a Tanzi family investment company.

THE MONITORING STRUCTURE: WHEN THE MONITORED CONTROLS THE MONITORS

The monitoring structure in Italian listed companies is characterised by the presence of two key gatekeepers: the board of statutory auditors and the external auditing firm. While the former is a particularly Italian device, the latter is certainly a widespread gatekeeper around the world.

The Role of the Board of Statutory Auditors

Italian law required listed (and unlisted) companies to set up a board of statutory auditors.[3] This board acts as the fundamental monitor inside the company. After the Draghi Reform (1998, Art. 149) its main tasks and responsibilities include:

- to check the compliance of acts and decisions of the board of directors with the law and the corporate bylaws and the observance of the so-called "principles of correct administration" by the executive directors and the board of directors;

- to review the adequacy of the corporate organisational structure for matters such as the internal control system, the administrative and accounting system as well as the reliability of the latter in correctly representing any company's transactions;

- to ensure that the instructions given by the company to its subsidiaries concerning the provision on all the information necessary to comply with the information requirements established by the law are adequate.

The Draghi Reform (1998, Art. 148) also requires corporate by-laws to provide the number of auditors (not less than three), the number of alternates (not less than two), the criteria and procedures for appointing the chairman of the board of statutory auditors and the limits on the accumulation of positions. Corporate by-laws shall also ensure that one (or two, when the board is composed of more than three auditors) of the members of the board of statutory auditors is appointed by the minority shareholders, so that the composition of the board reflects the will of all shareholders.

Parmalat Finanziaria's board of statutory auditors was composed of three members, i.e. the legal minimum requirement. This is not unusual among Italian listed companies. Consob (2002) reported that approx. 92 per cent of the boards of statutory auditors of listed companies were composed of three members. Even among the largest companies that are listed in the MIB30[4] (as Parmalat Finanziaria was from 1994 to 1999 and again from 2003), only approximately 30 per cent of the companies have set up a board of statutory auditors with more than three members. In such a case companies always choose a five-member board (see Figure C15.2).

As underlined in Melis (2004), the size of the board of statutory auditors has a direct influence over the level of protection on minority shareholders because some powers (e.g. the power to convene a shareholders' meeting because of a directors' decision) may be exercised only by at least two members of the board jointly. Only when the board of statutory auditors is composed of more than three members can minority shareholders appoint two statutory auditors.

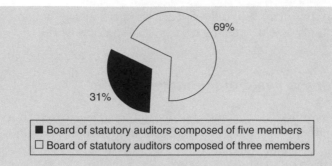

Figure C15.2   Size of the board of statutory directors among Italian MIB30
listed companies
Source: Elaborated with data based on CONSOB database. Data updated at December
2003. One company listed on MIB30 has not set up a board of statutory auditors. Being
based in the Netherlands it has chosen a two-tier board structure, with a supervisory
council

The Parmalat Finanziaria board of statutory auditors never reported anything wrong in their reports, nor to courts or to CONSOB[5] (Cardia, 2004).
Nor did the statutory auditors at Parmalat S.p.A. or any of its subsidiaries.
Even when, in December 2002, a minority shareholder (Hermes Focus Asset
Management Europe Ltd) filed a claim (pursuant to clause 2408 of the Italian
civil code) regarding, among other issues, related-parties transactions, the
board of statutory auditors answered that "no irregularity was found either
de facto or *de jure*".

This seems to confirm the argument (see Melis, 2004) that in a corporate
governance system characterised by the presence of a strong blockholder,
like Parmalat (and most Italian companies), the board of statutory auditors
seems to provide a legitimating device, rather than a substantive monitoring
mechanism.

The inefficiency of the board of statutory auditors as a monitor has been
attributed to (a) its lack of access to information related to shareholders'
activities, and (b) its lack of independence from the controlling shareholders (for a further analysis of these issues see Melis, 2004).

The Role of the External Auditing Firm

In Italy, the external auditing firm is appointed by the shareholders' meeting,
although the board of statutory auditors has a voice on the choice of the firm.
Its appointment lasts three years. After three appointments (i.e. nine years)
the law (Draghi Reform, 1998, Art. 159) requires the company to rotate its
lead audit firm. Italy is the only large economy to have made auditor rotation compulsory.

Grant Thornton S.p.A. served as auditors for Parmalat Finanziaria from 1990 to 1998, when the company changed auditors to comply with the mandatory auditor rotation. In 1999 Deloitte & Touche S.p.A. took over as chief auditors.

It seems difficult to argue that auditor rotation contributed to the discovery of the accounting fraud, since Deloitte & Touche S.p.A. did not discover it during its prior audits since 1999. In fact, they never claimed any problems regarding the financial position of Parmalat in any of their reports, nor directly to CONSOB (Cardia, 2004) until they issued a review report (published on 31 October 2003) on the interim financial information for the six months ended June 2003 in which they claimed to be unable to verify the carrying value of Parmalat's investment in the Epicurum Fund, as the fund had available no published accounts nor any marked to market valuation of its assets (Parmalat Finanziaria S.p.A., 2003).

Deloitte & Touche always rendered a "nonstandard" report underlying that up to 49 per cent of total assets of the group and 30 per cent of the consolidated revenues came from subsidiaries which were audited by other auditors (see Table C15.2).

In relation to the above-mentioned amounts, Deloitte & Touche stated that their opinion was basely solely upon other auditors' reports. In fact, mandatory audit rotation was not completely effective: Grant Thornton S.p.A. continued as auditor of Parmalat S.p.A. as well as certain Parmalat off-shore subsidiaries even after 1999. This means that Deloitte & Touche had been relying on Grant Thornton's work to give their opinion about Parmalat Finanziaria consolidated financial statements.

Among other subsidiaries, Grant Thornton, specifically two of their partners who had been auditing companies related to the Tanzi groups since the 1980s,[6] audited the Cayman Islands based Bonlat Financing Corporation. The latter was the wholly owned subsidiary, set up in 1998, that held the now well-known fictitious Bank of America account.

This nonexistent bank account raises fundamental questions about the role of the external auditor.

Grant Thornton claimed to have sent a request to Bank of America in December 2002 asking for confirmation of the bank account. The latter denied

Table C15.2 Total assets and consolidated revenues audited by the chief auditor and other auditors

	1999	2000	2001	2002
Total assets of the group non audited by the chief auditor	22%	40%	42%	49%
Total assets of the group audited by the chief auditor	78%	60%	58%	51%
Consolidated revenues non audited by the chief auditor	16%	23%	23%	30%
Consolidated revenues audited by the chief auditor	84%	77%	77%	70%

Source: Elaborated with data based on auditor's reports (see Parmalat Finanziaria S.p.A. 1999, 2000, 2001, 2002)

that they had received the request. Grant Thornton received a reply in March 2003, which was printed on Bank of America letterhead and signed by a bank employee. It is now believed that this confirmation letter was forged by Parmalat management. Grant Thornton publicly claimed that its staff acted correctly, and that the forged document made them a victim of fraud.

Nevertheless, even if the letter was a forgery, auditors may not label themselves as victims. Cash deposits are not complicated to evaluate, since they may be easily matched to a bank statement as part of a company's reconciliation procedures. The purpose of the third party confirmation is to ensure that bank statements received directly by the client and used in the reconciliation process have not been altered. When confirmation replies are not received on a timely basis, auditors should either send second requests or ask the client to provide a bank contact, so that they may reach the contact directly.

It is not clear whether Grant Thornton sent a second confirmation request given the time lag between the confirmation request and the response. However, they acknowledged that the request to Bank of America was done via the Parmalat chief finance director rather than getting in contact with Bank of America directly. Therefore, it seems reasonable to argue that they could have discovered the fraud if they had acted according to general auditing standards and exhibited the proper degree of professional "scepticism" in executing their audit procedures.

Prosecutors believe that the Grant Thornton auditors were too "involved" in the Bonlat issues, since the setting up of the latter was allegedly their idea to keep concealed the Parmalat financial crisis from the eyes of the incoming chief auditor Deloitte & Touche.

With regard to the Enron case, Palepu and Healy (2003) argue that the auditing firm firstly failed to exercise sound business judgement in reviewing transactions that were in fact creative accounting, i.e. only designed for financial reporting rather than business purposes. Then they "succumbed" to pressures from Enron's management. *Mutatis mutandis*, the Parmalat case does recall the Enron case with regard to the failure of the role of the external auditor at Parmalat as a gatekeeper, who was either not competent or (more likely in the case of Grant Thornton) not "independent".

This side of the story seems to fit perfectly into the global corporate governance issues. Thus it is against the argument of Parmalat as a particularly Italian case.

A REVIEW OF PARMALAT'S COMPLIANCE WITH THE ITALIAN CODE OF BEST PRACTICE

In civil law based countries (like Italy), the effectiveness of codes of best practice is limited because of the lower enforceability of their recommendations in comparison with Anglo-Saxon common law based countries (Cuervo, 2002).

Even taking this limitation into account, a review of the compliance of Parmalat with some key recommendations of the Preda Code (1999, 2002) is still useful to understand to what extent Parmalat complied, at least formally, with the highest standards of corporate governance in Italy. A high level of compliance would support the "Parmalat as a particularly Italian case" hypothesis, while a low level of compliance would not support such a hypothesis.

The Role of the Board of Directors

The Preda Code (1999, 2002, para. 1) recommends that matters of special importance should be reserved for the exclusive competence of the board of directors. These include (a) the examination and approval of the company's strategic, operational and financial plans and the corporate structure of the group, and (b) the examination and approval of transactions having a significant impact on the company's profitability, assets and liabilities or financial position, with special reference to transactions involving related parties.

Cavallari *et al.* (2003) report that, on a sample of Italian listed companies which represented 85 per cent of total capitalisation of the markets, 85 per cent of the companies fully complied with these recommendations. Eleven per cent of the sample complied partially, and only 4 per cent did not declare explicitly to reserve any of these functions to the board of directors.

According to its company reports on corporate governance, Parmalat Finanziaria, the listed holding company of the group, had complied with these recommendations since 2001.

The Composition of the Board of Directors

The Preda Code (2002, para. 2.1) also recommends the board of directors to be composed of executive and non-executive directors. The non-executive directors should, for their number and authority, carry a significant weight in the board's decision-making process.

The board of directors of Parmalat Finanziaria was composed of 13 members. Four of them, including the Chairman-CEO, were linked by family ties.

Parmalat Finanziaria, in its 2003 report on corporate governance, claimed that among the members of its board of directors, five were to be considered as non-executive directors. The fact that non-executive directors are less than executive directors is rather unusual among Italian listed companies (see Table C15.3).

At Parmalat Finanziaria, an executive committee was set up and composed of seven directors, including three Tanzi family members. One of the allegedly non-executive directors (Barili) belonged to the executive

Table C15.3 Composition of board of directors by type of control of listed companies

Type of control (1)	Executive	Non-executive	Total
Majority control	3.1	6.3	9.4
Working control	3.4	7.5	10.9
Under shareholders' agreement	4.5	7.1	11.6
No controlling shareholder(s)	4.7	8.1	12.8
Total	3.5	6.8	10.3

Source: Elaborated from CONSOB (2003). Data updated at December 2002. (1) Percentage ratio of the market share value of the ordinary share capital of the companies subject to each type of control to the market value of the ordinary share capital of all the companies listed at the Italian Stock Exchange

committee, and had been working in Parmalat as senior manager from 1963 until 2000.

With regard to the composition of the board, it is also interesting to observe that eight Parmalat Finanziaria directors also sat on the board of directors of Parmalat S.p.A., including all the members of the executive committee and one non-executive director.

The Independent Directors

The Preda Code (2002, para. 3) also recommends that an adequate number of non-executive directors should be independent in order to ensure the protection of the minority shareholders. An independent director is defined as a director who meets the following criteria:

■ s/he does not entertain, directly, indirectly or on behalf of third parties, nor has s/he recently entertained, with the company, its subsidiaries, the executive directors or the shareholder or group of shareholders who control the company, business relationships of a significance able to influence their autonomous judgement;

■ s/he does not own, directly or indirectly, or on behalf of third parties, a quantity of shares enabling them to control or notably influence the company or participate in shareholders' agreements to control the company;

■ s/he is not close family of executive directors of the company or a person who is in the situations referred to in the above paragraphs.

Cavallari *et al.* (2003) report that, among the Italian listed companies, the board of directors is generally composed of five directors that may be considered as independent. Parmalat Finanziaria claimed to have three independent directors on its board.

The Separation Between the Chairperson and CEO Positions

The Preda Code (1999, 2002, para. 4, p. 9) does not explicitly recommend that the Chairperson position should be held by a non-executive director, rather it acknowledges that "it is not infrequent in Italy for the same person to hold both positions or for some management powers to be delegated to the Chairman". When the two positions are not separated or the Chairman is delegated some executive powers, the board of directors is only recommended to provide adequate information in its annual report about the duties and responsibilities of the Chairperson and the executive directors.

Empirical evidence shows that among MIB30-listed companies the two positions are often separated (approx. 90 per cent of the cases). However, even when the positions are separated, the division of roles between Chairperson and CEO is often not adequately clear (Melis, 1999, 2000) since the Chairperson is often given some executive powers. In fact, in total 53 per cent[7] of the companies do delegate some executive powers to their Chairperson (see Figure C15.3).

At Parmalat Finanziaria, the Chairman and Chief executive director positions were not separated. Both positions were held by Tanzi. This situation led to a huge concentration of powers considering that the same person was the major shareholder of the company.

Although the separation between CEO and Chairperson is recommended by most international corporate governance codes of best practice since the Cadbury report (1992), Parmalat Finanziaria did comply with the Italian code of conduct since adequate information on the powers delegated to the Chairman/CEO was disclosed in its annual report.

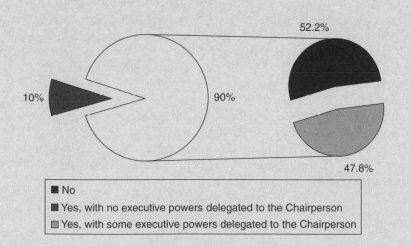

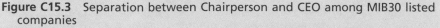

Figure C15.3   Separation between Chairperson and CEO among MIB30 listed companies
Source: Elaborated with data based on CONSOB database. Data updated at December 2003

The Preda Code (1999, 2002, para. 5) recommends that the Chairperson of the executive committee periodically report to the board of directors on the activities performed in the exercise of his/her powers. At Parmalat Finanziaria this report was done quarterly. Thus it complied with this recommendation.

Confidential Information

The Preda Code (1999, 2002, para. 6) deals with the handling of confidential information and recommends companies adopt internal procedures for the internal handling and disclosure of price-sensitive information, as well as information concerning transactions that involve financial instruments, carried out by persons who have access to relevant information.

Cavallari *et al.* (2003) report that the great majority (90 per cent in 2003, 81 per cent in 2002 and 58 per cent in 2001) of the Italian listed companies analysed complied with this provision.

Parmalat Finanziaria had informal internal procedures until 2002, when it set up a more structured system, under the responsibility of the Chairman/ CEO Tanzi. Thus it formally complied with the Preda Code on this issue. In fact, empirical evidence shows clearly that the above-mentioned procedures that dealt with confidential information were only used to keep concealed the accounting fraud for more than a decade.

The Appointment of Directors and the Nomination Committee

With regard to the nomination process, the Preda Code (1999, 2002, para. 7.2) recommends companies set up a nomination committee to propose candidates for election in cases when the board of directors believes that it is difficult for shareholders to make proposals. This may happen in cases when the corporate ownership and control structure is dispersed.

Parmalat Finanziaria did not comply with this recommendation and explained that shareholders never faced difficulties in proposing candidates for elections. This may be considered an adequate explanation given the concentrated control structure of the company.

The choice of not setting up a nomination committee is not uncommon among Italian listed companies. Only approximately 10 per cent set up such a committee (Cavallari *et al.*, 2003).

The Remuneration Committee

The Preda Code (1999, 2002, para. 8.1) recommends that companies set up a remuneration committee, which should be composed of mainly non-executive directors, in order to guarantee the body's impartiality. It is given the task of formulating proposals for the remuneration of managing directors and directors appointed to special offices.

Cavallari *et al.* (2003) reports that remuneration committees have been set up by more than 80 per cent of the companies analysed. In 95 per cent of cases these committees have mostly been composed of non-executive directors.

Parmalat Finanziaria set up the remuneration committee, which was composed of three members. Although one of them was also a member of the executive committee, the remaining two were non-executive directors. Both of them were also claimed as independent directors by the company reports. Therefore this recommendation was complied with.

Internal Control and the Role and Composition of the Internal Control Committee

The internal control committee is recommended by the Preda Code (1999, 2002, para. 10.2) to (a) assess the adequacy of the internal control system, (b) monitor the work of the corporate internal auditing staff, (c) report to the board of directors on its activity at least every six months and (d) deal with the external auditing firm. It has a similar role to that of British audit committees (see Spira, 1998; Windram and Song, 2004). It is appointed by the board of directors and should be composed of non-executive directors in order to be able to carry out its functions autonomously and independently.

The Preda Code (2002, para. 10.1) recommends that the majority of its members should be independent directors.

Cavallari *et al.* (2003) report that almost 90 per cent of the sample analysed adopted an internal control committee, which in over 82 per cent of the cases is entirely composed of non-executive directors, who are almost always independent.

At Parmalat Finanziaria, the internal control committee was composed of three members. Two of these members also sat in the executive committee. Thus, non-executive directors did not represent the majority of the committee. The recommendation of the Preda Code was not complied with, but no adequate explanation was given by the company in its corporate governance report.

It is also worth noting that one of the internal control committee members (Tonna) had been the chief finance director from 1987 until March 2003. He also held the Chairman position at Coloniale S.p.A., the Tanzi family holding company which was also the major shareholder of Parmalat Finanziaria.

The third member of the internal control committee, who was also the Chairman of the committee, was allegedly an independent director. However, further analysis (based on data not provided by the company) shows that he was the chartered certified accountant of the Tanzi family (as well as an old personal friend of Tanzi). Claiming that this relationship is not significant enough to influence his autonomous judgement seems difficult to argue and/or believe.

Therefore, it may be argued that none of the members of the internal control committee could have actually been considered as independent.

The Preda Code (1999, 2002, para. 3.2) acknowledges that when a group of shareholders controls a company, the need for some directors to be independent from the controlling shareholders is even more crucial. Parmalat Finanziaria failed to comply with this important recommendation, and did not give any adequate explanation for not complying.

Transactions with Related Parties

The Preda Code (1999, 2002, para. 11) recommends that transactions with related parties[8] should be treated according to criteria of "substantial" and "procedural" fairness. Companies are recommended to set up a procedure to deal with these transactions. In its corporate governance report, Parmalat Finanziaria claimed to comply with this provision, although empirical evidence clearly shows that such transactions were not treated according to the above-mentioned criteria.

Relations with Institutional Investors and Other Shareholders

With regard to the relations with institutional investors and other shareholders, it is recommended (Preda Code, 1999, 2002, para. 12) to designate a person or create a corporate structure to be responsible for this function.

In its corporate governance report Parmalat Finanziaria claimed to have set up an investor relations' structure since 2001. Thus, it complied with this recommendation.

CONCLUDING REMARKS

The paper examined and discussed to what extent Parmalat may be considered a particularly Italian case, or rather a case that fits into the global corporate governance argument.

The paper has looked at the role of the information supply agents (board of directors, board of statutory auditors, internal control committee, senior management and external auditing firm) in the Parmalat case.

Empirical evidence seems to confirm the lack of a monitoring structure making corporate insiders accountable in the presence of a corporate governance system characterised by a controlling shareholder.

The roles of the ownership and control structure (with special regard to the controlling shareholder's role), and of the board of statutory auditors, do have Italian traits and might suggest that Parmalat is a particularly Italian corporate governance case.

Moreover, the controlling shareholder was able to hold the positions of Chairman and CEO of Parmalat Finanziaria, which led to a huge concentration of powers. Although this concentration of positions is unusual among large Italian listed companies, the separation between the two positions is not explicitly recommended by the Italian code of best practice, so that Parmalat formally complied with it.

Although Italian corporate governance standards are not the highest at an international level, and might need improving, the standards themselves were not at fault in the Parmalat case, at least not completely.

In fact, Parmalat's corporate governance structure failed to comply with some of the key existing Italian corporate governance standards of best practice, such as the presence of independent directors, the composition of the board of directors and, especially, of the internal control committee (i.e. the audit committee).

Besides, the roles of the external auditor as well as the internal control committee as non-effective monitors seem to suggest that the Parmalat case fits, to some extent, into the global corporate governance argument and is not very different from Enron or other Anglo-American or continental European corporate scandals.

Whilst the Parmalat case may be considered to some extent a particularly Italian case, this does not imply that the corporate governance problems that emerged at Parmalat should be disregarded and catalogued as country-specific, since they may also surface at other firms around the world.

NOTES

1. Pyramidal groups, which are very widespread in Italy, have been defined as "organisations where legally independent firms are controlled by the same entrepreneur (the head of the group) through a chain of ownership relations" (Bianco and Casavola, 1999, p. 1059).
2. Prosecutors believe that Tanzi funnelled over €1.500 million to Parmatour and some other million to other Tanzi family-owned companies.
3. Since 2004 the new company law allows companies to choose between a unitary board structure (with an audit committee within the board of directors), a two-tier board structure (with a management committee and a supervisory council), and the traditional board structure with the board of statutory auditors.
4. MIB30 is the Italian equity share market segment that includes companies with a capitalisation above €800 million.
5. CONSOB (Commissione Nazionale per le Società e la Borsa) is the public authority that is responsible for regulating and controlling the Italian securities markets.
6. Mr Pecca, the President of Grant Thornton in Italy, and Mr Bianchi audited Parmalat from the 1980s, first as auditors of Hodgson Landau Brands, then as Grant Thornton.

7. In total 53 per cent of MIB30-listed companies delegate some powers to their Chairperson: 10 per cent of these companies do not separate the Chairperson and CEO positions and 43 per cent do separate the two positions.
8. See IAS 24 (IASB, 2003) for a definition of "transaction for related parties".

REFERENCES

Becht, M. (1997) Strong Blockholders, Weak Owners and the Need of European Mandatory Disclosure. In European Corporate Governance Network (ed.), *The Separation of Ownership and Control: A Survey of 7 European Countries. Preliminary Report to the European Commission.* Brussels: ECGN.

Bianco, M. and Casavola, P. (1999) Italian Corporate Governance: Effects on Financial Structure and Firm Performance, *European Economic Review*, 43, 1057–1069.

Cadbury Report (1992) *The Financial Aspects of Corporate Governance.* London: Gee.

Cardia, L. (2004) *I rapporti tra il sistema delle imprese, i mercati finanziari e la tutela del risparmio*, Testimony of the CONSOB President at Parliament Committees VI "Finanze" and X "Attivita produttive, Commercio e Turismo", della Camera and 6° "Finanze e Tesoro" and 10° "Industria, Commercio e Turismo" del Senato, 20 January.

Cavallari, A., Goos, E., Laorenti, F. and Sivori, M. (2003) *Corporate Governance in the Italian Listed Companies.* Milan: Borsa Italiana (http://www.borsaitalia.it).

CONSOB (2002) *Relazione annuale 2001.* Commissione Nazionale per le Società e la Borsa.

CONSOB (2003) *Relazione annuale 2002.* Commissione Nazionale per le Società e la Borsa.

CONSOB (2004) *Relazione annuale 2003.* Commissione Nazionale per le Società e la Borsa.

Cuervo, A. (2002) Corporate Governance Mechanisms: A Plea for Less Code of Good Governance and More Market Control, *Corporate Governance – An International Review*, 10(2), 84–93.

Draghi Reform (1998) Testo unico delle disposizioni in materia di intermediazione finanziaria, Legislative decree N. 58/1998.

Heller, R. (2003) Parmalat: A Particularly Italian Scandal, *Forbes*, 30 December (http://www.forbes.com).

IASB (2003) *International Financial Reporting Standards – IAS 24 Related Parties Disclosures.* London: IASCF.

Johnson, S., La Porta, R., Lopez-de-Sinales, F. and Shleifer, A. (2000) Tunnelling, *American Economic Review Papers and Proceedings*, 90(2), 22–27.

La Porta, R., Lopez-de-Sinales, F., Shleifer, A. and Vishny, R. (1997) Legal Determinants of External Finance, *Journal of Finance*, 52(3), 1131–1150.

La Porta, R., Lopez-de-Sinales, F., Shleifer, A. and Vishny, R. (2000) Investor Protection and Corporate Governance, *Journal of Financial Economics*, 58(1), 3–27.

Lyman, E. (2004) Parmalat's Problems: An Italian Drama, *The Washington Times*, 12 January.

Macey, J. (1998) Italian Corporate Governance: One American's Perspective, *Columbia Business Law Review*, 1, 121–144.

Melis, A. (1999) *Corporate Governance. Un'analisi empirica della realtà italiana in un'ottica europea*. Torino: Giappichelli.

Melis, A. (2000) Corporate Governance in Italy, *Corporate Governance – An International Review*, 8(4), 347–355.

Melis, A. (2004) On the Role of the Board of Statutory Auditors in Italian Listed Companies, *Corporate Governance – An International Review*, 12(1), 74–84.

Melis, G. and Melis, A. (2004) Financial Reporting, Corporate Governance and Parmalat. Was it a Financial Reporting Failure? University of Cagliari Dipartimento di Ricerche aziendali working paper.

Molteni, M. (ed.) (1997) *I sistemi di corporate governance nelle grandi imprese italiane*. Milan: EGEA.

Mulligan, M. and Munchau, W. (2003) Comment: Parmalat Affair has Plenty of Blame to go Round, *Financial Times*, 29 December.

Palepu, K. and Healy, P. (2003) The Fall of Enron, *Journal of Economic Perspectives*, 17(2), 3–26.

Parmalat Finanziaria S.p.A. (1999, 2000, 2001, 2002) *Relazione e bilancio d'esercizio* (Annual report).

Parmalat Finanziaria S.p.A. (2001, 2002, 2003) *Informativa sul sistema di Corporate Governance ai sensi della sezione IA.2.12 delle istruzioni al Regolamento di Borsa Italiana spa* (Report on Corporate Governance).

Parmalat Finanziaria S.p.A. (2003) *Interim reports*.

Parmalat S.p.A. (2002) *Relazione e bilancio d'esercizio 2002* (Annual report).

Preda Code (1999, 2002) *Codice di Autodisciplina*. Milano: Borsa Italiana.

Roe, M. (1994) *Strong Managers, Weak Owners. The Political Roots of American Corporate Finance*. Princeton: Princeton University Press.

Shleifer, A. and Vishny, R. (1986) Large Shareholders and Corporate Control, *Journal of Political Economy*, Part 1, June, 461–489.

Spira, L. F. (1998) An Evolutionary Perspective on Audit Committee Effectiveness, *Corporate Governance – An International Review*, 6(1), 29–38.

Stanghellini, L. (1999) Family and Government-owned Firms in Italy: Some Reflections on an Alternative System of Corporate Governance, Columbia Law School project on Corporate Governance, Mimeo, June.

Windram, B. and Song, J. (2004) Non-Executive Directors and the Changing Nature of Audit Committees: Evidence from UK Audit Committee Chairmen, *Corporate Ownership and Control*, 1(3), 108–115.

Reproduced from *Corporate Governance*, Vol. 13, No. 4 (July 2005), pp. 478–88.

Companies Still Failing to Fill the Funding Gap

Lucy Warwick-Ching

The dire state of Britain's pensions system was highlighted this week as new figures revealed that the black hole in company pension schemes is getting deeper in spite of a steady rise in equity markets.

Pension fund contributions by companies in the FTSE 100 index were at a similar level in 2004 to the previous year, at £11.4 bn. But after meeting the cost of new pension promises and interest on last year's deficit, less than £1 bn was left to reduce the £60 bn underlying deficit, according to research from RBC Capital Markets.

John Ralfe, an independent pension consultant and author of the research note, says although many companies have been increasing contributions, they have often done so after a full or partial contributions holiday. "This stops the deficit increasing but does nothing to reduce it," he says.

The size of the companies' pension liability is particularly important when seen in relation to the assets held by that company. "Many companies have huge pension liabilities – far bigger than the assets they have to pay them," says Donna Bradshaw, independent financial adviser at IFG Group. "This could leave thousands of workers in a parlous state if their employers suffer prolonged bad trading and go under – as has happened with MG Rover."

Five companies – British Airways, BAE Systems, ICI, Rolls-Royce and British Telecommunications – account for 20 per cent of the overall FTSE 100 liabilities and deficit under FRS17 accounting guidelines.

BA, which a couple of years ago had a market capitalisation smaller than the deficit on its pension fund, had a deficit equal to 66 per cent of its market cap in June this year. While its shares were worth £3 bn, the deficit was almost £2 bn. Like many other companies it no longer lets new employees join its final salary schemes, but existing employees can still contribute.

"The biggest risk for pension schemes, aside from equities crashing, or longevity of pensioners, is whether the company will be around in five or ten years' time to pay the benefits," says Tom McPhail, pensions expert at Hargreaves Lansdown. "Companies have overreached themselves with their promises over the past decades and they could find these promises very difficult to fulfil."

Pension funds have been battling a double whammy of falling stock markets that reduced the value of their assets, which are largely invested in equities and historically low bond yields, which effectively raise the cost of funding pension payments and therefore increase their liabilities. This, combined with increased life expectancy, means that companies are having to contribute about 50 per cent more to their pension funds than they did 15 years ago.

The RBC Capital Markets research preceded an announcement from the government on Wednesday that its new pensions safety net is now likely to cost more to fund than the £300 m a year originally estimated. The pension protection fund is designed to safeguard staff pension entitlements if an employer goes bust.

The fund also confirmed this week that companies in danger of going bankrupt, or whose pension schemes were underfunded, would have to contribute much more to the fund than stronger firms.

Of the five companies mentioned in the RBC Capital Markets research as having the weakest pension funds, not one has a credit rating higher than BBB+, two notches above the lowest investment-grade debt.

Ralfe believes that the continued high weighting in equities for many of the pension funds is partly to blame for the huge pension fund deficits. He says FTSE 100 companies for the most part appear to be hoping that strong rises in equities markets will bail them out.

"Some companies act as though a pension deficit can be plugged by holding a high level of equities and hoping for the best," he says. "Holding equities is not a substitute for increasing contributions."

He believes that UK pension schemes still hold too little in long-dated and index-linked bonds and says that a pension scheme should "hold matching bonds to back the pensions already being paid". He makes the point that "simply to match the pensions in payment today, UK pension schemes need to make a switch, of 20 per cent, or £125 bn, from equities to bonds," says Ralfe.

But not everyone agrees. "The notion that you can switch the risk by switching from equities into bonds is dangerous," says Ros Altmann, a pensions specialist and former adviser to the government on pensions. "The most important thing is to create a diversified portfolio so as to protect the downside as well as allow for any possible upside."

The good news is that the dramatic deficits are not uniformly spread among FTSE 100 companies. About 30 companies account for the bulk of the problem while the rest, making up 75 per cent of the FTSE 100 market cap, have a deficit of just 5 per cent or less of their market cap.

"Although many companies have recently increased their regular contributions, more should be following GlaxoSmithKline's lead in making consistent contributions to reducing pension deficits," says Ralfe. "Over the last three years, it has quietly made a total contribution of £1.6 bn, a net reduction in its underlying deficit of £650 m, leaving the latest deficit at £1.5 bn."

He expects more large one-off contributions from the stronger companies over the next few years, leaving pension holes increasingly concentrated in the weaker FTSE 100 companies.

Experts hope to see an increase in deficit contributions once the protection fund moves to a risk-based levy, which will impose an explicit cost on companies running a pension deficit. The Pensions Act 2004 which comes into effect in September is also expected to increase contributions. The new regime represents a dramatic shift in the balance of power in determining pension scheme funding with pension trustees being given greater powers to decide a company's contributions to its pension scheme.

"There will be a two-pronged approach to increasing contributions," says Steve Leake, principal at Punter Southall. "Companies will have to provide an estimate of the assets needed to make provision for the benefits when they fall due. They will have to come up with a recovery plan which will set out the manner and time-frame in which the deficit is to be eliminated."

He says that trustees will be encouraged to remove any deficit as soon as practicable. "Under the new rules, where trustees and employers cannot agree on an acceptable funding plan, the regulator [The Pensions Regulator] will be able to intervene. The body's powers include setting the contributions, stopping or changing the future accrual of benefits and even winding up the scheme," says Leake. These pressures could prove the last straw for those companies who still offer defined benefit pension schemes. Some 68 per cent of defined benefit schemes are closed to new entrants and 10 per cent closed to new accrual of benefits, according to a recent survey by the Association of Consulting Actuaries. "From September it will become obvious to the workforce what state their pensions are in and will cause a lot of alarm," says Leake. "Unless companies appear to be doing everything they can to close the gap between liabilities and deficits there will be an outcry from members."

Index